LEADING ILLINOIS ATTORNEYS
CONSUMER LAW GUIDEBOOK

1ST EDITION PUBLISHED JULY 1996

LEADING ILLINOIS ATTORNEYS

Illinois' Most Respected Legal Counsel As Selected By Their Peers.

The hiring of an attorney is an important decision that should not be based solely on advertisements. Before you decide to hire a lawyer to whom you are referred, ask that lawyer for written information about that lawyer's qualifications and experience.

© COPYRIGHT 1996 BY AMERICAN RESEARCH CORPORATION ALL RIGHTS RESERVED.

No part of this publication may be reproduced, stored in a retrieval system or transmitted in any form or by any means, electric, mechanical, photocopying, recording or otherwise, without the permission of the publisher.

The information contained herein is presumed to be accurate at the time of publication. The publisher is not liable for damages from errors or omissions. This publication is designed to provide accurate and authoritative information in regard to the subject matter covered. It is published with the understanding that the publisher is not engaged in providing legal advice, legal service, or instructions on the practice of law. For legal advice, consult an attorney, such as one of those listed in this book.

ISBN   1-885573-02-2
ISSN   1076-111X
UPC   94175-73024

AMERICAN RESEARCH CORPORATION
527 MARQUETTE AVENUE, SUITE 2100
MINNEAPOLIS, MN 55402
Phone: (612) 904-3200
Fax: (612) 334-3447
E-Mail: staff@lawlead.com
Web Site: http://www.lawlead.com

LEADING ILLINOIS ATTORNEYS

Illinois' Most Respected Legal Counsel As Selected By Their Peers.

This book is printed using soy-based inks on paper which is 50% recycled with a minimum of 10% post-consumer fiber. The entire book is recyclable.

PURPOSE:

The purpose of the *Leading Illinois Attorneys Consumer Law Guidebook* is to provide consumers with the names of Leading Illinois Attorneys who can handle their legal challenges, along with information about the law to assist in an understanding of a variety of legal issues.

TABLE OF CONTENTS

PART I

ABOUT THE PUBLISHER vii
ACKNOWLEDGMENTS ix
INTRODUCTION x
METHODOLOGY xi
ALPHABETICAL LISTING OF LEADING ILLINOIS ATTORNEYS xii
USING THE CONSUMER LAW GUIDEBOOK xviii

PART II

1. HOW TO HIRE AN ATTORNEY 1
   Preparing a List; Researching Attorneys on the List; Interviewing the Attorneys; Cost Considerations; Questions to Ask.

2. ILLINOIS' JUDICIAL SYSTEMS 8
   Jurisdiction; Venue; State and Federal Courts.

3. PROCESS OF A CASE: CIVIL & CRIMINAL 11
   Civil Process; Criminal Process; Trial Process; Small Claims Court.

4. CONSTITUTIONAL LAW & CIVIL RIGHTS 15
   Role of Constitutions; Civil Rights; Equal Protections; Due Process; Military; State Action; Freedom of Speech; Freedom of Religion.

5. CONSUMER PROTECTION 21
   Automobile Buyer Protection; Telephone and Mail Fraud; Credit Card Scams; Home Solicitations; Get-Rich-Quick Schemes; Specific Businesses.

6. CONTRACT LAW 27
   Contract Components; Defenses to Contract; Contract Termination; Damages.

PART III
INCLUDING LEADING ILLINOIS ATTORNEY LISTINGS AND BIOGRAPHICAL PROFILES

7. ADOPTION LAW 30
   What Is Adoption; Open Versus Closed Adoption; Who May Adopt; Adoption Placements and Procedures; Intercountry Adoptions.

8. ALTERNATIVE DISPUTE RESOLUTION 38
   ADR Options; Mediation; Arbitration; Mediation-Arbitration; Mini-Trial; Neutral Fact-Finding; Summary Jury Trial; Finding an ADR Provider; Costs.

9. ARTS, ENTERTAINMENT & INTELLECTUAL PROPERTY LAW 49
   Protecting Creative Work; Copyright; Patent; Trademark; Artists' Rights and Obligations; Contracts; Shopping, Management, Performance, and Mutual Release Agreements; Forming a Business.

10. BANKRUPTCY LAW 62
    Bankruptcy Code; Chapter 7; Chapter 13; Involuntary Bankruptcy; Effects of Declaring Bankruptcy; Transfers to Avoid Losing an Asset in Bankruptcy; Collection Agencies and the Law; Alternatives to Bankruptcy.

11. CIVIL APPELLATE LAW 77
    What Is an Appeal; Requirements for Appealing a Decision; Federal Appellate Structure; Illinois' Appellate Structure.

12. CRIMINAL LAW: DUI & MISDEMEANORS 88
    Criminal Codes; Attempt, Conspiracy, Aiding and Abetting; Misdemeanors; Alcohol and Drug-Related Traffic Offenses; Juveniles and the Law; Crime Victims' Rights.

TABLE OF CONTENTS

13. CRIMINAL LAW: FELONIES & WHITE COLLAR CRIME 99
Criminal Codes; Attempt, Conspiracy, Aiding and Abetting; Felonies; White Collar Crimes; Computer Crime; Defenses and Punishment; Crime Victims' Rights.

14. ELDER LAW 118
Age Discrimination in Employment; Health Care Decisions and Protective Arrangements; Living Wills; Power of Attorney for Health Care; Guardianship; Social Security; Medicare/Medical Assistance.

15. EMPLOYMENT LAW 131
The Employment Relationship; Government Administered Benefits; Civil Rights in the Workplace; Other Workplace Rights and Responsibilities.

16. ESTATE PLANNING, WILLS & TRUSTS LAW 151
Wills; Trusts; Probate; Avoiding Death Taxes.

17. FAMILY LAW 167
Marriage in Illinois; Termination of Marriage; Minimizing Litigation and Attorney Fees in Divorce Cases; Custody; Support; Legal Separation; Paternity; Abuse.

18. IMMIGRATION LAW 219
United States Citizenship; Aliens, Immigrants, Nonimmigrants, and Residents; The Visa System; Nonimmigrant Visas; Entry and Exclusion; Getting a Green Card and Becoming a Naturalized Citizen; Deportation.

19. PERSONAL INJURY LAW: GENERAL 228
General Concepts of Tort Law; Degree of Fault; Defenses; Damages; Product Liability; General Accidents and Injuries.

20. PERSONAL INJURY LAW: MEDICAL & PROFESSIONAL MALPRACTICE 259
Legal and Medical Malpractice; Duty; Breach; Injury.

21. PERSONAL INJURY LAW: TRANSPORTATION 275
Automobile, Maritime, Railroad, and Aviation Accidents.

22. REAL ESTATE LAW 285
Real Estate Ownership; Residential Real Estate; Buying or Selling a Home; Landlord-Tenant Issues; Discrimination in Housing.

23. SMALL BUSINESS LAW 299
Sole Proprietorship; Partnership; Corporation; Subchapter S Corporation; Nonprofit Corporation; Franchise; General Business Issues.

24. SOCIAL SECURITY LAW 310
Social Security Act; Benefits for Retirees; Railroad Retirement System; Disability Benefits; Medicare; Medicaid; Other State Assistance; Applying for Benefits.

25. TAX LAW 320
Understanding Tax Law; Federal Tax Disputes; IRS Audit; Taxpayer Rights in an IRS Audit; Appealing an Audit; Illinois Tax Disputes.

26. WORKERS' COMPENSATION LAW 331
Who Is Covered; Available Benefits; Employer Responsibilities; Reporting an Injury and Collecting Benefits; When an Employer or Carrier Refuses Benefits.

APPENDIX A: Profiled Attorneys & Law Firms
  by Region 347
APPENDIX B: Legal Resources 368
APPENDIX C: Community Resources 375
APPENDIX D: State Bar Associations 379
APPENDIX E: Glossary of Legal Terms & Phrases ... 382

INDEX F: Subject Matter Index 387
INDEX G: Attorney Extensive Experience Index 395
INDEX H: Profiled Attorneys Index 398

AMERICAN RESEARCH CORPORATION WOULD LIKE TO THANK THE FOLLOWING ATTORNEYS FOR EDITORIAL ASSISTANCE IN THE DEVELOPMENT OF THE LEADING ILLINOIS ATTORNEYS CONSUMER LAW GUIDEBOOK

Criminal Law: DUI & Misdemeanors: *David E. Camic*
Criminal Law: Felonies & White Collar Crime: *David E. Camic*
Family Law: *Edward I. Stein*

AMERICAN RESEARCH CORPORATION

President & CEO: *Brett R. Johnson*
Vice President, Marketing & Business Development: *Jeffrey T. Carroll*
Vice President, General Manager: *E. Hervey Evans III*
Vice President of Sales: *Scott C. Anderson*
Legal Marketing Executives: *Cindy Baertschi, J.D., Kate J. Swingle, John P. Shaul, J.D., Connie M. Bell, Robert McCollar, J.D., Kelly LeRoy.*
Illinois State Director: *Mike Evers, J.D.*
Florida State Director: *John L. Remsen, Jr.*
Florida Consumer Guidebook Director: *Jana S. Murphy, J.D.*
Production Manager: *Dawn M. Finger*
Managing Editor: *Katy M. Podolinsky*
Biographies Editor: *Joan Bettinger*
Director of Research: *Virginia A. Murphrey, Esq.*
Legal Research Specialists: *Holly Sitzmann, Jeanna M. Shepherd, Sheila Phillips, Daniel Mesnik, Sarah Fleming*
Information Systems Director: *Laura Gallup*
Director of Public Relations: *Marne E. Brooks, Esq.*
Marketing Intern: *Angela Horn*
Circulation Manager: *Brindley B. McGowan II*
Paralegal & Business Manager: *Pamela Schindler*
Human Resources Director: *Tom Felling*
Receptionist: *Tracy Swank*

AMERICAN RESEARCH CORPORATION WOULD LIKE TO THANK THE FOLLOWING FOR ASSISTANCE IN THE DEVELOPMENT OF THE GUIDEBOOKS

Mary Boyum
Michael Gutierres
Kate Houst
Tom Kaul
Kurtis Lange
Jennifer Leiseth

Robin Monty
Chas Porter
Julie Toman
Judy Finger
Lawrence Schmidt

AMERICAN RESEARCH CORPORATION WOULD LIKE TO THANK

Legal Research Center (LRC®)

for research and editorial in this edition of *Leading Illinois Attorneys Consumer Law Guidebook*. Since 1978, LRC has provided legal and factual research and writing services to attorneys in corporate and private practice. For further information, call (800) 776-9377.

ABOUT THE PUBLISHER

American Research Corporation (ARC) conducts market research and develops innovative communications strategies for select groups of professional services clients nationally and internationally.

Through its operating divisions of Leading Minnesota Attorneys, Leading Illinois Attorneys and Leading Florida Attorneys, the company is bridging the communications gap between those in need of exceptional legal advice and attorneys qualified to help.

The cornerstone of the company's strategy is its extensive research process. ARC identifies those attorneys most highly regarded by their peers by geographic region and area of practice. ARC then compiles and presents its research results in a variety of targeted formats.

ARC's initial research revealed that consumers lacked the means to locate legal counsel efficiently and with confidence. In addition, attorneys lacked the means to differentiate themselves and provide access to consumers in a dignified and effective manner.

ARC's products provide an invaluable service by communicating to those in need of focused legal assistance the names and credentials of preeminent attorneys.

Leading Illinois Attorneys Consumer Law Guidebook is a product users can trust. Consumers can consult a Leading Illinois Attorney with confidence, knowing that he or she is peer-recommended as exceptional in his or her area of practice.

ARC is continually evaluating and enhancing its ever-evolving range of innovative communication vehicles, including publishing, graphics and design, public relations, electronic media, Internet, and advertising services, as well as network affiliations to help bring useful information to the public.

Visit our Web Site at http://www.lawlead.com

ACKNOWLEDGMENTS

The *Leading Illinois Attorneys Consumer Law Guidebook* is intended to provide readers with an understanding of legal issues and an intelligent approach to finding the right lawyer for their legal needs. Along with its sister publication, *Leading Illinois Attorneys Business Law Guidebook*, the *Guidebooks'* objective is to offer Illinois consumers and businesses greater and more efficient access to the law and the legal community.

Many thanks are in order, beginning with the thousands of attorneys who took time to offer thoughtful recommendations in our research. Our only regret is that the research process, however rigorous, cannot possibly recognize the able and talented practitioners who may have been overlooked. In this sense, the list found in this *Guidebook* is not complete, nor could it ever be. It is, however, an excellent resource of exceptional attorneys.

This book was made possible only through the diverse contributions made by the many individuals listed on page *vi*. In addition, particular thanks must go to the attorneys who reviewed, advised and assisted in developing the individual chapters.

Our greatest appreciation is reserved for the Leading Illinois Attorneys whose biographical profiles appear at the end of each chapter. Without their support, this book would not be possible. They recognize the public's need for accessible legal information and the favorable impact such information can have in helping people resolve their legal matters. More importantly, these attorneys have demonstrated a willingness to support a new and innovative venture. For this, we are truly thankful.

Brett R. Johnson
Publisher

INTRODUCTION

Leading Illinois Attorneys Consumer Law Guidebook is a resource for people to use to address their legal issues efficiently and intelligently.

Along with the basics on law and the legal system, this *Guidebook* provides information on major issues in specific areas of Illinois law. At the end of each chapter of legal information are biographies of Leading Illinois Attorneys regarded by their peers as among the most reputable and qualified in that specific area of law.

The *Guidebook*'s purpose is to equip readers with the informational tools they need to address specific legal matters and to provide the names of Illinois legal professionals who are among the most qualified to help.

Our legal editors and researchers are continually collecting relevant legal information which they summarize and distill to provide readers a concise resource of Illinois law and legal resources.

However, American Research Corporation does not provide legal advice. This *Guidebook* cannot replace or diminish the importance of legal counsel. It is, however, a valuable starting point.

Selecting the right attorney may be the single most important factor in obtaining a favorable legal outcome. We recommend reading Chapter One, How to Hire an Attorney, and then carefully reviewing the attorneys' biographies in the applicable area of law before selecting attorneys to interview. Many listed attorneys excel in multiple areas and are referenced in chapters other than the chapter in which each attorney's biography appears. The Profiled Attorneys Index provides the names of all attorneys whose biographies can be found in this *Guidebook*.

The appendices, covering firm profiles, legal and community resources, and a glossary, provide a wealth of information. Resources are organized by region and interest group.

The Leading Illinois Attorneys sections at the end of each chapter provide the names of all Leading Illinois Attorneys in the specific area of law and professional biographies of many of these highly regarded legal experts—Illinois attorneys considered among the best in their fields. This information is designed to help one find the most appropriate legal counsel.

The attorneys who qualified to appear in this book were chosen through research conducted by American Research Corporation (see Methodology below).

Each attorney who was selected as a Leading Illinois Attorney was offered the opportunity to publish his or her biographical profile in this *Guidebook*. Those who chose to do so paid a standard fee to underwrite the cost of publishing and distributing this book.

This *Guidebook* does not rank its listing attorneys; it is not a "best of." Certainly there are qualified and reputable attorneys not listed (note: additional exceptional attorneys may be found in the *Leading Illinois Attorneys Business Law Guidebook*). However, all of the attorneys listed in this book are among the most highly qualified and reputable in Illinois as determined by their peers in an extensive statewide survey.

The production of this *Guidebook* is an ongoing effort. Subsequent editions will include biographies of attorneys not included in earlier versions, as well as updates on Illinois law and other useful resources. Based on reader feedback, we will make other changes to make this *Guidebook* more useful and to help it become the important legal education resource we envision.

METHODOLOGY

The Leading Illinois Attorneys listings found at the end of most chapters provide information on qualified, reputable Illinois attorneys. These lists of Leading Illinois Attorneys are the result of research conducted with attorneys throughout the state. To create the complete list, thousands of licensed Illinois attorneys were mailed questionnaires that inquired, "To whom would you refer a close friend or relative in need of legal help in a certain area of law?"

> We asked Illinois attorneys to whom they would refer a close friend or relative in need of legal assistance.

This list represents only a small percentage of the reputable and qualified attorneys in Illinois and does not include the names of attorneys who are listed in the Leading Illinois Attorneys Business Law Guidebook.

These phase-one survey recipients were selected using a random sort by zip code to ensure geographic balance. After self-nominations were removed, an attempt was made to contact each peer-recommended attorney. In phase two, we again sought names of individuals in their practice area whom they held in highest regard. Additional calls were then made to those recommended during this second phase. All partner or same-firm nominations were removed.

A third phase involved contacting those attorneys regarded as outstanding by their peers as indicated by multiple independent nominations during the second phase. Altogether, over 5,700 Illinois attorneys were interviewed. The resulting nominated group represents less than three percent of all Illinois attorneys. A complete list of all 1631 attorneys nominated for the *Illinois Consumer Law Guidebook* is found below (this list does not include attorneys nominated for the *Leading Illinois Attorneys Business Law Guidebook*).

Note: American Research Corporation made every effort to verify that all nominees listed below are lawfully engaged in the practice of law. To this end, all nominated attorneys were checked with the Attorney Registration and Disciplinary Commission. Whereas American Research Corporation can only rely on the most recent information available at the time of publication, it can make no guarantee as to the continuing status of any attorney in the alphabetical listing below.

ALPHABETICAL LISTING OF LEADING ILLINOIS ATTORNEYS

Abate, Alex M.
Ackerman, Allan A.
Adam, Sam
Adams Murphy, Jennifer
Adelman, Ronald S.
Agnew, Patrick H.
Ahern, James J.
Ahlgren, Robert D.
Aiello, Chris J.
Aimen, Julie B.
Albright, Christine L.
Aleksy, Richard E.
Alexander, Ellen J.
Alexander, Peter
Allegretti, James
Allen, Benjamin B.
Allen, Gemma B.
Alschuler, Benjamin P.
Alt, Leo F.
Altamore, Albert A.
Amari, Leonard F.
Angelini, Phil
Ansel, Marc J.

Antonik, Douglas A.
Anvaripour, Mark
Applegate, Steven D.
Applehans, Stephen G.
Arfa, Jack A.
Argento, Vincent C.
Ariano, Frank V.
Arnoff, Alisa
Arnold, Joel D.
Arnold, Nancy Jo
Arshonsky, Paul C.
Asonye, Uche O.
Auler, Robert I.
Austin, William W.
Avgeris, George N.
Axelrod, David A.
Azulay, J. Daniel
Azulay, Y. Judd
Badesch, Robert T.
Badgley, Brad L.
Bailey, James M.
Baime, Stephen G.
Baizer, Robert S.

Baker, David A.
Baker, James P.
Balbach, Stanley B.
Balch, Bruce L.
Ballard Bostick, Shelley
Balsley, Stephen G.
Balsley, William L.
Barash, Barry M.
Barder, Fredrick B.
Barnard, Morton J.
Barr, John
Barr, Richard J., Jr.
Barrett, Gregory E.
Bartholomew, Joseph
Bass, Renee F.
Bass, Richard I.
Batcher, Richard M.
Bateman, Philip L.
Bauer, Wendy S.
Baum, David M.
Bayard, Forrest S.
Bazos, Peter C.
Beck, Jeffrey

xii

Beckett, J. Steven
Beeman, Bruce A.
Beermann, Jon L.
Beermann, Miles N.
Bell, Brigitte Schmidt
Bell, Gregory S.
Bell, Joel M.
Bellatti, Robert M.
Belz, Edwin J.
Benassi, A. Lou
Benassi, Patricia C.
Benedick, Thomas F.
Beninati, Francis A.
Benjamin, Fred I.
Bennett, Jim A.
Bennett, Margaret A.
Bensinger, Ethan
Benson, Peter
Berdelle, Richard L., Jr.
Berg, Gershon S.
Berg, Royal F.
Berg, Steven W.
Berger, Michael J.
Berk, Keith H.
Berkemann, Rosemary L.
Berkson, Dennis A.
Berman, Arthur M.
Berman, Edward A.
Berman, Peter J.
Bernardi, John A.
Berning, Larry D.
Bernstein, Arnold
Bers, Alan B.
Bertrand, Louis L.
Beu, William R.
Biallas, John S.
Bingle, Robert J.
Binsbacher, Valroy
Bitterman, Patrick J.
Black, James F.
Black, Robert G.
Black, Terry R.
Blade, Thomas A.
Blake, Edward J., Jr.
Blan, Kennith W., Jr.
Block, Michael D.
Blomquist, Ernest R., III
Blood, Curtis L.
Bloom, Kenneth M.
Bloom, Marvin
Blum, Alan A.
Blumenfeld, Barry E.
Bobb, Patricia C.
Bochenek, Stephen J.
Bogusz, Richard P., Sr.
Boie, Wesley L.
Bollman, Robert M.
Bone, Maurice E.
Bongiorno, Salvatore J.
Bonifield, Jerald J.
Bonjean, Robert V., Jr.
Booth, Edward
Boreen, John M.
Botti, Stephen R.
Bourey, Alan D.
Bourque, Starr
Bower, Brian L.
Bowles, James E.
Bowman, John T.
Boylan, William E.
Boyle, Charles A.
Boyne, Kevin M.
Braden, Glenn A.
Brady, Gerald, Jr.
Brady, John C.
Bramfeld, John F.
Brandon, Wm. Kent
Brankey, Edward
Brannon, James S.

Brassfield, Eugene E.
Braud, Walter D.
Bravos, Zachary M.
Breen, Joseph R.
Breen, Thomas M.
Breen, Thomas
Brezina, David C.
Brill, Aaron P.
Brill, Kevin M.
Briscoe, Thomas A.
Bristol, Douglas
Brittingham, Francis M.
Brodsky, Joel A.
Broecker, Howard W.
Broida, Ronald J.
Brooks, Jack L.
Broom, William L., III
Brosterhous, Patricia
Brown, Alan C.
Brown, Joseph R., Jr.
Brown, Kenneth H.
Brown, Richard M.
Brown, Robert E.
Brown, Ronald M.
Brown, W. Campbell
Bruce, Joseph J.
Brunell, Alan R.
Bruno, Thomas A.
Bryan, George G.
Bryant, David R.
Bua, Nicholas J.
Bucklin, Bradford C.
Buckrop, Bruce A.
Buege, Robert M.
Bugos, Joseph T.
Burke, Dennis J.
Burke, John M.
Burke, William J.
Burkhardt, Craig S.
Burton, R. Nicholas
Busch, Kevin T.
Bush, Anna Markley
Bush, John R.
Bush, Robert A.
Bute, Daniel J.
Butera, Richard M.
Butler, David W.
Cacciatore, William T.
Cain, Daniel J.
Callis, Lance
Calvo, Larry A.
Camic, David E.
Campbell, David A.
Campbell, Michael I.
Campbell, Richard A.
Canel, James H.
Cannady, Thomas B.
Capron, Daniel F.
Carey, Jack
Carlson, Jon G.
Carlson, Ray M.
Carpenter, Robert T.
Carper, Nancy
Carr, Rex
Carroll, Brenda M.
Carroll, Gwen V.
Carroll, James J.
Carroll, Jane S.
Carroll, Timothy G.
Carter, Andrew M.
Casady-Trimble, Carolyn
Cass, Neil E.
Cassel, Jamie J. Swenson
Castaneda, John J.
Cates, Judy L.
Caulk, David A.
Chamberlin, Darcy J.
Chapman, Morris B.
Chapski, Robert A.

Chesley, George L.
Chill, Max
Chin, Davis
Christenson, Paul
Churchill, Daniel
Churchill, William A.
Cicero, Paul R.
Cirignani, Thomas R.
Clancy, Thomas A.
Clancy, Wendell W.
Clark, Gary L.
Clark, Robert H.
Clark, Stephen R.
Clark, William G., Jr.
Clayton, Fay
Clifford, Robert A.
Close, Henry J.
Cobb, Ronald W., Jr.
Coffel, Ron D.
Coffey, Gary R.
Coffield, Michael W.
Cogan, Michael P.
Cohen, Aaron
Cohen, Joseph E.
Cohen, Matthew D.
Cohen, Michael S.
Cohn, Frederick F.
Coladarci, Peter R.
Cole, Melvin J.
Cole, Paul R.
Coletta, Robert J.
Collander, Dan M.
Collins, George B.
Colombik, Richard M.
Colton, Kathleen
Conick, Harold W.
Connelly, Vincent J.
Connor, William C.
Constance, Michael B.
Conway, Kevin J.
Cook, Bruce N.
Cooley, John W.
Cooney, Robert J., Jr.
Cooper, Scott F.
Corboy, Philip Harnett, Jr.
Cornfield, Gilbert A.
Corsentino, Anthony P.
Corti, Peter D.
Coryell, James R.
Costello, Michael J.
Costello, Stephen J.
Cotiguala, Jac A.
Cotsirilos, George J.
Covey, Andrew W.
Covey, Charles E.
Cox, A. Clay
Cox, John W., Jr.
Crane, Eugene
Cronin, John J.
Cronin, Thomas G.
Crosby, Thomas F., III
Crowder, Barbara
Crowe, Brian L.
Cueto, Amiel
Cullen, George J.
Culver, Richard W.
Cunningham, Roscoe D.
Curcio, Joseph R.
Cusack, Daniel P.
Daley, Thomas M.
DaRosa, Ronald A.
Davenport, Linda E.
Davidson, Keith L.
Davidson, Mark S.
Davis, Larry
Davis, Michael J.
Davis, Muller
Davis, W. Keith
Day, Scott M.

De Jong, David J.
De Leon, John R.
Dean, Kenneth A.
DeArmond, Craig H.
DeCarlo, Vito D.
Decker, David A.
Decker, Thomas D.
DeDoncker, David
Dees, Richard L.
DeFranco, Leonard S.
Deitsch, Stephen M.
Delano, Charles H., III
Dembicki, Pauline G.
Demetrio, Michael K.
Demetrio, Thomas A.
Demos, James T.
Denny, Steven A.
Dentino, Michael P.
DeSanto, James J.
Devens, Charles J.
Dicker, Steven M.
Dickson, Fred H.
Dienes, Mary Ellen
DiMaggio, Debra A.
Dobben, Brian L.
Dobosz, Glen T.
Dolci, Dominick P.
Donahue, John F.
Donatelli, Mark R.
Donenfeld, J. Douglas
Donoghue, Lawrence M.
Donohue, James L.
Dorris, David V.
Douglas, Robert L.
Downs, Robert K.
Drendel, Gilbert X., Jr.
Drone, R. Michael
DuCanto, Joseph N.
Duffy, John M.
Duke, Patrick L.
Dukes, Carroll W.
Durkin, Kevin P.
Durkin, Thomas Anthony
Durree, Edward D.
Dutenhauer, Katheryn M.
Dutton, Janna S.
Dwyer, Edward W.
Eagle, Warren E.
Eaton, J. Timothy
Eberspacher, David Y.
Ebner, Deborah K.
Ecker, Lori D.
Ecklund, Gary L.
Edwards, Frank R.
Eglit, Howard C.
Ehrenreich, Richard F.
Eichner, Andrew D.
Einstein, Jean M.
Ekl, Terry A.
Elliott, Ivan A., Jr.
Elmore, James E.
Elsener, George M.
English, John D.
Enichen, Edward J.
Enloe, Douglas A.
Enright, Karen A.
Ephraim, Donald M.
Episcope, Paul B.
Epstein, Edna S.
Epstein, James R.
Erb, John C.
Erickson, Frederick P.
Erwin, Sam
Esposito, Kathleen C.
Esposito, Paul V.
Esrig, Jerry A.
Faber, William C., Jr.
Fairbanks, William J.
Falconer, Michael J.

Farina, James L.
Farrell, John A.
Farrell, John E.
Farrow, Mark R.
Favaro, Dennis R.
Fawell, Jeffrey B.
Feiertag, Terry Yale
Feinberg, Barry A.
Feinberg, Joy M.
Feiwell, George S.
Felch, Patricia A.
Feld, Edwin L.
Feldman, Howard W.
Feldman, James H.
Feldman, Lynne R.
Feldman, Mark I.
Felice, Richard D.
Ferguson, James R.
Ferguson, Mark E.
Ferracuti, Peter F.
Ferri, Richard H.
Field, Harold G.
Fields, Jane F.
Fieweger, Peter C.
Fifer, Samuel
Finkel, Leon I.
Finn, Newton E.
Finnegan, Frank R.
Fischer, Bella
Fisher, John W.
Fisher, Robert A.
Flaherty, Patrick M.
Flanagan, Leo M., Jr.
Flanders, Gary
Flanigan, Frank L.
Flanigan, Wayne B.
Flaxman, Kenneth D.
Fleck, Charles J.
Fleischer, Larry L.
Fleisher, Richard S.
Fleming, Michael A.
Fleming, Michael W.
Flood, James
Flynn, James R.
Flynn, Leonard T.
Flynn, Michael J.
Fombelle, Norman J.
Foote, Robert M.
Foran, Thomas A.
Ford, Christopher
Forde, Kevin M.
Foreman, Fred
Fortino, Susan R.
Foster, Chester H., Jr.
Fox, Barbara N.
Fox, Dennis R.
Fox, Leon
Fox, Robert J.
Frandsen, Roger K.
Frankel, Scott
Frankel, William H.
Frankland, David K.
Frazer, Quin R.
Frederick, Jeffrey D.
Fredrickson, Robert A.
Friedberg, Michael R.
Friedman, James J.
Friedman, James T.
Friedman, Linda D.
Friedman, Roselyn L.
Frischmeyer, Linda E.
Frisse, David M.
Frost, Michael J.
Fuller, Glenn O.
Gaber, Kathleen M.
Gabric, Ralph A.
Gadau, John E.
Gaertner, Kent A.
Gaffney, Glenn R.

Gaines, George L.
Galland, George F., Jr.
Galliani, William R.
Galvin, Frank J.
Garcia, Martha A.
Garrison, James T.
Garst, Steven L.
Gaubas, Robert D.
Gaziano, Mary J.
Gaziano, Paul E.
Gehlbach, Gary
Geiger, Donald H.
Geiler, Lorna K.
Geisler, Asher O.
Geisler, Gary F.
Gelman, Andrew R.
Geman, Kenneth Y.
Gensburg, Lane M.
Genson, Edward
Geraghty, Miriam
Gerber, Jacqueline M.
Germeraad, John H.
Gerske, Janet F.
Gertz, Theodore G.
Gesas, Michael L.
Geslewitz, Irving M.
Gesmer, James A.
Gesmer, Jason N.
Getzendanner, Susan
Gevirtz, Robert L.
Giacchetti, Cynthia
Giamanco, Paul D.
Gibson, Robert L.
Gibson, Scott B.
Gifford, Geoffrey L.
Giganti, Adam
Giganti, Francis J.
Gilbert, Howard E.
Gilfillan, Joseph P.
Gillespie, Terence P.
Giovannini, Dennis
Gitlin, H. Joseph
Gittler, Marvin
Given, Kenneth R.
Glass, Mark
Glassberg, Donald A.
Glenn, Ralph D.
Glenn, Robert J.
Glenn, Ronda B.
Glieberman, Herbert A.
Glimco, Joseph P., III
Glink, Martin
Goggin, Michael J.
Gold, Nan M.
Goldberg, Barry D.
Goldberg, Herbert
Goldberg, Jeffrey M.
Goldstein, Bernard
Goldstein, Louis S.
Goldstein, William M.
Gomric, James J.
Gonzalez, Richard
Good, Neil H.
Goodman, Bruce D.
Goodman, Lee H.
Gordon, Mark L.
Gordon, Stuart I.
Gore, Kenneth B.
Gorecki, Robert
Gorey, John J.
Gorman, H. Candace
Gorman, Mary P.
Gossage, Roza
Grach, Brian S.
Graham, Hugh J., III
Graham, James A.
Graham, William M.
Grandy, Laura K.
Granneman, Faye M.

Grant, Burton F.
Gray, Jonathan K.
Grebe, James R.
Green, Richard A.
Greenberg, Sharran R.
Greenberg, Steven A.
GreenLeaf, John L., Jr.
Greenlee, Cheri N.
Greenwald, Thomas E.
Greer, Daniel J.
Grimbau, Rochelle
Grimsley, Gregg N.
Grochocinski, David F.
Groshong, Donald E.
Grosso, J. Michael
Grounds, David K.
Groupe, Leonard M.
Grund, David I.
Guerard, Richard M.
Gurewitz, Thomas M.
Guth, Glenn J.
Guymon, David E.
Gzesh, Susan R.
Habiger, Richard J.
Haddad, Susan C.
Haddon, James T.
Hagen, Henry C.
Hagle, James J.
Hakeem, Ayesha S.
Haldeman, Richard R.
Hall, Charles C.
Hall, Robert C.
Hallagan, James E.
Halliday, Ronald E.
Hamilton, Robert E.
Hamm, Ronald L.
Hammer, Don C.
Hanagan, Michael J.
Hanagan, Steven F.
Hanagan, William D.
Hanna, Ronald
Hannigan, Richard D.
Hanno, Diana J.
Hanrahan, Donald J.
Hanrahan, Thomas P.
Hanson, David L.
Hanus, Richard
Hardy, Ralph C., Jr.
Harrington, Carol A.
Harris, Steven M.
Harrison, Louis S.
Harte, William J.
Hartmann, H. Michael
Hartsock, Allan
Harvey, Morris Lane
Haskin, Lyle B.
Haskins, Charles G., Jr.
Hassakis, Mark D.
Hasselberg, Eric E.
Hasselberg, Michael R.
Haughey, Roger E.
Hauser, Robert J.
Havrilesko, Michael K.
Hawkins, Robert J.
Healy, Bernard F., Jr.
Healy, Martin J., Jr.
Heavner, Richard L.
Hebeisen, Keith A.
Hedin, Craig R.
Hefner, M. John, Jr.
Hegarty, Terrence K.
Heiligenstein, C. E.
Heiple, Jeremy H.
Heller, Edward J.
Heller, Harlan
Heller, J. Brian
Heller, Stephen J.
Hellige, James R.
Hem, Ronald M.

Henbest, Barton L.
Henderson, Susan M.
Hendren, Paul C.
Hendricks, Scott P.
Henry, Kenneth A.
Henry, Thomas M.
Heriaud, Neal
Hess, Frederick J.
Hetherington, W. Joseph
Heyman, Glenn R.
Hierl, Michael A.
Higgins, Patricia M.
Higgs, David L.
Hilfman, Louis
Hirsch, John B.
Hirschfeld, John C.
Hodes, Scott D.
Hodge, Gerald K.
Hodge, Katherine D.
Hofeld, Albert F.
Hogan, Judy L.
Hogan Morrison, Kathleen
Holcomb, Barbara L.
Holley, Grady E.
Holloway, William J.
Holmes, Brent D.
Holzgrafe, Roger E.
Holzrichter, Linda M.
Hoogendoorn, Case
hooks, william h.
Hoover, Marsha K.
Hopkins, David H.
Hopp, Richard W.
Horberg, Kurt J.
Horn, Jerold I.
Horwood, Richard M.
Hoscheit, John J.
Houchen, Vernon H.
Howard, George C.
Howard, Timothy J.
Howard, William J.
Howerton, Robert H.
Hubbard, Elizabeth L.
Huck, James M.
Huck, Kevin J.
Huffman, John W.
Hughes, R. Courtney
Hunt, Mark B., Jr.
Hunt, Thomas C.
Hunter, Eugenia C.
Huntoon, H. Karl
Hupp, Robert B.
Hurley, Christopher T.
Hyman, Lawrence H.
Hyzer, Keith
Hyzer, Nancy
Ialongo, A. Mark
Indomenico, Sal
Jackman, Philip A.
Jacknewitz, Dennis J.
Jacobs, Alan
Jacobs, Allen F.
Jacobs, Jeff
Janssen, Jay H.
Jarvis, James S.
Jeep, Markham M.
Jennings, Harold M.
Jennings, Robert L.
Jensen, Philip F.
Jeske, John D.
Jiganti, John J.
Johnson, Don E.
Johnson, Dorothy B.
Johnson, Evan H.
Johnson, Gary V.
Johnson, James W.
Johnson, Raymond E.
Johnson, Thomas E.
Johnston, Jay J.

xiv

Jones, Gregory C.
Jones, Lance T.
Jones, Larry B.
Jones, Richard T.
Jones, Robert E.
Jones, W. Clyde, III
Jordan, Holly W.
Joseph, Jack
Joy, Richard M.
Jumes, Leon P.
Jutila, Gerald D.
Kadison, Steven J.
Kaergard, Kenneth L.
Kagan, Linda S.
Kagawa, Carlton M.
Kahan, Penny Nathan
Kahn, Bennett A.
Kahn, Donald W.
Kaiser, Daniel J.
Kalcheim, Michael W.
Kane, Larry R.
Kaplan, Henry S.
Kaplan, James L.
Kaplan, Melvin J.
Kaplan, Sidney M.
Karahalios, James N.
Karchmar, Larry
Karr, Robert W.
Katz, Bruce M.
Katz, Julie K.
Katz, Michael A.
Katz, Stephen H.
Kaufhold, Kevin C.
Kavensky, Craig L.
Kavensky, Harrison
Keefe, Thomas Q., Jr.
Keeling, James W.
Keith, John R.
Keller, K. Rick
Kelley, Randall W.
Kelly, E. Michael
Kelly, James D.
Kelly, John P.
Kelly, Roger H.
Kelly, Roger J.
Kelly, Timothy
Kempster, Donald
Kennelly, Matthew F.
Kesler, William R.
Kibler, Keith W.
Kilberg, Howard E.
Kilbride, Thomas L.
Kim, Ben H.
Kimnach, Richard A.
Kincaid, John B.
King, John P.
Kingery, Arthur
Kinnally, Patrick
Kinoy, Joanne
Kionka, Edward J.
Kirchner, Robert G.
Kirsh, Sanford
Kleinmuntz, Ira M.
Kling, Richard
Knight, Anne S.
Knippen, James H.
Knorr, Alfred L.
Knox, E. Phillips
Koenig, Philip E.
Kohen, Bruce M.
Kohn, William Irwin
Komie, Stephen M.
Kominsky, Robert
Konetski, James J.
Koonmen, Karl C.
Kopsick, Richard S.
Korein, Sandor
Korrub, Lawrence
Korstad, Dorothy C.

Kostelny, Marmarie J.
Koukios, Steven S.
Kouri, Stephen A.
Koutsky, Kenneth F.
Kowalczyk, Mark E.
Kralovec, John B.
Kralovec, Michael J.
Kramer, Henry E.
Kramer, Jack L.
Kraus, Grace M.
Krchak, David E.
Kreckman, Alfred H., Jr.
Kreitlow, Margaret
Kremin, David K.
Krengel, Ellen D.
Krentz, Paul G.
Kriezelman, Jeffrey A.
Krol, Gina B.
Kroll, Jeffrey J.
Kuczma, Linda A.
Kuhlman, Richard S.
Kuhn, Daniel L.
Kuhn, Richard W.
Kuleck, Edward J., Jr.
Kulwin, Shelly B.
Kulys, Margarita T.
Kunin, Joel A.
Kunkle, William J., Jr.
Kuppler, Karl B.
Kurowski, John J.
Kurz, Jerry B.
Kutsunis, Theodore G.
Lafer Abrahamson, Vicki
Laff, Charles A.
Lake, Steven R.
Lakernick, Harriette
Lakin, L. Thomas
Laks, Perry M.
LaMarca, William
Lambert, J. Laird
Lambert, Jerry
Lambert, Richard G.
Lamont, John M.
Lane, Fred
Lane, Stephen I.
Lansky, Marvin S.
Laraia, Joseph M.
Lasko, William E., II
Latherow, Jerry A.
Laukitis, Richard V.
Lauter, Richard S.
Lavin, Terrence J.
Lawless, J. Martin
Lawrence, Paul G.
Leahy, Mary Lee
Leahy, Tom
Leahy, W. Daniel
Leavitt, Marvin
LeChien, Thomas A.
Lee, Thomas J.
LeFevour, Terrence P.
Leff, Sherwin H.
Lefstein, Stuart R.
Lemon, Steven J.
Lengle, Philip J.
Leopold, Valerie A.
Lerner, Arthur M.
Lessman, Sarah P.
Lestikow, James M.
Levin, Jerome S.
Levin, Steven M.
Levine, Harold I.
Levine, Samuel H.
Levine, Sidney M.
Levine Levy, Elizabeth
Leving, Jeffery M.
Levo, Bonnie
Levy, David H.
Levy, Steven B.

Lewis, Kenneth S.
Lichter, Sally
Lied, Michael R.
Lierman, Joseph H.
Lietz, Gary R.
Lifshitz, Richard A.
Lindner, George P.
Lindstedt, Norman E.
Linklater, William J.
Linn, Craig M.
Lipton, Mark D.
Liss, Mark J.
Little, Thomas E.
Litwin, Stuart N.
Loats, J. Timothy
Locher, Bruce D.
Lockwood, Brocton D.
Logan, Michael J.
Loggans, Susan E.
London, Howard A.
Londrigan, Thomas F.
Lonergan, Susan M.
Longwell, Marilyn F.
Lorch, Kenneth F.
Lousberg, Peter H.
LoVallo, Michael A.
Loveless, R. Craig
Lowrey, John J.
Luby, Joseph K.
Lucco, J. William
Luchetti, Thomas D.
Lunardi, Steven B.
Lutz, Lonnie L.
Lyman, William D.
Lynch, David M.
Lynch, George J.
Lynch, George P.
MacKay, Karen K.
Maclean Snyder, Jean
MacRae, Roderick E.
Magee, James T.
Mager, T. Richard
Maggio, Frank P.
Magidson, Sherman C.
Maher, Edward M.
Maher, Jerelyn D.
Mahoney, Patrick E.
Mahoney, Terence J.
Malato, Stephen A.
Malkin, Earle A.
Mamer, Stuart M.
Manetti, Mark D.
Manion, Paul T.
Mann, Arthur L.
Mann, Richard E.
Mannix, Gerald J.
Mansfield, Thomas W.
Marcus, Dorene
Marcus, James I.
Margolis, Edward S.
Marifian, George E.
Marinaccio, Lee A.
Marino, Frank C.
Marks, Kenneth E.
Marsh, C. Stephen
Marsh, Roger A.
Marszalek, James J.
Marszalek, John E.
Martenson, David L.
Martin, John F.
Martin, Mary C.
Martin, Royal B.
Martin, William J.
Martinez, Francis M.
Marutzky, William F.
Mason, Mary Anne
Masur, W. Mark
Mathein, Veronica B.
Mathis, J. Michael

Mathis, Patrick B.
McAndrews, George P.
McCaleb, Malcolm, Jr.
McCarthy, D. Douglas
McCarthy, David H.
McCarthy, Edward T.
McCarthy, Kitty M.
McCarthy, Robert W.
McCarthy, Suzanne
McCormick, Margaret H.
McCue, Howard M., III
McCue, Judith W.
McCulloch, Thomas O.
McElvain, Mike
McGann-Ryan, Maureen J.
McGivern, Gerald
McGrath, William T.
McHugh, Timothy
McIntyre, Robert J.
McJoynt, Timothy
McKenzie, Robert E.
McKeown, Denis J.
McMillan, Bradley S.
McNamara, William B.
McNeely, Charles
McNish, Robert J., Jr.
McParland, James E.
McTavish, G. Alexander
McWilliams, Clare
Meachum, Bruce J.
Meachum, Clyde
Meczyk, Ralph E.
Meehan, Gerald J.
Meites, Thomas R.
Melber, Michael D.
Mellen, Thomas J., II
Menaker, Ronald D.
Mendelson, Michael S.
Mendenhall, Douglas R.
Mendillo, James R.
Mensch, Linda S.
Mescher, Gregory A.
Metnick, Michael B.
Metzger, Donald L.
Meyer, Lydia S.
Meyer, Michael J.
Meyers, Peter R.
Meyers, Ted A.
Meyers, William B.
Mielke, Craig S.
Mikva, Mary L.
Miller, Irving
Miller, Kenneth C.
Miller, Robin
Miller, Rochelle C.
Millon, Kevin H.
Minchella, Erica Crohn
Mindrup, Nancy H.
Miner, Judson H.
Minetz, Robert S.
Mirabella, Joseph F., Jr.
Mirabelli, Enrico J.
Miroballi, Joseph J.
Mirza, Jerome
Miselman, Michael D.
Misevich, Allyson
Mitchell, A. Ben
Mitchell, Bruce W.
Mitchell, Randall L.
Mitchell, Sam C.
Mitzner, Scott L.
Mollet, Chris J.
Molo, Steven F.
Moltz, Marshall J.
Monaco, Mark C.
Monahan, Joseph T.
Monco, Dean A.
Monco, Walter J.
Monico, Michael D.

Montroy, Gerald L.
Moore, Carl E., Jr.
Moore, Daniel M., Jr.
Moore, John G.
Moos, Patrick T.
Mooty, Brian D.
Moran, Katherine M.
Moran, Terence J.
Morelli, Fred M., Jr.
Morgan, Donna E.
Morgen, Perry
Morrison, John J.
Morrissey, Joseph A.
Morse, Keith S.
Mortimer, John
Moss, Thom W.
Motel, Robert
Motherway, Nicholas J.
Mott, Lorri
Mottaz, Steven N.
Motto, Patricia A.
Mozer, Stefan I.
Mudge, William A.
Mueller, William A.
Mullen, John C.
Mullen, Michael T.
Muller, Kurt A.
Mulryan, Rosemary
Munday, John J.
Murphy, G. Edward
Murphy, G. Patrick
Murphy, Sandra R.
Murphy, William C.
Murphy, William P.
Murray, James E.
Murtaugh, George J., Jr.
Musburger, Todd W.
Myler, Charles J.
Nack, Joseph E.
Nadler, Floyd N.
Nardulli, Steven
Narmont, John S.
Nash, Thomas
Natale, Bernard J.
Nathan, Thomas J.
Neighbour, Hubbard B.
Nelson, Richard F.
Nelson, Robert C.
Nelson, Steven L.
Neppl, James L.
Nepple, James A.
Nessler, Frederic W.
Neubauer, Terry J.
Neubauer, Timothy R.
Neville, Ronald F.
Newquist, Elaine T.
Nicoara, John P.
Niro, Cheryl I.
Niro, William L.
Nitikman, Franklin W.
Noble, Kent A.
Noe, Robert J.
Nolan, Donald J.
Nolan, Francis A.
Nolan, Nan R.
Noll, Jon
Nolte, Peter B.
Nottage, Rosaire
Novak, Anthony E.
Novoselsky, David A.
Nowak, Michael K.
O'Brien, Daniel R.
O'Brien, Timothy M.
O'Connor, John
O'Day, Daniel G.
O'Donnell, Terry
O'Neal Johnson, Susan
O'Neill, Treva H.
Oberhardt, William P.

Ogar, Helen E.
Ohlander, Jan H.
Oliver, Robert J.
Olsen, Joseph D.
Oney, Claudia
Opferman, Thomas G.
Ores, Nicholas H.
Ory, Christine
Osborne, Stephen M.
Ostrow, Joel S.
Otis, Lorri E.
Otto, John H.
Owen, Robert M.
Owens, John E., Jr.
Ozmon, Laird M.
Ozmon, Nat P.
Page, Robin A.
Palmer, Charles L.
Palmieri, Vincent L.
Panichi, William T.
Panter, Michael R.
Pappas, James
Parker, Drew
Parker, Julie
Parkhurst, Todd S.
Pasquesi, Theodore A.
Passen, Stephen M.
Pasulka, David P.
Patke, Marshall P.
Patterson, Robert B.
Pautsch, Charles W.
Pavalon, Eugene
Pavia, Joseph D.
Pavich, Robert J.
Pawlan, Mitchell D.
Pearl, Howard M.
Peck, Kerry R.
Peel, Gary E.
Peithmann, William A.
Pekala, Beverly A.
Pelton, Russell
Penn, Thomas J., Jr.
Peregrine, Michael W.
Perlis, Steven C.
Perrecone, Frank A.
Perrone, Mathew, Jr.
Peskind, Steven N.
Peters, Donald F., Jr.
Peters, Kenneth D.
Petro, Nerino J., Jr.
Pfaff, Bruce R.
Phares, William T.
Phebus, Joseph W.
Phillips, John G.
Phillips, Stephen D.
Phipps, John T.
Picl, Frank M.
Pietsch, Leigh R.
Pike, Harold K., III
Pincham, R. Eugene
Pinelli, Anthony
Piper, John A.
Pisoni, Jeanine M.
Platt, L. Steven
Polisky, Joel S.
Postilion, Michael H.
Potter, James R.
Potter, Robin B.
Poulos, Michael D.
Powell, W. Thomas
Power, Joseph A., Jr.
Powers, Michael E.
Prendergast, Richard J.
Presbrey, Kim E.
Presney, Paul E., Jr.
Pretnar, Alan
Prillaman, Roger L.
Prillaman, Terry S., Jr.
Primack, Ronald N.

Prince, Mark D.
Pritikin, James B.
Proctor, Janet C.
Provenza, James C.
Provenzano, William J.
Pryor, William A.
Puchalski, Donald E.
Puchalski, Richard J.
Pusey, John R.
Quigg, Leo W., Jr.
Raccuglia, Anthony C.
Radley, David B.
Rafool, Gary T.
Raleigh, Thomas
Ralph, Michael L.
Randle, Craig A.
Rantis, Nicholas S.
Rapoport, David E.
Rath, William W.
Rathsack, Michael W.
Ravitz, Gary J.
Rawles, Edward H.
Ray, Loraine A.
Raymond, E. James
Reagan, Michael J.
Reda, Edward E., Jr.
Redfield, John H.
Reed, Daniel A.
Reed, Gerald S.
Reed, John A.
Reed, Mike
Reese, Randall K.
Reid, William D.
Reidy, Daniel E.
Renzi, Constance J.
Resch, Marilyn B.
Resnick, Kalman D.
Reuland, Timothy J.
Rice, Stephen R.
Rice, T. Patrick
Rich, Thomas C.
Richards, G. William
Richards, Van R., Jr.
Richardson, Jeffrey D.
Richter, Harold
Richter, Kevin J.
Riebman, Hyman
Rikli, Donald C.
Rimland, Jack P.
Rinella, Bernard B.
Ripplinger, George R.
Ritt, Norbert C.
Ritz, Kenneth F.
Rivkin-Carothers, Anita
Robbins, Elliott H.
Roberts, Douglas R.
Roberts, J. William
Roberts, Keith E., Jr.
Roberts, Robert H.
Robertson, John W.
Robeson, J. Jay
Robin, Neil A.
Robinson, Jon D.
Roddy, Joseph V.
Rodes, Theodore, Jr.
Rodin, Curt N.
Rogers, Jeffrey E.
Rogers, Larry R., Sr.
Rogich, Richard B.
Rolewick, David F.
Rose, Mark A.
Rose, Raymond
Roseborough, Kathleen
Rosenberg, Herbert B.
Rosenberg, Russell S.
Rosenberg, Steven J.
Rosenfeld, Howard H.
Rosing, William G.
Ross, Gilbert J.

Ross, Jay B.
Ross-Shannon, Bruce
Roth, Robert R.
Rothman, Joel S.
Rothschild, Donald S.
Rotman, Michael H.
Rouhandeh, Mary Lou
Rovner, Jack A.
Rowder, William
Rubens, James L.
Rubin, Arnold G.
Rubman, David
Rudasill, Mary C.
Ruddy, C. John
Rudy, Sharon R.
Rumsey, Richard L.
Russo, Richard D.
Ruud, Glenn F.
Ryan, Catherine M.
Ryan, David J.
Ryan, Michael D.
Ryan, Richard P.
Ryan, Roger E.
Ryan, Stephen R.
Saavedra, Carlos A.
Sachs, Leonard W.
Sadowski, Ronald W.
Sahlstrom, R. Craig
Saint, Gale W.
Saltzberg, Gerald B.
Salvi, Albert J.
Salvi, Patrick A.
Salzetta, Paul L.
Samson, Donald M.
Samuels, Elliott M.
Samuelson, Joseph L.
Sanderman, Arthur P.
Savaiano, Anthony A.
Scanlan, Edmund J.
Schaffner, Harry
Schaffner, Howard S.
Schanlaber, William C.
Schick, William G.
Schiever, Carey J.
Schiff, Matthew B.
Schiller, Donald C.
Schiller, Richard D.
Schillerstrom, Robert J.
Schindel, Donald M.
Schirmer, Robin L.
Schlack, David A.
Schlesinger, Gary L.
Schneider, Gregg D.
Schrager, Leonard J.
Schroeder, Carl F.
Schuman, Joseph
Schur, Jerome
Schwartz, Allen N.
Schwartz, John B.
Schwarz, Benedict, II
Scott, Daniel P.
Scott, Gregory A.
Scott, Lisa
Scott, R. Stephen
Scott, William J., Jr.
Scovil, Douglas C.
Segal, Alan F.
Seigler, Darrell K.
Seliger, Stephen G.
Selin, Paul E.
Sgro, Gregory P.
Shadid, James E.
Shancer, Jeffrey M.
Shapiro, Jay M.
Sharp, John P.
Sharp, Terrell Lee
Shaw, Matthew G.
Shawler, Omer T.
Shayne, David

Sheehan, Patrick J.
Sheehan, William J.
Sheffler, Stephen K.
Sheppard, Barry D.
Sherman, Barbara
Shevlin, Gregory L.
Shovlain, Peter T.
Siebert, William Newell
Siegal, Barry P.
Siegel, Carole
Sigman, Helen
Silkwood, Larry R.
Silverman, Brian C.
Simon, Arthur G.
Simonian, Stephen M.
Sinars, Theodore A.
Skelnik, Josette
Skelton, Steven B.
Skipper, Robert
Sklarsky, Charles B.
Sklodowski, Robert
Slemer, Ronald R.
Slevin, John A.
Sloan, Mel
Slover, John A., Jr.
Slutsky, Mark G.
Smeeton, Jack C.
Smirl, Dale L.
Smith, Barbara W.
Smith, L. Lee
Smith, Robert S., Jr.
Smith, S. Craig
Smith, Timothy O.
Smith, Todd A.
Smith, Webb H.
Smith Anderson, Claudia
Smoot, Carolyn B.
Smythe, Terry J.
Solls, Joseph J.
Solon, Joseph
Solotorovsky, Julian
Somers, Kathryn M.
Soroka, Walter
Sorosky, Sheldon M.
Soskin, Rollin J.
Sostrin, Ellis M.
Spadoro, Mark A.
Sparkman, James D.
Spector, Barry A.
Speers, Robert L.
Spelman, James C.
Speroni, John
Spinak, Michael D.
Stanko, Glenn A.
Stark, Blooma
Statland, Donald A.
Stein, Arnold
Stein, David M.
Stein, Edward I.
Stein, Steven G.
Steinback, Jeffrey B.
Steinke, Edward B.
Stelle, Lori J.
Stephens, G. Douglas
Stephenson, Robert M.
Sterling, Harry J.
Stern, Gregory K.
Stetler, David J.
Stevens, James E.
Stine, Robert E.
Stogsdill, William J., Jr.
Stojan, Clark J.
Stone, Howard L.
Stone, Jed
Stone, Jeffrey E.

Stowell, Mary
Strange, Jeffrey
Straub, Marcia
Streicker, James R.
Streit, Thomas J.
Strodel, Robert C.
Strom, Neal B.
Strongin, Stuart J.
Stuart, Robert A., Jr.
Stubblefield, Timothy C.
Stumpe, Karen M.
Sturm, Timothy
Sugar, Richard A.
Sullivan, Donald P.
Sullivan, James R.
Sullivan, Peter T.
Sullivan, Terry
Sullivan, Thomas E.
Sullivan, Thomas P.
Summers, Holten D.
Susler, Marshall A.
Sussman, Jeffrey B.
Sutkowski, Edward F.
Sutterfield, David W.
Swartz, John L.
Swee, Jean A.
Switzer, Peter S.
Szesny, Henry C.
Tagge, Stephen A.
Talbot, Earl A.
Tallis, Jeffrey J.
Tapia-Ruano, Carlina
Taradash, Randall M.
Taren, Jeffrey L.
Tarun, Robert W.
Tatnall, Susan B.
Taylor, Jeffrey C.
Taylor, John C.
Tchen, Christina M.
Tecson, Andrew P.
Telander, Brian F.
Tenzer, Steven J.
Tepper, Michael
Terlizzi, Eric L.
Thayer, Steven J.
Theis, John T.
Thomas, David
Thomas, Henry I.
Thomas, Lott H.
Thomas, Mark Jacob
Thompson, Charles F., Jr.
Thorstenson, Craig R.
Tietz, Christopher M.
Tighe, Ann C.
Tighe, Mary Beth S.
Tillery, Stephen M.
Timoney, Patrick T.
Tinaglia, Michael L.
Tinney, Sarah B.
Toback, Alan J.
Tobin, Craig D.
Toner, Hugh F., III
Touhy, Timothy J.
Tracy, Keith M.
Trafelet, Janet
Trapp, James M.
Trentman, Brian K.
Trevino, Fern Niehuss
Trone, D. Kent
Truemper, William J.
Truitt, John R.
Tueth, James E.
Tuite, Gregory E.
Tuite, Patrick A.
Tulin, Ronald

Tully, Thomas M.
Turner, Harold L.
Turner, Mercer
Turner, Ralph T.
Turow, Scott
Tyrrell, Ross
Tyrrell, Thomas J.
Underhill, Frederick H., Jr.
Urban, Tod M.
Urdangen, Jeffrey
Valukas, Anton R.
Van Der Kamp, Roy W.
Van Der Snick, J. Brick
Van Winkle, Theodore
VanDemark, Ruth E.
VanHooreweghe, Francis R.
Vassen, John J.
Vella, Frank P., Jr.
Veltman, R. Edward
Veon, Leslie L.
Verity, Duane P.
Vickrey, Paul K.
Vieira, Michelle
Vigneri, Joseph W.
Vincent, James B.
Viverito, Lou J.
Voiland, Joseph R.
von Mandel, Michael J.
Vosicky, Joseph F., Jr.
Wadington, Robert N.
Wagner, Irvin J.
Wagner, Paul A.
Walker, James G.
Wall, Bernard T.
Walsh, Carl M.
Walsh, Edward J., Jr.
Walsh, Michael D.
Walther, M. Jacqueline
Walvoord, David J.
Warnecke, Michael O.
Warner, Michael J.
Washkuhn, Wilson C.
Wasko, Steven E.
Wasser, Stanley N.
Wasserman, Laurie J.
Waters, M. Michael
Watschke, David R.
Webb, Dan K.
Webber, Carl M.
Weihl, Donald E.
Weiler, Daniel A.
Weiler, Rory T.
Weilmuenster, J. Michael
Weinsheimer, William C.
Weinstein, Melvin A.
Weintraub, Alan I.
Weisman, Joel D.
Weissberg, Ariel
Weith, Glenna J.
Welch, David K.
Welch, Kay A.
Welch, Lyman W.
Wells, Robert E., Jr.
Wessels, Richard H.
West, Richard T.
Westensee, John H.
Wexler, Leon C.
Wham, Fred L., III
Wham, James B.
White, Francine B.
White, Richard E.
White, Roger A.
Whitmire, James E., Jr.
Whittington, Rebecca A.
Wilcox, Barbara L.

Will, Robert P., Jr.
Williams, Daniel T., Jr.
Williams, Guy E.
Williams, Jeffrey
Williams, Michael A.
Williams, Robert E.
Williams, Tamalou M.
Williamson, Carol A.
Willis, Standish E.
Willoughby, Stephen O.
Wilson, Clarence S., Jr.
Wilson, Michael J.
Wilson, Peter K., Jr.
Wilson, Susan P.
Wimmer, John R.
Windham, Danny L.
Winget, Walter W.
Winkler, Charles R.
Winkler, Karl F.
Winstein, Arthur R.
Winstein, Stewart R.
Winter, Arthur
Winter, Bernard R.
Winter-Black, Janett S.
Wirth, Andrea
Wishnick, Neal K.
Witcoff, David L.
Wittenberg, David M.
Wittenberg, Michael P.
Wognum, James P.
Wojtecki, Leonard J.
Wolf, Ilene M.
Wolf, Thomas J., Jr.
Wolf-Friestedt, Betsy J.
Wolff, Dale F.
Wolgamot, John P.
Womick, John
Wong, Betsy P.
Wood, George C.
Woodcock, George W.
Woodruff, Casey
Yavitz, David B.
York, Mary M.
Zaideman, Robert J.
Zaluda, Jeffrey A.
Zavett, Errol
Zazove, Neal C.
Zeit, Daniel R.
Zimmerman, Robert J.
Zimmerman, Steven P.
Zopf, Michael J.
Zuckerman, Richard Wayne
Zulkie, Paul L.

*Allen, Frederick
*Crowe, Robert W.
§Everhart, Millard S.
ΔHelm, Steven N.
*Keefe, Thomas Q., Sr.
+Leavitt, Marvin
+Mueller, Thomas E.
†Niemann, Ronald, A.
+O'Brien, Gregory M.
§Parsons, Richard H.
†Sargis, David R.
*Saunders, Joanne H.
+Sheen, Terence M.
+Shields, Karen G.
+Stewart, Bruce D.
§Tassef, George

Indicates retired
† Indicates deceased
+ Indicates judicial appointment
§ Indicates state's attorney or public defender
Δ Moved out of state

xvii

USING THE CONSUMER LAW GUIDEBOOK

The *Leading Illinois Attorneys Consumer Law Guidebook*'s first six chapters discuss general legal topics, including How to Hire an Attorney, Illinois' Judicial Systems, and Process of a Lawsuit: Civil & Criminal. Chapters 7 through 26 cover specific areas of law and include listings and biographical profiles of Leading Illinois Attorneys who practice in each area. The *Guidebook* concludes with five appendices and three indices for further information and cross-referencing. In addition to other helpful information, the *Guidebook* appendices and indices include pertinent legal and community resources, a glossary of legal terms and phrases, firm profiles, an attorney "extensive experience index," a profiled attorneys index and a subject matter index.

If the services of an attorney are necessary, we advise that you review the biographical profiles at the end of each chapter to identify attorneys whose areas of experience match your need. The following is a guide to the format of biographical profiles:

Shaded area indicates region in which an attorney's office is located.

Because many attorneys practice in multiple areas of law, the short "See Also" listings are of attorneys who practice in the specific areas but whose full biographical profiles appear in other chapters of the Guidebook.

Bullet (•) indicates attorney was nominated in this specific area of law.

STEPHEN Z. ERGAN - *Ergan Roberts & Wilson* - 221 North First Street - Anytown, US 55454 - Phone: (111) 343-8989, Fax: (111) 343-8023 - *See complete biographical profile in Elder Law Chapter, page 127.*

•**ROBERT T. GANNON** - *Marx & Thomas* - 3000 Norwest Center - Anytown, US 55454 - Phone: (111) 554-8809, Fax: (111) 544-8097 - *See complete biographical profile in Adoption Law Chapter, page 89.*

Practice profile describes the attorney's practice and experience.

These sections provide insight into the attorney's background and interests.

Information about the attorney's firm provides insight into resources the attorney can draw upon.

• **SUSAN T. JOERG:** Susan Joerg practices primarily family law, concentrating in all aspects of matrimonial law. She has successfully represented individual clients in issues arising out of divorce and legal separation proceedings, spousal maintenance, child support, child custody and visitation, domestic and child abuse, antenuptial agreements, paternity and third party child custody proceedings. Emanating from her focus on child custody, Ms. Joerg has also developed a significant practice representing mental health professionals in disputes with their respective state licensing boards.
Education: JD 1980, DePaul University; BA 1976, Smith College.
Admitted: 1978 Illinois; 1979 U.S. Dist. Ct. (N. Dist. IL).
Employment History: 1991-present, Masters & Joerg; Partner 1987-90, Mey, Alling & Killman; Sole Practitioner 1981-87; Attorney 1980-81, Anytown City Attorney's Office.
Representative Clients: Family and Children Social Services; Catholic Charities; City of Lakes Mental Health Center; Newton Extended Care, Inc.
Professional Associations: American Academy of Matrimonial Lawyers; ABA; ISBA [Family Law Section; (Family Law Rules Committee, Chair)]; McHenry County Bar Assn. (Family Law Section); Illinois Assn. for Women Lawyers.
Community Involvement: United Board of Directors 1990-present; Anystate Dept. of Human Services Committee 1989-93; YWCA (Board of Directors 1987-present).
Firm: Formed in January 1991, Masters & Joerg brings to the community unique knowledge and varied experience in all areas of family and children issues. The firm has over 25 years' combined experience representing clients in matters of marriage dissolution, custody, adoption, delinquency, paternity, appeals, and personal estate planning. The firm strengthens its commitment to the community through active participation in bar activities, teaching, and speaking at public forums and seminars. *Ms. Joerg also practices Arts, Entertainment & Intellectual Property Law.*

SUSAN T. JOERG

Masters & Joerg
400 Fourth Avenue North
Suite 230
Anytown, US 55415

Phone: (111) 555-2220
Fax: (111) 555-2244

Extensive Experience In:
• Custody
• Grandparents Visitation
• Paternity Issues

Quick reference information, cross-referenced in specialized index.

xviii

CHAPTER

1

HOW TO HIRE AN ATTORNEY

Perhaps the first question many readers of this book will have is, "Do I have a legal claim?" Our legal system provides a number of remedies for people who have been injured, but the legal system limits the kinds of cases it addresses. Not everyone who has been injured by someone has a legal case. Although one may be harmed by another, many factors must be present to assert a legal claim.

The next question may be, "Do I need a lawyer to handle my legal claim?" The shortest answer is "no," an individual has the right to represent himself or herself in court in any type of case, but as an old saying goes, "He who represents himself has a fool for a client." Simply put, our legal system can be too complex and specialized for the average layperson to represent himself or herself effectively. Even a lawyer may be unable to handle a particular legal question as most lawyers specialize in a narrow area of practice rather than attempt to master all areas of law. In anything other than the simplest of matters, it is advisable for an individual to seek the consultation of and be represented by an attorney competent in the particular area of law in which the legal claim arises.

Given that each year so many people need to employ lawyers, it is surprising how few consumers make informed choices when selecting legal services. Many consumers find lawyers intimidating, so they fail to use the same common sense in selecting a lawyer as they would use in making any other major consumer purchase. As a result, they often make inappropriate choices and end up confused and unhappy. Given the importance of the issues our society trusts lawyers to handle and the amount of money spent on their services, consumers have a right to be satisfied with the representation they receive.

No one should fall into the trap of believing the tired old saying that, "lawyers are all alike." Lawyers are not all alike. Every lawyer must have a four-year college degree before being admitted to law school. However, the degree can be in any area, so a particular lawyer might have a degree in English, accounting, biology, or any other academic subject. In law school, students study many required subjects but they also have the opportunity to study areas of special interest, such as environmental law, family law, or tax law. After law school, law students must pass a state bar exam to practice law in that state. The United States is broken down into many different systems of courts, known as bars. Each bar sets its own requirements for lawyers who practice there. A lawyer who is not a member of the Illinois bar cannot practice law in Illinois absent special permission. Bars may also have special categories of lawyers who are certified to practice in a particular area.

The consumer who exercises care in choosing a lawyer intelligently can be satisfied because there is a right way to choose legal services and it does make a difference. The following three-step process can help the consumer find the right attorney for his or her particular legal needs.

STEP 1: PREPARING A LIST

The first step any consumer faces in choosing a lawyer is generating a list of potential prospects. This is usually an easy step. There are thousands of lawyers in Illinois alone, and most people know of at least one lawyer to whom they could refer someone. The quality of referrals can vary greatly, however, depending on the source.

ADVERTISING

Ever since the United States Supreme Court lifted the ban on attorney advertising, there has been an explosion in the amount of print and broadcast advertising done by the thousands of Illinois lawyers eager to reach new clients. However, not all forms of lawyer advertising are permitted. For example, a lawyer is never allowed to solicit business from an accident victim in the hospital unless specifically invited there by the victim. But while some forms of advertising are banned, the range of permissible forms of advertising is quite broad and can include some fairly outlandish forms of self-promotion.

Given the amount of advertising that is done by lawyers, the average consumer could easily rattle off the names of at least a few lawyers who practice in his or her community. The trouble, of course, is that the best known attorneys are not necessarily the best practitioners of their profession. While it may be easiest to look up the section on attorneys in the phone book or call a telephone number broadcasted on radio or television, it often pays to use other sources of information such as the *Martindale-Hubbell Law Directory,* a list of many attorneys in the United States, or the book, *The Best Lawyers in America,* which is published annually. A local bar association may be another source of names. And of course, it is hoped that this book, *Leading Illinois Attorneys Consumer Law Guidebook,* will be of great use in helping consumers find competent, peer-referred attorneys to handle their legal affairs. Consulting one or more of the lawyers listed at the end of the chapters is an excellent way to start the search for a good lawyer.

PERSONAL REFERRALS

Another good source of attorney names is personal referrals. Friends and relatives are often able to recommend a lawyer. Business associates may also be a good source of names. A trusted accountant, insurance agent, or employer might also be able to recommend a competent lawyer. The benefit of a recommendation from a business associate is that, unlike a recommendation from a friend or relative, accountants, insurance agents, and employers regularly consult with attorneys on a broad variety of issues and may be in a better position to steer the consumer toward the best lawyer for his or her needs.

Regardless of who recommends a name, ask specific questions about the lawyer. How does the person know the lawyer? Has the person ever consulted the lawyer? If so, for what reason? What are the lawyer's strengths and weaknesses? Does he or she return phone calls promptly and keep the client informed of the process of the case? What outcome was the lawyer able to get? Is the lawyer a member of the Illinois State Bar Association? A referral that seems promising at first may not help much if it turns out that the lawyer practices a different area of law, the lawyer is not a member of the Illinois bar, or if the person recommending the lawyer knows very little about him or her.

REFERRAL SERVICES

A consumer who would be more comfortable talking with someone who shares a similar background should not hesitate to seek out such an attorney. Some women may turn to other women to handle their legal affairs because they believe that another woman may better empathize with the unique legal problems women face. A person of color might prefer to give business to another person of color, or someone in the gay and lesbian community might believe that a person from their community can best represent their interests. Law schools have made tremendous strides in recruiting more diverse student bodies in the past two decades and consequently, the ranks of lawyers today have swelled with competent practitioners of every race, gender, ethnicity, and lifestyle. In order to make the legal community more responsive to our changing society, several organizations have sprung up in Illinois that refer consumers to lawyers sensitive to the needs of women, Hispanic-Americans, African-Americans, Asian-Americans, gays, lesbians, and others. A consumer who would feel more comfortable hiring a lawyer from a particular background should not hesitate to seek out names from one of these special referral organizations. Most of these organizations have no fee associated with their services or their fees are paid by the lawyer, not the consumer. The Legal Resources and Community Resources Appendices of this *Guidebook* contain information and telephone numbers for several of these organizations.

Once the consumer has a list of a few potential lawyers it is time to think about the next step—researching the attorneys on the list.

STEP 2: RESEARCHING THE ATTORNEYS ON THE LIST

Once a consumer has gathered the names of a number of possible attorneys, there are many issues to consider. Some questions can be answered by a quick phone call to the lawyer's office but others can only be answered by talking to other consumers. Some of the more important issues to research about the lawyers on the list include the items below.

REPUTATION

An attorney's reputation for technical skill is important, but only the individual can determine its relevance to a particular legal matter. Consider that a lawyer who has built a sterling reputation for his or her competent handling of complex litigated probate disputes may be overqualified to draft a simple will. Similarly, a lawyer whose head is full of knowledge gained from representing large corporations may need to start researching from scratch if asked to represent an individual. Savvy individuals with a variety of legal concerns often employ different lawyers to work on different matters because they realize no lawyer can be all things to all people, for every type of legal question. Certainly, if a case involves a lot of money or if personal freedom is at stake, as is the case when someone is accused of a felony and risks being sent to prison, then the consumer wants to find the very best attorney there is to handle the matter. For more routine matters, where smaller dollar amounts are at stake, a less experienced lawyer may actually be a better fit as well as more affordable.

As important as a lawyer's technical reputation is, his or her ethical reputation may be even more important. It pays to ask around about a lawyer's ethical reputation, for a lawyer's reputation is well known among other professionals. To find out about an attorney's reputation, one should ask others with similar needs or problems for references—perhaps someone who has gone through a similar situation. Lawyers should be willing to provide references or a list of past clients whom the prospective client can contact. Beware of lawyers with poor ethical reputations. The State of Illinois maintains the Attorney Registration and Disciplinary Commission, with locations in both Chicago and Springfield. The commission investigates charges of unethical conduct against attorneys and may seek disciplinary action against attorneys. Potential clients may contact the commission to inquire into an attorney's disciplinary history. A lawyer who does not follow the rules of his or her own profession may not handle your case properly either. To contact the Attorney Registration and Disciplinary Commission in Chicago, call (312) 565-2600 or (800) 826-8625. In Springfield, call (217) 522-6838 or (800) 252-8048.

Despite the considerable criticism they get in the media, lawyers are held to very high ethical standards. For every example of misconduct reported in the media, there are literally thousands of honest and reputable attorneys that will do the right and ethical thing. Putting effort into choosing a lawyer can go a long way towards eliminating the risk of retaining an unethical attorney.

SPECIALIZATION

Following trends in other professions, many lawyers today devote themselves to one area of law and present themselves as "experts" or "specialists" in that area. Because it is wise to get an attorney whose experience matches a consumer's particular need, many consumers will be tempted to hire a lawyer described as an expert or specialist in his or her area of law. Illinois does not certify legal specialists. In communicating fields of practice, references to such terms require the disclaimer: "The Supreme Court of Illinois does not recognize certifications of specialties in the practice of law and that the certificate, award or recognition is not a requirement to practice law in Illinois" (Illinois Supreme Court Rules of Professional Conduct).

In addition, it is wise to be aware that one attorney may call herself a tax expert because she has handled tax matters for over twenty years, while another attorney may call himself a tax expert because, although he only passed the bar last month and is still quite inexperienced, he plans to devote himself exclusively to tax matters. Clearly one expert is not equal to another. Buyer beware!

Another important point to keep in mind is that not all legal matters require the attention of a "specialist." Just as one would not automatically turn to a medical specialist for a common cold, one need not turn to a legal specialist for every routine legal matter. Chances are good that if a local attorney engaged in the general practice of law has done a fine job on a variety of legal matters in the past, he or she can be counted on to handle routine legal matters in the future. Also, because most specialists will be clustered in larger cities, a consumer in a small community may choose to hire a generalist practicing locally for the ease and convenience of being able to work with a member of the community.

FIRM SIZE

Another important issue to consider is whether to choose a solo practitioner, a lawyer in a small firm, or a lawyer in a large firm. Recognize that in most cases it is an individual attorney who will work on a particular file and with whom the client will have the most interaction. An individual may not immediately notice a difference between a solo practitioner, a lawyer at a small firm, and a lawyer at a large firm. A solo practitioner or a lawyer practicing in a small group may be able to provide more personalized attention to a file but a larger firm can bring a depth of resources that most small firms cannot. Lawyers at large firms typically charge more for their services, however, so an individual may not want or need to pay extra for a relatively straightforward legal problem. Again, it all depends on the needs of the particular individual.

LOCATION

A lawyer's location is another obvious consideration. A lawyer in the client's hometown may not always be the best choice. If many meetings will take place in a city other than where the client lives, it may be advantageous to hire an attorney who lives in the other city. Most larger firms in Illinois are centrally located in downtown office buildings in major cities. While these locations may provide the most convenient access to courthouses, banks, and corporate headquarters, they may not be the most convenient for the individual client. Most lawyers charge for transportation time and the time necessary for them to get to and from meetings and court appearances, so it may be wise to choose someone located near the courthouse or any other location where meetings will take place. If a particular matter will not require many meetings or trips to the courthouse, the convenience of a downtown office may be unnecessary. Of course, because nice office space downtown is usually more expensive than office space in a suburb or small town, downtown lawyers may have higher overhead expenses that they pass along to their clients.

STEP 3: INTERVIEWING THE ATTORNEYS

Once an individual has narrowed down his or her list to a few attorneys, he or she should then phone them individually and seek a personal consultation with each one. It is wise to ask on the phone whether the lawyer charges a fee for the initial consultation. As with any major consumer purchase, a consumer of legal services is not obligated to hire the first attorney he or she sees.

INITIAL CONSULTATION

It is not reasonable for a consumer to expect free advice from a lawyer, though top-notch attorneys will welcome opportunities to spend time with potential clients answering questions and being compared with their peers because they know their knowledge and experience will show through.

An initial consultation can be more productive if the individual takes contracts, photographs, other relevant documents, and a list of questions to the meeting. At the initial interview the individual should be open and honest with the attorney. It is best not to embellish or hide facts because they may dilute the strength of a case. Some facts, such as the events in a dispute occurring some time ago, may make a case impossible to win because of the statute of limitations, and the lawyer can explain that any money spent pursuing the claim would be money wasted. Some facts are less damaging than the individual assumes, and the lawyer can minimize their effect by acting quickly. The attorney may feel that a conflict of interest prevents him or her from representing the client. For example, the lawyer may already represent the opposite party in a dispute. Most of what an individual tells a lawyer in an interview is confidential and protected by the attorney-client privilege.

Consulting a lawyer does not obligate the consumer to employ or to retain that lawyer. Most initial consultations are either free of charge or available for a nominal fee, especially if the consumer decides not to employ the attorney consulted. Some attorneys will charge for the initial consultation if they are subsequently hired.

It is important to note an important distinction between consulting an attorney and retaining that attorney. Only retaining an attorney obligates him or her to act on behalf of the client. Many Illinois residents have learned this lesson the hard way, thinking that consulting a lawyer about their legal problem meant that their case was being handled, so they stopped taking steps to pursue a claim. Meanwhile the lawyer they consulted allowed the statute of limitations to run out on the claim because the lawyer believed that he or she had not been retained to act on the client's behalf. Many legal malpractice suits have centered on whether an original office visit with a lawyer constituted a consultation or a hiring. The lesson to learn is that before leaving a lawyer's office, the individual and the lawyer should be absolutely clear as to whether the lawyer has or has not been hired.

PERSONAL CHEMISTRY

So much of being a good attorney has to do with responsiveness, understanding of a client's particular situation, and the ability to communicate. The lawyer who has bad rapport with a client may not be an effective representative of the client's interests. Because each person is different, the chemistry between a client and an attorney is one of the most important elements of their relationship. Smart shoppers should ask many questions. Does the lawyer listen to the client's story or does he interrupt in the middle of sentences? Does she present a variety of options to pursue or does she insist there is only one right way to do everything? Does the lawyer try to dominate the conversation? Is this someone the client wants to spend time with? Gut feelings at this stage of the process can tell someone much about what it would be like to hire this person.

MALPRACTICE INSURANCE

It may be an uncomfortable subject to raise with an attorney whom one has just met, but it is important to determine whether the attorney carries malpractice insurance. The financial losses stemming from a poorly handled case can be quite large. If the lawyer does not carry malpractice insurance, it may be impossible to recover any losses if the lawyer commits legal malpractice.

EXPERIENCE

Many individuals naïvely assume that the longer a lawyer has been in practice the more experience he or she has. This assumption is frequently unfounded. Relevant experience in a particular area of law is far more important than the total number of years that a person has practiced law. A young attorney whose practice has been narrowly focused on one area of law may have far more insight into how a problem should be handled than an attorney with more years of practice in a broad variety of legal matters. In addition, because laws change so quickly, in some cases, a recent graduate may have greater knowledge of a particular area of law than a more senior attorney. The consumer should ask pointed questions about a lawyer's specific experience handling similar cases.

In some large firms, a senior partner may agree to handle a matter, then assign most of the work to less experienced associates. It pays to ask who is going to work on a file and to discuss that person's experience and his or her success in representing cases or doing similar work. Still, other lawyers may be eager to take on cases in areas of law in which they have little experience, reasoning that they can simply learn the relevant law as they go along. Not having experience in the relevant area of law need not rule out a lawyer. A lawyer inexperienced in one area of law may still be a terrific choice to handle a case, but it is appropriate to ask how long it will take the lawyer to learn the relevant laws and whether the client is expected to pay for the educational time.

ESTIMATE OF TIME

A lawyer ought to be able to estimate a timetable for completing a case. This will depend on many variables, including the complexity of the matter, whether the lawyer expects to go to trial, how cooperative all parties are, and the lawyer's workload. Asking for a timetable is likely to bring all of these issues into the open. A relatively simple matter may take a long time to complete if a particular lawyer is too busy to devote his or her full attention to it. A lawyer with very little experience may reveal that inexperience if he or she cannot describe the steps necessary to complete a task and estimate how long each will take.

COST

Money should be discussed at the initial meeting with an attorney. It is important to know what will and what will not be charged and at what rates. Although a lawyer may not be able to give an exact cost, a lawyer with experience should be able to provide a ballpark estimate of his or her fees.

An individual should not feel uncomfortable comparison shopping for a lawyer. Hiring an attorney can require a major outlay of resources so, like any other expenditure, a consumer should find out such details as how and how often bills are sent out, whether the firm requires a retainer, and whether the firm has minimum billing increments. Find out how often the lawyer sends out status reports about a case or matter. Finally, as with any business arrangement, get your agreement in writing.

Lawyers have several different ways that a client may pay the fees for their services:

Flat Fees

The simplest fee payment option is the flat fee. A lawyer charging a flat fee simply quotes a fee for which he or she will do the work. Flat rates were once quite rare. A lawyer often has no way of knowing for certain how complex a matter is until investigating it and can be understandably adverse to committing to a flat fee in advance. Recently, the flat fee has been growing in popularity. Much of this growth is client driven and stems from clients' desire to better predict and control the rising cost of legal representation. Today, lawyers are increasingly willing to discuss the possibility of a flat fee for relatively simple legal matters, such as simple wills or uncontested divorces. The consumer should bear in mind, however, that some lawyers who advertise low flat fees for simple wills or uncontested divorces rarely ever find that a client needs only a simple will or uncontested divorce. Sometimes the low advertised flat fees are merely a ploy to get a potential client in the door in hopes that, once in the office, the client can be convinced that his or her needs are actually far more complex and therefore justify much higher fees.

Hourly Rates

For many matters, a lawyer will charge an hourly rate for time spent on a file. The hourly rate is usually a reflection of the lawyer's competence, experience, and overhead expenses. The lowest hourly rate is not necessarily the best deal for the consumer. An experienced lawyer with higher rates will usually be able to complete a matter more quickly than a less experienced lawyer with lower rates. A common complaint about hourly rates is that they give the lawyer no incentive to handle a matter in a timely fashion. After all, who wants to work quickly and efficiently if it means making less money? Paying for legal services at hourly rates is a time-honored tradition at American law firms that is unlikely to disappear soon, and can unfortunately open the door to much disagreement over how long it should have taken a lawyer to complete a task. Before agreeing to hire a lawyer to work for an hourly rate, it is appropriate to request a written estimate of the hours that will be needed, as well as an estimate of how much money will be necessary for miscellaneous expenses.

Retainer Fees

There are actually two kinds of retainer fees used in the legal community. The first is a variation of the flat fee. Rather than paying a lawyer a flat fee to handle a specific matter, some wealthy individuals or large corporations will simply pay an attorney a lump sum each year to retain that attorney for the year. In return for this kind of retainer fee, the lawyer agrees to be on call for any legal problems that arise or to manage routine day-to-day legal affairs. The average consumer does not have a sufficient volume of legal questions to require this type of set-up.

Chapter 1: How to Hire an Attorney

The more common retainer fee is actually just an advance on the hourly rate, described above. If it is the first time that a lawyer has represented a particular client or if there is any question about the client's ability to pay, the lawyer may insist upon the payment of a large retainer up front. This money is then placed in a special account and the costs of legal services provided are deducted from that account. A client who agrees to pay this type of retainer is still entitled to periodic written statements detailing how much has been deducted from the account for legal services and, of course, the client is entitled to any money remaining in the account when legal representation has been concluded.

Contingent Fees

Another common legal fee arrangement is the contingent fee. The contingent fee is most common among personal injury attorneys who charge for their services by taking a percentage (the going rate is one-third) of whatever damages are recovered or the amount of money saved for the client, whether through an out-of-court settlement or a jury award. The percentage that a lawyer asks for depends on the difficulty of the issues, the amount of money at stake, and the skill and experience of the attorney. Essentially, when an individual asks a lawyer to take a case on a contingency basis, the lawyer is being asked to gamble on the outcome of the case. A case with only a very slight chance of success can consume a great deal of the lawyer's time and energy and yield no fee if the case is lost. In that case, an individual may need to offer a lawyer a larger percentage of the award in order to convince him or her to take that risk. Conversely, an individual with a case that is very likely to result in a large award and that presents few procedural difficulties may be able to bargain down the contingent fee to a smaller percentage of the award.

A person may be better off with a more experienced attorney because, although the fee will be higher, so will the award. If a less experienced attorney handles a lawsuit, and wins a $300,000 award, using the usual contingency rate of one-third, the client keeps $200,000 and the lawyer gets $100,000. But if an attorney with superior legal talents wins an award of $600,000, the client keeps $400,000 and the attorney gets $200,000. Hiring the less experienced attorney would therefore cost the consumer the extra $200,000 he or she would have received if the more experienced lawyer had handled the case.

There are several reasons to be especially careful when hiring a personal injury lawyer to work on a contingent fee basis. Many law firms specializing in these kinds of cases make their money by handling a large number of personal injury cases and settling them quickly. Because of the typical contingent fee arrangement, some lawyers are motivated to accept early settlement offers made by insurance companies, the usual defendants in personal injury lawsuits.

By settling early, these firms make a lot of money very quickly. This tactic is popular with some lawyers, as they take a cut of the settlement at a time when they have few expenses and because they have not spent the time and money to fully prepare a case. Be wary of such firms. The client has the right to refuse any settlement offer made and should consider doing so, especially if the case is a strong one that may cause a jury to award a large sum of money. Remember that the law gives an individual only one chance to make a case before a jury. Only under very special circumstances can someone go back to court to ask a jury for more money just because the original award money ran out after a period of several years. This is an especially important point to consider if someone has an injury that will require medical care and medical bills for the rest of his or her life.

Although contingent fee agreements are quite popular with some attorneys, they are inappropriate in some types of cases, and ethics rules forbid lawyers from accepting contingent fee arrangements in criminal cases and some divorce cases.

Variable Contingent Fees

A third payment option becoming fairly popular among some lawyers is the variable contingent fee arrangement. In this situation, the attorney's fees vary depending upon when the case is settled. Typical arrangements specify that the attorney collect 20 percent if the case settles before initiating a formal lawsuit, 25 percent if the case settles within a year after a lawsuit is filed, and 33 percent of any damage award received any time after a year. With this type of arrangement, the lawyer has an incentive not to settle too early because the fee will be greater if a larger settlement can be won by going to trial.

It is wise to clarify the exact terms of a contingent fee arrangement before signing it. Almost all contingent fee agreements stipulate that the attorney's expenses are first deducted from any award won, and the remainder of the money is then split on the one-third/two-thirds basis. Thus the statement common in the advertisements of many personal injury lawyers, "no fee unless we win your case," does not mean that a client pays nothing for legal representation. A personal injury lawyer's fee will be a percentage of any award and therefore may be nothing, but win or lose, a client is almost always responsible for the attorney's costs. A client must make sure, therefore, that he or she fully understands what kind of costs he or she is expected to pay before signing a contingent fee agreement.

Miscellaneous Expenses

Many disputes that clients have with lawyers over money stem from a misunderstanding of the difference between "fees" and "expenses." Regardless of which type of fee plan discussed above a client chooses, most lawyers will charge for their expenses in addition to their fees, regardless of the outcome of the case. Many contingent fee clients, lured by attorneys claiming, "no fees unless we recover for you," have been shocked to find out, after failing to recover any money on their claims, that they owe money to their lawyers. The client may indeed pay no fees unless the case is successful but may still be responsible for sizable expenses incurred handling the case, regardless of its outcome. For example, an attorney might charge for travel time, secretarial overtime, delivery services, court costs, filing fees, deposition fees, expert witness fees, investigation expenses, and the initial consultation. Many law firms bill incidentals, such as photocopying and postage, at rates far higher than what those services would cost at an independent copy center or post office, so it is important to discuss specific details. The client should also ask about referral fees. Some lawyers refer clients only to other lawyers who will split the fees with them. Thus, the individual who employs a lawyer referred by another lawyer may be inadvertently paying for two attorneys but getting the services of only one.

LEGAL AID

If someone cannot afford a lawyer at all, he or she should contact a local legal aid association or another organization dedicated to representing the needy. Many local legal aid societies have attorneys who volunteer their advice and services to the needy. Each organization has its own rules for who it will represent and which types of cases it will agree to take. More information about these organizations can be found in the Legal Resources Appendix of this *Guidebook*.

BENEFITS OF THE PROCESS

The point of this three-step process is to educate the individual to become a more sophisticated consumer of legal services. The three-step process described above should begin with a list of names and, after diligent research and meetings, conclude with one name standing out among the others as the best choice. The consumer should be able to cross some names off the list before actually meeting the lawyers, because after researching the names, it will become apparent that some attorneys are inappropriate for the legal matter at hand. It is even possible that every name on the list will be crossed off for one reason or another, and the consumer will have to return to step one and seek more names. For example, if it becomes apparent that a particular legal matter will require the services of a lawyer who litigates matters regularly in a courtroom and all of the attorneys on the list rarely see the inside of a courtroom, a consumer should go back to a referral agency or to this book and specifically look for names of lawyers whose practices include litigation. Unless the consumer is under extreme pressure to resolve a legal matter immediately, it is far better to spend time choosing a good lawyer than trying to undo a poor decision later. It is always the privilege of the client to change lawyers before a legal matter has been concluded, but doing so can be costly and time consuming. If a client fires his or her attorney before a matter is settled, the attorney is owed for the reasonable value of the time that has been spent on the matter, even if a contingent fee agreement stated that the attorney would be paid only if the case were won. All of the files on the matter belong to the client and must be turned over to the client on termination of the lawyer's services. A new attorney will have to spend time becoming newly acquainted with the facts in the file.

RESOURCES

Chairman of Ethics Board, 100 West Randolph, #3-300, Chicago, IL 60601, phone: (312) 814-4340.

Illinois State Bar Association, 424 South Second Street, Springfield, IL 62701, phone: (217) 525-1760, fax: (217) 525-0712.

The Chicago Bar Association, 321 South Plymouth Court, Chicago, IL 60604, phone: (312) 554-2000, fax: (312) 554-2054.

The Chicago Council of Lawyers, Room 800, 220 South State Street, Chicago, IL 60604, phone: (312) 427-0710.

CHAPTER 2

ILLINOIS' JUDICIAL SYSTEMS

It may be useful for a person thinking about initiating a legal action to understand the legal and judicial systems that exist in Illinois. One of the most confusing aspects of the judicial system is that there are two separate systems: state and federal. The majority of cases are filed in state courts. This chapter discusses the state and federal systems and summarizes the jurisdictions of both. The Process of a Case: Civil & Criminal Chapter outlines how a case goes through the state civil and criminal processes. Claims that arise on Native American land may be subject to tribal courts and not the state or federal courts.

As one may remember from civics class, there are three branches of government: legislative, executive, and judicial. The legislative branch creates the laws, the executive branch enforces the laws, and the judicial branch interprets the laws. Laws are also called statutes or codes. The executive branch can create rules or regulations to govern its administrative procedures and the judicial branch may also interpret these regulations.

When a case is brought before a court, the court applies the law to the facts of the case and a decision is made. There are many sources of law the court uses in making its decision: the Constitutions of both the United States and Illinois, statutes, regulations, and prior decisions of its own or of other higher courts (case law). The way in which a higher state court answers a legal question is binding on all other lower courts within that jurisdiction when faced with the same legal question. For example, if the Illinois Supreme Court decides a legal question, all state courts in Illinois must follow that decision. However, state courts in Michigan would not have to follow the Illinois decision because they are in a different jurisdiction.

JURISDICTION

When a person decides to file a legal action, he or she must decide where to file the case. Where a person files a case depends on which court has jurisdiction in such cases. Jurisdiction determines whether a particular court has the power and authority to decide a case. This is subject matter jurisdiction. If a court does not have subject matter jurisdiction, it may not decide a case. A court must also have personal jurisdiction over the defendant in a case. There are different ways to have personal jurisdiction, including if a defendant resides or has a business within the court's geographical region. For example, an Illinois plaintiff cannot bring an action in Illinois circuit court against a defendant who lives and works in another state if that defendant has no contact with the state of Illinois. Jurisdiction is set in law, constitutions, or case law. It is possible to have courts with overlapping jurisdiction and a person has a choice of which court to file an action in. There are three types of subject matter jurisdiction: exclusive, general, and limited.

EXCLUSIVE JURISDICTION

Exclusive jurisdiction means that only a particular court can decide a case. An example of exclusive subject matter jurisdiction is bankruptcy court. Only in a federal bankruptcy court can a person file a bankruptcy action. State courts have no jurisdiction in bankruptcy cases.

GENERAL JURISDICTION

General jurisdiction means that a court has the ability to hear and decide a wide range of cases. Unless a law or constitutional provision denies them jurisdiction, courts of general jurisdiction can handle any kind of case. The Illinois circuit courts are general jurisdiction courts.

LIMITED JURISDICTION

Limited jurisdiction means that a court has restrictions on the cases it can decide. Small claims court is a court of limited jurisdiction. It can only hear and decide cases which claim damages of $2,500 or less.

VENUE

Venue deals with the location of a legal action and designates the particular county in which a court with jurisdiction may hear and decide a case. In Illinois, a case is brought in the county in which the claim originates or where one or more defendants resides. For example, if a person is hit by a car in Chicago, and the car was driven by a person from Joliet, an action against the driver could be filed in either Cook County (Chicago) or in Will County (Joliet).

STATE AND FEDERAL COURTS

As previously mentioned, there are two separate court systems: state and federal. Which court system a person enters depends on a number of factors: whether a court has exclusive jurisdiction over the subject matter of the case, the amount of damages involved, and the locations of the parties in the case.

STATE COURTS

Illinois has three levels to its court system: circuit courts, the Appellate Court, and the Illinois Supreme Court. The court of claims is not in the judicial system, but was created solely to hear claims against the State of Illinois.

Illinois Circuit Courts

Illinois' 102 counties are divided into 22 judicial circuits. Each judicial circuit is composed of one or more counties. As previously mentioned, the circuit court has general subject matter jurisdiction and handles a wide variety of cases, both civil and criminal. The circuit courts are courts of original jurisdiction, that is, cases start there. That is where trials are held, witnesses testify, evidence is presented, and judgments are rendered. Small claims court is a division of circuit court. A person who loses a case in circuit court may appeal it. Appeals from circuit court are typically brought to the Illinois Appellate Court.

Illinois Appellate Court

There are five districts of the Illinois Appellate Court, each with four to eighteen judges. Cook County comprises the whole of the First District, and Chicago is the district seat. Elgin is the seat of the Second District; Ottawa, the seat of the Third District; Springfield, the seat of the Fourth District; and Mount Vernon, the seat of the Fifth District. Unlike the circuit courts, which hear trials with witnesses, jurors, and evidence, the Appellate Court's primary function is to determine whether there has been an error at the circuit court level, and if so, to remedy it. The Appellate Court reviews the transcript from the circuit court and may also consider written and oral arguments. The Appellate Court can reverse or affirm a circuit court ruling or send it back to the circuit court for additional action. The Appellate Court hears most appeals from the circuit courts unless the law specifically states that a particular appeal goes directly to the Illinois Supreme Court. Appeals from the Appellate Court are sent to the Illinois Supreme Court.

Illinois Supreme Court

The Illinois Supreme Court is the highest court in the state. Located in Springfield, it has seven justices. Like the Appellate Court, the Illinois Supreme Court does not hold trials but reviews transcripts, takes written and oral arguments, and determines whether there has been an error at the circuit court level. It may also reverse, affirm, or remand a case. The Supreme Court is the rule-making body for the state courts and has administrative responsibility for the operation of the state court system. An Illinois Supreme Court decision is a final decision in Illinois and may be appealed to the U.S. Supreme Court only if there is a federal issue involved.

FEDERAL COURTS

The federal court system hears both civil and criminal cases and is also broken down into three levels. There are generally three ways a case can be filed in federal court: the case involves federal law, the case raises a question of U.S. Constitution interpretation, or the case involves parties from more than one state and the amount in question is more than $50,000.

Federal District Court

The federal government has divided the United States into federal judicial districts. The state of Illinois makes up three judicial districts, designated as the Northern, Central and Southern Districts. The Northern District's main office is in Chicago, with an additional location in Rockford. The Central District has offices in Rock Island, Danville and Peoria, with its main office in Springfield. The Southern District has its main office in East St. Louis, with an additional location in Benton. Like the state circuit courts, the federal district court holds trials on issues over which it has jurisdiction. Appeals from the federal district court go to the Seventh Circuit Court of Appeals.

The bankruptcy court is also in the federal system. This court has exclusive jurisdiction over bankruptcy matters. There are U.S. bankruptcy courts in Chicago, Danville, Peoria, Rockford, Benton, Springfield, and East St. Louis.

Federal Court of Appeals

The federal government groups the U.S. federal judicial districts into circuits, and each circuit has a court of appeals. Illinois is in the Seventh Circuit, along with Indiana and Wisconsin. The Seventh Circuit Court of Appeals hears the appeals from federal district courts within its circuit. As in the Illinois Appellate Court, the Seventh Circuit Court of Appeals does not try cases, but only reviews cases from the federal district courts. The Seventh Circuit Court of Appeals has its main office in Chicago. Appeals from the Seventh Circuit Court of Appeals are heard at the U.S. Supreme Court.

U.S. Supreme Court

The U.S. Supreme Court is the only court created by the U.S. Constitution. It hears appeals from the circuit courts of appeal and states' supreme courts, and other cases in which it has jurisdiction—cases between states, for example. The Court is made up of nine justices and is based in Washington, D.C. Only a small percentage of the cases appealed to the U.S. Supreme Court are actually heard. As with other appellate courts, the refusal to hear an appeal lets stand the lower court's ruling.

CHAPTER 3

PROCESS OF A CASE: CIVIL & CRIMINAL

Our legal system is based on the adversary system. This system allows opposing parties to present their case to an impartial third party who renders a decision. The adversary process determines the facts of the case, determines the governing law, applies the law to the facts, and provides a judgment.

There are two kinds of cases: civil and criminal. Civil cases resolve private conflicts between people, businesses, and the government. Criminal cases involve the enforcement of a law by the government. Most disputes are resolved before trial. Disputes may be resolved before any legal action is filed, after legal action is filed in court, or while a trial is in process but before the judge or jury renders a decision. Most cases have to be filed within the time limits set by law. These limits are known as the statutes of limitations. The time limitations vary depending on the type of legal claim filed. If a person does not file a case within the time period set by law, he or she loses the right to file the legal claim.

This chapter will outline the process of a case through the civil and criminal circuit court system. It will also outline the trial process. Finally, it will discuss the use of small claims court.

The Illinois' Judicial Systems Chapter discusses the state and federal court systems in Illinois. Also see the specific subject matter chapters for more information, including the Criminal Law Chapters and the Personal Injury Law Chapters. The Alternative Dispute Resolution Chapter discusses options that exist outside the courtroom.

CIVIL PROCESS

Civil cases make up the majority of the cases filed. Examples of civil cases include personal injuries, contract disputes, landlord-tenant disputes, adoptions, and divorce. In civil cases where damage is done to a party, that party can claim money damages. However, depending on the case, a party may ask for something other than money damages. (For a discussion of damages in contract disputes, see the Contract Law Chapter.) A person may ask the court to issue an injunction against another party. An injunction bars a person from doing a specific act. The court may issue a restraining order restricting the defendant's actions until the case is resolved. For example, a person signs a contract to buy a house from the homeowner and the owner turns around and sells the house for a second time to another person. The first buyer may ask the court to restrain the seller from completing the sale to the second buyer until the case between the first buyer and the seller is resolved.

On rare occasions, civil cases may be filed as class actions. Class actions arise when there is a common question of law and fact for a large number of persons. There is a special process to go through to establish a class action. This certification process can be lengthy. Recent examples of class actions include breast implant cases and real estate dual agency cases.

The burden of proof in a civil case is on the party who initiates the case (the plaintiff). The plaintiff must prove the case by a preponderance of evidence. This means that the party in a case who presents the more convincing evidence wins the case. The plaintiff's evidence must be more convincing than the evidence presented by the opposing party (the defendant).

Civil jury trials usually include only 6 jurors where the claim for damages is less than $15,000, although either party may demand a jury of 12. All other civil trials have 12 jurors. Civil juries are not required to reach a unanimous verdict. If 11 of the 12 jurors agree on a case resolution, it may be enough for a verdict. A person is limited to bringing one legal action for damages arising from the same circumstances.

CIVIL PRETRIAL PROCESS

As previously mentioned, a civil case is a private dispute between two or more parties. The following is an outline of the steps one may take if a civil action is filed in a Illinois circuit court.

The plaintiff's attorney prepares a document called a complaint. The complaint states what the dispute is about, why the defendant is responsible, and asks the court to take a stated action, such as awarding damages. The complaint, along with a summons, is delivered to the party the action has been filed against. A summons is a written order stating that a defendant must answer the plaintiff's complaint. There are requirements for serving a summons. The party served is the defendant. The defendant has a specific period of time to respond to the complaint. This written response is an answer. The answer admits or denies allegations in the complaint, states any defenses to the plaintiff's complaint, and asks the court to decide in favor of the defendant. The defendant may also state claims he or she has against the plaintiff. These claims by the defendant against the plaintiff are counterclaims. The plaintiff must respond to the defendant's counterclaims. If the defendant does not respond to the complaint, the plaintiff can win the case by default. The complaint, answer, and any counterclaims are called the pleadings. These documents are eventually filed in circuit court.

There are several steps before a case goes to trial. To assist the parties in preparing their cases and learning about the other side's case, a process called discovery occurs. During discovery, each side may ask the other to answer written questions (interrogatories), provide copies of documents, or answer questions orally under oath (deposition). A deposition is usually held in an attorney's office and recorded by a stenographer. A deposition can be used to impeach a witness during the trial if testimony at trial is different from the testimony given at the deposition. Each side may also make motions to the court asking it to settle legal questions that arise.

During the pretrial process, a settlement might be arranged. Six circuit courts, including the Cook County Circuit Court, require mandatory arbitration in cases where the sole claim is for an amount of money not in excess of $50,000. This is an effort to settle cases before they go to trial. For more information on the arbitration process, see the Alternative Dispute Resolution Chapter.

CRIMINAL PROCESS

Unlike a civil case, which is a private dispute, criminal cases involve persons who are charged by the government with a violation of the law. Examples of criminal cases are assault, burglary, embezzlement, rape, and murder. Crimes in Illinois are divided into categories ranging from the most serious crimes to less serious crimes. The most serious crimes are called felonies. Murder and arson are felonies. Felonies are further classified to reflect the seriousness of the crime, with five different classes of felonies. A person convicted of first degree murder, which is the most serious class of felonies, may be sent to prison for life. A person convicted of one of the lesser classes of felonies may be sent to prison to serve time ranging from one to thirty years. A person convicted of a felony may also be required to pay a substantial fine.

The next level of crime is called a misdemeanor. Like felonies, misdemeanors are also classified to reflect the seriousness of the crime. A person convicted of a misdemeanor may be sent to jail for up to a year and may also be required to pay a fine. Other violations, such as parking tickets and moving violations, are called petty offenses. A person guilty of these offenses cannot be sent to jail but can be required to pay a fine of up to $500.

The burden of proving a case against a person in a criminal proceeding (the defendant) is on the party bringing the charges (the prosecutor). A criminal defendant does not have to prove his or her innocence; the prosecutor must prove that the defendant is guilty. Decisions in a criminal proceeding are based upon a different standard than civil cases. In order for a person to be found guilty of a crime, the prosecution must prove the defendant is guilty beyond a reasonable doubt.

There are 12 jurors in a criminal case, and unlike a civil proceeding, all jurors must reach a guilty or not guilty verdict. If a jury fails to reach a unanimous verdict, it is a hung jury and a mistrial is declared. If a mistrial is declared, a new trial may be held.

CRIMINAL PRETRIAL PROCESS

The following is an outline of the pretrial procedures for a felony criminal case filed in Illinois circuit court.

When a crime is committed, the police conduct an investigation. When a person has been identified as the probable perpetrator of the crime, the evidence linking that person to the crime is presented to either a prosecutor (county attorney) or in some instances, a grand jury. The prosecutor can file a complaint against the defendant or the grand jury can indict a person. Based upon the complaint or indictment, a warrant for arrest or a summons to appear in court are issued to the suspect. Once a suspect is arrested, the suspect is charged with the crime. If police wish to question the suspect, the suspect must be given a Miranda warning, which advises the suspect of the right to not answer questions and the right to an attorney.

Soon after an arrest, a defendant must be taken before a judge, where the defendant is informed of the charge against him or her. The judge again informs the defendant of the right to an attorney. At that time, if the defendant cannot afford an attorney, a public defender is appointed. Although defendants have the right to represent themselves in court, most prefer to be represented by an attorney. Finally, at this initial hearing, the judge determines whether the defendant should be released on bail or kept in custody.

A defendant will be released on bail only if the judge determines that the defendant does not pose a threat to any person or the community. The amount of bail set depends on many factors, including the likelihood that the defendant will return for future proceedings and the nature and circumstances of the charged offense. If a defendant fails to report for a subsequent court appearance, the defendant forfeits the amount of the bail, and may also be punished with contempt of court or with criminal sanctions.

At the next court appearance, the judge reviews the evidence against the defendant to make sure there is probable cause to believe the defendant committed the offense. The next step is the defendant's arraignment. At the arraignment, the judge reads the charges to the defendant, and the defendant must make a plea. In Illinois, the only pleas available are guilty, not guilty, or guilty but mentally ill. If the defendant pleads guilty, the court will not accept the plea until the judge fully explains to the defendant the consequences of such a plea and the maximum penalty provided by law. If the defendant persists in the guilty plea after the explanation, the plea is accepted, and the next step is sentencing. If the defendant pleads guilty but mentally ill, the court will not accept the plea until the defendant has undergone an examination by a clinical psychologists or psychiatrists. If the defendant pleads not guilty, the case proceeds to trial.

At any stage in the proceeding, the defendant and prosecutor can engage in plea bargaining. During plea bargaining, a defendant may agree to plead guilty to a lesser criminal charge in exchange for dropping the more serious charge.

Before a defendant is sentenced, there is a pre-sentence investigation. This investigation examines many factors, such as the defendant's criminal history, physical and mental condition, and family situation and background. At the sentencing hearing, the court considers the pre-sentence report, any trial evidence, evidence of aggravating or mitigating circumstances, and statements of the defendant and the defendant's victim(s), if any. Depending on the crime, a sentence may consist of a fine, a term of imprisonment, probation, or some combination thereof. The possible sentencing alternatives for a particular crime are defined by statute, but the judge is free to sentence a defendant anywhere within the statutory range, depending on the evidence presented.

If a defendant does not plead guilty along the way and charges are not dropped by the prosecutor, the next step is a trial.

TRIAL PROCESS

Whether a case is civil or criminal, the basic outline of a trial is similar. The decision maker in a trial can be either a judge or a jury. There are rights to a jury trial in many cases, but this right may be waived by the parties.

If a jury trial is requested, the first step is selecting a jury. A group of persons selected for jury duty is brought into the courtroom and asked questions by the judge and attorneys for both sides. The questioning is to determine whether a person can be a fair and impartial juror. A person who cannot be fair may be removed for cause. Others may be eliminated from the jury by the attorneys without reason. This is known as a peremptory challenge. Each attorney has a limited number of peremptory challenges that he or she may make. When a jury is selected, the members are sworn in.

The next step is the opening statement. The opening statement allows each side to tell the jurors about the case, what to expect, and what they intend to prove. The plaintiff in a civil case and the prosecutor in a criminal case give their opening statements first.

After the opening statements, testimony begins. The plaintiff or prosecutor, whichever the case may be, calls witnesses to the stand and begins questioning them. The questioning of a witness by the party who asked that witness to testify is called direct examination. The opposing side also has the opportunity to question the witnesses; this questioning is called cross-examination. After cross-examination, the first party may question the witness again in rebuttal.

After the plaintiff or prosecution is done presenting its case, it is the defendant's turn. This time, the defense calls and questions witnesses, and the other side cross-examines them. Attorneys for either side may make objections to questions that the opposing side asks or evidence the opposing side wants to introduce. There are rules on what information is admissible in court, and the judge follows these rules when resolving any objections.

After both sides have presented their cases, attorneys give closing arguments. In closing, each attorney summarizes the facts of the case and states why his or her side should prevail. Finally, the judge gives instructions to the jury on the law to be applied in the case. After receiving the judge's instructions, the jury retires to decide the issues in the case. As mentioned before, a unanimous decision is not required in a civil case, but is required in a criminal case. If a party believes that there was an error at trial, he or she can appeal the decision to a higher (appeals) court. However, a prosecutor cannot appeal a not guilty verdict. Discussion of courts of appeals is contained in the Illinois' Judicial Systems Chapter.

SMALL CLAIMS COURT

An option for consumers thinking about pursuing a civil claim is small claims court. Any individual or corporation doing business in Illinois can be a party to an action in small claims court, although the court may require the appointment of a guardian for a party who is under 18 years old. Small claims court has limited jurisdiction and only hears cases if the amount of damages claimed is $2,500 or less. A person does not need to be represented by an attorney in small claims court, although representation by an attorney is allowed. The procedures have been simplified so one can represent oneself. Common issues resolved in small claims court include property damage, nonpayment of debts, and evictions.

A person who wishes to file a claim in small claims court (the plaintiff) must fill out a standard small claims court form in the county where the defendant lives or where the claim arose. The filing fee must be paid at that time. The fee varies from county to county. If the plaintiff requests that the case be heard by a jury, rather than only a judge, the plaintiff must pay an additional fee. If the plaintiff wins the case, the plaintiff may request that the court require the defendant to reimburse the plaintiff for these fees.

After the form is filled out and the fee is paid, the small claims court clerk will mail notice of the hearing to the plaintiff and defendant. The defendant does not have to answer the complaint, but must appear in court at the appointed time. If a defendant fails to appear at the hearing, the plaintiff may win the case by default.

A party who wins a small claims court case must collect the money himself. The court does not force the defendant to pay the prevailing party. If the losing party does not pay what is owed, the prevailing party may need to garnish the other party's wages through the small claims court, or may need to commence other legal action to collect the money due. A party who is dissatisfied with the judge's decision may appeal the decision.

The Office of the Illinois Attorney General, Consumer Fraud Bureau, publishes a pamphlet that describes the small claims court process. The pamphlet is available free of charge by calling (217) 782-1090 in Springfield, (312) 814-3000 in Chicago, or (800) 252-8666 toll-free.

CHAPTER 4

CONSTITUTIONAL LAW & CIVIL RIGHTS

THE ROLE OF CONSTITUTIONS

Constitutions are important documents in this country's system of government. The United States Constitution establishes the three branches of the federal government: Congress (the legislative branch); the courts, including the Supreme Court (the judicial branch); and the President (the executive branch). It also defines the powers that each of these branches have and the limitations placed on those powers.

The Illinois Constitution plays a similar role in state government. The federal Constitution is the supreme law of the land, and the Illinois Constitution must provide at least as much protection for civil rights as the federal Constitution. Accordingly, this chapter focuses primarily on the law of the federal Constitution.

Constitutional law is very broad and very complex. It includes the actual text of the U.S. Constitution or state constitution, including amendments, and a huge number of cases which attempt to interpret the words of the Constitution. In constitutional law, more than in any other area of law, there has been a great deal of interpretation of the original documents. Often, reading the Constitution itself is only the very beginning of understanding the law of the Constitution on a particular subject. In constitutional law, it is essential to become acquainted with the way courts interpret the documents' provisions. Because constitutions are such important documents, and because the courts play such a key role in understanding what the documents say, the nomination of justices to sit on the federal and states' Supreme Courts is an important issue. People care about constitutions and who interprets them because they know that constitutions matter.

Despite the importance of constitutional law in our legal system, many of the thorniest issues in constitutional law are of limited interest to the average consumer. Some areas of law that are affected by constitutional analysis are discussed in separate chapters in this *Guidebook:* the Employment Law, Elder Law, Criminal Law, and Arts, Entertainment & Intellectual Property Law Chapters. Of great interest to everyone, however, is the constitutional law of civil rights. Thus, this chapter focuses primarily on the civil rights guaranteed by the federal Constitution, and the limitations that government can place on those rights.

CIVIL RIGHTS

Civil rights include, but are not limited to, the right to practice a religion freely, the right to be free from discrimination, the right to privacy, the right to travel freely, the right to free speech, the right to assemble peacefully, and the right to express opinions against the government. Most of the civil rights United States citizens enjoy today first were granted more than 200 years ago when the original 13 states ratified the Constitution's first ten amendments, known as the Bill of Rights. Consequently, much of what we call civil rights law is constitutional law. In a some areas, civil rights are based on statutes rather than the Constitution.

One of the most important concepts in constitutional law is that the rights granted in the Constitution are not absolute. Many rights have limits placed upon them. The rights granted in the Constitution must be exercised responsibly or else they conflict with other rights. Most constitutional law is about defining the limits of powers granted in the Constitution or balancing the rights of individuals whose rights are in conflict.

EQUAL PROTECTIONS

The Fourteenth Amendment to the United States Constitution says that no state government can deny any person within its jurisdiction the equal protection of the law. There is no identical provision applicable to the federal government. However, the Fifth Amendment guarantees that the federal government shall not deprive a person of life, liberty, or property without due process of law. Courts have understood the Fifth Amendment to require the federal government to give equal protection. Equal protection, in its simplest definition, means that laws are supposed to protect people equally. For obvious reasons, however, laws cannot always treat people equally. Government programs to benefit the poor, for example, obviously treat the poor differently from the wealthy, just as programs to benefit children treat children differently than adults, or they have no effect. The government often needs to classify people in order for laws to be effective.

Standards of Scrutiny

Equal protection analysis by courts focuses on whether the classifications the government makes are so unfair as to violate the Constitution. In reviewing a classification, a court applies one of three different standards to a law or governmental action. Each of these standards asks what the goal of a law is and how well the government has chosen a method to reach that goal.

Rational Basis

Rational basis scrutiny is the lowest level of scrutiny the court can apply. Applying this test, the courts decide a government classification is acceptable so long as it is rationally related to a legitimate government interest. The government interest need not be a particularly good one, so long as it is a goal that the government may legitimately pursue. The classification chosen need not be an especially effective way of reaching that goal, so long as there is a rational connection between the classification and its goal. Laws that classify people on the basis of economics typically are scrutinized by courts using rational basis. For example, if a state offers public assistance to people whose income is below the poverty line, but not to people with higher incomes, the law will be subject to this analysis. Because this standard is so low, courts applying this standard almost never overturn the government's classification.

Intermediate Scrutiny

Intermediate scrutiny is used infrequently by courts. Courts applying this standard overturn a government classification unless it is substantially related to an important government interest. Here, the government's interest must be more than merely legitimate as required by the rational basis test, and the classification chosen must be more carefully tailored to meet that goal.

Strict Scrutiny

Strict scrutiny is the highest standard a court can apply in deciding whether a government classification violates a person's right to equal protection. To withstand strict scrutiny, a challenged classification must be necessary to a compelling government interest. Here, the means chosen must be so carefully tailored that the action is absolutely necessary and no less restrictive means exist. Also, the government's interest must be compelling, not just optional or important. Courts applying this standard rarely uphold the challenged classification.

Classifications

Given these three very different standards, the most important question in most equal protection cases is which of these standards the court applies in reviewing a classification. Plaintiffs alleging that a classification violates equal protection almost always lose if the court applies a rational basis test and they almost always win if the court applies strict scrutiny. The standard that applies is determined by the kind of classification the court reviews. Most challenged classifications receive rational basis scrutiny. The following classifications receive special treatment.

Suspect Classifications

Suspect classifications are subject to strict scrutiny. A classification is called suspect because it is likely to be based on illegal discrimination. The clearest example of a suspect classification is race. History shows that most laws that use race as a way to classify people are based on racial discrimination and have no legitimate purpose. Racial classifications are automatically suspect, so courts apply the highest level of scrutiny and almost always strike down racial classifications. There is no fixed list of which classifications are suspect, but the Supreme Court typically treats as suspect any classification of people who

- Have a trait that cannot be changed
- Have a trait that is highly visible
- Historically have been disadvantaged
- Historically have lacked effective political representation

Racial and ethnic classifications are the two suspect classifications most often given strict scrutiny. For example, suppose the State of Illinois creates a law that says African-Americans have to pay more for driver's licenses than non-African-Americans. The state might claim it passed the law simply to raise more money, but a court reviewing the law under strict scrutiny would strike it down because the classification is not necessary to a compelling purpose. The need for more money might be a compelling interest, but a racial classification is not necessary to raise those revenues. The state has other ways it can raise revenues, perhaps by increasing the cost of driver's licenses for everyone.

Suppose, instead, the state passes a law that says people over age 40 have to pay more for driver's licenses than people under age 40. Age is not a suspect classification, so a court reviewing the law would not apply strict scrutiny. A court applying a lower standard would likely find the law constitutional because it is rationally related to the legitimate government interest in raising more revenues.

Classifications That Infringe Upon Fundamental Rights

When a government classification limits these so-called fundamental rights, a court will review the classification using strict scrutiny. Fundamental interests include most voting rights, marriage, and procreation. For example, suppose a state decides to reduce the amount of money spent on public education by refusing to enroll children in families with more than two children. A court reviewing this law would strike it down. Limiting public spending might be a compelling government interest but discouraging people from having children is not necessary to achieve that goal. There are other ways to limit spending that do not infringe upon the fundamental right to procreate.

Semi-Suspect Classifications

Courts apply intermediate scrutiny to a limited number of classifications. Gender classifications, classifications that distinguish between legitimate and illegitimate children, and racial classifications intended to benefit a disadvantaged racial group are examples of semi-suspect classifications. For example, suppose a state decides to create an affirmative action program for Asian-American firefighters because it had discriminated against Asian-American firefighters in the past. A court reviewing this classification likely would apply intermediate scrutiny and ask whether the program is substantially related to the important government interest in remedying its past discrimination. The court's decision would turn on how well the state tailored the program to meet this goal and whether it implemented its provisions fairly.

DUE PROCESS

The Fourteenth Amendment to the United States Constitution says that no state shall deprive a person of life, liberty, or property without due process of law. As mentioned earlier, the Fifth Amendment has similar wording, but it applies to the federal government. The right to due process is actually two separate guarantees: procedural due process and substantive due process.

Procedural Due Process

Procedural due process is the guarantee that the government will not deprive a person of life, liberty, or property without first giving the person some amount of legal process. Legal process means some kind of legal notice or opportunity for a hearing. Courts use a two-step balancing analysis to decide procedural due process claims. First, they ask whether there is a property or liberty interest at stake. The government is not required to give due process unless a person has a liberty or property interest at stake. If a court finds that there is a liberty or property interest at stake, it then asks what process the individual deserves, weighing the private interest, the public interest, and the risk of error from the method chosen by the government. The following examples can illustrate this analysis:

- Example 1: A person applies for a job with the federal government and is turned down with no opportunity for appeal. The applicant claims she was denied procedural due process. The court determines that the applicant was not denied procedural due process because she had no liberty or property interest in the job yet. Merely hoping for a job does not equal having a property interest in it, so no procedural process is due from the government.
- Example 2: A person working for a state agency is fired after receiving repeated warnings about inadequate job performance and being given opportunities to improve. He claims a denial of procedural due process. Here the court rules that the employee has a legally protected interest in keeping his job. The court asks whether the employee received adequate process. It weighs the public interest in the state having competent employees, the employee's interest in keeping his job, and the risk that if the employee is not given the right amount of legal process, his termination may be unfair. States are aware of their obligation to provide procedural due process, so they establish detailed procedures for employee evaluations. If the person actually received warnings and reviews were fairly done, the court is likely to find there was no denial of procedural due process.

- Example 3: A person receiving food stamps suddenly is denied benefits without any right to appeal. The person claims a denial of procedural due process. The court rules that the recipient has a legitimate property interest in continuing to receive assistance and that the risk of unfair termination was high because the recipient received no legal process at all. It decides the person's procedural due process rights were denied.

SUBSTANTIVE DUE PROCESS

Substantive due process is the right to be free from arbitrary or unreasonable government actions. Modern Supreme Court decisions have used substantive due process analysis to decide challenges to government restrictions on personal rights.

Privacy

There is no right to privacy mentioned specifically in the Constitution, nor do the words "privacy," "abortion," and "contraception" appear in the text of the Constitution. However, some court decisions have understood other explicit guarantees, such as freedom of association and freedom from unreasonable searches, to mean people have the right of privacy. The right of privacy includes a right to abortion and contraception. Decisions affecting the right of privacy are almost always controversial and recent cases have cast doubt on how future courts will analyze substantive due process challenges to these rights, but the following general points stand out:

- Laws that forbid exercise of a fundamental right always are struck down as a violation of substantive due process. For example, a law making all abortions illegal would be struck down.
- Laws that make it more difficult to exercise a right without making it impossible usually are upheld. For example, a government putting a tax on contraceptives may make it more difficult for some people to exercise the right to contraception, but such a tax still is permissible.
- Minors have fewer protections of their fundamental rights than do adults. For example, it is permissible to limit the sale of contraceptives to minors, and a minor can be required to receive parental permission before having an abortion.

Sexual Orientation

Courts do not interpret the right of privacy to include all forms of sexual activity and personal autonomy. For example, the Supreme Court upheld one state's law criminalizing homosexual activity. Thus, the right of privacy is not broad enough to protect homosexual activity. This is an area in which some state laws provide greater protection for a person's civil rights than the federal Constitution provides.

REFUSING MEDICAL TREATMENT

Courts have decided that the right to refuse medical treatment for oneself is a fundamental right. For example, many states, including Illinois, have passed legislation governing living wills, which limit the amount of medical treatment a person will receive if he or she becomes terminally ill. Living wills are discussed in the Elder Law Chapter. Refusing medical treatment is discussed further in this chapter under free exercise of religion.

MILITARY

People serving in the military have less protection of their civil rights. Courts use more lenient standards when reviewing actions taken by the United States military, because the law says that the military should be given broad deference in order to function. Thus, many actions that would be unconstitutional if taken by private parties or a civilian branch of government are not unconstitutional when taken by the military. This explains why the military is allowed to exclude women from many combat positions. The military also can seize and hold military personnel without extending many of the civil rights protections offered to suspects arrested by state police. Because the courts are reluctant to overturn military decisions, civil rights advocates sometimes to turn to the President, who is Commander-in-Chief of the military, to change military policy.

STATE ACTION

The Fourteenth and Fifteenth Amendments to the Constitution limit what states can do. These amendments do not reach the actions of private parties. Thus, in order to strike down an action under these amendments, a plaintiff must show that the action is state action. Some examples of state action are clear. When the state, its counties, municipalities, or state-operated institutions act, those actions are clearly state action. Other examples are less clear. Sometimes actions by private institutions that receive public funds are considered state action.

FREEDOM OF SPEECH

The First Amendment to the United States Constitution guarantees the right to free speech. Like other rights already discussed, the right to free speech is not absolute but must be measured against other rights. Following are some examples of how the right of free speech may be limited.

OBSCENITY

Obscenity is not a protected form of free speech. This means that people do not have complete freedom of speech when it comes to obscene materials. The reason obscenity is such a controversial area of constitutional law is that people disagree on where the line is between obscene and non-obscene communications. Courts consider a communication obscene if it meets the following three-part test:

- Prurient interest: Would a person, applying contemporary community standards and taking the work as a whole, find that the work appeals to the prurient interest in sex?
- Patently offensive: Is sexual conduct depicted in a way that is patently offensive?
- Lack of serious value: Does the work lack serious value?

The definition permits different decisions in different parts of the country or state and at different times, because it uses contemporary community standards to judge communications. An item might be obscene in Joliet but acceptable in Chicago. An item considered obscene a decade ago might be legally protected speech today.

Private possession of obscene material is not punishable, because it is protected by the right of privacy. States cannot punish possession, although they are free to punish the distribution or display of obscene material.

ZONING

States can regulate where bookstores, movie theaters, and places of live entertainment can operate. Here the right of free speech conflicts with the state interest in orderly planning, so the two interests must be accommodated.

CHILD PORNOGRAPHY

The Supreme Court recognizes that the government has an important interest in protecting children from sexual exploitation. Therefore, any depictions that use actual children in a sexually explicit manner can be prohibited, even though this puts a limit on free speech. Depictions that use older actors pretending to be children or that use idealized drawings are protected speech.

COMMERCIAL SPEECH

Commercial speech is speech that advertises a product or service for profit or for a business purpose. Commercial speech is entitled to much less protection than non-commercial speech. Specifically, misleading commercial speech or commercial speech which proposes unlawful actions has no protection under the law.

FREEDOM OF RELIGION

Many people have the mistaken belief that the federal Constitution requires a wall of separation between church and state, and are surprised to learn that the Constitution does not mandate a complete separation between church and state. Clergy persons can hold public office, religious colleges can receive public grants, and the government can require a church to install smoke detectors or other safety equipment.

The Constitution guarantees religious freedom, and this guarantee has two branches. The federal government is forbidden to establish a state church and individuals are guaranteed the right to exercise their religion freely. Like the other rights discussed in this chapter, these rights are not absolute.

ESTABLISHMENT CLAUSE

The Establishment Clause forbids the establishment of a state church. Cases arising in this area frequently involve whether the state can give aid to a religiously affiliated institution, such as a Christian grade school or a Jewish hospital. Courts usually ask the following three questions when hearing challenges to government support of religiously affiliated institutions:

- Does the aid have a secular purpose?
- Does the aid have a primarily secular effect?
- Does the aid require excessive government entanglement in the affairs of the religious body?

Using this test, courts have upheld programs that have only an incidental benefit to religious schools, such as free busing, but have struck down programs that directly benefit the schools, such as paying the salaries of parochial school teachers.

FREE EXERCISE

Courts deciding whether there has been an infringement of the right to freely exercise one's religion use a three-part balancing test that considers the following:

- Weight of the government interest
- Degree of interference
- Availability of alternate means to achieve the goal

Cases decided in this area have produced a few general principles. First, strong government interests can completely override a religious belief. For example, a strong government interest in encouraging monogamy was enough to allow the government to forbid polygamy in the 19th century, even though some Mormons believed in polygamy as part of their religion. Second, free exercise claims are stronger when they involve one's own actions than when they involve one's children. For example, freedom of religion allows adults to refuse medical treatment, but a state may intervene on behalf of children and force parents to seek medical treatment for their children, even if the medical treatment violates the parent's religious beliefs.

CHAPTER 5

CONSUMER PROTECTION

Consumers enter into transactions every day. From buying a car to contracting for lawn care services, it is important that consumers be smart shoppers to avoid being taken advantage of. Every year, thousands of Illinois residents lose money to consumer frauds. Consumer complaints are as varied as the people who make them, but most consumer problems could be avoided if consumers made more informed decisions. This chapter covers the most common consumer complaints and laws designed to protect consumers.

AUTOMOBILE BUYER PROTECTION

Automobiles are one of the most common consumer purchases. Purchasing an automobile is one of the most expensive transactions most consumers ever make aside from a house purchase. Yet, despite the frequency of car sales and the large amount of money spent on cars each year, most consumers know very little about the vehicles they buy. The average car today is too complex, with too many systems and parts, for the consumer to master. Add to this the wide variety of models available, and most consumers are forced to rely on the seller's representation that a car is in good working order. Recognizing that car buyers are often at the mercy of car sellers, the State of Illinois has enacted two principal laws to protect car buyers.

ILLINOIS LEMON LAW

Illinois' New Vehicle Buyer Protection Act, commonly known as the Illinois Lemon Law, protects consumers who buy or lease new cars, pickup trucks, and vans in Illinois. The law contains no warranties of its own. Instead, it puts teeth into the warranties manufacturers and dealers provide by giving consumers a remedy if a dealer or manufacturer fails to honor its written warranties. Illinois has a similar law that enforces express written warranties for the purchase of new farm implements.

Automobiles Covered

The Illinois Lemon Law covers new cars, pickup trucks, vans under 8,000 pounds and recreational vehicles purchased in Illinois. A new vehicle is also covered if it is leased for at least four months. The vehicles must be used at least 40 percent of the time for personal, family, or household use.

Coverage

The law applies to any written express warranty on the vehicle for one year or 12,000 miles driven, whichever is shorter. If the warranty has already expired, the Lemon Law does not apply. The manufacturer or dealer must repair a vehicle in accordance with the warranty if the defect or problem is covered by the warranty and the owner reports it within the warranty period or 12 months after delivery of the vehicle, whichever comes first. As long as the problem is reported within the warranty period, the manufacturer or dealer must make repairs, even if the warranty subsequently runs out.

The law has special provisions for vehicles with serious problems—the real lemons. If the dealer or manufacturer is unable to repair a vehicle's problem after a reasonable number of attempts, the buyer or person leasing the vehicle has a right to go to the manufacturer's arbitration program or to court and seek a replacement vehicle or a full refund of the purchase or lease price. What constitutes a reasonable number of attempts depends on the problem. A reasonable number is four or more unsuccessful attempts to correct the same problem, more than one unsuccessful attempt to correct a problem that causes a complete failure of the steering or braking system if the defect is likely to cause death or serious bodily harm, or any warranty repairs that cause the vehicle to be out of service for repairs for 30 or more business days.

Exceptions to Coverage

The Illinois Lemon Law does not apply to problems that do not substantially impair either the use or market value of the car. The law does not cover problems resulting from abuse, neglect, or unauthorized alterations to the car.

ILLINOIS USED CAR WARRANTY LAW

Illinois also has a warranty law that covers the power train on new or used vehicles. The power train includes the engine block, engine head, internal engine parts, oil pan, gaskets, water pump, intake manifold, transmission and internal transmission parts, torque converter drive shaft, U-joints, rear axle and its internal parts and rear wheel bearings. Unless repairs are required as a result of abuse, negligence or collision, a retail automobile dealer in Illinois is liable for a portion of the cost of repairs on power train components for 30 days from the date of delivery. For cars up to two years old, the dealer is liable for 50 percent of the cost of repairs, cars over two years old but fewer than three years old carry a 25 percent liability to the dealer and cars between three and four years old require 10 percent coverage by the dealer. Cars older than four years are not covered.

FEDERAL USED CAR RULE

There is a Federal Used Motor Vehicle Trade Regulation Rule that requires a dealer to (1) properly represent the condition of a used vehicle; and (2) properly represent the terms of any warranty offered, if any. Any vehicle offered for sale by a dealer must be clearly marked "AS IS—NO WARRANTY," if no warranty will be offered. The dealer must also disclose the history of the vehicle if that history would affect the buyer's decision to purchase.

Warranty Providers

The warranty described above applies only if the consumer buys from a used car dealer. Anyone in the business of selling used cars who sells more than five used cars a year is considered a dealer and is required to get a license from the state. A person who sells more than five used cars a year but does not get a license from the state is still considered a dealer even though unlicensed.

TELEPHONE AND MAIL FRAUD

While many reputable firms use the telephone and the postal service to do business, these tools may be used to defraud consumers. The following scams frequently cross many lines. For example, telephone frauds can use promises of prizes, or mail frauds can attempt to get consumers' credit card numbers. The important lesson is for consumers to be aware of attempts to defraud them. If a consumer wants his or her name removed from direct marketing lists, a request can be made to either the Mail Preference Service, Direct Marketing Association, P.O. Box 9008, Farmingdale, NY 11735-9008 (junk mail), or the Telephone Preference Service, Direct Marketing Association, P.O. Box 9014, Farmingdale, NY 11735-9014 (telemarketing calls). Both services could significantly reduce the amount of unwanted mail or telephone calls received.

TELEMARKETING FRAUD

It is wise to be skeptical about offers made over the telephone, because the telephone can be used for a variety of scams. Often, telemarketing scams are versions of other scams described in this section. Illinois limits the lawful hours for telephone solicitation to 8:00 a.m. to 9:00 p.m. Legitimate businesses using the telephone to reach customers should be willing to take the time to explain the product or service and to send information in the mail if a consumer is truly interested in an offer. Sure signs that an offer is not legitimate include pressuring a consumer to act quickly, offering to send someone to the consumer's home to pick up a check or cash immediately, insisting on a credit card number or checking account number, and offering prizes only after the consumer buys a product from the company.

The Illinois Attorney General gives this advice to consumers to protect themselves against telemarketing fraud: (1) don't buy from unfamiliar companies; (2) always take your time making a decision; (3) never send money or give out your credit card or bank account number to unfamiliar companies; (4) always be suspicious of companies that ask you to send payment by courier or overnight delivery; and (5) contact the Illinois Secretary of State, Division of Securities to see if an investment company is registered by calling (217) 782-2256.

CREDIT CARD SCAMS

Credit cards are popular with shoppers because they provide a convenient, easy way to make purchases without carrying money. Unfortunately, credit card holders are also an easy target for fraud. Anyone who obtains a credit card number can instantly use that number to defraud its owner and the credit card issuer, so it is wise to guard one's credit card numbers at all times. A common method used by crooks to get credit card numbers is to convince innocent cardholders to give the numbers over the telephone. To combat telephone credit card fraud, a person should never give out a credit card number over the telephone unless he or she initiates the call and is purchasing something.

A very common credit card scam is for con artists to phone a home, telling the person who answers that he or she has won a prize and need only provide a credit card number to verify his or her identity. Another common scam is for a con artist to phone a consumer and claim to be an employee of a credit card company seeking cooperation from the cardholder to catch a con artist. In this scam, the caller claims to be investigating credit card scams and asks for the victim's credit card number in order to set a trap to catch the con artist. Of course, no credit card company actually does this, and no one should ever give his or her credit card number to anyone using this scam.

Illinois law gives consumers specific rights regarding requests for identification when paying by check. A seller may ask to see a credit card for verification, however, the seller may only record the type of card and its expiration date. Regarding the credit card number in connection with any payment by check or draft is illegal and can carry a fine of up to $500 per occurrence.

PRIZE MAILINGS

Every year, thousands of Illinois residents receive letters telling them they have won a prize in a contest. These letters often sound too good to be true and probably are. The letters usually seem quite believable, because they are printed on good stationery, sound very convincing, and are sent by organizations with official-sounding names. What the victim does not realize is that, in order to claim a prize, he or she must pay inflated delivery costs or processing fees, give out a credit card number, or make an expensive long-distance telephone call. Often the prizes are either nonexistent or of very little value. A legitimate prize has no strings attached and is otherwise accompanied by all material terms and conditions of the offer. Illinois has an Unsolicited Merchandise Act, which gives the recipient of a prize an absolute right to refuse delivery and no obligation to return unsolicited goods to the sender.

HOME SOLICITATIONS

While legitimate businesses use home solicitations to reach new customers, this method of doing business may attract unscrupulous people.

DOOR-TO-DOOR SALES

The intent behind many door-to-door cons is to pressure the consumer into an impulse purchase. Anyone trying to con a consumer does not want the consumer to think about an offer or to compare prices. Most door-to-door salespeople can be politely refused. No one should feel obligated to let a stranger into their home simply because the stranger appears at the door claiming to be selling a product. If someone wants to do business with a door-to-door salesperson, it is best to get all the terms of the deal and any guarantees in writing.

INSURANCE FRAUD

Every year, the State of Illinois receives many complaints about fraudulent insurance agents who visit their victims' homes. To sell insurance legally, a person must have a license from the state and an appointment from a legitimate insurance company. Some of the worst scams occur when a person who was formerly a licensed and appointed agent attempts to swindle consumers and then disappears before the fraud is discovered. These frauds are convincing because the seller has legitimate experience selling insurance policies legally. When such persons decide to operate outside the law, they seem virtually indistinguishable from legitimate agents.

Anyone suspecting that they may not be dealing with a legitimate insurance agent should check with both the state and the insurance company about the agent's status. In Illinois, questions about insurance fraud should be directed to the Illinois Office of the Attorney General.

THREE-DAY COOLING-OFF LAW

In response to the fraud so commonly associated with home solicitations, Illinois has passed laws that protect consumers from home solicitation and other fraud, including campground memberships. The most important of these protection laws is commonly called the three-day cooling-off law. This law covers anyone offering consumer goods or services away from their traditional place of doing business. This includes traditional door-to-door solicitations and other sales made at temporary locations, such as county fairs or in hotel or motel rooms. Phone solicitations and person-to-person solicitations may also be covered. A salesperson covered by this law is required to tell the consumer, before saying anything else, his or her name, the name of the company represented, and the product or service he or she is selling. It is against the law to misrepresent one's identity as a salesperson. A salesperson cannot misrepresent the true purpose of the deal or the true identity of the company and cannot misrepresent the true cost of the good or service by failing to mention additional hidden but required costs. The seller is required to provide a copy of any contract the consumer signs and must give notice of the buyer's right to cancel the contract (if for more than $25) within three business days. To cancel the contract, the buyer must give written notice to the seller within three days. Written notice of cancellation is best sent by certified mail with return receipt requested so that the consumer has proof that the cancellation was sent and received. The three-day cooling-off law does not apply to real estate, insurance, or securities or commodities by a registered broker-dealer.

GET-RICH-QUICK SCHEMES

Many scams take advantage of the get-rich-quick dream with very little effort.

Work-at-Home Scams

Illinois residents are frequently victims of work-at-home schemes that promise to pay a lot of money in return for easy, no-experience-required work that can be done at home, such as light assembly or addressing labels. Senior citizens and the disabled are especially vulnerable to such scams because the scams appear to offer a way to supplement one's income without leaving home. Many work-at-home schemes are frauds requiring the victims to purchase expensive materials from the company with no guarantee that the finished product will be purchased. Often they are pyramid schemes as described below. Anyone interested in work at home should first contact the Illinois Office of the Attorney General or the Better Business Bureau.

Pyramid Schemes

A pyramid scheme is an illegal plan in which a large number of people at the bottom of a pyramid pay money to relatively few people at the top. New participants are recruited with the promise that, if they pay now, they can move up the pyramid and profit from later recruits. Pyramid schemes are illegal and deceptive because they are mathematically doomed to failure. No matter how long the scheme continues, eventually the majority of participants are cheated. Most people are smart enough to stay away from pure pyramid schemes that ask new recruits to pay money to be included in a pyramid. To hide the true nature of the rip-off, pyramid creators often hide a pyramid scheme behind what looks like a legitimate business. Rather than simply ask a new recruit to pay money to join a pyramid, a recruiter might claim to be selling a product to the new recruit. In exchange for paying an inflated price for a product, the new recruit is given the chance to become a dealer or distributor of the product. In this way, the new recruit winds up paying money to the people at the top of the pyramid and recruiting others for the lower level of the pyramid. The distinguishing feature of these scams is that those at the top of the pyramid make more money from their own distributors than from the sale of products. The emphasis in such organizations is on maintaining a steady stream of new dealers and distributors rather than actually marketing a product.

SPECIFIC BUSINESSES

There are many different ways to make money legitimately in Illinois. Unfortunately, certain businesses have been particularly plagued by unscrupulous business practices. While the majority of people involved in the following businesses are honest, the State of Illinois has passed special legislation to curb abuses in these businesses.

Hearing Aid Sales

Illinois has laws specifically designed to protect consumers of hearing aids against fraud. Anyone selling hearing aids must hold a permit from the Illinois Department of Health. Prohibited practices include engaging in conduct likely to deceive or defraud, fee-splitting, abusive or fraudulent selling procedures, and high-pressure sales tactics. Buyers must have a recommendation or a prescription to purchase a hearing aid. The seller of mail order hearing aids in Illinois must provide a 45-day money-back guarantee that permits the buyer to cancel the sale for any reason during that time. Anyone repairing a hearing aid must provide the consumer with an itemized bill. Penalties for violating hearing aid sales laws include criminal prosecution and civil penalties.

Funerals, Burial and Cremation

Illinois residents spend millions of dollars on funeral services each year, making the funeral business a very big industry. Yet for all the money spent each year on funeral goods and services, the average consumer knows very little about the goods and services offered or the laws regulating their sale. It is wise to shop around for burial and funeral services just like any other consumer purchase. Most funeral directors in Illinois are hard-working professionals who strive to provide a needed service to their customers for a fair price. Unfortunately, the industry has attracted a few unscrupulous people who take advantage of people at a time when they are particularly vulnerable.

The Federal Trade Commission's Funeral Practices Trade Regulation Rule, as well as a number of Illinois state regulations, regulate this industry. These laws are designed to prevent fraud by making members of the general public better educated consumers of funeral goods and services. The federal rule is complicated, but there are some important points to know. Funeral directors must make their prices available over the phone and a general price list available at the start of any discussions with a consumer. At the conclusion of discussions, a funeral director must provide an itemized statement reflecting the goods and services chosen by the consumer.

Unless required by law, a funeral director must first obtain permission before embalming. A funeral director may not require a casket before a cremation, although a simple container is required. The federal rule forbids a funeral director from representing that state or local laws require embalming or a casket for cremation when they do not. It is an unfair or deceptive act for a provider of funeral goods and services to fail to furnish price information on each of the specific goods or services offered. Written complaints can be made to the Comptroller's Office, State of Illinois, Director of Cemetery Care and Trust, State of Illinois Center, #15-500, 100 Randolph Street West, Chicago, IL 60601, phone: (312) 814-5921.

DEBT COLLECTION AGENCIES

State and federal laws limit the kinds of activities that a collection agency can engage in as it tries to collect a debt. These laws only apply to third-party collection agencies and not to in-house collections. That is, if the XYZ Dress Shop tries on its own to induce its delinquent customers to pay overdue bills, it is not required to obey the laws governing collection agencies. But if XYZ's owner turns collection matters over to ABC Collection Agency, ABC's employees must follow the rules outlined below.

Collection agencies are usually paid on commission and only make money if they collect from debtors. Collection agencies typically keep between 30 and 50 percent of what they collect. There is a powerful incentive to be very aggressive in trying to induce someone to pay an overdue bill. Debt collection laws are designed to ensure that an agency's natural aggressiveness does not cross over the line into harassment or manipulation.

Anyone weary of a collection agency's efforts can stop future contact by writing the agency a letter stating that he or she no longer wishes to be contacted about the debt. The agency must stop contacting the debtor, except to tell the debtor that it is stopping its collection efforts or that it will sue to collect the debt. A major drawback to taking this route is that it might cause the agency to initiate legal action, in which case the debtor may have to pay court fees and attorney fees in order to defend himself or herself. If a debtor disputes the amount of money owed, he or she can write the collection agency requesting that it provide proof of the debt. The agency must then verify the debt before it can resume efforts to collect the debt.

Debt collectors must be discreet when contacting a debtor about a debt. They may not call a debtor at work unless the debtor is at least 30 days in default and the debt collector provides at least five days prior written notice of the intent to call the debtor's place of employment. If a collector calls someone at work, the collector cannot tell a boss or leave a message with a secretary that he or she is trying to collect a debt. Finally, debt collectors cannot harass a debtor, for example, they cannot call in the middle of the night, use vulgar language, or threaten physical harm to someone.

Most collection agencies know these laws and obey them because the penalties for not doing so are rather severe. Anyone with good evidence that a collection agency has violated any of these laws can sue the agency. If the debtor wins, the court can make the collection agency pay the debtor the money lost as a result of the agency's illegal actions. In addition, the court can punish the agency by making it pay up to $1,000. The court may even make the agency reimburse the debtor for the money spent to hire an attorney.

CONSUMER REPORTING AGENCIES

Many consumer reporting agencies collect and disseminate information on an individual's credit history, arrest record, and whether the person has ever filed for bankruptcy. The most common type of consumer report is the credit report. Consumer reports can be used by creditors, insurers, and employers in deciding whether to extend credit, underwrite insurance policies, or to employ a job applicant. Illinois laws and the Federal Fair Credit Reporting Act give consumers rights in dealing with consumer reporting agencies. The laws are designed to curb abuses in credit reporting and enable individuals to have mistakes in their credit reports corrected. The federal law is more extensive than the state law and provides greater protection for the consumer. The federal law limits who can receive copies of reports, limits what reports can be used for, and provides federal civil penalties for non-compliance.

Under the federal law, if a consumer application for credit is denied, the creditor must tell the applicant if the application was denied because of information contained in a credit report. The creditor is required to tell the consumer which reporting agency issued the report. In many situations, the consumer can get a copy of the information in his or her report and the sources of that information. If employment, credit, or insurance is denied on the basis of information contained in a consumer report, the consumer has a right to receive a copy of the report free of charge. The consumer is given an opportunity to dispute items contained in a consumer report.

Under the state law, the consumer has a right to request a copy of his or her report once every 12 months. The consumer can be required to pay for reasonable copying charges, not to exceed eight dollars, and has a right to dispute items in the report. The primary benefit of the state law is that it gives consumers a state cause of action for non-compliance.

HOME REPAIR FRAUD ACT

The Illinois Home Repair Fraud Act protects consumers against misrepresentations in home repair contracts, false pretenses to induce home repair contracts, unreasonable prices charged for the value of contracts over $4,000, misrepresentation of the person or business, and damages to property while performing under a home repair contract. Penalties for violating the Home Repair Fraud Act can be civil or criminal. Penalties are enhanced when made against persons over 60 years old.

PAY-PER-CALL SERVICES CONSUMER PROTECTION ACT

With the increase in the number of pay-per-call telephone services, the Illinois legislature passed laws requiring certain disclosures in advertising pay-per-call numbers. All advertising of pay-per-call services in Illinois must include (1) the cost for each call or fee per minute; (2) any availability limitations; (3) disclosure that callers under 12 must request parental or guardian permission; (3) callers under 12 must be allowed 12 seconds to hang up with no charge; and (4) introduction for the call must inform the consumer of the permission requirement for minors, a description of the service, an accurate summation of costs for the call and a notice that billing will begin three seconds following the introductory announcement. Some calls are exempt from the introduction requirement. Violations of the Pay-Per-Call Services Consumer Protection Act should be reported to the Office of the Attorney General for the State of Illinois.

RESOURCES

National Futures Association, Public Affairs and Education, 200 Madison Street West, #1600, Chicago, IL 60606-3447. Call this association for information or to order *Swindlers Are Calling, Alliance Against Fraud in Telemarketing*.

Contact the Board of Governors of the Federal Reserve System, Washington, D.C. 20551, for information or to order the *Consumer Handbook to Credit Protection Laws*.

Contact the Office of the Attorney General, Consumer Fraud Bureau, 500 Second Street South, Springfield, IL 62706, phone: (218) 782-9011, TDD: (217) 785-2771 or 100 Randolph Street West, Chicago, IL 60601, phone: (321) 814-3000, TDD: (312) 814-3374, toll-free: (800) 252-8666, for information or to order free brochures.

CHAPTER 6

CONTRACT LAW

A contract is simply a legally binding agreement between parties to do or not do something. Consumers enter into contracts for many reasons. An agreement to buy a car or buy a home typically involves a contract. If one hires a service to maintain his or her lawn, a contract is created. There are several factors to look at to determine whether a contract has been made. Once a contract has been created, it must be determined if there are any issues on the contract's validity. Finally, if there has been a breach of the contract, there is a question of whether damages have occurred.

This chapter summarizes the elements of a contract, factors that may affect the validity of a contract, and damages if a contract is breached. One should always read and understand a document before agreeing to be held to its contents. Before one enters into a contract with major implications, an attorney experienced in the subject matter of the contract should be consulted.

CONTRACT COMPONENTS

There are three elements that must be present for a contract to exist: offer; acceptance; and consideration.

OFFER

The first step to a contract is an offer. An offer is a statement, written or spoken, by a party of his or her intention to be held to a commitment upon the acceptance of the offer. There are a number of factors to look at to determine whether a statement constitutes an offer:

- Is the person making the offer serious? A person who jokingly states that he will sell his new house for $100 is not making an offer.
- Does the statement show a willingness of the party to be held to its contents? A person requesting a price quote or opening negotiations is not making an offer. Advertisements are usually seen as invitations to offers.
- Does the statement contain definite terms regarding subject matter? Is the subject matter identified, are parties identified, is the price set, are quantities determined, and is time for performance stated? There should be enough information contained in the statement that, if needed, a court would be able to enforce the contract or determine the damages.

ACCEPTANCE

In order for an acceptance of an offer to be valid, the acceptance must be made while the offer is still open. In some situations, the person making the offer gives a definite time frame (I will sell you my car for $200 but you must decide whether to buy it within two days). Other ways an offer may end include: the person making the offer withdraws the offer, the person who receives the offer rejects it, or a reasonable amount of time passes after the offer is made. Also, if the subject matter of the offer is destroyed before acceptance, the offer terminates.

If a person changes the conditions of the offer in responding, the offer is rejected and a counteroffer is made (I will buy your car, but I will pay only $150 for it). In this scenario, the person who made the original offer responds to the new offer by accepting or rejecting it, or proposing yet another offer.

There are two ways a person can accept an offer, either by promising to do or not do something, or by performing the desired act. In the first type, a person promises to pay $150 for a car. This is a bilateral contract. In the second type, a homeowner offers a neighbor $10 to cut his grass and the neighbor cuts his grass; the neighbor accepts the offer by performing the act requested. This is a unilateral contract.

Consideration

Consideration is a legal concept which describes something of value that is given in exchange for a performance or a promise to perform. Consideration can be a promise to do something there is no legal obligation to do, or a promise to not do something there is a legal right to do. Promises to exchange money, goods, or services are forms of consideration. All parties in an agreement must give consideration in order to create a contract; it is consideration that distinguishes contracts from gifts. Courts typically do not look at the adequacy of consideration unless there is evidence of some type of wrongdoing by the party benefiting most from the contract.

DEFENSES TO CONTRACT

Once it is determined that there is a contract, it must be determined whether there are any defenses that call into question the validity of the contract. There are some defenses that make the contract unenforceable (void) and other defenses that may give the parties the option to enforce the contract or not (voidable).

Legality of the Contract

Although two persons may exchange an offer, acceptance, and consideration, if the subject matter of the contract is illegal, a valid, enforceable contract does not exist. For example, if a person offers to pay another person money for illegal drugs, this is a void contract.

Capacity of the Parties

In order to be bound to a contract, the parties must be competent to enter into such a legal arrangement. Underage persons, persons who are mentally ill, and intoxicated persons are usually not held to the contracts they enter. However, a minor may have the option of enforcing the contract.

Mistake, Duress and Fraud

A mutual mistake by both parties to a contract on an important issue makes the contract unenforceable. However, a mistake by only one party does not necessarily make the contract void.

Duress is the use of force or pressure by one party to make the other party agree to the contract. The force does not have to be physical—one could be put under mental duress. The use of duress makes the contract voidable by the party under duress.

Fraud is the intentional misrepresentation of an important issue of the contract. The presence of fraud in a contractual proceeding makes the contract voidable by the party upon whom the fraud was perpetrated.

Unconscionability

A contract may be unenforceable if it is found by a court to be flagrantly unfair. This defense is usually found in consumer cases in which a person buys an item under terms so grossly unfair to the customer that the court refuses to enforce the contract.

Statute of Frauds

Contracts, in many instances, do not have to be in writing to be legally binding. However, a law known as the Statute of Frauds requires that some contracts must be written to be valid. Contracts involving the sale of real estate, contracts concerning the sale of goods worth more than $500, contracts that cannot be performed within one year, contracts to pay off someone else's debts, leases for more than one year, and contracts concerning a marriage must be in writing.

Parol Evidence Rule

Although not a defense to a contract, the parol evidence rule may affect the contents of a contract and how a contract is enforced. The parol evidence rule applies once parties have come to a final, written contract. Once there is a final, written contract between the parties, the parol evidence rule forbids the introduction in a court proceeding of any previous agreements between the parties on the subject matter of the contract. The parol evidence rule permits the judge or jury in a contract dispute to only look at the written contract and not any previous discussions between the parties. The impact of the parol evidence rule is that all factors which are important to the contract and have been decided by the parties should be stated in the final, written contract. The parol evidence rule does not forbid the introduction of subsequent agreements between the parties.

CONTRACT TERMINATION

Once there is a valid contract between parties, it can end in several ways. A contract may have a limited time span and finish at the end of the stated time. If a person is hired to work for two weeks, the contract concludes at the end of two weeks. In many instances, where there is a specific time frame stated in the contract, parties to the contract may have the option to extend the contract for a longer period of time. Contracts may also be project, not time, specific. Goods or services may be contracted for a project and upon the completion of the project, the contract for these goods or services ends. Parties to a contract may mutually agree to rescind the contract. In that case, the parties may agree on the duties and responsibilities of each party after the rescission.

A contract also may end because of a breach. A breach occurs when a person does not fulfill his or her responsibilities as promised in the contract. A breach may be minor or major. A minor breach is one that affects small, minor details of the agreement and may not affect the outcome of the contract. However, a major breach is one that does affect the subject matter of the contract and may affect the outcome of the contract. This is also known as a breach of a material issue. When there has been a breach in a contract, the question of damages is raised.

DAMAGES

The damages due to a party when there is a contract breach depend on many factors, including which party breached, what damages were incurred, what the contract states with regard to damages, whether the breach material or not, and the subject matter of the contract. When a person is damaged by a contract breach, courts usually award only foreseeable damages. Foreseeable damages are those damages that the parties anticipate or should anticipate at the time the contract is formed.

Money Damages

In most cases when an injury results from a contract breach, the injured party receives money damages. The court places the person in the position he would have been in if the contract had been performed. For example, if a homeowner contracts with a person to paint a house for $500, the painter might stop in the middle of the job and refuse to finish painting. If the homeowner finds another painter to finish the job at an additional cost of $150, the damages are $150. Although one is entitled to the money difference between what was promised and what it costs to complete the promise, the injured party must mitigate to collect damages. Mitigation means the injured party takes reasonable steps to limit the extent of the injury and finish the job. So in the previous example, the homeowner could not hire a famous painter from Italy to finish painting the house and expect the first painter to pay for the extra expense of plane fare and room and board.

Specific Performance

There are some situations where money damages are inadequate. Typically in contracts involving the sale of land, awarding money damages for a breach does not put the nonbreaching party in the same position he or she would have been in if the contract were fulfilled. Because real estate is unique, one cannot simply go out and buy property that is the same as originally contracted. In cases such as this, a remedy called specific performance may be awarded by the court. The court may order the breaching party to perform the duties required by the contract. The use of specific performance is rare. Only in cases in which the subject matter of the contract is unique, and it is difficult to put a monetary amount on the damage incurred as a result of the breach, is specific performance ordered. Specific performance is not awarded in personal service contracts. So in the previous example, the court would not order the original painter to complete the job.

Liquidated Damages

In an attempt to set monetary damage amounts in cases where it may be difficult, some contracts have provisions that specify the amount of damages in event of a breach. Such predetermined damages are called liquidated damages. An example is when a person puts down earnest money for a house and later changes his mind. In a real estate contract with a liquidated damages provision, the buyer may forfeit the earnest money to the seller as a damage award.

Rescission

In most contract disputes, a court puts the nonbreaching party in the position he or she would have been in if the contract had not been breached. However, there are times when the court may place the party in the position he was in before the contract was executed. In cases where there was a mutual mistake on the subject matter of the contract, the parties may be returned to their positions before the contract. In this case, if the parties have exchanged goods or money, those items are returned to the other party. This remedy may also be selected in cases where there was an intentional misrepresentation of a material fact by one party.

CHAPTER 7

ADOPTION LAW

Adoption policy in the United States is undergoing a great deal of public scrutiny. News reports in recent years have featured dramatic stories of conflict between biological and adoptive parents, raising questions about how to balance the rights of both families and about which policies further the best interests of the adopted child. These cases have helped clarify important legal and social questions surrounding adoption. Although adoption remains a hotly debated and legislated area of the law, most adoptions proceed through the legal system with little, if any, conflict. For many families, adoption is a perfect way for adults to provide love and care to a child whose biological parents are not able to do so.

Adoption law, like most family law, is state law; there is very little federal regulation of adoption. Each state has the authority to create adoption laws and to regulate adoption agencies. One major exception to this rule concerns adoption of a child from another country. The United States Immigration and Naturalization Service (INS) imposes regulations on such adoptions in addition to those imposed by the state; the adoptive parents must be United States citizens, for example. Adoption in Illinois is governed by the Illinois Adoption Act.

WHAT IS ADOPTION?

In an adoption, parental rights are transferred from the natural or birth parents to the adoptive parents. Adoption is a legal transaction; the adoptive parents become legally responsible for the child they adopt and they obtain all legal parental rights with regard to the child. This legal proceeding is so complete that a new birth certificate is issued for the child. It shows the adoptive parents' names as the child's mother and father at the time of birth. The original birth certificate is retained but sealed, so it can be accessed only by court order.

Adoption may take place within a family. This kind of adoption sometimes is called a relative adoption. A stepparent who is responsible for providing the care, love, discipline, and guidance for the children of his or her spouse may formalize the relationship by adopting the stepchildren. As with any adoption, this can happen only if both natural parents agree.

It is possible for an adult to be adopted in Illinois. If the person being adopted is 14 years of age or older, that person must consent to the adoption. In addition, the adopted person either must be related to one of the adopting parents, or must have lived with his or her new family for at least two years prior to the adoption.

Most of the laws and regulations concerning adoptions are applicable to so-called stranger adoption or unrelated adoption. That is, people seek out a child to adopt through an acquaintance or an agency.

OPEN VERSUS CLOSED ADOPTION

If the adoptive and birth parents know each other and remain in touch after the adoption, the adoption is said to be open. If they do not know each other and do not stay in touch after the adoption, it is said to be closed.

Open and closed adoptions are not the only two options available to parents; they exist at opposite ends of a continuum of choices. The degree of openness in an adoption is determined by the parties involved and may be quite complex. Most important to a successful adoption is that all expectations regarding openness and the role both sets of parents will play are clearly communicated and understood by all parties. Adoption facilitators or attorneys can assist in ensuring the most secure adoption plan in the best interests of the child.

WHO MAY ADOPT?

People seeking to adopt in Illinois must reside in Illinois for at least six months prior to commencing the adoption proceedings. Commonly, married couples apply to become adoptive parents, although single or divorced people do have the right to adopt in Illinois. Married people must adopt together, however; one spouse may not seek to adopt a child without the consent and joint petition of the other spouse. If a person gets married while in the process of adopting a child, the new spouse must join in the adoption petition.

As a practical matter, it is easier for some people to adopt than for others. Agencies tend to prefer placing children with couples who have been married for a considerable length of time (generally at least three years) and who have financial security. People who are healthy and under 40 years of age usually will have an easier time also. People who do not fall within these general guidelines may be required to provide additional information to an agency considering their application. For instance, a single person may be asked whether there are family members who will be available to help with child care.

ADOPTION PLACEMENTS AND PROCEDURES

An agency placement of a child for adoption is one made through a private or public state-licensed adoption agency. An independent placement is one arranged between the adoptive and birth parents without assistance of an agency. In this situation, the parties have come together through other means—usually through mutual friends. Approximately two-thirds of all adoptions in the United States are arranged through agencies.

In Illinois, all agencies specializing in adoption must be licensed as child welfare agencies under the Illinois Child Care Act. A hospital that is not licensed as a child welfare agency, for example, may not legally facilitate adoptions. In order to adopt in Illinois from an agency in another state, the agency must be licensed in accordance with the Interstate Compact on the Placement of Children, or the agency must provide other means of showing it is a reputable organization that will take responsibility if the adoption fails.

Even with these regulations, however, not all licensed agencies are equal. Agencies differ in the services offered, adoptive clients served, geographic area served, fees charged, and age of child sought to be adopted. When dealing with an adoption agency, it is best to ask questions to determine whether the needs of the adoptive parents and the birth parents fit the services offered by the agency.

INITIATING AN ADOPTION

Before an adoption of a child under the age of 14 can commence, the child's birth parents must voluntarily give up their parental rights by signing a document relinquishing all legal rights with regard to the child. Another way parental rights are terminated is involuntarily: the parents are declared unfit by a court of law. For example, a court may find that a parent has abandoned the child, severely abused the child, or has shown such little interest in caring for the child that he or she is not competent to be a parent. Usually, however, when birth parents relinquish their right to raise a child they do so consensually. The right to care for the child and make decisions on his or her behalf may be given over to an adoption agency (discussed below) prior to the child's placement with his or her adoptive parents.

Both birth parents must relinquish parental rights. Without this consent, an adoption may not occur, with one exception: If the child was born out of wedlock, the Illinois Department of Children and Family Services must provide notice of the adoption proceeding to the person presumed to be the father. If the father comes forward, his right to be the parent may be terminated only if he voluntarily consents or if he is declared unfit. If he does not respond to the notice, the adoption can proceed with the biological mother's consent only.

In Illinois, as in all other states, it is illegal to buy a baby. This means not only that adoptive parents may not pay a parent or a third person for the right to adopt a child, but the parents are prohibited from giving gifts to the birth mother, paying her living expenses, or doing anything else that could be considered buying the right to adopt a particular baby. This law does not prohibit adoption agencies or intermediaries such as attorneys from charging fees for their services. Most states, including Illinois, do allow the adoptive parents to pay for the birth mother's medical expenses related to the birth of the child.

QUALIFICATION

Adoption agencies conduct a rather extensive examination of people who wish to adopt, to ensure that they are fit to do so. Agency workers perform a "home study," going into the potential parents' home to investigate that it is an appropriate place for a child. The home study also includes an interview, the purpose of which is to ascertain whether the potential parents are ready for the responsibilities of parenting. Some of the issues covered in the home study include the following:

- Is the house clean and safe?
- Is there room for the child?
- How long have the applicants been married?
- Are both people eager to adopt?
- Do the applicants have any experience with children?
- Can they afford to have the child?
- Will one parent stay home with the child or will they use day care?

The goal of the interview and examination process is not to make sure the applicants have a lot of money, a big house, or a great deal of education. It is meant to verify that adoption is the appropriate choice for the couple and that they will be able to meet the specific needs of the child they are seeking to adopt. The home study also is an opportunity for the potential parents to obtain information from the agency worker and to have their questions answered.

FINALIZING THE ADOPTION

Once the applicants have been approved to be adoptive parents and to adopt a particular child, the child is placed in the home on a tentative basis. This probationary period, which lasts six months, is designed to make sure that the placement is appropriate and that the new relationship will be successful. If problems arise, or if the parents change their minds about adopting, the adoption agency removes the child from the home and seeks a new home for the child.

If the tentative placement is successful, a court enters a final adoption order. At this point, the new birth certificate is issued, and the legal rights and responsibilities of parenting go into effect. A final order of adoption is—as its sounds—final. It may not be challenged by the birth parents or other parties (although the adoptive parents' fitness, if it became an issue, could be challenged in a separate court proceeding).

INTERCOUNTRY ADOPTIONS

As noted earlier, adopting a child from another country is regulated not only by Illinois law but by federal law, as well. The INS determines, according to its guidelines, whether a person or couple is qualified to adopt, approves the child for adoption based on a number of factors, including country of origin and level of health, and requires that all requisites for immigration to the United States be met. Although it is possible to adopt a child from another country independently, it is much better to go through an agency. Private agencies (public agencies do not facilitate intercountry adoptions) are experienced in avoiding the special problems that can arise when attempting to adopt in another country.

Intercountry adoptions can be quite a bit more expensive than domestic adoptions. In addition to travel expenses, INS fees, and fees for additional documentation, agency fees usually are higher, as are foreign court fees. Many people work with a foreign agency, as well, which is an additional expense. Intercountry adoptions also can be more difficult. The waiting period both before and after the adoptive parents qualify is longer, and there is more risk of medical and social factors becoming problematic.

All of this said, however, intercountry adoption is a perfect option for many people. Some people prefer to adopt a healthy infant, which is much more of a possibility because waiting lists in the United States are quite long. Finally, many of the procedures for adopting a child from another country—such as home studies, investigations of the birth and adoptive parents, forms, fees, and court petitions—are not much different than the procedures required in any adoption.

OTHER ADOPTION SERVICES

In addition to coordinating placement of a child with adoptive parents, most public and private adoption agencies provide other services to both sets of parents. Adoption facilitators may be available to provide personal assistance throughout the adoption, including facilitating communication between the parties. Directories, including photographs and background information, are maintained by adoption agencies. These lists are provided to assist the adoptive parents in choosing a child. Most agencies also maintain an attorney referral service, which can be an additional source for locating an adoption attorney.

Counseling frequently is offered to support birth parents through the decision to place their child for adoption. Larger agencies may even have counseling for relatives of birth parents who have decided not to raise a child themselves. Many agencies provide classes about adopting, which are designed to educate people about adoption laws and procedures. Some classes are tailored specifically to the parents' or child's situation; information about parenting a child of a different race, a child who is HIV-positive, or a child who has been abused may be available, for example. Other classes may function almost like support groups, in which people wishing to adopt exchange information and experiences. Some agencies provide classes, counseling, or even financial assistance for adoptive parents after the home placement, or even after the adoption is final.

Private and public adoption agencies and support groups in Illinois are too numerous to list here. Contact one of the agencies below for agency and resource information.

RESOURCES

Contact the Illinois Department of Children and Family Services, Adoption and Guardianship Section, 100 Randolph Street West, Sixth Floor, Chicago, IL 60601, phone: (312) 814-6864, for information on Illinois adoptions, the Interstate Compact on Adoption, and state adoption agencies.

The Adoption Information Center of Illinois, 188 Randolph Street West, #600, Chicago, IL 60606, phone: (312) 346-1516 or toll-free: (800) 572-2390, is the location for the state adoption exchange and photo listing.

The Illinois Department of Public Health, Office of Vital Records, 605 Jefferson Street West, Springfield, IL 62702-5097, phone: (217) 782-6553, is the repository for Illinois birth, divorce, death, and marriage records.

To order the free pamphlet entitled *Adoption,* contact the Illinois State Bar Association, Illinois Bar Center, Springfield, IL 62701-1779, phone: (217) 525-1760.

The National Adoption Information Clearinghouse was established by Congress as an information center for consumers, professionals, and the general public. It is funded by the United States Department of Health and Human Services. While it does not provide information on or assist in specific adoptions, nor provide counseling, it does make referrals and publish numerous fact sheets and directories. For general information, to obtain free publications such as *Adoption: Where Do I Start?; Intercountry Adoption;* or *Open Adoption;* or to purchase the National Adoption Directory (a listing by state of all adoption agencies), contact the National Adoption Information Clearinghouse, 5640 Nicholson Lane, #300, Rockville, MD 20852, phone: (301) 231-6512.

Adoption Law Leading Illinois Attorneys

The Leading Illinois Attorneys listed below were nominated as exceptional by their peers in a statewide survey conducted by American Research Corporation (ARC). ARC asked several thousand licensed Illinois attorneys to name the lawyer to whom they would send a close friend or family member in need of legal assistance in specific areas of law. The attorneys below were nominated in the area of Adoption Law.

Because the survey results (all practice area results combined) represent less than three percent of Illinois' practicing attorneys, this list should not be construed as a complete list. Nevertheless, it is an excellent source of highly qualified and reputable Illinois attorneys.

For information on ARC's survey methodology, see page *xi*.
For the complete list of Leading Illinois Consumer Attorneys, see page *xii*.

The Leading Illinois Attorneys below are listed alphabetically in accordance with the geographic region in which their offices are located. Note that attorneys may handle clients from a broad geographic area; attorneys are not restricted to only serving clients residing within the cities in which their offices are located.

An attorney whose name appears in bold has included a biographical profile in this chapter.

LEADING ILLINOIS ATTORNEYS

Illinois' Most Respected Legal Counsel As Selected By Their Peers.

The Leading Illinois Attorneys below were recommended by their peers in a statewide survey.

Cook & Collar Counties

Downs, Robert K. - Oak Park (Chicago), page 36
Hogan, Judy L. - Geneva
Hogan Morrison, Kathleen - Chicago
Skelnik, Josette - Elgin

Northwestern Illinois Including Rockford & Quad Cities

Blade, Thomas A. - Moline

Central Illinois

Weith, Glenna J. - Champaign

Southern Illinois

Smoot, Carolyn B. - Marion

Biographical Profiles of Adoption Law Leading Illinois Attorneys

The Leading Illinois Attorneys profiled below were nominated as exceptional by their peers in a statewide survey conducted by American Research Corporation (ARC). ARC asked several thousand licensed Illinois attorneys to name the lawyer to whom they would send a close friend or family member in need of legal assistance in specific areas of law. The attorneys below were nominated in the area of Adoption Law.

Because the survey results (all practice area results combined) represent less than three percent of Illinois' practicing attorneys, this list should not be construed as a complete list. Nevertheless, it is an excellent source of highly qualified and reputable Illinois attorneys.

For information on ARC's survey methodology, see page *xl*.
For the complete list of Leading Illinois Consumer Attorneys, see page *xii*.
For the list of Leading Illinois Adoption Law Attorneys, see page 34.

The Leading Illinois Attorneys below are listed alphabetically in accordance with the geographic region in which their offices are located. Note that attorneys may handle clients from a broad geographic area; attorneys are not limited to only serving clients residing within the cities in which their offices are located.

The two-line attorney listings in this section are of attorneys who practice in this area but whose full biographical profiles appear in other sections of this book. A bullet "•" preceding a name indicates the attorney was nominated in this particular area of law.

For information on the format of the full biographical profiles, consult the "Using the Consumer Guidebook" section on page *xviii*.

The following abbreviations are used throughout these profiles:

App.	Appellate
Cir.	Circuit
Ct.	Court
Dist.	District
Sup.	Supreme
JD	Juris Doctor (Doctor of Law)
LLB	Legum Baccalaureus (Bachelor of Laws)
LLD	Legum Doctor (Doctor of Laws)
LLM	Legum Magister (Master of Laws)
ADR	Alternative Dispute Resolution
ABA	American Bar Association
ABOTA	American Board of Trial Advocates
ATLA	Association of Trial Lawyers of America
CBA	Chicago Bar Association
ISBA	Illinois State Bar Association
ITLA	Illinois Trial Lawyers Association
NBTA	National Board of Trial Advocacy

Cook & Collar Counties

ROBERT K. DOWNS

Downs & Downs, P.C.
1010 Lake Street
Suite 620
Oak Park (Chicago), IL 60301

Phone: (708) 848-0700
Fax: (708) 848-0029

Extensive Experience In:

- Adoption Law & Custody Litigation
- Family Law Litigation
- Child/Guardian Ad Litem Matters

•**ROBERT K. DOWNS:** Mr. Downs concentrates full-time in family law and adoption, with extensive trial and hearing experience. He is frequently court appointed attorney for the minor child and guardian ad litem in custody and visitation disputes. He is active in reform efforts for the Cook County Domestic Relations Courts. He served as a state representative in the Illinois House of Representatives, receiving the Ethel Parker and the Best Legislator awards from the Independent Voters of Illinois, as well as numerous other honors. He has been a frequent lecturer at Illinois State and Chicago Bar Associations seminars on topics including "Role of Attorney for the Minor Child," "Substitution of Judge," "Legislative Updates," and "Civil and Professionalism." He has recently appeared on several cable television programs, discussing current adoption issues.

Education: JD 1965, Stetson University; BA 1957, Grinnell College.
Admitted: 1966 Illinois; 1965 Florida.
Employment History: Partner 1985-present, Downs & Downs, P.C.
Professional Associations: ISBA 1992-present [Family Law Section Council (Chair 1996-97); Legislative Relations Subcommittee (past Chair); Assembly 1992-present]; CBA [Matrimonial Law Committee (Vice Chair); Attorney for the Minor Child Subcommittee (Cochair); Legislation Subcommittee to Revise Proposed "Income Shares" Legislation (Chair); Court Liaison Committee; Domestic Relations Subcommittees, Circuit Court of Cook County]; ABA [National Pro Bono Service Award (Recipient 1995)]; Illinois Board of Managers (Fellow); American Academy of Matrimonial Lawyers [Divorce and Custody Mediation Service (President)]; West Suburban Bar Assn.; DuPage County Bar Assn.; Assn. of Family and Conciliation Courts; National Assn. of Counsel for Children; Mediation Council of Illinois.
Community Involvement: *Wednesday Journal, Inc.* [Board of Directors (Chair)]; Oak Park-River Forest Community Foundation (Board of Directors).
Firm: Downs & Downs, P.C., also has attorneys who handle general legal issues, including estate planning and real estate matters. *See complete firm profile in Appendix A.*

•**JUDY L. HOGAN** - *Judy L. Hogan, P.C., Attorneys and Mediators* - 115 Cambell, Suite 100A - Geneva, IL 60134 - Phone: (630) 232-1886, Fax: (630) 232-1890 - *See complete biographical profile in the Alternative Dispute Resolution Chapter, page 46.*

SUSAN M. LONERGAN - *Susan M. Lonergan, Attorney at Law, P.C.* - 1450 West Main Street, Suite C - P.O. Box 1416 - St. Charles, IL 60174 - Phone: (630) 513-8600, Fax: (630) 513-8602 - *See complete biographical profile in the Family Law Chapter, page 194.*

GARY L. SCHLESINGER - *Law Office of Gary L. Schlesinger* - 1512 Artaius Parkway, Suite 300 - P.O. Box 6229 - Libertyville, IL 60048 - Phone: (847) 680-4970, Fax: (847) 680-5459 - *See complete biographical profile in the Family Law Chapter, page 202.*

ROBERT S. SMITH, JR. - *Law Offices of Robert S. Smith, Jr.* - 747 Deerfield Road, Suite 310 - P.O. Box 231 - Deerfield, IL 60015 - Phone: (847) 945-3455, Fax: (847) 945-6795 - *See complete biographical profile in the Estate Planning, Wills & Trusts Law Chapter, page 163.*

WILLIAM J. TRUEMPER - *Truemper, Hollingsworth, Wojtecki, Courtin & Titiner* - 1700 North Farnsworth Avenue, Suite 11 - Aurora, IL 60505 - Phone: (630) 820-8400, Fax: (630) 820-8582 - *See complete biographical profile in the Family Law Chapter, page 205.*

CENTRAL ILLINOIS

DON C. HAMMER - *Hayes, Hammer, Miles, Cox & Ginzkey* - 202 North Center Street - P.O. Box 3067 - Bloomington, IL 61702-3067 - Phone: (309) 828-7331, Fax: (309) 827-7423 - *See complete biographical profile in the Family Law Chapter, page 211.*

DAVID M. LYNCH - *Lynch & Bloom, P.C.* - 411 Hamilton Boulevard, Suite 1300 - Peoria, IL 61602 - Phone: (309) 673-7415, Fax: (309) 673-3189 - *See complete biographical profile in the Family Law Chapter, page 211.*

DAVID H. MC CARTHY - *Attorney at Law* - 1820 First Financial Plaza - Peoria, IL 61602 - Phone: (309) 674-4508, Fax: (309) 674-4546 - *See complete biographical profile in the Family Law Chapter, page 212.*

STEVEN NARDULLI - *Stratton and Nardulli* - 725 South Fourth Street - Springfield, IL 62703 - Phone: (217) 528-2183, Fax: (217) 528-1874 - *See complete biographical profile in the Family Law Chapter, page 213.*

RICHARD WAYNE ZUCKERMAN - *Law Offices of Richard W. Zuckerman* - 124 SW Adams, Suite 520 - Peoria, IL 61602 - Phone: (309) 637-3732, Fax: (309) 637-5788 - *See complete biographical profile in the Family Law Chapter, page 215.*

SOUTHERN ILLINOIS

ROZA GOSSAGE - *Roza Gossage, P.C.* - 525 West Main Street, Suite 130 - Belleville, IL 62220 - Phone: (618) 277-6800, Fax: (618) 277-6820 - *See complete biographical profile in the Family Law Chapter, page 216.*

TREVA H. O'NEILL - *O'Neill & Proctor* - 818 West Main Street - P.O. Box 878 - Carbondale, IL 62903-0878 - Phone: (618) 457-3561, Fax: (618) 549-5267 - *See complete biographical profile in the Family Law Chapter, page 217.*

CHAPTER 8

ALTERNATIVE DISPUTE RESOLUTION

Alternative Dispute Resolution (ADR) is an increasingly popular trend that allows people to solve disputes outside court in a cooperative manner rather than through litigation. ADR techniques have been used successfully in disputes involving small and large businesses, the government, and the general public. ADR is becoming very popular in family law cases. It can be faster and cheaper than litigation. Because the parties settle out of court, expenses for depositions and clerical costs can be substantially reduced, and there is little or no waiting for trial dates. The use of ADR can also improve client satisfaction with the way disputes are resolved.

ADR OPTIONS

ADR may involve the use of mediation, arbitration, mediation-arbitration, neutral fact-finding, mini-trials, or summary jury trials instead of litigation and other formal, adversarial proceedings.

Dispute resolution processes can be voluntary, mandatory, binding, or advisory. These dispute resolution options can be used at any point during a dispute. Some parties might choose to use ADR from the very beginning of a dispute, while others will turn to ADR after more traditional dispute resolution options become too lengthy or costly.

MEDIATION

Mediation is an informal method of ADR that involves a trained third party (mediator or mediation panel) helping disputing parties negotiate a settlement to their conflict. Instead of presenting cases in a courtroom, each side meets privately with the mediator, as well as in joint sessions with the mediator and the other side. Mediation is nonbinding because the mediator does not have the power to impose a resolution upon the parties. Rather, the role of the mediator or mediation panel is to help the parties reach their own resolution. Mediation seeks solutions that satisfy all parties, and because the parties are empowered to control the outcome, the potential exists for a solution that addresses the interests of all parties. While courts are limited by law to specific remedies, mediation is limited only by the nature of the problem and the parties' own creativity.

Although participation in some mediation programs may be mandatory, reaching agreement usually is voluntary. Mediation gives the parties a sense of involvement in the dispute resolution process, making compliance with the result more likely than in the case of an imposed solution. Parties sometimes stipulate beforehand that any agreement reached will be enforceable as a contract. However, if the parties do not reach agreement between themselves, there is no agreement to enforce and the parties are free to use other methods to solve their dispute. Even in cases in which the parties cannot reach an agreement, the process of mediation may better define the dispute and help each party understand how a judge or jury might react to the case in court. Agreement can be reached on some issues while the parties agree to seek an advisory or binding judgment on the issues that remain in dispute.

Parties who use ADR successfully can learn valuable skills to help them address future conflicts more creatively. Mediated cases are usually settled in less time than litigated cases, and both parties can achieve considerable cost and time savings. Even people who believe they could win a court case sometimes prefer to mediate rather than incur court costs and lawyers' fees, which could swallow a large part of any award received. With the exception of some disputes involving public interest, mediation is considered to be private and confidential. Pursuant to the Illinois Not-For-Profit Dispute Resolution Center Act, all communications and documents, including work notes made and used during mediation, are confidential and cannot be used in a court of law should there be subsequent litigation.

Mediation currently is used to resolve disputes in a wide variety of settings. Whether the dispute is between students, neighbors, family members, businesses, or parties to an accident, whether it involves a claim, governmental agencies, or nations, the mediation process is an effective tool for achieving solutions by mutual agreement rather than by court order.

MINI-TRIAL

In a mini-trial, each party presents its position in trial-like fashion before a panel that can include selected representatives for both parties (such as managers or executives), neutral third parties, or both. Every panel has one neutral advisor. Mini-trials help to define the issues and develop a basis for realistic settlement negotiations. The representatives from the two sides provide an overview of their positions and arguments to the panel. As a result, each party becomes more knowledgeable about the other party's position. After hearing each side's presentation, the panel, including the advisor, meets to develop a compromise solution, as in the mediation process. The neutral advisor also may issue an advisory opinion regarding the merits of the case. The advisory opinion is not binding unless the parties agree beforehand that it will be binding and enter into a written settlement agreement. The primary benefit of a mini-trial is that both parties have an opportunity to develop solutions, because each side has representation and access to detailed information.

ARBITRATION

Like a mini-trial, arbitration allows both parties to present their cases to a neutral third party or a panel of third parties who are experts in a particular area. An arbitration panel differs from a mediation panel because it is chosen by both sides, much like attorneys choose members of a jury. The parties stipulate in advance as to whether the decision of the arbitrator will be binding or nonbinding. If binding, the decision is enforceable in court in the same manner as any other contractual obligation.

Arbitration is best used in cases involving factual conflicts that can be resolved by experts on a particular subject. For many, this is a distinct advantage to arbitration. Many people feel more comfortable knowing their dispute is settled by an expert who is knowledgeable in a particular field, rather than by a judge who is accustomed to handling a wide variety of diverse cases.

Some arbitration cases can be as complex and expensive as litigated cases; however, usually they are settled without much publicity. This can be a significant advantage if a dispute involves sensitive issues, such as trade secrets or future business plans, or if the parties prefer to remain out of the public eye.

Illinois has adopted the Uniform Arbitration Act, which declares valid and enforceable an agreement to arbitrate. The act regulates how the time and place of the hearing is determined, how the arbitrator will decide the matter, and how the award delivered, if these details are not set forth in the contract. It also states that Illinois courts will enforce arbitration awards.

MEDIATION-ARBITRATION

Mediation-arbitration combines mediation and arbitration. The parties agree in advance that if they are unable to resolve their dispute using mediation, they will seek arbitration and receive an advisory or binding judgment on all or part of the issues that remain in dispute. In these instances, the mediator typically will switch roles and, as the arbitrator, provide the judgment.

The mediation-arbitration process has advantages over using arbitration or mediation alone. There is greater incentive for parties to cooperate in the mediation stage of the process because they know if they are unable to come to an agreement voluntarily, they may have a solution imposed upon them in the arbitration stage. Also, mediation-arbitration can be less expensive, because the same person usually acts as both the mediator and the arbitrator. This saves time and money that would otherwise be spent educating a new arbitrator or taking a dispute to court.

NEUTRAL FACT-FINDING

Neutral fact-finding is an informal process in which an agreed-upon neutral third party is asked to investigate a dispute, usually one involving complex or technical issues. The third party analyzes the facts in the dispute and issues his or her findings in a nonbinding report or recommendation. This process can be especially useful in handling allegations of gender or racial discrimination within a company, for a variety of reasons. Such cases often provoke strong emotions and internal division within a company. If both parties are employees of the same company, there may be conflicts of interest that would interfere with a supervisor's or manager's ability to conduct a fair and impartial investigation of an allegation. To avoid the appearance of unfairness, a company may turn to the outside neutral third party in hopes of reaching a settlement all employees will respect.

A variation of neutral fact-finding is Early Neutral Evaluation (ENE). Parties using ENE have their attorneys present the core of the dispute to a neutral evaluator in the presence of the parties. This occurs after the case is filed in court but before discovery of facts is conducted. The neutral evaluator then gives a candid assessment of the strengths and weaknesses of the case. If the parties cannot settle, the neutral evaluator helps narrow the dispute and suggests guidelines for managing discovery.

Chapter 8: Alternative Dispute Resolution

SUMMARY JURY TRIAL

Summary jury trial is a court-managed process which takes place after a case has been filed but before it reaches trial. In a summary jury trial, each party presents its arguments to a six-person jury. Abbreviated opening and closing arguments, as well as an overview of arguments, are presented. Counsel are usually given one hour each for their presentations, and are limited to presenting information that would be admissible at trial. No testimony is taken from sworn witnesses, and proceedings generally are not recorded. Because the proceedings are nonbinding, rules of evidence and procedure are more flexible than at a normal trial.

The jury renders an advisory, nonbinding decision based on the information provided. The verdict in this setting serves to give counsel and their clients insight into their case, and may suggest a fair basis for settlement of the dispute. If the dispute is not resolved by counsel at or immediately following the summary jury trial proceeding, a pretrial is held before the court to discuss settlement.

A summary jury trial proceeding typically concludes in less than a day, but will, on rare occasion, extend beyond a full day. The proceedings may be presided over by either a district court judge or a magistrate assigned by the judge.

ADR TRAINING AND EDUCATION

Under the Illinois Not-For-Profit Dispute Resolution Center Act, all mediators must have at least 30 hours of training in conflict resolution techniques, and they are subject to ongoing peer review. These mediators are volunteers, and the mediation process prescribed by the Illinois General Assembly is voluntary. However, the method for dispute resolution is formalized under the act. Each judicial circuit has funding for a dispute resolution center, which is organized to provide free mediation services. The disputes mediated at these centers include, but are not limited to, those referred from the courts. Illinois has recognized that ADR has the potential to lift a burden from an overworked judicial system, as well as to resolve disputes more efficiently and amicably.

FINDING AN ADR PROVIDER

As noted, Illinois has numerous dispute resolution centers which provide mediation services. Courts also will provide lists of licensed attorneys who are trained as arbitrators to parties wishing to resolve a dispute through arbitration. Other ADR providers are listed in the Legal Resources Appendix of the *Leading Illinois Attorneys Business Law Guidebook*.

Several steps should be taken when choosing a provider. Parties should ask potential mediators about their mediation training and about their substantive knowledge of the issues in dispute. If, after selecting a mediator, a party to the dispute genuinely feels that the mediator has shown bias, has a conflict of interest, or lacks the skills or experience necessary to mediate the case, he or she should voice the concern.

There is a wide range of ADR providers with varying levels of specialization, expertise, ability, and quality. The kind of ADR provider appropriate to a particular dispute depends on the kind of dispute, the parties, how much money is involved, the level of expertise necessary to handle a matter, and how far the parties are into the dispute. Some community dispute resolution programs offer juvenile mediation, victim-offender mediation, and post-divorce visitation mediation. ADR providers offer dispute resolution services for these conflicts as well as for large, multi-party disputes. Some providers have special areas of expertise, such as corporate or environmental dispute resolution. Many ADR providers specialize in the area of divorce and family law. Because of the sensitive issues involved, family and divorce mediators must meet more stringent requirements to be recognized by the court.

COSTS

The costs of ADR vary depending on the type of dispute, the type of ADR process chosen, and the experience and expertise of the ADR provider. Because Illinois dispute resolution centers use trained, volunteer mediators, usually there is no charge for their ADR services. Arbitrators appointed by the court under the Uniform Arbitration Act are compensated for their services and reimbursed for expenses; these costs usually are divided among the parties. The costs of for-profit ADR providers vary depending upon the experience and expertise of the provider chosen. Some ADR providers charge an hourly rate while others charge a flat fee for handling an entire matter from initiation to resolution. Even if a given ADR provider charges a substantial hourly rate, using ADR can often resolve a dispute quickly, saving the client time and money.

Alternative Dispute Resolution
Leading Illinois Attorneys

The Leading Illinois Attorneys listed below were nominated as exceptional by their peers in a statewide survey conducted by American Research Corporation (ARC). ARC asked several thousand licensed Illinois attorneys to name the lawyer to whom they would send a close friend or family member in need of legal assistance in specific areas of law. The attorneys below were nominated in the area of Alternative Dispute Resolution.

Because the survey results (all practice area results combined) represent less than three percent of Illinois' practicing attorneys, this list should not be construed as a complete list. Nevertheless, it is an excellent source of highly qualified and reputable Illinois attorneys.

For information on ARC's survey methodology, see page *xi*.
For the complete list of Leading Illinois Consumer Attorneys, see page *xii*.

The Leading Illinois Attorneys below are listed alphabetically in accordance with the geographic region in which their offices are located. Note that attorneys may handle clients from a broad geographic area; attorneys are not restricted to only serving clients residing within the cities in which their offices are located.

An attorney whose name appears in bold has included a biographical profile in this chapter.

LEADING ILLINOIS ATTORNEYS

Illinois' Most Respected Legal Counsel As Selected By Their Peers.

The Leading Illinois Attorneys below were recommended by their peers in a statewide survey.

Cook & Collar Counties

Aimen, Julie B. - Chicago
Alexander, Ellen J. - Evanston
Amari, Leonard F. - Chicago
Ariano, Frank V. - Elgin
Axelrod, David A. - Chicago
Bailey, James M. - Chicago
Bayard, Forrest S. - Chicago
Bell, Brigitte Schmidt - Chicago, page 44
Benjamin, Fred I. - Chicago
Berman, Edward A. - Chicago
Berman, Peter J. - Chicago, page 45
Bernstein, Arnold - Arlington Heights
Bobb, Patricia C. - Chicago
Broecker, Howard W. - Chicago, page 45
Bua, Nicholas J. - Chicago
Coffield, Michael W. - Chicago
Cooley, John W. - Evanston
Cornfield, Gilbert A. - Chicago
Crowe, Brian L. - Chicago
Dutenhauer, Katheryn M. - Chicago
Finn, Newton E. - Lake Bluff
Getzendanner, Susan - Chicago
Goodman, Lee H. - Northbrook
Haskin, Lyle B. - Wheaton

Hogan, Judy L. - Geneva, page 46
Hubbard, Elizabeth L. - Chicago
Hunt, Thomas C. - Bensenville
Korstad, Dorothy C. - Wheaton
Levin, Jerome S. - Skokie
Lonergan, Susan M. - St. Charles
McNish, Robert J., Jr. - Chicago
Meyers, Peter R. - Chicago
Miller, Robin - Wheaton
Monaco, Mark C. - Batavia
Munday, John J. - Chicago
Neville, Ronald F. - Chicago
Niro, Cheryl I. - Chicago, page 47
Oberhardt, William P. - Chicago
Saltzberg, Gerald B. - Chicago
Schrager, Leonard J. - Chicago
Schwarz, Benedict, II - West Dundee
Sklodowski, Robert - Chicago
Somers, Kathryn M. - Chicago
Sullivan, James R. - Oak Brook
Tyrrell, Ross - Chicago
Valukas, Anton R. - Chicago
Wimmer, John R. - Downers Grove, page 47

July 1996 41

Northwestern Illinois Including Rockford & Quad Cities

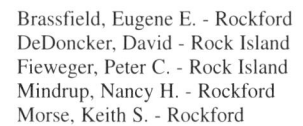

Brassfield, Eugene E. - Rockford
DeDoncker, David - Rock Island
Fieweger, Peter C. - Rock Island
Mindrup, Nancy H. - Rockford
Morse, Keith S. - Rockford

Natale, Bernard J. - Rockford
Perrecone, Frank A. - Rockford
Smith, Barbara W. - Rockford
Switzer, Peter S. - Rockford
Turner, Harold L. - Rockford

Central Illinois

Davis, W. Keith - Bloomington
Geiler, Lorna K. - Champaign
Gibson, Robert L. - Paris
Goldstein, William M. - Urbana
Hammer, Don C. - Bloomington
Hendren, Paul C. - Champaign
Lipton, Mark D. - Champaign
Mann, Richard E. - Winchester
Phipps, John T. - Champaign

Ryan, Stephen R. - Mattoon
Silverman, Brian C. - Urbana
Solls, Joseph J. - Peoria
Stine, Robert E. - Springfield
Sturm, Timothy - Springfield
Susler, Marshall A. - Decatur
Taylor, John C. - Champaign
Tinney, Sarah B. - Champaign
Wong, Betsy P. - Urbana

Southern Illinois

Brandon, Wm. Kent - Carbondale
Crowder, Barbara - Edwardsville
Green, Richard A. - Carbondale
Levine Levy, Elizabeth - Edwardsville
Lockwood, Brocton D. - Marion

McGivern, Gerald - Alton
Smith, Webb H. - Carbondale
Terlizzi, Eric L. - Salem
Wilson, Susan P. - Belleville

BIOGRAPHICAL PROFILES OF ALTERNATIVE DISPUTE RESOLUTION LEADING ILLINOIS ATTORNEYS

The Leading Illinois Attorneys profiled below were nominated as exceptional by their peers in a statewide survey conducted by American Research Corporation (ARC). ARC asked several thousand licensed Illinois attorneys to name the lawyer to whom they would send a close friend or family member in need of legal assistance in specific areas of law. The attorneys below were nominated in the area of Alternative Dispute Resolution.

Because the survey results (all practice area results combined) represent less than three percent of Illinois' practicing attorneys, this list should not be construed as a complete list. Nevertheless, it is an excellent source of highly qualified and reputable Illinois attorneys.

For information on ARC's survey methodology, see page *xi*.
For the complete list of Leading Illinois Consumer Attorneys, see page *xii*.
For the list of Leading Illinois Alternative Dispute Resolution Attorneys, see page 41.

The Leading Illinois Attorneys below are listed alphabetically in accordance with the geographic region in which their offices are located. Note that attorneys may handle clients from a broad geographic area; attorneys are not limited to only serving clients residing within the cities in which their offices are located.

The two-line attorney listings in this section are of attorneys who practice in this area but whose full biographical profiles appear in other sections of this book. A bullet "•" preceding a name indicates the attorney was nominated in this particular area of law.

For information on the format of the full biographical profiles, consult the "Using the Consumer Guidebook" section on page *xviii*.

The following abbreviations are used throughout these profiles:

App.	Appellate
Cir.	Circuit
Ct.	Court
Dist.	District
Sup.	Supreme
JD	Juris Doctor (Doctor of Law)
LLB	Legum Baccalaureus (Bachelor of Laws)
LLD	Legum Doctor (Doctor of Laws)
LLM	Legum Magister (Master of Laws)
ADR	Alternative Dispute Resolution
ABA	American Bar Association
ABOTA	American Board of Trial Advocates
ATLA	Association of Trial Lawyers of America
CBA	Chicago Bar Association
ISBA	Illinois State Bar Association
ITLA	Illinois Trial Lawyers Association
NBTA	National Board of Trial Advocacy

Chapter 8: Alternative Dispute Resolution

Cook & Collar Counties

•**JULIE B. AIMEN** - *Attorney at Law* 343 South Dearborn Street, Suite 1400 - Chicago, IL 60604 - Phone: (312) 697-0022, Fax: (312) 697-0812 - *See complete biographical profile in the Criminal Law: Felonies & White Collar Crime Chapter, page 110.*

•**FORREST S. BAYARD** - *Law Offices of Forrest S. Bayard* - 150 North Wacker Drive, Suite 2570 - Chicago, IL 60606 - Phone: (312) 236-3828, Fax: (312) 704-6746 - *See complete biographical profile in the Family Law Chapter, page 182.*

BRIGITTE SCHMIDT BELL

Brigitte Schmidt Bell, P.C.
53 West Jackson Boulevard
Suite 702
Chicago, IL 60604

Phone: (312) 360-1124
Fax: (312) 360-1126

Extensive Experience In:

- Family & Divorce Mediation
- Employment Mediation
- Business Disputes

•**BRIGITTE SCHMIDT BELL:** Ms. Bell is in private practice as a mediator and divorce attorney. She previously worked at several large firms in the Chicago area, both as a litigator and a tax and ERISA attorney. She has been teaching mediation and consensual dispute resolution at Loyola Law School as an adjunct professor each semester since 1987, and in 1992, began teaching a course in mediation at The School for New Learning at DePaul University. She is a volunteer mediator and trainer, and serves on the Board of Directors and as General Counsel for The Center for Conflict Resolution. In private practice, Ms. Bell conducts mediations and represents people who are in mediation in areas including premarital agreements, dissolution/divorce, custody, post-decree disputes, adoptions, parenting planning, employment, clergy sexual misconduct, business relationships, and the distribution of family property in contexts other than divorce. She speaks both locally and nationally on issues in mediation and family law.

Education: JD 1979, University of Chicago; Graduate Work 1979, University of Iowa; BA 1970 with high honors, Swarthmore College.

Admitted: 1979 Illinois; 1979 U.S. Dist. Ct. (N. Dist. IL); 1981 U.S. Ct. App. (7th Cir.); 1982 U.S. Tax Ct.

Employment History: Private Practice 1993-present, Brigitte Schmidt Bell, P.C.; Officer 1990-93, Pretzel & Stouffer, Chartered; Litigation Associate 1987-90, McDermott, Will & Emery; Litigation Associate 1979-82, 1985-87, Jenner & Block; Litigation Associate 1982-85, Butler, Rubin, Newcomer, Saltarelli & Boyd.

Professional Associations: ABA (Family Law Committee; Dispute Resolution Committee); CBA (Family Law Committee 1990-present; ADR Subcommittee 1993-present; Guardian Ad Litem Subcommittee 1993-present); Legal Assistance Foundation [Children's Rights Project Advisory Board 1985-90 (Chair 1985-86)]; Circuit Court of Cook County (Court Appointed Guardian Ad Litem Program 1990-present); American Academy of Family Mediators (Associate Member); Assn. of Family and Conciliation Courts 1990-present (Associate Member); Mediation Council of Illinois 1987-present (Board of Directors 1994-present).

Firm: The firm of Brigitte Schmidt Bell, P.C., was founded in 1993. Lynn A. Gaffigan, a trained mediator and former litigator in a large firm practice, joined the firm in 1995. Ms. Gaffigan shares the firm's objective to resolve cases in an efficient and cost-effective way by focusing on the needs of the parties and their children and encouraging mediation whenever possible. *Ms. Bell and Ms. Gaffigan also practice Family Law.*

MARGARET A. BENNETT - *Law Offices of Bennett & Bennett, Ltd.* - 720 Enterprise Drive - Oak Brook, IL 60521 - Phone: (630) 573-8800, Fax: (630) 573-9810 - *See complete biographical profile in the Family Law Chapter, page 183.*

•PETER J. BERMAN: Mr. Berman represents clients in need of legal assistance in the resolution of business disputes, through litigation, arbitration, and mediation. He handles disputes involving closely held corporations, shareholder disagreements, partnership dissolutions, brokers/dealers and commodity brokers, commercial real estate, banking, fidelity bonds, and directors' and officers' liability insurance matters. Although he is not a mediator or an arbitrator, he encourages his clients, as well as opposing counsel, to consider the benefits of using ADR to settle disputes. When necessary, Mr. Berman tries cases before federal and state courts and before various arbitration bodies. His articles include "How to Resolve Business Disputes Without Going Broke," *AM&G Ledger,* Summer 1994; "The Attorney/Client Privilege and the IRS: Assessing the Currency Transaction Reporting Regulations," *Illinois State Bar Association Journal,* June 1989. Other articles have appeared in *Certified Public Accountants Journal, The Journal of Futures Markets* and various trade journals.
Education: JD 1974 cum laude, DePaul University (*Law Review*); BA 1968, University of Wisconsin.
Admitted: 1974 Illinois; 1974 U.S. Dist. Ct. (N. Dist. IL); 1975 U.S. Ct. App. (7th Cir.); 1979 U.S. Sup. Ct.; 1991 U.S. Ct. App. (3rd Cir.).
Professional Associations: CBA [Futures Trading Committee 1978-present; Litigation Subcommittee (Chair 1986); Securities Law Committee 1985-present; Professional Responsibility Committee 1985-present]; ABA (Business Law Section; Commodities Law Committee 1979-present); Chicago Council of Lawyers; National Futures Assn. (Arbitrator).

PETER J. BERMAN
Peter J. Berman, Ltd.
332 South Michigan Avenue
Suite 1000
Chicago, IL 60604-4398

Phone: (312) 408-1114
Fax: (312) 939-4661

Extensive Experience In:
• Securities & Commodities Law

•HOWARD W. BROECKER: Mr. Broecker's practice is concentrated in the areas of family law and family law mediation. He has lectured extensively in the area of family law for the Kane and DuPage County Bar Associations, Illinois State Bar Association, American Academy of Matrimonial Lawyers, and the Law Education Institute of Milwaukee, Wisconsin. Mr. Broecker has completed several courses on mediation, including a 40-hour program at the Center for Dispute Resolution in Boulder, Colorado. He is a faculty member of the Academy's Mediation Study Committee and has participated in the training of over 200 academy members. Mr. Broecker lectures and writes for the Illinois Institute for Continuing Legal Education and other publications. His articles include "Cross-Examination of a Business Valuation Expert Witness," *The Connecticut Family Law Journal,* Vol. 8, No. 4; "The Use of Financial Experts in Marital Litigation: The Attorney's Viewpoint and the Expert's Viewpoint," *American Journal of Family Law,* Fall 1987; "Mediation vs. Settlement Conference," *Chicago Daily Law Bulletin,* November 16, 1994; "The Automated Attorney: Your Law Office and Computers," *Law Education Institute,* January 1992; and "The Role of the Attorney in Mediation," *DuPage County Bar Journal,* Spring 1995.
Education: JD 1966, Illinois Institute of Technology, Chicago-Kent.
Admitted: 1966 Illinois.
Employment History: Panelist 1995-present, J•A•M•S/Endispute; Partner 1992-present, Johnson, Westra, Broecker, Whittaker & Newitt; Senior Vice President/Chief Operating Officer 1994-96, Judicial Resolutions Illinois, Inc.; 1982-92, Howard W. Broecker & Associates, Ltd.; 1966-82, Ehrlich, Bundesen & Broecker.
Professional Associations: American Academy of Matrimonial Lawyers [Fellow; Illinois Chapter (Vice President)]; American Academy [Mediation Study Committee (Faculty Member; Trainer)].
Community Involvement: Illinois Institute of Technology, Chicago-Kent College of Law [Alumni Assn. (past President); Partnership Program (Chair)]; Sunny Ridge Family Center (Board Member); Daystar University, Nairobi, Kenya (Board Member); Media Associates International (Board Member). *See complete firm profile in Appendix A. Mr. Broecker also practices Family Law.*

HOWARD W. BROECKER
J•A•M•S/Endispute
Three First National Plaza
Suite 200
Chicago, IL 60602

Phone: (312) 739-0200
Fax: (312) 739-0617

Extensive Experience In:
• Divorce Mediation
• Divorce Litigation

PATRICIA A. FELCH - *ARTSLaw Offices of Patricia A. Felch, P.C.* - Three First National Plaza, Suite 3600 - 70 West Madison - Chicago, IL 60602 - Phone: (312) 236-0404, Fax: (312) 236-0403 - *See complete biographical profile in the Arts, Entertainment & Intellectual Property Law Chapter, page 60.*

JOSEPH P. GLIMCO III - *Law Offices of Joseph P. Glimco III* - 6900 South Main Street, Suite 204 - Downers Grove, IL 60515 - Phone: (630) 852-3636, Fax: (630) 852-3880 - *See complete biographical profile in the Family Law Chapter, page 188.*

•LYLE B. HASKIN - *Lyle B. Haskin & Associates* - 310 South County Farm Road - P.O. Box 31 - Wheaton, IL 60189-0031 - Phone: (630) 665-0800, Fax: (630) 665-1289 - *See complete biographical profile in the Family Law Chapter, page 190.*

Chapter 8: Alternative Dispute Resolution

JUDY L. HOGAN

Judy L. Hogan, P.C.
Attorneys and Mediators
115 Cambell
Suite 100A
Geneva, IL 60134

Phone: (630) 232-1886
Fax: (630) 232-1890

Extensive Experience In:

- Training of Mediators
- Custody Mediation
- Conflict Resolution Plan Development

•**JUDY L. HOGAN:** Ms. Hogan is a family law attorney who has primarily devoted the past seven years to mediation and alternative dispute resolution. She serves the Chicagoland area as a family mediator, designing and implementing mediation training and intervention programs for corporations, the state and federal government, and the private sector. She offers mediation and arbitration services, and is the Project Director of two pilot mediation programs for the Illinois Department of Children and Family Services. Ms. Hogan is a nationally approved trainer of basic and advanced mediation skills for the Academy of Family Mediators, holding its highest membership as a Practitioner Member, and serves as an Academy Consultant. She is a Senior Lecturer for Aurora University's New College, teaching at its Conflict Resolution and Divorce Mediation Institute.

Education: JD 1984, Oklahoma City University School of Law (Business Editor, *Law Review;* Highest Grade 1983, Labor Law; Outstanding Fraternity Member 1984); BSW 1978, George Williams College.

Admitted: 1984 Illinois; 1991 U.S. Dist. Ct. (N. Dist. IL).

Employment History: President 1995-present, Judy L. Hogan, P.C.; Director 1995-present, Resource Alliance, Inc.; Sole Practitioner 1991-95, Judy L. Hogan; Contractual, Mediation and Arbitration Services 1987-present, Illinois Department of Children and Family Services; Arbitrator 1990-present, Circuit Court of Cook and Kane Counties; Staff Attorney 1985-87, Illinois Coalition Against Sexual Assault; Associate 1984-85, Ronald R. Carped, Ltd.

Representative Clients: Ms. Hogan primarily handles family law, guardianship and child welfare matters.

Professional Associations: Academy of Family Mediators 1991-present; Mediation Council of Illinois, Inc. (Board of Directors 1993-present); Society of Professionals in Dispute Resolution 1991-present; Assn. of Family and Conciliation Courts 1994-present; ABA 1984-present; ISBA 1984-present; Kane County Bar Assn. 1990-present; Government Bar Assn. 1989-94.

Community Involvement: Chicago Junior School, Elgin [Parent Support Assn. (Board of Directors; Secretary; President)]; American Assn. of University Women [Executive Board (Vice President)]; Macon County Mental Health Assn. (Board of Directors); Big Brothers/Big Sisters (Volunteer Advocate); Omni House Youth Services (Youth Advocate Volunteer).

Firm: Ms. Hogan takes the team approach in handling cases, recognizing the core of the team is the client, her staff, and herself. She believes in regular client contact and consultation in decision making. She readily defers to the client for elements of the case that he or she can perform to keep down costs. *Ms. Hogan also practices Family Law and Adoption Law.*

FRED LANE - *Lane & Lane* - 33 North Dearborn Street, Suite 2300 - Chicago, IL 60602 - Phone: (312) 332-1400, Fax: (312) 899-8003 - *See complete biographical profile in the Personal Injury Law: General Chapter, page 243.*

•**SUSAN M. LONERGAN** - *Susan M. Lonergan, Attorney at Law, P.C.* - 1450 West Main Street, Suite C - P.O. Box 1416 - St. Charles, IL 60174 - Phone: (630) 513-8600, Fax: (630) 513-8602 - *See complete biographical profile in the Family Law Chapter, page 194.*

EARLE A. MALKIN - *Law Offices of Earle A. Malkin* - 33 North Dearborn Street, Suite 2300 - Chicago, IL 60602 - Phone: (312) 372-6150, Fax: (312) 236-4725 - *See complete biographical profile in the Family Law Chapter, page 195.*

KURT A. MULLER - *The Muller Firm, Ltd.* - 200 North Dearborn Street, Suite 4602 - Chicago, IL 60601 - Phone: (312) 855-9558, Fax: (312) 855-9362 - *See complete biographical profile in the Family Law Chapter, page 196.*

•**CHERYL I. NIRO:** Ms. Niro is an experienced attorney, mediator, arbitrator, and ADR consultant. She has resolved commercial, employment, real estate, personal injury, family, school, health care-related and community-based disputes. A recognized leader in alternative dispute resolution, she is a consultant to the U.S. Department of Justice and has taught Mediation and Negotiation Workshops at the Harvard Law School Program of Instruction for Lawyers. Recent publications in the field of ADR include "The Decision Tree: A Systematic Approach to Settlement Decisions," *Illinois Bar Journal,* March 1994. Ms. Niro is a leader of the Illinois State Bar Association and will serve as the second woman President in 1999. A recipient of many awards, Ms. Niro is a Fellow of the American Bar Foundation and Illinois Bar Foundation. She is also a Founder of the Illinois Institute for Dispute Resolution, which provides conflict resolution training and consulting.
Education: JD 1980, Northern Illinois University (Dean's List; Teaching Assistant to Dean); BS 1972 summa cum laude, University of Illinois-Urbana.
Admitted: 1981 Illinois; 1981 U.S. Dist. Ct. (N. Dist. IL); 1990 U.S. Ct. App. (7th Cir.).
Employment History: Partner 1996-present, Partridge & Niro, P.C.; President 1993-present, Associates in Dispute Resolution, Inc.; Director of Legal Programs 1993-present, Illinois Institute for Dispute Resolution; Principal 1988-92, Law Office of Cheryl Niro.
Professional Associations: ISBA [Third Vice President 1996-97; Treasurer 1995-96; Board of Governors 1993-present; Assembly 1992-present; Mutual Insurance Company (Board of Directors)]; ABA [ADR Section (Training Committee); House of Delegates 1996-present]; Society for Professionals in Dispute Resolution (Full Member 1992-present); CBA (Alliance for Women 1992-present); Our Children in the Courts Foundation (Board of Directors); Cook County Legal Assistance Foundation (President; Board of Directors 1993-94); Illinois Supreme Court Legal Historical Society (Founding Director).
Community Involvement: Oak Park/River Forest Children's Chorus (Founder).
Firm: Partridge & Niro is dedicated to innovative, efficient, custom-designed service for its clients. The firm evaluates the facts, the law, and the business goals of each action, and with the client, develops a strategy tailored to best advance the interests of the client. One client's solution may be avoiding litigation, another client's solution may be a litigated victory, and still another client's solution may be a negotiated win for all sides. The firm's experience in both litigation and mediation allows use of all approaches to reach an appropriate resolution for each client. *Ms. Niro also practices Employment Law and Family Law.*

CHERYL I. NIRO
Partridge & Niro, P.C.
Associates in Dispute Resolution, Inc.
900 West Jackson Boulevard
Suite Five East
Chicago, IL 60607

Phone: (312) 850-1906
Fax: (312) 850-1901
E-mail: cniro@aol.com

Extensive Experience In:

• Labor & Employment Matters
• Multi-Party Disputes
• ADR Process Advice

•**BENEDICT SCHWARZ II** - *Law Offices of Benedict Schwarz II, Ltd.* - 303 West Main Street - West Dundee, IL 60118 - Phone: (847) 428-7725, Fax: (847) 428-7750 - *See complete biographical profile in the Family Law Chapter, page 202.*

WILLIAM J. TRUEMPER - *Truemper, Hollingsworth, Wojtecki, Courtin & Titiner* - 1700 North Farnsworth Avenue, Suite 11 - Aurora, IL 60505 - Phone: (630) 820-8400, Fax: (630) 820-8582 - *See complete biographical profile in the Family Law Chapter, page 205.*

•**JOHN R. WIMMER:** Mr. Wimmer is a trial and appellate lawyer practicing in the Chicago metropolitan area. He has argued many appeals, civil and criminal, and he has orally argued cases before the Illinois Supreme Court. Mr. Wimmer also tries cases, civil and criminal, in courts throughout the Chicago metropolitan area, and is a member of the Trial Bar of the United States District Court for the Northern District of Illinois, Eastern Division.
Education: JD 1979, University of Illinois; BA 1976, Cornell University (Graduated with Distinction in all subjects).
Admitted: 1979 Illinois; 1981 U.S. Dist. Ct. (N. Dist. IL); 1987 U.S. Ct. App. (7th Cir.).
Employment History: Sole Practitioner 1990-96, The Law Offices of John R. Wimmer; Associate 1986-89, Botti, Marinaccio, DeSalvo & Pieper; Law Clerk 1984-86, Honorable Paul W. Schnake, Appellate Court of Illinois; Staff Attorney 1981-84, Office of the State Appellate Defender; Associate 1980-81, Richard E. Alexander, Ltd.; Law Clerk 1979-80, Honorable Richard Stengel, Appellate Court of Illinois.
Professional Associations: CBA; ISBA.
Community Involvement: St. Matthew Evangelical Lutheran Church, Lemont, Illinois; Cross of Christ Lutheran Church, Downers Grove, Illinois (former Congregation Member; past President); Autism Society of America. *Mr. Wimmer also practices Civil Appellate Law and Criminal Law: Felonies & White Collar Crime.*

JOHN R. WIMMER
The Law Offices of John R. Wimmer
928 Warren Avenue
Downers Grove, IL 60515

Phone: (630) 810-0005
Fax: (630) 960-5852
E-mail: jwimmerlaw@aol.com

Extensive Experience In:

• Civil Appeals
• Defamation Against Media Defendants
• Federal Civil Rights

NORTHWESTERN ILLINOIS
INCLUDING ROCKFORD & QUAD CITIES

ROBERT A. FREDRICKSON - *Reno, Zahm, Folgate, Lindberg & Powell* - 1415 East State Street, Suite 900 - Rockford, IL 61104 - Phone: (815) 987-4050, Fax: (815) 987-4092 - *See complete biographical profile in the Personal Injury Law: General Chapter, page 250.*

•KEITH S. MORSE - *Attorney at Law* - 810 East State Street, Suite 101 - Rockford, IL 61104 - Phone: (815) 967-5000, Fax: (815) 967-5002 - *See complete biographical profile in the Family Law Chapter, page 208.*

•PETER S. SWITZER - *Barrick, Switzer, Long, Balsley & Van Evera* - One Madison Street - Rockford, IL 61104 - Phone: (815) 962-6611, Fax: (815) 962-0687 - *See complete biographical profile in the Family Law Chapter, page 208.*

CENTRAL ILLINOIS

•DON C. HAMMER - *Hayes, Hammer, Miles, Cox & Ginzkey* - 202 North Center Street - P.O. Box 3067 - Bloomington, IL 61702-3067 - Phone: (309) 828-7331, Fax: (309) 827-7423 - *See complete biographical profile in the Family Law Chapter, page 211.*

MARY LEE LEAHY - *Leahy Law Offices* - 308 East Canedy Street - Springfield, IL 62703 - Phone: (217) 522-4411, Fax: (217) 522-7119 - *See complete biographical profile in the Employment Law Chapter, page 149.*

JOHN P. NICOARA - *Nicoara & Steagall* - 416 Main Street, Suite 815 - Peoria, IL 61602 - Phone: (309) 674-6085, Fax: (309) 674-6032 - *See complete biographical profile in the Personal Injury Law: General Chapter, page 254.*

CHAPTER 9

Arts, Entertainment & Intellectual Property Law

Whether a person is an aspiring author, a musician in a band, or a tinkerer who hopes to invent an indispensable product, arts, entertainment, and intellectual property issues and accompanying legal rights will arise.

The law of arts, entertainment, and intellectual property crosses over many lines. A person involved in one of these areas may be confronted with contract, copyright, trademark, business organization, or tax issues. This chapter will highlight some of the specific issues a person may encounter in these areas. Other chapters in this *Guidebook* also may be useful, including Small Business Law, Constitutional Law & Civil Rights, and Contract Law.

PROTECTING CREATIVE WORK

Intellectual property is a creation such as a song, poem, company logo, or invention through which the creator has expressed an idea and in which he or she has certain rights under the law. Although an author or inventor may be granted these rights, it is up to the person, not the court system, to protect his or her interest. If infringement—the unauthorized use of subject matter—occurs, the person who has the right may go to court to seek a remedy for the infringement.

There are different categories of intellectual property. Which category is applicable depends on the particular subject matter in question. A copyright protects the interests in an original writing, while a patent protects the interests in an invention.

Intellectual property law can be very technical and complicated. An attorney with experience in the particular intellectual property area should be consulted to adequately protect one's intellectual property rights.

COPYRIGHT

A copyright is the exclusive legal right given to a creator of original literary or artistic work. Copyright protection is provided by federal law, and is granted to original works of authorship fixed in a tangible form of expression. Authorship includes literary works, such as novels, poems, and short stories; musical works, including any accompanying words; dramatic works, including any accompanying music, dance works, paintings, photographs, sculptures, movies and sound recordings; and architectural works. Copyright protection applies to a wide range of expression, from computer software to advertisements. What all these items have in common is an original expression of an idea. Copyright applies to the expression of the idea, not the idea itself. Copyright is separate from the subject matter of the copyright. For example, if a person buys a painting from an artist, he or she buys the painting only and not the copyright. If the buyer makes copies of the painting and sells them, he or she is infringing on the artist's copyright.

Copyright protection originates from the time the work is created. A work does not have to be published in order to receive copyright protection. Copyright gives the creator of the work the exclusive right to perform, display, reproduce, and distribute copies of the work, and to prepare other works based upon the copyrighted work. An owner of a copyright can sell one, some, or all of these exclusive rights. For example, an author of a novel can sell the movie rights to one person and the paperback rights to another.

The owner of a copyright is typically the creator of the work. However, when a person is employed by another and creates the work while doing his or her job, the copyright is owned by the employer, not the employee. This is known as work made-for-hire. If an independent contractor contracts to create a work, he or she should address the copyright ownership issue up front.

There are no applications to fill out in order to have copyright protection. As stated previously, copyright is created when a work is created. However, a person may give notice that a work is copyrighted and register a copyright. For works created after March 1, 1989, it is no longer necessary to place a copyright notice on the work. However, it is a good idea to place the copyright notice on all creative works to give notice of the copyright claim. If there is an infringement of a copyright, a court will not allow the infringer to claim that he or she did not know the work was copyrighted if a notice was placed on the work.

A copyright notice contains the following three parts:

- The word "Copyright," the abbreviation "Copr.," or the © symbol
- The year the work first was published
- The name of the copyright owner

The federal law states that notice should be in a manner and location to give reasonable notice of the copyright claim. A copyright notice on a work should be in a conspicuous location.

A person also may register a copyright, which is not required, but provides several benefits. Registration creates a presumption that the copyright claim is valid and the potential for an award of attorney fees and statutory damages in an infringement case. Copyright registration also is a prerequisite to bringing an action for copyright infringement.

Registering a copyright is relatively straightforward. In general, a person should register within three months of publication. To register, a person must complete an application supplied by the Copyright Office of the Library of Congress and return the form to the office with a filing fee and copies of the work. The number of copies to be supplied depends on whether the work has been published, whether the work has been published outside the United States, and whether the work is a contribution to a collective work.

Copyright protection lasts a limited time. The time period depends on when the work was created and whether it was published. Generally, works created on or after January 1, 1978, have copyright protection from the time of creation throughout the creator's life, plus an additional 50 years. For works made during the course of employment, the duration of copyright is 75 years from publication or 100 years from creation, whichever is shorter.

When a party uses a copyrighted work without authorization, copyright infringement occurs. The owner of the copyright can bring a federal civil action against the infringer. The plaintiff in an infringement action must prove that he or she is the owner of the copyright and that the defendant infringed upon one of the plaintiff's exclusive rights. If the plaintiff has registered as the owner of the copyright, the law presumes that the plaintiff is the owner of the copyright. The plaintiff has the burden of proving that the defendant had access to the plaintiff's work and the defendant's work is substantially similar to the plaintiff's work. Once the plaintiff proves these elements, the burden shifts to the defendant to prove that the defendant's work was created independently. An innocent infringer—a person who relied on an authorized copy in which the copyright notice was omitted and who had no reason to believe the work was protected—may have a defense to an infringement claim. An innocent infringer is not liable for actual or statutory damages.

Before the infringement issue is resolved through a trial or settlement, a copyright owner can go to court and ask for a restraining order against the defendant to prevent the defendant from continuing the alleged infringement activity. If the activity is determined to be infringement by the court, it may grant an injunction, permanently barring the defendant's actions. A plaintiff who prevails in an infringement case can recover money damages as provided by statute or actual damages incurred as a result of the infringement, plus any profits made by the infringer. The choice of damages is made by the plaintiff. Attorney fees may be granted by the court in a successful infringement case.

Although a copyright gives its owner exclusive rights, "fair use" of a copyrighted work is not considered an infringement of copyright. Fair use includes copying for purposes such as news reporting, teaching, research, and comments and criticisms. Factors to be considered in determining whether use is fair use include the purpose of the use, whether the use was for profit, the amount of the work used, and the effect of the use upon the value of the work. There also are exceptions for libraries and teachers.

PATENTS

A patent is a right granted by the federal government to an inventor to exclude others from making, using, or selling an invention. The rationale behind the patent is to reward an inventor for the time and effort used in the creation of an invention. A patent is granted for a limited time period. After a patent expires, the inventor loses the exclusive rights to the invention. A patent protects an invention only in this country. If an inventor wishes to have protection in other countries, those countries patent procedures must be followed. An invention must be new, useful (except for a design patent, which must be ornamental), and not obvious in order to be granted a patent.

There are three categories of patents. A utility patent is granted to anyone who invents or discovers any new or useful process, machine, manufacture, composition of matter, or any improvement thereof. A new industrial or technical process may be patented. A utility patent is granted for a term of 17 years. A design patent is granted to anyone who invents a new, original, and ornamental design for an article of manufacture. The appearance of the article is protected under this patent. A design patent is granted for a term of 14 years. A plant patent is granted to any person who invents or discovers and asexually reproduces a distinct and new variety of plant. A plant may be a mutant, hybrid, or newly found seedling, except a tuber propagated plant or a plant found in an uncultivated state. A plant patent is granted for a term of 17 years.

In order for a patent to be granted, an application must be filed. A patent application is made to the United States Patent and Trademark Office, which is part of the Department of Commerce. A patent application is confidential; however, if a patent is granted, the application becomes public information.

The application includes three components. First, the applicant must submit a written document that describes the invention and states the claims of the inventor. The statement must be in such detail that a person knowledgeable in the subject matter area could build and use the invention based upon the information provided. The claims state the patented characteristics of the invention. This document also must contain a declaration by the inventor that he or she believes himself or herself to be the original and first inventor of the application's subject matter. The declaration must be notarized. The second component of the application is drawings illustrating the invention. An inventor should supply as many drawings as necessary to describe the invention. The third requirement is the filing fee. The fees may be reduced by 50 percent if the patent applicant is an individual, small business, or a nonprofit organization.

After a patent application is filed, a patent examiner reviews the application. The examiner may allow the patent, reject the application, or object to the application. A rejection means that the examiner believes the invention should not be granted a patent, while an objection means that there is a problem with the application, which can be fixed. The inventor can amend his or her patent application to address the concerns raised by the examiner. An inventor may appeal a patent rejection.

A patent will not be granted if the invention was in public use or on sale in the United States, or was the subject of a patent application in another country that had matured for more than one year prior to the filing of a patent application. An inventor's own use of the invention may bar him or her from receiving a patent if the invention was used for more than one year prior to application.

Patents are granted only to the inventor; however, an inventor may sell his or her rights to the patent or sell licenses under which another pays a fee to use the patent. A license may be exclusive or nonexclusive. If the rights to a patent are assigned, this assignment should be registered with the Patent and Trademark Office.

Before an inventor applies for a patent, a search should be done to determine whether a patent already has been granted for the invention. This search may be expensive. The Public Search Room of the Patent and Trademark Office is the primary source of information. Also, Patent and Trademark Depository Libraries have been established at the Illinois State Library in Springfield and at the Chicago Public Library.

When a patent is granted, an inventor must pay an issuance fee. Also, maintenance fees for the patent are paid three times during the patent period to keep the patent in force.

The Patent and Trademark Office maintains a register of attorneys and agents who meet the legal, scientific, and technical requirements to practice patent law, and who agree to uphold high standards of professional conduct. A person seeking to have his or her invention patented should contact a patent law attorney.

TRADEMARK

A trademark is a word, phrase, symbol, or design, or a combination of these items, that identifies and distinguishes the source of the goods of one party from those of another. A service mark is the same as a trademark except that it identifies and distinguishes the source of a service rather than a product. This section will use the terms "trademark" and "mark" to refer to both trademarks and service marks.

Rights to a trademark arise when a trademark is used or an application to register is made and the applicant intends to use the mark. A trademark gives the owner exclusive use of the trademark as long as it is used to identify goods or services.

Registering a trademark is not required; however, registration of a trademark, like registration of a copyright, provides benefits that make it worthwhile. The owner of a federal trademark registration is presumed to be the owner of the trademark and is entitled to use the trademark nationwide. A trademark may be registered with either the Patent and Trademark Office or the Illinois Secretary of State. Registration in one office does not register the trademark in the other office.

An application for federal trademark registration is in two stages. First, the application must be accepted. Once the application has been accepted, the process to determine trademark registration begins. An application to register a trademark is filed in the name of the owner, who can be an individual, partnership, or corporation. An owner who has not yet used the trademark may make an application based on an intention to use the trademark. Use of a trademark in promotion or advertising before the trademark is used with products or goods does not qualify as use. If an owner files an application based on intent to use the trademark, he or she must use the trademark and submit proof of this use to the Patent and Trademark Office before the trademark will be registered.

The application consists of a completed application form, a drawing of the mark, and a filing fee. There is a separate filing fee for each class of goods or services listed. The Patent and Trademark Office maintains a list of over 40 class categories, from furniture to clothing to chemicals. If the application is based on the use of the trademark, the application must include three examples per class showing actual use of the trademark. A separate application must be filed for each trademark a person wishes to register. The applicant must be careful when identifying goods and services, because an application may not be amended later to add goods or services not within the scope of the original identification.

After an application is filed, it is reviewed to determine if it meets the minimum requirements. If it does, the application is given a serial number and the applicant is sent a receipt. If minimum requirements are not met, the application and the fee are returned to the applicant. After an application is accepted, an examining patent and trademark attorney reviews the application to determine whether the trademark should be registered. If the attorney decides that the trademark should not be registered, he or she sends a letter to the applicant stating the grounds for refusal. The applicant must respond with objections within six months or the application will be abandoned. If the applicant's response does not overcome the attorney's objections, a final refusal will be issued. A common reason for refusing to register a trademark is the likelihood of confusion between the applicant's trademark and a trademark that already has been registered.

If there are no objections to the application or the objections have been overcome, the attorney will approve the trademark for publication in the *Official/Gazette*, a weekly publication of the Patent and Trademark Office. Any party who believes that it may be harmed by registration of the trademark has 30 days to file an opposition to the trademark with the Trademark Trial and Appeal Board.

If no oppositions are raised, the application continues in the registration process. The next step depends on whether the application is based on actual use of the trademark or intent to use the trademark. If the application is based on the actual use of the mark, the Patent and Trademark Office registers the mark and issues a registration certificate. If the application is based on the party's intent to use the trademark, the office issues a Notice of Allowance. The applicant has six months from the date of the notice either to use the trademark and send to the office a Statement of Use with three samples of use per class, or to request an extension of time. If the Statement of Use is filed and approved, the Patent and Trademark Office then issues a registration certificate. There is an additional fee per class for these filings. The term of a federal trademark registration is ten years, with ten-year renewal terms.

Before a person applies for federal registration of a trademark, a search should be done to determine whether there are any conflicting trademarks. The application fee is not refunded if a conflicting trademark is found. Also, one would not want to spend resources on a trademark that is not available. The Public Search Library of the Patent and Trademark Office and the Patent and Trademark Depository Libraries at the Illinois State Library in Springfield and the Chicago Public Library are sources of trademark information.

Besides registering a trademark claim, a person also may give notice to the public that trademark rights are claimed. The "TM" symbol or the "SM" symbol may be used to notify the public of the claim. Use of the registration symbol ® is permitted only when the trademark has been registered with the Patent and Trademark Office.

A trademark also may be registered with the Illinois Secretary of State's Office. A state trademark registration is not equivalent to federal registration. A trademark that is registered with the United States Patent and Trademark Office does not need to be registered with a state because federal registration gives the owner the rights to that trademark nationally. However, a party who has not registered a trademark federally may wish to file the trademark with the state. For example, if a person is operating a small business in Illinois and has no intention of expanding the business, he or she may consider registering the trademark with the Secretary of State to protect his or her interests only in the state of Illinois. State registration only provides protection in that state, so a person can have a trademark registered in Illinois and another person legally could use the same trademark in Michigan.

A trademark registration in Illinois costs less time and money than the federal registration. A party must submit an application to the Secretary of State's Office with the appropriate filing fee. A trademark registered in Illinois is protected as long as the trademark continues to be used. The initial term of a trademark registration is ten years, with subsequent renewal periods. Registering an assumed name or a corporate name in Illinois is not trademark registration and does not provide trademark protection. See the Small Business Law Chapter for further information on assumed name registration.

ARTISTS' RIGHTS AND OBLIGATIONS

It is believed that there is a unique bond between an artist and the work he or she creates. Based on this belief, artists have specific rights. These rights are known as moral rights (in French, *droit moral*). Moral rights protect, among other things, the integrity of an artist's work so that it cannot be changed without his or her permission. Moral rights originated in France and are recognized in a number of countries including, in a limited way, the United States. However, the United States does not recognize all moral rights. There are also differences between states in protecting artists' moral rights. If an artist wants to ensure certain rights that are not provided by law, one option is to put these rights into a contract. Contracts are discussed below.

The right of an artist to create or not create a work is included in moral rights. Disputes over the right to create usually arise when an artist refuses to create or complete a work for which he or she was commissioned. Artists rarely are forced to create because courts are reluctant to force the performance of services and because the party contracting for the work also may be reluctant to have the artist forced to finish the work. However, an artist who fails to fulfill his or her duties under a contract is liable for damages.

In 1990, the federal Visual Artists Rights Act (VARA) was passed. This act applies to paintings, drawings, prints, or sculptures, and amends federal copyright law by providing certain artists with attribution and integrity rights. VARA permits an artist to claim credit for the work he or she has created. If an artist's work is distorted, mutilated, or modified, the artist also has the right to stop the use of his or her name as the artist if such use becomes prejudicial to the artist's honor or reputation.

VARA also provides the artist the right to prevent destruction of a work of recognized stature. What constitutes a work of recognized stature is determined by scholars, curators, and collectors. This protection may be limited if the work is placed on a building.

An artist's economic rights give the artist the right to receive profits from resale of his or her work. Authors and entertainers typically enjoy royalty payments from subsequent reproduction and syndication. Fine artists, on the other hand, receive payment upon the initial sale only and, unfortunately, fail to receive profits from resale. Neither the United States nor Illinois provide statutory economic rights to artists. If an artist includes in a sales contract a provision requiring a share of profits from any resale, enforcement of such a provision may be a problem.

Although the United States Constitution guarantees the freedom of expression, this right has limitations, some of which are especially applicable to artists and entertainers. Obscene material is not entitled to constitutional protection. The United States Supreme Court created the following test to use in determining whether material is obscene: the average person applying contemporary community standards would find that the work, taken as a whole, appeals to the prurient interest; the work depicts or describes, in a patently offensive way, sexual conduct specifically defined by the applicable state law; and the work, taken as a whole, lacks serious literary, artistic, political, or scientific value. This standard is difficult to apply in the abstract, and can vary widely from community to community.

Injudicious speech sometimes can lead to a defamation suit. Defamation is a false statement that damages another person's reputation or character, such as false accusation of a crime, dishonesty in business, or unchastity. Libel is written defamation and slander is spoken defamation.

A defamatory statement must be a statement of fact, not a statement of opinion, to be actionable. There is a difference between stating a person is "a jerk" (opinion) and stating a person is "a convicted murderer" (fact). No matter how damaging a statement may be, if the statement is true there is no action for defamation (although there may be grounds for a different lawsuit, such as harassment). The defamatory statement must be communicated to a third party (publication), and must identify the party being defamed.

Once a plaintiff in a defamation case has proven that the defendant published a false, defamatory statement of fact about the plaintiff, the plaintiff must prove that the statement was made with actual malice or with negligence. The standard used depends on whether the plaintiff is considered a public figure or a private person. A public figure is a celebrity, politician, police officer, or citizen active in public policy. If the plaintiff is a public figure, he or she must prove that the defendant acted maliciously by deliberately failing to verify the defamatory statement. A plaintiff who is a private person only must prove that the defendant was negligent in publishing the statement and should have known that the statement was false.

Chapter 9: Arts, Entertainment & Intellectual Property Law

CONTRACTS

Artists and entertainers have many reasons to make contracts. They may enter contracts for performances, consignment agreements, recording agreements, or booking agreements. The following is a list of some of the common contracts an artist or entertainer is likely to encounter in his or her career. (For more information on contracts, see the Contract Law Chapter).

SHOPPING AGREEMENT

A shopping agreement is an agreement that an artist or a group of artists (such as a musical band) makes with an agent or manager who then "shops" around trying to find work for the artist(s). A shopping agreement should clearly spell out how long the contract is in effect. The time period should be long enough to give both parties time to evaluate each other, but not so long as to restrict the parties to a clearly unsatisfactory arrangement. A shopping agreement also should state in what manner the agent or manager is to be paid (usually a 10 to 20 percent commission) and who is responsible for expenses.

MANAGEMENT OR BOOKING CONTRACT

When an artist or group of artists is managed and/or promoted by another party, the parties should execute a management or booking contract. The agreement should sufficiently define all the rights and responsibilities of each party. Items of particular importance include specific commitments by the manager or agent to promote the artist's or group of artists' career; the management fee or commission; how the manager or agent will settle any disputes regarding conflicting booking obligations; and how the agreement will be affected if a group changes its name, members, or artistic style.

PERFORMANCE AGREEMENT

A performance agreement is an agreement between a performer and an organization or person producing (paying for) the performance. A performance agreement should at least state the basics: who will perform; where and when the performance will take place; the manner and hours of the performance; amount of compensation for the performance; and the manner and form of promotion of the performance. A more detailed agreement may include who will pay attorney fees for any disputes and the manner in which disputes will be settled (e.g., arbitration, mediation). Performers also should make certain that the person signing the contract is the person responsible for making payment after the performance, or an authorized representative thereof.

MUTUAL RELEASE AGREEMENT

A mutual release agreement outlines how to manage the legal and financial aspects of an artistic group's break-up. Having a mutual release agreement is especially important if the departure of a member is not voluntary. Important elements include the departing member's rights to use the group's material; the departing member's right to future royalties; and which member, if any, has the right to continue using the group's name.

CONSIGNMENT AGREEMENT

A consignment agreement is an agreement between an artist and an art dealer (or gallery owner) whereby the artist delivers a work of art to an art dealer for the purpose of sale. Upon selling the artwork, the art dealer usually receives a commission or some other form of compensation. In an effort to protect artists from bankrupt or unscrupulous gallery owners or art dealers, Illinois law requires that all consignment agreements be in written form and include the following provisions:

- The proceeds of the sale must be delivered to the artist at a schedule agreed to by the artist and the art dealer
- The art dealer is responsible for the stated value of the artwork in the event of loss or damage while the artwork is in possession of the art dealer
- The artwork will only be sold by the art dealer for an amount at least equal to that agreed to by the artist in writing
- The artwork may be used or displayed by the art dealer only with prior written consent of the artist and only if the artist is acknowledged in such use or display
- An artwork delivered to an art dealer for the purpose of sale or exhibition, and the artist's share of the proceeds of any sale by the art dealer creates a priority in favor of the artist over any claims, liens, or security interests in the artwork by creditors of the art dealer

After delivering the artwork to the art dealer, the artist should place a tag on the artwork giving notice that the work of art is being sold on a consignment basis (or the art dealer can post a sign in his or her place of business stating that some of the artworks being sold are consignment pieces). Adhering to the above provisions better enables artists to protect themselves against possible loss.

FORMING A BUSINESS

In order to adequately protect any assets, artists and entertainers should give careful consideration to business formation. A person may want to form a corporation, a partnership, or remain a sole proprietor. There are definite advantages and disadvantages to each business form. For more information, see the Small Business Law Chapter.

RESOURCES

Lawyers for the Creative Arts, 213 Institute Place West, #411, Chicago, IL 60610-3125, phone: (312) 944-ARTS, toll-free: (800) 525-ARTS.

Volunteer Lawyers for the Arts, One 53rd Street East, Sixth Floor, New York, NY 10022, phone: (212) 319-2787 ext. 25, publishes the following publications:

> *The Musician's Business and Legal Guide*
> *VLA Guide to Copyright for Musicians and Composers*
> *A Writer's Guide to Copyright*
> *The Writer's Legal Companion*
> *The Rights of Authors, Artists, and Other Creative People*
> *VLA Guide to Copyright for the Performing Arts*
> *VLA Guide to Copyright for Visual Artists*
> *Trademark: How to Name a Business and Product*
> *Licensing Art and Design*

Copyright Office, Library of Congress, Washington, D.C. 20554-6000, Public Information Office phone: (202) 707-3000. To order copyright application forms, call (202) 707-9100. In addition, frequently requested Copyright Office circulars, announcements, and the most recently proposed as well as final regulations are now available on the Internet. These documents may be examined and downloaded through the Library of Congress campus-wide information system, LC MARVEL, which can be reached through Telnet (marvel.loc.gov), Gopher (marvel.loc.gov), and the World Wide Web (http://www.lcweb.loc.gov/copyright).

United States Department of Commerce, Patent and Trademark Office, Washington, D.C. 20231. For General Information, call (703) 308-HELP; for Automated Information, call (703) 557-INFO, TDD: (703) 305-4487.

For Illinois trademark registration information, contact the Illinois Secretary of State, Department of Business Services, Trademarks Section, 213 State Capitol, Springfield, IL 62756, phone: (217) 782-9520.

Patent and Trademark Depository Libraries, where searches can be made for conflicting patents or trademarks, are located at the Chicago Public Library, 400 South State Street, Chicago, IL 60605, phone: (312) 269-2865, and in Springfield at the Illinois State Library, 300 South Second Street, Springfield, IL 62701-1976, phone: (217) 782-5659.

Arts, Entertainment & Intellectual Property Law
Leading Illinois Attorneys

LEADING ILLINOIS ATTORNEYS

Illinois' Most Respected Legal Counsel As Selected By Their Peers.

The Leading Illinois Attorneys below were recommended by their peers in a statewide survey.

The Leading Illinois Attorneys listed below were nominated as exceptional by their peers in a statewide survey conducted by American Research Corporation (ARC). ARC asked several thousand licensed Illinois attorneys to name the lawyer to whom they would send a close friend or family member in need of legal assistance in specific areas of law. The attorneys below were nominated in the area of Arts, Entertainment & Intellectual Property Law.

Because the survey results (all practice area results combined) represent less than three percent of Illinois' practicing attorneys, this list should not be construed as a complete list. Nevertheless, it is an excellent source of highly qualified and reputable Illinois attorneys.

For information on ARC's survey methodology, see page *xi*.
For the complete list of Leading Illinois Consumer Attorneys, see page *xii*.

The Leading Illinois Attorneys below are listed alphabetically in accordance with the geographic region in which their offices are located. Note that attorneys may handle clients from a broad geographic area; attorneys are not restricted to only serving clients residing within the cities in which their offices are located.

An attorney whose name appears in bold has included a biographical profile in this chapter.

Cook & Collar Counties

Applehans, Stephen G. - Waukegan
Azulay, Y. Judd - Chicago
Brezina, David C. - Chicago, page 59
Chin, Davis - Chicago
Ephraim, Donald M. - Chicago
Felch, Patricia A. - Chicago, page 60
Feldman, Mark I. - Chicago
Fifer, Samuel - Chicago
Frankel, William H. - Chicago
Gordon, Mark L. - Chicago
Hartmann, H. Michael - Chicago
Henderson, Susan M. - Arlington Heights
Hierl, Michael A. - Chicago
Hodes, Scott D. - Chicago
Hoover, Marsha K. - Chicago
Jacobs, Jeff - Chicago
Kaplan, Henry S. - Chicago
Kuczma, Linda A. - Chicago
Kuhlman, Richard S. - Chicago
Laff, Charles A. - Chicago
Liss, Mark J. - Chicago
Maclean Snyder, Jean - Chicago

McAndrews, George P. - Chicago
McCaleb, Malcolm, Jr. - Chicago
McGrath, William T. - Chicago
Mendelson, Michael S. - Chicago
Mensch, Linda S. - Chicago
Meyers, William B. - Chicago
Monco, Dean A. - Chicago
Moore, Carl E., Jr. - Chicago
Mortimer, John - Chicago
Musburger, Todd W. - Chicago
Niro, William L. - Chicago
Oberhardt, William P. - Chicago
Parkhurst, Todd S. - Chicago
Perrone, Mathew, Jr. - Algonquin
Pisoni, Jeanine M. - Chicago
Ross, Jay B. - Chicago, page 61
Sullivan, Terry - Rolling Meadows
Thomas, Henry I. - Chicago
Warnecke, Michael O. - Chicago
Weisman, Joel D. - Chicago
Wilson, Clarence S., Jr. - Chicago
Witcoff, David L. - Chicago

CENTRAL ILLINOIS

Ansel, Marc J. - Champaign
Bateman, Philip L. - Decatur
Keith, John R. - Springfield
Prillaman, Roger L. - Urbana

SOUTHERN ILLINOIS

Applegate, Steven D. - Carbondale
Hess, Frederick J. - Belleville
Rouhandeh, Mary Lou - Carbondale

Chapter 9: Arts, Entertainment & Intellectual Property Law

BIOGRAPHICAL PROFILES OF ARTS, ENTERTAINMENT & INTELLECTUAL PROPERTY LAW LEADING ILLINOIS ATTORNEYS

The Leading Illinois Attorneys profiled below were nominated as exceptional by their peers in a statewide survey conducted by American Research Corporation (ARC). ARC asked several thousand licensed Illinois attorneys to name the lawyer to whom they would send a close friend or family member in need of legal assistance in specific areas of law. The attorneys below were nominated in the area of Arts, Entertainment & Intellectual Property Law.

Because the survey results (all practice area results combined) represent less than three percent of Illinois' practicing attorneys, this list should not be construed as a complete list. Nevertheless, it is an excellent source of highly qualified and reputable Illinois attorneys.

For information on ARC's survey methodology, see page *xi*.
For the complete list of Leading Illinois Consumer Attorneys, see page *xii*.
For the list of Leading Illinois Arts, Entertainment & Intellectual Property Law Attorneys, see page 56.

The Leading Illinois Attorneys below are listed alphabetically in accordance with the geographic region in which their offices are located. Note that attorneys may handle clients from a broad geographic area; attorneys are not limited to only serving clients residing within the cities in which their offices are located.

The two-line attorney listings in this section are of attorneys who practice in this area but whose full biographical profiles appear in other sections of this book. A bullet "•" preceding a name indicates the attorney was nominated in this particular area of law.

For information on the format of the full biographical profiles, consult the "Using the Consumer Guidebook" section on page *xviii*.

The following abbreviations are used throughout these profiles:

App.	Appellate
Cir.	Circuit
Ct.	Court
Dist.	District
Sup.	Supreme
JD	Juris Doctor (Doctor of Law)
LLB	Legum Baccalaureus (Bachelor of Laws)
LLD	Legum Doctor (Doctor of Laws)
LLM	Legum Magister (Master of Laws)
ADR	Alternative Dispute Resolution
ABA	American Bar Association
ABOTA	American Board of Trial Advocates
ATLA	Association of Trial Lawyers of America
CBA	Chicago Bar Association
ISBA	Illinois State Bar Association
ITLA	Illinois Trial Lawyers Association
NBTA	National Board of Trial Advocacy

Cook & Collar Counties

•DAVID C. BREZINA: Since beginning private practice, Mr. Brezina has handled a broad range of practice in all aspects of patent, trademark and copyright law, including applications, litigation, counseling, and negotiating agreements in all these areas. Mr. Brezina is both a Registered Patent Attorney and a member of the Trial Bar. His undergraduate scientific training was in oceanography. He served as a legislative intern in the Iowa State General Assembly in the 66th Legislative Session. Beginning in 1983, Mr. Brezina taught undergraduate "Legal Aspects of Entertainment, Publishing and the Arts" and "Entrepreneurship: Basic Business Principles"; and graduate "Entertainment Law" in the Management Department of Columbia College in Chicago. Mr. Brezina compiled the text for *Legal Aspects* from 1984 to 1987. Since 1993, Mr. Brezina has been an adjunct professor at the Center for Intellectual Property Law of the John Marshall Law School in Chicago, where he teaches "Antitrust and Misuse Aspects of Intellectual Property." He has also participated in other academic activities, including judging intellectual property trial advocacy classes and judging papers for the Gerald Rose Memorial Legal Writing Competition. Mr. Brezina has made presentations on patents, trademarks, copyrights and other topics to bar committees and continuing education programs, law school clubs, law fraternities, trade associations, and computer user groups, and has published articles in various scholarly and trade publications.
Education: LLM Intellectual Property Law 1988, John Marshall Law School; JD 1978 with honors, Illinois Institute of Technology, Chicago-Kent; BSS 1975, Cornell College.
Admitted: Illinois 1978; 1978 U.S. Ct. App. (7th Cir.); 1978 U.S. Dist. Ct. (N. Dist. IL); 1981 U.S. Sup. Ct.; 1982 U.S. Dist. Ct. (N. Dist. IL, Trial Bar); 1982 U.S. Ct. App. (Fed. Cir.); 1988 U.S. Dist. Ct. (N. Dist. IN).
Professional Associations: CBA [Patent, Trademark and Copyright Committee (Chair 1994); Patent Subcommittee (Chair 1990)]; ISBA (Intellectual Property Section; Antitrust Section; Local Government and School Law Section); ABA (Intellectual Property Section; Antitrust Section; Management Section); Intellectual Property Law Assn. of Chicago; Bohemian Lawyers Assn. of Chicago; Lawyers for the Creative Arts; Society of Naval Architects and Marine Engineers (Associate Member).
Community Involvement: Mr. Brezina's community activity includes non-partisan citizens groups, poll watching, and participation in political campaigns for qualified and successful candidates. Mr. Brezina is a private pilot. He played and coached for the Lincoln Park Rugby Football Club and coached his son's American Youth Soccer Organization soccer team. He is active in the Chicago Corinthian Yacht Club and has built his own sailboat. *Mr. Brezina also practices Consumer Protection Law.*

DAVID C. BREZINA
Lee, Mann, Smith, McWilliams, Sweeny & Ohlson
209 South LaSalle Street
Suite 410
Chicago, IL 60604
Phone: (312) 368-1300
Fax: (312) 368-0034
Firm Web: http://www.intelpro.com

Extensive Experience In:
- Patent/Trademark/Copyright Law
- Patent/Trademark/Copyright Litigation
- Patent/Trademark/Copyright Application

Patricia A. Felch

ARTSLaw Offices of
Patricia A. Felch, P.C.
Three First National Plaza
Suite 3600
70 West Madison
Chicago, IL 60602

Phone: (312) 236-0404
Fax: (312) 236-0403
E-mail: artslawp@aol.com

Extensive Experience In:

- Copyright Litigation
- Publishing Contracts
- Intellectual Property Insurance Coverage

•**PATRICIA A. FELCH:** Ms. Felch represents clients with creative properties, including graphic designs, films, videos, plays, books, screenplays and teleplays, fine art, music, lyrics, poetry, computer programs, names, and logos. Although she does not serve as an agent, Ms. Felch assists her clients in protecting their properties through copyright and trademark registrations, clearances and licensing; simple contracts or multiparty deals; formations of appropriate business entities; and, if necessary, in all stages of litigation, including settlement negotiations, mediation, injunctive proceedings, pretrial litigation, trials, and appeals. She also teaches Entertainment and Sports Law at Loyola University School of Law, and the Arts and Entertainment Law Seminar at Columbia College. She serves on bar association committees and on the boards of several arts organizations. She is Of Counsel to a number of arts and nonprofit corporations and estates, and speaks and publishes widely on the legal aspects of the arts.

Education: JD 1987, Loyola University (Leadership and Service Award); MA 1973, University of Denver (Harriet E. Howe Scholarship); MAL 1973, University of Denver (Beta Phi Mu); BA 1969, University of Denver; AA 1967, Pine Manor College.

Admitted: 1987 Illinois; 1987 U.S. Dist. Ct. (N. Dist. IL, General Bar); 1987 U.S. Ct. App. (7th Cir.); 1990 U.S. Dist. Ct. (N. Dist. IL, Trial Bar).

Employment History: Owner 1993-present, ARTSLaw Offices of Patricia A. Felch, P.C.; Associate 1987-92, Gessler, Flynn, Fleischmann, Hughes & Socol, Ltd.; Law Clerk 1986-87, Joyce & Kubasiak; Summer Associate 1986, Hosier & Sufrin; Law Librarian 1981-86, Coffield, Ungaretti, Harris & Slavin.

Professional Associations: ABA (Forum Committee on the Entertainment and Sports Industries 1987-present); ISBA [Intellectual Property Section Council 1995-96 (Chair); Assembly Budget Committee 1992-93 (Chair); Legal Education, Admissions and Competence Committee 1991-92 (Chair)]; CBA [Creative Arts Committee 1989-90 (Chair); Entertainment Law Committee 1992-93 (Chair)]; Lawyers for the Creative Arts 1984-present (Volunteer 1987-present; Board Member 1988-present; Secretary 1992-94; President 1994-96); CARPLS, Coordinated Advice and Referral Program for Legal Services (Board Member 1993-present); Illinois Alliance for Arts Education (Board Member 1991-present).

Firm: Established in 1993, ARTSLaw focuses on clients in the arts, entertainment, publishing, and advertising industries. The main goal of the firm is to assist creative companies and individuals in protecting their creative properties through copyright and trademark registrations, contracts, incorporations and, if necessary, litigation. The firm offers other services and advice in many other areas of law, including employment, commercial, real and personal property, personal injury, and personality rights matters. *Ms. Felch also practices Alternative Dispute Resolution and Small Business Law.*

KURT A. MULLER - *The Muller Firm, Ltd.* - 200 North Dearborn Street, Suite 4602 - Chicago, IL 60601 - Phone: (312) 855-9558, Fax: (312) 855-9362, Cable: MULLAW - *See complete biographical profile in the Family Law Chapter, page 196.*

•**JAY B. ROSS:** Mr. Ross is a seasoned negotiator in contract law, concentrating in entertainment law. He consults for and/or handles negotiations on recordings, licensing, and publishing deals with every major record company and with most of the prominent television and film corporations. Mr. Ross consults for or negotiates at least one recording contract per month. He was the guiding force behind one of the largest artist shares secured for a pay-per-view (James Brown/Warner Brothers). Mr. Ross has handled numerous contract creations for independent companies, customizing each to fit the client's needs. He helped draft a law on the contracting of minors in the entertainment industry that protects both the company and the minor. Mr. Ross has represented many non-entertainment corporations in their negotiations with performers and entertainment companies for tour support, corporate sponsorship, contracting with corporate spokespeople and other entertainment-related activities. He was instrumental in developing the precedents that now protect artists whose material is sampled without permission. He has written articles for *The Entertainment Law and Finance Newsletter, The Blues Heaven Foundation Newsletter, Hollywood East Magazine, The Daily Law Bulletin, Screen Magazine,* and *The Illinois Entertainer,* among others. Mr. Ross hosted a radio program about entertainment law on WYTZ-FM for five years and produced and hosted the ultimate insiders' television show, *Backstage with Jay B. Ross.* He is the producer of a series of blues videos and a Christmas record released last year by Two Flight Records. Mr. Ross is an adjunct professor presently teaching entertainment law at the Chicago-Kent University School of Law.

Education: JD 1967, University of Illinois; BS 1964, University of Wisconsin.
Admitted: 1967 Illinois; 1987 New York.
Employment History: 1987-present, Jay B. Ross and Associates, P.C.
Representative Clients: Mr. Ross represents actors, comedians, radio personalities, screen writers, television and film score producers, CD-Rom manufacturers, and performers in all areas of music. He handles estates and rights of publicity for artists, including Dinah Washington, Willie Dixon, Howling Wolf, Charlie Parker, T-Bone Walker, Leadbelly, and Wes Montgomery. He is currently working with the former president of Tri-Star Pictures and the former entertainment president of CBS-TV to help their respective film and television companies.
Community Involvement: Blues Heaven Foundation (Board Member); Jay B. Ross Foundation for Charitable Endeavors (Director); National Academy of Recording Arts and Sciences [Chicago Chapter (President)]; Comedy Hall of Fame (Founder; Executive Director); Variety Club (Board Member).

JAY B. ROSS

Jay B. Ross and Associates, P.C.
838 West Grand Avenue
Suite 2W
Chicago, IL 60622-6565

Phone: (312) 633-9000
Fax: (312) 633-9090
Web Site: http://ww1.msen.com/
~stoff/entertainment_law
E-mail: music_law@msn.com

Extensive Experience In:

• Negotiation of Entertainment Contracts
• Rights to Publicity & Packaging
• Retrieving Monies Due Artists

CHAPTER 10

BANKRUPTCY LAW

If a person falls behind in paying off debts and it appears that the person will not be able to make payments as they come due, it is better to take action rather than let one's financial situation deteriorate. For many people, the answer to financial problems is to declare bankruptcy, a legal proceeding in federal court that allows a person to be released from the obligation of paying some or all debts.

It is often said that bankruptcy gives a debtor a fresh start, but filing bankruptcy is not a panacea for all financial problems because it is not painless. Declaring bankruptcy can seriously damage a person's credit rating, making it difficult to establish credit or take out loans. Many people can work themselves out of even very serious debt without ever going near a bankruptcy court, so declaring bankruptcy should not be an automatic first step for someone experiencing financial problems.

THE BANKRUPTCY CODE

Bankruptcy law is federal law. The United States Constitution grants to the federal government the exclusive right to make bankruptcy laws. Pursuant to this authority, the federal government created the Bankruptcy Code, Bankruptcy Rules of Procedure, and a system of bankruptcy courts to handle bankruptcies throughout the country. This is not to say that bankruptcy law is uniform throughout the nation, however. Although the federal government has final authority to make all bankruptcy laws, in some instances the Bankruptcy Code grants to individual states the power to deviate from federal rules in limited circumstances. For instance, the Bankruptcy Code allows a debtor to keep certain assets, known as exempt assets, that creditors cannot reach to satisfy a debt. The Bankruptcy Code gives states the authority to expand the categories of exempt assets if they choose. Thus, the amount of assets beyond the reach of creditors differs depending upon the state where the debtor files for bankruptcy.

The Bankruptcy Code creates different categories of bankruptcy, known as chapters, appropriate for different debtors. The two most common forms of consumer bankruptcy are Chapter 7 and Chapter 13.

CHAPTER 7

The vast majority of bankruptcy cases are Chapter 7 cases. Chapter 7 is often called liquidation bankruptcy. Chapter 7 is commonly used by individuals who want to walk away from their debt simply, but it may also be used by businesses that want to terminate their operations and liquidate their assets. When a debtor files Chapter 7, the bankruptcy court appoints a person to administer the case. This person is called the trustee. The debtor turns over some or all debts and assets to the trustee. The trustee then liquidates the property by selling it off and dividing the resulting cash among the creditors.

Under Illinois law, a person who files for Chapter 7 bankruptcy is permitted to retain up to $7,500 of equity in the person's residence; up to $1,200 in equity in the person's car; up to $2,000 in personal property such as cash and furniture; all necessary clothing, books and family pictures; up to $750 in implements, professional books or tools of the trade; and all professionally prescribed health aids for the person or one of the person's family members. These assets are called exempt assets. A person filing for bankruptcy must properly request these exempt assets in a bankruptcy case.

STEP 1: PETITION AND SCHEDULES

A Chapter 7 case begins when the debtor files a petition with the bankruptcy court. Any individual, partnership, or corporation can file Chapter 7 regardless of the amount of debt or whether the debtor is solvent or insolvent. The petition should be filed with the court serving the area where the debtor lives or where the debtor's principal place of business or assets are located.

Along with the petition, or shortly thereafter, the debtor files with the court several schedules listing current income and expenditures, a statement of financial affairs, all executor contracts, existing or potential lawsuits by or against the debtor, and any recent transfers of assets. If a debtor does not reveal a debt in these schedules, the bankruptcy court cannot discharge or cancel that debt. Any debt omitted from these schedules is called a non-scheduled debt and is not affected by the bankruptcy.

Step 2: Stay

Filing the petition automatically stops (stays) all of the listed creditors from trying to collect the money owed them. The stay arises automatically, without any judicial action, although the court usually does notify creditors of the filing of the petition. The stay is effective from the time of filing, even if the creditors do not receive notice until much later. As long as the stay is in effect, creditors cannot generally start or continue actions against the debtor to collect on the debt. Lawsuits, garnishment actions, even telephone calls to the debtor must cease.

Step 3: Creditors Meeting

After the debtor files a Chapter 7 petition, the court appoints a trustee to administer the case and liquidate assets. The trustee usually calls a meeting of the debtor, the debtor's attorney, and the creditors. The debtor must attend this meeting. Creditors may attend in order to ask questions, and examine documents concerning the debtor's financial affairs and property. In most consumer bankruptcies, all of the debtor's assets are either exempt or subject to valid liens, so there are no assets for creditors to pursue. In these cases, known as "no asset" cases, it is likely that no creditors show up at the creditors meeting. If it appears that a case will have assets to pursue, creditors usually show up at this meeting to gather information about the case because they plan to ask the bankruptcy judge to declare some of the debts non-dischargeable, they plan to challenge the exempt status of some asset, or they plan to file claims.

Step 4: Claims

After the creditors meeting, the creditors can file a claim against the debtor with the court. If the case has non-exempt assets free of security interests, these will be used to satisfy valid claims.

Step 5: Liquidation, Discharge and Reaffirmation

The trustee's primary role is to sell off the debtor's non-exempt assets in a way that maximizes the amount the creditors receive for their claims. Revenues from assets subject to security interests, such as property subject to a mortgage, is used to satisfy the debt on the particular asset. A Chapter 7 bankruptcy concludes when the trustee sells the debtor's property, distributes the cash to the creditors, and discharges the remaining debt. The discharge extinguishes the debtor's remaining personal liability on the debt. Certain items are non-dischargeable and thus unaffected by the bankruptcy. Non-dischargeable debts include

- Alimony and child support
- Most tax obligations
- Most student loans
- Liability for damages resulting from willful or malicious acts

Creditors can ask the court to deny an individual debtor a discharge. The grounds for denial of discharge are extremely narrow and requests for denial are rarely granted. Grounds for denial include:

- The debtor fails to adequately explain the loss of assets
- The debtor perjured himself or herself or failed to obey lawful orders of the court
- The debtor fraudulently transfers, conceals, or destroys property that should be in the estate

Because a secured creditor has rights that permit the creditor to seize pledged property, a debtor may want to reaffirm a debt even after it has been discharged if the debtor wants to keep the property. A reaffirmation is an agreement between the debtor and the secured creditor that the creditor will not exercise the creditor's right to take back the asset so long as the debtor makes payments.

A debtor must wait six years before the debtor can file for Chapter 7 again.

CHAPTER 13

Chapter 13 bankruptcy is often referred to as a "wage-earner plan," because it is generally used by people with stable incomes who want to repay at least some of their debts but are currently unable to do so. A debtor may file Chapter 13 bankruptcy if the debtor's financial crisis is temporary and the debtor expects income will grow enough in the next few years to pay off all debts. The main advantage to Chapter 13 is that the debtor is allowed to keep the debtor's property while a court-approved repayment plan is in effect. However, only an individual with less than

$100,000 in unsecured debts and less than $350,000 in secured debts is eligible to file a Chapter 13 bankruptcy. Corporations and partnerships cannot file Chapter 13 bankruptcies, although this option is available to a small business operated by a sole proprietor. In addition, the debtor must have a job or prove to the court that the debtor has the ability to earn stable income.

STEP 1: PETITION

The petition required for a Chapter 13 bankruptcy is similar to that described above for Chapter 7. The debtor provides the court with the following:

- Lists of all creditors, including the amount and nature of claims
- The source, amount and frequency of debtor income
- Lists of all property
- Detailed descriptions of the debtor's monthly living expenses, including food, clothing, shelter, utilities, taxes, transportation, and medical care

STEP 2: STAY

Filing a Chapter 13 petition automatically stays most actions against the debtor. So long as the stay is in effect, creditors generally cannot start or continue lawsuits or garnishment actions, or even phone the debtor demanding repayment. Chapter 13 also has a special stay provision that prohibits creditors from collecting consumer debt owed to the debtor by a third person.

STEP 3: PLAN

Within 15 working days of filing a Chapter 13 bankruptcy, the debtor presents a plan to the court that spells out how the debtor proposes to pay off debts over a three-year period or, by permission, over a five-year period. The plan must provide for the full payment of claims entitled to priority. For reasons of public policy, the Bankruptcy Code has several categories of unsecured claims that have priority over other unsecured claims, including the following:

- Costs of administering the bankruptcy
- Employees' wages, salaries, and commissions
- Contributions to employee benefit plans
- Deposits accepted by the debtor for personal items or services that the debtor did not deliver
- Taxes

STEP 4: CREDITORS MEETING

A creditors meeting is usually held about 20 to 40 days after the petition is filed. The debtor and trustee must attend the conference, but creditors have the option to attend. Trustee and creditors can question the debtor about financial affairs and terms of the plan. Any problems with the plan are usually solved during or shortly after this meeting.

STEP 5: CONFIRMATION HEARING

After the creditors meeting, the bankruptcy court determines at a bankruptcy hearing whether the plan is feasible and meets the standards for confirmation set by the Bankruptcy Code. Creditors are allowed to object to confirmation. The most common objections are that the debtor has not pledged sufficient disposable income to the plan or that the creditors receive less than they would if the debtors assets were liquidated in a Chapter 7 proceeding.

For most plans in Illinois, the bankruptcy court allows a five-year repayment plan. The court occasionally reduces the size of some of the dischargeable debts. During this five-year period, a portion of the debtor's paycheck goes to a court-appointed trustee who divides the money among the debtor's creditors.

If approved by the bankruptcy court, the plan prevents a debtor's creditors from garnishing wages or repossessing property.

STEP 6: DISCHARGE

A Chapter 13 debtor is entitled to a discharge if the debtor successfully completes all payments under an approved plan. The discharge releases the debtor from all debts provided for or disallowed under the plan. Creditors provided for under the plan may not start or continue actions against the debtor to collect a discharged obligation.

ADVANTAGES OF CHAPTER 13 OVER CHAPTER 7

Filing a Chapter 13 bankruptcy has advantages over a Chapter 7 liquidation. Unlike a Chapter 7 bankruptcy, there is not a six-year waiting period before the debtor can file bankruptcy again. Thus, with only a few exceptions, the debtor can file a Chapter 7 bankruptcy at any time after filing Chapter 13 bankruptcy. This means that if the debtor is unable to make the payments specified in a Chapter 13 bankruptcy plan, the debtor can still act to discharge debts through a Chapter 7 liquidation.

The non-dischargeable debts under a Chapter 13 bankruptcy are generally the same as the non-dischargeable debts in a Chapter 7 bankruptcy. However, a Chapter 13 bankruptcy allows the debtor to discharge a few more types of debts than does a Chapter 7 bankruptcy.

If the debtor owns an unincorporated business, such as a freelance consulting business, the debtor can continue to own and operate the business under a Chapter 13 plan. Under a Chapter 7 liquidation, a bankruptcy court may order that such a business or its assets be sold. Also, the automatic stay of a Chapter 13 bankruptcy protects any co-signers of consumer debts, whereas Chapter 7 offers only very limited protection of others who may share the debtor's obligation.

Finally, certain homeowners may prefer a Chapter 13 bankruptcy, because in many instances it allows them to make up past payments on their mortgage. When someone falls behind in making mortgage payments or is in actual default, a lender quite often "accelerates" the payments. For a debtor in this situation, filing a Chapter 13 bankruptcy may allow the debtor to "decelerate" or reduce those monthly payments and may even reinstate the mortgage by wiping out a prior default. However, if saving a house is the primary reason for filing bankruptcy, the homeowner should talk through all the possibilities with an attorney, because the laws governing this area are extremely complicated and it is easy to make a costly misstep.

CONVERSION

The Bankruptcy Code allows a debtor to convert a Chapter 7 case to Chapter 13 or vice versa as long as the debtor meets the eligibility requirements of the new chapter and the case has not previously been converted from the new chapter. In other words, the debtor is not allowed to repeatedly convert the case from one chapter to another.

INVOLUNTARY BANKRUPTCY

Unlike the types of situations described above, in which the debtor decides whether to file bankruptcy, in an involuntary bankruptcy creditors force the debtor into bankruptcy. Under certain conditions, creditors can petition the bankruptcy court to initiate a Chapter 7 or 11 (but not a Chapter 13) bankruptcy against a debtor (see the *Leading Illinois Attorneys Business Law Guidebook* for a discussion of Chapter 11 bankruptcy). The court will only accept such a petition if it is signed by at least three creditors who are owed a total of at least $5,000 in unsecured debt. If a debtor has fewer than 12 unsecured creditors, however, just one unsecured creditor owed at least $5,000 can file an involuntary bankruptcy petition.

Involuntary bankruptcy is rare, but if someone does file a petition against a debtor in bankruptcy court, the debtor has an opportunity to file an answer to the petition and refute any charges made by creditors in the petition. If the judge sides with the debtor, the court dismisses the petition and can make the creditors pay reasonable attorney fees and any money the debtor loses in defending the case. In addition, if the judge decides that the petition was filed in bad faith the court may also award the debtor punitive damages.

EFFECTS OF DECLARING BANKRUPTCY

The old adage that it is better to know how to swim before jumping into deep water applies to anyone considering filing bankruptcy. Although under federal law it is illegal for an employer to discharge or discriminate against an employee who has filed a bankruptcy case, there are other potentially adverse effects of which to be aware.

POOR CREDIT RATING

Consumer laws allow credit agencies to list on reports of a person's credit history all of that person's bankruptcy filings in the preceding ten years. This means that mortgage companies, banks, credit card companies, landlords, employers, and all others who can legally obtain a copy of a person's credit report will know about that person's troubled financial past. Filing bankruptcy can make it difficult to obtain credit for those ten years.

According to the Illinois State Bar Association, while each case is different, some people find that obtaining future credit is easier if they file a Chapter 13 bankruptcy and attempt to repay some of their debts, rather than file a Chapter 7 bankruptcy and make no attempt to repay.

CREDITOR SCRUTINY

One of the first events in a bankruptcy is a meeting between the debtor and all the debtor's creditors. At this meeting, the creditors and a court-appointed trustee are allowed to examine all of the debtor's financial records, such as bank statements and loan documents, and ask questions about how money has been spent. For anyone with anything unsavory or illegal to hide, such as gambling debts with a bookie, a bankruptcy proceeding can be incriminating.

COST

Understandably, bankruptcy attorneys are very careful about a client's ability to pay legal bills. A bankruptcy attorney will usually collect enough money in advance from a near-bankrupt client to handle a typical bankruptcy filing. This may be more than some clients can pay, especially if there is any contest with creditors. In addition, the trustee in charge of a bankruptcy case is paid by commission, a percentage of the money that the trustee distributes to pay creditors.

OTHER FORMS OF BANKRUPTCY

There are three other kinds of bankruptcy filings that are not discussed more fully in this chapter because of their limited relevance to consumers. Knowing about them can help one better understand bankruptcy options.

CHAPTER 9

Chapter 9 is a very rare form of bankruptcy available only to municipalities.

CHAPTER 11

Chapter 11 is available for corporations, partnerships, and individuals but is mostly used by troubled corporations and partnerships. Chapter 11 allows the debtor to remain in operation while being sheltered from some of its debts. Chapter 11 bankruptcy is discussed more fully in the *Leading Illinois Attorneys Business Law Guidebook*.

FARM BANKRUPTCIES

Chapter 12 is available only to family farmers and is designed to allow farmers to stay in business while attempting to pay off their debts. Chapter 12 offers several advantages over other bankruptcy chapters because it recognizes the seasonal nature of most agricultural income, the difficulty of predicting in advance how much a farmer will profit from a crop, and the fact that most farmers need much more credit than do most individuals. Chapter 12 was originally scheduled to be repealed on October 1, 1993, but the repeal date was pushed back to October 1, 1998. Chapter 12 bankruptcy is discussed more fully in the *Leading Illinois Attorneys Business Law Guidebook*.

TRANSFERS TO AVOID LOSING AN ASSET IN BANKRUPTCY

Some transfers that are valid outside the context of bankruptcy are invalid in bankruptcy. The Bankruptcy Code empowers a bankruptcy trustee to invalidate certain transfers made prior to a bankruptcy filing.

FRAUDULENT CONVEYANCES

The Uniform Fraudulent Transfer Act is designed to remove any temptation a debtor may have to hide property, by giving it to a relative, for example, before declaring bankruptcy. Any transfer of the debtor's assets made within 90 days of filing bankruptcy, or one year if a relative or business associate is involved, is carefully scrutinized by the bankruptcy court. If the court determines that the debtor attempted to defraud creditors by selling property at a below-market price, the court can order that property or other assets be given over to the trustee. Anything sold at a reasonable market value before a bankruptcy filing cannot be recovered by the court under the rules of the Uniform Fraudulent Transfer Act.

PREFERENCES

A preference occurs when a debtor treats one creditor more favorably than another. For instance, if a debtor with only $100 owes $100 each to creditors A and B and pays A completely, leaving nothing for B, then A has received a preference. Bankruptcy condemns preferences if the following conditions exist:

- Transfer is for the benefit of a creditor
- Transfer is made for debt owed prior to the initiation of bankruptcy
- Debtor is insolvent at the time of transfer
- Transfer is made 90 days before filing of the bankruptcy or one year before filing if made to an insider such as a relative or director of a corporate debtor

Creditors receiving preferences can be forced to return them to the debtor's estate.

COLLECTION AGENCIES AND THE LAW

Although not a part of Bankruptcy Code, laws regulating collection agencies are usually of concern to anyone experiencing financial difficulties. Both state and federal laws limit the kinds of activities that a collection agency can engage in as it tries to collect a debt. These laws only apply to third-party collection agencies and not to in-house collections. That is, if a creditor tries on its own to induce its delinquent accounts to pay their overdue bills, it is not required to follow the laws governing collection agencies. But if a creditor turns collection matters over to a collection agency, the collection agency's employees must follow the rules. Laws regulating debt collection agencies are discussed more fully in the Consumer Protection Chapter.

ALTERNATIVES TO BANKRUPTCY

Anyone in financial trouble has undoubtedly received many letters from creditors demanding payment on debts owed. Even a very demanding creditor may have a change of heart once a debtor mentions the possibility of filing bankruptcy, because creditors know that bankruptcy means that they may only get a fraction of what is owed them.

Anyone confident that existing financial problems are only temporary may want to consider asking major creditors to accept reduced payments for a short period or asking for a short delay in making payments. Provided that the debtor has not already given creditors reason to doubt the debtor's sincerity, e.g., by completely ignoring their letters or by consistently breaking promises, chances are good that creditors will agree to one of these plans.

As mentioned above, creditors know that bankruptcy means they will probably get just a small fraction of the total sum owed them. A creditor also knows that if it sues to collect its money, it must ask a judge to issue a court order to garnish the debtor's wages. This is time-consuming and costly. All these factors make it more likely that a creditor will agree to a repayment plan.

Many creditors can be understanding if approached with a reduced or delayed payment plan accurately spelling out the debtor's financial situation and showing that the debtor is trying to spread out meager resources in a way that tries to please everyone. A consumer credit counselor can help set up such a plan. Credit counselors can help to analyze and organize one's finances to set up a deferred or reduced payment plan.

In a typical case, a credit counselor devises a repayment plan that is then described in a form letter to be mailed to the debtor's major creditors. There are both advantages and disadvantages to using credit counselors, however. On the plus side, creditors who see that a debtor has taken the effort to consult with a credit advisor may be more likely to accept a repayment plan because seeing a credit counselor shows that the debtor is serious about getting out of debt. But credit counseling services also charge fees for their work, which may be more than an already-stressed budget can handle. However, there are some nonprofit agencies that offer credit counseling for a sliding-scale fee.

RESOURCES

Office of the Illinois Attorney General, Consumer Fraud Bureau, 500 South Second Street, Springfield, IL 62706, phone: (217) 782-1090 or 100 West Randolph Street, Chicago, IL 60601, phone: (312) 814-3000, toll-free: (800) 252-8666. Call or write to receive the free brochure, *Bankruptcy.*

Illinois State Bar Association, Illinois Bar Center, Springfield, IL 62701, phone: (217) 525-1760. Call or write for the free brochure, *Bankruptcy for Individuals.*

Money Troubles: Legal Strategies to Cope with Your Debts, Robin Leonard, Nolo Press, Berkeley, CA, 1991.

Chapter 10: Bankruptcy Law

BANKRUPTCY LAW LEADING ILLINOIS ATTORNEYS

LEADING ILLINOIS ATTORNEYS

Illinois' Most Respected Legal Counsel As Selected By Their Peers.

The Leading Illinois Attorneys below were recommended by their peers in a statewide survey.

The Leading Illinois Attorneys listed below were nominated as exceptional by their peers in a statewide survey conducted by American Research Corporation (ARC). ARC asked several thousand licensed Illinois attorneys to name the lawyer to whom they would send a close friend or family member in need of legal assistance in specific areas of law. The attorneys below were nominated in the area of Bankruptcy Law.

Because the survey results (all practice area results combined) represent less than three percent of Illinois' practicing attorneys, this list should not be construed as a complete list. Nevertheless, it is an excellent source of highly qualified and reputable Illinois attorneys.

For information on ARC's survey methodology, see page *xi*.
For the complete list of Leading Illinois Consumer Attorneys, see page *xiii*.

The Leading Illinois Attorneys below are listed alphabetically in accordance with the geographic region in which their offices are located. Note that attorneys may handle clients from a broad geographic area; attorneys are not restricted to only serving clients residing within the cities in which their offices are located.

An attorney whose name appears in bold has included a biographical profile in this chapter.

COOK & COLLAR COUNTIES

Aiello, Chris J. - Villa Park
Bass, Richard I. - Chicago
Biallas, John S. - St. Charles, page 71
Brill, Kevin M. - Chicago
Brodsky, Joel A. - Chicago
Brown, Kenneth H. - Highland Park
Brown, Ronald M. - Chicago
Chill, Max - Chicago
Cohen, Joseph E. - Chicago
Costello, Stephen J. - Carpentersville
Crane, Eugene - Chicago
Davis, Michael J. - Oak Brook
Ebner, Deborah K. - Chicago
Feld, Edwin L. - Chicago
Foster, Chester H., Jr. - Homewood
Gaertner, Kent A. - Naperville
Geiger, Donald H. - Waukegan
Gesas, Michael L. - Chicago
Grochocinski, David E. - Palos Heights
Groupe, Leonard M. - Chicago
Heyman, Glenn R. - Chicago
Holzrichter, Linda M. - Aurora
Jones, Richard T. - Woodstock
Kahn, Bennett A. - Chicago
Kaplan, Melvin J. - Chicago, page 71
Katz, Bruce M. - Chicago
Kohn, William Irwin - Chicago
Korrub, Lawrence - Chicago
Koukios, Steven S. - Park Ridge, page 72
Krol, Gina B. - Chicago
Lauter, Richard S. - Chicago

Magee, James T. - Round Lake
Margolis, Edward S. - Chicago
Marutzky, William F. - Chicago
McTavish, G. Alexander - Aurora
Minchella, Erica Crohn - Chicago, page 72
Mitzner, Scott L. - Westmont
Myler, Charles J. - Aurora
O'Donnell, Terry - Elmhurst
Pappas, James - Flossmoor
Pawlan, Mitchell D. - Northbrook
Raleigh, Thomas - Chicago
Ralph, Michael L. - Vernon Hills
Rath, William W. - Wheaton
Redfield, John H. - Skokie, page 72
Reed, John A. - Joliet
Ruddy, C. John - Aurora
Sanderman, Arthur P. - Palatine
Simon, Arthur G. - Chicago
Smirl, Dale L. - Chicago
Soroka, Walter - Chicago
Spadoro, Mark A. - Chicago
Stern, Gregory K. - Chicago
Strange, Jeffrey - Wilmette
Tracy, Keith M. - Schaumburg
Voiland, Joseph R. - Aurora
Wagner, Irvin J. - Chicago
Watschke, David R. - Elmhurst
Weissberg, Ariel - Chicago, page 73
Welch, David K. - Chicago
Windham, Danny L. - Chicago
Wognum, James P. - Chicago

68 *Leading Illinois Attorneys Consumer Law Guidebook*

Bankruptcy Law Leading Illinois Attorneys

Northwestern Illinois Including Rockford & Quad Cities

Balsley, Stephen G. - Rockford
Balsley, William L. - Loves Park
Buckrop, Bruce A. - Rock Island
Cassel, Jamie J. Swenson - Rockford, page 73
Flanders, Gary - Rockford
Gorman, Mary P. - Rockford
Howard, William J. - Rockford
Jackman, Philip A. - Galena
Kutsunis, Theodore G. - Rock Island

Meyer, Lydia S. - Loves Park
Natale, Bernard J. - Rockford
Nelson, Steven L. - Rock Island
Olsen, Joseph D. - Rockford
Ritz, Kenneth F. - Rockford, page 74
Stevens, James E. - Rockford
Whitmire, James E., Jr. - Silvis
Williams, Michael A. - Rock Island

Central Illinois

Barash, Barry M. - Galesburg
Barr, John - Decatur
Bonjean, Robert V., Jr. - Jacksonville
Bourey, Alan D. - Decatur
Bramfeld, John F. - Urbana
Brankey, Edward - Charleston
Brannon, James S. - Peoria
Chesley, George L. - Bloomington
Cole, Paul R. - Champaign
Covey, Andrew W. - Peoria
Covey, Charles E. - Peoria
Cox, A. Clay - Bloomington
Davis, W. Keith - Bloomington
Feldman, Howard W. - Springfield
Frisse, David M. - Paris
Germeraad, John H. - Springfield
Giganti, Francis J. - Springfield
GreenLeaf, John L., Jr. - Decatur
Grimsley, Gregg N. - Peoria, page 74
Howard, Timothy J. - Peoria
Johnson, James W. - Decatur

Keller, K. Rick - Effingham
Kelly, James D. - Springfield
Mann, Arthur L. - Champaign
Mann, Richard E. - Winchester
McNeely, Charles - Jacksonville
Meachum, Bruce J. - Danville
Meachum, Clyde - Danville
Moss, Thom W. - Decatur
Narmont, John S. - Springfield
Prillaman, Roger L. - Urbana
Quigg, Leo W., Jr. - Decatur
Rafool, Gary T. - Peoria
Richardson, Jeffrey D. - Decatur
Scott, Gregory A. - Springfield
Scott, R. Stephen - Springfield
Sheffler, Stephen K. - Champaign, page 75
Swartz, John L. - Springfield
Tagge, Stephen A. - Springfield
Taylor, Jeffrey C. - Decatur
Vigneri, Joseph W. - Decatur

Southern Illinois

Antonik, Douglas A. - Mt. Vernon
Blake, Edward J., Jr. - Belleville
Clark, Stephen R. - Belleville
Grandy, Laura K. - Belleville
Groshong, Donald E. - Alton
Hendricks, Scott P. - Carbondale
Katz, Michael A. - Collinsville
Kibler, Keith W. - Marion
Kunin, Joel A. - Belleville
McCarthy, Edward T. - Edwardsville

Mottaz, Steven N. - Alton
Mueller, William A. - Belleville, page 75
Reed, Mike - Centralia, page 76
Samson, Donald M. - Belleville
Sharp, Terrell Lee - Mt. Vernon, page 76
Smith, Webb H. - Carbondale
Veltman, R. Edward - Centralia
Vieira, Michelle - Marion
Williams, Tamalou M. - West Frankfort

10

July 1996 69

Biographical Profiles of Bankruptcy Law Leading Illinois Attorneys

The Leading Illinois Attorneys profiled below were nominated as exceptional by their peers in a statewide survey conducted by American Research Corporation (ARC). ARC asked several thousand licensed Illinois attorneys to name the lawyer to whom they would send a close friend or family member in need of legal assistance in specific areas of law. The attorneys below were nominated in the area of Bankruptcy Law.

Because the survey results (all practice area results combined) represent less than three percent of Illinois' practicing attorneys, this list should not be construed as a complete list. Nevertheless, it is an excellent source of highly qualified and reputable Illinois attorneys.

For information on ARC's survey methodology, see page *xi*.
For the complete list of Leading Illinois Consumer Attorneys, see page *xii*.
For the list of Leading Illinois Bankruptcy Law Attorneys, see page 68.

The Leading Illinois Attorneys below are listed alphabetically in accordance with the geographic region in which their offices are located. Note that attorneys may handle clients from a broad geographic area; attorneys are not limited to only serving clients residing within the cities in which their offices are located.

The two-line attorney listings in this section are of attorneys who practice in this area but whose full biographical profiles appear in other sections of this book. A bullet "•" preceding a name indicates the attorney was nominated in this particular area of law.

For information on the format of the full biographical profiles, consult the "Using the Consumer Guidebook" section on page *xviii*.

The following abbreviations are used throughout these profiles:

App.	Appellate
Cir.	Circuit
Ct.	Court
Dist.	District
Sup.	Supreme
JD	Juris Doctor (Doctor of Law)
LLB	Legum Baccalaureus (Bachelor of Laws)
LLD	Legum Doctor (Doctor of Laws)
LLM	Legum Magister (Master of Laws)
ADR	Alternative Dispute Resolution
ABA	American Bar Association
ABOTA	American Board of Trial Advocates
ATLA	Association of Trial Lawyers of America
CBA	Chicago Bar Association
ISBA	Illinois State Bar Association
ITLA	Illinois Trial Lawyers Association
NBTA	National Board of Trial Advocacy

Cook & Collar Counties

•JOHN S. BIALLAS: Mr. Biallas is a sole practitioner with an active practice in Kane, DuPage, DeKalb, McHenry, and Kendall Counties of Illinois. His work is concentrated principally in the areas of commercial/business-related Chapter 7 (liquidation) and Chapter 11 (reorganization) bankruptcy cases. He also handles consumer-related individual and joint Chapter 7 cases. A former member of the Panel of Private Trustees for the Northern District of Illinois, Eastern Division, Mr. Biallas has successfully handled virtually all types of bankruptcy cases and related adversary proceedings in U.S. Bankruptcy Court, as well as many types of collection-related cases in state court. He is the author of "Practitioner's Bankruptcy Forms for the Macintosh Computer." Mr. Biallas also has extensive experience in banking law, including customer workouts, commercial collections, and receiverships for both businesses and individuals. In addition, he has experience in foreclosure of mechanic's liens and mortgages; real estate development and closings.
Education: JD 1975, John Marshall Law School; BA 1972, Southern Illinois University; Class of 1970, United States Naval Academy, Annapolis, Maryland.
Admitted: 1975 Illinois; 1975 U.S. Dist. Ct. (N. Dist. IL, General Bar); 1975 U.S. Ct. App. (7th Cir.); 1980 U.S. Dist. Ct. (N. Dist. IL, Trial Bar).
Employment History: Sole Practitioner 1980-present; Associate 1978-80, Benson, Mair & Gosselin; Law Clerk 1975-78, Honorable William Guild, Illinois Second District Court of Appeals; Intern/Assistant Corporation Counsel 1974-75, Department of Law, City of Chicago.
Representative Clients: First State Bank of Maple Park.
Professional Associations: Kane County Bar Assn. 1975-94.
Community Involvement: Raymond B. Miller Charitable Trust (Co-Trustee); United States Naval Academy Alumni Assn.; United States Naval Institute.
Firm: As a sole practitioner, Mr. Biallas concentrates in his practice area. He is part of a mutual referral network providing clients with other types of legal services from highly qualified attorneys in his geographic area. *Mr. Biallas also practices Real Estate Law and Small Business Law.*

JOHN S. BIALLAS
Attorney at Law
2020 West Dean Street
Unit F
St. Charles, IL 60174

Phone: (630) 513-7878
Fax: (630) 513-7880
E-mail: jsb70@aol.com

Extensive Experience In:
- Chapter 7 Cases
- Chapter 11 Cases
- Foreclosure Law

•MELVIN J. KAPLAN: Mr. Kaplan exclusively practices consumer bankruptcy law. Over the past 38 years, Mr. Kaplan has helped thousands of Chicago-area families save their homes and find dignified solutions to their financial problems. He is the only attorney in the Chicago area to be *Certified by the American Bankruptcy Institute as a Consumer Bankruptcy Specialist. Mr. Kaplan is the author of *Out of Debt Through Chapter 13; How to Get Completely Out of Debt Through Chapter 13;* and *How to Get Your Creditors Off Your Back Without Losing Your Shirt.* He is a frequent lecturer at professional association seminars and community service programs.
Education: BA 1958, Roosevelt University; JD 1958, Illinois Institute of Technology, Chicago-Kent.
Admitted: 1958 Illinois; 1981 New York; 1985 Colorado; 1959 U.S. Dist. Ct. (N. Dist. IL); 1974 U.S. Sup. Ct.; 1982 U.S. Ct. App. (7th Cir.).
Professional Associations: National Assn. of Consumer Bankruptcy Attorneys (Board of Directors; Founding Member); ISBA; CBA [Bankruptcy and Reorganization Committee (past Chair)]; Bankruptcy Referral Service (Panel Member)]; ABA; Federal Trial Bar; Atticus Finch Inn of Court (Master of the Bench); AFL-CIO [Legal Service Plan (Panel Member)].
Firm: The law firm of Melvin J. Kaplan & Associates helps people who, due to a variety of circumstances, must consider the possibility of bankruptcy. For the past 25 years, consumer bankruptcy has been the firm's only business. All critical junctures of a client's case are handled by a highly qualified attorney. Paralegals help efficiently expedite paperwork, allowing the firm to provide an effective, professional service for a reasonable fee. A staff attorney attends the required court hearing on the client's behalf and personally reviews all bankruptcy paperwork filed. Appointment times are flexible, with evening and Saturday hours available.

*The Supreme Court of Illinois does not recognize certifications of specialties in the practice of law. A certificate, award or recognition is not a requirement to practice law in Illinois.

MELVIN J. KAPLAN
Melvin J. Kaplan & Associates
14 East Jackson Boulevard
Suite 1200
Chicago, IL 60604

Phone: (312) 294-8989
Fax: (312) 294-8995

Extensive Experience In:
- Chapter 7, Consumer & Corporation
- Chapter 13, Consumer & Business
- Corporate Assignments

Chapter 10: Bankruptcy Law

STEVEN S. KOUKIOS

Koukios & Associates
1480 Northwest Highway
Suite 203
Park Ridge, IL 60068

Phone: (847) 299-4440
Fax: (847) 299-4468

•**STEVEN S. KOUKIOS:** Mr. Koukios practices primarily bankruptcy law, including matters involving collections and mechanic's liens. He also handles real estate law, personal injury law, trusts and estates, traffic violations, and wrongful death. His experience includes numerous trials and contested hearings in Bankruptcy Court.
Education: JD 1986, DePaul University; BS 1982, Northern University of Illinois.
Admitted: 1986 Illinois.
Employment History: Partner, Koukios & Associates.
Representative Clients: Mr. Koukios represents debtors, creditors, and trustees in consumer and business bankruptcy proceedings.
Professional Associations: ITLA; CBA.
Community Involvement: Park Ridge City Chamber of Commerce.
Firm: Along with his associate, Panagiota Fortsas, Mr. Koukios has extensive experience in all matters related to bankruptcy law. *Mr. Koukios also practices Personal Injury Law: General and Real Estate Law.*

ROBERT E. MC KENZIE - *McKenzie & McKenzie, P.C.* - 5450 North Cumberland Avenue, Suite 120 - Chicago, IL 60656 - Phone: (312) 714-8040, Fax: (312) 714-8055 - *See complete biographical profile in the Tax Law Chapter, page 329.*

ERICA CROHN MINCHELLA

Minchella & Porter, Ltd.
19 South LaSalle Street
Suite 1500
Chicago, IL 60603-1403

Phone: (312) 759-1700
Fax: (312) 759-8813

•**ERICA CROHN MINCHELLA:** Ms. Minchella has represented small businesses and their owners for over 16 years. Her areas of practice include representation of debtors and creditors in business and dischargeability litigation, debtor-creditor remedies, commercial law, with particular emphasis on Chapter 11 reorganizations, and loan workouts and financial restructuring. Ms. Minchella also has extensive experience in negotiating and analyzing alternatives for restructuring and managing crisis situations. She is a member of the Federal Trial Bar. Ms. Minchella has been invited to lecture throughout the Chicago area and has been published nationally and locally on topics of concern to the public and the legal community on bankruptcy-related issues.
Education: JD 1981, Loyola University of Chicago; BA 1975, University of Illinois.
Admitted: 1981 Illinois; 1981 U.S. Dist. Ct. (N. Dist. IL); 1995 U.S. Dist. Ct. (W. Dist. WI).
Professional Associations: ABA; Commercial Law League of America (Bankruptcy and Insolvency Section); ISBA; CBA [Solo and Small Firm Practitioners Committee (Chair 1995-96)].
Firm: Minchella & Porter, Ltd., is the merger of the solo practices of Erica Crohn Minchella, which dates back to 1984, and Karen Jackson Porter, former law clerk to Bankruptcy Judge Thomas James and staff attorney to the Bankruptcy Judges of the Northern District of Illinois. The firm of four attorneys concentrates in bankruptcy and related practice areas, including construction and mechanic's liens law. The principals of the firm have combined experience of over 30 years in bankruptcy law. *Ms. Minchella also practices Small Business Law and Real Estate Law.*

JOHN H. REDFIELD

Attorney at Law
5420 Old Orchard Road
#A-205
Skokie, IL 60077

Phone: (847) 966-9920
Fax: (847) 966-6638

Extensive Experience In:

• Chapters 7, 11 & 13
• Bankruptcy Litigation & Appeals
• Liquidations & Reorganizations

•**JOHN H. REDFIELD:** Mr. Redfield is an attorney with a master's degree in taxation law and he is a Certified Public Accountant. He represents banks and other financial institutions as well as corporations and individuals—effectively, efficiently and at an economical hourly rate. The counsel and representation provided by Mr. Redfield draws on almost 20 years of experience as a trustee in bankruptcy, an attorney representing bankruptcy trustees, and as legal counsel for a group of Chicago and suburban banks. Having both prosecuted and defended cases in the Bankruptcy Court, he has handled numerous Chapter 11 cases, preference actions, dischargeability questions, alter ego cases, dissolutions, liquidations, and sophisticated collections and workouts over the years. He is an experienced practitioner and speaker on bankruptcy topics, having addressed educational programs of the professional associations of Certified Public Accountants and paralegals, as well as a lecturer at the John Marshall Law School.
Education: LLM 1983, DePaul University; JD 1976, John Marshall Law School; BA 1973, University of Michigan; Certified Public Accountant.
Admitted: 1976 Illinois.
Employment History: Private Practice 1976-present; Of Counsel 1994-present, Howard E. Gilbert & Associates, Ltd.
Professional Associations: CBA (Bankruptcy Committee).
Community Involvement: Jewish United Fund [Lawyers Division Committee (Chair)]; Landmark Education Corporation.
Firm: Mr. Redfield has devoted his career to developing a good professional reputation and good working relationships with his clients. It is his policy to handle each client's case or matter personally, in a thorough, meticulous and professional manner. He keeps each client advised of the progress or status of his or her case, including providing copies of all documents prepared or filed on the client's behalf. *Mr. Redfield also practices Estate Planning, Wills & Trusts Law and Tax Law.*

•**ARIEL WEISSBERG:** Mr. Weissberg insists on big firm quality within a small firm, delivering "hands-on" services with a team approach. Trained as the only associate in a small business law firm, he was responsible for every partner's chosen tasks (litigation, buying/selling property, and businesses, and insolvencies). He later honed this broad foundation with big firm experience. As such, he brings this broad base of business experience and training into his private practice, with the ability to litigate, reorganize businesses, and structure or close business deals. His experience, coupled with a strong clientele of financial institutions, mortgage bankers, and equipment lessors, enhances Mr. Weissberg's success in providing positive results for his clients. He is a frequent lecturer to professional associations, industry groups, and community associations on insolvencies, creditor rights, and real estate and business reorganizations. He is widely recognized for his knowledge in fraudulent conveyance law.
Education: JD 1979, St. Louis University; BA 1976, Washington University.
Admitted: 1979 Illinois; 1979 U.S. Dist. Ct. (N. Dist. IL); 1985 U.S. Dist. Ct. (E. Dist. WI).
Employment History: 1984-present, Weissberg and Associates, Ltd.; 1983-84, Berman, Fagel, et al; 1981-83, Schwartz, Cooper, Kolb & Gaynor; 1979-81, Boorstein & Weismann.
Representative Clients: Mr. Weissberg represents privately held business organizations, mortgage bankers, equipment lessors, and middle-market banks.
Professional Associations: CBA; ISBA; Decalogue Society of Lawyers.
Community Involvement: Mr. Weissberg has been an Officer and Board Member of his local synagogue for 16 years, a Cub Scout Leader, and a board member with various local and national Jewish charitable organizations.
Firm: The firm of Weissberg and Associates, Ltd., now consisting of three lawyers, was organized in 1984. The firm's business philosophy is to rehabilitate and salvage, rather than destroy; to work with clients as a team member to achieve the most cost-efficient positive results; and to reject the "volume-shop" approach to lawyering. The firm embraces the building of long-standing and broad-based relationships with its clients. The firm represents privately held business organizations, equipment lessors, mortgage bankers (prime and non-conforming credit), and is the counsel to over 65 closely held corporations. *Mr. Weissberg also practices Small Business Law and Real Estate Law.*

ARIEL WEISSBERG
Weissberg and Associates, Ltd.
401 South LaSalle Street
Suite 403
Chicago, IL 60605
Phone: (312) 663-0004
Fax: (312) 663-1514

Extensive Experience In:
• Real Estate Reorganization
• Trial Work
• Mortgage Banking

NORTHWESTERN ILLINOIS
INCLUDING ROCKFORD & QUAD CITIES

•**JAMIE J. SWENSON CASSEL:** Ms. Cassel has a civil practice emphasizing business matters, bankruptcy, and related state and federal commercial litigation. She has represented creditors, debtors, and trustees in both consumer and business bankruptcy proceedings. As a bankruptcy lawyer, Ms. Cassel's representation begins with pre-bankruptcy negotiations and court actions, and continues through the entire bankruptcy process to include ancillary and related deficiency/guaranty litigation. She writes and lectures frequently in the areas of bankruptcy, transactions, and debtor-creditor matters. Ms. Cassel, who has excellent negotiating skills, also has considerable experience in real estate, business matters, and commercial litigation involving contract claims, construction and shareholder/partner disputes, fiduciary matters, and real estate issues.
Education: JD 1986, University of Wyoming; BS 1982, University of Wyoming.
Admitted: 1986 Utah; 1989 Illinois; 1986 U.S. Dist. Ct. (Dist. of UT); 1989 U.S. Dist. Ct. (N. Dist. IL); 1993 U.S. Dist. Ct. (Dist. of NE); 1994 U.S. Ct. App. (7th Cir.).
Employment History: Partner 1992-present, Associate 1989-91, Reno, Zahm, Folgate, Lindberg & Powell; Associate 1986-89, Hansen & Anderson, Salt Lake City, Utah.
Professional Associations: Winnebago County Bar Assn. 1989-present [Board of Directors 1995-present; Bankruptcy Section 1993-present (Chair 1994-95); Federal Trial Section 1989-present (Chair 1995-96)]; ISBA 1989-present; Utah State Bar Assn. 1986-present; ABA 1989-present; American Bankruptcy Institute 1993-present.
Community Involvement: On The Waterfront, Inc. (Board of Directors); First Night Rockford (Steering Committee); P.E.O.; Pi Beta Phi Alumni Club; Ducks Unlimited; University of Wyoming Alumni Assn.; Rotary.
Firm: Reno, Zahm, Folgate, Lindberg & Powell has served clients throughout Illinois and Wisconsin since 1923. The firm provides clients with established experience in all phases of trial law, business law, real estate law, employment law, and tax law, as well as other subspecialties. The firm has successfully tried a wide variety of cases including all types of injury cases and complex business disputes. As a local firm comprised of attorneys with a strong commitment to its community, Reno, Zahm, Folgate, Lindberg & Powell serves its clients at the highest standard of legal representation. *See complete firm profile in Appendix A. Ms. Cassel also practices Small Business Law and Real Estate Law.*

JAMIE J. SWENSON CASSEL
Reno, Zahm, Folgate, Lindberg & Powell
1415 East State Street
Suite 900
Rockford, IL 61104
Phone: (815) 987-4050
Fax: (815) 987-4092

Extensive Experience In:
• Nondischargeability/Denial of Discharge
• Preferential Transfers
• Lien & Mortgage Matters

Chapter 10: Bankruptcy Law

KENNETH F. RITZ

Ritz, Willette & Hampilos
728 North Court Street
Rockford, IL 61103

Phone: (815) 968-1807
Fax: (815) 961-1917
E-mail: kenritz@aol.com

Extensive Experience In:
- Bankruptcy-Creditors
- Bankruptcy-Debtors

•**KENNETH F. RITZ:** Mr. Ritz has a practice that is heavily concentrated in the areas of collection and bankruptcy, especially the representation of creditors and debtors in Chapter 11 proceedings. He authored the textbook, *Chapter 11—Bankruptcy for Rich People;* has authored and lectured for the Illinois Institute for Continuing Legal Education in the state of Illinois on various banking and bankruptcy-related problems, and has written and spoken for the National Business Institute.
Education: JD 1959, University of Illinois (Board of Editors, *Law Review*); BA 1957, University of Toledo.
Admitted: 1959 Illinois; 1965 U.S. Ct. App. (7th Cir.); 1965 U.S. Dist. Ct. (N. Dist. IL, General Bar, Trial Bar).
Professional Associations: Winnebago County Bar Assn.; ISBA; ABA.
Firm: The firm consists of Kenneth F. Ritz, Craig A. Willette, George P. Hampilos, and Thomas E. Laughlin. Mr. Willette graduated from the University of Illinois in 1977 and was admitted to practice in the State of Illinois and the Federal Courts of the Northern District of Illinois in that year. Mr. Hampilos graduated from Syracuse University, cum laude 1992, and is licensed in the State of Illinois and the Federal Courts of the Northern District of Illinois. Mr. Laughlin graduated from the University of Illinois in 1972 and has been licensed to practice law in the State of Illinois and the Federal Courts of the Northern District of Illinois and the Seventh Circuit Court of Appeals since 1975. The firm engages in a wide practice involving all civil and bankruptcy matters. *Mr. Ritz also practices Small Business Law and Real Estate Law.*

CENTRAL ILLINOIS

GREGG N. GRIMSLEY

Carter & Grimsley
1500 Commerce Bank Building
Peoria, IL 61602

Phone: (309) 673-3517
Fax: (309) 673-3318

Extensive Experience In:
- Business Reorganization
- Debt Restructure
- Complex Bankruptcy Litigation

•**GREGG N. GRIMSLEY:** Mr. Grimsley has a diverse practice in most areas of commercial and civil litigation. In addition, he has developed an extensive bankruptcy practice, representing both debtors and creditors. Mr. Grimsley has, over the past 15 years, successfully reorganized many farming operations and businesses. He is the only attorney in the state of Illinois *Certified by the American Bankruptcy Board of Certification as a Specialist in both consumer and business Bankruptcy Law.
Education: JD 1976, Vanderbilt Law School (*Law Review* Award); BA 1973, Northwestern University.
Admitted: 1976 Illinois; 1976 U.S. Dist. Ct. (C. Dist. IL); 1977 U.S. Ct. App. (7th Cir.); 1989 U.S. Dist. Ct. (N. Dist. IL).
Employment History: Partner 1995-present, Carter & Grimsley; Associate/Partner 1976-94, Vonachen, Lawless, Trager & Slevin.
Representative Clients: Mr. Grimsley represents individuals, small and closely held corporations, financial institutions, and bankruptcy trustees.
Professional Associations: American Bankruptcy Institute; ISBA [Assembly 1988-92; Bankruptcy Law Section Council (Chair 1988-89)]; Illinois Bankers Assn. [Committee on Bank Council (Chair 1990)]; Illinois Bar Foundation (Fellow 1986-present).
Community Involvement: Father Sweeney School (Board Member; Treasurer 1988-95); Peoria Ballet Company (Director/Treasurer 1994-present); Diocese of Quincy (Vice Chancellor 1992-present); Illinois Farmers Legal Assistance Foundation (Director 1987-present).
Firm: Founded in 1995, the firm of Carter & Grimsley has over 45 years of combined legal experience in all forms of civil litigation, concentrating in personal injury, employment discrimination, divorce, and bankruptcy. The firm's goal is to provide its clients with quality representation at a reasonable cost. Carter & Grimsley strengthens its commitment to the community through active participation in civic and professional societies. The firm's members lecture and write frequently on their respective areas of practice. *Mr. Grimsley also practices Personal Injury Law: General and Family Law.*

*The Supreme Court of Illinois does not recognize certifications of specialties in the practice of law. A certificate, award or recognition is not a requirement to practice law in Illinois.

•**STEPHEN K. SHEFFLER:** Mr. Sheffler is currently engaged in the general practice of law. He has been located in the Champaign-Urbana, Illinois, community since July of 1979. He has concentrated his practice in the areas of bankruptcy, real estate, and financial and business matters. He was a faculty member for a presentation of creditors rights and protection of security interests in a bankruptcy seminar for the National Business Institute, Inc., in 1986.
Education: JD 1976, University of Illinois; AB 1973 with highest honors, Illinois College.
Admitted: 1976 Illinois; 1979 U.S. Dist. Ct. (C. Dist. IL); 1983 U.S. Sup. Ct.; 1985 U.S. Ct. App. (7th Cir.).
Employment History: Partner 1979-present, Pelini & Sheffler and predecessor partnerships; Associate 1976-79, Hartzell, Glidden, Tucker & Neff.
Representative Clients: Mr. Sheffler served as Bankruptcy Trustee, *In re: Wandell's Nursery, Inc.*; and as attorney for Creditors' Committee, *In re: C & S Grain Company, Inc.* He has represented numerous consumer and business debtors in bankruptcy proceedings under Chapters 7, 11 and 13 since 1980.
Professional Associations: Champaign County Bar Assn. 1979-present (Real Estate Committee 1994-present); ISBA 1976-present (Commercial Banking and Bankruptcy Law Section 1990-present); Champaign County Assn. of Realtors (Affiliate Member).
Community Involvement: Prairie Center 1986 92 (Board of Directors; President 1989-91).
Firm: Pelini & Sheffler is a small law firm which offers legal representation in a number of areas. The practice emphasizes personal client service. Stephen K. Sheffler concentrates his area of practice primarily in bankruptcy and related real estate, financial and business matters. Current staff includes an office manager/secretary who served as a Clerk in the Office of the Champaign County Circuit Clerk, Urbana, Illinois, for 14 years (12 years in a supervisory capacity); and a part-time law clerk who is a full-time University of Illinois law student. The firm has historically hired law clerks to facilitate more timely and efficient delivery of services to clients. *Mr. Sheffler also practices Real Estate Law and Estate Planning, Wills & Trusts Law.*

STEPHEN K. SHEFFLER
Pelini & Sheffler
501 West Church Street
P.O. Box 1486
Champaign, IL 61820

Phone: (217) 359-6242
Fax: (217) 359-6271

RICHARD WAYNE ZUCKERMAN - *Law Offices of Richard W. Zuckerman* - 124 SW Adams, Suite 520 - Peoria, IL 61602 - Phone: (309) 637-3732, Fax: (309) 637-5788 - *See complete biographical profile in the Family Law Chapter, page 215.*

SOUTHERN ILLINOIS

•**WILLIAM A. MUELLER:** Mr. Mueller, operating under the name, The Bankruptcy Center, practices exclusively in consumer bankruptcy law. Mr. Mueller has 11 years of bankruptcy experience, and his firm currently files a larger percentage of Chapter 7s and Chapter 13s than any other firm in the Southern District of Illinois. He is a frequent lecturer at local bankruptcy seminars. Mr. Mueller's philosophy of providing clients with a personal approach, reasonable fees, and prompt service has resulted in the rapid growth of his practice.
Education: JD 1984 cum laude, St. Louis University; BA 1981 magna cum laude, Eastern Illinois University.
Admitted: 1984 Illinois; 1985 Missouri; 1984 U.S. Dist. Ct. (S. Dist. IL).
Employment History: Owner 1992-present, The Bankruptcy Center; Associate 1989-92, Ripplinger, Dixon & Johnston; Associate 1984-89, Law Office of Charles Kolker.
Representative Clients: In 1995, The Bankruptcy Center represented approximately one-third of all consumer debtors in Chapter 7s and Chapter 13s filed in the Southern District of Illinois.
Professional Associations: National Association of Chapter 13 Trustees (Associate 1991-present); Southern Illinois Bankruptcy Institute 1990-present; ISBA 1984-present (Banking and Bankruptcy Section Council 1990-94); St. Clair County Bar Assn. 1984-present.
Firm: The Bankruptcy Center has four associate attorneys, and offices in Belleville, Edwardsville, Mt. Vernon, and Carbondale for client convenience. Some evening and weekend appointments are available and the initial consultation with an attorney is free.

WILLIAM A. MUELLER
The Bankruptcy Center
7805 West Main Street
Belleville, IL 62223

Phone: (618) 394-0713
Fax: (618) 394-1497

Extensive Experience In:
• Chapter 7 Bankruptcy
• Chapter 13 Wage Earner Plan

MIKE REED

Law Office of Mike Reed
423 South Poplar Street
Centralia, IL 62801

Phone: (618) 533-0122
Fax: (618) 533-7541
800: (800) 693-4471

Extensive Experience In:

- Chapter 11
- Lender Liability

•**MIKE REED:** Mr. Reed practices primarily in bankruptcy matters. He has 14 years' experience in handling consumer and business matters and transactions. While the majority of his practice involves consumer Chapter 7 liquidations and Chapter 13 wage earner cases, he has represented farmers in successful Chapter 12 reorganization cases and business interests in Chapter 7, 11 and 13 cases. Mr. Reed has significant trial experience in both state and federal courts, including bench and jury trials and civil appeals. He has been a speaker for a Small Business Administration-sponsored class, designed to teach individuals how to establish a small business. Mr. Reed has also been a speaker for his local bar association lecture series on bankruptcy matters to the general public and to other attorneys. His accomplishments include confirmed reorganization plans involving significant reductions in debt to banks to offset lender liability problems. He has also attended various seminars, including a three-day intensive trial course sponsored by the Illinois Institute for Continuing Legal Education, and a course entitled "Effective Negotiation Techniques for Lawyers," a three-day seminar sponsored by the Law Education Institute. He is also experienced in computer legal research with Westlaw and Laserlaw.

Education: JD 1981, John Marshall Law School (Moot Court; Labor Law Moot Court); BA 1976 with honors, Western Illinois University (Scholarship Award; Student Government President).

Admitted: 1982 Illinois; 1981 U.S. Dist. Ct. (N. Dist. IL); 1982 U.S. Dist. Ct. (S. Dist. IL).

Employment History: 1990-present, Law Office of Mike Reed; Attorney 1982-86, Partner 1986-90, Crain, Cooksey and Veltman, Ltd.

Representative Clients: Mr. Reed represents local banks for bankruptcy matters and disputes between banks; Chapter 7 Trustee, Donald Hoagland; Chapter 12 and 13 Trustee, Robert Kearney.

Professional Associations: Marion County Bar Assn. (President 1995-present); ISBA.

Community Involvement: Optimist Club [Annual Fishing Derby (Vice President; Chair)]; football, soccer and basketball coach. *Mr. Reed also practices Real Estate Law and Family Law.*

TERRELL "TERRY" LEE SHARP

Law Office of Terry Sharp, P.C.
1115 Harrison Street
P.O. Box 906
Mt. Vernon, IL 62864

Phone: (618) 242-0246
Fax: (618) 242-1170
800: (800) 769-7000

Extensive Experience In:

- Shareholder Litigation
- UCC Article 9
- Mortgage Foreclosure

•**TERRELL "TERRY" LEE SHARP:** Mr. Sharp practices bankruptcy law and real estate law and represents numerous real estate developers in all phases of real estate development. He is a Certified Fraud Examiner, Certified Public Accountant, and has lectured for the Illinois State Bar Association, Illinois Institute for Continuing Legal Education, Illinois Bankers Association, and trade and community seminars. He has published several articles dealing with bankruptcy issues, including coauthoring "Defining Value" in the January 1996 edition of *Journal of Lending and Credit Risk Management,* a monthly publication distributed to 23,000 banks and lending institutions.

Education: JD 1973, University of Illinois; BS 1970, University of Illinois.

Admitted: 1973 U.S. Dist. Ct. (S. Dist. IL); 1986 U.S. Ct. App. (7th Cir.); 1991 U.S. Sup. Ct.; 1996 U.S. Dist. Ct. (C. Dist. IL).

Employment History: Senior Attorney 1973-present, Law Office of Terry Sharp, P.C.

Representative Clients: Banterra Bank Group; Housing Authority of the City of Mt. Vernon; FS Credit Corporation; Heidelberg; Harris, Inc. The firm is the issuing agent for Lawyers Title Insurance Company, Attorneys Title Guaranty Fund, and National Land Title Insurance Company.

Professional Associations: Jefferson County Bar Assn. (President 1975); ISBA; ABA; ITLA.

Community Involvement: Rotary Club (President); Jefferson County Chamber of Commerce (President 1984-95); United Fund (Vice President).

Firm: The Law Office of Terry Sharp, P.C., established in 1973, has extensive experience in creditors' remedies, inside and outside of bankruptcy. The firm represents numerous banks and agricultural financing agencies on a recurring basis, protecting the rights of its clients in circuit and bankruptcy court litigation throughout the geographic region. The firm also provides representation to bankruptcy trustees and debtors in Chapters 7, 11, 12 and 13 on a case-by-case basis and represents numerous real estate developers in all phases of real estate development. The firm also practices in the areas of commercial, banking, corporate, probate and estate planning laws. The firm makes extensive use of paralegals and law clerks to provide prompt and less expensive service to the firm's clients. *Mr. Sharp also practices Real Estate Law and Estate Planning, Wills & Trusts Law.*

CHAPTER 11

CIVIL APPELLATE LAW

After a decision is rendered in a civil case by a trial judge or jury, the party who "loses" has the right to have the decision reviewed by a higher court. This process, known as the appeals or appellate process, is the subject of this chapter. Court proceedings prior to appeal are outlined in the Process of a Case: Civil & Criminal Chapter. The court system in general is covered in the Illinois' Judicial Systems Chapter.

Appellate courts are set up just to make appellate decisions. So, too, many lawyers practice only appellate law. One reason for this area of practice is that arguing an appeal is quite different from representing a party in a trial.

A party who disagrees with a judge's or jury's decision should seek the advice of an appellate lawyer regarding the prospects of a better outcome on appeal. A party served with a notice that the opposing party is appealing the decision likewise should contact an appellate attorney.

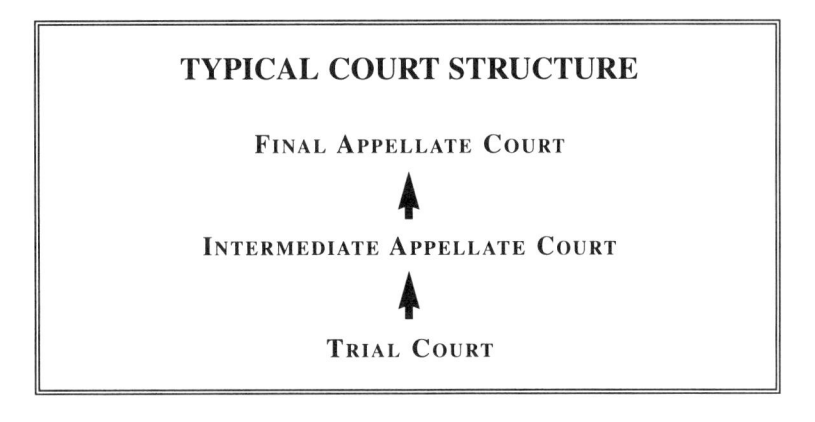

TYPICAL COURT STRUCTURE

FINAL APPELLATE COURT
↑
INTERMEDIATE APPELLATE COURT
↑
TRIAL COURT

WHAT IS AN APPEAL?

Appeal is the term used to describe the process by which a higher court reviews the decision of a lower (trial) court. The right to appeal an adverse legal decision is granted by the United States Constitution and the Illinois Constitution. This appeals system provides a check on the power of a judge or jury. Judges who interpret the law erroneously will have their decisions overturned by a court with authority to do so. Judges know that their governance over every case may be checked by an appellate court.

Some appeals are granted only at the discretion of the appellate court. The United States Supreme Court, because it cannot review every single case decided in the federal system, hears appeals only at its discretion.

A party who had a court decision made against him or her is the party with the right to appeal. (Only under very rare circumstances can a party appeal a favorable decision on the ground that he or she disagrees with the reasoning of the decision.) The party who appeals is known as the appellant. In opposition to the appellant is the appellee, the party who agrees with the outcome of the trial and who will argue during the appeal that the judge's or jury's decision should be left alone.

Chapter 11: Civil Appellate Law

REQUIREMENTS FOR APPEALING A DECISION

FINALITY

Not every determination made by a judge is appealable. Only final judgments, decisions that conclude the case in that court once and for all, are appealable. If a particular decision was not final, it is not time for an appeal.

Throughout the course of any civil trial, the trial judge may make numerous decisions. The judge may rule on a motion to limit the scope of questions that may be asked in a deposition, or may grant or deny a request that the case be dismissed on the ground that there is insufficient evidence of wrongdoing. Any court order that does not complete the case is not considered a final order. For example, if the judge denies a motion to dismiss, the proceedings will continue and the order denying the motion is considered an interim or interlocutory order, not a final order. On the other hand, if the judge grants the motion to dismiss the case, that order is final. A decision regarding the subject matter of the case has been made: sufficient grounds do not exist for the case to continue. The final decision (also called a final disposition, final judgment, or final order) disposes of the case as far as that court is concerned.

Generally, a final decision is made after a hearing. The judge or jury has heard all the evidence, and it makes a decision. A finding that the plaintiff proved or failed to prove his or her case ends the litigation at that stage. The final order is appealable.

TIMELINESS

If the lower court has not yet rendered its final decision, the appeal is not appropriate. For another court to give its input into the proceedings while they are still going on would be confusing and inefficient for everyone involved.

Thus, only a final decision is appealable. The right to appeal, though, does not last forever. Parties are bound to keep things moving along by exercising the right to appeal within a reasonable length of time after the final judgment is rendered. Like a statute of limitations, every court has a rule dictating the length of time after the final judgment during which an appeal may be made. For example, in the federal system, a federal district court's final decision generally must be appealed within 30 days (or 60 days if the United States or its agent or officer is a party) or the party who wishes to appeal loses that right forever.

Sometimes, there is a question as to when the final judgment of the trial court was entered. In an employment discrimination case in which a plaintiff sought back pay and other damages, a court issued an order setting forth its findings of fact and conclusions of law and stating that judgment was for the plaintiff and against the defendant. Some months later, the court issued another order awarding back pay and a retroactive promotion to the plaintiff. Yet another order was entered in the next month, in which the court granted the plaintiff attorney fees and litigation expenses. A question arose about when the clock started ticking for the defendant to file a notice of appeal. Which order was the final order for purposes of appeal? The appeals court held that the last order, granting fees and expenses, was the final judgment in the case, because it dispensed with the last of the issues raised in the plaintiff's complaint.

THE SCOPE OF REVIEW

What an appeals court has authority to decide is limited. The appellant must outline the specific question it wants answered by the appeals court. The question may be as broad as, "Did the trial court err in deciding in favor of the plaintiff?" or it may be very specific. Usually, the appellant asks that several critical questions be answered. Historically, rather than "filing an appeal" a party was said to file a "writ of error." The writ of error was a request to a higher court to overturn the lower court's final decision based on a critical error in reasoning or, simply, because the decision was wrong.

A plaintiff who loses an age discrimination case, for instance, may file an appeal challenging the bases upon which the trial judge made his or her decision. This appeal might be structured as follows:

- Did the trial judge err when she ruled that the Age Discrimination in Employment Act did not apply?
- Did the trial judge err when she ruled that the plaintiff was required to show that he was replaced by a worker outside the protected age group?
- Did the trial judge err when she ruled that the plaintiff failed to establish a prima facie case?

Because appeals are structured in this way, it is sometimes said that the actions of the trial judge are on trial, not the actions of the parties to the original litigation.

In fact, the parties do not have a chance to re-litigate the case before the appeals court. The trial level is the only opportunity to submit evidence, examine and cross-examine witnesses, and argue the facts and the law of the case. The appeals court only considers whether the trial was conducted properly and whether the outcome was reached by proper application of the law to the facts. As noted above, the only question for an appeals court may be very specific, such as whether a particular document should have been submitted. But only issues that were raised originally in the trial court can be challenged at the appellate level.

The body of evidence—argument, testimony, and objections considered in the trial court—is all that may be considered by the appeals panel. This body of evidence is called the record. Every piece of evidence and every argument made by the parties' lawyers is recorded into one big document, the record, which is said to "close" once the trial is over. Once the record is closed, no more evidence can be included. Also, no more objections to evidence can be made.

At the appeals level, the court is restricted to review of the record. A party cannot offer new evidence or new objections for the appellate court to consider. The age discrimination plaintiff, for example, may not ask the appellate court to overturn the decision of the trial judge based on a new document that the trial judge never saw. The trial was the only opportunity to present the document. On the other hand, the plaintiff may argue on appeal that the judge should have allowed his coworker to testify, as long as the plaintiff made that argument in his original case. He may give the appellate court an indication of what the coworker would have said, so the court can weigh whether the exclusion of the testimony was harmful to the plaintiff's case.

THE APPELLATE DECISION

Because the appeals court only reviews the actions of the lower court—not the actions of the parties—its decision is couched in terms of whether the lower court made the right decision. The following are the options for an appeals court:

- *Affirm:* The appeals court may affirm the lower court's decree, judgment, or order, which is a declaration that the decision of the lower court was right and it will stand.
- *Error:* If the appellate court holds that the lower court's decision was erroneous, it will reverse, modify, or remand (see below). It may rule that the mistake was a harmless error, which means that even though there was an error, it did not affect the outcome of the case enough to make a difference. Maybe a particular witness should have been allowed to testify, but the testimony would have been similar to that of a witness who did take the stand and whose testimony did not carry much weight, so the jury probably would not have found the excluded testimony very compelling. Excluding the witness was harmless error.
- *Modify:* A final trial court decision may be affirmed by a higher court with minor modification that does not affect the substance or general findings of the decision.
- *Remand:* The remand of a case is the sending it back to the lower court with instructions about what the lower court should do. Usually, a remand means there were errors in the trial court's decision to such an extent that the appellate court cannot correct the errors itself. The lower court must reconsider the case based on the appellate court's instructions.
- *Reverse:* An appeals court decision to reverse a case is a ruling that the trial court should have reached the opposite conclusion. A finding for the plaintiff should have been a finding that the defendant was not liable; a finding for the defendant should have been a ruling that there was enough evidence to find the defendant liable. Unlike a remand, the appeals court has enough evidence in the record to make a determination to reverse. Sometimes, the appeals court reverses and remands at the same time. In this situation, the court has enough information to reverse the trial court's bottom line, its ultimate decision, but some questions (such as the amount of damages) still need to be worked out on remand.

In addition to these different options, appeals courts often hand down decisions that combine several different rulings. A court may reverse in part and affirm in part, or it may affirm a judgment as modified by the points described in its opinion.

APPEALS COURTS AND APPELLATE PROCEDURE

THE FEDERAL APPELLATE STRUCTURE

The federal appellate system consists of 13 federal circuits, each of which has one appellate court, called a court of appeals, and the United States Supreme Court. Within each of the federal circuits are several federal district courts that serve as trial courts for issues of federal concern. Parties who are dissatisfied with the outcome of a district court case have the right to appeal to the court of appeals encompassing that district. Illinois is located in the Seventh Circuit; thus, a case heard in a federal district court in Illinois (such as the Federal District Court for the Northern District of Illinois) would be appealed to the Court of Appeals for the Seventh Circuit, which is located in Chicago. (Indiana and Wisconsin are in the Seventh Circuit also.)

Chapter 11: Civil Appellate Law

THE THIRTEEN FEDERAL JUDICIAL CIRCUITS

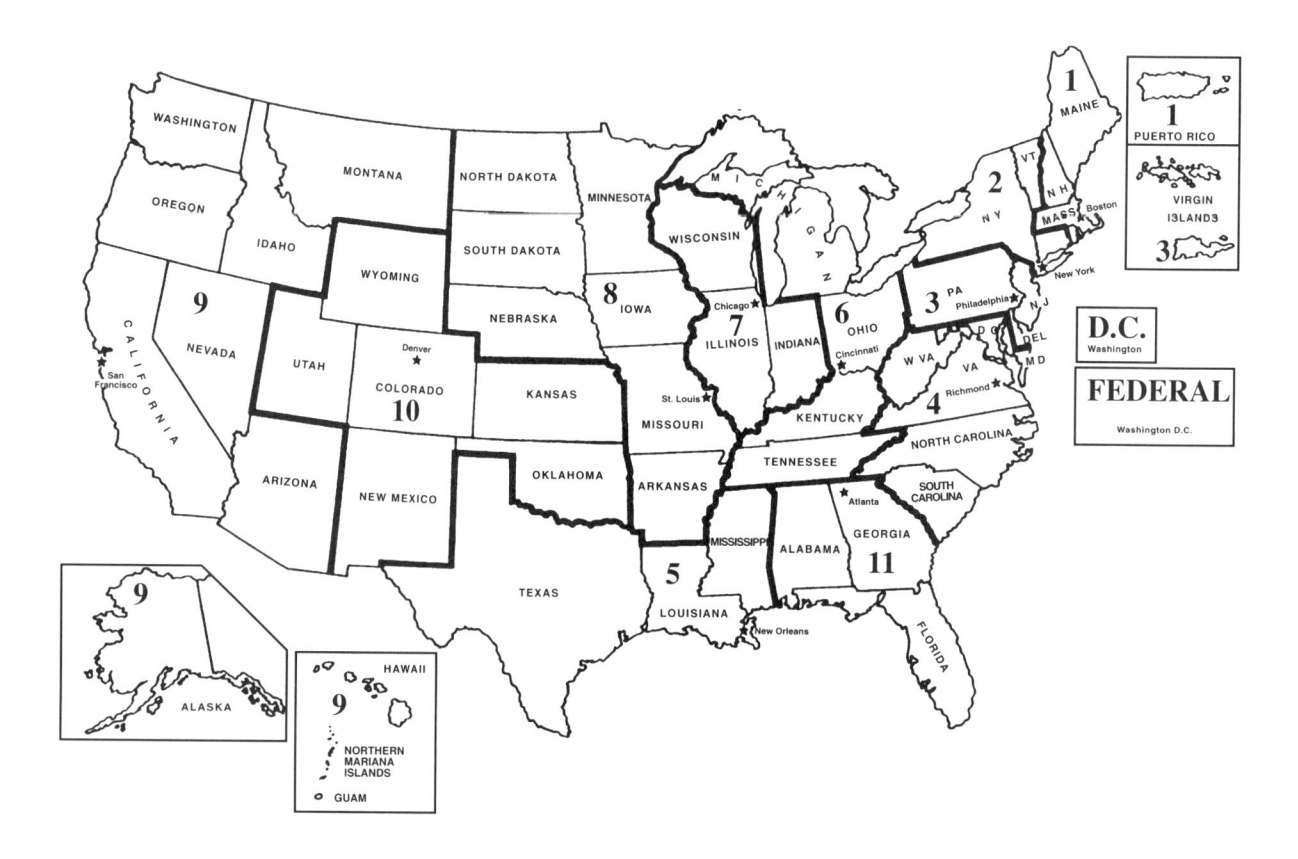

The United States Supreme Court hears some cases that are appealed "as of right." Mandatory appeals to the Supreme Court are made only in cases decided by a district court composed of three judges, chiefly in actions to enjoin legislative apportionments on constitutional grounds. Most cases reach the Court by an application process known as petitioning for certiorari. Review by the United States Supreme Court requires more than just the belief by a party that the wrong decision was made in his or her case; the case must be of important enough concern to federal law that its issues should be decided by the Court.

ILLINOIS' APPELLATE STRUCTURE

Like the federal judicial system, the Illinois court system has three tiers, two of which are appellate. Illinois' judicial circuit courts are the trial level courts in which actions are filed. There are 22 judicial circuits in Illinois. Circuit courts also have some appellate authority, as final orders of lower tribunals and administrative actions sometimes are appealable to the circuit courts. There are five judicial districts, each of which has an appellate court—the court with appellate jurisdiction in standard cases. The judicial districts have courts in Chicago, Elgin, Ottawa, Springfield, and Mount Vernon. The Illinois Supreme Court is the highest court for determining important questions of Illinois law. Located in Springfield, the Illinois Supreme Court directly reviews the final decisions of the appellate courts.

The right to appeal an adverse decision is granted by the Illinois Constitution. Generally, the appellant must file a Notice of Appeal and pay a filing fee within 30 days of the final order.

Civil Appellate Law Leading Illinois Attorneys

The Leading Illinois Attorneys listed below were nominated as exceptional by their peers in a statewide survey conducted by American Research Corporation (ARC). ARC asked several thousand licensed Illinois attorneys to name the lawyer to whom they would send a close friend or family member in need of legal assistance in specific areas of law. The attorneys below were nominated in the area of Civil Appellate Law.

Because the survey results (all practice area results combined) represent less than three percent of Illinois' practicing attorneys, this list should not be construed as a complete list. Nevertheless, it is an excellent source of highly qualified and reputable Illinois attorneys.

For information on ARC's survey methodology, see page *xi*.
For the complete list of Leading Illinois Consumer Attorneys, see page *xii*.

The Leading Illinois Attorneys below are listed alphabetically in accordance with the geographic region in which their offices are located. Note that attorneys may handle clients from a broad geographic area; attorneys are not restricted to only serving clients residing within the cities in which their offices are located.

An attorney whose name appears in bold has included a biographical profile in this chapter.

LEADING ILLINOIS ATTORNEYS

Illinois' Most Respected Legal Counsel As Selected By Their Peers.

The Leading Illinois Attorneys below were recommended by their peers in a statewide survey.

Cook & Collar Counties

Adelman, Ronald S. - Chicago
Applehans, Stephen G. - Waukegan
Arnold, Nancy Jo - Chicago
Axelrod, David A. - Chicago
Black, Robert G. - Naperville
Clayton, Fay - Chicago
Cooley, John W. - Evanston
Cornfield, Gilbert A. - Chicago
Dienes, Mary Ellen - Northfield
Eaton, J. Timothy - Chicago
Epstein, Edna S. - Chicago
Esposito, Paul V. - Chicago
Farina, James L. - Chicago
Ferguson, James R. - Chicago
Forde, Kevin M. - Chicago
Galland, George F., Jr. - Chicago
Harte, William J. - Chicago
Johnson, Thomas E. - Chicago
Kagan, Linda S. - Chicago
Kulys, Margarita T. - Chicago
Levine, Samuel H. - Chicago
London, Howard A. - Chicago
Maclean Snyder, Jean - Chicago
Mason, Mary Anne - Chicago
Moran, Terence J. - Chicago
Novoselsky, David A. - Chicago
Ostrow, Joel S. - Chicago
Pincham, R. Eugene - Chicago
Prendergast, Richard J. - Chicago
Rathsack, Michael W. - Chicago
Reuland, Timothy J. - Aurora
Skelnik, Josette - Elgin
Sullivan, Thomas E. - Wheaton
Sullivan, Thomas P. - Chicago
Tchen, Christina M. - Chicago
VanDemark, Ruth E. - Chicago, page 84
Walther, M. Jacqueline - Chicago
Wilson, Peter K., Jr. - Aurora
Wimmer, John R. - Downers Grove, page 85

Northwestern Illinois Including Rockford & Quad Cities

Blade, Thomas A. - Moline
Kilbride, Thomas L. - Rock Island
Lefstein, Stuart R. - Rock Island
Misevich, Allyson - Rockford
Nolte, Peter B. - Rockford, page 85
Oliver, Robert J. - Rockford

Chapter 11: Civil Appellate Law

CENTRAL ILLINOIS

Ansel, Marc J. - Champaign
Bell, Gregory S. - Peoria
DeArmond, Craig H. - Danville
Feldman, Howard W. - Springfield
Fleming, Michael A. - Peoria
Hall, Charles C. - Danville
Heiple, Jeremy H. - Peoria
Kirchner, Robert G. - Champaign
Kreckman, Alfred H., Jr. - Paris

Leahy, Mary Lee - Springfield
McMillan, Bradley S. - Peoria
Palmer, Charles L. - Champaign
Pusey, John R. - Peoria
Stanko, Glenn A. - Champaign
Susler, Marshall A. - Decatur
Swartz, John L. - Springfield
Tietz, Christopher M. - Decatur

SOUTHERN ILLINOIS

Blood, Curtis L. - Collinsville
Carr, Rex - East St. Louis
Cook, Bruce N. - Belleville
Elliott, Ivan A., Jr. - Carmi
Howerton, Robert H. - Marion

Kionka, Edward J. - Carbondale, page 86
Sterling, Harry J. - Fairview Heights
Stubblefield, Timothy C. - Belleville, page 87
Whittington, Rebecca A. - Carbondale

82 *Leading Illinois Attorneys Consumer Law Guidebook*

BIOGRAPHICAL PROFILES OF CIVIL APPELLATE LAW LEADING ILLINOIS ATTORNEYS

The Leading Illinois Attorneys profiled below were nominated as exceptional by their peers in a statewide survey conducted by American Research Corporation (ARC). ARC asked several thousand licensed Illinois attorneys to name the lawyer to whom they would send a close friend or family member in need of legal assistance in specific areas of law. The attorneys below were nominated in the area of Civil Appellate Law.

Because the survey results (all practice area results combined) represent less than three percent of Illinois' practicing attorneys, this list should not be construed as a complete list. Nevertheless, it is an excellent source of highly qualified and reputable Illinois attorneys.

For information on ARC's survey methodology, see page *xi*.
For the complete list of Leading Illinois Consumer Attorneys, see page *xii*.
For the list of Leading Illinois Civil Appellate Law Attorneys, see page 81.

The Leading Illinois Attorneys below are listed alphabetically in accordance with the geographic region in which their offices are located. Note that attorneys may handle clients from a broad geographic area; attorneys are not limited to only serving clients residing within the cities in which their offices are located.

The two-line attorney listings in this section are of attorneys who practice in this area but whose full biographical profiles appear in other sections of this book. A bullet "•" preceding a name indicates the attorney was nominated in this particular area of law.

For information on the format of the full biographical profiles, consult the "Using the Consumer Guidebook" section on page *xviii*.

The following abbreviations are used throughout these profiles:

App.	Appellate
Cir.	Circuit
Ct.	Court
Dist.	District
Sup.	Supreme
JD	Juris Doctor (Doctor of Law)
LLB	Legum Baccalaureus (Bachelor of Laws)
LLD	Legum Doctor (Doctor of Laws)
LLM	Legum Magister (Master of Laws)
ADR	Alternative Dispute Resolution
ABA	American Bar Association
ABOTA	American Board of Trial Advocates
ATLA	Association of Trial Lawyers of America
CBA	Chicago Bar Association
ISBA	Illinois State Bar Association
ITLA	Illinois Trial Lawyers Association
NBTA	National Board of Trial Advocacy

Chapter 11: Civil Appellate Law

Cook & Collar Counties

•**WILLIAM J. HARTE** - *William J. Harte, Ltd.* - 111 West Washington Street, Suite 1100 - Chicago, IL 60602 - Phone: (312) 726-5015, Fax: (312) 641-2455 - *See complete biographical profile in the Personal Injury Law: General Chapter, page 241.*

LYLE B. HASKIN - *Lyle B. Haskin & Associates* - 310 South County Farm Road - P.O. Box 31 - Wheaton, IL 60189-0031 - Phone: (630) 665-0800, Fax: (630) 665-1289 - *See complete biographical profile in the Family Law Chapter, page 190.*

RUTH E. VANDEMARK

Law Offices of Ruth E. VanDemark
225 West Washington Street
Suite 2200
Chicago, IL 60606

Phone: (312) 419-7162
Fax: (312) 419-7285

Extensive Experience In:

- Product Liability Defense
- Medical Malpractice Defense
- Computer Law

•**RUTH E. VAN DEMARK:** Ms. VanDemark concentrates in appellate practice, including civil rights, commercial, constitutional, environmental, general tort, medical malpractice, labor, landlord-tenant, probate, product liability, tax, and federal and state procedural and evidentiary appeals. She also concentrates in intellectual property law, focusing on computer software and hardware licensing and contracting. She is the author of "The Illinois Supreme Court's 1994 Season: From Obscurity to Household Word," *Illinois Bar Journal,* July 1995; "The Illinois Supreme Court's 1993 Season: The New Team in the Civil Field," *Illinois Bar Journal,* June 1994; "The Illinois Supreme Court's 1992 Season: The Civil Arena," *Illinois Bar Journal,* June 1993; and many other publications. She has been a speaker at numerous seminars and meetings, including those sponsored by the Illinois Institute for Continuing Legal Education and the American Bar Association. She was an Associate Editor of the *Connecticut Law Review.*

Education: JD 1976 with honors, University of Connecticut (Associate Editor, *Law Review*); MTS 1969, Harvard University; AB 1966, Vassar College.

Admitted: 1976 Connecticut; 1977 Illinois; 1976 U.S. Dist. Ct. (Dist. CT); 1977 U.S. Dist. Ct. (N. Dist. IL); 1983 U.S. Sup. Ct.; 1984 U.S. Ct. App. (7th Cir.).

Employment History: Principal 1995-present, Law Offices of Ruth E. VanDemark; Associate/Partner/Appellate Practice Group Chair 1977-94, Wildman, Harrold, Allen & Dixon.

Professional Associations: Illinois Supreme Court Rules Committee 1996-present; Pro Bono Advocates (Director 1993-present; Development Chair 1993, 1995); Appellate Lawyers Assn. of Illinois (President 1992-93; Vice President 1991-92; Secretary 1990-91; Treasurer 1989-90; Director 1985-87); ABA [Litigation Section (Appellate Practice Committee, past Program Chair)]; ISBA; CBA (Chicago Council of Lawyers); Computer Law Assn.; Seventh Circuit Bar Assn.; Copyright Society.

Community Involvement: Chicago Vassar Club (Advisory Board 1981-present; President 1979-81); Horizon Hospice (Advisory Board 1978-present); Harvard Divinity School Alumni/ae Council 1988-91; Piven Theater Workshop (Director 1987-89); Junior Leagues of Illinois (State Public Affairs Committee 1987-88); Friends of Battered Women and Their Children (Founding Director 1986-87); Evanston YWCA/North Shore Battered Women's Shelter (Advisory Board 1984-86); New Voice Productions (Director 1984-86); Junior League of Evanston (Volunteer of the Year Award 1983-84); White House Conference on Families, Los Angeles (Delegate-at-Large 1980). *Ms. VanDemark also practices Computer Software Law.*

•**JOHN R. WIMMER:** Mr. Wimmer is a trial and appellate lawyer practicing in the Chicago metropolitan area. He has argued many appeals, civil and criminal, and he has orally argued cases before the Illinois Supreme Court. Mr. Wimmer also tries cases, civil and criminal, in courts throughout the Chicago metropolitan area, and is a member of the Trial Bar of the United States District Court for the Northern District of Illinois, Eastern Division.
Education: JD 1979, University of Illinois; BA 1976, Cornell University (Graduated with Distinction in all subjects).
Admitted: 1979 Illinois; 1981 U.S. Dist. Ct. (N. Dist. IL); 1987 U.S. Ct. App. (7th Cir.).
Employment History: Sole Practitioner 1990-96, The Law Offices of John R. Wimmer; Associate 1986-89, Botti, Marinaccio, DeSalvo & Pieper; Law Clerk 1984-86, Honorable Paul W. Schnake, Appellate Court of Illinois; Staff Attorney 1981-84, Office of the State Appellate Defender; Associate 1980-81, Richard E. Alexander, Ltd.; Law Clerk 1979-80, Honorable Richard Stengel, Appellate Court of Illinois.
Professional Associations: CBA; ISBA.
Community Involvement: St. Matthew Evangelical Lutheran Church, Lemont, Illinois; Cross of Christ Lutheran Church, Downers Grove, Illinois (former Congregation Member; past President); Autism Society of America. *Mr. Wimmer also practices Alternative Dispute Resolution and Criminal Law: Felonies & White Collar Crime.*

JOHN R. WIMMER
The Law Offices of John R. Wimmer
928 Warren Avenue
Downers Grove, IL 60515

Phone: (630) 810-0005
Fax: (630) 960-5852
E-mail: jwimmerlaw@aol.com

Extensive Experience In:
• Civil Appeals
• Defamation Against Media Defendants
• Federal Civil Rights

NORTHWESTERN ILLINOIS
INCLUDING ROCKFORD & QUAD CITIES

•**PETER B. NOLTE:** Mr. Nolte concentrates in appellate law, handling cases in the Appeals Courts of Illinois and the Seventh Circuit. He has focused in appellate practice since 1974, and has handled numerous cases in various reviewing courts, including the United States Supreme Court and Appellate Courts of Illinois. He has lectured at many bar association seminars on appellate advocacy and procedures.
Education: JD 1974, Illinois Institute of Technology, Chicago-Kent; BA 1971, Kent State University.
Admitted: 1974 Illinois; 1975 U.S. Dist. Ct. (N. Dist. IL); 1979 U.S. Sup. Ct.; 1987 U.S. Ct. App. (7th Cir.).
Employment History: Sole Practitioner 1990-present; Of Counsel 1984-90, Sreenan & Cain, P.C.; Sole Practitioner 1977-84; 1974-77, Office of the State Appellate Defender.
Representative Clients: Civil Service Commission, City of Loves Park.
Community Involvement: Center for Sight and Hearing Impaired (Volunteer Counsel); Blackhawk Valley Riding for the Handicapped (Volunteer Counsel).
Firm: Mr. Nolte maintains, with a secretary, a sole practice in order to provide close, personal attention to his clients' legal needs. He is available to practice in all state and federal courts in Illinois. *Mr. Nolte also practices Criminal Law: Felonies & White Collar Crime and Family Law.*

PETER B. NOLTE
Attorney at Law
312 West State Street
Suite 1201
Rockford, IL 61101

Phone: (815) 965-2647
Fax: (815) 965-3820

Chapter 11: Civil Appellate Law

CENTRAL ILLINOIS

STANLEY N. WASSER - *Feldman & Wasser* - 1307 South Seventh Street P.O. Box 2418 - Springfield, IL 62705 - Phone. (217) 544-3403, Fax: (217) 544-1593 - *See complete biographical profile in the Employment Law Chapter, page 150.*

SOUTHERN ILLINOIS

MORRIS LANE HARVEY - *Law Offices of Morris Lane Harvey* - 215 SE Third Street, Suite 100 - P.O. Box 820 - Fairfield, IL 62837 - Phone: (618) 842-5117, Fax: (618) 842-5773 - *See complete biographical profile in the Family Law Chapter, page 216.*

EDWARD J. KIONKA
Professor of Law
Southern Illinois University
School of Law
218 Lesar Law Building
Carbondale, IL 62901-6804

Phone: (618) 453-8755
Fax: (618) 453-3317
E-mail: ejkionka@siu.edu
tedkionka@aol.com

•**EDWARD J. KIONKA:** Professor Kionka limits his practice to civil appeals and trial consultation. He has been teaching law courses at the Southern Illinois University Law School since 1973. He is the author of *Torts in a Nutshell,* 1992; *Torts Black Letter,* 1993; *Materials for the Study of Evidence,* with Michie Butterworth, 1991; and *Appeals to the Illinois Supreme and Appellate Courts,* Illinois State Bar Association, 1994. In addition, Professor Kionka has written numerous articles and book chapters on torts, evidence, civil practice, and appellate practice.

Education: LLM 1974, Columbia University; JD 1962, University of Illinois (Order of the Coif); BS 1960, University of Illinois.

Admitted: 1962 Illinois; 1977 Missouri; 1963 U.S. Dist. Ct. (N. Dist. IL, General Bar); 1970 U.S. Ct. App. (7th Cir.); 1971 U.S. Sup. Ct.; 1975 U.S. Ct. App. (5th Cir.); 1975 U.S. Dist. Ct. (C. Dist. IL); 1978 U.S. Dist. Ct. (S. Dist. IL).

Employment History: Professor of Law 1973-present, Associate Dean 1984-85, Acting Dean, Summer 1985, Southern Illinois University School of Law; Private Practice 1971-73, Norton & Kionka; Assistant Dean/Assistant Professor of Law 1967-71, University of Illinois College of Law; Executive Director 1965-67, Illinois Institute for Continuing Legal Education; Instructor 1964-65, University of Michigan Law School; Private Practice 1962-64, Leibman, Williams, Bennett & Baird (now Sidley & Austin); Instructor 1962, Columbia University Law School; Visiting Professor, Summer 1992, University of San Diego School of Law; 1989, Emory University School of Law, Atlanta; 1985-86, McGeorge School of Law; 1979-80, Washington University Law School; 1983, University of Hawaii Law School; 1976, St. Louis University Law School.

Professional Associations: Illinois Supreme Court Committee on Jury Instructions in Civil Cases (Reporter 1979-95); Illinois Supreme Court Committee on Rules of Evidence 1976-79; Illinois Institute for Continuing Legal Education [Board Member 1967-72, 1973-85 (Chair 1983-84); Executive Committee 1967-71, 1980-85]; ISBA 1963-present [Assembly 1990-92; Publications Committee 1979-85 (Chair 1984-85); Special Committee on the Standards of Judicial Conduct (Chair 1980-82)]; ABA 1963-present; Scribes (Board of Directors 1990-94; Secretary 1993-94); American Academy of Appellate Lawyers 1991-present (Board of Directors 1992-present); Appellate Lawyers Assn. (President 1977-78; Vice President 1976-77; Secretary 1975-76; Treasurer 1974-75); Illinois Judicial Conference (Professor Reporter 1976, 1979, 1980, 1984, 1986, 1987, 1991).

•**TIMOTHY C. STUBBLEFIELD:** Mr. Stubblefield practices primarily in areas of law which involve litigation, specifically family law, workers' compensation, and personal injury. He has successfully represented clients in all areas of family law, including divorce, maintenance and support, child support, visitation, grandparent visitation, child custody, and child abuse cases. He has also successfully represented disabled children and adults in matters concerning employment, education, and guardianships.
Education: JD 1983, St. Louis University (Phipps Scholar; Vice President, Moot Court Board); BA 1980, Northwestern University.
Admitted: 1983 Illinois.
Employment History: Partner 1989-present, Nelson, Bement, Stubblefield & Levenhagen, P.C.; Partner 1983-89, Hillsbrand & Stubblefield, P.C.
Representative Clients: The firm concentrates in the representation of individual clients, as opposed to businesses or corporations.
Professional Associations: Monroe County Bar Assn. (President 1993; Vice President 1992); Attorney General's Advisory Committee for Disabled Adults 1985-89; St. Clair County Bar Assn. 1983-present; ISBA 1983-present.
Community Involvement: Epilepsy Assn. of Southern Illinois (Board of Directors 1986-94; President 1988-91; Vice President 1987).
Firm: Nelson, Bement, Stubblefield & Levenhagen, P.C., is a litigation-oriented law firm. The majority of the firm's clients are individuals, as opposed to businesses or corporations. The firm provides a full range of legal services in family law, wills and estates, workers' compensation, and personal injury cases. *See complete firm profile in Appendix A. Mr. Stubblefield also practices Family Law, Personal Injury Law: General and Workers' Compensation Law.*

TIMOTHY C. STUBBLEFIELD
Nelson, Bement, Stubblefield & Levenhagen, P.C.
420 North High Street
P.O. Box Y
Belleville, IL 62222

Phone:	(618) 277-4000
	(618) 277-8260
Fax:	(618) 277-1136

CHAPTER 12

Criminal Law: DUI & Misdemeanors

This chapter outlines some criminal law issues and focuses on misdemeanors, for which punishments are relatively less severe than for felonies. Felonies are covered in the Criminal Law: Felonies & White Collar Crime Chapter, along with white collar crimes, the rights of persons accused of crimes, and the rights of crime victims.

This chapter also discusses driving-under-the-influence violations, as well as the juvenile justice system. The Family Law Chapter covers domestic abuse and protective orders, and the Process of a Case: Civil & Criminal Chapter describes criminal procedure. Private causes of action that result from criminal conduct are covered in the Personal Injury Law Chapters.

CRIMINAL CODES

Criminal law defines conduct that is prohibited by the government and the range of penalties that can be imposed for violating these prohibitions. Depending on the nature of the crime, a person who violates a criminal law incurs penalties including fines and/or imprisonment. By definition, misdemeanors are crimes for which a person may be committed to no more than one year of imprisonment. Illinois also has laws that allow the authorities to seize property connected with the commission of a crime. For example, a person convicted for driving under the influence of alcohol will have his or her driver's license revoked by the government. Similarly, a person charged with violating laws connected with controlled substances must forfeit the substances as well as the raw materials used to make the drugs, vehicles and real property used to further the crime, and any money or other proceeds from the sale of the controlled substances.

Every crime is defined by a list of elements. In a criminal trial, the prosecutor attempts to prove all the elements of the crime the person is accused of committing. If all elements are proven, the judge or the jury finds the person guilty of the crime. However, even for minor criminal violations, the accused may not be found guilty unless the jury or judge finds him or her guilty "beyond a reasonable doubt."

ATTEMPT, CONSPIRACY, AIDING AND ABETTING

Anyone who, with intent to commit a crime, takes a substantial step toward committing the crime may be guilty of attempt to commit a crime. Merely thinking about committing a crime, or even preparing to commit a crime, is not an attempt; there must be a substantial step. For example, if a group of teenagers talks about how easy they think it would be to walk out of a store with a pair of jeans, they have not committed a crime, nor have they committed an attempted crime. However, if they deactivate a store's alarm system so it cannot detect what passes through the doors, they probably have committed a tampering or vandalism crime as well as attempted theft. They have taken a substantial step toward the commission of the theft.

The law of conspiracy and the law of aiding and abetting are other general doctrines that apply to a wide range of offenses. Conspiracy is an agreement between two or more persons to commit a crime. For example, if three people conspire to preclude all potential renters who fall within a protected group from renting apartments in their building, and if the apartment manager actually rejects those people, they all can be charged with both conspiracy and violating the civil rights law. Even if a conspirator backs out of the conspiracy, but the other conspirators commit the crime, all conspirators may be criminally liable if the acts were reasonably foreseeable.

A person who aids or advises another in committing a crime may be guilty of aiding and abetting, and may be criminally liable for the acts of the other person, as well. Thus, if someone intentionally advises another how to commit a crime, both people are equally liable under the law.

MISDEMEANORS

Criminal codes penalize a variety of activities, and many offenses are listed as violations of the law under the Illinois Criminal Code. Under the Criminal Code, misdemeanors range from unlawfully interfering with a public utility to criminal trespass to a residence, a vehicle, or real property, to intentionally damaging a traffic sign or traffic light. Under the law, many crimes are misdemeanors on the first offense, but become felonies on the second offense. This means that, for example, retail theft of property valued at less than $150 is a misdemeanor the first time. If a person already has been convicted of retail theft (shoplifting) and is arrested again for a similar action, the person will be charged with felony retail theft.

As mentioned, misdemeanors carry a maximum punishment of a fine and less than one year of incarceration. Crimes for which a person may be punished by more than one year in jail or in prison are categorized in Illinois as felonies.

CRIMES CAUSING HARM TO PROPERTY

Theft, burglary, and robbery are felonies in Illinois unless the value of the property taken is under $300. Similarly, whether a crime against property is charged as a misdemeanor or a felony depends on the value of the property taken or damaged. The statute prohibiting criminal damage to property, for example, proscribes knowingly or recklessly damaging another's property, setting a fire on another's property, injuring another's domestic animal, and setting a stink bomb or other offensive-smelling compound on another's property. If the damage to the property is no more than $300, these crimes are misdemeanors; if the damage equals more than $300, the crimes are felonies. Similarly, criminal defacement of property is knowingly damaging another's property with paint, an etching tool, a writing instrument, or a similar device; the severity of punishment depends on the level of offense, which is a misdemeanor or felony depending on whether the property damage exceeds $300. In contrast, trespass to another person's property generally is a misdemeanor, while arson is always a felony.

CIVIL RIGHTS CRIMES

The Illinois Human Rights Act forbids discrimination in employment, housing, financial credit, and public accommodations on the basis of age, ancestry, citizenship, color, disability, marital status, national origin, race, religion, sex, or unfavorable military discharge. Violation of these prohibitions can subject the violator to criminal prosecution.

SEX CRIMES

Some actions involving sex are illegal misdemeanors under Illinois law, unless the person charged has been convicted of a previous offense or unless a child is involved, in which case they are felonies that carry more severe punishment. Prostitution, pimping, and solicitation are misdemeanors.

It is criminal sexual abuse, sometimes called statutory rape, for anyone to have sexual penetration or sexual conduct with a victim under the age of 17. If the accused is over five years older, it is a felony. Criminal sexual abuse also can be sexual conduct other than sexual penetration in which force is used or the victim was unable to consent.

ALCOHOL AND DRUG-RELATED TRAFFIC OFFENSES

Alcohol and drug-related traffic offenses, commonly known as driving under the influence (DUI) are frequently prosecuted crimes in Illinois. If a person's blood alcohol concentration (BAC) is .10 or greater and the person is in physical control of a motor vehicle, he or she is presumed to be driving under the influence. Even if a person's BAC is more than .05 but less than .10, the person may face DUI charges if there is other evidence to show DUI. It is a DUI-related offense to carry alcoholic beverages in a vehicle, unless the beverages are sealed in the original containers. A person also can be held liable for serving alcohol to someone who commits a DUI offense.

A person age 21 or over who is convicted of DUI the first time faces a mandatory sentence of losing driving privileges for at least one year, as well as possible imprisonment. If the person had a child in the car at the time of the arrest, the judge must add to the punishment a fine of $500 to $1,000 and five days of community service. Subsequent convictions carry increased jail time, higher fines, mandatory community service for ten days, and/or loss of driving privileges for up to six years.

Illinois recently began a "zero tolerance" campaign to address the problem of DUI, especially among drivers under age 21. The first time a person under age 21 is convicted of DUI, he or she automatically loses driving privileges for two years and may face imprisonment and a fine, as well. Subsequent convictions have more severe mandatory penalties. For drivers under age 21, "zero tolerance" means it is illegal to drive with a BAC of more than .00, even if the BAC is not as high as what some people consider enough to make them intoxicated. For the first such offense, a driver automatically loses his or her license for three months; for subsequent offenses he or she loses driving privileges for one year. Refusing to submit to chemical testing for BAC also carries with it a mandatory suspension of driving privileges.

Other alcohol or drug-related traffic offenses include reckless homicide (discussed in the Criminal Law: Felonies & White Collar Crime Chapter) under the influence and aggravated DUI. Aggravated DUI is committed if the offender

- Has three or more DUI arrests
- Commits DUI while driving a school bus full of children
- Is convicted of DUI after a collision that caused great bodily harm or permanent disfigurement or disability
- Has a second DUI conviction after a DUI conviction that caused reckless homicide or great bodily injury

Aggravated DUI carries with it a loss of driving privileges for one year, a minimum fine of $10,000, and possible imprisonment for one to three years.

Numerous other offenses connected to DUI are misdemeanors in Illinois. Offenses include

- Falsifying a driver's license
- Failing to carry valid automobile insurance
- Allowing one's residence to be used by children under the age of 21 to drink
- Selling alcohol to a minor or an intoxicated person
- Knowingly renting a hotel or motel room to a person under the age of 21 who is drinking alcoholic beverages
- Allowing a person under the influence of alcohol to operate one's vehicle

JUVENILES AND THE LAW

Illinois has a juvenile court system for minors that operates separately from other courts. The purpose of this separate system is to help serve the best interests of juveniles, rather than simply punish them. Generally, minors under age 17 who run afoul of the law are said to commit delinquent acts rather than crimes. The distinction is one of words only. Delinquent acts committed by a minor are called crimes if committed by an adult. Minors between the ages of 15 and 17 who commit certain crimes, such as first degree murder, are prosecuted as if they are adults.

The most significant distinction between the juvenile court system and adult criminal courts is in courtroom procedures. Juvenile courts generally are less formal than other courts. For example, minors being adjudicated or giving courtroom testimony in some cases can have a supportive person present during their testimony. Juvenile cases are heard in an adjudication hearing by a judge who determines the guilt or innocence of a minor accused of committing a delinquent act. Sometimes these hearings are closed to the public. Records made by law enforcement officers about delinquent minors must be kept confidential and separate from other arrest records. Under certain circumstances, records from juvenile court may be used in other legal proceedings, depending on the seriousness of the offense.

Illinois has strict laws that seek to address juvenile gang violence. When the state seeks to try a violent juvenile delinquent on criminal charges, it may include in its petition evidence that the criminal activity was gang-related, and the judge may consider this evidence and order the minor tried as an adult. For example, if a 16-year-old minor allegedly committed a forcible felony that was part of criminal gang activity, and the minor already was declared a juvenile delinquent, the judge will order the case to be heard in criminal court.

CRIME VICTIMS' RIGHTS

Some crime victims have the right to compensation for the crimes committed against them. This means that a crime victim may receive compensation for certain expenses or losses such as medical expenses or loss of support if the crime victim becomes unable to support dependents. There are requirements that must be met for a victim to get reimbursement, and victims must file an application for consideration with the Illinois Court of Claims for compensation. The maximum amount a victim can receive from the Court of Claims is $25,000.

Under Illinois law, the victim may receive compensation from the person who committed the crime. This is called restitution. For example, a person whose vehicle is stolen may be able to receive compensation for the vehicle. In this case, the state arranges to collect the money from the criminal and sends a check to the victim when all the restitution has been made.

The Illinois Victims Rights Constitutional Amendment gives all victims the right to be treated with fairness, the right to privacy, the right to make a statement at sentencing, and the right to reasonable protection from the accused during the criminal justice proceedings. Victims of the most violent crimes also have the right to be notified of the status of the investigation, whether an indictment has been brought, the time and place of any hearings, and when the defendant is released from custody.

If the court does not order restitution, or if a prosecutor does not press charges, the victim still has the option to seek compensation directly by suing the offender in civil court. This option is discussed more fully in the Process of a Case: Civil & Criminal Chapter.

RESOURCES

Mothers Against Drunk Driving (MADD). Call 1-800-GET-MADD for information about local MADD chapters.

Illinois State Bar Association, Illinois Bar Center, Springfield, IL 62701-1779. Call (217) 525-1760 for information or to order the free pamphlet, *Your Rights if Arrested*.

Secretary of State, Traffic Safety Division, 2701 Dirksen Parkway South, Springfield, IL 62723, phone: (217) 785-1444, TTY: (800) 252-2904. Contact the Traffic Safety Division to order the free pamphlet, *DUI Law: Making Progress, Getting Results* or the free booklet, *DUI 1994 Fact Book*.

Crime victims who wish to apply for compensation should apply to the Illinois Court of Claims, Capitol Building, Room 213, Springfield, IL 62756, phone: (217) 782-7101.

Illinois Crime Victims Reparation Board, 100 Randolph Street West, Chicago, IL 60601, phone: (312) 814-2581.

This chapter was reviewed and edited by Leading Illinois Attorney David E. Camic.

Criminal Law: DUI & Misdemeanors
Leading Illinois Attorneys

LEADING ILLINOIS ATTORNEYS

Illinois' Most Respected Legal Counsel As Selected By Their Peers.

The Leading Illinois Attorneys below were recommended by their peers in a statewide survey.

The Leading Illinois Attorneys listed below were nominated as exceptional by their peers in a statewide survey conducted by American Research Corporation (ARC). ARC asked several thousand licensed Illinois attorneys to name the lawyer to whom they would send a close friend or family member in need of legal assistance in specific areas of law. The attorneys below were nominated in the area of Criminal Law: DUI & Misdemeanors.

Because the survey results (all practice area results combined) represent less than three percent of Illinois' practicing attorneys, this list should not be construed as a complete list. Nevertheless, it is an excellent source of highly qualified and reputable Illinois attorneys.

For information on ARC's survey methodology, see page *xi*.
For the complete list of Leading Illinois Consumer Attorneys, see page *xii*.

The Leading Illinois Attorneys below are listed alphabetically in accordance with the geographic region in which their offices are located. Note that attorneys may handle clients from a broad geographic area; attorneys are not restricted to only serving clients residing within the cities in which their offices are located.

An attorney whose name appears in bold has included a biographical profile in this chapter.

Cook & Collar Counties

Adam, Sam - Chicago
Ahern, James J. - Skokie
Aimen, Julie B. - Chicago
Allegretti, James - Chicago
Angelini, Phil - Oak Brook
Baime, Stephen G. - Chicago
Belz, Edwin J. - Chicago
Berkson, Dennis A. - Chicago
Blomquist, Ernest R., III - Arlington Heights
Bloom, Marvin - Chicago
Breen, Thomas - Chicago
Briscoe, Thomas A. - Waukegan
Brodsky, Joel A. - Chicago
Bugos, Joseph T. - Lisle
Busch, Kevin T. - Aurora
Camic, David E. - Aurora, page 96
Carlson, Ray M. - Mundelein
Collins, George B. - Chicago
Colton, Kathleen - Batavia
Connelly, Vincent J. - Chicago
Cotsirilos, George J. - Chicago
Davis, Larry - Des Plaines
De Leon, John R. - Chicago
Decker, Thomas D. - Chicago
Dolci, Dominick P. - Oakbrook Terrace
Donahue, John F. - Lisle
Durkin, Thomas Anthony - Chicago
Ekl, Terry A. - Clarendon Hills
Epstein, James R. - Chicago
Fawell, Jeffrey B. - Wheaton
Fischer, Bella - Lake Bluff
Fisher, Robert A. - Chicago

Fleisher, Richard S. - Chicago
Fleming, Michael W. - Elmhurst
Fox, Robert J. - Waukegan
Genson, Edward - Chicago
Gevirtz, Robert L. - Northfield
Gillespie, Terence P. - Chicago
Giovannini, Dennis - Chicago
Goggin, Michael J. - Oak Park
Goldberg, Herbert - Chicago
Greenberg, Steven A. - Chicago
Hartmann, H. Michael - Chicago
Hauser, Robert J. - Waukegan
Howard, George C. - Chicago
Johnson, Gary V. - Aurora, page 97
Kaplan, Sidney M. - Chicago
Kennelly, Matthew F. - Chicago
Kling, Richard - Chicago
Komie, Stephen M. - Chicago
Kopsick, Richard S. - Waukegan
Kowalczyk, Mark E. - Glen Ellyn
Kulwin, Shelly B. - Chicago
Kunkle, William J., Jr. - Chicago
Kurz, Jerry B. - Chicago
Laraia, Joseph M. - Wheaton
LeFevour, Terrence P. - Chicago
Luby, Joseph K. - Mt. Prospect
Lunardi, Steven B. - Waukegan
Lynch, George J. - Chicago
Lynch, George P. - Downers Grove
Magidson, Sherman C. - Chicago
Marcus, James I. - Chicago

Martin, Royal B. - Chicago
Martin, William J. - Oak Park
McCulloch, Thomas O. - St. Charles
McWilliams, Clare - Palatine
Melber, Michael D. - Chicago
Menaker, Ronald D. - Chicago
Miller, Irving - Chicago
Minetz, Robert S. - Chicago
Molo, Steven F. - Chicago
Monaco, Mark C. - Batavia
Monico, Michael D. - Chicago
Morelli, Fred M., Jr. - Aurora
Murphy, William P. - Chicago
Murtaugh, George J., Jr. - Chicago
Nolan, Francis A. - Chicago
Nolan, Nan R. - Chicago
Pearl, Howard M. - Chicago
Pinelli, Anthony - Chicago
Powers, Michael E. - Oak Brook
Rantis, Nicholas S. - Oakbrook Terrace
Rath, William W. - Wheaton
Ravitz, Gary J. - Chicago
Ray, Loraine A. - Chicago
Reidy, Daniel E. - Chicago
Richards, Van R., Jr. - Elgin
Riebman, Hyman - Des Plaines
Rimland, Jack P. - Chicago
Roberts, Douglas R. - Waukegan
Russo, Richard D. - Wheaton
Ryan, Richard P. - Chicago
Sadowski, Ronald W. - Oak Brook
Samuels, Elliott M. - Chicago
Schillerstrom, Robert J. - Naperville
Sheppard, Barry D. - Chicago
Simonian, Stephen M. - Waukegan
Skipper, Robert - Chicago
Sklarsky, Charles B. - Chicago
Smeeton, Jack C. - Evanston
Smirl, Dale L. - Chicago
Sorosky, Sheldon M. - Chicago
Spector, Barry A. - Chicago
Steinke, Edward B. - St. Charles
Stephenson, Robert M. - Chicago
Stetler, David J. - Chicago
Stone, Jeffrey E. - Chicago
Streicker, James R. - Chicago
Sullivan, Thomas P. - Chicago
Tallis, Jeffrey J. - Chicago
Tarun, Robert W. - Chicago
Telander, Brian F. - Glen Ellyn
Theis, John T. - Chicago
Thomas, David - Chicago
Tighe, Ann C. - Chicago
Tuite, Patrick A. - Chicago
Urban, Tod M. - Chicago
Urdangen, Jeffrey - Chicago
Valukas, Anton R. - Chicago
Van Der Snick, J. Brick - Geneva
Wagner, Paul A. - Chicago
Walsh, Carl M. - Chicago
Walsh, Michael D. - Chicago
Webb, Dan K. - Chicago
Will, Robert P., Jr. - Waukegan
Williams, Jeffrey - Chicago
Willis, Standish E. - Chicago
Wojtecki, Leonard J. - Aurora
Zeit, Daniel R. - Waukegan

NORTHWESTERN ILLINOIS INCLUDING ROCKFORD & QUAD CITIES

Altamore, Albert A. - Rockford
Beu, William R. - Rockford
Bush, Robert A. - Elizabeth
Bute, Daniel J. - Ottawa
Cain, Daniel J. - Rockford
Caulk, David A. - Rockford
Gaziano, Paul E. - Rockford
Henbest, Barton L. - Loves Park
Kelly, Roger H. - Galena
Koonmen, Karl C. - Loves Park
Kreitlow, Margaret - Rockford
Kuleck, Edward J., Jr. - Ottawa
Marsh, C. Stephen - Rock Island
Martinez, Francis M. - Rockford
Nack, Joseph E. - Galena
Ruud, Glenn F. - Rock Island
Schick, William G. - Rock Island
Seigler, Darrell K. - Ottawa
Truitt, John R. - Rockford
Vella, Frank P., Jr. - Rockford

CENTRAL ILLINOIS

Beckett, J. Steven - Urbana
Brady, Gerald, Jr. - Peoria
Bruno, Thomas A. - Urbana
Butler, David W. - Bloomington
Coryell, James R. - Decatur
Costello, Michael J. - Springfield
DeArmond, Craig H. - Danville
Dukes, Carroll W. - Danville
Eberspacher, David Y. - Mattoon
Elmore, James E. - Springfield
Erickson, Frederick P. - Decatur
Fuller, Glenn O. - Decatur
Geisler, Asher O. - Decatur
Geisler, Gary F. - Decatur
Giganti, Adam - Springfield
Halliday, Ronald E. - Peoria
Hamm, Ronald L. - Peoria
Hanna, Ronald - Peoria
Heller, Harlan - Mattoon
Holmes, Brent D. - Mattoon
Jennings, Harold M. - Bloomington
Johnson, James W. - Decatur
Kagawa, Carlton M. - Danville
Keller, K. Rick - Effingham
Lawrence, Paul G. - Bloomington
Lerner, Arthur M. - Champaign

Chapter 12: Criminal Law: DUI & Misdemeanors

Lipton, Mark D. - Champaign
Locher, Bruce D. - Springfield
Lutz, Lonnie L. - Charleston
McNamara, William B. - Danville
Metnick, Michael B. - Springfield
Meyer, Michael J. - Effingham
Murphy, G. Edward - Peoria
Novak, Anthony E. - Urbana
O'Day, Daniel G. - Peoria
Parker, Drew - Peoria
Penn, Thomas J., Jr. - Peoria
Pretnar, Alan - Taylor Springs
Pryor, William A. - Springfield
Reid, William D. - Springfield

Rose, Mark A. - Peoria
Ryan, David J. - Danville
Ryan, Stephen R. - Mattoon
Sharp, John P. - Springfield
Silkwood, Larry R. - Urbana
Smith, L. Lee - Peoria
Stanko, Glenn A. - Champaign
Timoney, Patrick T. - Springfield
Toner, Hugh F., III - Peoria
Tulin, Ronald - Charleston
Viverito, Lou J. - Effingham
Winter-Black, Janett S. - Mattoon
Wood, George C. - Bloomington
Zopf, Michael J. - Urbana

Southern Illinois

Applegate, Steven D. - Carbondale
Daley, Thomas M. - Belleville
Douglas, Robert L. - Robinson
Groshong, Donald E. - Alton
Grounds, David K. - Wood River
Kelley, Randall W. - Belleville
Lucco, J. William - Edwardsville

Mansfield, Thomas W. - Murphysboro
Mudge, William A. - Edwardsville
Slemer, Ronald R. - Edwardsville
Trentman, Brian K. - Belleville
Veltman, R. Edward - Centralia
White, Richard E. - Murphysboro

CRIMINAL LAW: DUI & MISDEMEANORS LEADING ILLINOIS ATTORNEYS

The Leading Illinois Attorneys profiled below were nominated as exceptional by their peers in a statewide survey conducted by American Research Corporation (ARC). ARC asked several thousand licensed Illinois attorneys to name the lawyer to whom they would send a close friend or family member in need of legal assistance in specific areas of law. The attorneys below were nominated in the area of Criminal Law: DUI & Misdemeanors.

Because the survey results (all practice area results combined) represent less than three percent of Illinois' practicing attorneys, this list should not be construed as a complete list. Nevertheless, it is an excellent source of highly qualified and reputable Illinois attorneys.

For information on ARC's survey methodology, see page *xi*.
For the complete list of Leading Illinois Consumer Attorneys, see page *xii*.
For the list of Leading Illinois Criminal Law: DUI & Misdemeanors Attorneys, see page 92.

The Leading Illinois Attorneys below are listed alphabetically in accordance with the geographic region in which their offices are located. Note that attorneys may handle clients from a broad geographic area; attorneys are not limited to only serving clients residing within the cities in which their offices are located.

The two-line attorney listings in this section are of attorneys who practice in this area but whose full biographical profiles appear in other sections of this book. A bullet "•" preceding a name indicates the attorney was nominated in this particular area of law.

For information on the format of the full biographical profiles, consult the "Using the Consumer Guidebook" section on page *xviii*.

The following abbreviations are used throughout these profiles:

App.	Appellate
Cir.	Circuit
Ct.	Court
Dist.	District
Sup.	Supreme
JD	Juris Doctor (Doctor of Law)
LLB	Legum Baccalaureus (Bachelor of Laws)
LLD	Legum Doctor (Doctor of Laws)
LLM	Legum Magister (Master of Laws)
ADR	Alternative Dispute Resolution
ABA	American Bar Association
ABOTA	American Board of Trial Advocates
ATLA	Association of Trial Lawyers of America
CBA	Chicago Bar Association
ISBA	Illinois State Bar Association
ITLA	Illinois Trial Lawyers Association
NBTA	National Board of Trial Advocacy

COOK & COLLAR COUNTIES

•**JULIE B. AIMEN** - *Attorney at Law* - 343 South Dearborn Street, Suite 1400 - Chicago, IL 60604 - Phone: (312) 697-0022, Fax: (312) 697-0812 - *See complete biographical profile in the Criminal Law: Felonies & White Collar Crime Chapter, page 110.*

•**EDWIN J. BELZ** - *Belz & McWilliams* - 4407 North Elston Avenue - Chicago, IL 60630 - Phone: (312) 282-9129, Fax: (312) 282-9811 - *See complete biographical profile in the Criminal Law: Felonies & White Collar Crime Chapter, page 111.*

•**MARVIN BLOOM** - *Marvin Bloom & Associates* - 53 West Jackson, Suite 1430 - Chicago, IL 60604 - Phone: (312) 641-1044, Fax: (312) 554-8780 - *See complete biographical profile in the Criminal Law: Felonies & White Collar Crime Chapter, page 111.*

David E. Camic

Camic, Johnson, Wilson & Bloom, P.C.
546 West Galena Boulevard
Aurora, IL 60506

Phone: (630) 859-0135
Fax: (630) 859-1910
800: (800) 750-0135

Extensive Experience In:
- Violent Felonies/Narcotics Felonies
- Complex Criminal Matters
- DUI & Misdemeanors

•**DAVID E. CAMIC:** Mr. Camic represents clients in criminal trials, including felonies and misdemeanors, in Illinois state and federal courts. His practice includes both bench and jury trials and he holds the record for one of the shortest jury acquittals in Illinois: seven minutes. Mr. Camic is a frequent speaker at seminars and programs for professional associations and the general public. He has lectured for many professional associations and several local schools and organizations. Mr. Camic is on the faculty of Aurora University where he teaches an introductory course in criminal law, and he previously taught courses at Elgin Community College. He has lectured to police officers on the law of arrest, including DUI, for Illinois Northeast Multi-Regional Police Training. He is the author of "Rights of Pre-Trial Detainees in Illinois," *Illinois Police Association Official Journal,* 1987; has researched information for the Illinois Institute for Continuing Legal Education's Handbook, *Federal Civil Practice,* Chapter 5S, 1987; wrote on sentencing for the *Kane County Bar Journal;* and contributed case notes for the Illinois Bar Association's *Criminal Justice Newsletter.* In addition, Mr. Camic assisted in the editing of the two Criminal Law Chapters of this book. He has represented clients in several high-profile cases, and has acted as lead counsel on death penalty cases and complex narcotics cases. He is often retained by clients who have previously been represented by other attorneys and has been able to successfully vacate convictions in both the trial and appellate courts.

Education: JD 1987 with distinction, John Marshall Law School (Order of John Marshall; Phi Delta Phi Honors Fraternity; Faculty Merit Scholarship); Graduate Studies 1982-83, DePaul University; BA 1982, Aurora College.

Admitted: 1987 Illinois; 1987 U.S. Dist. Ct. (N. Dist. IL, General Bar); 1990 U.S. Dist. Ct. (N. Dist. IL, Trial Bar); 1996 New York.

Employment History: Partner 1987-present, law firm currently known as Camic, Johnson, Wilson & Bloom, P.C.; Police Officer 1977-87, Aurora Police Department; Research Assistant 1985, John Marshall Law School.

Representative Clients: Police officers, a priest, doctors, gang leaders, lawyers, teachers, and corporations.

Professional Associations: NACDL; ABA; ISBA [Criminal Justice Section Council (Secretary)]; Illinois Attorneys for Criminal Justice (Treasurer); Kane County Bar Assn. [Criminal Practice Committee (Chair 1991-96)]; DuPage County Bar Assn.

Community Involvement: People's Law School; High School trial competitions; Legislative testimony.

Firm: The firm's criminal trial partners, Mr. Camic, Gary V. Johnson, and Marvin Bloom, are all listed in this *Guidebook. See complete firm profile in Appendix A. Mr. Camic also practices Criminal Law: Felonies & White Collar Crime and Personal Injury Law: General.*

•GARY V. JOHNSON: Mr. Johnson represents clients in criminal trials, including felonies and misdemeanors, in Illinois state and federal courts. His practice includes both bench and jury trials. Mr. Johnson took part in one of the longest criminal trials in Illinois, when he defended Steve Buckley in the first Nicarico prosecution. Mr. Buckley was the only defendant not convicted in that trial. Mr. Johnson is a frequent speaker at seminars and for professional associations, including the Kane County Bar Association, Cook County Public Defender, People's Law School, and local schools and organizations. He was previously elected the State's Attorney of Kane County. Mr. Johnson served for four years prior to reentering private practice. Since his reentry into private practice, Mr. Johnson has successfully represented several clients charged with murder and capital murder. He has been specially appointed by trial courts to assist a convicted capital murder defendant on his post-conviction petition. He was recently given special mention by the Illinois State Appellate Defender for obtaining an acquittal for a defendant in a complex capital murder case. Mr. Johnson has extensive experience in complex and high-profile criminal cases.

Education: JD 1978 with honors, Drake University (Order of the Coif); BA 1975, Wesleyan University, Illinois.

Admitted: 1978 Illinois; 1978 U.S. Dist. Ct. (N. Dist. IL, General Bar, Trial Bar); 1980 U.S. Ct. App. (7th Cir.).

Employment History: 1994-present, Camic, Johnson, Wilson & Bloom, P.C.; Sole Practitioner 1993-94; Elected Kane County State's Attorney 1988-92; Sole Practitioner 1988; 1983-88, Clancy & McGuirk; Assistant State's Attorney 1979-82, Kane County.

Representative Clients: Gang leaders, school officials, lawyers, judges, capital murder cases, and complex narcotics cases.

Professional Associations: NACDL; ABA; ISBA (Criminal Justice Section Council); Illinois Attorneys for Criminal Justice (Executive Board); Kane County Bar Assn. [Criminal Practice Committee (Chair 1987-88)]; DuPage County Bar Assn.

Community Involvement: Mr. Johnson is active in People's Law School and St. Charles Township.

Firm: Camic, Johnson, Wilson & Bloom, P.C., evolved from a firm started in 1987. The firm has extensive criminal trial experience involving capital murder cases, high-profile cases, white collar defense, and environmental crimes. The firm's criminal trial partners, Mr. Johnson, David E. Camic, and Marvin Bloom, are all listed in this *Guidebook. See complete firm profile in Appendix A. Mr. Johnson also practices Criminal Law: Felonies & White Collar Crime and Personal Injury Law: General.*

GARY V. JOHNSON
Camic, Johnson, Wilson & Bloom, P.C.
546 West Galena Boulevard
Aurora, IL 60506

Phone: (630) 859-0135
Fax: (630) 859-1910
800: (800) 750-0135

Extensive Experience In:
- Murder/Capital Murder
- Narcotics/Violent Crimes
- DUI & Misdemeanors

CATHERINE M. RYAN - *Ryan, Miller & Trafelet, P.C.* - 120 South Riverside Plaza, Suite 1150 - Chicago, IL 60606-3910 - Phone: (312) 207-1700, Fax: (312) 207-1332 - *See complete biographical profile in the Family Law Chapter, page 200.*

NORTHWESTERN ILLINOIS
INCLUDING ROCKFORD & QUAD CITIES

KEITH S. MORSE - *Attorney at Law* - 810 East State Street, Suite 101 - Rockford, IL 61104 - Phone: (815) 967-5000, Fax: (815) 967-5002 - *See complete biographical profile in the Family Law Chapter, page 208.*

R. CRAIG SAHLSTROM - *Attorney and Counsellor at Law* - One Court Place, Suite 301 - Rockford, IL 61101 - Phone: (815) 964-4601, Fax: (815) 964-3292 - *See complete biographical profile in the Criminal Law: Felonies & White Collar Crime Chapter, page 116.*

Chapter 12: Criminal Law: DUI & Misdemeanors

CENTRAL ILLINOIS

NICHOLAS H. ORES - *Attorney at Law* - 1720 First Financial Plaza - Peoria, IL 61602 - Phone: (309) 674-5297, Fax: (309) 674-5299 - *See complete biographical profile in the Family Law Chapter, page 213.*

CHAPTER 13

CRIMINAL LAW: FELONIES & WHITE COLLAR CRIME

This chapter outlines how the criminal justice system operates and describes the most serious criminal violations—felonies and white collar crime. It also includes information about the rights of persons accused of crimes and the rights of crime victims. Domestic abuse and protective orders are covered in the Family Law Chapter. Criminal procedure is covered in the Process of a Case: Civil & Criminal Chapter. Private causes of action that result from criminal conduct are covered in the Personal Injury Law Chapters. Finally, misdemeanors, the juvenile justice system, and driving-under-the-influence violations are covered in the Criminal Law: DUI & Misdemeanors Chapter.

CRIMINAL CODES

Criminal law defines conduct that is prohibited by the government and the range of penalties that can be imposed for violating these prohibitions. Persons who violate criminal laws incur penalties ranging from fines to imprisonment or, in some states, execution. All crimes are defined by statutes. These statutes are collected and organized into books of rules known as criminal codes. In addition to the Illinois State Criminal Code, which applies only in Illinois, the federal government has a criminal code that regulates certain crimes nationwide. Most criminal activity violates either a state law or a federal law, not both; however, an important exception is drug crimes, which can be prosecuted in either state or federal court or both.

Every crime is defined by a list of elements. In a criminal trial, the prosecutor attempts to prove all the elements of the crime the person is accused of committing. If the judge or the jury decides all the elements of the crime have been proven beyond a reasonable doubt, the accused person is guilty of the crime. If the prosecutor cannot prove all the elements, the accused cannot be found guilty of the crime.

ATTEMPT, CONSPIRACY, AIDING AND ABETTING

Anyone who, with intent to commit a crime, takes a substantial step toward committing the crime may be guilty of attempt to commit a crime. Merely thinking about committing a crime is not a crime; even preparation for a crime is not a substantial step. For example, if someone buys a gun with intent to kill another person, the act of buying is mere preparation. However, going to a person's house after buying a gun with intent to kill the person may be a substantial step that is enough to charge a person with attempting to commit a crime.

The law of conspiracy and the law of aiding and abetting are other general doctrines that apply to a wide range of offenses. A conspiracy is an agreement between two or more persons to commit a crime. For example, if three people conspire to commit murder, at least one of them takes action to further the conspiracy, and the murder actually occurs, they all can be charged with both conspiracy and murder. Even if a conspirator backs out of the conspiracy, but the other conspirators commit the crime, all conspirators may be criminally liable if the acts were reasonably foreseeable.

A person who intentionally aids or advises another in committing a crime may be guilty of aiding and abetting, and may be criminally liable for the acts of the other person, as well. Thus, if someone intentionally advises another how to commit robbery and lends the robber a car to use in the getaway, both people are equally liable under the law.

OFFENSES

Criminal codes penalize a variety of activities. Generally, an offense is any violation of the Illinois Criminal Code. The Criminal Code makes a major distinction between felonies and misdemeanors. A felony is a crime for which a person can be sentenced to one year or more in the penitentiary, or to death. A misdemeanor is a crime for which a person can be sentenced to less than one year in jail.

FELONIES

The most violent crimes, such as murder and rape, as well as so-called white collar crimes, generally are felonies under the Illinois Criminal Code.

CRIMES CAUSING HARM TO PERSONS

Homicide and Suicide

Homicide is the unlawful killing of another human being. There are several types of homicide: murder, manslaughter, and reckless homicide. All forms of homicide are felonies.

Murder is the unlawful killing of another with intent to kill. Murder is divided into subcategories by degree of seriousness. First degree murder is killing someone with intent to kill or to cause great bodily harm, or knowing that one's actions will cause death or create a strong probability of death or great bodily harm. First degree murder also includes unlawful killing during the commission of a forcible felony. Second degree murder is similar to first degree murder, except at the time of the killing the offender has the unreasonable belief that the killing is justified, or the offender is acting under an intense and sudden passion resulting from being provoked.

Manslaughter and reckless homicide differ from murder because these crimes do not require proof of intent. Under Illinois law, involuntary manslaughter is unintentionally killing another person while engaged in an action that is likely to cause death or great bodily harm if the action is done recklessly. However, if the cause of death is by a person recklessly driving a motor vehicle, the crime is called reckless homicide.

Suicide is taking one's own life. Suicide and attempted suicide no longer are crimes in Illinois. However, it is a crime to induce another to commit suicide.

Assault and Battery

Under Illinois law, assault and battery are separate crimes. Assault is defined as an act that makes another person have reasonable apprehension of battery. Battery means intentionally or knowingly and without legal justification causing bodily harm to another person, or making an insulting or provoking physical contact with a person. Examples of aggravated assault are assault with a mask or a weapon, or assault against a person the offender knows is a government employee, a person with a disability, a police officer, or a senior citizen. Aggravated battery is a battery committed under the same particular circumstances as aggravated assault. Other laws make battery of particular people, such as family members, criminal acts. These laws include domestic battery, battery or aggravated battery of an unborn child, aggravated battery of a child or institutionalized mentally retarded person, and aggravated battery of a senior citizen. A separate statute makes transmission of HIV a crime if the person knows he or she is infected with HIV and contaminates another person through sexual contact, donation of blood or other body fluids, or sells or shares drug paraphernalia.

Rape

Criminal sexual assault—also known as rape—is a felony that carries with it severe penalties. Criminal sexual assault is sexual penetration by force or threat of force, without consent of the victim, or against a minor. Aggravated criminal sexual assault is criminal sexual assault when one of the following occurs:

- A dangerous weapon is used or displayed
- The offender causes bodily harm
- The rape occurs during the course of another felony
- The victim is over 60 years of age
- The victim has a physical disability
- The victim is under nine years of age
- The victim is institutionalized and severely mentally retarded

It is criminal sexual abuse, sometimes called statutory rape, for anyone to have sexual penetration or sexual conduct with a victim under the age of 17. If the accused is over 5 years older, it is a felony. Criminal sexual abuse also can be sexual conduct other than sexual penetration in which force is used or the victim was unable to consent.

Kidnapping

Kidnapping is secretly and knowingly confining a person against his or her will, or using deceit, enticement, force, or threat of force to cause a person to go from one place to another with the intention of secretly and knowingly confining that person against his or her will. Confining a child 12 years old or younger without the consent of the child's parent also constitutes kidnapping. Aggravated kidnapping is kidnapping under additional circumstances or with additional actions, such as kidnapping while wearing a mask or with a dangerous weapon, or kidnapping for ransom. All forms of kidnapping are felonies.

Intimidation

The crime of intimidation is defined as intending to cause another person to act a certain way by threatening the person by phone, by mail, or in person. The threats can include threatening to

- Hurt the person, another person, or property
- Physically confine or restrain the person
- Commit a crime or accuse the other person of committing a crime
- Expose the person to hatred or ridicule
- Cause a strike or boycott

In Illinois, intimidation is a felony.

Stalking

Stalking also is a felony. Stalking is the crime of knowingly following a person or putting a person under surveillance without justification, combined with threatening the person or causing the person to believe the stalker will harm him or her physically. The acts of following or watching must occur on at least two separate occasions to be stalking. A person commits aggravated stalking by actually causing physical harm. Another form of aggravated stalking is stalking that violates an order of protection. Orders of protection are described in detail in the Family Law Chapter.

Hate Crime

Illinois law prohibits hate crime, which is defined as a crime such as assault, battery, or theft committed against a person because of his or her ancestry, color, disability, gender, national origin, race, or sexual orientation. For example, a group of white youths who chased and beat two black youths, referring to them using racial insults, were guilty of a hate crime in Illinois.

FEDERAL DRUG AND GUN LAWS

Federal laws contain harsh penalties for distributing controlled substances, especially if firearms are even remotely involved. For example, any person who possesses, with intent to distribute, five grams of crack cocaine is subject to a mandatory sentence of five years without parole. If a gun is available for use or is being carried during a drug transaction—even if it is not used—a mandatory five-year sentence must be imposed consecutively to a conviction for the drug offense. Thus, the person with five grams of crack cocaine with intent to distribute would receive a mandatory ten-year sentence without parole if he or she was carrying a gun. In most circumstances, federal judges cannot depart from these mandatory sentences. Penalties for controlled substance offenses become even harsher as quantities of the contraband increase.

CRIMES CAUSING HARM TO PROPERTY

Depending on the value of the property involved, as well as the level of violence, most property crimes are felonies in Illinois. The legal definition of theft is obtaining, exerting control over, and intending to deprive; or knowingly using, concealing, or abandoning so as to deprive a person of his or her property. This definition is much broader than what most people think of as theft. It can include writing bad checks, keeping found property without making a reasonable attempt to find its rightful owner, misusing trade secrets, unlawfully tapping into cable television or other television services, interfering with public utilities, or taking large sums of money by deception from persons over age 60. Unless the value of the property taken is $300 or less, the crime of theft is a felony. Additionally, theft always is a felony if a firearm is involved or if the accused has been convicted previously of theft, burglary, or robbery. Burglary, because it involves entering or remaining in a building or dwelling without authority and with the intent to commit theft or a felony there, generally is a felony. Not only is it burglary to enter a house unlawfully with the intent to steal money or property, but it also is burglary to enter with the intent to commit a felony such as arson or murder. Similarly, robbery almost always is felonious. Robbery is unlawfully taking personal property from another person or in the presence of the other person while using or threatening to use force against the person. Aggravated robbery is robbery committed with a dangerous weapon.

Chapter 13: Criminal Law: Felonies & White Collar Crime

WHITE COLLAR CRIMES

Although there is no fixed definition of white collar crime, a number of nonviolent crimes frequently are grouped together as white collar crimes. The term "white collar crime" generally is used to describe crimes that have cheating or dishonesty as their common basis. These crimes typically are committed by professionals or entrepreneurs under cover of legitimate business activity. Such crimes may be difficult to prosecute because of their complexity. Often they carry lesser penalties because they are not associated with violence. However, defendants convicted of white collar crimes may incur enormous fines, be ordered to pay restitution, or spend time in jail. Today, there is a trend toward stricter punishment for white collar crimes, as people recognize the financial damage white collar criminals inflict on society.

As a practical matter, it is impossible to describe every activity that fits within the definition of white collar crime, because white collar crime takes many forms. Some criminal actions are prohibited by specific laws narrowly drawn to outlaw a particular activity. Other actions are not covered by specific laws but instead are prosecuted under one or more "catch-all" laws criminalizing dishonest behavior generally.

BRIBERY

Federal law and Illinois law both prohibit bribery. The purpose of most bribery statutes is to prevent people from seeking preferential treatment from public officials and to prevent public officers from using their offices for personal gain. Specifically, if a government official is offered or seeks anything of value for himself or herself in exchange for performing an official act, a fraudulent action, or any action in violation of his or her official duty, the elements of bribery may be met.

COMPUTER CRIME

Computer crime is an area of the law in which the government appears to be playing catch-up with the growth in new technologies. Some variations of computer crime are so new that there are no specific laws to address them, and general laws in existence do not seem adequate in proscribing the particular illicit activities.

Generally, the conduct specifically outlawed by federal statute includes

- Knowingly accessing a computer, without authorization or exceeding authorization, and thereby obtaining confidential national security information
- Intentionally accessing a computer, without authorization or exceeding authorization, and thereby obtaining the financial information of a financial institution or of a credit card issuer
- Intentionally accessing, without authorization, a computer of a federal department or agency used exclusively by that department or agency or affecting the government's use thereof
- Knowingly, and with intent to defraud, accessing a federal interest computer, without authorization or exceeding authorization, to further a fraud or obtain anything of value
- Intentionally accessing a federal interest computer, without authorization, to alter, damage, or destroy information and thereby causing a loss of $1,000 or, if medical information is affected, any amount
- Knowingly, and with intent to defraud, trafficking in any password or similar information through which a computer is accessed, without authorization, if such computer affects interstate or foreign commerce or is used by or for the government

Illinois law also recognizes the crimes of computer tampering, aggravated computer tampering, and computer fraud. Computer tampering occurs when a person knowingly and without authorization

- Accesses a computer, program, or data, whether or not the person obtains data or services
- Accesses a computer, program, or data, and damages or destroys the computer, program, or data
- Inserts a "program" into a computer knowing that it contains information or commands that will damage or destroy that computer or other computers, or that will alter, delete, or remove a program or data

Aggravated computer tampering occurs when a person commits computer tampering and knowingly disrupts government or other public services or causes great bodily harm to a person.

A person commits computer fraud when he or she knowingly accesses, uses, damages, or destroys a computer, program, or data, or obtains money, property, or services of another in connection with a scheme to defraud. Computer crimes carry severe penalties, especially as the value of the property damaged or stolen increases.

EMBEZZLEMENT

To embezzle means to take another's money or property through abuse of an official job or position of trust. Embezzlement can take many forms. An accountant might use sophisticated methods to falsify records and skim profits. A bank teller might walk home with an extra 20 dollars from his or her drawer. Both of these actions constitute embezzlement.

FALSE STATEMENTS

The crime of making false statements is not specific to white collar criminals, but this crime is broad enough to encompass activities that might not be unlawful if not for associated false statements. To convict someone of false statements requires proof of a statement made willfully and knowingly that contains a false material fact or conceals a material fact.

FRAUD

Fraud is intentionally lying in order to induce someone into relying upon the lie to part with something of value. Like embezzlement, fraud can be either complex or simple. The federal government has three general anti-fraud statutes for mail fraud, bank fraud, and wire fraud. Mail fraud has two elements: (1) a scheme devised or intending to defraud or for obtaining property or money by fraudulent means, and (2) using the mails in furtherance of that fraudulent scheme. The "scheme to defraud" element of mail fraud is deliberately broad. It encompasses a wide variety of criminal activity, including credit card fraud, securities fraud, medical drug fraud, and frauds based on political malfeasance. Because the mail fraud statute uses such broad language and because it is relatively easy to prove, mail fraud is one of the most common charges brought by federal prosecutors. Charges of mail fraud frequently are made even in cases in which more specific crimes have been charged.

The federal wire fraud statute is similar to the mail fraud statute, but requires an interstate or foreign transmittal of a communication by wire, radio, or television. The federal bank fraud statute criminalizes the conduct of any party who "knowingly executes, or attempts to execute, a scheme or artifice to defraud a financial institution, by means of false or fraudulent pretenses, representations, or promises."

In addition, Illinois law prohibits fraud generally, as well as specific fraudulent acts. In Illinois, fraud includes such crimes as public aid wire fraud and deceptive collections practices. The crime of deceptive practices occurs when a person who has an intent to defraud uses a threat or deception for an unlawful purpose, such as to

- Sign a document transferring property or creating a financial obligation
- Use his or her position as an officer or manager to receive an investment
- Issue a false check to pay taxes, buy property, or pay for services

Although generally the crime of deceptive practices is a misdemeanor, if the property at issue is worth $150 or several transactions within a 90-day period exceed $150, the crime becomes a felony. Check fraud, deception of financial institutions, false personation, forgery, and possessing another's identification card (such as a card for an automated teller machine) also are crimes under Illinois law.

OBSTRUCTION OF JUSTICE

Obstruction of justice is a category of offenses of interference in one of the three branches of government. Obstruction of justice can take many forms, including assaulting a process server, improperly influencing a juror, stealing or altering a record of process, and obstructing a criminal investigation by officers of a financial institution. Picketing, parading, or using sound amplification devices in front of a courthouse, a building or residence occupied by a judge, juror, witness, or court officer, may be prosecuted as obstruction of justice.

PERJURY

Federal perjury laws penalize anyone who willfully or knowingly makes false statements under oath. The sworn statements may be written or oral and need not be made in court; a person may perjure himself or herself in deposition or written testimony. A related law against subornation of perjury makes it illegal for anyone to procure another person to commit perjury.

RACKETEER INFLUENCED AND CORRUPT ORGANIZATIONS ACT

The Racketeer Influenced and Corrupt Organizations Act (RICO) was established to fight the influence of organized crime on legitimate businesses. Under federal criminal law, defendants may be found guilty of violating RICO if they engage in "racketeering activity" under the auspices of an enterprise that affects interstate commerce, or if they are involved in the collection of an unlawful debt. There are 9 state and 35 federal offenses specifically listed as racketeering activity. The 9 listed state offenses are murder, kidnapping, gambling, robbery, arson, bribery, dealing in obscene materials, and dealing in narcotics or other dangerous drugs. While drug smuggling, murder, bribery, and extortion of "protection money" are examples of the activities to which RICO originally was applied, more recently it has been used to prosecute an increasing variety of criminal actions.

Securities Fraud and Insider Trading

A broad range of illegal behavior is prosecuted under securities fraud statutes. Criminal prosecutions require the prosecutor to show that the accused acted willfully; if the accused is found in violation, he or she is subject to criminal penalties, civil penalties, or both. The securities fraud statutes recognize that deception may take many forms and thus are worded broadly to prohibit "any device, scheme or artifice to defraud" in securities sales.

There are two general categories of securities fraud. The first involves the sale of securities to investors for far more than their actual value. The second involves the sale of legitimate securities for illegal purposes. An example of the first type of fraud is selling shares in dry oil wells. An example of the second type of fraud is sale of legitimate stock by a broker who conceals information about his or her own involvement with the brokerage company. These acts are prohibited by rules established by the Securities and Exchange Commission.

Insider trading prosecutions have been some of the most publicized white collar prosecutions of the 1980s and 1990s. Surprisingly, "insider trading" is not defined in any specific statute; it is a term used to describe insiders (such as officers of a corporation) taking unfair advantage of information to make money or avoid losing money in securities. Generally, insider trading means that an insider with material, non-public information engages in trading without disclosing that information to the public first. These crimes typically are prosecuted under the Securities and Exchange Act of 1934. However, prosecutors are not confined to using specific securities fraud statutes to prosecute securities fraud. General anti-fraud statutes may be used instead of, or in addition to, specific securities fraud laws. For example, parties engaged in securities fraud may be charged with violating mail and wire fraud statutes.

Tax Crimes

Often, people charged with other white collar crimes are accused of committing a tax crime also. Failing to file a tax return or filing a false tax return is a crime, as is interfering with the administration of the internal revenue laws. Specific laws prohibit obstruction, extortion, or bribery with regard to a tax official.

DEFENSES AND PUNISHMENT

In some criminal trials, the prosecutor proves all the elements of a crime but the person accused is not punished because he or she has a valid defense.

Self-defense sometimes is used as a defense. The general rule for self-defense is that a person may use any amount of force—except deadly force—that he or she reasonably believes is necessary to prevent immediate unlawful harm to a person. Using deadly force is permissible only when it reasonably appears to be necessary to avoid immediate death or serious injury to a person, or to prevent the commission of a felony in the actor's dwelling. If a person claims that he or she acted in self-defense, the prosecutor must prove beyond a reasonable doubt that self-defense was not the reason for the crime.

By itself, intoxication is not a defense to a crime. In rare cases, intoxication works like a defense if there is proof that the person accused of the crime was unable to form the necessary intent to commit a crime. Someone who is intoxicated may not be found guilty of a crime that requires he or she acted intentionally, but the intoxicated person may be guilty of another crime that does not require intentional actions.

In the area of white collar crime, the same defenses are available to defendants as those available in crimes generally. Some people accused of white collar crimes also claim entrapment by the government; they argue they were induced to act, and would not have acted unlawfully otherwise. Another common defense by businesses is that a particular businessperson was acting alone, without the authority of the company behind him or her. Businesses further argue that once it was discovered that an officer or employee was acting unlawfully, the business acted immediately to resolve the situation. Sometimes a business avoids criminal liability altogether if it shows that it took proper action to correct a situation as soon as managers were made aware of a problem.

Felonies and white collar crimes carry the strictest punishments, such as lengthy imprisonment, heavy fines, or even death. Federal sentencing guidelines contain a method for calculating fines to be paid by organizations that commit crimes. Businesses that are found guilty of operating for a primarily criminal purpose incur fines equal to their total assets.

Illinois also has laws that allow the authorities to seize property connected with the commission of a crime. For example, any money or other profits connected with computer fraud may be seized by the government. Similarly, a person charged with violating laws connected with controlled substances must forfeit the substances as well as the raw materials used to make the drugs, vehicles and real property used to further the crime, and any money or other proceeds from the sale of the controlled substances.

CRIME VICTIMS' RIGHTS

Victims of the most violent crimes have rights in the Illinois criminal justice system. Under the Bill of Rights for Victims and Witnesses of Violent Crime Act, a victim of violent crime generally has the right to be notified of the status of the investigation, whether an indictment has been brought, the time and place of any hearings, and when the defendant is released from custody. The Illinois Victims Rights Constitutional Amendment also gives all victims the right to be treated with fairness, the right to privacy, the right to make a statement at sentencing, and the right to reasonable protection from the accused during the criminal justice proceedings.

Some crime victims also have a right to compensation for the crimes committed against them. This means that a crime victim may receive compensation for certain expenses or losses such as medical expenses or loss of support if the crime victim becomes unable to support dependents. There are requirements that must be met for a victim to get reimbursement, and a victim must file an application for consideration with the Illinois Court of Claims for compensation. The maximum amount a victim can receive from the Court of Claims is $25,000.

Under some Illinois laws, the victim may receive compensation from the person who committed the crime. This is called restitution. For example, a person whose vehicle is stolen may be able to receive compensation for the vehicle. In this case, the state arranges to collect the money from the criminal and sends a check to the victim when all the restitution has been made.

If the court does not order restitution, or if a prosecutor does not press charges, the victim still has the option to seek compensation directly by suing the offender in civil court. This option is discussed more fully in the Process of a Case: Civil & Criminal Chapter.

RESOURCES

Business Crime: Criminal Liability of the Business Community, Stanley S. Arkin, et al, Matthew Bender, New York, NY, 1994.

Illinois Crime Victims Reparation Board, 100 Randolph Street West, Chicago, IL 60601, phone: (312) 814-2581.

National Coalition Against Sexual Assault, P.O. Box 21378, Washington, D.C. 20009, phone: (202) 483-7165.

National Organization for Victim Assistance, 1757 Park Road NW, Washington, D.C. 20010, phone: (202) 232-6682.

To obtain the free pamphlet, *Your Rights if Arrested,* contact the Illinois State Bar Association, Illinois Bar Center, Springfield, IL 62701-1779, phone: (217) 525-1760.

Crime victims who wish to apply for compensation should apply to the Illinois Court of Claims, Capitol Building, Room 213, Springfield, IL 62756, phone: (217) 782-7101.

This chapter was reviewed and edited by Leading Illinois Attorney David E. Camic.

Criminal Law: Felonies & White Collar Crime
Leading Illinois Attorneys

Illinois' Most Respected Legal Counsel As Selected By Their Peers.

The Leading Illinois Attorneys below were recommended by their peers in a statewide survey.

The Leading Illinois Attorneys listed below were nominated as exceptional by their peers in a statewide survey conducted by American Research Corporation (ARC). ARC asked several thousand licensed Illinois attorneys to name the lawyer to whom they would send a close friend or family member in need of legal assistance in specific areas of law. The attorneys below were nominated in the area of Criminal Law: Felonies & White Collar Crime.

Because the survey results (all practice area results combined) represent less than three percent of Illinois' practicing attorneys, this list should not be construed as a complete list. Nevertheless, it is an excellent source of highly qualified and reputable Illinois attorneys.

For information on ARC's survey methodology, see page *xi*.
For the complete list of Leading Illinois Consumer Attorneys, see page *xii*.

The Leading Illinois Attorneys below are listed alphabetically in accordance with the geographic region in which their offices are located. Note that attorneys may handle clients from a broad geographic area; attorneys are not restricted to only serving clients residing within the cities in which their offices are located.

An attorney whose name appears in bold has included a biographical profile in this chapter.

Cook & Collar Counties

Ackerman, Allan A. - Chicago, page 110
Adam, Sam - Chicago
Aimen, Julie B. - Chicago, page 110
Angelini, Phil - Oak Brook
Belz, Edwin J. - Chicago, page 111
Berkson, Dennis A. - Chicago
Blomquist, Ernest R., III - Arlington Heights
Bloom, Marvin - Chicago, page 111
Breen, Thomas - Chicago
Briscoe, Thomas A. - Waukegan
Brunell, Alan R. - Chicago
Bugos, Joseph T. - Lisle
Busch, Kevin T. - Aurora
Camic, David E. - Aurora, page 112
Coffield, Michael W. - Chicago
Cohn, Frederick F. - Chicago
Collins, George B. - Chicago
Colton, Kathleen - Batavia
Connelly, Vincent J. - Chicago
Cotsirilos, George J. - Chicago
Crowe, Brian L. - Chicago
De Leon, John R. - Chicago
Decker, Thomas D. - Chicago
Dolci, Dominick P. - Oakbrook Terrace
Donahue, John F. - Lisle
Duffy, John M. - Chicago
Durkin, Thomas Anthony - Chicago
Ekl, Terry A. - Clarendon Hills
Epstein, James R. - Chicago
Falconer, Michael J. - Chicago

Farrell, John E. - Chicago
Fawell, Jeffrey B. - Wheaton
Ferguson, James R. - Chicago
Fischer, Bella - Lake Bluff
Fisher, Robert A. - Chicago
Fleischer, Larry L. - Chicago
Fleisher, Richard S. - Chicago
Fleming, Michael W. - Elmhurst
Flood, James - Des Plaines
Foran, Thomas A. - Chicago
Foreman, Fred - Chicago
Fox, Robert J. - Waukegan
Frankel, Scott J. - Chicago, page 112
Genson, Edward - Chicago
Gevirtz, Robert L. - Northfield
Giacchetti, Cynthia - Chicago
Gillespie, Terence P. - Chicago
Goggin, Michael J. - Oak Park
Goldberg, Herbert - Chicago
Graham, James A. - Chicago
Harte, William J. - Chicago
Hauser, Robert J. - Waukegan, page 113
hooks, william h. - Chicago, page 114
Howard, George C. - Chicago
Hyman, Lawrence H. - Chicago
Johnson, Gary V. - Aurora, page 114
Jones, Gregory C. - Chicago
Kaplan, Sidney M. - Chicago
Kennelly, Matthew F. - Chicago
Kling, Richard - Chicago

106 *Leading Illinois Attorneys Consumer Law Guidebook*

Komie, Stephen M. - Chicago
Kopsick, Richard S. - Waukegan
Kowalczyk, Mark E. - Glen Ellyn
Kulwin, Shelly B. - Chicago
Kunkle, William J., Jr. - Chicago
Kurz, Jerry B. - Chicago
Laraia, Joseph M. - Wheaton
LeFevour, Terrence P. - Chicago
Linklater, William J. - Chicago
Lunardi, Steven B. - Waukegan
Lynch, George J. - Chicago
Lynch, George P. - Downers Grove
Magidson, Sherman C. - Chicago
Marcus, James I. - Chicago
Martin, Royal B. - Chicago, page 115
Martin, William J. - Oak Park
McCulloch, Thomas O. - St. Charles
McWilliams, Clare - Palatine
Meczyk, Ralph E. - Chicago
Melber, Michael D. - Chicago
Menaker, Ronald D. - Chicago
Miller, Irving - Chicago
Molo, Steven F. - Chicago
Monaco, Mark C. - Batavia
Monico, Michael D. - Chicago
Morelli, Fred M., Jr. - Aurora
Murphy, William P. - Chicago
Murtaugh, George J., Jr. - Chicago
Neville, Ronald F. - Chicago
Nolan, Francis A. - Chicago
Nolan, Nan R. - Chicago
Pearl, Howard M. - Chicago
Pincham, R. Eugene - Chicago
Pinelli, Anthony - Chicago
Poulos, Michael D. - Evanston
Powers, Michael E. - Oak Brook
Rantis, Nicholas S. - Oakbrook Terrace
Ravitz, Gary J. - Chicago
Ray, Loraine A. - Chicago
Reidy, Daniel E. - Chicago
Richards, Van R., Jr. - Elgin
Riebman, Hyman - Des Plaines
Rimland, Jack P. - Chicago
Rivkin-Carothers, Anita - Chicago
Roberts, Douglas R. - Waukegan
Roddy, Joseph V. - Chicago
Rogers, Jeffrey E. - Chicago

Russo, Richard D. - Wheaton
Ryan, Richard P. - Chicago
Sadowski, Ronald W. - Oak Brook
Samuels, Elliott M. - Chicago
Schillerstrom, Robert J. - Naperville
Sheppard, Barry D. - Chicago
Simonian, Stephen M. - Waukegan
Sklarsky, Charles B. - Chicago
Smeeton, Jack C. - Evanston
Smirl, Dale L. - Chicago
Solotorovsky, Julian - Chicago
Sorosky, Sheldon M. - Chicago
Spector, Barry A. - Chicago
Steinback, Jeffrey B. - Chicago
Stephenson, Robert M. - Chicago
Stetler, David J. - Chicago
Stone, Jed - Chicago, page 115
Stone, Jeffrey E. - Chicago
Streicker, James R. - Chicago
Sullivan, Terry - Rolling Meadows
Sullivan, Thomas E. - Wheaton
Sullivan, Thomas P. - Chicago
Tallis, Jeffrey J. - Chicago
Tarun, Robert W. - Chicago
Telander, Brian F. - Glen Ellyn
Theis, John T. - Chicago
Thomas, David - Chicago
Tighe, Ann C. - Chicago
Tobin, Craig D. - Chicago, page 116
Tuite, Patrick A. - Chicago
Turow, Scott - Chicago
Tyrrell, Thomas J. - Chicago
Urban, Tod M. - Chicago
Urdangen, Jeffrey - Chicago
Valukas, Anton R. - Chicago
Van Der Snick, J. Brick - Geneva
von Mandel, Michael J. - Chicago
Wagner, Paul A. - Chicago
Walsh, Carl M. - Chicago
Walther, M. Jacqueline - Chicago
Watschke, David R. - Elmhurst
Webb, Dan K. - Chicago
Will, Robert P., Jr. - Waukegan
Williams, Jeffrey - Chicago
Willis, Standish E. - Chicago
Wojtecki, Leonard J. - Aurora
Zeit, Daniel R. - Waukegan

NORTHWESTERN ILLINOIS INCLUDING ROCKFORD & QUAD CITIES

Altamore, Albert A. - Rockford
Beu, William R. - Rockford
Braud, Walter D. - Rock Island
Bush, Robert A. - Elizabeth
Bute, Daniel J. - Ottawa
Butera, Richard M. - Rockford
Cain, Daniel J. - Rockford
Caulk, David A. - Rockford
Gaziano, Paul E. - Rockford
Kelly, Roger H. - Galena
Koonmen, Karl C. - Loves Park

Kreitlow, Margaret - Rockford
Marsh, C. Stephen - Rock Island
Martinez, Francis M. - Rockford
Nack, Joseph E. - Galena
Ruud, Glenn F. - Rock Island
Sahlstrom, R. Craig - Rockford, page 116
Schick, William G. - Rock Island
Seigler, Darrell K. - Ottawa
Sparkman, James D. - Rockford
Vella, Frank P., Jr. - Rockford

Chapter 13: Criminal Law: Felonies & White Collar Crime

CENTRAL ILLINOIS

Auler, Robert I. - Urbana
Beckett, J. Steven - Urbana
Brady, Gerald, Jr. - Peoria
Bruno, Thomas A. - Urbana
Butler, David W. - Bloomington
Costello, Michael J. - Springfield
DeArmond, Craig H. - Danville
Dukes, Carroll W. - Danville
Elmore, James E. - Springfield
Erickson, Frederick P. - Decatur
Feldman, Howard W. - Springfield
Fuller, Glenn O. - Decatur
Gaubas, Robert D. - Peoria
Geisler, Asher O. - Decatur
Geisler, Gary F. - Decatur
Giganti, Adam - Springfield
Halliday, Ronald E. - Peoria
Hamm, Ronald L. - Peoria
Hanna, Ronald - Peoria
Hefner, M. John, Jr. - Mattoon
Holmes, Brent D. - Mattoon
Jennings, Harold M. - Bloomington
Kagawa, Carlton M. - Danville
Keller, K. Rick - Effingham
Kirchner, Robert G. - Champaign
Lawrence, Paul G. - Bloomington
Lerner, Arthur M. - Champaign
Lipton, Mark D. - Champaign

Locher, Bruce D. - Springfield
Lutz, Lonnie L. - Charleston
Metnick, Michael B. - Springfield, page 117
Meyer, Michael J. - Effingham
Murphy, G. Edward - Peoria
Noll, Jon - Springfield
Novak, Anthony E. - Urbana
O'Day, Daniel G. - Peoria
Parker, Drew - Peoria
Penn, Thomas J., Jr. - Peoria
Picl, Frank M. - Peoria
Potter, James R. - Springfield
Reid, William D. - Springfield
Roberts, J. William - Springfield
Rose, Mark A. - Peoria
Ryan, David J. - Danville
Ryan, Stephen R. - Mattoon
Shadid, James E. - Peoria
Silkwood, Larry R. - Urbana
Silverman, Brian C. - Urbana
Skelton, Steven B. - Bloomington
Smith, L. Lee - Peoria
Stanko, Glenn A. - Champaign
Timoney, Patrick T. - Springfield
Toner, Hugh F., III - Peoria
Tulin, Ronald - Charleston
Viverito, Lou J. - Effingham
Winter-Black, Janett S. - Mattoon

SOUTHERN ILLINOIS

Allen, Benjamin B. - Alton
Applegate, Steven D. - Carbondale
Christenson, Paul - Murphysboro
Cunningham, Roscoe D. - Lawrenceville
Daley, Thomas M. - Belleville
Gomric, James J. - Belleville
Groshong, Donald E. - Alton
Hess, Frederick J. - Belleville
Kelley, Randall W. - Belleville
Lockwood, Brocton D. - Marion

Lucco, J. William - Edwardsville
Mansfield, Thomas W. - Murphysboro
Rice, Stephen R. - Belleville
Slemer, Ronald R. - Edwardsville
Speroni, John - Marion
Trentman, Brian K. - Belleville
Veltman, R. Edward - Centralia
Verity, Duane P. - Marion
White, Richard E. - Murphysboro

Biographical Profiles of Criminal Law: Felonies & White Collar Crime Leading Illinois Attorneys

The Leading Illinois Attorneys profiled below were nominated as exceptional by their peers in a statewide survey conducted by American Research Corporation (ARC). ARC asked several thousand licensed Illinois attorneys to name the lawyer to whom they would send a close friend or family member in need of legal assistance in specific areas of law. The attorneys below were nominated in the area of Criminal Law: Felonies & White Collar Crime.

Because the survey results (all practice area results combined) represent less than three percent of Illinois' practicing attorneys, this list should not be construed as a complete list. Nevertheless, it is an excellent source of highly qualified and reputable Illinois attorneys.

For information on ARC's survey methodology, see page *xi*.
For the complete list of Leading Illinois Consumer Attorneys, see page *xii*.
For the list of Leading Illinois Criminal Law: Felonies & White Collar Crime Attorneys, see page 106.

The Leading Illinois Attorneys below are listed alphabetically in accordance with the geographic region in which their offices are located. Note that attorneys may handle clients from a broad geographic area; attorneys are not limited to only serving clients residing within the cities in which their offices are located.

The two-line attorney listings in this section are of attorneys who practice in this area but whose full biographical profiles appear in other sections of this book. A bullet "•" preceding a name indicates the attorney was nominated in this particular area of law.

For information on the format of the full biographical profiles, consult the "Using the Consumer Guidebook" section on page *xviii*.

The following abbreviations are used throughout these profiles:

App.	Appellate
Cir.	Circuit
Ct.	Court
Dist.	District
Sup.	Supreme
JD	Juris Doctor (Doctor of Law)
LLB	Legum Baccalaureus (Bachelor of Laws)
LLD	Legum Doctor (Doctor of Laws)
LLM	Legum Magister (Master of Laws)
ADR	Alternative Dispute Resolution
ABA	American Bar Association
ABOTA	American Board of Trial Advocates
ATLA	Association of Trial Lawyers of America
CBA	Chicago Bar Association
ISBA	Illinois State Bar Association
ITLA	Illinois Trial Lawyers Association
NBTA	National Board of Trial Advocacy

COOK & COLLAR COUNTIES

ALLAN A. ACKERMAN

Allan A. Ackerman, P.C.
2000 North Clifton
Chicago, IL 60614

Phone: (312) 332-2891
Fax: (312) 871-3304

•**ALLAN A. ACKERMAN:** Nationally recognized and respected for innovative and ingenious defense strategies, Mr. Ackerman practices almost exclusively in the area of criminal defense, both at the trial and appellate levels. As a trial lawyer, he has successfully defended some of the country's most problematic cases, including major racketeering (RICO), drug and white collar prosecutions. As an appellate advocate, he has successfully briefed and argued countless cases before the United States Supreme Court and most federal appellate courts in the country. His work is the subject of study in law schools throughout the nation and has been covered by both the local and national media, including the *Chicago Tribune, Time magazine,* and *The Wall Street Journal.* He frequently lectures on trial and appellate stratagem to both law students and attorneys.

Education: JD 1961, John Marshall Law School; Undergraduate, University of Chicago; Wright Jr. College.

Admitted: 1961 Illinois; 1972 U.S. Ct. App. (7th Cir.); 1978 U.S. Sup. Ct.; 1978 U.S. Ct. App. (1st Cir.; 4th Cir.); 1985 U.S. Ct. App. (5th Cir.); 1986 U.S. Ct. App. (8th Cir.); 1987 U.S. Ct. App. (11th Cir.); 1991 U.S. Ct. App. (6th Cir.); 1995 U.S. Ct. App. (9th Cir.); Multiple U.S. Dist. Ct. Admissions.

Employment History: Sole Practitioner 1985-present, Allan A. Ackerman, P.C.; Partner 1977-85, Ackerman & Egan; Partner 1969-77, Ackerman, Durkin & Egan.

Representative Clients: Mr. Ackerman represents clients accused of the full range of federal and state criminal offenses, including RICO and drug offenses, IRS violations, fraud, embezzlement, murder, arson, bribery, illegal gambling activities, white collar crimes, and other offenses. Mr. Ackerman generally refuses to identify his clients unless their names appear in either federal or state legal publications. Mr. Ackerman has represented selected plaintiffs in federal civil rights cases, including Title VII employment discrimination litigation.

Professional Associations: NACDL; ATLA; ABA; CBA; ISBA; Federal Bar Assn.; Fifth Circuit Bar Assn.; Seventh Circuit Bar Assn.

JULIE B. AIMEN

Attorney at Law
343 South Dearborn Street
Suite 1400
Chicago, IL 60604

Phone: (312) 697-0022
Fax: (312) 697-0812

•**JULIE B. AIMEN:** Ms. Aimen is a sole practitioner concentrating in the areas of criminal defense and family law. Ms. Aimen's practice in the criminal area includes both trial and appellate work. She accepts appointed cases from the circuit court, as well as handles an active private practice. In family law, Ms. Aimen's previous background in arbitration and social work give her the unique skills to successfully arbitrate many matters. She has attended the National Criminal Defense College and teaches an intensive trial advocacy program annually at the University of Chicago, Mandel Legal Clinic. As Cochair of the NACDL Forensic Committee, Ms. Aimen handles a national forensic hotline, referring attorneys to forensic experts. She is a coauthor of "Pretrial Procedures and Practice," *Illinois Criminal Procedure.*

Admitted: 1984 Illinois; 1984 U.S. Dist. Ct. (N. Dist. IL).

Education: JD 1984 with honors, Illinois Institute of Technology, Chicago-Kent; BASW 1979 with honors, University of Wisconsin.

Employment History: Sole Practitioner 1986-present; Hearing Officer 1992-present, Vehicle Impoundment Program; Panel Attorney 1991-present, Capitol Resource Center; Arbitration Officer 1990-present, Circuit Court of Cook County; Assistant Appellate Defender 1984-86, Office of the State Appellate Defender, Chicago.

Representative Clients: Ms. Aimen represents a broad range of clients.

Professional Associations: NACDL [Board of Directors 1995-present; Forensic Committee and Hotline (Cochair); New Member Recruitment and Services (Cochair)]; Chicago Council of Lawyers [Board of Governors 1995-present, 1987-93; Indigency Panel and State Evaluation Committee (Cochair)]; CBA 1984-present (past Chair; past Vice Chair); ISBA; National Lawyers Guild.

Community Involvement: Segundo Ruis Belvis Westtown Legal Clinic 1987-90 (Board of Directors); Fund for Justice 1984-85.

Firm: Ms. Aimen is first and foremost a trial attorney who concentrates in litigation. However, as head of a full-service law office, Ms. Aimen tries to provide a holistic approach to dispute resolution. Special counseling services are sought for the family when necessary. Pretrial sentencing and mediation professionals are employed when possible. Ms. Aimen's background in social work gives her a unique approach to criminal cases. *Ms. Aimen also practices Criminal Law: DUI & Misdemeanors and Alternative Dispute Resolution.*

•**EDWIN J. BELZ:** Mr. Belz started practicing law in the Cook County State's Attorney's Office in 1961. He handled criminal cases, including appeals. He was one of only five attorneys to participate in the Federal Defender Program in 1965. Since that time, Mr. Belz has been defending clients charged with criminal felonies and misdemeanors, including DUI cases. In addition, he handles corporate and personal injury litigation. Mr. Belz is committed to his law practice, and enjoys the effort and unity between himself and his clients that litigation requires.
Education: JD 1961, DePaul University (*Law Review*); BS 1958, St. Vincent College.
Admitted: 1961 Illinois; 1966 U.S. Dist. Ct.
Employment History: 1980-present, Belz & McWilliams; 1966-80, Belz & Kohl; Trial Attorney 1965-66, Vaccarello Law Firm; Assistant State's Attorney 1961-64, State's Attorney's Office, Cook County.
Representative Clients: Mr. Belz represents criminal and civil litigants.
Professional Associations: CBA; Northwest Suburban Bar Assn. (Board of Governors 1980-81).
Community Involvement: Damien House in Ecuador (Founder); Norwood Park Historical Society; Edison Park Chamber of Commerce 1961-67; Norwood Park Youth Baseball Assn.
Firm: Belz & McWilliams seeks fair trials and justice for its clients. The firm mainly concentrates in all aspects of criminal law, personal injury, and corporate law. Mr. Belz also has an office at 6125 North Northwest Highway, Chicago, IL 60631. Phone: (312) 775-7000, Fax: (312) 775-7685.

EDWIN J. BELZ
Belz & McWilliams
4407 North Elston Avenue
Chicago, IL 60630

Phone: (312) 282-9129
Fax: (312) 282-9811

•**MARVIN BLOOM:** Mr. Bloom practices criminal law as a sole practitioner in both state and federal courts. He has obtained numerous acquittals for clients in a broad range of serious criminal cases, including homicides, drug offenses, and various white collar crimes. He was recently featured in the *Chicago Tribune* for having obtained numerous consecutive jury acquittals. He has long been associated with several local law schools as an adjunct faculty member, teaching trial practice, and has lectured on cross-examination techniques.
Education: JD 1978, Loyola University (Finals, National Trial Practice Competition 1978); BA 1975, University of Iowa (Phi Beta Kappa).
Admitted: 1978 Illinois; 1978 U.S. Dist. Ct. (N. Dist. IL); 1978 U.S. Ct. App. (7th Cir.); 1992 U.S. Dist. Ct. (N. Dist. MI); 1992 U.S. Dist. Ct. (N. Dist. IN).
Employment History: Sole Practitioner 1978-present; Of Counsel 1994-present, Camic, Johnson, Wilson & Bloom.
Representative Clients: Mr. Bloom represents clients charged with a wide range of federal and state felonies, including murder, drug offenses, fraud, and official corruption.
Professional Associations: NACDL 1994-present; ISBA 1994-present.
Community Involvement: Misericordia Home for Disabled Children, Chicago (President). *Mr. Bloom also practices Personal Injury Law: General and Criminal Law: DUI & Misdemeanors.*

MARVIN BLOOM
Marvin Bloom & Associates
53 West Jackson
Suite 1430
Chicago, IL 60604

Phone: (312) 641-1044
Fax: (312) 554-8780

Chapter 13: Criminal Law: Felonies & White Collar Crime

DAVID E. CAMIC

Camic, Johnson, Wilson & Bloom, P.C.
546 West Galena Boulevard
Aurora, IL 60506

Phone: (630) 859-0135
Fax: (630) 859-1910
800: (800) 750-0135

Extensive Experience In:

- Violent Felonies/Narcotics Felonies
- Complex Criminal Matters
- DUI & Misdemeanors

•**DAVID E. CAMIC:** Mr. Camic represents clients in criminal trials, including felonies and misdemeanors, in Illinois state and federal courts. His practice includes both bench and jury trials and he holds the record for one of the shortest jury acquittals in Illinois: seven minutes. Mr. Camic is a frequent speaker at seminars and programs for professional associations and the general public. He has lectured for many professional associations and several local schools and organizations. Mr. Camic is on the faculty of Aurora University where he teaches an introductory course in criminal law, and he previously taught courses at Elgin Community College. He has lectured to police officers on the law of arrest, including DUI, for Illinois Northeast Multi-Regional Police Training. He is the author of "Rights of Pre-Trial Detainees in Illinois," *Illinois Police Association Official Journal,* 1987; has researched information for the Illinois Institute for Continuing Legal Education's Handbook, *Federal Civil Practice,* Chapter 5S, 1987; wrote on sentencing for the *Kane County Bar Journal;* and contributed case notes for the Illinois Bar Association's *Criminal Justice Newsletter.* In addition, Mr. Camic assisted in the editing of the two Criminal Law Chapters of this book. He has represented clients in several high-profile cases, and has acted as lead counsel on death penalty cases and complex narcotics cases. He is often retained by clients who have previously been represented by other attorneys and has been able to successfully vacate convictions in both the trial and appellate courts.

Education: JD 1987 with distinction, John Marshall Law School (Order of John Marshall; Phi Delta Phi Honors Fraternity; Faculty Merit Scholarship); Graduate Studies 1982-83, DePaul University; BA 1982, Aurora College.

Admitted: 1987 Illinois; 1987 U.S. Dist. Ct. (N. Dist. IL, General Bar); 1990 U.S. Dist. Ct. (N. Dist. IL, Trial Bar); 1996 New York.

Employment History: Partner 1987-present, law firm currently known as Camic, Johnson, Wilson & Bloom, P.C.; Police Officer 1977-87, Aurora Police Department; Research Assistant 1985, John Marshall Law School.

Representative Clients: Police officers, a priest, doctors, gang leaders, lawyers, teachers, and corporations.

Professional Associations: NACDL; ABA; ISBA [Criminal Justice Section Council (Secretary)]; Illinois Attorneys for Criminal Justice (Treasurer); Kane County Bar Assn. [Criminal Practice Committee (Chair 1991-96)]; DuPage County Bar Assn.

Community Involvement: People's Law School; High School trial competitions; Legislative testimony.

Firm: The firm's criminal trial partners, Mr. Camic, Gary V. Johnson, and Marvin Bloom, are all listed in this *Guidebook. See complete firm profile in Appendix A. Mr. Camic also practices Criminal Law: DUI & Misdemeanors and Personal Injury Law: General.*

SCOTT J. FRANKEL

Frankel & Cohen
Attorneys at Law
77 West Washington Street
Suite 1711
Chicago, IL 60602

Phone: (312) 759-9600
Fax: (312) 759-9603

Extensive Experience In:

- Murder & Other Violent Felonies
- Narcotics Felonies
- Fraud

•**SCOTT J. FRANKEL:** Mr. Frankel practices criminal law in all state and federal courts, representing clients at trial, on appeal, and in post-conviction proceedings. Mr. Frankel's experience includes litigating hundreds of bench and jury trials in state and federal court. Mr. Frankel has handled cases ranging from theft to murder, as well as complex, multiple defendant narcotics conspiracies and white collar bank fraud cases.

Education: JD 1985 with honors, Ohio State University (Editor-in-Chief, *Law Journal;* Awards for Leadership and Scholarship); BA 1981, Oberlin College.

Admitted: 1985 Ohio; 1986 U.S. Dist. Ct. (S. Dist. OH); 1987 Illinois; 1987 U.S. Dist. Ct. (N. Dist. IL); 1992 U.S. Ct. App. (7th Cir.); 1995 U.S. Dist. Ct. (C. Dist. IL).

Employment History: Partner 1992-present, Frankel & Cohen; Assistant Public Defender 1988-92, Cook County Public Defender's Office; Associate 1987-88, Mayer, Brown & Platt; Law Clerk 1985-87, U.S. District Court, Southern District Ohio.

Representative Clients: Mr. Frankel represents clients accused of capital murder, murder, attempted murder, gun-related offenses, narcotics cases, including multi-million dollar narcotics conspiracies, theft-related offenses, and fraud and forgery cases, including complex white collar bank fraud.

Professional Associations: CBA [Young Lawyers Section (Director 1994-present); Criminal Justice Committee (Chair 1993-94); Federal Trial Bar Course (Cochair 1992-93)]; NACDL 1992-present; ISBA 1995-present.

Firm: Frankel & Cohen advises and represents both individuals and businesses in all areas of litigation, with particular concentration in the areas of labor, employment law, and criminal defense. In the general civil litigation practice area, Frankel & Cohen advises and represents clients in all types of civil litigation, including contract, tort, and statutory-related causes of action. In the labor and employment practice area, Frankel & Cohen advises and represents clients in all labor and employment-related matters, including arbitration hearings, employment discrimination, retaliatory and wrongful discharge, and breach of contract. In the area of criminal defense, the firm advises and represents clients in all criminal-related matters, including both federal and state criminal matters, at trial, on appeal, and in post-conviction proceedings. *See complete firm profile in Appendix A. Mr. Frankel also practices Employment Law.*

•**WILLIAM J. HARTE** - *William J. Harte, Ltd.* - 111 West Washington Street, Suite 1100 - Chicago, IL 60602 - Phone: (312) 726-5015, Fax: (312) 641-2455 - *See complete biographical profile in the Personal Injury Law: General Chapter, page 241.*

•**ROBERT J. HAUSER:** Recognized and highly respected for creative and innovative defense strategies in problematic criminal cases, Mr. Hauser is a trial attorney with extensive courtroom experience. He has achieved successful outcomes in numerous complex, high-profile criminal cases. His post-conviction petition on behalf of Robert Kubat, then on Illinois' Death Row, resulted in the reversal of Kubat's death sentence, with the post-conviction petition now being used as a model in Illinois jurisprudence. He has appeared and been successful before the Illinois Supreme Court in making new law protecting and expanding defendants' rights. His class action on behalf of prisoners resulted in the construction of a "state-of-the-art" jail in Lake County. His cases have been covered by *Court TV* and at least two of his cases have been used as plots by the TV show, *Law and Order*. In addition to his criminal representation, Mr. Hauser has achieved success in the civil area. He represents numerous injured parties in personal injury and wrongful death actions arising from airplane crashes, accidental electrocution, products liability, medical, legal and general malpractice, and automobile accidents. He represents individuals against insurance companies and his efforts have expanded insurance coverage for injured individuals who were initially denied such coverage.

Education: JD 1970, Harvard University; BA 1967 with honors, University of Illinois.
Admitted: 1970 Illinois; 1970 U.S. Dist. Ct. (N. Dist. IL); 1996 U.S. Sup. Ct.
Employment History: Currently, Sullivan, Smith, Hauser & Noonan, Ltd.; Assistant Professor 1995-present, DePaul University (Trial Advocacy); Associate Professor 1974-82, College of Lake County (Criminal Law).
Professional Associations: NACDL; ISBA; ATLA; ITLA; ABA; Lake County Bar Assn.; Lake County Trial Lawyers Assn.; Jefferson Inns of Court.
Community Involvement: National Assn. for Down's Syndrome; Northern Illinois Council on Alcoholism and Substance Abuse (Board of Directors).
Firm: The law firm of Sullivan, Smith, Hauser & Noonan, Ltd., was formed in 1970 and has expanded to its present size of nine partners, and associates. The firm's practice includes personal injury and wrongful death cases, business and professional disputes, civil appeals and other types of civil actions, plus representation in felonies, misdemeanors, DUIs and juvenile traffic offenses. The firm litigates in state and federal court, with each partner focusing on a separate area of law so that the clients can receive maximum representation. *Mr. Hauser also practices Personal Injury Law: General and Personal Injury Law: Medical & Professional Malpractice.*

ROBERT J. HAUSER
Sullivan, Smith, Hauser & Noonan, Ltd.
25 North County Street
Waukegan, IL 60085-4342
Phone: (847) 244-0111
Fax: (847) 244-0513

Chapter 13: Criminal Law: Felonies & White Collar Crime

william h. hooks

Hooks Law Offices, P.C.
Three First National Plaza
52nd Floor
70 West Madison Street
Suite 5200
Chicago, IL 60602

Phone: (312) 553-5252
Fax: (312) 553-1510

Extensive Experience In:

- Search & Seizure Matters
- Trials Involving Credibility Issues
- Professionals & Felonies/Misdemeanors

•**WILLIAM H. HOOKS:** Mr. Hooks has successfully defended or prosecuted persons facing criminal charges involving drug conspiracy, illegal kickbacks, violence, sexual offenses, theft, illegal possession of drugs, credit cards, bank fraud, mail fraud, forgery, counterfeiting, weapons, arson, and espionage. He represents persons and companies facing grand jury investigations, and provides pretrial and trial representation in state, federal and military courts. He also handles complex civil litigation, including medical malpractice, commercial law, and serious personal injury litigation. Mr. Hooks established his reputation as an aggressive trial lawyer while serving as a U.S. Marine Corps criminal defense counsel and later as a Marine prosecutor in Quantico, Virginia, and Washington, D.C. In 1993, he received the Cook County Bar Association's Award for Legal Excellence and was later awarded its Westbrook Criminal Law Practitioner of the Year Distinction. One of his winning closing arguments is featured in ten sections of Stein's *Closing Arguments*. Mr. Hooks is an adjunct law school advanced trial practice instructor and a frequent speaker and legal commentator on criminal law, evidence, and trial advocacy for radio, television, community and bar groups, and legal publications.
Education: JD 1981, Illinois Institute of Technology, Chicago-Kent (Dean's List); BA 1975, DePaul University (Ford Foundation Scholar; Dean's List).
Admitted: 1981 Illinois; 1981 U.S. Dist. Ct. (N. Dist. IL, General Bar, 1985 Trial Bar); 1981 U.S. Ct. App. (7th Cir.); 1982 U.S. Ct. App. (Military); 1982 U.S. Tax Ct.; 1995 U.S. Sup. Ct.
Employment History: Owner, Hooks Law Offices, P.C.; Adjunct Faculty, DePaul College of Law; Hinshaw & Culbertson; Pretzel & Stouffer Chartered; Office of the Staff Judge Advocate, USMC.
Representative Clients: Mr. Hooks' clients have included lawyers, investment professionals, law enforcement agents, civil rights activists, corporate officers, business owners, and religious leaders. Other clients have simply been hard working citizens in the wrong place at the wrong time.
Professional Associations: Illinois Supreme Court [Attorney Disciplinary Commission Hearing Board (Commissioner 1991-present; Chair 1994-present)]; U.S. District Court, N. Dist. IL (Study of Rules of Practice and Internal Operating Procedures Advisory Committee 1990-99); Federal Bar Assn. [Federal Litigation Section (Secretary; Editor-in-Chief, *Sidebar*); National Council (Presidential Appointee); Chicago Chapter (Vice President; Board of Directors)]; Cook County Bar Assn. (Vice President; Board of Directors); NACDL; ABA (Criminal Justice Section; Litigation Section); Million Dollar Advocates Forum; ISBA; National Bar Assn.; South Suburban Bar Assn.; Illinois Lawyers for Criminal Justice.
Community Involvement: NAACP; U.S. Marine Corps [Reserves (Lieutenant Colonel, ret.)]; Chicago Area Council (Board of Directors); National Eagle Scout Assn. (Life Member). *Mr. Hooks also practices Personal Injury Law: Medical & Professional Malpractice and Personal Injury Law: General.*

Gary V. Johnson

Camic, Johnson, Wilson & Bloom, P.C.
546 West Galena Boulevard
Aurora, IL 60506

Phone: (630) 859-0135
Fax: (630) 859-1910
800: (800) 750-0135

Extensive Experience In:

- Murder/Capital Murder
- Narcotics/Violent Crimes
- DUI & Misdemeanors

•**GARY V. JOHNSON:** Mr. Johnson represents clients in criminal trials, including felonies and misdemeanors, in Illinois state and federal courts. His practice includes both bench and jury trials. Mr. Johnson took part in one of the longest criminal trials in Illinois, when he defended Steve Buckley in the first Nicarico prosecution. Mr. Buckley was the only defendant not convicted in that trial. Mr. Johnson is a frequent speaker at seminars and for professional associations, including the Kane County Bar Association, Cook County Public Defender, People's Law School, and local schools and organizations. He was previously elected the State's Attorney of Kane County. Mr. Johnson served for four years prior to reentering private practice. Since his reentry into private practice, Mr. Johnson has successfully represented several clients charged with murder and capital murder. He has been specially appointed by trial courts to assist a convicted capital murder defendant on his post-conviction petition. He was recently given special mention by the Illinois State Appellate Defender for obtaining an acquittal for a defendant in a complex capital murder case. Mr. Johnson has extensive experience in complex and high-profile criminal cases.
Education: JD 1978 with honors, Drake University (Order of the Coif); BA 1975, Wesleyan University, Illinois.
Admitted: 1978 Illinois; 1978 U.S. Dist. Ct. (N. Dist. IL, General Bar, Trial Bar); 1980 U.S. Ct. App. (7th Cir.).
Employment History: 1994-present, Camic, Johnson, Wilson & Bloom, P.C.; Sole Practitioner 1993-94; Elected Kane County State's Attorney 1988-92; Sole Practitioner 1988; 1983-88, Clancy & McGuirk; Assistant State's Attorney 1979-82, Kane County.
Representative Clients: Gang leaders, school officials, lawyers, judges, capital murder cases, and complex narcotics cases.
Professional Associations: NACDL; ABA; ISBA (Criminal Justice Section Council); Illinois Attorneys for Criminal Justice (Executive Board); Kane County Bar Assn. [Criminal Practice Committee (Chair 1987-88)]; DuPage County Bar Assn.
Community Involvement: Mr. Johnson is active in People's Law School and St. Charles Township.
Firm: Camic, Johnson, Wilson & Bloom, P.C., evolved from a firm started in 1987. The firm has extensive criminal trial experience involving capital murder cases, high-profile cases, white collar defense, and environmental crimes. The firm's criminal trial partners, Mr. Johnson, David E. Camic, and Marvin Bloom, are all listed in this *Guidebook. See complete firm profile in Appendix A. Mr. Johnson also practices Criminal Law: DUI & Misdemeanors and Personal Injury Law: General.*

•**ROYAL B. MARTIN:** Mr. Martin concentrates primarily in the representation of companies or executives under criminal investigation or subsequent to the return of indictment, including criminal tax defense, health care fraud, public corruption defense and other white collar complex business fraud cases. Mr. Martin was an Assistant United States Attorney for the Northern District of Illinois from 1970 until 1975, and in 1974 was the recipient of a Special Commendation for Outstanding Service from the Department of Justice. Mr. Martin was the Chair of the Illinois State Appellate Defender Commission from 1977 to 1983, and has lectured and written extensively in the area of criminal tax fraud defense.
Education: JD 1970, University of Washington; BA 1967, University of San Francisco.
Admitted: 1970 Washington; 1970 Illinois; 1971 U.S. Dist. Ct. (N. Dist. IL); 1972 U.S. Ct. App. (7th Cir.); 1976 U.S. Tax Ct.; 1977 U.S. Ct. App. (2nd Cir.); 1981 U.S. Ct. App. (5th Cir.); 1984 U.S. Ct. App. (11th Cir.); 1989 U.S. Dist. Ct. (C. Dist. IL); 1989 U.S. Ct. App. (8th Cir.).
Employment History: President/Partner 1992-present, Martin, Brown & Sullivan, Ltd.; Partner 1979-92, Silets & Martin, Ltd.; Associate 1975-79, Harris, Burman & Silets; Assistant U.S. Attorney 1970-75, U.S. Attorney's Office, Northern District of Illinois.
Representative Clients: Joseph Herring in *United States v. Caremark, Inc.* (criminal health care fraud charges); Sheldon Schneider in *United States v. Dempsey* (RICO, mail fraud, commodities fraud charges); Jon Kneen in *United States v. Jon Kneen* (tax fraud, false statements charges); Mark Shyres in *United States v. Shyres* (conspiracy, mail fraud, tax fraud charges).
Professional Associations: American College of Trial Lawyers; ABA; CBA; ISBA; NACDL.
Community Involvement: Saints Faith, Hope and Charity School Board (President; Board Member); Regina Dominican High School [Board of Directors; Athletic Board (Chair; Vice Chair)].
Firm: Martin, Brown & Sullivan, Ltd., provides individuals and corporations with representation in government controversy matters. The firm represents plaintiffs and defendants across a wide spectrum of commercial disputes, including contract disputes, consumer fraud, banking and financial industry controversies, partnership and shareholder litigation, and debtor/creditor litigation. *See complete firm profile in Appendix A. Mr. Martin also practices Tax Law and Health Law.*

ROYAL B. MARTIN

Martin, Brown & Sullivan, Ltd.
321 South Plymouth Court
Tenth Floor
Chicago, IL 60604

Phone: (312) 360-5000
Fax: (312) 360-5026

JOHN J. MORRISON - *Law Office of John J. Morrison, Ltd.* - 135 South LaSalle Street, Suite 3600 - Chicago, IL 60603 - Phone: (312) 641-3484, Fax: (312) 641-0727 - *See complete biographical profile in the Tax Law Chapter, page 329.*

•**JED STONE:** Mr. Stone is a criminal defense lawyer in Chicago and is a Diplomate of the National Board of Trial Advocacy. He is a frequent lecturer on criminal law and constitutional issues. Mr. Stone is the author of "Preserving the Record" in *Defending Illinois Criminal Cases;* "A Lawyer's Reflection on Death," *The Chicago Bar Record,* Chicago Bar Association, October 1992; and the newly revised *Illinois Criminal Defense Motions,* West Publishing, 1995. Mr. Stone serves on the faculties of the National College of Criminal Defense, Mercer Law School, Macon, Georgia; the New York State Defender Institute; and the University of Chicago, Mandel Clinic Trial Advocacy Program as a visiting faculty member. He is listed in *Who's Who in American Law.*
Education: JD 1975, Illinois Institute of Technology, Chicago-Kent; BA 1971, Lake Forest College.
Admitted: 1976 Illinois; 1984 Wisconsin; 1976 U.S. Dist. Ct. (N. Dist. IL); 1976 U.S. Ct. App. (7th Cir.); 1980 U.S. Ct. App. (11th Cir.); 1983 U.S. Ct. App. (5th Cir.); 1984 U.S. Sup. Ct.; 1990 U.S. Dist. Ct. (C. Dist. IL).
Employment History: Principal 1977-present, Law Offices of Jed Stone, Ltd.
Professional Associations: Illinois Attorneys for Criminal Justice (President 1995; Board of Directors 1986); NACDL 1976-present (Lawyers Assistance Strike Force; Death Penalty Task Force); National Criminal Defense College (Faculty 1994-present); ABA; ISBA; Texas Criminal Defense Lawyers Assn. (Honorary Member 1994); The Bar Assn. of St. Petersburg, Russia (Honorary Member 1995); American Academy of Forensic Science (Jurisprudence Section); Lake County Bar Assn. [Criminal Law Committee (Chair 1984-86)]; ATLA; ITLA.
Community Involvement: Illinois Coalition Against the Death Penalty (President); American Civil Liberties Union; American College of Forensic Psychiatry. Mr. Stone is on the faculty of the National Criminal Defense College, where he teaches and writes about criminal law.
Firm: The Law Offices of Jed Stone, Ltd., is a boutique criminal defense firm concentrating in the representation of persons charged with serious crimes in state and federal courts. Mr. Stone has acquired a nationwide reputation for vigorous advocacy on behalf of persons accused of crimes.

JED STONE

Law Offices of Jed Stone, Ltd.
1415 North Dayton Street
Chicago, IL 60622

Phone: (312) 943-7881
Fax: (312) 943-7978

MARY STOWELL - *Leng Stowell Friedman & Vernon* - 321 South Plymouth Court, 14th Floor - Chicago, IL 60604 - Phone: (312) 431-0888, Fax: (312) 431-0228 - *See complete biographical profile in the Employment Law Chapter, page 146.*

Chapter 13: Criminal Law: Felonies & White Collar Crime

CRAIG D. TOBIN

Craig D. Tobin & Associates
70 West Madison Street
Suite 535
Chicago, IL 60602

Phone: (312) 641-1321
Fax: (312) 641-5220

•**CRAIG D. TOBIN:** Mr. Tobin has extensive federal and state court trial experience. He represents businesses as well as individuals in white collar prosecutions, murder cases and other selected felonies. Mr. Tobin has represented individuals as well as businesses under governmental investigation for violations of regulatory matters. Mr. Tobin has achieved landmark decisions in complex civil cases as well as criminal cases. He has been featured in numerous periodicals, including the *Chicago Tribune* and the *American Bar Journal.* Mr. Tobin is an instructor and faculty member for the National Institute for Trial Advocacy. He has given numerous lectures on the art of cross-examination, closing arguments, and other trial-related matters.

Education: JD 1980 with high honors, Illinois Institute of Technology, Chicago-Kent; BA 1976 with honors, University of Illinois.

Admitted: 1980 Illinois; 1980 U.S. Dist. Ct. (N. Dist. IL); 1980 U.S. Ct. App. (7th Cir.); 1985 U.S. Dist. Ct. (IN).

Employment History: 1995-present, Craig D. Tobin & Associates; 1980-85, Cook County Public Defender's Office, Felony Trial Division, Murder Task Force.

Representative Clients: Mr. Tobin represents lawyers, doctors, other professionals, high-profile community leaders, and businesses.

Professional Associations: ATLA; CBA; ABA; ISBA.

Firm: Craig D. Tobin & Associates was founded in 1985, when Craig Tobin left the Murder Task Force of the Cook County Public Defender's Office and went into private practice. Mr. Tobin was joined by the Honorable Robert J. Collins. Mr. Collins was a well-respected criminal court judge called by the *Chicago Tribune,* "the standard by which all other judges are to be measured." The firm is dedicated to the highest quality of litigation services available. The firm invests in its clients' representation by maintaining state-of-the-art computer hardware and software specially designed to assist in the delivery of litigation services. Advanced technology coupled with experience allow the firm to provide unprecedented legal services.

JOHN R. WIMMER - *The Law Offices of John R. Wimmer* - 928 Warren Avenue - Downers Grove, IL 60515 - Phone: (630) 810-0005, Fax: (630) 960-5852 - *See complete biographical profiles in the Alternative Dispute Resolution Chapter, page 47 and Civil Appellate Law Chapter, page 85.*

NORTHWESTERN ILLINOIS
INCLUDING ROCKFORD & QUAD CITIES

PETER B. NOLTE - *Attorney at Law* - 312 West State Street, Suite 1201 - Rockford, IL 61101 - Phone: (815) 965-2647, Fax: (815) 965-3820 - *See complete biographical profile in the Civil Appellate Law Chapter, page 85.*

R. CRAIG SAHLSTROM

Attorney and Counsellor at Law
One Court Place
Suite 301
Rockford, IL 61101

Phone: (815) 964-4601
Fax: (815) 964-3292

•**R. CRAIG SAHLSTROM:** Mr. Sahlstrom practices criminal law. He is a well known, respected and accomplished trial lawyer. Mr. Sahlstrom represents individuals charged with a wide range of criminal offenses, from first degree murder, aggravated battery, felony theft, and drug offenses, through driving under the influence of alcohol and traffic offenses. He began his career as a State Prosecutor prior to entering private practice. Mr. Sahlstrom has experience in other areas of law and is active in community affairs.

Education: JD 1979, John Marshall Law School; BS 1976, Drake University.

Admitted: 1979 Illinois; 1980 U.S. Dist. Ct. (N. Dist. IL); U.S. Ct. App. (7th Cir.).

Employment History: 1992-present, R. Craig Sahlstrom, Attorney and Counsellor at Law; Appointed Public Defender 1994-present, 17th Judicial Circuit, Boone County; 1985-92, Ring and Nash, P.C.; Assistant State's Attorney 1980-85, State's Attorney's Office, Winnebago County, Illinois.

Professional Associations: ISBA 1980-present; Winnebago County Bar Assn. 1980-present [Young Lawyers Section (President 1988-89)]. *Mr. Sahlstrom also practices Criminal Law: DUI & Misdemeanors, Personal Injury Law: General and Small Business Law.*

ARTHUR R. WINSTEIN - *Winstein, Kavensky & Wallace* - 224 18th Street, Fourth Floor - Rock Island, IL 61201 - Phone: (309) 794-1515, Fax: (309) 794-9929, 800: (800) 747-1527 - *See complete biographical profile in the Family Law Chapter, page 209.*

CENTRAL ILLINOIS

•**HOWARD W. FELDMAN** - *Feldman & Wasser* - 1307 South Seventh Street - P.O. Box 2418 - Springfield, IL 62705 - Phone: (217) 544-3403, Fax: (217) 544-1593 - *See complete biographical profile in the Family Law Chapter, page 210.*

LANCE T. JONES - *Reid & Jones Law Offices* - 2041 West Iles, Suite A - Springfield, IL 62704 - Phone: (217) 546-1001, Fax: (217) 546-1771 - *See complete biographical profile in the Employment Law Chapter, page 148.*

•**MICHAEL B. METNICK:** Mr. Metnick is the founding partner of the law firm of Metnick, Wise, Cherry & Frazier. He is a prolific trial attorney with a statewide practice. As one of only three down-state Illinois attorneys listed in Barry Tarlow's *National Directory of Criminal Lawyers,* Mr. Metnick has distinguished himself by representing individuals in both criminal and civil cases. During his 20 years of practice, Mr. Metnick has successfully handled high-profile drug, homicide, and white collar cases throughout the state. He has been appointed by the Illinois Supreme Court to represent individuals accused of capital crimes. In recent years, Mr. Metnick has received commendations from the Illinois Public Defenders Association, National Association of Criminal Defense Attorneys, and the Illinois State Bar Association. He is a contributor to the Illinois Institute for Continuing Legal Education's Handbook, *Defending Criminal Cases,* and has written articles in numerous legal publications. Mr. Metnick has lectured to Illinois attorneys on topics ranging from "The Defense of DNA Cases" to "Handling Criminal Cases on a Shoestring Budget."
Education: JD 1975, John Marshall Law School; BA 1970, University of Oklahoma.
Admitted: 1975 Illinois; 1975 U.S. Ct. App. (7th Cir.); 1975 U.S. Dist. Ct. (C. Dist. IL).
Professional Associations: ISBA [Criminal Justice Section Council (Chair 1994-95)]; Illinois Attorneys for Criminal Justice [Board of Directors (President 1988-91)]; Lincoln-Douglas Inn of Courts; ITLA [Criminal Defense Section (Chair 1983-84)]; ATLA.
Firm: Metnick, Wise, Cherry & Frazier represents clients in civil and criminal cases in state and federal courts. The firm's practice includes personal injury and malpractice cases; civil appeals and other civil actions; dissolution and custody matters; criminal felonies; misdemeanors, reckless homicide, murder, DUIs and other traffic offenses; financial cases; and employment law. The firm litigates in state and federal courts and argues criminal appeals in the U.S. and Illinois Supreme Courts. *Mr. Metnick also practices Family Law and Personal Injury Law: General.*

MICHAEL B. METNICK

Metnick, Wise, Cherry & Frazier
Number One West Old State Capital Plaza
Myers Building
Suite 200
Springfield, IL 62701

Phone: (217) 753-4242
Fax: (217) 753-4642
800: (800) 500-4242
E-mail: mwcf@aol.com

Extensive Experience In:

• First & Second Degree Murder
• Reckless Homicide
• Drug Offenses

NICHOLAS H. ORES - *Attorney at Law* - 1720 First Financial Plaza - Peoria, IL 61602 - Phone: (309) 674-5297, Fax: (309) 674-5299 - *See complete biographical profile in the Family Law Chapter, page 213.*

•**DREW PARKER** - *Parker & Halliday* - 414 Hamilton Boulevard, Suite 300 - Peoria, IL 61602 - Phone: (309) 673-0069, Fax: (309) 673-8791 - *See complete biographical profile in the Family Law Chapter, page 214.*

•**GLENN A. STANKO** - *Rawles, O'Byrne, Stanko & Kepley, P.C.* - 501 West Church Street - P.O. Box 800 - Champaign, IL 61824 - Phone: (217) 352-7661, Fax: (217) 352-2169 - *See complete biographical profile in the Employment Law Chapter, page 149.*

ROBERT C. STRODEL - *Law Offices of Robert C. Strodel, Ltd.* - 927 Commerce Bank Building - Peoria, IL 61602 - Phone: (309) 676-4500, Fax: (309) 676-4566 - *See complete biographical profile in the Personal Injury Law: Medical & Professional Malpractice Chapter, page 273.*

CHAPTER 14

ELDER LAW

Elder law is one of the fastest-growing specialty areas of legal practice today. As recently as ten years ago, almost no one would have described their legal practice as an elder law practice, because most lawyers assumed that the concerns of elderly clients were indistinguishable from the interests of any other group. Because few lawyers focused their practices on senior citizens, many seniors felt their unique concerns were ignored by the legal profession.

All this is changing rapidly. As the average age of Americans rises, society is becoming increasingly aware of the unique problems facing elderly people, as well as the professional opportunities available in serving them. Governments have responded with a wide array of state and federal programs designed to guarantee financial and physical well-being for the elderly and to fight age-based discrimination. As senior citizens take a more active role in asserting their rights, an increasing number of the elderly have sought legal representation from lawyers sensitive to their needs.

Elder law is not a well-defined area of legal specialization. Elder law borrows from many other areas such as health, probate, estate planning and trusts, civil rights, and even consumer protection. Each of these areas is discussed fully in separate chapters of this *Guidebook*.

AGE DISCRIMINATION IN EMPLOYMENT

With longer life expectancies and better access to health care, more people are staying active longer and want to remain in the work force past traditional retirement age. Also, many elderly people need the income from employment. Consequently, employers have far more elderly employees, and the number of elderly job applicants is higher than at any other time in history. Unfortunately, incidents of age-based job discrimination are also on the rise.

Seniors in Illinois have two basic means—one state, one federal—with which to counter age discrimination in the workplace: the Illinois Human Rights Act and the federal Age Discrimination in Employment Act of 1967.

ILLINOIS HUMAN RIGHTS ACT

The Illinois Human Rights Act (IHRA) is a comprehensive anti-discrimination law prohibiting labor organizations, employers and employment agencies from discriminating based on age (over the age of 40), ancestry, arrest record, citizenship, color, disability, marital status, national origin, race, religion, sex, or unfavorable military discharge. Under IHRA, it is illegal in most instances for an employer to use a person's age as a basis for decisions regarding hiring, recruitment, pay, promotion, transfer, discharge, discipline or privileges if the person is over the age of 40. For example, an employer cannot replace an older worker with a younger worker simply because the employer wants a young work force. Involuntary retirement before the age of 70 generally is prohibited. IHRA does permit an employer to offer various insurance plans or other fringe benefits to an employee based on age as long as the cost to the employer is reasonably equivalent for all employees.

Any person who feels victimized by a violation of IHRA may bring a civil action directly against the employer or may file a charge with the Illinois Department of Human Rights. If a person files a charge of discrimination with the Department of Human Rights, he or she must do so within 180 days of the discriminatory act. For example, if an older person is fired and believes the motive was age discrimination, the charge must be filed within 180 days of the employer's notice of termination.

Any individual who files an employment discrimination lawsuit must show

- That the employee is a member of the protected class (in this case, the protected age group)
- That he or she is qualified to do the job
- That he or she was rejected for the job or was fired from the job despite being qualified
- That the employer filled the job with someone with similar qualifications

Elder Law

The limitation period for filing a lawsuit directly against the employer is two years from the date of the discriminatory act.

AGE DISCRIMINATION IN EMPLOYMENT ACT OF 1967

The federal Age Discrimination in Employment Act of 1967 (ADEA) also prohibits age-based discrimination by labor organizations, employers, and employment agencies. Under ADEA, employers are prohibited from using age as a basis for making hiring, firing, promotion, or compensation decisions, or from limiting, segregating, or classifying employees in any way that would deprive or tend to deprive an individual of employment opportunities or otherwise adversely affect his or her status. ADEA specifically prohibits the use of job advertisements that specify an applicant should be "young," a "recent graduate," or that use terms such as "retired" or "over 65."

ADEA has five major exceptions to its coverage. Employers accused of violating ADEA usually invoke one or more of the following exceptions as a defense for their actions:

- Tenured Faculty Members: Until recently, ADEA did not prohibit compulsory retirement at age 70 for tenured faculty members at institutions of higher learning. This exception expired on December 31, 1993, so compulsory retirement ages for tenured faculty are no longer permissible.
- Executives and Policy Makers: A small number of high-level employees with substantial executive authority are not covered by ADEA and can be subjected to compulsory retirement at age 70. This exception is a very narrow one and does not allow for compulsory retirement policies for mid-level managers.
- Good Cause: An employer is permitted to discharge an employee for "good cause," a catch-all category that includes many different forms of failure to do a job adequately.
- Occupational Requirement: In certain narrowly defined situations, an action otherwise impermissible under ADEA may be legal if the employer's action is "reasonably necessary to the operation of the business" or is based on "reasonable factors other than age." For example, employers may have mandatory retirement policies for firefighters and airplane pilots.
- Bona Fide Seniority Systems and Employee Benefit Plans: Generally, it is permissible for an employer to adopt a bona fide seniority system or employee benefit plan as long as the system or plan is not intended to evade the purposes of ADEA.

A victim of age-based discrimination can bring an action under ADEA against his or her employer within two years of a non-willful violation or within three years of a willful violation.

RELATIONSHIP BETWEEN IHRA AND ADEA

The relationship between IHRA and ADEA is complex, primarily because ADEA was not intended to supersede or replace existing state regulations regarding age-based discrimination. Both laws cover age discrimination in employment. An aggrieved person may file a charge with the Illinois Department of Human Rights for relief under IHRA, or may file a charge with the federal Equal Employment Opportunity Commission (EEOC) based on discrimination in employment under the ADEA. However, there are rules concerning the relationship between the state and federal systems. Because of the complex interplay between the two laws and because they have different statutes of limitation, a lawyer or representative of the EEOC or Illinois Department of Human Rights can advise a victim of age discrimination how, when, and where to proceed against an employer.

HEALTH CARE DECISIONS AND PROTECTIVE ARRANGEMENTS

With people living longer than ever before and medical technology advancing at a rapid pace, more people are beginning to plan now for their future health care. Illinois law provides for different arrangements in which people set forth in advance what will happen should they become incapacitated and unable to make health care decisions. These arrangements are designed to protect individuals who, in varying degrees, are unable to care for themselves. Because much of the law in this area is new and is evolving rapidly, it can appear confusing, even contradictory, at times. This is one area of law for which it is especially important to hire good legal counsel who can be relied upon to stay abreast of important new laws and recommend appropriate changes.

Living wills and powers of attorney for health are two written documents covering decisions in this area. If people do not create these documents, their health care decisions may be covered by the Illinois Health Care Surrogate Act. Under this act, a surrogate or a guardian—usually a family member—may be appointed to make important decisions about a person's health care if he or she becomes unable to do so. When a patient becomes unable to make a decision about life-sustaining treatment, and is diagnosed with a condition that will require such a decision, the health care provider must inquire about the existence of a living will or power or attorney for health

Chapter 14: Elder Law

care. If neither of these documents exists, the physician is authorized to rely upon a surrogate to make the decision. The patient must be informed that a surrogate has been appointed and who the surrogate is. Any decision made by the surrogate decision maker should be made in accordance with the patient's wishes.

LIVING WILL

Despite its popular name, a living will is not actually a will at all. A living will is a document spelling out how much and what kind of medical care its writer (declarant) wants if he or she becomes terminally ill and incapable of communicating his or her wishes. "Terminally ill" means the person has an incurable or irreversible condition and the use of medical procedures only delays and prolongs the dying process. Living wills are controversial and, although many states refuse to recognize them, they are recognized in Illinois.

Any competent adult can make a living will. Although many people have living wills drafted by their lawyers at the same time they have traditional wills drafted, living wills do not need to be drafted by lawyers. Illinois has a suggested living will form, which people can use if they wish. Many people seek advice from a doctor before drafting a living will so they can describe their wishes specifically, taking into account the kinds of medical technology currently available to them. Also, it is useful for a person who signs a living will to inform his or her doctor of what the living will says. The most important point about a living will is that the individual decides how much and what kind of health care he or she wants.

LIVING WILL

Declaration

This declaration is made this .... day of .... (month, year). I, ..., being of sound mind, willfully and voluntarily make known my desires that my moment of death shall not be artificially postponed.

If at any time I should have an incurable and irreversible injury, disease, or illness judged to be a terminal condition by my attending physician who has personally examined me and has determined that my death is imminent except for death delaying procedures, I direct that such procedures which would only prolong the dying process be withheld or withdrawn, and that I be permitted to die naturally with only the administration of medication, sustenance, or the performance of any medical procedure deemed necessary by my attending physician to provide me with comfort care.

In the absence of my ability to give directions regarding the use of such death delaying procedures, it is my intention that this declaration shall be honored by my family and physician as the final expression of my legal right to refuse medical or surgical treatment and accept the consequences from such refusal.

Signed ....

City, County and State of Residence ....

The declarant is personally known to me and I believe him or her to be of sound mind. I saw the declarant sign the declaration in my presence (or the declarant acknowledged in my presence that he or she had signed the declaration) and I signed the declaration as a witness in the presence of the declarant. I did not sign the declarant's signature above for or at the direction of the declarant. At the date of this instrument, I am not entitled to any portion of the estate of the declarant according to the laws of intestate succession or, to the best of my knowledge and belief, under any will of declarant or other instrument taking effect at declarant's death, or directly financially responsible for declarant's medical care.

Witness ....

POWER OF ATTORNEY FOR HEALTH CARE

Living wills can be used only for terminal illnesses. Treatment decisions for non-terminal illness can be addressed by the creation of a power of attorney for health care. A power of attorney for health care is a document that one person (principal) signs in order to give another person (agent) authority to make health care decisions if the principal becomes incapacitated. Unlike a living will, a person's health condition does not have to be terminal for a power of attorney for health care to be effective.

The power of attorney for health care sets out exactly what the agent will do if the principal becomes unable to make health care decisions. It may state that the agent has complete authority to make health care decisions based on what the agent believes is best, or it may state specifically what the health care decisions should be. For example, the principal may declare that every measure should be used to keep him or her alive, or that medical treatment should be stopped under certain circumstances.

A principal must be at least 18 years old in order to create a power of attorney for health care. Illinois has a suggested short form power of attorney for health care, or a principal may write his or her own power of attorney for health care as long as it contains certain information required by law. The power of attorney for health care must name the agent, describe the power the agent will have, and be signed by the principal and dated while the principal still is able to make his or her own decisions.

GUARDIANSHIP

The Illinois Guardians for Disabled Adults Act provides that a court may appoint a guardian, if a person (ward) becomes mentally or physically incapable of making personal or financial decisions. The guardian may be appointed as a guardian of the person or guardian of the person's estate, or both. The purpose of guardianship is to promote the well-being of disabled adults, and to prevent abuse, neglect, and exploitation.

To create a guardianship, any person can petition the court, whether that person is a potential guardian, a potential ward, or a third person. Usually a petition is made by a family member or close friend concerned about the person's competence to manage property or make personal decisions. A petition must include the name and other information about the person, the value of the person's property, and the name and other information about the proposed guardian. It also must set forth the reasons why guardianship is needed. The petitioner has the burden of proving the ward's incapacity and the court applies a standard of the best interest of the ward in making its decision.

A ward can be restored to capacity by petition to the court. Anyone can bring a petition and must show by a preponderance of the evidence that the ward no longer is incapacitated and is able to make provisions for personal care or management of his or her property.

For many families, guardianship causes a drastic change in the family relationship, especially if not all family members agree that a petition for guardianship should be filed. Some of this potential stress can be avoided if an aging person creates a living will or power of attorney for health care while still legally competent. Another option is to create a living trust, which is discussed in the Estate Planning, Wills & Trusts Law Chapter of this *Guidebook*.

COMMITMENT TO A STATE INSTITUTION

There are three ways an individual in Illinois can be committed to an institution for mentally ill persons. Commitment sometimes becomes an issue for elderly people.

Voluntary Commitment

A person 18 years of age or older in Illinois may request voluntary admission to a mental health facility. This voluntary admission may be done very informally without application. The facility director will deem the individual suitable to be admitted after an examination. Voluntary admission also may be requested formally by filing an application with the facility director. Any person admitted voluntarily to a mental health facility must be informed of his or her right to be discharged. Persons admitted informally may be discharged at any time during normal day-shift hours starting from the first day after admission. People who are admitted by way of the formal voluntary admission procedure must apply for discharge in writing, and will be discharged within five days of the request.

Emergency Hold

Any adult may petition the director of a mental health facility to admit someone on an emergency basis. The hospitalization must be necessary to protect the admitted person from hurting himself or herself or others. The petition must be accompanied by a certificate from a physician or a clinical psychologist, and it must state the reasons why the person should be admitted involuntarily. The person held under an emergency admission has the right to a medical examination within 24 hours and a right to a hearing within five days.

Judicial Commitment

Any adult may petition a court for judicial admission of another individual to a mental health facility. The person petitioning for involuntary judicial admission must file the petition in the county where the person sought to be admitted resides. The petition must state the facts that make commitment necessary and the names and addresses of witnesses to these facts. Upon the filing of a petition for commitment, the court will set the matter for hearing or, if the petition does not contain physicians' certificates, will order an examination. The proposed patient receives notice of the hearing and a written summary of his or her rights. No involuntary admission may be made unless the court finds that the person is unable to care for himself or herself, or that the person is a danger to himself or herself or others. A judge may involuntarily commit someone to a state institution for an initial period of up to 180 days. After that period, the patient is entitled to periodic review of his or her case and possible release.

SOCIAL SECURITY

Congress passed the Social Security Act in 1935 to create a very broad social safety net for all United States workers and their families. The Social Security Act and its amendments started several public benefit programs. Most of these programs are financed by taxes levied on workers. Employers automatically deduct a portion of each worker's paycheck and match that amount with money from their business or organization. Self-employed workers are responsible for paying the entire amount themselves.

The three largest programs within the Social Security Act are Retirement, Survivors, and Disability Health Insurance (RSDHI); Supplemental Security Income (SSI); and Medicaid. RSDHI is the name of the federal government's benefits program for workers and retirees, and therefore is of special interest to seniors.

RSDHI itself contains three separate programs to cover retirement, disability, and health insurance (Medicare).

These three programs are extremely complex. Although detailed descriptions are beyond the space limitations of this book, a general familiarity with them is helpful for understanding one's entitlements.

Retirement and Survivors Insurance

Despite the fact that Retirement and Survivors Insurance (RSI) is only one branch of RSDHI, which in turn is only one branch of the Social Security Act, when most people refer to Social Security they actually mean RSI. Payments from RSI are the Social Security checks that millions of Americans receive each month. Social Security was not intended to be a person's sole source of income, but to supplement other income sources such as pensions, insurance, savings, and investments. However, for many, RSI is their only source of income.

A worker gains RSI coverage by performing covered employment for a certain amount of time. The term "covered employment" means most types of work including full- or part-time wage or salaried work, self-employment, farm work, membership in the United States Armed Services, employment in private nonprofit organizations, most domestic work, and most federal, state, and local government employment. The only major exceptions are railroad employees separately covered by the Railroad Retirement System, federal workers hired before 1984, and certain religious workers. The rules of eligibility and benefit amount are quite complex and provide limited coverage for spouses, children, and survivors.

Generally, a person begins receiving RSI benefits at age 65; however, a worker has the option of initiating benefits at age 62. All benefits are based on what is called the primary insurance amount (PIA): the amount a worker is entitled to if he or she retires exactly at age 65. The amount of the monthly check varies depending on how much the worker made each year. The higher his or her pay, the higher the benefits, up to a maximum dollar amount. A person who initiates benefits at age 62 receives a reduced monthly amount equal to a percentage of his or her PIA. This is a permanent reduction that amounts to approximately seven percent of the PIA for each year a person receives benefits before age 65. Postponing the receipt of benefits until after age 65 can entitle a worker to receive higher monthly amounts. Cost-of-living increases are built into the system so that the monthly amount automatically increases each year as the national cost of living rises.

Family members receive benefits based on the worker's retirement benefits. The spouse of an eligible worker draws spousal benefits on the worker's account—usually one-half of the worker's PIA—if the spouse is at least 62 years old or cares for a child eligible for child's benefits on the worker's account. Other bases for family eligibility are

- Spousal benefits for a divorced spouse if he or she was married to the insured worker for at least ten continuous years and has not remarried
- Full benefits for a surviving widow or widower of a fully insured worker from age 65
- A one-time death benefit (currently $255) for surviving relatives of fully insured workers who apply within two years of the worker's death
- Benefits for the child or grandchild of an insured worker if he or she was dependent on the worker when benefits began, is unmarried, and
    - Is 18 years old or younger
    - Is 19 years old or younger but enrolled as a full-time elementary or secondary school student, or
    - Is older than 18 years but became disabled before reaching age 22

As a general rule, an eligible individual must apply for RSI benefits in order to receive them. It is wise to apply at least two months before the desired start of payments, because completing paperwork takes some time. Failure to apply for benefits as soon as one is entitled to them can forfeit earned benefits. Anyone interested in learning how much he or she is likely to receive in RSI benefits can visit a local Social Security Office and request an estimate of future benefits based on one's earnings.

Railroad Retirement System

The Railroad Retirement System is a federal income insurance program specifically for workers in the railroad industry. Originally, this system was independent of the Social Security Administration, but in 1974 its provisions were integrated into the Social Security System. The integration was not entirely smooth, however, which has led to complex and confusing rules that are often the source of errors in awarding benefits.

Most of the rules for Railroad Retirement closely parallel those for RSI. A retired railroad worker is eligible for monthly benefits if he or she worked for a railroad employer for at least ten years before reaching age 65. As with RSI, a worker can opt to retire earlier, at age 62, but will receive reduced benefits. Anyone with fewer than ten years employment in the railroad industry is ineligible for railroad benefits, but the years of railroad employment can be added to years of non-railroad employment for purposes of calculating RSI benefits.

Some railroad workers who retired before January 1, 1975, are entitled to draw both full RSI benefits and full Railroad Retirement benefits. Most other workers, however, have their RSI benefits reduced by the amount of the Railroad benefits.

Disability Benefits

The federal government has two disability benefit programs administered by the Social Security Administration for qualified applicants: RSDHI Disability Insurance and Supplemental Security Income (SSI). These two programs are similar and are governed by many of the same rules. An individual who qualifies for one program occasionally can receive benefits from both programs simultaneously.

Both RSDHI and SSI programs define disability as "inability to engage in any substantial gainful activity by reason of any medically determined physical or mental impairment which can be expected to last for a continuous period of not less than 12 months." The physical or mental disability must be "of such severity" that an applicant not only is unable to do the work he or she did previously, but is unable to engage in any kind of gainful work.

The applicant for either RSDHI disability or SSI has the burden of proving by medical evidence that he or she is disabled or blind. Most applicants must wait five full months before their benefits begin. Each applicant's case is reviewed periodically to determine whether his or her condition has improved to the point that he or she is able to resume working.

RSDHI Disability Insurance

RSDHI Disability Insurance provides benefits for workers with substantial work histories in covered employment who are unable to continue work because they became disabled before reaching age 25. The term "covered employment" includes most types of work. The disabled worker and his or her dependents usually are eligible for RSDHI disability benefits. In some cases, disabled survivors of an insured worker can receive benefits.

Supplemental Security Income

SSI is a nationwide income maintenance program designed to help persons with limited income and assets who are elderly, blind, or disabled. Although SSI is administered by the Social Security Administration, it is not funded by Social Security taxes. SSI differs from RSI because it is based on financial need only. A person's work record is not relevant in determining eligibility for SSI. Thus, a disabled person under age 65 who has not worked a sufficient amount of time to qualify for RSDHI disability may be eligible to receive SSI disability benefits.

To receive SSI, a person must be 65 or older, be blind or disabled, and have financial need. The formula for determining SSI eligibility and benefits takes into account both income level and assets. A person qualifying on the basis of blindness or disability must be referred to vocational rehabilitation services. If the disability is related to alcohol or drug dependency, the applicant may be required to enroll in an appropriate treatment program or risk losing eligibility. Residence in a public institution, such as a prison or certain hospitals, disqualifies an applicant. These people should take appropriate steps to get any pensions, annuities, retirement, disability benefits, worker's compensation benefits, unemployment insurance, or veterans benefits to which they may be entitled.

When the federal government created SSI, it replaced many state-administered welfare programs for the elderly, blind, and disabled. The State of Illinois chose to continue its own program to supplement SSI benefits. This program is known as State Supplemental Payments (SSP). SSP provides additional assistance to qualified elderly, blind, and disabled persons, including those whose income levels are above the SSI standards. The purpose of SSP is to help very poor Illinois residents who are unable to work but whose needs are not met by other federal or state programs.

Medicare

Medicare—also called Medical Assistance in Illinois—is a federal program administered by the Social Security Administration designed to cover some basic medical and health care costs of eligible individuals over age 65 as well as many people with disabilities. Medicare has become an enormous federal program, providing billions of dollars in coverage every year.

Medicare should not be confused with Medicaid. Medicaid is a program administered by the Social Security Administration to pay doctor and hospital bills of people with limited income and assets. Medicare benefits are available to qualified individuals regardless of financial need. Because Medicare is closely linked to RSI, Disability Insurance, and Railroad Disability benefits, a basic understanding of the eligibility requirements and application procedures for those programs is helpful for an understanding of Medicare.

Medicare Parts A and B

Medicare has two basic divisions, called Part A and Part B. Medicare Part A, commonly known as Hospital Insurance, covers medically necessary hospital and related health care. Included in Part A are costs for such expenses as inpatient hospital care necessitated by acute illness, skilled nursing home care, certified hospice care for the terminally ill, inpatient psychiatric care, and care in the home by a certified home health care provider. People qualify for Hospital Insurance when they turn 65 or if they are covered by Social Security or Railroad Retirement benefits.

Medicare Part B, commonly known as Medical Insurance, is a voluntary health insurance program designed to cover some of the costs not covered by Medicare Part A, such as outpatient hospital services, outpatient physical therapy, speech pathology services, necessary ambulance service, and medical equipment. Unlike Part A, which is paid for out of Social Security taxes and is free to anyone who qualifies, Part B is an optional program that carries a monthly premium of under $50.

The federal government contracts with private insurance companies to handle routine claims processing, payment, and other functions under Parts A and B.

Costs Not Covered by Medicare

Medicare never was intended to provide comprehensive coverage for all medical needs of America's elderly population, but rather was intended to supplement private resources. Many health services are not covered by Medicare. For example, Medicare does not pay for

- Custodial care provided by someone without medical training and intended to help the patient with his or her daily living needs, such as help with bathing, walking, or exercising
- Dentures or routine dental care
- Eyeglasses, hearing aids, and examinations to prescribe or fit them
- Nursing home care (except skilled nursing care)
- Prescription drugs
- Routine physical checkups and related tests

Insurance Issues Related to Medicare

Many seniors look for some form of private insurance to supplement Medicare coverage. Some seniors are able to get continuation or conversion coverage from group policies they had through their jobs. Another popular option for seniors is to join a Health Maintenance Organization (HMO). HMO coverage is similar to continuation or conversion coverage, but many HMOs have more complicated rules for persons who are covered by Medicare, so it pays to learn about a particular HMO's policies regarding Medicare benefits before signing up.

Illinois seniors who are refused health insurance by private health insurance companies, or who can obtain insurance but only at an excessive rate may be able to get coverage under the Illinois Comprehensive Health Insurance Plan. This program was intended as an alternative to traditional health insurance, and provides coverage for medically necessary treatment such as hospital services.

In Illinois, two additional programs help older people and people with disabilities pay for their Medicare coverage. In order to be eligible for these programs, an individual must have assets of no more than $4,000 and must live in Illinois. The Qualified Medicare Beneficiary Program (QMB) assists those who have Part A Hospital Insurance and whose income is at 100 percent or less than the federal poverty level. The Specified Low-Income Medicare Beneficiary Program (SLMB) covers Part B Medical Insurance for individuals with incomes between 100 percent and 110 percent of the poverty level. These programs are run by the Illinois Department of Public Aid.

RESOURCES

Commission on Legal Problems for the Elderly, American Bar Association, 740 15th Street NW, Washington, D.C. 20005, phone: (202) 662-8690.

Illinois Attorney General, Senior Citizens Advocacy, toll-free phone: (800) 252-2518.

Contact the Illinois Department of Human Rights, State of Illinois Center, 100 Randolph Street West, #10-100, Chicago, IL 60601, phone: (312) 814-6200, TDD: (312) 263-1579 or 222 College South, #101, Springfield, IL 62706, phone: (217) 785-5100, TDD: (217) 785-5125, for information on age discrimination or to file a charge.

Contact the Illinois Department of Public Aid, Division of Medical Programs, Prescott E. Bloom Building, 201 South Grand Avenue East, Springfield, IL 62763, phone: (217) 782-2570, toll-free: (800) 252-8635, for information about Medicaid, Medicare, SSI, or SSP.

Contact the Illinois Department on Aging, Division of Older American Services, 421 Capitol Avenue East, #100, Springfield, IL 62701-1789, phone: (217) 785-3356 or (312) 917-2630 or toll-free: (800) 252-8966 for information about elder services and protective services or to order the free pamphlet, *Partners in Aging: A Guide to Programs, Services and Advocacy Organizations Serving Older Adults in Illinois,* 1993-94, or other publications.

The Illinois Secretary of State, Department of Human Services, Senior Citizen Division, 450 Howlett Building, Springfield, IL 62756, phone: (800) 252-2904 (voice or TTY) offers services for seniors.

Illinois Securities Department, Secretary of State, Lincoln Tower, 520 Second South, #200, Springfield, IL 62701, phone: (217) 782-2256. Call to order the free pamphlet, *Senior Citizens Securities Fraud.*

Illinois State Bar Association, Illinois Bar Center, Springfield, IL 62701-1779. Call (217) 525-1760 to order the free pamphlets, *Estate Planning & Living Wills* and *Your Health Care: Who Decides?*

Call the Social Security Administration at (800) 772-1213 to order the free pamphlets, *Understanding Social Security* and *You May Be Able to Get SSI.*

United States Equal Employment Opportunity Commission, Chicago District Office, 930A Federal Building, 536 Clark Street South, Chicago, IL 60605, phone: (312) 353-2713.

Elder Law Leading Illinois Attorneys

LEADING ILLINOIS ATTORNEYS

Illinois' Most Respected Legal Counsel As Selected By Their Peers.

The Leading Illinois Attorneys below were recommended by their peers in a statewide survey.

The Leading Illinois Attorneys listed below were nominated as exceptional by their peers in a statewide survey conducted by American Research Corporation (ARC). ARC asked several thousand licensed Illinois attorneys to name the lawyer to whom they would send a close friend or family member in need of legal assistance in specific areas of law. The attorneys below were nominated in the area of Elder Law.

Because the survey results (all practice area results combined) represent less than three percent of Illinois' practicing attorneys, this list should not be construed as a complete list. Nevertheless, it is an excellent source of highly qualified and reputable Illinois attorneys.

For information on ARC's survey methodology, see page *xi*.
For the complete list of Leading Illinois Consumer Attorneys, see page *xii*.

The Leading Illinois Attorneys below are listed alphabetically in accordance with the geographic region in which their offices are located. Note that attorneys may handle clients from a broad geographic area; attorneys are not restricted to only serving clients residing within the cities in which their offices are located.

An attorney whose name appears in bold has included a biographical profile in this chapter.

Cook & Collar Counties

Arshonsky, Paul C. - Northbrook
Bourque, Starr - Wheaton
Bryant, David R. - Chicago
Carroll, Brenda M. - Wheaton
Chamberlin, Darcy J. - Oak Brook
Conick, Harold W. - Downers Grove
Dembicki, Pauline G. - Evanston
Dickson, Fred H. - Aurora
Dolci, Dominick P. - Oakbrook Terrace
Dutton, Janna S. - Chicago, page 129
Eglit, Howard C. - Chicago
Fox, Barbara N. - Chicago
Friedman, James J. - Rolling Meadows
Gorecki, Robert - St. Charles
Hanson, David L. - Chicago
Heller, Stephen J. - Chicago
Hem, Ronald M. - Aurora
Hodge, Gerald K. - Aurora
Karchmar, Larry - Chicago
Knight, Anne S. - Chicago
Kraus, Grace M. - Elmhurst
LoVallo, Michael A. - Chicago
McCue, Judith W. - Chicago
McWilliams, Clare - Palatine
Monahan, Joseph T. - Chicago
Motel, Robert - Lincolnwood
Peck, Kerry R. - Chicago
Peregrine, Michael W. - Chicago
Perlis, Steven C. - Arlington Heights
Renzi, Constance J. - Aurora
Steinke, Edward B. - St. Charles
Wall, Bernard T. - Chicago
Wilcox, Barbara L. - Chicago
Wilson, Peter K., Jr. - Aurora

Northwestern Illinois Including Rockford & Quad Cities

Beck, Jeffrey - Rockford
Gaziano, Mary J. - Rockford
Gorman, Mary P. - Rockford
Granneman, Faye M. - Rockford
Kilbride, Thomas L. - Rock Island
Rudy, Sharon R. - Rockford
Smith, Barbara W. - Rockford
Stojan, Clark J. - Rock Island
Vincent, James B. - Galena

Central Illinois

Balbach, Stanley B. - Urbana
Bauer, Wendy S. - Champaign
Bellatti, Robert M. - Springfield
Casady-Trimble, Carolyn - Urbana
Hanrahan, Donald J. - Springfield
Henry, Thomas M. - Peoria
Mathis, J. Michael - Peoria, page 130
Moore, Daniel M., Jr. - Decatur
O'Neal Johnson, Susan - Peoria
Pavia, Joseph D. - Urbana
Saint, Gale W. - Bloomington
Summers, Holten D. - Urbana
Susler, Marshall A. - Decatur
Sutterfield, David W. - Effingham
Tepper, Michael - Urbana
Thomas, Lott H. - Champaign
Tueth, James E. - Decatur
Walvoord, David J. - Peoria

Southern Illinois

Boie, Wesley L. - Anna
Elliott, Ivan A., Jr. - Carmi
Guymon, David E. - Belleville
Habiger, Richard J. - Carbondale
Jacknewitz, Dennis J. - Belleville
Kibler, Keith W. - Marion
Marifian, George E. - Belleville
Proctor, Janet C. - Carbondale
Rikli, Donald C. - Highland
Rudasill, Mary C. - Carbondale

Biographical Profiles of Elder Law Leading Illinois Attorneys

The Leading Illinois Attorneys profiled below were nominated as exceptional by their peers in a statewide survey conducted by American Research Corporation (ARC). ARC asked several thousand licensed Illinois attorneys to name the lawyer to whom they would send a close friend or family member in need of legal assistance in specific areas of law. The attorneys below were nominated in the area of Elder Law.

Because the survey results (all practice area results combined) represent less than three percent of Illinois practicing attorneys, this list should not be construed as a complete list. Nevertheless, it is an excellent source of highly qualified and reputable Illinois attorneys.

For information on ARC's survey methodology, see page *xi*.
For the complete list of Leading Illinois Consumer Attorneys, see page *xii*.
For the list of Leading Illinois Elder Law Attorneys, see page 126.

The Leading Illinois Attorneys below are listed alphabetically in accordance with the geographic region in which their offices are located. Note that attorneys may handle clients from a broad geographic area; attorneys are not limited to only serving clients residing within the cities in which their offices are located.

The two-line attorney listings in this section are of attorneys who practice in this area but whose full biographical profiles appear in other sections of this book. A bullet "•" preceding a name indicates the attorney was nominated in this particular area of law.

For information on the format of the full biographical profiles, consult the "Using the Consumer Guidebook" section on page *xviii*.

The following abbreviations are used throughout these profiles:

App.	Appellate
Cir.	Circuit
Ct.	Court
Dist.	District
Sup.	Supreme
JD	Juris Doctor (Doctor of Law)
LLB	Legum Baccalaureus (Bachelor of Laws)
LLD	Legum Doctor (Doctor of Laws)
LLM	Legum Magister (Master of Laws)
ADR	Alternative Dispute Resolution
ABA	American Bar Association
ABOTA	American Board of Trial Advocates
ATLA	Association of Trial Lawyers of America
CBA	Chicago Bar Association
ISBA	Illinois State Bar Association
ITLA	Illinois Trial Lawyers Association
NBTA	National Board of Trial Advocacy

COOK & COLLAR COUNTIES

•DARCY J. CHAMBERLIN - *Attorney at Law* - 1211 West 22nd Street, Suite 1006 - Oak Brook, IL 60521 - Phone: (630) 447-2478, Fax: (630) 572-1432 - *See complete biographical profile in the Estate Planning, Wills & Trusts Law Chapter, page 160.*

•JANNA S. DUTTON: Ms. Dutton is a *Certified Elder Law Attorney and concentrates her practice in the area of elder law. She advises and represents individuals and their families in the areas of estate planning, trusts, asset protection, health care decision making, guardianship, planning for incapacity, probate, and nursing home issues. She has successfully represented spouses of persons residing in nursing homes in obtaining increased asset allowances for Medicaid eligibility. In addition, she represents agencies and individuals seeking to protect the elderly from abuse and neglect. Her publications include a chapter on Medicaid in the manual, *Advising the Elderly Client and Their Families,* published by the Illinois Institute for Continuing Legal Education. She is the General Editor of the Lawyers Cooperative Publishing Company's reference manual, *Counseling the Elderly Client in Illinois.* Ms. Dutton serves on the Public Policy Committee of the Chicago Area Chapter of the Alzheimer's Association and is the Chair of the Elder Law Committee of the Chicago Bar Association. She is a frequent lecturer on elder law topics both to lay and attorney audiences.
Education: JD 1979, DePaul University; BA 1975, Wheaton College.
Employment History: Of Counsel 1991-present, Monahan & Cohen; Principal 1989-91, Law Office of Janna Dutton; Project Director 1985-89, Senior Citizens Legal Services, Cook County Legal Assistance Foundation, Oak Park; Staff Attorney 1982-85, Senior Citizens Legal Services, Cook County Legal Assistance Foundation; Adjunct Clinical Professor 1980-82, Chicago-Kent College of Law; Staff Attorney 1979-80, Buffalo Neighborhood Legal Services, Buffalo, New York; Law Clerk 1976-80, Legal Assistance Foundation of Chicago.
Professional Associations: Alzheimer's Disease and Related Disorders Assn. [Chicago Area Chapter (Public Policy Committee)]; National Academy of Elder Law Attorneys [National Chapter; Illinois Chapter (Treasurer 1995-96)]; CBA [Trust Law Committee; Elder Law Committee (Chair 1995-96)].
Firm: Ms. Dutton also has an office at 225 West Washington Street, Suite 2300, Chicago, Illinois 60606. Phone: (312) 419-0252.

*The Supreme Court of Illinois does not recognize certifications of specialties in the practice of law. A certificate, award or recognition is not a requirement to practice law in Illinois.

JANNA S. DUTTON
Monahan & Cohen
7257 West Touhy
Chicago, IL 60631

Phone: (312) 774-5220
Fax: (312) 419-7428
E-mail: jsdutton@aol.com

Extensive Experience In:
• Spousal Impoverishment
• Guardianship
• Medicaid Issues

•KERRY R. PECK - *Kerry R. Peck & Associates* - 105 West Adams Street, 31st Floor - Chicago, IL 60603 - Phone: (312) 201-0900, Fax: (312) 201-0803 - *See complete biographical profile in the Estate Planning, Wills & Trusts Law Chapter, page 161.*

CATHERINE M. RYAN - *Ryan, Miller & Trafelet, P.C.* - 120 South Riverside Plaza, Suite 1150 - Chicago, IL 60606-3910 - Phone: (312) 207-1700, Fax: (312) 207-1332 - *See complete biographical profile in the Family Law Chapter, page 200.*

ROBERT S. SMITH, JR. - *Law Offices of Robert S. Smith, Jr.* - 747 Deerfield Road, Suite 310 - P.O. Box 231 - Deerfield, IL 60015 - Phone: (847) 945-3455, Fax: (847) 945-6795 - *See complete biographical profile in the Estate Planning, Wills & Trusts Law Chapter, page 163.*

NORTHWESTERN ILLINOIS
INCLUDING ROCKFORD & QUAD CITIES

J. LAIRD LAMBERT - *Attorney at Law* - 910 Second Avenue, Suite 300 - Rockford, IL 61104 - Phone: (815) 969-8800, Fax: (815) 969-8821 - *See complete biographical profile in the Real Estate Law Chapter, page 297.*

Central Illinois

•J. MICHAEL MATHIS: Mr. Mathis has been an attorney in private practice in the Peoria area since 1959. He was responsible for the Civil Division of the Peoria County State's Attorney's Office from 1960 through 1968, and continued to represent Peoria County with regard to federal matters through 1976. Mr. Mathis is a frequent lecturer and author in the areas of elder law and estate planning for bar groups, colleges, civic and professional organizations, and the National Business Institute. While representation of counties and municipalities, particularly in matters of taxation and development, has been a major area of practice, estate planning, probate, and counseling closely held businesses formed the bulk of his practice during the 1980s.
Education: JD 1959, University of Illinois.
Admitted: 1959 Illinois; 1959 U.S. Dist. Ct. (C. Dist. IL).
Employment History: Senior Partner 1959-present, The Mathis Law Firm.
Professional Associations: National Academy of Elder Law Attorneys; ISBA; ABA.
Firm: The explosion in the area of elder law and living trust planning, combined with the satisfaction of working with caring people, led to the creation, by Mr. Mathis and his three sons, who are also attorneys, of The Mathis Law Firm. This unique law firm provides a broad range of legal services to mature clients and their families. Concentrating exclusively on estate planning and the special legal problems of the elderly, the firm is especially sensitive to the stresses that our confusing health care and taxation systems can place on older Americans and their families. *Mr. Mathis also practices Estate Planning, Wills & Trusts Law and Social Security Law.*

J. MICHAEL MATHIS
The Mathis Law Firm
7707 Knoxville Avenue
Suite 105
Peoria, IL 61614

Phone: (309) 692-2600
Fax: (309) 692-2633
800: (800) 2-MATHIS
E-mail: hhcv08a@prodigy.com

•DAVID W. SUTTERFIELD - *Sutterfield & Johnson, P.C.* - 208 South Second Street - P.O. Box 836 - Effingham, IL 62401 - Phone: (217) 342-3100, Fax: (217) 347-8723 - *See complete biographical profile in the Social Security Law Chapter, page 318.*

Southern Illinois

•JANET C. PROCTOR - *O'Neill & Proctor* - 818 West Main Street - P.O. Box 878 - Carbondale, IL 62901 - Phone: (618) 457-3561, Fax: (618) 549-5267 - *See complete biographical profile in the Family Law Chapter, page 218.*

•DONALD C. RIKLI - *Attorney at Law* - 914 Broadway - Highland, IL 62249-1897 - Phone: (618) 654-2364, Fax: (618) 654-4752, 800: (800) 24-RIKLI (247-4554) - *See complete biographical profile in the Estate Planning, Wills & Trusts Law Chapter, page 166.*

CHAPTER 15

EMPLOYMENT LAW

Workers enjoy many rights designed to make the workplace safe and free from illegal discrimination and harassment. This chapter outlines some of the important federal and state laws governing the legal relationships and problems between employers and employees.

THE EMPLOYMENT RELATIONSHIP

The extent of a worker's rights depends upon the legal relationship between the worker and his or her employer.

INDEPENDENT CONTRACTOR VERSUS EMPLOYEE

When a worker gets paid to do a task or provide a service for another person, the worker is an independent contractor or an employee. The distinction is important both for the business and the worker, but it is not always clear. For a worker, the classification determines the benefits to which he or she is entitled, whether the worker is covered by workers' compensation, and whether the worker is protected by federal and state wage and hour regulations. Employees enjoy substantially more protection in the workplace than do independent contractors.

Whether a worker is an independent contractor or an employee is based on the work performed, not the worker's title. The more control an employer has over a worker, the more likely it is the worker is an employee. On the other hand, the more a worker acts like an independent business enterprise, the more likely the worker is an independent contractor. In some cases, the status is clear: A worker who arrives at a set time every day, is trained by the employer, uses the boss's tools or equipment, and is paid by the hour, week, or month, most likely is an employee. Someone who works for more than one company at a time, sets his or her own hours, and realizes a profit or risks a loss, probably is an independent contractor.

A worker or an employer who is unsure about the legal status of his or her employment relationship can seek advice from the Internal Revenue Service, the Illinois Department of Revenue, the Illinois Department of Employment Security, or the Illinois Department of Labor.

EMPLOYMENT AT WILL

The State of Illinois recognizes the traditional rule of employment at will. This means that all workers in Illinois are at-will employees unless the employer takes some action to create a different relationship. There are several ways an employer can alter the relationship. An employer might enter into an oral or written contract guaranteeing to employ someone for a specific period of time or promising to terminate the employee only for specified reasons. An employee handbook or collective bargaining agreement may limit the employer's right to terminate employees. Sometimes employers inadvertently limit their right to fire employees if, by their actions, the employers give the employees reason to believe their jobs will continue. For example, if an employer promises a job to someone from out of state and that person moves to Illinois specifically to take the job, the employer probably has changed the employment relationship. The employment is not at will because the employee has gone to the trouble and expense of moving after reasonably relying on the promise of new employment.

The implications of the at-will relationship are far-reaching. Unless there is an agreement to the contrary, an employer may discharge an employee at any time for any legal reason. As long as an employee is not fired for an illegal reason—such as racial or gender discrimination—an employer does not need a good reason to fire someone. Even a silly reason is enough. It also means that an employee may resign at any time, for any reason, with or without giving notice. The employee is free to leave for any reason at all, even if by doing so he or she greatly inconveniences the employer.

GOVERNMENT ADMINISTERED BENEFITS

Three programs administered by the state and federal governments are of particular interest to workers: Unemployment Compensation Insurance, Workers' Compensation Insurance, and Social Security. The benefits a worker enjoys under any of these programs depends upon the terms and conditions of employment.

UNEMPLOYMENT INSURANCE

Unemployment insurance provides benefits to employees who are laid off, fired, or forced to leave their jobs. Most employees are covered by unemployment insurance, a program administered by the state and funded by employer contributions.

Application

Unemployment benefits are not automatic; the worker must apply for them from the Illinois Department of Employment Security. After gathering information about an applicant, the department makes an initial determination whether the person is eligible to receive benefits. If the department's decision is that the employee is eligible, it informs the former employer. Because the former employer contributes to pay the benefits, the employer has the right to some of the information given by the former employee to the department and has an opportunity to present information.

Eligibility

To be eligible to receive unemployment benefits, the employee must have worked for the employer for a certain length of time and must have made a certain amount of money in wages. The time period is called a base period, and it is based on the calendar quarter system. Eligible employees must have made at least $1,600 in wages during the base period. To collect unemployment benefits, a person also must be available for work, have registered for work with the Illinois Job Service, and meet a few other provisions.

Not everyone who leaves a job is eligible to receive unemployment benefits. An applicant is not entitled to receive benefits if the applicant

- Is an independent contractor or a commission-only salesperson
- Is a student hired by the educational institution in which he or she was enrolled
- Is fired for misconduct
- Quits for any reason other than an illegal or intolerable work environment
- Participates in a labor strike
- Refuses an offer to work again for the former employer
- Fails to seek, apply for, or accept suitable work

Because employers and employees often have different ideas of what constitutes a reasonable work environment, the issue in most disputed unemployment claims is whether the employer created an intolerable workplace environment. Only certain kinds of employer actions give an employee a legitimate reason to quit a job and still collect unemployment benefits. Some of these valid reasons include

- Sexual harassment by an employer, or inaction by an employer who was informed of instances of sexual harassment
- A substantial cut in pay or benefits
- Drastic changes in working conditions or hours without an employee's consent
- Requiring an employee to break the law or work under obviously unsafe conditions

Demotions, modest decreases in wages or benefits, disagreements over management policy, and reasonable changes in workplace hours or employee regulations are conditions of employment that do not create an intolerable working environment for purposes of eligibility to collect unemployment benefits.

Unemployment Benefits

If the department decides that an applicant is eligible to receive benefits, the former employee receives a weekly benefit of a percentage of his or her previous average weekly salary. The benefit cannot exceed a maximum ceiling amount determined by the average statewide salary calculated each year. Benefits are paid for up to 26 weeks or until an applicant has received the maximum amount allowed, whichever is sooner. As long as the recipient continues to look for permanent work, working a part-time or temporary job will not terminate unemployment benefits. The recipient keeps a portion of his or her weekly income, and the benefits are reduced by any income in excess of a designated amount.

WORKERS' COMPENSATION

Workers' compensation provides benefits to employees injured in the workplace, regardless of how the injury happened. With few exceptions, all Illinois employees are covered by workers' compensation administered by the Illinois Industrial Commission.

The benefits available to workers include death benefits, permanent or temporary total disability, permanent or temporary partial disability, and medical and related expenses. The benefit amounts are determined by state guidelines and can be as high as two-thirds of a worker's salary at the time of the injury.

Workers' compensation is discussed further in the Workers' Compensation Law Chapter.

SOCIAL SECURITY

Social Security provides benefits for retired workers. A worker gains Social Security coverage by performing "covered employment," which includes full- or part-time wage or salary work, self-employment, farm work, service in the United States Armed Services, work in private nonprofit organizations, most domestic work, and most federal, state, and local government work. The covered employment must be for a certain amount of time each quarter of the year.

The usual age to begin receiving Social Security benefits is 65; however, a worker has the option of initiating benefits at age 62. The amount of each monthly check depends on how much the worker made each year. The higher his or her pay, the higher the benefits, up to a maximum dollar amount.

Social Security is discussed in greater detail in the Social Security Law and Elder Law Chapters.

CIVIL RIGHTS IN THE WORKPLACE

Four major federal laws—the Civil Rights Act of 1964; the Civil Rights Act of 1991; the Age Discrimination in Employment Act of 1967; and the Americans with Disabilities Act of 1990—protect the rights of workers to be free from workplace discrimination in the United States. Illinois workers have additional protection under the Illinois Human Rights Act. For example, the Americans with Disabilities Act only applies to employers with 15 or more employees after July 26, 1994. But the Illinois Human Rights Act covers alleged discrimination based on physical, mental or perceived handicap by any Illinois employers with one or more employees. In addition, the Illinois law covers more types of discrimination than the federal laws. Employees also should be aware that there may be local anti-discrimination laws applicable to their employment situation. For example, Cook County and the City of Chicago both have employment rights laws that apply to all employers with employees. That is, even an employer with one employee in Chicago or Cook County is subject to local employment laws.

IN GENERAL

Most employment discrimination is outlawed by the two major civil rights acts passed by Congress in 1964 and 1991 and by the Illinois Human Rights Act. Through a combination of these laws, Illinois workers are protected against discrimination based on age, ancestry, arrest record, citizenship, color, creed, disability, marital status, national origin, race, religion, sex, or unfavorable military discharge.

People frequently refer to "Title VII" rights when they are talking about a particular section of the Civil Rights Act of 1964. Title VII prohibits discrimination in a wide number of employment areas, including advertisements for jobs, apprenticeship programs, benefits, firing, hiring, layoffs, promotions, recalls, recruitment, testing, training and transfers. Title VII also prohibits retaliation against a person who files a charge of discrimination, participates in an investigation of discrimination, or opposes an unlawful employment practice.

Under certain extremely limited circumstances employers are allowed to base their employment decisions or practices on a person's marital status, race, sex, etc., if the employer can demonstrate a truly legitimate need. For example, it is legal to hire only women to be attendants in women's locker rooms. Religious institutions may refuse to hire individuals based on their religious beliefs, but only for positions that are directly related to the performance of religious duties; they generally are not allowed to discriminate when hiring individuals for secular tasks such as secretarial or janitorial work.

Certain employers, such as police departments, may base some employment decisions on an applicant's physical abilities. Other types of hiring criteria are allowed if they measure skills that are truly essential for an applicant to have in order to perform a particular job, and if they are not applied in a selective or discriminatory way. For example, an employer may require applicants for administrative jobs to pass typing or computer skills examinations.

Proving discrimination in the workplace depends on the specifics of each situation. Generally, it is easier to prove discrimination from a repeated pattern of behavior rather than an isolated incident. For example, if several Mexican immigrants are passed over for promotions in favor of nonimmigrants, and all the people involved have the same qualifications, a good case may be made to charge unlawful discrimination. In addition, any documented evidence showing an employer is prejudiced against a class of people can strengthen a discrimination case. If an employer makes statements such as "blacks don't take orders well" or "women aren't capable of making tough management decisions," this likely will increase an applicant's chances of proving discrimination, especially if the statements are made repeatedly and in the presence of witnesses.

A person who feels that he or she has been unfairly discriminated against or harassed in the workplace may file a complaint with the Illinois Department of Human Rights or the federal Equal Employment Opportunity Commission (EEOC). The Illinois Department of Human Rights enforces the Illinois Human Rights Act, and the EEOC enforces the federal civil rights acts that apply to the workplace. When a person files a complaint with one agency, that agency cross-files with the other agency. A victim of discrimination only has 180 days to file a complaint with either agency. Another option for a victim of discrimination is to hire a private attorney to pursue a claim against an employer. A civil action for violation of the Illinois Human Rights Act must be filed within two years of the termination or other occurrence.

Age Discrimination

The Age Discrimination in Employment Act (ADEA) expands Title VII prohibitions against age discrimination. Most employers may not enforce mandatory retirement policies, except under a few very specific circumstances in which age is a valid qualification for doing a particular job, such as firefighting, police work, or flying airplanes. Anyone age 40 or over who works for an employer with 20 or more employees is protected by the ADEA and cannot be retired against his or her will, regardless of age, as long as he or she can do the job. The Illinois Human Rights Act contains similar provisions that apply to Illinois employers with only one employee. Other federal and state laws prevent discrimination based on age, with some exceptions allowing employers to force an employee age 70 or older to retire.

Discrimination Against Persons with Disabilities

The Americans with Disabilities Act of 1990 (ADA) is a federal law that prohibits discrimination based on a person's physical or mental ability. The ADA makes it illegal to fire or to refuse to hire someone because that person lacks physical or mental abilities that are not essential to the job; the ADA does not change an employer's right to employ only people who have the skills to perform the "essential duties" of a job. For example, an employer may not refuse to hire as a daycare provider a person with epilepsy, simply because the potential employee cannot drive to a hospital in an emergency. In this example, driving is not an essential duty of the job, so it is not a valid reason to discriminate against an applicant who is unable to get a driver's license because of his or her epilepsy.

The ADA requires employers to make "reasonable accommodations" for applicants or employees with disabilities. The employer must do whatever is reasonable to accommodate a person's disability, including modifying work schedules, providing special training, changing the work environment, buying or modifying special equipment, or reassigning to another position an employee who no longer is able to do the "essential duties" of a job. A reasonable accommodation is one that does not place an undue burden on the employer. Using pre-employment tests that identify and exclude applicants with disabilities is permissible only if the tests are unequivocally job-related.

The ADA only protects from discrimination people with permanent conditions that limit a major life activity. Thus, the ADA does not cover an employee who has a sprained ankle that is expected to heal fully, even though that employee is disabled for a period of time. A person with a permanent disabling condition that is controlled by drugs, physical therapy, or by some other treatment is covered by the ADA, such as an epileptic whose seizures are controlled by medication. The ADA also prohibits discriminating against individuals with AIDS or HIV, or people who have completed or are still participating in drug rehabilitation programs. However, an applicant or employee currently using illegal drugs is not protected by the ADA.

The ADA is administered by the EEOC. Discrimination against persons with disabilities also is prohibited by the Illinois Human Rights Act.

Sexual Harassment

Everyone has the right to be free from sexual harassment in the workplace. Sexual harassment is prohibited by the Illinois Human Rights Act and is punishable as an illegal form of sex discrimination under Title VII of the Civil Rights Act of 1964. Sexual harassment can take many forms, including the following:

- Sexual or sexist comments about a coworker's appearance
- A mandatory dress code that provokes others to make sexually explicit comments
- Unwanted sexual contact or touching

- Sexual suggestions or pressure to have sexual contact
- Sexual jokes or explicit sexual comments that embarrass a coworker
- Sexual or pornographic pictures displayed or passed around

Sexual harassment is illegal if participation in any of the above activities is required to get or keep a job, to be promoted, or to qualify for benefits, or if the activity makes it harder for a worker to do his or her job by creating a hostile environment. The behavior must be unwelcome, undesirable, and offensive to be considered sexual harassment. The law uses the "reasonable person" standard to determine what is offensive: If a reasonable person would find an action offensive, then it is offensive under the law.

Determining what kind of behavior constitutes sexual harassment may depend on the circumstances; however, some general descriptions of sexual harassment can be made. A single, or occasional, sexual joke or sexual comment is not sexual harassment unless the comment unequivocally offers workplace advancement in return for sexual favors. Unwanted touching of someone else's body is sexual harassment. Someone who repeatedly tells lewd or obscene jokes that make other employees uncomfortable may be guilty of sexual harassment, especially if the person has been told that he or she makes the workplace uncomfortable. A case for sexual harassment in this example would be weakened if the person claiming harassment participates in the joke-telling.

In addition to laws designed to give victims a civil remedy against sexual harassment, criminal laws provide remedies against the most serious forms of unwanted sexual contact.

People who believe they are victims of sexual harassment should contact the EEOC, the Illinois Department of Human Rights, or the Illinois Human Rights Commission.

If a harasser's behavior crosses the line into assault, battery, or rape, the victim may file criminal charges against the perpetrator. These crimes are discussed in the Criminal Law Chapters.

Anyone fired or forced to leave a job because of sexual harassment may be entitled to receive unemployment insurance benefits while searching for a new job.

Pregnancy Discrimination

Title VII protects pregnant workers and job applicants from discrimination. Employers may not refuse to hire a woman because she is pregnant, fire a woman because she is pregnant, take away benefits or accrued seniority because a woman takes maternity leave, take away benefits from a single woman who has a baby, or fire or refuse to hire a woman who has an abortion.

Generally, an employer must treat pregnant women the same as other workers who cannot perform their jobs for short periods of time. Thus, if an employer allows employees to take leave for a broken leg or short-term illness, the employer must allow pregnant women to take leave under the same terms and conditions. Pregnancy leave also is protected under the Family and Medical Leave Act (discussed below).

OTHER WORKPLACE RIGHTS AND RESPONSIBILITIES

Wages and Hours

The federal minimum wage for adult workers age 18 and over is $4.25 per hour. Employers must pay at least the minimum wage, even to employees who earn tips, and employers may not force employees to share their tips with other workers or managers, although employees may do so voluntarily. There are some exceptions to the minimum wage law. For example, workers under 18 years of age must be paid a minimum wage of $3.75 per hour. Generally, employers also must pay hourly employees one-and-a-half times their regular rate for every hour over 40 hours worked in a week.

Certain salaried workers are exempt from minimum wage standards and overtime regulations. To be exempt, an employee must be in an executive, administrative, or professional position and receive at least $250 each week in salary or fee. The employee must supervise at least two other workers, manage an office or a business operation, be a skilled artistic performer or a teacher, or work in a profession requiring advanced knowledge, such as engineering.

Employment laws also regulate child labor. For example, no child under the age of 12 is allowed to work, except for children who are members of farm families and who live and work on farms. Students who are 14 or 15 years old may work only three hours per day during the school year, and only eight hours per day during school vacations. All child workers under the age of 16 must have employment certificates.

Substance Abuse in the Workplace

Under certain circumstances, employers in Illinois may compel employees to pass drug and alcohol tests as a condition of employment. These tests must not be given in a discriminatory way, and if passing a drug or alcohol test is a job requirement, then all employees performing that job must be subject to the testing requirement.

An employer may test an employee for drugs and alcohol only if the test is part of a reasonable policy that seeks to prohibit the use of alcohol or illegal drugs in the workplace. For example, an individual who has undergone treatment for the illegal use of drugs may be tested subsequently under reasonable circumstances to ensure that he or she remains rehabilitated. A reasonable policy also may include testing of all employees in safety-sensitive positions. Federal law governs and allows workplace testing for use of alcohol and illegal use of drugs in the defense, nuclear, and transportation industries.

Parenting, Family and Medical Leave

The federal government requires certain employers to provide parenting, family, and medical leave to qualified employees. The Family and Medical Leave Act of 1993 (FMLA) allows qualified employees to take up to 12 weeks of unpaid leave to attend to family matters, including health emergencies. Under the act, a qualified employee may take an unpaid leave following the birth or adoption of a child, after acquiring a foster child, to care for an immediate family member with a serious health condition, or to care for his or her own serious health condition.

Men and women are entitled equally to this leave, but not every worker is qualified. A person must be a full-time government employee, or an employee of a company with 50 or more employees who has worked for the company at least 12 months and at least 1,250 hours during the 12 months immediately prior to taking leave.

Under most circumstances, an employee may elect or the employer may require the use of any accrued paid leave for periods of unpaid leave under the FMLA.

When the leave is foreseeable, an employee must provide the employer with at least 30 days' notice of the need for the leave. If the leave is not foreseeable, the notice must be given as soon as it is practical. An employer may require medical certification of a serious health condition from the employee and may require periodic reports during the period of leave of the employee's status and intent to return to work. In addition, an employer may require a fitness for duty certification upon return to work in appropriate situations.

The employee is not entitled to accrue benefits such as vacation time or sick leave during a leave under the FMLA. Any benefits accrued by the employee at the time of the leave, however, stay with the employee. During the leave, the employer must maintain the health benefits the employee was receiving at the time leave began, at the same level and in the same manner as if the employee had continued to work.

When an employee returns from leave under the FMLA, the employee is entitled to be restored to the same job the employee left when the leave began. If the same job is not available, the employer must place the employee in an equivalent job with equivalent pay, benefits, duties, and responsibilities. Under the act, employers are prohibited from discriminating against or interfering with employees who take FMLA leaves.

Privacy

Employees' right to privacy at work is a hotly debated issue today as increasing numbers of employers are using searches, surveillance, and eavesdropping in an attempt to better monitor their employees' activities. The law in this area is evolving and is largely unsettled, but it is fair to say that an employee surrenders some of his or her right to privacy at the workplace door. Employers have more of a legal right to monitor employees than governments have to monitor citizens.

When a court must determine whether an employee's right to privacy was violated, it looks at whether the employee's expectation of privacy in a particular situation was reasonable. For example, the expectation of privacy is more reasonable for items in a locked desk drawer than for items left out on a desk. Similarly, it is more reasonable to expect privacy during a personal phone call made on a pay phone than for a work-related call on the employer's phone.

The reasonable expectation standard is not a very strong guarantor of employee privacy. An employer may expand his or her right to search or monitor simply by giving notice to employees. Once an employee receives notice that the employer reserves the right to monitor calls, search offices, read electronic mail, or film the workplace, there is very little reasonable expectation of privacy.

Whistleblowing

It is illegal for an employer to fire a worker in retaliation for reporting a violation of law or for refusing to participate in activity the employee believes to be illegal. If an employee acts in good faith and reports suspected illegal activities to the employer, a governmental agency, or law enforcement officer, the employee cannot be fired or be treated adversely. This workplace right is covered by workers' compensation laws. An employee who is terminated for whistleblowing may sue the employer for retaliatory discharge.

EMPLOYEE ACCESS TO PERSONNEL RECORDS

Illinois law gives employees the right to inspect personnel records. The right to inspection means each employee may review records kept about him or her regarding employment qualifications, promotions, transfers, compensation, discharge, and disciplinary actions. Employees are allowed to obtain the final score of any examinations required for employment. They may not access reference letters or specific portions of employment examinations. Employers are not required to keep personnel records, so the right to inspect records only applies if the records exist.

RESOURCES

Empowered at Forty: How to Negotiate the Best Terms and Time of Your Retirement, Robert Coulson, HarperBusiness, New York, NY, 1990.

Illinois Department of Revenue, 101 Jefferson Street West, P.O. Box 19044, Springfield, IL 62794-9044, phone: (217) 785-7100 or Illinois Department of Revenue, State of Illinois Center, #7-100, 100 Randolph Street West, Chicago, IL 60601, toll-free: (800) 732-8866.

Internal Revenue Service, 1111 Constitution Avenue NW, Washington, D.C. 20224, toll-free: (800) 829-3676.

National Organization on Disability (NOD), 910 16th Street NW, #600, Washington, D.C. 20006, phone: (202) 293-5960, TDD: (202) 293-5968.

For information or to order the free pamphlets, *Filing a Charge of Discrimination Under the Illinois Human Rights Act* or *Illinois Law Prohibits Sexual Harassment,* contact the Illinois Department of Human Rights, 222 College South, #101-A, Springfield, IL 62704, phone: (217) 785-5100, TDD: (217) 785-5125 or Illinois Department of Human Rights, 100 Randolph Street West, #10-100, Chicago, IL 60601, phone: (312) 814-6200, TDD: (312) 263-1579.

The Illinois Department of Labor has information on wages, hours, and overtime, and a free poster called *Notice to Employers and Employees.* Contact the Illinois Department of Labor, State of Illinois Building, 160 LaSalle Street North, #C1300, Chicago, IL 60601-3150, phone: (312) 793-2800, toll-free: (800) 654-4620 or Illinois Department of Labor, One Old State Capitol Plaza West, #300, Springfield, IL 62701 or Illinois Department of Labor, 2209 Main Street West, Marion, IL 62959.

For information, unemployment insurance claimant services, forms, or to order the free publications, *Summary of Services* or *Guide to the Illinois Unemployment Insurance Act,* contact the Illinois Employment Security Department, 401 State Street South, Sixth Floor, Chicago, IL 60605, phone: (312) 793-5280, TTY: (800) 662-3943.

For public hearing or appeal rights information, contact the Illinois Human Rights Commission, State of Illinois Center, 100 Randolph Street West, #5-100, Chicago, IL 60601, phone: (312) 814-6269 or Illinois Human Rights Commission, Stratton Building, #404, Springfield, IL 62706, phone: (217) 785-4350.

The Illinois Industrial Commission, 100 Randolph Street West, Eighth Floor, Room 200, Chicago, IL 60601, phone: (312) 814-6611, has information on workers' compensation rights.

The Illinois Secretary of State, Springfield, IL 62756, phone: (217) 782-5763, has a free pamphlet entitled *Sexual Harassment Is Against the Law: An Explanation of the Secretary of State's Office Policy to Prevent Sexual Harassment.*

Free publications also may be obtained from the United States Department of Labor, Women's Bureau, Region V, 230 Dearborn Street South, #1022, Chicago, IL 60604, phone: (312) 353-6985. These pamphlets include *Family and Medical Leave: Know Your Rights; Pregnancy Discrimination: Know Your Rights;* and *Sexual Harassment: Know Your Rights.*

For information about the Americans with Disabilities Act or to order the free booklets, *The Americans with Disabilities Act: Questions and Answers* and *Your Employment Rights as an Individual with a Disability,* contact the United States Equal Employment Opportunity Commission, Chicago District Office, 500 Madison Street West, #2800, Chicago, IL 60661, phone: (312) 353-2713; Region IV Disability and Business Technical Assistance Center, phone: (404) 888-0022, TDD: (404) 888-9098; 1801 L Street NW, Washington, D.C. 20507, phone: (202) 663-4900, TDD: (800) 872-3302.

For information or to order the free pamphlets, *Compliance Guide to the Family and Medical Leave Act* (June 1993) or *Handy Reference Guide to the Fair Labor Standards Act* (October 1994), contact the Wage and Hour Division, Employment Standards Administration, United States Department of Labor Regional Administrator, 230 Dearborn Street South, Chicago, IL 60604, phone: (312) 353-7280 or (202) 219-8743 (headquarters), TDD: (800) 326-2577.

The Cook County Commission on Human Relations can be reached at (312) 443-3456.

The Chicago Commission on Human Rights can be reached at (312) 744-4111.

Employment Law Leading Illinois Attorneys

The Leading Illinois Attorneys listed below were nominated as exceptional by their peers in a statewide survey conducted by American Research Corporation (ARC). ARC asked several thousand licensed Illinois attorneys to name the lawyer to whom they would send a close friend or family member in need of legal assistance in specific areas of law. The attorneys below were nominated in the area of Employment Law.

Because the survey results (all practice area results combined) represent less than three percent of Illinois' practicing attorneys, this list should not be construed as a complete list. Nevertheless, it is an excellent source of highly qualified and reputable Illinois attorneys.

For information on ARC's survey methodology, see page *xi*.
For the complete list of Leading Illinois Consumer Attorneys, see page *xii*.

The Leading Illinois Attorneys below are listed alphabetically in accordance with the geographic region in which their offices are located. Note that attorneys may handle clients from a broad geographic area; attorneys are not restricted to only serving clients residing within the cities in which their offices are located.

An attorney whose name appears in bold has included a biographical profile in this chapter.

LEADING ILLINOIS ATTORNEYS

Illinois' Most Respected Legal Counsel As Selected By Their Peers.

The Leading Illinois Attorneys below were recommended by their peers in a statewide survey.

Cook & Collar Counties

Adams Murphy, Jennifer - Chicago
Argento, Vincent C. - Elgin
Arnoff, Alisa - Chicago
Asonye, Uche O. - Chicago, page 142
Carroll, Gwen V. - Chicago
Clayton, Fay - Chicago
Cotiguala, Jac A. - Chicago
Dolci, Dominick P. - Oakbrook Terrace
Donoghue, Lawrence M. - Skokie
Eagle, Warren E. - Chicago
Ecker, Lori D. - Chicago, page 142
Epstein, Edna S. - Chicago
Esposito, Paul V. - Chicago
Esrig, Jerry A. - Chicago
Favaro, Dennis R. - Palatine, page 143
Flaxman, Kenneth D. - Chicago
Frankel, Scott J. - Chicago, page 143
Friedman, Linda D. - Chicago, page 144
Gaffney, Glenn R. - Glendale Heights
Galland, George F., Jr. - Chicago
Geraghty, Miriam - Chicago
Gerske, Janet F. - Chicago
Geslewitz, Irving M. - Chicago
Gittler, Marvin - Chicago
Gonzalez, Richard - Chicago
Gorman, H. Candace - Chicago
Hakeem, Ayesha S. - Chicago
Henry, Kenneth A. - Chicago
Holcomb, Barbara L. - Chicago
Holloway, William J. - Chicago

Hubbard, Elizabeth L. - Chicago
Jeske, John D. - Chicago
Kahan, Penny Nathan - Chicago, page 144
Kelly, Roger J. - Chicago, page 145
Kinnally, Patrick - Aurora
Kinoy, Joanne - Chicago
Knight, Anne S. - Chicago
Kralovec, Michael J. - Chicago
Lafer Abrahamson, Vicki - Chicago
Lambert, Jerry - Flossmoor
Longwell, Marilyn F. - Chicago
McCarthy, Suzanne - Chicago
Meites, Thomas R. - Chicago
Meyers, Ted A. - Elgin
Mikva, Mary L. - Chicago
Miner, Judson H. - Chicago
Minetz, Robert S. - Chicago
Mitchell, Randall L. - Chicago
Moran, Katherine M. - Aurora
Motto, Patricia A. - Chicago
Nelson, Richard F. - Chicago
O'Connor, John - Chicago
Oney, Claudia - Chicago, page 145
Pautsch, Charles W. - St. Charles
Pelton, Russell - Chicago
Peters, Donald F., Jr. - Chicago
Pinelli, Anthony - Chicago
Platt, L. Steven - Chicago
Potter, Robin B. - Chicago
Provenzano, William J. - Libertyville

Chapter 15: Employment Law

Puchalski, Richard J. - Chicago
Resnick, Kalman D. - Chicago
Rothschild, Donald S. - Summit
Rubman, David - Chicago
Seliger, Stephen G. - Chicago
Stein, Edward I. - Northbrook
Stowell, Mary - Chicago, page 146
Szesny, Henry C. - Chicago
Taren, Jeffrey L. - Chicago
Tatnall, Susan B. - Batavia
Thorstenson, Craig R. - Chicago
Tinaglia, Michael L. - Park Ridge
Trevino, Fern Niehuss - Chicago, page 146
Wasserman, Laurie J. - Skokie, page 147
Wessels, Richard H. - St. Charles

Northwestern Illinois Including Rockford & Quad Cities

Batcher, Richard M. - Moline
Braud, Walter D. - Rock Island
Close, Henry J. - Rockford
Fieweger, Peter C. - Rock Island
Frischmeyer, Linda E. - Rock Island
Havrilesko, Michael K. - Rockford
Kilbride, Thomas L. - Rock Island
Lefstein, Stuart R. - Rock Island
Luchetti, Thomas D. - Rockford
Martenson, David L. - Rockford
Meehan, Gerald J. - Rock Island
Neighbour, Hubbard B. - Moline
Ohlander, Jan H. - Rockford
Winstein, Arthur R. - Rock Island
Winstein, Stewart R. - Rock Island
Zimmerman, Steven P. - Rockford

Central Illinois

Ansel, Marc J. - Champaign
Baker, James P. - Springfield
Bell, Gregory S. - Peoria
Benassi, A. Lou - Peoria
Benassi, Patricia C. - Peoria
Durree, Edward D. - Peoria
Feldman, Howard W. - Springfield
Geiler, Lorna K. - Champaign
Gibson, Robert L. - Paris
Jones, Lance T. - Springfield, page 148
Krchak, David E. - Champaign
Leahy, Mary Lee - Springfield, page 149
Lied, Michael R. - Peoria
Manion, Paul T. - Danville
McMillan, Bradley S. - Peoria
Otto, John H. - Champaign
Owen, Robert M. - Decatur
Piper, John A. - Paris
Potter, James R. - Springfield
Sachs, Leonard W. - Peoria
Stanko, Glenn A. - Champaign, page 149
Straub, Marcia - Peoria
Susler, Marshall A. - Decatur
Tulin, Ronald - Charleston
Wasser, Stanley N. - Springfield, page 150
Wolgamot, John P. - Danville
Wong, Betsy P. - Urbana
Wood, George C. - Bloomington

Southern Illinois

Bartholomew, Joseph - Belleville
Carey, Jack - Belleville
Crosby, Thomas F., III - Marion
Giamanco, Paul D. - Mt. Vernon
Hassakis, Mark D. - Mt. Vernon
Hendricks, Scott P. - Carbondale
Huffman, John W. - Carbondale
Kaufhold, Kevin C. - Belleville
Lambert, Richard G. - Marion
Mendillo, James R. - Belleville
Mitchell, Bruce W. - Marion
O'Neill, Treva H. - Carbondale
Richter, Kevin J. - Belleville
Whittington, Rebecca A. - Carbondale
Wirth, Andrea - Belleville

BIOGRAPHICAL PROFILES OF EMPLOYMENT LAW LEADING ILLINOIS ATTORNEYS

The Leading Illinois Attorneys profiled below were nominated as exceptional by their peers in a statewide survey conducted by American Research Corporation (ARC). ARC asked several thousand licensed Illinois attorneys to name the lawyer to whom they would send a close friend or family member in need of legal assistance in specific areas of law. The attorneys below were nominated in the area of Employment Law.

Because the survey results (all practice area results combined) represent less than three percent of Illinois' practicing attorneys, this list should not be construed as a complete list. Nevertheless, it is an excellent source of highly qualified and reputable Illinois attorneys.

For information on ARC's survey methodology, see page *xi*.
For the complete list of Leading Illinois Consumer Attorneys, see page *xii*.
For the list of Leading Illinois Employment Law Attorneys, see page 139.

The Leading Illinois Attorneys below are listed alphabetically in accordance with the geographic region in which their offices are located. Note that attorneys may handle clients from a broad geographic area; attorneys are not limited to only serving clients residing within the cities in which their offices are located.

The two-line attorney listings in this section are of attorneys who practice in this area but whose full biographical profiles appear in other sections of this book. A bullet "•" preceding a name indicates the attorney was nominated in this particular area of law.

For information on the format of the full biographical profiles, consult the "Using the Consumer Guidebook" section on page *xviii*.

The following abbreviations are used throughout these profiles:

App.	Appellate
Cir.	Circuit
Ct.	Court
Dist.	District
Sup.	Supreme
JD	Juris Doctor (Doctor of Law)
LLB	Legum Baccalaureus (Bachelor of Laws)
LLD	Legum Doctor (Doctor of Laws)
LLM	Legum Magister (Master of Laws)
ADR	Alternative Dispute Resolution
ABA	American Bar Association
ABOTA	American Board of Trial Advocates
ATLA	Association of Trial Lawyers of America
CBA	Chicago Bar Association
ISBA	Illinois State Bar Association
ITLA	Illinois Trial Lawyers Association
NBTA	National Board of Trial Advocacy

Cook & Collar Counties

UCHE O. ASONYE

Asonye & Associates
203 North LaSalle Street
Suite 2100
Chicago, IL 60601

Phone: (312) 558-1792
Fax: (312) 558-1787

Extensive Experience In:

- Litigation of Employment Cases
- Cases Before Human Rights Commission

•**UCHE O. ASONYE:** Mr. Asonye concentrates his practice in employment litigation, including sex discrimination, sexual harassment, race discrimination, age discrimination, and retaliation. He represents individuals and institutions in employment litigation in front of the Illinois Human Rights Commission and federal court. He also represents clients in administrative proceedings of the Equal Employment Opportunity Commission, Illinois Department of Human Rights, Chicago Commission on Human Relations, and the Cook County Commission on Human Rights.
Education: JD 1992, Loyola University; Certified Public Accountant 1987, Illinois; BSC 1985 with honors, DePaul University.
Admitted: 1992 Illinois; 1992 U.S. Dist. Ct. (N. Dist. IL); 1995 U.S. Tax Ct.
Employment History: 1994-present, Asonye & Associates; 1992-93, Lindner, Speers & Reuland, P.C.; Summer Associate 1991, Baker & McKenzie; Tax/Computer Consultant 1986-91, Arthur Anderson & Co.
Representative Clients: Mr. Asonye's clients include individuals and small companies, including those seeking redress from sex discrimination, age discrimination, breach of contract, retaliation, and disability discrimination.
Professional Associations: ABA; National Employment Lawyers Assn.; CBA; Cook County Bar Assn.; ATLA.
Community Involvement: Campus Green Assn. (Board of Directors 1993-95). In addition, Mr. Asonye accepts pro bono cases on a regular basis.
Firm: Asonye & Associates is dedicated to providing competent and individualized legal services. The firm represents individuals and small companies in litigation involving sexual harassment, race discrimination, sex discrimination, age discrimination, retaliation, and breach of contract. *Mr. Asonye also practices Immigration Law and Tax Law.*

LORI D. ECKER

Kahan & Ecker
180 North LaSalle Street
Suite 2323
Chicago, IL 60601

Phone: (312) 855-1660
Fax: (312) 855-1431

•**LORI D. ECKER:** An experienced trial attorney practicing since 1982, Ms. Ecker has concentrated her practice in the area of employment-related disputes for the past eight years. She represents employees exclusively in cases arising under local, state, and federal anti-discrimination laws and in matters involving unemployment compensation, the Family Medical Leave Act, restrictive covenants, severance agreements, employment contracts, and employment torts. She is on the list of employment law attorneys of the Chicago Bar Association's Lawyer Referral Program and is listed in *Who's Who in American Law.* A frequent lecturer, Ms. Ecker has spoken and written on a wide variety of employment law topics, including employment torts, sexual harassment, and age discrimination. Recently, she was a panelist for "The Latest and the Greatest in Employment Litigation: Past, Present and Future" presented by the Labor and Employment Law Committee of the Young Lawyers Section of the Chicago Bar Association, February 1996; a faculty member of the Illinois Institute for Continuing Legal Education's Fall 1995 program, "Winning Pre-Trial Preparation in the New World of Illinois Civil Litigation"; a speaker at the 1995 Annual Meeting of the American Bar Association's "Multiple Claims Available to Injured Employees"; and a panelist on the topic of "Winning Employment Tort Cases" at the Annual Convention of the National Employment Lawyers Association in Waterville Valley, New Hampshire.
Education: JD 1982, DePaul University; BA 1979, Lake Forest College.
Admitted: 1982 Illinois; 1982 U.S. Dist. Ct. (N. Dist. IL); 1986 U.S. Dist. Ct. (N. Dist. IL, Trial Bar).
Professional Associations: National Employment Lawyers Assn. [Illinois Affiliate (Chair 1995-present)]; ATLA; ISBA; CBA [Labor and Employment Law Committee (Vice Chair 1996-present); Young Lawyers Section (Labor and Employment Law Committee, Cochair 1991-93)].
Firm: Kahan & Ecker is an employment law firm. The firm offers consultation and legal services for individual employees on a wide variety of employment issues. The firm is committed to providing the highest quality legal representation to its clients. *See complete firm profile in Appendix A.*

•**DENNIS R. FAVARO:** Mr. Favaro concentrates his practice in employment law and civil litigation. He has represented employers and employees in state and federal litigation and before administrative agencies of the Illinois Department of Human Rights Commission and Equal Employment Opportunities Commission. His representation of clients' interests has included negotiation, mediation, and litigation of employment disputes involving discrimination, sexual harassment, retaliatory discharge, breach of contract, and other employment law actions. Mr. Favaro has been a guest on numerous local cable television and radio programs concerning employment law topics. He is a frequent lecturer for continuing legal education seminars for lawyers and paralegals. Mr. Favaro is an adjunct faculty member of William Rainey Harper College, where he teaches employment and business law courses. In recognition of his work, his biography is included in *Who's Who in American Law*. Mr. Favaro has *Certification in Trial Advocacy from the National Institute of Trial Advocacy and is a graduate of the American College of Trial Advocacy.
Education: JD 1986, Valparaiso University; BA 1983, Illinois Wesleyan University.
Admitted: 1986 Illinois; 1987 U.S. Dist. Ct. (N. Dist. IL, General Bar); 1987 U.S. Ct. App. (7th Cir.); 1989 U.S. Dist. Ct. (N. Dist. IL, Trial Bar).
Employment History: Principal 1989-present, Thill, Kolodz & Favaro, Ltd.; 1987-89, Law Offices of Dennis R. Favaro; Associate 1986-87, Cowlin & Poehlmann.
Professional Associations: Northwest Suburban Bar Assn. [Board of Governors 1995-present; Employment Law Committee (Chair; Vice Chair 1988-present)]; McHenry County Bar Assn. 1986-present; National Employment Lawyers Assn. 1994-present.
Community Involvement: Mr. Favaro has served on numerous Boards of Directors of charitable organizations, including the American Cancer Society (Northwest); CEDA (Northwest); Public Action to Deliver Shelter (PADS); and Illinois Youth and Government. He is active with his church, serving on its Board of Education. Mr. Favaro has successfully coordinated county political campaigns for congressional and attorney general candidates for elected office.
Firm: With offices in Chicago, Palatine, and Crystal Lake, Mr. Favaro's objective is to provide both the individual and corporate client with personal and quality representation. Although an accomplished litigator and trial attorney, Mr. Favaro strives to avoid litigation and expenses associated with litigation by exploring with the client alternative dispute resolution opportunities. He views litigation as the last avenue for redress of the dispute. *Mr. Favaro also practices Personal Injury Law: General.*

*The Supreme Court of Illinois does not recognize certifications of specialties in the practice of law. A certificate, award, or recognition is not a requirement to practice law in Illinois.

DENNIS R. FAVARO
Thill, Kolodz & Favaro, Ltd.
835 Sterling Avenue
Suite 100
Palatine, IL 60067

Phone: (847) 934-0060
Fax: (847) 934-6899

•**SCOTT J. FRANKEL:** Mr. Frankel and his partner, Robert Cohen, represent individuals with disputes arising from their employment. Mr. Frankel represents individuals in all types of wrongful discharge and employment discrimination claims, including discrimination claims based on age, sex (including sexual harassment), race, disability, religion, and national origin. He also represents individuals in other employment-related claims, including claims for retaliatory discharge, breach of contract, and unemployment compensation. Mr. Frankel represents individuals in federal and state courts and administrative agencies.
Education: JD 1985 with honors, Ohio State University (Editor-in-Chief, *Law Journal;* Awards for Leadership and Scholarship); BA 1981, Oberlin College.
Admitted: 1985 Ohio; 1987 Illinois; 1986 U.S. Dist. Ct. (S. Dist. OH); 1987 U.S. Dist. Ct. (N. Dist. IL); 1992 U.S. Ct. App. (7th Cir.); 1995 U.S. Dist. Ct. (C. Dist. IL).
Employment History: Partner 1992-present, Frankel & Cohen; Assistant Public Defender 1988-92, Cook County Public Defender's Office; Associate 1987-88, Mayer, Brown & Platt; Law Clerk 1985-87, U.S. District Court, Southern District Ohio.
Representative Clients: Mr. Frankel represents individuals in all types of wrongful discharge and employment discrimination claims, including discrimination claims based on race, sex (including sexual harassment), disability, age, religion, and national origin. He also represents individuals in other employment-related claims, including claims for retaliatory discharge, breach of contract, and unemployment compensation.
Professional Associations: CBA [Young Lawyers Section (Director 1994-present); Criminal Justice Committee (Chair 1993-94); Federal Trial Bar Course (Cochair 1992-93)]; NACDL 1992-present; ISBA 1995-present.
Firm: Along with his partner, Robert Cohen, Mr. Frankel advises and represents both individuals and businesses in all areas of litigation, with particular concentration in the areas of labor, employment law, and criminal defense. Mr. Cohen was a Clinical Lecturer in Law at the University of Chicago Law School, 1987-92, concentrating in employment discrimination cases. Mr. Cohen is a part-time hearing officer at the City of Chicago and Cook County Human Rights Commissions, and was the Chair of the Civil Rights Committee of the Chicago Bar Association, 1993-95. *See complete firm profile in Appendix A. Mr. Frankel also practices Criminal Law: Felonies & White Collar Crime.*

SCOTT J. FRANKEL
Frankel & Cohen
Attorneys at Law
77 West Washington Street
Suite 1711
Chicago, IL 60602

Phone: (312) 759-9600
Fax: (312) 759-9603

Extensive Experience In:
• Employment Discrimination
• Sexual Harassment
• Wrongful Discharge

Linda D. Friedman

Leng Stowell Friedman & Vernon
321 South Plymouth Court
14th Floor
Chicago, IL 60604

Phone: (312) 431-0888
Fax: (312) 431-0228

•**LINDA D. FRIEDMAN:** Ms. Friedman's practice is limited primarily to employment discrimination and civil rights matters, including sexual discrimination, sexual harassment, racial discrimination, age and disability discrimination, First Amendment issues, and due process. She represents class and individual plaintiffs.
Education: JD 1985, DePaul University.
Admitted: 1985 Illinois; 1985 U.S. Dist. Ct. (N. Dist. IL); 1990 U.S. Ct. App. (7th Cir.); 1991 U.S. Ct. App. (4th Cir.).
Employment History: Founding Partner 1989-present, Leng Stowell Friedman & Vernon; Law Clerk 1986-87, United States District Court for the Northern District of Illinois.
Professional Associations: CBA; National Employment Lawyers Assn.; Women's Bar Assn.
Firm: Leng Stowell Friedman & Vernon is a litigation firm with a national practice, whose partners have a wealth of experience in a wide range of matters, including employment discrimination, civil rights, product liability, white collar criminal law, securities law, commodities regulation, antitrust and trade regulation, unfair competition, employment covenants, and personal injury. *See complete firm profile in Appendix A.*

Penny Nathan Kahan

Kahan & Ecker
180 North LaSalle Street
Suite 2323
Chicago, IL 60601

Phone: (312) 855-1660
Fax: (312) 855-1431

Extensive Experience In:

- Employment Litigation
- Negotiations of Employment Contracts
- Negotiations of Separation Agreements

•**PENNY NATHAN KAHAN:** Ms. Kahan has concentrated her practice in employment-related issues since 1981, and began her own plaintiffs' employment practice in 1983. She represents individual employees in a wide variety of employment disputes, including wrongful discharge, sexual harassment, and employment discrimination litigation. Ms. Kahan is a very experienced litigator and trial attorney. She has been particularly effective in negotiating and drafting employment contracts, severance packages and settlement agreements, primarily at the executive level. Ms. Kahan also advises and assists employers in drafting and implementing personnel policies and procedures which minimize the risk of employee-instituted lawsuits, and she has been retained by other law firms to do independent investigations of sexual harassment claims, as well as make recommendations for resolution of other kinds of workplace disputes. She has been quoted on a number of occasions as a nationally recognized employment lawyer in publications such as the *Chicago Tribune* and *The Wall Street Journal*. Ms. Kahan is actively involved with the National Employment Lawyers Association and is the Founder of NELA/Illinois. In addition to her practice and bar activities, she writes extensively on the field of employment law and is frequently asked to lecture on a wide variety of employment topics. Recently, she spoke for the Illinois Institute for Continuing Legal Education, "Retaliatory Discharge: An Analysis of Illinois Law," April 1996; and for the Chicago Bar Association, "Choice of Forum: An Analysis of Pros and Cons of *State v. Federal Court,*" December 1995. She is a coauthor of "Evaluation and Investigation of Discharge Claims: Employee's Perspective," *Employment Termination Handbook,* Illinois Institute for Continuing Legal Education, 1994; contributing author of *Employment Litigation: Forms and Practices,* Matthew Bender, 1991; and *Civil Rights Litigation and Attorneys Fees Annual Handbook,* Volume VI, Clark Boardman Co., Ltd., 1990.
Education: JD 1978, University of California-Berkeley; Graduate Studies 1968-69, University of Chicago; BA 1966, Roosevelt University.
Admitted: 1979 Illinois; 1979 U.S. Dist. Ct. (N. Dist. IL, Trial Bar); 1992 U.S. Ct. App. (7th Cir.).
Professional Associations: CBA (Labor and Employment Law Committee); ISBA; ABA; Women's Bar Assn.; National Employment Lawyers Assn. [Executive Board 1985-96; Treasurer 1991-96; Illinois Affiliate 1985-92 (Founder; Chair)].
Firm: Kahan & Ecker is an employment law firm. The firm offers consultation and legal services for individual employees on a wide variety of employment issues. The firm is committed to providing the highest quality legal representation to its clients. *See complete firm profile in Appendix A.*

•**ROGER J. KELLY:** Mr. Kelly's practice focuses on the legal problems and issues of individuals and their families. He has extensive experience in the area of employment discrimination litigation. This includes cases of disability discrimination, sexual harassment, age discrimination, retaliatory discharge, gender discrimination, and race discrimination. Mr. Kelly also represents injured persons and their families in a wide variety of claims involving personal injury, medical malpractice, and business torts. Mr. Kelly was a lecturer at Loyola University of Chicago Law School and continues to lecture on employment-related matters before high school, undergraduate, and community groups. To complement his litigation practice, Mr. Kelly also provides legal advice regarding real estate transactions and estate planning.
Education: JD 1983, Loyola University; BA 1977, University of Notre Dame.
Admitted: 1983 Illinois; 1984 U.S. Dist. Ct. (N. Dist. IL, General Bar); 1984 U.S. Dist. Ct. (N. Dist. IL, Trial Bar); 1989 U.S. Ct. App. (7th Cir.).
Employment History: Principal 1994-present, Law Offices of Roger J. Kelly; Partner 1991-94, O'Connor & Kelly, P.C.; Associate 1985-91, Zukowski, Rogers and Flood; Lecturer 1983-85, Loyola University of Chicago Law School.
Professional Associations: CBA (Labor and Employment Law Committee; Real Estate Committee); ISBA (Real Property Section; Employment Law Section; Trial Section); Loyola University of Chicago (Board of Governors 1990-93); Federal Trial Bar.
Community Involvement: Children's Memorial Hospital (Volunteer); St. Josaphat's Grammar School (Youth Sports Coach); Misericordia and Maryville Academy (Volunteer). *Mr. Kelly also practices Real Estate Law and Personal Injury Law: General.*

ROGER J. KELLY

Law Offices of Roger J. Kelly
53 West Jackson Boulevard
Suite 1252
Chicago, IL 60604

Phone: (312) 663-3699
Fax: (312) 663-3689

Extensive Experience In:
• Disability Discrimination
• Sexual Harassment
• Age/Race/Gender Discrimination

CHERYL I. NIRO - *Partridge & Niro, P.C.; Associates in Dispute Resolution, Inc.* - 900 West Jackson Boulevard, Suite Five East - Chicago, IL 60607 - Phone: (312) 850-1906, Fax: (312) 850-1901 - *See complete biographical profile in the Alternative Dispute Resolution Chapter, page 47.*

•**CLAUDIA ONEY:** Ms. Oney has concentrated in employment law for the past 17 years, specifically in the areas of age, race, and sex discrimination in federal courts. She has practiced continually before the Federal Equal Employment Opportunity Commission; Illinois Department of Human Rights; Illinois Human Rights Commission; Cook County Circuit Court (Law Division and Chancery Division); U.S. District Court; and Seventh Circuit Court of Appeals. She also has been involved in Illinois State Court actions against employers; state claims of contract pursuant to an employment manual; and state claims of assault and battery, defamation, and retaliation. Ms. Oney has represented clients who were fired, defamed, not promoted, or not hired for a variety of reasons. Sometimes such treatment is illegal and sometimes it is not. Following an initial consultation, Ms. Oney believes it is her job to advise a client whether or not their case has merit, based on a complicated array of circumstances. She ensures that each client understands the law as it relates to his or her particular circumstances, and she does not believe in making unrealistic promises. Since starting her own firm in 1978, most of her clients have been referrals from other clients. Ms. Oney utilizes a written retainer and her clients are thoroughly advised as to potential fees.
Education: JD 1978, DePaul University; BA 1968, University of Texas.
Admitted: 1978 Illinois; 1978 U.S. Ct. App. (7th Cir.); 1981 U.S. Dist. Ct. (N. Dist. IL, Trial Bar); 1983 U.S. Sup. Ct.
Employment History: 1978-present, Claudia Oney, P.C.
Professional Associations: ISBA; CBA; National Employment Lawyers' Assn.
Firm: Ms. Oney has recently invested in the latest computer hardware and software and has a connection to Lexis/Nexis; Lexis Counsel Connect; a direct internet connection; and a variety of CD-ROM materials, including the Illinois Annotated Statutes and Illinois Case Law, published by West Publishing Company. These extensive resources give Ms. Oney and her associates immediate access to constantly changing information databases, enabling them to serve clients efficiently and with accuracy. *Ms. Oney also practices Family Law.*

CLAUDIA ONEY

Claudia Oney, P.C.
55 East Monroe Street
Suite 2920
Chicago, IL 60603

Phone: (312) 782-1900
Fax: (312) 782-1965

KIM E. PRESBREY - *Presbrey and Associates, P.C.* - 821 West Galena Boulevard - Aurora, IL 60506 - Phone: (630) 264-7300, Fax: (630) 897-8637, 800: (800) 552-8622 - *See complete biographical profile in the Workers' Compensation Law Chapter, page 342.*

Chapter 15: Employment Law

MARY STOWELL

Leng Stowell Friedman & Vernon
321 South Plymouth Court
14th Floor
Chicago, IL 60604

Phone: (312) 431-0888
Fax: (312) 431-0228

Extensive Experience In:

- Employment Discrimination

•**MARY STOWELL:** An experienced trial lawyer for 20 years, with extensive experience before juries, and a member of the American College of Trial Lawyers, Ms. Stowell's practice is primarily in the areas of civil rights and employment discrimination. Ms. Stowell has handled high-profile single and multiple plaintiff cases, including class actions. She has obtained judgments and/or substantial settlements for clients on claims for age, race, sex and pregnancy discrimination, sexual harassment, retaliation, wrongful discharge, Fair Labor Standards Act violations, First Amendment and Due Process Constitutional claims, W.A.R.N. Act, disability, breach of contract, and defamation actions. Further, she has developed a concentration in sex discrimination, sexual harassment, pregnancy and glass ceiling issues in the securities industry. In addition to litigating claims, Ms. Stowell provides counseling in matters related to employment disputes, including negotiating separation agreements and buyouts. Ms. Stowell has taught at both the Advocacy Institute, sponsored by the Department of Justice, while an Assistant United States Attorney, and at the National Institute of Trial Advocacy.

Education: JD 1974, Northwestern University; BA 1971, University of Missouri, Kansas City (top five percent of class; Outstanding Student in Political Science Award).
Admitted: 1974 Illinois; 1974 U.S. Dist. Ct. (N. Dist. IL); 1980 U.S. Sup. Ct.; 1990 U.S. Dist. Ct. (C. Dist. IL); 1992 U.S. Ct. App. (7th Cir.).
Employment History: Partner 1989-present, Leng Stowell Friedman & Vernon; Assistant U.S. Attorney 1976-85, U.S. Attorney's Office.
Representative Clients: Ms. Stowell has represented employees from a broad range of corporations, including employees of major securities companies, financial institutions, medical institutions, the computer software industry, privately held corporations, and public institutions.
Professional Associations: American College of Trial Lawyers; CBA; Women's Bar Assn.
Firm: The partners of Leng Stowell Friedman & Vernon are two former Assistant United States Attorneys, a former clerk to a United States District Court Judge, and a former partner in a major firm. The firm handles a variety of litigation matters, from employment discrimination and white collar criminal defense cases to product liability defense and corporate litigation. *See complete firm profile in Appendix A. Ms. Stowell also practices Criminal Law: Felonies & White Collar Crime.*

FERN NIEHUSS TREVINO

Law Office of Fern N. Trevino
Chicago Bar Association Building
321 South Plymouth Court
Suite 800
Chicago, IL 60604

Phone: (312) 408-2751
Fax: (312) 408-1770
E-mail: fntrevino@aol.com

Extensive Experience In:

- Discrimination
- Sexual Harassment
- Retaliatory Discharge

•**FERN NIEHUSS TREVINO:** Ms. Trevino has practiced employment law exclusively since 1983. She has represented employees, small- to medium-sized businesses and international corporations in federal and state court and before federal, state, and local civil rights agencies, thus bringing a comprehensive perspective to each case. Since 1992, she has represented primarily plaintiff employees in negotiation and litigation of employment disputes involving discrimination, sexual harassment, breach of contract, retaliatory discharge, defamation, and other employment law torts. In addition, Ms. Trevino addresses employment law issues as a public speaker for the Chicago Bar Association's Speaker's Bureau, and as a guest lecturer. Representative presentations include "Employment Discrimination: The Pitfalls of Management," Chief Financial Officers' Round Table at Altschuler, Melvoin & Glasser, 1993; "Update on Sexual Harassment" sponsored by A. E. Roberts Company, 1994; and "Employee Rights," Law at the Library Lectures, sponsored by the Chicago Bar Association, 1995. She has appeared on radio programs such as WBEZ's *Talk of the City* and USFM 99's *Chicago Up Close* to discuss wrongful termination, 1995. In January 1996, she provided in-service training to Lane Technical High School's staff. She is actively involved in the Labor and Employment Law Committees of the Chicago Bar Association and the Women's Bar Association of Illinois and she has been approved by both associations for the Labor and Employment Law Specialty Referral Panels. In 1988 and 1989, Ms. Trevino was the recipient of a Merit Service Award from the Regional Counsel's Office of the Internal Revenue Service. She is also fluent in Spanish.

Education: JD 1983, Loyola University; BA 1968, Loyola University.
Admitted: 1983 Illinois; 1983 U.S. Dist. Ct. (N. Dist. IL, Trial Bar); 1992 U.S. Dist. Ct. (N. Dist. CA).
Employment History: 1992-present, Law Office of Fern N. Trevino; 1990-92, Banta Cox & Hennessy; Employment Law Attorney 1987-90, Regional Counsel's Office, Internal Revenue Service; Assistant Corporation Counsel 1983-87, City of Chicago Law Department, Employment Litigation Division.
Professional Associations: CBA (Labor and Employment Law Committee; Speaker's Bureau); Women's Bar Assn. of Illinois [Labor and Employment Law Committee (Cochair)]; ISBA.
Community Involvement: National Assn. of Women Business Owners, Chicago Chapter [Board of Directors 1993-present; Membership Retention Committee (Chair 1993-present)]; Toastmasters (Treasurer).

•**LAURIE J. WASSERMAN:** Ms. Wasserman primarily devotes her practice to employment law, including representing employees and employers in all phases of employment discrimination cases. Employees can receive consultations concerning their legal rights, clarify their alternatives, and be represented in administrative agencies and, where appropriate, in court. Employers consult with Ms. Wasserman to ensure their compliance with the various federal, state and local employment laws and for advice concerning problem employees and situations. Ms. Wasserman audits employment practices, drafts employee handbooks, employment contracts, and other similar documents, and provides training in various employment-related areas such as sexual harassment. She represents individuals and employers before the Illinois and U.S. Departments of Labor, and in court on wage and hour issues. Ms. Wasserman is a frequent lecturer to bar associations, employers' groups, and civic groups, concerning various aspects of employment law.
Education: JD 1974, Northwestern University (*Law Review*); PhD 1981, Northwestern University; AB 1970, University of Chicago.
Admitted: 1979 Illinois; 1979 U.S. Dist. Ct. (N. Dist. IL).
Employment History: Principal 1980-present, Law Offices of Laurie J. Wasserman.
Representative Clients: Ms. Wasserman represents employees with claims against their present or former employers for discrimination based on age, race, sex, religion, national origin, disability, marital status, and wage claims. She advises small- to medium-sized employers on discrimination issues, including sexual harassment training, and litigates on behalf of employees and employers.
Professional Associations: CBA [Labor and Employment Law Committee (Liaison to Illinois Department of Human Rights and Illinois Human Rights Commission 1991-present)]; Women's Bar Assn. of Illinois 1980-present; ISBA 1980-present; ITLA 1988-present; ATLA 1988-present; National Employment Lawyers' Assn. 1985-present; North Suburban Bar Assn. 1980-present; Northwest Suburban Bar Assn. 1985-present; Chicago Council of Lawyers 1980-present; Decalogue Society of Lawyers 1980-present.
Community Involvement: Chicago Chay Commission (President 1995-present); Habonim, Camp Tavor (Board of Directors 1993-present); Hadassah [Chicago Chapter (Board Member; Legal Advisor 1985-present)]; American Jewish Congress 1985-present.
Firm: The primary focus of the Law Offices of Laurie J. Wasserman is to provide legal representation to businesses and individuals relating to employment discrimination laws, drafting employee handbooks and employment agreements, wage claims, and consultations with employers concerning how to comply with the various employment laws. The firm also prepares wills, trusts, powers of attorney, and living wills, and provides legal representation in probate and guardianship proceedings and litigation. *Ms. Wasserman also practices Estate Planning, Wills & Trusts Law.*

LAURIE J. WASSERMAN
Law Offices of Laurie J. Wasserman
9933 Lawler Avenue
Suite 312
Skokie, IL 60077-3706

Phone: (847) 674-7324
Fax: (847) 674-8938

NORTHWESTERN ILLINOIS
INCLUDING ROCKFORD & QUAD CITIES

•**ARTHUR R. WINSTEIN** - *Winstein, Kavensky & Wallace* - 224 18th Street, Fourth Floor - Rock Island, IL 61201 - Phone: (309) 794-1515, Fax: (309) 794-9929, 800: (800) 747-1527 - *See complete biographical profile in the Family Law Chapter, page 209.*

CENTRAL ILLINOIS

LANCE T. JONES
Reid & Jones Law Offices
2041 West Iles
Suite A
Springfield, IL 62704

Phone: (217) 546-1001
Fax: (217) 546-1771
E-mail: ltj@cnsnet.net

Extensive Experience In:
- Employment Discrimination
- Civil Rights
- Wrongful Discharge

•**LANCE T. JONES:** Mr. Jones is a trial lawyer practicing extensively in employment and business disputes in state and federal courts and agencies. Prior to entering private practice, Mr. Jones served the State of Illinois for over six years as an Assistant Attorney General. He defended Illinois and its agencies, officials, and employees in scores of civil rights suits and employment discrimination actions brought in every federal trial court in Illinois.

Education: JD 1984, DePaul University; BA 1981, Eastern Illinois University.

Admitted: 1984 Illinois; 1984 U.S. Dist. Ct. (N. Dist. IL, General Bar); 1986 U.S. Dist. Ct. (N. Dist. IL, Trial Bar); 1988 U.S. Dist. Ct. (C. Dist. IL); 1989 U.S. Dist. Ct. (S. Dist. IL); 1991 U.S. Ct. App. (6th Cir.; 7th Cir.); 1994 U.S. Sup. Ct.

Employment History: Partner 1996-present, Reid & Jones Law Offices; Sole Practitioner 1993-96, Lance T. Jones; Of Counsel 1994-96, Hodge & Dwyer; 1990-93, Gordon & Glickson, P.C.; Office of the Attorney General: Executive Director 1990-91, Illinois Asbestos Abatement Authority, Springfield; Chief 1990, Asbestos Litigation Division, Springfield; Section Chief 1988-90, Court of Claims Unit, Springfield; Assistant Attorney General 1984-90, General Law Division; Chief Law Clerk/Law Clerk to Division Chief 1983-84, Chicago. Illinois State Senate Majority Staff/Legislative Staff/Internship Program 1980-81, Senate Majority Staff, Springfield.

Representative Clients: St. Nicholas Apartments; Allied Design, Inc.; Karmak, Inc.; various state agencies including the Illinois Secretary of State, Illinois Department of Public Health, Illinois Department of Labor, Illinois State Appellate Prosecutor's Office, Illinois Department of Revenue, and Illinois Attorney General, and various administrators, directors, and employees of these agencies; a number of employees with disputes against their employers.

Professional Associations: ISBA (Administrative Law Council 1992-present); ABA; Sangamon County Bar Assn.; ATLA; Seventh Circuit Bar Assn.; Central Illinois Business Network (Vice President 1996).

Community Involvement: Springfield Redevelopment Corporation (Secretary; Board Member); Westminster Presbyterian Church (Deacon; Youth Advisor); Springfield Chamber of Commerce; Rochester Youth Athletic Assn. (Sponsor; Volunteer).

Firm: The firm of Reid & Jones is committed to providing each client individualized attention and the best legal services available, particularly in the field of litigation and small business. Recognizing that the client is the lifeblood of its business, Reid & Jones strives to be the best possible resource for resolving conflicts and finding alternative solutions to a client's problem, including, if necessary, aggressive litigation. The firm has up-to-date computerized services and equipment, allowing it to respond to concerns quickly and to produce documents efficiently and accurately. By delivering extraordinary service, building trust and confidence, and creating value, the firm strives to earn the right to serve its clients in long-term relationships. *Mr. Jones also practices Criminal Law: Felonies & White Collar Crime and Small Business Law.*

•**MARY LEE LEAHY:** Since 1966, Mrs. Leahy has represented numerous plaintiffs in employment discrimination cases. She has assisted employers in establishing anti-discrimination policies and has trained employees in various businesses so as to prevent discrimination in the workplace. Mrs. Leahy has won significant victories from the trial court to the United States Supreme Court, establishing important rights for employees, including *Rutan v. Republican Party*, 497 U.S. 62, 110S.Ct. 2729 (1990). She has also written *amicus* briefs in important appellate employment cases, including ones on behalf of the American Federation of Teachers, AFL-CIO, and the National Employment Lawyers Association (NELA). Mrs. Leahy practices throughout the state of Illinois, particularly in the central and southern parts of the state. She also practices in all aspects of family law, drafts wills, and handles probate matters.
Education: JD 1966, University of Chicago (*Law Review*); MA 1964, Manchester University (Fulbright Scholar; won British-style Debate Championship); BS 1962 with honors, Loyola University (First in Class; Best Female Debater by *Saturday Evening Post*).
Admitted: 1966 Illinois; 1966 U.S. Dist. Ct. (N. Dist. IL); 1966 U.S. Ct. App. (7th Cir.); 1972 U.S. Sup. Ct.; 1977 U.S. Dist. Ct. (C. Dist. IL); 1977 U.S. Dist. Ct. (S. Dist. IL); 1995 U.S. Ct. App. (6th Cir.).
Employment History: Owner 1977-present, Leahy Law Offices; Director 1974-77, Illinois Department of Children and Family Services; Assistant to Governor of Illinois 1973-74, State of Illinois; Professor 1971-72, Illinois Institute of Technology, Chicago-Kent; Delegate 1969-70, Sixth Illinois Constitutional Convention; Associate 1966-69, Ligtenberg, Goebel & Dejong.
Representative Clients: Mrs. Leahy represents plaintiffs in employment discrimination matters brought under 42 U.S.C. 1983, Title VII, ADA, ADEA, the Illinois Human Rights Act, and under common law causes of action. She represents unions in arbitration matters. Mrs. Leahy also represents clients in marital matters, child custody cases and post-divorce matters. She writes wills and handles simple probate matters.
Professional Associations: ISBA 1966-present [Individual Rights and Responsibilities Committee (Secretary 1995-96); Section Council (Vice Chair 1996-97)]; National Employment Lawyers Assn. 1990-present; ITLA 1992-present; Central Illinois Women's Bar Assn. (Co-Founder; President).
Community Involvement: St. Joseph's Grammar School (Annual Fund Committee 1992-present).
Firm: Leahy Law Offices strives to understand the particular problems facing its individual clients and to keep its clients apprised of the status of their cases. In advising employers on employment discrimination matters, Mrs. Leahy attempts to anticipate problems and prevent them from occurring, in an effort to eliminate litigation. *Mrs. Leahy also practices Family Law and Alternative Dispute Resolution.*

MARY LEE LEAHY
Leahy Law Offices
308 East Canedy Street
Springfield, IL 62703

Phone: (217) 522-4411
Fax: (217) 522-7119

EDWARD H. RAWLES - *Rawles, O'Byrne, Stanko & Kepley, P.C.* - *501 West Church Street - Champaign, IL 61820 - Phone: (217) 352-7661, Fax: (217) 352-2169 - See complete biographical profile in the Personal Injury Law: General Chapter, page 255.*

•**GLENN A. STANKO:** Mr. Stanko has a general litigation practice. He concentrates in employment law, employment discrimination cases, plaintiffs' personal injury suits, and criminal defense. Mr. Stanko also has extensive appellate experience in state and federal courts. In 1987, he argued a criminal case involving First Amendment issues, *Pope v. Illinois,* before the United States Supreme Court.
Education: JD 1976, University of Illinois; BS 1971 with honors, Western Illinois University.
Admitted: 1976 Illinois; 1977 U.S. Dist. Ct. (C. Dist. IL); 1982 U.S. Sup. Ct.; 1986 U.S. Ct. App. (7th Cir.).
Employment History: Shareholder/Director/Officer 1995-present, Rawles, O'Byrne, Stanko & Kepley, P.C.; Shareholder/Director/Officer 1984-94, Reno, O'Byrne & Kepley, P.C.; Partner 1980-83, Reno, O'Byrne & Kepley; Associate 1976-79, Reno, O'Byrne & Kepley.
Representative Clients: Mr. Stanko has represented a variety of large and small employers in east central Illinois in employment-related matters, including employment discrimination cases. He also represents individual employees in employment discrimination cases and in civil rights suits.
Professional Associations: ATLA; ITLA; Appellate Lawyers' Assn.; First Amendment Lawyers' Assn.; ABA (Labor and Employment Law Section); ISBA (Criminal Justice Section; Tort Law Section; Civil Practice and Procedure Section); Champaign County Bar Assn. (Board of Governors 1988-90).
Community Involvement: Don Moyer Boys & Girls Club [Board of Directors 1989-present; President 1994-95; Personnel Committee (Chair 1992-94)]; Champaign County Bar Assn. People's Law School (Instructor, Sexual Harassment, March 1994); YMCA Youth and Government Program [Judicial Component (Mentor 1993-94)].
Firm: Rawles, O'Byrne, Stanko & Kepley, P.C., offers a full range of legal services, including estate planning and probate, health law, business and tax law, real estate, criminal law, civil litigation, and general counseling. The firm, which was founded in 1931, presently includes six attorneys and two certified legal assistants. *See complete firm profile in Appendix A. Mr. Stanko also practices Personal Injury Law: General and Criminal Law: Felonies & White Collar Crime.*

GLENN A. STANKO
Rawles, O'Byrne, Stanko & Kepley, P.C.
501 West Church Street
P.O. Box 800
Champaign, IL 61824

Phone: (217) 352-7661
Fax: (217) 352-2169

Extensive Experience In:

• Title VII & Human Rights Litigation
• Age Discrimination Claims
• Retaliatory Discharge

Chapter 15: Employment Law

STANLEY N. WASSER

Feldman & Wasser
1307 South Seventh Street
P.O. Box 2418
Springfield, IL 62705

Phone: (217) 544-3403
Fax: (217) 544-1593

•**STANLEY N. WASSER:** Mr. Wasser has a general law practice which includes civil and criminal trial and appellate cases. His practice concentrates in employment law, probate and contested estates, criminal law (federal and state), and construction law. He has tried numerous cases to verdict in both federal and state court and has argued appeals in both federal and state appellate courts.

Education: JD 1975, Catholic University, Washington, D.C.; BA 1972, Pennsylvania State University.

Admitted: 1976 Illinois; 1975 District of Columbia; 1977 U.S. Dist. Ct. (C. Dist. IL); 1978 U.S. Ct. App. (7th Cir.); 1992 U.S. Dist. Ct. (S. Dist. IL).

Employment History: Partner 1987-present, Feldman & Wasser; Chief Counsel 1985-86, Illinois Department of Transportation; General Counsel 1984-85, Illinois Bureau of Budget; Assistant Deputy Chief Counsel 1977-84, Illinois Department of Transportation; Assistant Attorney General 1977, Illinois Attorney General's Office; Staff Counsel 1975-76, Illinois Office of Comptroller.

Representative Clients: Williams Brothers Construction Company; Kinney Contractors, Inc.; R.L. Vollintine Construction, Inc.

Professional Associations: Sangamon County Bar Assn.; ISBA; ABA.

Community Involvement: March of Dimes [Local Chapter (Board Member; Advisory Board; past President 1990-91)]; Springfield Jewish Federation [Board Member; past President; past Treasurer; Endowment Fund (past President)].

Firm: Feldman & Wasser was founded in 1987 by Howard Feldman and Stanley Wasser for the general practice of law. The firm represents a diverse group of clients, from those charged with federal crimes to the preparation of corporate documents. The six lawyers in the firm concentrate in different areas of law, including family law, estate and probate law, construction litigation, criminal and civil trials and appeals, employment law, real estate and municipal law. The firm has a broad range of experience. *See complete firm profile in Appendix A. Mr. Wasser also practices Civil Appellate Law and Estate Planning, Wills & Trusts Law.*

SOUTHERN ILLINOIS

ROZA GOSSAGE - *Roza Gossage, P.C.* - 525 West Main Street, Suite 130 - Belleville, IL 62220 - Phone: (618) 277-6800, Fax: (618) 277-6820 - *See complete biographical profile in the Family Law Chapter, page 216.*

CHAPTER 16

ESTATE PLANNING, WILLS & TRUSTS LAW

Although no one likes to think about dying, there are good reasons to prepare for this inevitable event by setting up a plan to distribute one's estate after death. A person's estate consists of all his or her property and possessions, and includes bank accounts, real estate, furniture, automobiles, stocks, bonds, life insurance policies, retirement funds, pensions, and death benefits. If a person plans well, his or her estate can often be passed on after death quickly, easily, and subject to fewer taxes.

This chapter discusses the most common estate planning tools—wills and trusts. Living wills, guardianship, and conservatorship are discussed in the Elder Law Chapter.

WILLS

A will is the most common document used to specify how an estate should be handled after death. Anyone designated to receive property under a will (or trust) is called a beneficiary. A will can be simple or elaborate, depending upon the size of the estate and the wishes of the person who makes it, called the testator. Many types of post-death instructions can be described in a will. A will can describe who should receive specific items of furniture, artwork, or jewelry. A will can name a guardian who will take care of minor children should there be no surviving parent. A will can disinherit a child if the testator does not want the child to receive any part of the estate. The options for what a person can do with a will are varied but limited.

REQUIREMENTS FOR A VALID WILL

Each state sets slightly different formal requirements for the creation of a legal will. In Illinois, a person must be at least 18 years old and must be of sound mind and memory in order to make a legal will. Sound mind and memory means that the person has no disability that prevents the person from understanding the full nature of the will document. In Illinois, a will must be in writing and must be signed by the testator. The will must also be witnessed, in the special manner provided by law, by at least two other people. A handwritten will, often called a holographic will, is valid in Illinois provided that it is witnessed and signed by two people. Individuals must sign their own wills, but if they are illiterate or otherwise incapacitated, they can direct another person, in the presence of witnesses, to sign for them. A will is valid until it is revoked or superseded by a new will. An individual provision can be changed by a codicil, which is described in the section, Changing and Updating Wills.

It is not necessary to hire an attorney to create a will. A non-attorney can create a will, but he or she must pay close attention to the details outlined above. Smaller estates can be described simply, and making a will to disperse a smaller estate can be done by almost anyone. The simplest will in history ever to be declared valid by a court contained only three words: "All to wife." However, a lawyer's guidance is very helpful if the testator has complicated property holdings or an estate with many assets, especially if they are located in several different places. In these cases, an attorney's help can ensure that the transfer of property described in the will is done in a way that minimizes the survivor's tax liability. Also, a complicated estate may require documents in addition to the will, such as trust agreements, to ensure that all of the person's wishes are carried out.

PERSONAL REPRESENTATIVE

A will typically appoints someone called a personal representative to carry out the specific wishes of the person who has died—the decedent. The personal representative should be a trusted friend or family member who should be made fully aware of his or her duties before the decedent dies. Under state law, a personal representative appointed by a testator must be a resident of the United States, but need not be a resident of Illinois. A personal representative must do many things, including collecting and managing the decedent's assets; collecting any money owed at the time of death; selling assets, if necessary, to pay estate taxes or expenses; and filing all required tax returns. Because a personal representative is allowed to charge a fee for doing this work, choosing a friend or family member who is also a beneficiary to fill this role may be a good choice, as he or she may not charge the full amount allowed by law. It is wise for a testator to name one or more contingent personal representatives who can take over the responsibilities of the primary personal representative if the primary personal representative is unable to assume the responsibilities of the position.

If a person does not name a personal representative in his or her will, state law establishes the order in which a probate court appoints relatives to act as personal representative. If none of these family members agree to be the personal representative, the circuit court may appoint a professional administrator to do the job.

Appointing a Guardian for Children

A person with minor or dependent children can name in a will a guardian to care for those children should there be no surviving parent. If a person fails to name someone to assume the role of guardian, the probate court appoints someone. The person chosen by the court will usually be a close relative or friend, but it may not be the person the parent would have chosen. As with the selection of a personal representative, it is important that the potential guardian understand the provisions of the will and be willing to accept the responsibilities of being a guardian. Also, the testator should name an alternate guardian in case the primary guardian is unable to accept the responsibility. Of course, the selection of a guardian for children is likely to influence how the parent wants to distribute his or her property. Otherwise, a decedent's money might go to one person while his or her children go to another person. The parent may want to give property to someone only if the recipient accepts guardianship of a child. In this way, the guardian is given the financial resources to care for the child.

Planning for Incapacity

People drafting wills often use the opportunity to plan for the possibility of their own incapacity. By preparing a document called a power of attorney, they can give another person of their choosing full legal authority to act on their behalf should they become unable to handle their personal and financial affairs. Without a power of attorney, a person's family might need to go to court to have someone appointed to handle the person's legal affairs. If a power of attorney is made part of the will, it is essential that the will be made known to family members before the testator becomes incapacitated. If a will is kept secret, locked away in a safe deposit box until a person dies, it will be too late for the power of attorney provisions to be useful.

Some people also use a document called a power of attorney for health care to make health care decisions in advance in case they subsequently become incapacitated. Creating a power of attorney for health care is discussed in the Elder Law Chapter.

Restrictions on Wills

In order to protect spouses and dependent children, Illinois law prevents a person from entirely disinheriting a spouse or child without the consent of the one who is disinherited. Under Illinois law, a spouse is entitled to at least $10,000, plus $5,000 for each dependent child. This amount is intended to support the decedent's family for the first nine months following the death of the decedent. A spouse receives this amount of money whether or not there is a will. This spousal award is considered a preferred claim and a debt of the estate.

The provisions of this law may be overcome in two ways. First, a will may specifically state that its provisions are meant to stand in the place of the spousal award, *and* the spouse does not renounce the will. In this case, the terms of the will would govern distribution. Second, the spouse may renounce the will, and take an elective share of the estate. In this case, distribution of the estate would be governed by statute. Note, however, that renunciation would not be available to a spouse who had signed an agreement during the life of the decedent in which the spouse agreed to abide by the terms of the will. Occasionally this happens through a prenuptial agreement, for example, in which a second spouse agrees that an entire estate will go to children from a first marriage. A person may legally disinherit an *independent* child by clearly specifying in a will that the child not receive any of the estate.

There are other restrictions on wills. Anything owned in joint tenancy with another person will go to the surviving joint tenant. Arrangements must be made to end the joint tenancy before death if one joint tenant does not want the other to inherit the jointly held property. Because there may be significant tax consequences in doing so, these changes should be made only after consulting an attorney. Other possessions not considered part of an estate are those already promised to someone else. For example, a testator cannot specify in a will that someone other than the beneficiary of a life insurance policy gets the benefits described in that policy. However, a person can designate his or her estate as the beneficiary of a life insurance policy. In this case, the money from the policy will be added to other estate assets and will be distributed according to the will. Similarly, the money from a retirement plan goes to the persons named on the plan, regardless of whether they are beneficiaries in a will. Laws designed to uphold public policy also limit what can be done with a person's assets after death. For example, conditions in a will encouraging someone to do something illegal or immoral in order to inherit money or property would not be enforced.

Estate Planning, Wills & Trusts Law

CHANGING AND UPDATING WILLS

The provisions of a will are valid until they are changed, revoked, destroyed, or invalidated by the writing of a new will. Changes or additions to a will can be included in a document called a codicil. Codicils must be written, signed, and witnessed in the same way as a will. Wills cannot be changed simply by crossing out existing language or writing in new provisions. In order to avoid making a new will or codicil each time a person's possessions change, a will can specify that personal property is to be distributed according to instructions outlined in a separate document. A person can then revise the separate document as often as necessary, without observing all of the formalities required to change the will itself.

If someone dies with a will that is not up-to-date, people may not be provided for adequately. For example, a person chosen to be a personal representative or guardian may have died or fallen out of favor with the author of the will, or a favorite charity may no longer be in existence. A significant amount of case law has dealt with how a probate court is to proceed with a will that has become unenforceable because of changed circumstances. These headaches can be avoided if a will is reviewed at least every two years and revised for major changes in tax laws or for personal events such as births, deaths, marriages, divorces, or significant changes in the size of the estate. It is also a good idea to review a will if its author moves to another state, because the new state of residency may have different inheritance and tax laws.

THE RIGHT OF ELECTION

As discussed previously, Illinois' probate code protects surviving spouses from being entirely disinherited by a decedent spouse. A surviving spouse who is unsatisfied with his or her portion under a valid will is allowed to exercise the right of election and take a statutory share of the estate. If the decedent left no descendants, the spouse's statutory share is half of the decedent's estate. If the decedent left descendants, the spouse's statutory share is one-third of the decedent's estate. Thus, the one-third portion is the minimum amount a surviving spouse may receive. A will can give more to the surviving spouse, but if it gives less, the surviving spouse can simply elect to forego his or her share under the will in favor of this statutorily guaranteed one-half or one-third share. Note, however, that the statutory share is not available to a spouse who has entered a contract during the life of the descendent to accept the provisions of the will.

DYING WITHOUT A WILL

If a person does not have a will or has not adequately planned for the distribution of the person's estate at death, survivors can face a complicated, time-consuming, and costly process. Often, survivors wind up having to pay more taxes on their inheritance than they would have paid had there been a will or other estate planning tool. To provide for surviving friends and relatives, or to support favorite causes or charities, a person can plan for the distribution of his or her estate after death. With planning, an estate can be distributed as fairly as possible with as little tax burden as legally allowed.

When a decedent leaves no will or fails to dispose of all property through a will, the decedent is said to have died intestate. When a person dies intestate, the circuit court steps in to divide the decedent's estate among the decedent's surviving relatives, according to a formula set out in the state inheritance laws.

A circuit court applying the state inheritance laws first deducts from the estate the funeral expenses and administration costs, the surviving spouse and child's award, any money owed to the federal government, any money due to employees of the decedent, any unpaid medical bills or other expenses of the decedent's last illness, any money owing to state or local government, and any other debt owed (in that order of preference).

After all the claims against the estate are paid, and if the decedent has a surviving spouse and no children, the entire estate goes to the spouse. If there are children and no surviving spouse, the entire estate is divided equally among the children. If there is both a surviving spouse and children, half of the estate goes to the spouse, and the remaining half is divided equally among the children. If the decedent leaves neither a spouse nor children, the estate goes to the decedent's parents, brothers, sisters, nieces and nephews. If the decedent leaves none of these relatives, the estate goes to the decedent's grandparents, aunts, uncles and cousins. If none of these relatives exist, investigation continues down the line of inheritance in an attempt to locate the decedent's nearest kin. Illinois law does not distinguish between kin of whole or half-blood. If, however, the decedent leaves no kin, the estate goes to the county where the decedent lived or in which the estate property is located.

One problem with relying on a circuit court applying state inheritance laws to distribute one's estate is that it may not distribute the estate in the manner the decedent would have wanted. State inheritance laws only recognize relatives. The inheritance laws never permit the circuit court to support a decedent's close friend, lover, or favorite charities. Clearly, for most people, writing a will (or creating a trust) is advisable.

TRUSTS

A trust is another frequently used estate planning device that manages the distribution of a person's estate.

MECHANICS OF A TRUST

To create a trust, the owner of property (grantor) transfers the property to a person or institution (trustee) who holds legal title to the property and manages it for the benefit of a third party (beneficiary). The grantor can name himself or herself or another person as the trustee. A trust can be either a testamentary trust or a living trust. A testamentary trust transfers the property to the trust only after the death of the grantor. A living trust, sometimes called an *inter vivos* trust, is created during the life of the grantor and can be set up to continue after the grantor's death or to terminate and be distributed upon the grantor's death.

Unlike a will, which in some cases can be drafted without the help of an attorney, a person should never draft a trust without the aid of a lawyer. Many complex laws regulate trusts and trusts must be carefully structured if they are to take advantage of beneficial tax treatment. An experienced attorney should always assist a person in drafting a trust so that it is valid, meets the needs of the estate, and does not conflict with any previously drafted will.

ADVANTAGES AND DISADVANTAGES OF TRUSTS

Trusts have many advantages over wills. All trusts have the advantage of allowing the grantor to determine who receives the benefit of the money, when they receive it, and what conditions must be met. If a spouse is unable or unwilling to manage assets, if children are minors or unable to handle money responsibly, or if a beneficiary is disabled, creating a trust can be a better way of passing on assets. Both living and testamentary trusts are popular ways of providing for beneficiaries' future educational or medical costs.

Some advantages are particular to living trusts. First, a living trust can give its grantor substantial tax advantages. Second, possessions held in a living trust are not subject to estate administration by the circuit court after the grantor dies. Survivors do not have to reveal the details of any possessions held in trust through the public filing process that takes place during probate. In addition, if the grantor owns real estate in another state, establishing a living trust for the title to that property may allow survivors to avoid probate in the other state. A living trust can free the grantor from the burden of overseeing his or her financial affairs because a trustee manages all the assets of a living trust. More importantly, a living trust allows a trustee to manage the trust funds in the event that its creator becomes incapacitated or mentally or physically unable to oversee his or her possessions. If a living trust contains all of a person's assets, then he or she may not need a will, and his or her survivors may be able to avoid probate. If only part of a person's possessions are held in living trust, then a will is necessary to distribute those items in the estate not placed into a trust. However, a pour-over provision in a will can place any possessions remaining upon death into a pre-existing living trust.

The primary disadvantage of a living trust is that it involves the loss of some flexibility and control over one's assets. Unlike wills, which become effective only at death, a living trust becomes effective immediately upon its creation. For the person who wants to retain unrestricted control over his or her estate, a will or a testamentary trust is a better estate planning tool because it can be changed at any time prior to death.

The primary advantage of a testamentary trust is that it allows the grantor to retain unrestricted control over his or her estate. A testamentary trust becomes effective only upon the death of its grantor. Like a will, a testamentary trust can be changed at any time prior to death.

The primary disadvantage to testamentary trusts is that they do not take advantage of the beneficial tax treatment given to living trusts. Because a testamentary trust only takes effect when the grantor dies, the grantor cannot enjoy any tax advantage during his or her life. Also, most testamentary trusts must go through probate.

REVOCABLE AND IRREVOCABLE TRUSTS

A living trust can be either revocable or irrevocable. As implied by their names, a revocable trust can be changed or revoked after its creation, while an irrevocable trust cannot be changed or revoked. A revocable trust is quite often devised to supplement a will and/or to name someone to handle the grantor's affairs should the grantor become incapacitated. A trust usually must be made irrevocable if the grantor wants to avoid income or estate taxes. Tax authorities consider the grantor of a revocable trust to be the owner of the property because he or she still controls the property. For this reason, income from assets held in a revocable trust must be reported as income to the grantor for income tax purposes. At the death of the grantor, property in a revocable trust is included in the estate for calculating estate taxes.

An irrevocable trust is often designed to be the beneficiary of a life insurance policy. Such a life insurance trust can also spell out how the policy's money is distributed to survivors. In addition, irrevocable trusts are often set up to manage money given to minors and to charities. Finally, an irrevocable trust can be used to transfer assets to another person in the event that the grantor requires expensive medical care. Although doing so may protect the grantor's family by ensuring that the cost of medical care does not wipe out the family fortune, it may also make the grantor ineligible to receive federal and state Medical Assistance.

PROBATE

With few exceptions, the estate of a person who dies owning property in his or her name cannot be legally distributed without first going through probate. Only if all of a decedent's property is held in joint tenancy or in trust can survivors avoid probate. Probate can operate with court supervision, called supervised administration, or without court supervision, called independent administration. Some simple, small estates may be administered through summary administration.

Regardless of the type of administration, the first duty of the circuit court is to determine whether the decedent left a valid will. The person in possession of a decedent's will must file it with the clerk of the circuit court within 30 days of the decedent's death. If the decedent left a valid will, the court oversees the process of settling the estate according to the terms of the will. If the decedent did not leave a will or if the circuit court determines the will is invalid, the court applies the state inheritance laws, described earlier, to the estate.

Summary administration is available if the estate is $50,000 or less, all claims against the estate are known, there are no taxes due, and all the heirs and legatees consent to the process. In a summary administration, the circuit court determines the rights of the claimants, directs payments and distributes the estate at a single hearing.

Independent administration permits the personal representative to administer the estate without court orders or filings. Unless disputes arise between the beneficiaries or with third parties, or unless requested to intervene by the personal representative or an interested party, the court is involved only to open and close the estate. Independent administration increases family privacy, because no inventory or accounting is usually filed. The process also reduces the time involved in probate. If an interested person objects to independent administration, the court must supervise the administration.

Supervised administration requires the personal representative to file specific documents with the court, such as an estate inventory and periodic accountings. The personal representative must also obtain court approval to perform such duties as selling or leasing estate property.

AVOIDING DEATH TAXES

A carefully created estate plan can considerably reduce the tax burden on an estate. Illinois has no estate tax provisions. Other than income taxes, only the federal estate tax applies to decedents who were Illinois residents or whose property was located in Illinois. Under federal tax law, a person is allowed to leave $600,000 tax-free to one or more individuals, other than a surviving spouse. The surviving spouse is entitled to receive an unlimited amount tax-free. If the estate is a very large one, however, and the entire estate is left to the surviving spouse, that surviving spouse may lose the option of giving $600,000 tax-free to individuals of his or her own choosing. The federal government's inheritance tax scheme is quite complicated; however, an experienced tax attorney can help an individual avoid paying unnecessary estate taxes.

Regardless of whether the recipient pays state or federal estate taxes, there may be income tax consequences for the recipients under a will.

RESOURCES

Illinois State Bar Association, 424 South Second Street, Springfield, IL 62701, phone: (217) 525-1760. Contact the ISBA for the free booklet, *Estate Planning & Living Wills*.

Chicago Bar Association, 321 South Plymouth Court, Chicago, IL 60604, phone: (312) 554-2000. The Chicago Bar Association provides the free pamphlet, *The Senior Citizens Will Program*.

National Senior Citizens Law Center, 2025 M Street NW, #400, Washington, D.C. 20036, phone: (202) 887-5280.

Estate Planning, Wills & Trusts Law
Leading Illinois Attorneys

Illinois' Most Respected Legal Counsel As Selected By Their Peers.

The Leading Illinois Attorneys below were recommended by their peers in a statewide survey.

The Leading Illinois Attorneys listed below were nominated as exceptional by their peers in a statewide survey conducted by American Research Corporation (ARC). ARC asked several thousand licensed Illinois attorneys to name the lawyer to whom they would send a close friend or family member in need of legal assistance in specific areas of law. The attorneys below were nominated in the area of Estate Planning, Wills & Trusts Law.

Because the survey results (all practice area results combined) represent less than three percent of Illinois' practicing attorneys, this list should not be construed as a complete list. Nevertheless, it is an excellent source of highly qualified and reputable Illinois attorneys.

For information on ARC's survey methodology, see page *xi*.
For the complete list of Leading Illinois Consumer Attorneys, see page *xii*.

The Leading Illinois Attorneys below are listed alphabetically in accordance with the geographic region in which their offices are located. Note that attorneys may handle clients from a broad geographic area; attorneys are not restricted to only serving clients residing within the cities in which their offices are located.

An attorney whose name appears in bold has included a biographical profile in this chapter.

Cook & Collar Counties

Albright, Christine L. - Chicago
Alschuler, Benjamin P. - Aurora
Applehans, Stephen G. - Waukegan
Baker, David A. - Chicago
Barnard, Morton J. - Chicago
Beninati, Francis A. - Chicago
Berg, Gershon S. - Skokie
Berning, Larry D. - Chicago
Bitterman, Patrick J. - Chicago
Bloom, Kenneth M. - Chicago
Bollman, Robert M. - Waukegan
Boylan, William E. - Wheaton
Breen, Joseph R. - Chicago
Brosterhous, Patricia - Chicago
Brown, Alan C. - Chicago
Brown, Richard M. - Chicago
Campbell, Richard A. - Chicago
Carroll, James J. - Chicago
Carroll, Timothy G. - Chicago
Cass, Neil E. - Chicago
Chamberlin, Darcy J. - Oak Brook, page 160
Clark, William G., Jr. - Chicago
Cohen, Aaron - Chicago
Collander, Dan M. - Naperville
Colombik, Richard M. - Schaumburg, page 160
Dees, Richard L. - Chicago
Dembicki, Pauline G. - Evanston
Dickson, Fred H. - Aurora
Dobben, Brian L. - Chicago
Donatelli, Mark R. - Hinsdale
Dutton, Janna S. - Chicago
English, John D. - Chicago

Fairbanks, William J. - Chicago
Feinberg, Barry A. - Chicago
Flanagan, Leo M., Jr. - Elgin
Fleming, Michael W. - Elmhurst
Fox, Barbara N. - Chicago
Frazer, Quin R. - Chicago
Friedberg, Michael R. - Chicago
Friedman, Roselyn L. - Chicago
Gelman, Andrew R. - Chicago
Gertz, Theodore G. - Chicago
Gilbert, Howard E. - Skokie
Glassberg, Donald A. - Chicago
Gold, Nan M. - Skokie
Gorecki, Robert - St. Charles
Hamilton, Robert E. - Chicago
Hanson, David L. - Chicago
Hardy, Ralph C., Jr. - Elgin
Harrington, Carol A. - Chicago
Harris, Steven M. - Chicago
Harrison, Louis S. - Chicago
Hellige, James R. - Chicago
Hem, Ronald M. - Aurora
Heriaud, Neal - Chicago
Hirsch, John B. - Chicago
Hodge, Gerald K. - Aurora
Hoogendoorn, Case - Chicago
Howard, George C. - Chicago
Huck, James M. - Wheaton
Huck, Kevin J. - Wheaton
Hupp, Robert B. - Aurora
Jacobs, Alan - Chicago
Jacobs, Allen F. - Buffalo Grove

156 Leading Illinois Attorneys Consumer Law Guidebook

Jarvis, James S. - Chicago
Jones, W. Clyde, III - Geneva
Joseph, Jack - Chicago
Jumes, Leon P. - Chicago
Kimnach, Richard A. - Chicago
Levine, Sidney M. - Chicago
Levy, David H. - Chicago
Lorch, Kenneth F. - Chicago
LoVallo, Michael A. - Chicago
MacKay, Karen K. - Chicago
Mannix, Gerald J. - Park Ridge
McCue, Howard M., III - Chicago
McCue, Judith W. - Chicago
McHugh, Timothy - Elmhurst
Meyers, Ted A. - Elgin
Miller, Rochelle C. - Chicago
Monahan, Joseph T. - Chicago
Morgan, Donna E. - Chicago
Motel, Robert - Lincolnwood
Mozer, Stefan I. - Chicago
Mulryan, Rosemary - Chicago
Nitikman, Franklin W. - Chicago
Opferman, Thomas G. - Chicago
Otis, Lorri E. - Chicago
Owens, John E., Jr. - Park Ridge
Palmieri, Vincent L. - Libertyville
Pasquesi, Theodore A. - Highland Park
Peck, Kerry R. - Chicago, page 161
Polisky, Joel S. - Chicago
Powell, W. Thomas - Wheaton
Provenza, James C. - Glenview, page 161
Reda, Edward E., Jr. - Chicago, page 162
Reed, Daniel A. - Aurora

Ritt, Norbert C. - Elgin
Rodes, Theodore, Jr. - Chicago
Rolewick, David F. - Wheaton, page 162
Rosenberg, Herbert B. - Chicago
Rothman, Joel S. - Chicago
Rowder, William - Chicago
Schanlaber, William C. - Aurora
Schiever, Carey J. - Libertyville, page 163
Schindel, Donald M. - Chicago
Schuman, Joseph - Chicago
Segal, Alan F. - Chicago
Shayne, David - Chicago
Siegal, Barry P. - Chicago
Smith, Robert S., Jr. - Deerfield, page 163
Soskin, Rollin J. - Skokie
Stark, Blooma - Chicago
Sugar, Richard A. - Chicago
Talbot, Earl A. - Chicago
Thayer, Steven J. - Chicago
Trapp, James M. - Chicago
Tully, Thomas M. - Chicago
Vosicky, Joseph F., Jr. - Wheaton
Wall, Bernard T. - Chicago
Weiler, Daniel A. - Elgin
Weinsheimer, William C. - Chicago
Welch, Lyman W. - Chicago
Wilcox, Barbara L. - Chicago
Windham, Danny L. - Chicago
Winter, Arthur - Evanston
Winter, Bernard R. - Waukegan
Wittenberg, Michael P. - Homewood
Zaluda, Jeffrey A. - Chicago

NORTHWESTERN ILLINOIS INCLUDING ROCKFORD & QUAD CITIES

Agnew, Patrick H. - Rockford
Balch, Bruce L. - Rock Island
Beck, Jeffrey - Rockford
Churchill, Daniel - Moline
Cox, John W., Jr. - Galena
Edwards, Frank R. - Rock Island
Enichen, Edward J. - Rockford
Ferracuti, Peter F. - Ottawa
Gaziano, Mary J. - Rockford
Gehlbach, Gary - Dixon
Gorman, Mary P. - Rockford
Granneman, Faye M. - Rockford
Horberg, Kurt J. - Cambridge

Howard, William J. - Rockford
Huntoon, H. Karl - Moline
Johnson, Raymond E. - Rockford
Keeling, James W. - Rockford
Koenig, Philip E. - Rock Island, page 164
Oliver, Robert J. - Rockford
Phares, William T. - East Moline
Roth, Robert R. - Galena
Rudy, Sharon R. - Rockford
Slover, John A., Jr. - Moline
Stojan, Clark J. - Rock Island
Van Der Kamp, Roy W. - Rock Island
Vincent, James B. - Galena

CENTRAL ILLINOIS

Austin, William W. - Effingham
Balbach, Stanley B. - Urbana
Bauer, Wendy S. - Champaign
Bellatti, Robert M. - Springfield
Benassi, A. Lou - Peoria
Bennett, Jim A. - Mattoon
Booth, Edward - Decatur
Brady, John C. - Peoria
Brittingham, Francis M. - Danville
Burton, R. Nicholas - Decatur

Connor, William C. - Peoria
Erwin, Sam - Champaign
Flynn, Leonard T. - Champaign
Flynn, Michael J. - Bloomington
Garst, Steven L. - Paris
Gerber, Jacqueline M. - Springfield
Gibson, Robert L. - Paris
Gilfillan, Joseph P. - Peoria
Glenn, Ralph D. - Mattoon
Greer, Daniel J. - Springfield, page 165

Hagen, Henry C. - Springfield
Hall, Robert C. - Peoria
Hasselberg, Eric E. - Peoria
Haughey, Roger E. - Champaign
Hendren, Paul C. - Champaign
Holzgrafe, Roger E. - Peoria
Horn, Jerold I. - Peoria
Hunt, Mark B., Jr. - Mattoon
Kesler, William R. - Danville
Knox, E. Phillips - Urbana
Kramer, Henry E. - Charleston
Kuppler, Karl B. - Peoria
Lawless, J. Martin - Peoria
Lestikow, James M. - Springfield
Mamer, Stuart M. - Champaign
Meachum, Bruce J. - Danville
Mescher, Gregory A. - Peoria
Moore, Daniel M., Jr. - Decatur
Noble, Kent A. - Peoria
Osborne, Stephen M. - Springfield
Pavia, Joseph D. - Urbana
Peithmann, William A. - Farmer City, page 165

Roberts, Robert H. - Decatur
Saint, Gale W. - Bloomington, page 165
Shawler, Omer T. - Marshall
Sheehan, Patrick J. - Springfield
Sheehan, William J. - Springfield
Silkwood, Larry R. - Urbana
Stuart, Robert A., Jr. - Springfield
Stumpe, Karen M. - Peoria
Sturm, Timothy - Springfield
Summers, Holten D. - Urbana
Sutkowski, Edward F. - Peoria
Thomas, Lott H. - Champaign
Tietz, Christopher M. - Decatur
Tueth, James E. - Decatur
Turner, Mercer - Bloomington
Turner, Ralph T. - Bloomington
Walvoord, David J. - Peoria
Washkuhn, Wilson C. - Peoria
Webber, Carl M. - Urbana
Williams, Guy E. - Decatur
Wolff, Dale F. - Effingham
Wolgamot, John P. - Danville

Southern Illinois

Binsbacher, Valroy - Mascoutah
Blake, Edward J., Jr. - Belleville
Boie, Wesley L. - Anna
Brown, W. Campbell - West Frankfort
Coffey, Gary R. - Edwardsville
Drone, R. Michael - Carmi
Elliott, Ivan A., Jr. - Carmi
Farrell, John A. - Godfrey
Frankland, David K. - Albion
Grandy, Laura K. - Belleville
Guymon, David E. - Belleville
Habiger, Richard J. - Carbondale
Jennings, Robert L. - Belleville
Johnson, Don E. - Pinckneyville

LeChien, Thomas A. - Belleville
Mager, T. Richard - Carbondale
Marifian, George E. - Belleville
Mathis, Patrick B. - Belleville
Metzger, Donald L. - Edwardsville
Mitchell, A. Ben - Mt. Vernon
Richter, Kevin J. - Belleville
Rikli, Donald C. - Highland, page 166
Smith, Webb H. - Carbondale
Smoot, Carolyn B. - Marion
Weihl, Donald E. - Belleville
Welch, Kay A. - Belleville
Wells, Robert E., Jr. - Belleville
Whittington, Rebecca A. - Carbondale

BIOGRAPHICAL PROFILES OF ESTATE PLANNING, WILLS & TRUSTS LAW LEADING ILLINOIS ATTORNEYS

The Leading Illinois Attorneys profiled below were nominated as exceptional by their peers in a statewide survey conducted by American Research Corporation (ARC). ARC asked several thousand licensed Illinois attorneys to name the lawyer to whom they would send a close friend or family member in need of legal assistance in specific areas of law. The attorneys below were nominated in the area of Estate Planning, Wills & Trusts Law.

Because the survey results (all practice area results combined) represent less than three percent of Illinois' practicing attorneys, this list should not be construed as a complete list. Nevertheless, it is an excellent source of highly qualified and reputable Illinois attorneys.

For information on ARC's survey methodology, see page *xi*.
For the complete list of Leading Illinois Consumer Attorneys, see page *xii*.
For the list of Leading Illinois Estate Planning, Wills & Trusts Law Attorneys, see page 156.

The Leading Illinois Attorneys below are listed alphabetically in accordance with the geographic region in which their offices are located. Note that attorneys may handle clients from a broad geographic area; attorneys are not limited to only serving clients residing within the cities in which their offices are located.

The two-line attorney listings in this section are of attorneys who practice in this area but whose full biographical profiles appear in other sections of this book. A bullet "•" preceding a name indicates the attorney was nominated in this particular area of law.

For information on the format of the full biographical profiles, consult the "Using the Consumer Guidebook" section on page *xviii*.

The following abbreviations are used throughout these profiles:

App.	Appellate
Cir.	Circuit
Ct.	Court
Dist.	District
Sup.	Supreme
JD	Juris Doctor (Doctor of Law)
LLB	Legum Baccalaureus (Bachelor of Laws)
LLD	Legum Doctor (Doctor of Laws)
LLM	Legum Magister (Master of Laws)
ADR	Alternative Dispute Resolution
ABA	American Bar Association
ABOTA	American Board of Trial Advocates
ATLA	Association of Trial Lawyers of America
CBA	Chicago Bar Association
ISBA	Illinois State Bar Association
ITLA	Illinois Trial Lawyers Association
NBTA	National Board of Trial Advocacy

Cook & Collar Counties

•DARCY J. CHAMBERLIN: Ms. Chamberlin brings 17 years of experience to the areas of estate planning, probate and trust administration, and federal estate and fiduciary taxation. Her areas of concentration include estate tax analysis; the preparation of wills; advanced directives, including living wills and powers of attorney for health care; revocable living trusts; irrevocable trusts, dynasty or generation skipping trusts; education trusts and special needs trusts; charitable tax planning, including the preparation of charitable remainder trusts; gift giving techniques, including the preparation of qualified personal residence trusts and family limited partnerships; business succession planning; buy-sell agreements; prenuptial agreements; probate and trust administration; and estate and fiduciary income tax preparation. Ms. Chamberlin has a significant elder law practice, with an emphasis on meeting the estate planning needs of clients caring for a family member with a disability. She has assisted her clients in addressing Medicaid/Medicare issues; nursing home and retirement home contract review and negotiation; and guardianships of adults with disabilities. She has been a featured speaker at events hosted by the Chicagoland Chapters of the National Association of Down's Syndrome, the National Alzheimer's Association, and the Multiple Sclerosis Society. Ms. Chamberlin has authored a number of articles on estate planning in legal journals and continues to serve the legal and lay communities through active participation in bar activities and frequent speaking at public forums and seminars.

Education: JD 1979, Indiana University; BA 1976, Indiana University.
Admitted: 1979 Illinois; 1979 U.S. Dist. Ct. (N. Dist. IL).
Employment History: Sole Practitioner 1979-present.
Professional Associations: ISBA; CBA (Trust Law Section); National Academy of Elder Law Attorneys 1993.
Community Involvement: Ms. Chamberlin has been on the Advisory Board of Community Support Services in Brookfield, Illinois, since 1989. This organization serves families with developmental disabilities. *Ms. Chamberlin also practices Elder Law and Small Business Law.*

DARCY J. CHAMBERLIN
Attorney at Law
1211 West 22nd Street
Suite 1006
Oak Brook, IL 60521

Phone: (630) 447-2478
Fax: (630) 572-1432

•RICHARD M. COLOMBIK: Mr. Colombik is an estate planning, business, asset protection, and tax attorney. He has been the liaison to the District Director of the Internal Revenue Service for the Illinois State Bar Association since 1990. He previously chaired the Illinois State Bar Association's Federal Taxation Section Council, the Northwest Suburban Bar Association's Estate, Probate and Tax Section Council, and is a member of the ISBA Trusts and Estate Section Council. Mr. Colombik is a member of the Offshore Institute, relative to implementation of offshore and domestic asset protection planning. He has also recently authored a book, *Business Entity Selection Within Illinois*, as well as written a chapter in *Estate Planning Short Course*, both published by the Illinois Institute for Continuing Legal Education. From his initial background as one of the members on the private tax staff of one of the world's wealthiest families, Mr. Colombik's extensive tax experience was expanded by his additional education through law school. He later became a Tax Manager at Touche, Ross & Company, currently Deloitte & Touche. Mr. Colombik has been operating his own law firm since 1982. Its current size is ten people. Mr. Colombik has published approximately 100 articles on taxation, estate planning, business planning, and asset protection planning. He has appeared on television, radio, newspapers and magazines, relative to his estate planning and taxation experience, and asset protection planning. He is a sought-after lecturer for professional associations and corporations. He has been recognized by various associations for his contributions and extensive support through his publications and dedication.

Education: JD 1980 cum laude, John Marshall Law School; CPA 1977, University of Illinois; BS 1975, University of Colorado (Dean's List).
Employment History: 1982-present, Richard M. Colombik & Associates, P.C.; 1980-82, Touche, Ross & Co. (now Deloitte & Touche); Tax Manager 1977-78, Henry Crown and Company (Illinois).
Professional Associations: Northwest Suburban Bar Assn. [Vice President 1996; Probate, Estate Planning and Tax Committee (Chair 1989-90)]; ISBA [Federal Taxation Section Council 1990-94 (Chair 1993-94); Trusts and Estates Section Council 1995-96]; American Assn. of Attorney CPAs (Vice President 1992-96); ABA [Taxation Committee (Vice Chair); Section of General Practice Committee 1995]; North Shore Estate Planning Council 1990; Northwest Estate Planning Council 1992-96.

RICHARD M. COLOMBIK
Richard M. Colombik & Associates, P.C.
1111 Plaza Drive
Suite 430
Schaumburg, IL 60173

Phone: (847) 619-5700
Fax: (847) 619-0971
E-mail: rcolom29@starnetinc.com
Web: http://www.colombik.com

Extensive Experience In:
• Estate Planning
• Asset Protection
• Tax Structure & Planning

•HOWARD E. GILBERT - *Howard E. Gilbert & Associates, Ltd.* - 5420 Old Orchard Road, Suite A205 - Skokie, IL 60077 - Phone: (847) 966-6600, Fax: (847) 966-6638 - *See complete biographical profile in the Small Business Law Chapter, page 307.*

MICHAEL W. KALCHEIM - *Kalcheim, Schatz & Berger* - 161 North Clark, Suite 2800 - Chicago, IL 60601 - Phone: (312) 782-3456, Fax: (312) 782-8463 - *See complete biographical profile in the Family Law Chapter, page 191.*

JOHN J. MORRISON - *Law Office of John J. Morrison, Ltd.* - 135 South LaSalle Street, Suite 3600 - Chicago, IL 60603 - Phone: (312) 641-3484, Fax: (312) 641-0727 - *See complete biographical profile in the Tax Law Chapter, page 329.*

•**KERRY R. PECK:** Mr. Peck has an extensive law practice in the areas of probate, elder law, guardianship, estate planning (trusts and wills), estates, and chancery/probate litigation. He has taught courses for attorneys at seminars for the American Bar Association, the Chicago Bar Association, the North Suburban Bar Association, the Women's Bar Association of Illinois, and the Northwest Suburban Bar Association. He has presented seminars to the professional staffs of health care institutions, banks, savings and loans, and the City of Chicago, Department of Aging. He has been engaged by the U.S. Department of Health and Human Services, the Food and Drug Administration and others to present pre-retirement seminars to employees nearing retirement age. Mr. Peck's legal talent has been recognized by the television, radio, and print media. He has been quoted in the Business Section of the *Chicago Tribune* on estate planning and has appeared on several television and radio shows, including "Front and Center," *CLTV News;* "Will Fights," the *Oprah Winfrey Show;* on a cable television show regarding probate, chancery and estate planning, with Aurelia Pucinski, Clerk of the Circuit Court of Cook County; "Sunday Morning," *WJJD Talk Radio; ABC-TV News,* with Financial Reporter Andrew Leckey, regarding probate and wills; and monthly on CBS-WBBM radio's *Dave Baum Talk Show* for two-and-one-half years. He has authored numerous articles which have appeared in the Chicago Bar Association journals and other bar journals.
Education: JD 1978 with honors, Illinois Institute of Technology, Chicago-Kent; BS 1978, Northern Illinois University.
Admitted: 1978 Illinois; 1979 Florida.
Professional Associations: CBA [Treasurer; Board of Managers; Elder Law Committee (Founder; past Chair); Urban Affairs Committee (Crime Reduction Project with Roosevelt University Institute of Metropolitan Affairs); Young Lawyers Section (past Vice Chair)]; National Academy of Elder Law Attorneys [Illinois Chapter (Board of Directors)]; North Suburban Bar Assn. (Board of Managers).
Community Involvement: Legal Clinic for the Disabled (Board of Directors); Decalogue Society of Lawyers (Board of Managers).
Firm: Kerry R. Peck & Associates is a three-attorney law firm that represents senior citizens, families, financial institutions, health care providers, and guardianship agencies. *Mr. Peck also practices Elder Law and Tax Law.*

KERRY R. PECK
Kerry R. Peck & Associates
105 West Adams Street
31st Floor
Chicago, IL 60603
Phone: (312) 201-0900
Fax: (312) 201-0803

Extensive Experience In:
• Wills/Trusts Contests
• Contested Guardianships
• Living Trusts

•**JAMES C. PROVENZA:** Mr. Provenza practices law primarily in the areas of estate planning and probate, charitable giving, planning for disabled children, business succession, and Medicaid. He has represented individuals and families in planning for retirement and passing assets to the next generation. He has also helped families organize a deceased family member's affairs. Mr. Provenza has been a Certified Public Accountant since 1977. As Chair of the Estate Planning Committee for the Northwest Suburban Bar Association and as a member of the Lake County Bar Association, Mr. Provenza writes a monthly column on new developments in estate planning and speaks at these associations' annual estate planning seminars. He frequently speaks in conjunction with financial planners on estate and financial planning.
Education: JD 1980, John Marshall Law School; BS 1977, University of Illinois-Champaign.
Admitted: 1980 Illinois; 1980 U.S. Tax Ct.
Employment History: 1982-present, James C. Provenza, P.C.; Certified Public Accountant 1980-81, Ernst and Whinney (now Ernst and Young).
Representative Clients: Mr. Provenza represents all individual clients, with estates modest or large.
Professional Associations: Northwest Suburban Bar Assn. [Estate Planning Committee (Chair 1995-96)]; Lake County Bar Assn.
Community Involvement: Chicago Council on Planned Giving; Assn. of Lutheran Development Executives.
Firm: James C. Provenza, P.C., helps clients in both lifetime and after-death planning goals. The firm helps clients set goals for retirement, income tax reduction, disability, and other future, anticipated financial needs. The firm keeps clients informed of new ideas through a quarterly newsletter and periodic follow-up. *Mr. Provenza also practices Tax Law.*

JAMES C. PROVENZA
James C. Provenza, P.C.
1701 East Lake Avenue
Suite 407
Glenview, IL 60025
Phone: (847) 729-3939
Fax: (847) 657-6801

Chapter 16: Estate Planning, Wills & Trusts Law

EDWARD E. REDA, JR.
Reda, Ltd.
8501 West Higgins
Suite 440
Chicago, IL 60631
Phone: (312) 399-1122
Fax: (312) 399-1144

•**EDWARD E. REDA, JR.:** Mr. Reda is engaged in the general practice of law, with an emphasis on estate planning, probate and trust law. He also is involved in advising many small- to mid-size corporations. He has never lectured, written a book nor authored a law review article. His time is devoted to serving his clients and raising a family with four active children. Mr. Reda's personal philosophy is that he tries to practice law in an honest, caring, compassionate, and Christian way. He believes that by being a sole practitioner, he alone is totally responsible for the service provided to his clients. He accepts and enjoys that accountability.
Education: JD 1976 magna cum laude, DePaul University; BS 1973, DePaul University.
Admitted: 1976 Illinois.
Employment History: Sole Practitioner 1992-present, Reda, Ltd.; Partner 1985-92, Reda & Hennessy; Sole Practitioner 1978-85; Partner 1976-78, Reda, Haber and Reda.
Professional Associations: ABA; ISBA; CBA; Justinian Society of Lawyers.
Community Involvement: Athletic Committee at Mary Seat of Wisdom Grammar School; Park Ridge Youth Baseball Coach since 1987. *Mr. Reda also practices Real Estate Law and Small Business Law.*

JOHN H. REDFIELD - *Attorney at Law* - 5420 Old Orchard Road, #A-205 - Skokie, IL 60077 - Phone: (847) 966-9920, Fax: (847) 966-6638 - *See complete biographical profile in the Bankruptcy Law Chapter, page 72.*

DAVID F. ROLEWICK
Rolewick & Gutzke, P.C.
1776 South Naperville Road
Suite 104A
Wheaton, IL 60187
Phone: (630) 653-1577
Fax: (630) 653-1579

Extensive Experience In:
• Estate Planning
• Business Organizations
• Commercial Litigation

•**DAVID F. ROLEWICK:** Mr. Rolewick concentrates in estate planning, business planning and organization, trusts, corporate litigation, employment law, and professional standards and misconduct. Mr. Rolewick is the author of *A Short History of the Illinois Judicial Systems,* Illinois Bar Foundation, 1968; "Unconscionability Under the Uniform Commercial Code," 1 *Loyola University Law Journal* 313, 1971; "Voir Dire Examination of Jurors," 25 *DePaul University Law Review* 50, 1975; "Proving Oppression of the Minority Shareholders (Chancery Relief in Shareholder Disputes)," DuPage County Bar Association's *Brief,* May 1991.
Education: JD 1971, Loyola University (Law Alumni Award 1971, Alpha Sigma Nu National Honor Fraternity; Notes Editor 1970-71, *Law Journal*); BS 1968, Loyola University.
Admitted: 1971 Illinois; 1974 U.S. Dist. Ct. (N. Dist. IL); 1978 U.S. Ct. App. (7th Cir.); 1983 U.S. Dist. Ct. (N. Dist. IL, Trial Bar); 1984 U.S. Sup. Ct.
Employment History: Principal 1981-present, Rolewick & Gutzke, P.C.; Private Practice 1979-81, Law Offices of David F. Rolewick, P.C.; Associate 1975-79, O'Reilly & Cunningham, P.C.; Assistant Director 1973-75, Administrative Office of Illinois Courts; Clerk/Secretary to Justice Daniel Ward 1971-73, Illinois Supreme Court.
Representative Clients: Borg Mechanical Contractors, Inc.; Dugan & Lopatka, C.P.A.; First National Bank of Brookfield; Guarantee General Store, Inc.; Home Landscape Materials, Inc.; MacGregor & Company, Inc.; Phillips & Johnston, Inc.; Westlake Motors, Inc.
Professional Associations: ABA; ISBA [Corporations/Securities Law Section Council (Newsletter Editor 1989-91; Secretary 1992-93; Vice Chair 1993-94; Chair 1994-95); Liaison to ABA Committee on Uniform State Corporations Law 1992-94; Task Force on Public Protection from the Unauthorized Practice of Law 1995-present]; DuPage County Bar Assn. [Lawyer Referral Service 1991-present; Tax and Practice Committee (Vice Chair 1991; Chair 1992)]; ATLA; DuPage County Estate Planning Council; Attorney Registration and Disciplinary Commission of the Supreme Court of Illinois [Inquiry Board Member (Chair 1990-94; Hearing Board (Chair 1994-present)].
Firm: The firm was founded by David Rolewick in 1978. In the 15 years since its inception, the firm has grown from a one-man law office to a diversified firm consisting of seven full-time attorneys working closely with a very qualified and committed paralegal/secretarial staff. *See complete firm profile in Appendix A. Mr. Rolewick also practices Tax Law and Small Business Law.*

•**CAREY J. SCHIEVER:** Mr. Schiever practices in the areas of estate planning and administration, estate tax, corporate and business law, and real estate law. His 25 years of experience provide a unique combination of skills which enable him to represent clients in all facets of office practice.
Education: JD 1973, Washington University, St. Louis; BA 1970, DePauw University.
Admitted: 1973 Illinois; 1973 U.S. Dist. Ct. (N. Dist. IL).
Employment History: 1981-present, Carey J. Schiever, Ltd.; Partner 1981, Lang & Schiever; Attorney 1975-81, White & Roux, Ltd.; Trust Officer 1973-75, Continental Illinois National Bank, Chicago; Law Clerk 1970-73, Crowe, Schneider & Gioia, St. Louis, Missouri.
Representative Clients: Mr. Schiever represents a diversity of clients, including over 100 small corporations and businesses ranging from contractors and manufacturers to book sellers, restaurants (and their suppliers), a micro-brewery and many manufacturers' representatives. Clients include Interlacken Construction Company (builder), Maneval Construction Co. (road paver), Burke Products Co. (chocolate manufacturer), Libertyville Brewing Co., Unique Books, Inc., and Tru-Clean Filters, Inc.
Professional Associations: Lake County Bar Assn. [Trust and Estate Committee; Corporate Committee (Chair 1994)]; Lake County Estate Planning Council 1977-present (President 1982)]; ISBA 1975-present; Lake County Life Underwriters Assn. 1975-80 (Associate Member).
Community Involvement: Sunrise Rotary Club, Libertyville; Libertyville Soccer Assn.; Libertyville Little League 1992-present (Coach); Lake County March of Dimes (Fund Raiser).
Firm: Since clerking for the firm that represents the City of St. Louis Public Administrator and receiving extensive training at Continental Bank, Mr. Schiever has been involved in estate planning and administration processes for many years, and is frequently a speaker at classes on these subjects. He provides continual, personal, full service to his clients, and is proud to be the "family lawyer" to many closely held business owners. *Mr. Schiever also practices Real Estate Law and Small Business Law.*

CAREY J. SCHIEVER

Carey J. Schiever, Ltd.
1512 Artaius Parkway
Suite 300
Libertyville, IL 60048-5231

Phone: (847) 680-1123
Fax: (847) 680-1124

Extensive Experience In:

- Elder Law
- Estate Tax Returns & Tax Planning
- Disability & Minor's Trusts

•**ROBERT S. SMITH, JR.:** Mr. Smith practices probate and related law, concentrating in the areas of the resolution of estates for families and assisting them in probate, guardianship matters, minor's estates, contested wills and heirships, and resultant trusts stemming from estates or estate plans. He has lectured substantially at various seminars regarding estate and guardianship practice.
Education: JD 1971, Loyola University; MPS 1995, Loyola University; BA 1967, St. Meinrad College.
Admitted: 1971 Illinois; 1971 U.S. Dist. Ct. (N. Dist. IL).
Employment History: Private Practice 1978-present, Law Offices of Robert S. Smith, Jr.; Assistant State's Attorney 1972-77, State's Attorney's Office, Lake County.
Professional Associations: ISBA; Lake County Bar Assn. [Estate and Trust Committee (past Chair); Volunteer Lawyer Committee (past Chair)].
Community Involvement: Boy Scouts of America [Local District Committee; Explorer Post (Chair)]; Archdiocese of Chicago (Deacon).
Firm: Mr. Smith works actively with his clients and underscores the responsibilities the entrusted person has in probate procedures. Probate and guardianship cases are often emotionally difficult and wrenching matters when dealing with elder or disabled relatives or friends. He assists and counsels his clients during these times when responsible and complex decisions must be made for the welfare of family members or friends. *Mr. Smith also practices Adoption Law and Elder Law.*

ROBERT S. SMITH, JR.

Law Offices of Robert S. Smith, Jr.
747 Deerfield Road
Suite 310
P.O. Box 231
Deerfield, IL 60015

Phone: (847) 945-3455
Fax: (847) 945-6795

Extensive Experience In:

- Guardianship of Adults
- Contested Estates & Wills
- Contested Heirship

LAURIE J. WASSERMAN - *Law Offices of Laurie J. Wasserman* - 9933 Lawler Avenue, Suite 312 - Skokie, IL 60077-3706 - Phone: (847) 674-7324, Fax: (847) 674-8938 - *See complete biographical profile in the Employment Law Chapter, page 147.*

NORTHWESTERN ILLINOIS
INCLUDING ROCKFORD & QUAD CITIES

PHILIP E. KOENIG

Katz, McHard, Balch, Lefstein & Fieweger, P.C.
1705 Second Avenue
Suite 200
Rock Island, IL 61201

Phone: (309) 788-5661
Fax: (309) 788-5688

Extensive Experience In:
- Drafting of Wills & Trusts
- Estate Administration
- Farm & Business Estate Planning

•**PHILIP E. KOENIG:** Mr. Koenig has practiced in western Illinois for over 20 years, with a concentration in estate planning, probate, trust and real estate matters. He has handled many estates which have involved and required income tax planning and/or estate tax planning, as well as resolution of real estate title land aquisitions, and sale and financing transactions. He authored "Summary of Illinois Law—Real Estate Finance," 12 *Southern Illinois University Law Journal* 1157. For the last six years, he has been a speaker for, and contributor to, the annual law education series on real estate law offered by the Real Estate Law Section Council, Illinois State Bar Association. He has given presentations on federal tax liens, partition and quiet title suits, mortgage foreclosures, and recent judicial decisions. He is currently Chair of the Real Estate Law Section Council, Illinois State Bar Association. He has testified before the Illinois General Assembly and Senate on proposed legislation. He maintains membership in the Quad City Estate Planning Council.

Education: JD 1975, Southwestern University, Los Angeles; BA 1972, Southern Illinois University.

Admitted: 1975 Illinois; 1975 U.S. Dist. Ct. (C. Dist. IL); 1985 U.S. Dist. Ct. (N. Dist. IL); 1994 U.S. Ct. App. (7th Cir.); 1995 U.S. Tax Ct.

Employment History: Principal/Associate 1988-present, Katz, McHard, Balch, Lefstein & Fieweger, P.C.; Partner 1978-87, White & Koenig.

Professional Associations: ISBA [Real Estate Law Section Council 1979-83, 1988-present (Secretary 1994; Vice Chair 1995; Chair 1996); Commercial Banking and Bankruptcy Section Council 1984-87; Continuing Legal Education Committee 1996-present]; Illinois Bar Foundation (Charter Member); ABA [Real Property, Probate and Trust Law Section; Foreclosure Remedies Summary Committee (Contributor)].

Community Involvement: First Congregational United Church of Christ, Moline, Illinois [Diaconate Board 1988-95 (Chair 1994); Board of Trustees]; Moline Rotary Club; Trinity Medical Center Planned Giving (Advisory Council).

Firm: One of the largest law firms in its community, Katz, McHard, Balch, Lefstein & Fieweger, P.C., has maintained a diverse general practice for over 80 years. The firm has attorneys who concentrate in tax, labor, and other areas of business law, as well as a quality trial and appellate practice.

J. LAIRD LAMBERT - *Attorney at Law* - 910 Second Avenue, Suite 300 - Rockford, IL 61104 - Phone: (815) 969-8800, Fax: (815) 969-8821 - *See complete biographical profile in the Real Estate Law Chapter, page 297.*

FRED L. WHAM III - *Attorney at Law* - 124 North Water Street, Suite 202 - Rockford, IL 61107 - Phone: (815) 964-6717, Fax: (815) 962-6153 - *See complete biographical profile in the Family Law Chapter, page 209.*

CENTRAL ILLINOIS

A. CLAY COX - *Hayes, Hammer, Miles, Cox & Ginzkey* - 202 North Center Street - P.O. Box 3067 - Bloomington, IL 61702-3067 - Phone: (309) 828-7331, Fax: (309) 827-7423 - *See complete biographical profile in the Tax Law Chapter, page 330.*

•**DANIEL J. GREER:** Mr. Greer practices estate planning, wills and trusts law, real estate law, and tax law.
Education: JD 1966, University of Illinois; BA 1963, Ohio Wesleyan University.
Admitted: 1966 Illinois.
Employment History: 1987-present, Stine, Wolter & Greer; Sole Practitioner, 1968-86.
Professional Associations: ISBA; Sangamon County Bar Assn.
Community Involvement: Mr. Greer is active in his church, the Optimist Club, and Habitat for Humanity.
Firm: Stine, Wolter & Greer offers a wide scope of services. The firm's members concentrate in various areas of law. The firm emphasizes first-person contact with its clients throughout the period of representation. The office is centrally located near the state government complex and the courts. *See complete firm profile in Appendix A.*

DANIEL J. GREER
Stine, Wolter & Greer
426 South Fifth Street
Springfield, IL 62701
Phone: (217) 744-1000
Fax: (217) 744-1444

J. MICHAEL MATHIS - *The Mathis Law Firm* - 7707 Knoxville Avenue, Suite 105 - Peoria, IL 61614 - Phone: (309) 692-2600, Fax: (309) 692-2633, 800: (800) 2-MATHIS - *See complete biographical profile in the Elder Law Chapter, page 130.*

•**WILLIAM A. PEITHMANN:** Mr. Peithmann concentrates his practice in estate planning and administration and the connected areas of wealth management; closely held businesses, particularly farm operations; business succession planning; elder law; commercial and farm real estate; and gift, estate and income taxation of all types. Particular emphasis is on custom-designed business and estate plans employing advanced asset protection and tax avoidance techniques, including generation skipping transfer tax-exempt trusts. Mr. Peithmann is a frequent writer and lecturer on estate planning and administration for the Illinois State Bar Association, the Illinois Institute for Continuing Legal Education, and the American Bar Association on such topics as qualified disclaimers; powers of appointment; the practical use of living trusts; and the various features of the generation skipping transfer tax. He is a coauthor of the standard Illinois reference work, *Illinois Estate Administration* (Illinois Institute for Continuing Legal Education, 1993, Supp. 1995).
Education: JD 1978, University of Denver; BA 1975, Loretto Heights College.
Admitted: 1979 Illinois; 1978 Colorado; 1980 California.
Professional Associations: American College of Trust and Estate Counsel; ABA [Real Property, Probate and Trust Law Section (B-1 Generation Skipping Transfers Committee, Vice Chair 1994-present)]; ISBA [Board of Governors 1995-present; Assembly 1994-present; Special Committee on Living Trusts; Trusts and Estate Section Council 1988-96 (Chair 1994-95)].
Firm: The Peithmann Law Office was founded in 1948 by Ortheldo A. Peithmann. William Peithmann joined his father in 1985, after several years practicing international corporate and commercial law in Los Angeles and San Francisco. The firm has been providing personalized business, estate and tax counsel to central Illinois families for almost 50 years. The Peithmann Law Office accepts clients from all five Illinois judicial districts, and increasingly is retained to assist other Illinois attorneys on a special project basis. Other areas of law the firm concentrates in include tax, agriculture, real estate and small business.

WILLIAM A. PEITHMANN
Peithmann Law Office
111 South Main Street
P.O. Box 228
Farmer City, IL 61842
Phone: (309) 928-3390

Extensive Experience In:
• Wills & Probate
• Living Trusts
• Farm Estate Planning

•**GALE W. SAINT:** Mr. Saint has practiced in the areas of estate planning, trusts, and estate administration for over 25 years, including wills, trusts, estate, gift and generation skipping transfer planning, business transition arrangements, charitable trusts, and related techniques for wealth preservation and transfer. He has been a frequent lecturer for the Illinois Institute for Continuing Legal Education, Illinois State Bar Association Law Education Series, as well as related programs for CPAs, insurance and financial planners, as well as public estate planning educational forums.
Education: JD 1962, Valparaiso University; BA 1959, Valparaiso University.
Admitted: 1973 Illinois; 1962 Minnesota; 1973 U.S. Dist. Ct. (C. Dist. IL); 1974 U.S. Tax Ct.
Employment History: 1973-present, Saint & Carmichael, P.C.; Director of Insurance Planning 1967-73, County Life Insurance Company; Trust Officer 1971-73, IAA Trust Company, Bloomington, Illinois.
Professional Associations: American College of Trust and Estate Counsel (Fellow 1991-present); The American College of Life Underwriters (Chartered Life Underwriter 1969); Life Management Institute [Life Officers Management Assn. (Fellow 1971)]; American Academy of Hospital Attorneys (Fellow).
Community Involvement: Mennonite Hospital Assn. (Board of Directors; President 1978-83); various church and local charitable activities.
Firm: Saint & Carmichael, P.C., is a five-lawyer firm with offices in Bloomington and Pekin, Illinois. In addition to estate and trust work, the firm provides services in civil litigation, health and hospital law, business organization, and tax planning.

GALE W. SAINT
Saint & Carmichael, P.C.
115 West Jefferson Street
Suite 303
Bloomington, IL 61701
Phone: (309) 829-7086
Fax: (309) 827-5025
E-mail: saintlaw@saintlaw.com
Web: http://www.saintlaw.com

Extensive Experience In:
• Health Law

Chapter 16: Estate Planning, Wills & Trusts Law

STEPHEN K. SHEFFLER - *Pelini & Sheffler* - 501 West Church Street - P.O. Box 1486 - Champaign, IL 61820 - Phone: (217) 359-6242, Fax: (217) 359-6271 - *See complete biographical profile in the Bankruptcy Law Chapter, page 75.*

STANLEY N. WASSER - *Feldman & Wasser* - 1307 South Seventh Street - P.O. Box 2418 - Springfield, IL 62705 - Phone: (217) 544-3403, Fax: (217) 544-1593 - *See complete biographical profile in the Employment Law Chapter, page 150.*

SOUTHERN ILLINOIS

Donald C. Rikli

Attorney at Law
914 Broadway
Highland, IL 62249-1897

Phone: (618) 654-2364
Fax: (618) 654-4752
800: (800) 24-RIKLI
(247-4554)

Extensive Experience In:

- Living Trusts
- Charitable Remainder Trusts

•**DONALD C. RIKLI:** Mr. Rikli practices estate planning, probate, trust, real estate, and elder law. He handles probate administration and settlement of many estates of decedents, minors and disabled adults, will contests, trust contests, contested claims and other probate litigation, including appeals to the Illinois Appellate and Supreme Courts and the U.S. Supreme Court. Mr. Rikli is a frequent lecturer at law schools, bar association meetings and seminars, and continuing legal education institutes in 30 states and Canada. He has written more than 60 articles published in legal publications for attorneys, and the book, *The Illinois Probate System*. He has been the editor, or a member of the boards of editors, of nine legal publications. He was named Sole Practitioner of the Year by the American Bar Association, Section of General Practice, in 1990. He has received four Awards of Excellence from LawPhone, including Law Firm of the Year.
Education: JD 1953, University of Illinois; AB 1951, Illinois College.
Admitted: 1953 Illinois; 1961 U.S. Dist. Ct. (S. Dist. IL); 1968 U.S. Dist. Ct. (N. Dist. IL); 1968 U.S. Ct. App. (7th Cir.); 1968 U.S. Claims Ct.; 1968 U.S. Tax Ct.; 1974 U.S. Sup. Ct.; 1991 U.S. Ct. App. (Military); 1992 U.S. Dist. Ct. (C. Dist. IL).
Employment History: Attorney 1953-present, Donald C. Rikli.
Representative Clients: Gehrig's Store Company; O. J. Koehler Trucking Co.; The Chocolate Affair, Inc.; Highland Home; Illinois South Conference United Church of Christ; Eagle/Watson Farms; Gutzlers Tom-Boy Markets, Inc.; Kershaw Land Trust; Wicks Organ Co.; Helvetia Sharpshooters Society.
Professional Associations: ABA [House of Delegates 1991-93; Section of General Practice (Chair 1990-91; Council 1981-93)]; ISBA [Estate Planning, Probate, and Trust Law Section 1976-81 (Council 1976-81; Secretary 1978-80)]; Madison County Bar Assn. (President 1966-67); American College of Trust and Estate Counsel (Fellow 1967-present).
Community Involvement: Jennie Latzer Kaeser Educational Trust (Board of Overseers 1982-present); Dana Deibert Scholarship Trust (Scholarship Selection Board 1987-present); Friends of St. Joseph Hospital Foundation (Board of Directors 1986-91); Highland-Madison County Fair Assn. (Board of Directors 1954-65); Highland Chamber of Commerce (President 1960-62); Evangelical United Church of Christ, Highland (Consistory 1960-63, 1992-95).
Firm: Mr. Rikli's firm strives to provide quality services to individuals and families in the areas of estate planning, probate law, trust law, real estate law, and elder law in a time-efficient and cost-efficient manner. Each member keeps up-to-date on changes in the law by maintaining a current law library, attending frequent continuing legal education seminars, and frequently writing articles and lecturing to lawyers and lay audiences. *Mr. Rikli also practices Elder Law and Real Estate Law.*

TERRELL "TERRY" LEE SHARP - *Law Office of Terry Sharp, P.C.* - 1115 Harrison Street - P.O. Box 906 - Mt. Vernon, IL 62864 - Phone: (618) 242-0246, Fax: (618) 242-1170, 800: (800) 769-7000 - *See complete biographical profile in the Bankruptcy Law Chapter, page 76.*

CHAPTER 17

FAMILY LAW

Family law touches most people at least once in their lives. When getting married or dissolving a marriage, reaching adulthood, or having children, people need to be aware of how their legal status changes. Most family law is state law; there is very little federal regulation of families. Because each state has the authority to regulate families within its borders, this chapter is specific to Illinois.

REACHING THE AGE OF MAJORITY IN ILLINOIS

In Illinois, a person legally becomes an adult at age 18. With a person's 18th birthday come most of the rights, privileges, responsibilities, and obligations of adulthood. These rights include the right to vote, the right to make contracts, the right to marry without permission from parents or guardians, and the right to serve on a jury.

MARRIAGE IN ILLINOIS

Common law marriage is not recognized in Illinois. People must be legally married to be entitled to spousal rights and to be bound by spousal obligations. A legal marriage requires a marriage license and an exchange of vows before an official authorized to formalize the vows. Officials authorized to conduct weddings include clerks of court, judges, and licensed religious officials. The exchange of vows must be witnessed by at least two other individuals.

WHO MAY MARRY

In Illinois, an unmarried man and an unmarried woman, both of sound mind and both at least 18 years old, may marry without the permission of others. Men and women between 16 and 18 years old may marry if they have the consent of both parties' parents or guardians, or with judicial approval. Illinois law prohibits marriage of people who are already married, as well as marriage between an ancestor and descendant, brother and sister (even if siblings by adoption), aunt and nephew, and uncle and niece. First cousins are not allowed to marry each other unless they are both at least 50 years old or they can prove one of the parties to the marriage is permanently and irreversibly sterile. Illinois is obligated by the Constitution of the United States to give full faith and credit to any marriage recognized by any other state.

LICENSE REQUIREMENTS

Marriage licenses may be obtained through the clerk of court in any county in Illinois. Each applicant must provide his or her name, address, date and place of birth, gender, social security number, and occupation. If either party was married before, the application must include information concerning the previous marriage, and where and when it was dissolved or declared invalid, or the date and place of death of the former spouse. The application also must include the parents' names and addresses and a statement as to whether the parties are related to each other. Marriage license applications must be signed by the parties and accompanied by a licensing fee and proof that the parties are of legal age to marry and that the marriage is not prohibited for any reason.

When the county clerk provides the marriage license, he or she gives the couple written information regarding sexually transmitted diseases, inherited metabolic diseases, and fetal alcohol syndrome. Within ten days after the marriage is solemnized, the person officiating the marriage ceremony must complete the marriage certificate form and forward it to the county clerk, who then registers the marriage.

PRENUPTIAL AGREEMENTS

A prenuptial or premarital agreement, also known as an antenuptial agreement, is a contract between parties made before they are married regarding what rights each has to the other's property upon dissolution of the marriage, legal separation, or death. Prenuptial agreements made in Illinois after January 1, 1990, are governed by the Uniform Premarital Agreement Act. These contracts are valid and enforceable in Illinois if they are made voluntarily, are fair and reasonable, use precise words, are in writing, and are signed by both parties.

Chapter 17: Family Law

Rights Within Marriage

Spouses have an obligation to support one another and their children. Providing necessities such as food, clothing, and shelter is the responsibility of both spouses. Married individuals have the right to one's own earnings, to sue and be sued (including the right to sue each other), to make contracts, to act as each other's attorney in fact or agent, and to transfer property. Spouses are responsible for each other's contracts, debts, and damages, and must provide a home and support. When one spouse dies, the surviving spouse typically has the right to receive a certain percentage of his or her spouse's property. It is difficult, though not impossible, to disinherit a partner to a valid marriage.

TERMINATION OF MARRIAGE

Dissolution, also known as divorce, ends a marriage. A marriage is dissolved by a Judgment of Dissolution of Marriage issued by an Illinois state court. The court also decides related issues such as custody, visitation, child support, spousal maintenance, division of property, and responsibility for payment of marital debts.

Grounds for Dissolution

In order for an Illinois court to grant a divorce, at least one of the parties must be a resident of Illinois at the time the action is filed and must maintain that residency for a minimum of 90 days prior to the entry of the judgment. Divorce may be granted on no-fault grounds or on fault grounds.

A judge may grant a no-fault divorce if the parties have lived separately for a continuous period of more than two years, there has been an irretrievable breakdown of the marriage due to irreconcilable differences, and attempts to reconcile have failed or future attempts would not be in the best interest of the family. If the parties are in agreement that the marriage should be dissolved, and they have lived separately for six months, they may waive the two-year separation requirement by signing a written stipulation.

Divorce granted on fault grounds means that the dissolution of the marriage is based on one spouse's fault or misconduct. Although the fault of a party may not be considered by a judge in dividing property, awarding child support, or awarding spousal maintenance, wrongful behavior may be considered when the judge is determining child custody if the behavior is relevant to the child's or children's best interests. In Illinois, the grounds for a fault divorce include the following:

- Adultery (sexual intercourse with another person of the opposite sex)
- Attempted murder of the spouse
- Conviction of a felony
- Bigamy (the spouse was already married to another at the time of marriage)
- Desertion (the spouse has willfully left the home for one year or more)
- Extreme and repeated physical or mental cruelty
- Habitual drunkenness or excessive use of addictive drugs for two years or more
- Infection of the spouse with a communicable sexually transmitted disease
- Permanent impotence at the time of the marriage

The party alleging one of these grounds must also allege and prove that the ground occurred without any provocation on his or her part. For example, a wife who files for divorce based on desertion must also allege and prove that she did not provoke the husband to desert her.

Minimizing Litigation and Attorney Fees in Divorce Cases

Although Illinois law does not require that a person be represented by an attorney, due to the complexities of the substantive laws and procedural laws in divorce cases, each person should be represented by an attorney so that their rights can be protected. Prior to seeing an attorney for a divorce, a person should make a list of all assets and debts which they know exist, gather available information concerning those assets and debts, as well as the incomes of both spouses.

People who are going through a divorce may agree with one another as to the resolution of all of the issues that have or will arise in their case; in doing so, Illinois encourages the use of postnuptial agreements, commonly referred to as Marital Settlement Agreements. Such an agreement is a contract which adjusts, defines, and details all of the rights, duties, and obligations which will result when the marital relationship is dissolved. The contract usually becomes incorporated into and becomes part of the Judgment of Dissolution of Marriage, although in certain cases, only certain sections of the contract should be incorporated into the final Judgment of Dissolution.

Although these agreements may be oral, the better practice is that they be written. These agreements normally resolve such issues as child custody and visitation, child support, spousal maintenance, division of marital property and debts, allocation of attorney fees, as well as many other related issues. It is important to note that matters involving support and property division may have serious income tax consequences which need to be addressed.

Matters on which the parties disagree must be decided by a court. The litigation process may begin with court appearances to resolve temporary custody, visitation, child support, spousal maintenance, and attorney fee issues, as well as to have injunction orders entered to prevent dissipation of property. After the attorneys have discovered the existence of all of the property of the parties and the value thereof, have ascertained the income and debts of the parties, and have completed discovery regarding all other issues in the case, the parties may request a pretrial conference with a judge to try to settle all disputed issues. Any issues that are not settled at the pretrial conference must be decided by the court at a trial.

CHILD CUSTODY

Child custody is determined by a court based upon the best interests of the children. Some of the factors which the courts consider in determining what is in the best interests of the children are the sincerity of each parent's desire to have custody, the wishes of the children, the interaction and interrelationship of the children with their parents, siblings and others, the children's adjustment to their home, school, and community, the mental and physical health of the individuals involved, past physical violence on the part of each parent, the ongoing occurrence of domestic abuse, and the willingness and ability of each parent to encourage a close and continuing relationship between the other parent and the children.

Having custody of a minor child can mean sole legal custody, which is the right to make major decisions affecting the child's life (such as medical care, education and religion), and normally also includes physical custody, which is the actual possession and control of the child subject to reasonable visitation by the non-custodial parent. If the parents have joint legal custody, the children reside mostly with one parent, known as the residential parent, who is responsible for the routine decisions affecting the children, but both parents share the responsibility for and have a say in making the major decisions regarding the children. If they have joint physical custody, both parents are involved in even the day-to-day decisions affecting their children, and the children spend time with both parents, although not necessarily an equal amount of time with each. In matters where the parties have joint custody, the time each parent spends with their children is known as parenting time. Also, in order for a court to award joint custody, it must determine that the parents have the ability to cooperate effectively and consistently with each other in matters that directly affect the joint parenting of the children. The court must also order the parents to produce a Joint Parenting Agreement which, among other things, will normally provide for mediation of future disputes regarding the children. Child custody is modifiable by a court if changing circumstances warrant a modification.

VISITATION AND PARENTING TIME

Typically, the non-custodial parent is granted visitation rights unless the court feels that such visits would be detrimental to the children. Parents may make child visitation agreements themselves, but if a friendly agreement cannot be reached, the court sets a schedule for visitation, or it orders that the non-custodial parent be allowed reasonable visitation. Since the term "reasonable" is very subjective, the better practice is to have a detailed visitation provision so that the parties and the children have more certainty as to when the children will be with each parent. Certain other people, such as grandparents, who have close relationships with the children, may also be allowed some form of visitation. Visitation is modifiable by a court if changing circumstances warrant a modification.

CHILD SUPPORT

Child support is financial assistance provided by the non-custodial parent (or, in the case of joint custody, by the non-residential parent) to help support the children. Child support is not deductible by the paying parent and is not taxable to the recipient parent. The amount of child support a court orders is based on statutory guidelines which militate that a percentage of the payor's net income from all sources be paid depending on the number of children. For one child, the percentage is 20 percent, two children 25 percent, three children 32 percent, four children 40 percent, five children 45 percent, and six or more children 50 percent. The court can consider other factors affecting the amount of child support it will order, including each parent's income, the children's needs (including special needs such as medical and psychological needs), the needs of the parents, and the standard of living the children would have enjoyed if the parties remained married. Child support is an independent obligation and must be maintained despite any other problems between the parents, such as disagreements about visitation.

A recently enacted federal law requires employers to withhold wages from employees who are under a court order to provide child support after January 1, 1994. In Illinois, the law provides that if a court receives evidence that a parent is even one month behind in paying child support, the court must order the payment to be withheld from the person's income. The court may also enter an order requiring the paying parent's employer to withhold wages from the paying parent and pay that sum directly to the recipient parent or to the clerk of the court who sends it to the recipient parent. A court also may order an unemployed person who is obligated to pay child support to seek employment and to provide the court with proof that he or she is diligently looking for employment. Child support is modifiable by a court if changing circumstances warrant a modification. Child support can only be modified (increased, decreased or abated) by a court, and past due payments of child support accrue interest and are not dischargeable in bankruptcy.

Spousal Maintenance

Spousal maintenance, formerly known as alimony, is financial support provided by one ex-spouse to the other. Spousal maintenance is normally deductible by the paying parent and taxable to the recipient parent if certain criteria are met. Either spouse may seek spousal maintenance. Factors that a court evaluates in setting spousal maintenance include the income and property of each party, including marital property apportioned and non-marital property assigned to the parties; the needs of each party; the present and future earning capacity of each party; any impairment of the present and future earning capacity of the party seeking maintenance due to that party devoting time to domestic duties or having foregone or delayed education, training, employment, or career opportunities due to the marriage; the time necessary to enable the party seeking maintenance to acquire appropriate education, training, and employment, and whether that party is able to support himself or herself through appropriate employment or is the custodian of a child making it appropriate that the custodian not seek employment; the standard of living established during the marriage; the duration of the marriage; the age and the physical and emotional condition of both parties; the tax consequences of the property division upon the respective economic circumstances of the parties; and contributions and services by the party seeking maintenance to the education, training, career or career potential, or license of the other spouse. Maintenance may be either temporary or permanent. If a party agrees to give up a claim for maintenance, it may not be renewed at a later date unless the right to do so is reserved. Maintenance can only be modified (increased, decreased, or abated) by a court, and past due payments of maintenance are not dischargeable in bankruptcy.

Division of Property

In divorce actions, courts are authorized to fairly divide all marital property owned by either spouse alone, together with a third party or with the other spouse. Marital property is defined as all property acquired by either spouse during the marriage, except the following, which is known as non-marital property: property acquired before the marriage; property acquired by gift or inheritance; property acquired in exchange for property acquired before the marriage or in exchange for property acquired by gift or inheritance; property acquired by a spouse after a Judgment of Legal Separation; property excluded by valid agreement of the parties; and any judgment or property obtained by judgment awarded to one spouse from the other spouse. For purposes of distribution of property, all property acquired by either spouse after the marriage and before a Judgment of Dissolution of Marriage or Declaration of Invalidity of Marriage, including non-marital property transferred into some form of co-ownership between the spouses, is presumed to be marital property, regardless of whether title is held individually or by the spouses in some form of co-ownership.

In a divorce proceeding, the court will assign each spouse's non-marital property to that spouse and will also divide their marital property, without regard to marital misconduct, in fair and equitable proportions (not necessarily equally) considering all relevant factors, including the contribution of each party to the acquisition, preservation, or increase or decrease in value of the marital or non-marital property, including the contribution of a spouse as a homemaker or to the family unit; the dissipation by each party of the marital or non-marital property; the value of the property assigned to each spouse; the duration of the marriage; the relevant economic circumstances of each spouse when the division of property is to become effective, including the desirability of awarding the family home, or the right to live in it for reasonable periods, to the spouse having custody of the children; any obligations and rights arising from a prior marriage of either party; any valid antenuptial agreement of the parties; the age, health, station, occupation, amount and sources of income, vocational skills, employability, estate, liabilities, and needs of each of the parties; the custodial provisions for any children; whether the apportionment is in lieu of or in addition to maintenance; the reasonable opportunity of each spouse for future acquisition of capital assets and income; and the tax consequences of the property division upon the respective economic circumstances of the parties.

Special attention is paid to the particular needs of the parties in making the division. In the case of a business or another kind of property that cannot be split, the court will award the property to one spouse and order that party to pay the other for the lost interest in the property. Pensions and other retirement assets accumulated during the marriage are also subject to equitable distribution. In Illinois, a spouse who contributed support and financial resources while the other received an education is entitled to some compensation for his or her investment. It is important to note that marital debts must also be equitably apportioned between the parties.

INVALID MARRIAGES

A Declaration of Invalidity of Marriage (formerly called an annulment) is a judgment issued by a court finding that a couple's marriage is invalid and thus, never legally existed. A distinction must be made between void and voidable marriages. Void marriages are those which never legally existed for any purpose, such as bigamous marriages and marriages between certain family members too closely related by blood. Voidable marriages are those where one of the parties may bring an action to have the marriage declared invalid because of an impediment which existed at the time of the marriage. Voidable marriages may result in cases of fraud or when proper consent for the marriage was not obtained. For example, if one party engaged in fraud regarding his or her willingness to cohabit or to consummate the marriage, or was physically incapable of consummating the marriage, the marriage may be declared invalid. If a party has engaged in fraud regarding paternity or pregnancy, or was under age 18 and did not have parental consent or judicial approval at the time of the marriage, the court may declare the marriage invalid. It is important to note that there are time limits imposed by law wherein a party to a voidable marriage must seek to have the marriage declared invalid or they will be found to have ratified the marriage and have thus waived their right to invalidate the marriage. It is also important to note that a legal annulment is different from an annulment granted by a church. A religious annulment is spiritual, rather than legal in nature, and does not affect the legal status of the marriage. Likewise, a legal invalidation may not satisfy the requirements for a religious annulment. Also, children born during a marriage that later is declared invalid are legitimate. Finally, if a person has entered into an invalid marriage with the good faith belief that they entered into a valid marriage, they may be entitled to maintenance from the other party.

LEGAL SEPARATION

A legal separation involves many of the same procedures as dissolution. A court may make decisions regarding custody, visitation, child support, spousal maintenance, and attorney fees. However, the court does not decide the property rights of the parties. After a Judgment of Legal Separation, the couple remains legally married, and unless and until a Judgment of Dissolution is entered, remarriage is forbidden. A legal separation is granted on the basis of a party living separate and apart from their spouse without fault. Sometimes a legal separation is sought by those whose religious beliefs prohibit divorce but who still desire child support and spousal maintenance. It should be noted that any property acquired by a spouse after the entry of a Judgment of Legal Separation is excluded from marital property should the parties subsequently obtain a dissolution.

PATERNITY

Paternity is the condition of being the father of a child. While the identity of a child's mother usually is obvious from birth, the identity of the father may be unclear. Decisions regarding child custody, visitation, and child support frequently turn on whether a court has established a man's paternity of a child.

Illinois law presumes a man is the father of a child if any of the following elements apply:

- He and the child's mother were married to each other at the time the child was born or conceived
- He and the child's mother marry after the child is born, and he consents to being named as the child's father on the birth certificate
- He and the child's mother have signed an acknowledgment of paternity in accordance with Illinois Department of Public Aid rules
- He and the child's mother have signed a petition to establish the parent and child relationship by consent, in accordance with the Illinois Parentage Act

ABUSE

Abuse is not easily defined. The legal definition of abuse is evolving and changing in response to society's changing understanding of the problem. More members of society are becoming responsible for reporting and preventing abuse. For example, under Illinois law, health care workers are obligated to provide suspected victims of domestic abuse with immediate and detailed information about the services available to them. Other professionals must report abuse they know about or suspect. Abuse of family members is against the law, but different rules and standards apply to different categories of abuse.

DOMESTIC ABUSE

Domestic abuse—also called domestic violence—is defined by the Illinois Domestic Violence Act of 1986 as physical abuse, harassment, interference with personal liberty, willful deprivation, or intimidation of a family or household member. When people talk about domestic abuse they usually mean the abuse of a woman by her present or former husband or boyfriend; "child abuse" and "elder abuse" often are referred to separately. Domestic abuse includes actual or threatened physical harm, sexual abuse, and assault to the extent that immediate physical harm is feared. The term also includes emotional abuse, such as harassment, intimidation, and threats.

There are several options available to a victim of domestic abuse. A victim may file criminal charges, file a civil suit seeking damages, or seek an order of protection against the abuser. Usually, the first step is to seek an order of protection from a family or county court.

Orders of Protection

An order of protection is a court order prohibiting the abuser (the respondent) from continuing the abuse against the person bringing the action (the petitioner) or against any minor children in the household. The order forbids the offender from physically harming or causing fear of harm. The order is enforceable throughout the state of Illinois.

Requirements

Orders of protection can be obtained at the circuit courthouse in the county where the victim lives. To protect the victim and substantiate his or her claim against an abuser, it is important that application be made as soon as possible after the abuse occurs. The petition for an order of protection usually must be made by the victim; however, if the victim is unable to file the petition due to age, disability, or health, someone may file the petition on the victim's behalf.

For a court order to be granted, a petition must be supported with evidence of the abuse; thus, the abused person must fill out an affidavit describing the events or incidents surrounding the abuse, the effects of the abuse on the petitioner, and the need for protection. When completing the paperwork, it is helpful if the abused person provides a picture of the abuser. If a picture is unavailable, a description of the offender is needed along with the offender's work and home addresses. A prepared statement of all incidents of abuse, past and present, and including dates and notes, can help document the need for protection.

If necessary, the abused person may request an emergency order of protection. These orders also are called temporary or *ex parte* orders of protection. An emergency order might be necessary when an abused person is in danger and the protection is needed immediately. This kind of order of protection is valid only for up to 21 days but may be extended by the court for good cause shown.

Hearing

A hearing at which a judge will consider whether to issue a long-term (up to two years) plenary order of protection normally is set within 21 days but may be extended by the court for good cause shown. Further, upon two days' notice to the petitioner, a respondent subject to an emergency order of protection may appear and petition the court for a rehearing of the original *ex parte* order of protection. The hearing is held so that the abused person and the person accused of abuse can tell the judge about the events surrounding the alleged abuse. In order to notify the person accused of the abuse of the hearing, the sheriff of the county in which the accused lives serves the papers on the accused.

Regardless of whether the accused person attends the court hearing, the abused person—or a representative if he or she is unable to attend due to age or disability—must be present. The hearing is the opportunity to present evidence of abuse and for the person accused of the abuse to respond. At the hearing, the person alleging abuse should present medical records, police reports, and all other factual data which may be used as evidence of the abuse.

At this point, the judge usually rules on the matter by granting the petition or dismissing the matter. In order to grant the petition, the judge must believe that the petitioner needs protection for his or her safety. If the judge dismisses the matter, he or she does not believe that the request for protection is supported by the evidence.

Usually an order of protection prohibits the offender from contact with the victim, including visits to the victim's school or workplace when the victim is present. In some cases, the court may order a trial for cases in which the abuse is denied. A judge also may include other orders in the order for protection, such as temporarily changing child custody or visitation arrangements of children, granting the petitioner exclusive use of the residence, making the abuser pay restitution or receive counseling, or amending child support or spousal maintenance arrangements.

Violations of Orders of Protection

When an order of protection is granted and the offender attempts to violate the order, the police should be contacted through the 911 emergency system and notified of the order. Police officers must respond immediately, and they have a duty to do everything possible to prevent further abuse. Once an order of protection is enforced by the police (usually by removing the abuser from the premises), a complete police report should be filed documenting the incident. Police officers may arrest the abuser.

Violating an order is a criminal offense. Even if the officer does not make an arrest, he or she still must inform the victim of his or her right to request criminal proceedings, and advise the victim to seek medical help, take photographs to document the abuse, and keep evidence such as damaged clothing. Law enforcement officers also must file reports of every incident and investigate any believable allegations of abuse.

Changing an Order

If circumstances arise making a change in the order necessary, a petition must be filed to set another hearing in the same court. The process is similar to that described above. A modification of the order of protection may be made if the abuser has violated the order since it was issued, or if the petitioner wishes to add another provision to the order that was not included originally. If an extension of the protection period is needed, the petitioner should file a motion with the court stating there has been no significant change in circumstances since the order was issued.

CHILD ABUSE

Child abuse is a serious problem that may take many forms, including neglect, physical abuse, mental injury, and sexual abuse. Threatened injury, including any statement, overt act, condition, or status that would be considered a risk of child abuse, is also included in the definition of child abuse. Illinois has numerous laws concerned with protecting children from abuse, including the Abused and Neglected Child Reporting Act, the Children's Advocacy Center Act, and the Child Sexual Abuse Prevention Act.

Neglect is the failure of a person responsible for a child to supply necessary food, clothing, shelter, or medical care when that person is able to do so, or the failure to protect the child from imminent and serious danger to his or her physical or mental health. Neglect may only be charged against a person who is legally responsible for the child. Neglect does not, however, cover instances where a parent or guardian in good faith relies on spiritual prayer for a sick child.

Physical abuse is any physical injury, actual or threatened, inflicted upon a child by other than accidental means by a person responsible for the child's well-being. Physical abuse also includes any physical injury that cannot be explained by the child's medical history, and any means of discipline or control not authorized by law as acceptable for use with persons who are mentally challenged or impaired.

Mental injury is any harm done to a child's psychological capacity or emotional stability. Evidence of such harm is any observable or substantial impairment of a child's ability to function normally as compared with other children of the same culture. Repeated and habitual mental or emotional abuse by the person responsible for the care and nurturing of the child can cause serious problems in the child. Symptoms of mental injury may include emotionally disturbed behavior, low self-esteem, inappropriate interaction with others, inability to communicate with others, extreme hostility and anger, anti-social behavior, and speech and learning disorders.

Sexual abuse occurs when any person in a position of authority over a child has sexual contact with the child. Sexual contact includes any touching, fondling, or molestation, clothed or naked, of intimate parts of the child or the abuser. Intimate parts include the genitals, groin, inner thighs, buttocks or breasts. A person in a position of authority over a child includes a parent or person acting in the role or place of a parent. A person in a position of authority also includes anyone responsible for, either directly or through another person, the care, supervision, health or welfare of a child, no matter how brief, at the time of the abuse. Sexual abuse can also include involving a child in prostitution or pornography.

Reporting Child Abuse

Neglect and abuse are leading causes of death in children. By law, certain members of society, by virtue of their professions and positions, are required to report child abuse. Persons required to report abuse—known as mandatory reporters—include health care professionals, teachers, law enforcement officials, child care providers, and social workers. Virtually anyone who works directly with children to provide care, protection, and supervision is required to report instances, actual or suspected, of child abuse.

Mandatory reporters are obligated to report any abuse or neglect immediately to the Illinois Department of Children and Family Services (DCFS). Failure of a mandatory reporter to report suspected child abuse is a class A misdemeanor, unless the reporter is a physician, in which case the physician will be reported to the Illinois State Medical Disciplinary Board.

Persons who report abuse or neglect in good faith are immune from civil or criminal liability. This means that if an investigation shows there was no abuse, the reporter cannot be sued as long as he or she reported the alleged child abuse with an honest belief and without knowledge of any facts or events contradicting the abuse or neglect.

Contents of a Report of Child Abuse or Neglect

Child protective service workers must request information from a person reporting child abuse. To expedite the attention given to a child in an abusive or neglected situation, the reporter should have the following items ready for report:

- Names and addresses of the child and his or her parent(s) or guardian(s)
- Age, race, and sex of the child
- Events surrounding the known or suspected abuse, including the extent of injuries and any evidence of prior abuse
- Names and addresses of the alleged abuser(s)
- Information about the family of the victim, including information about other children in the home
- Name, occupation, and actions taken by the reporter
- Any other information regarding the child or family that might be helpful

If a child is in immediate danger, any person may report actual or suspected abuse to law enforcement through the emergency 911 system. The name of the individual reporting the abuse or neglect must be kept confidential by the DCFS and may only be released by consent of the reporter or by court order.

After an Abuse Report

Once a report is filed, the DCFS must protect the child and other children in the family while trying to keep the family together. Depending upon the urgency of the report, an investigation usually follows. If a child is in immediate danger, the child may be removed from the home, even against the parent's or guardian's wishes, on a temporary basis. If a DCFS worker believes the child should be kept away from the home for the child's safety, a court order is necessary.

Investigation of Child Abuse

In investigating a report of child abuse or neglect, DCFS workers are not required to obtain parental permission before interviewing the victim of the alleged abuse. By the time the investigation concludes, however, the parent or guardian must be informed that the child has been interviewed.

The initial objectives of the investigation by DCFS workers are to evaluate the existence of any physical or emotional damage to the child, identify the risk of harm to the child, determine the urgency of the claim, and decide whether immediate intervention is required. After these factors have been assessed, the goals are to determine whether or not the family is a candidate for treatment, and to initiate and monitor treatment and its progress. If the worker decides that judicial intervention is needed, an action is initiated in juvenile or family court.

HIGH-RISK ADULTS

Included in the Illinois Domestic Violence Act of 1986 are provisions dealing with the problem of abuse of high-risk adults with disabilities. A high-risk adult with a disability is someone over the age of 18 who has a physical or mental disability that prevents the adult from being able to protect himself or herself. The definition includes elderly people with disabilities. Family or household members are covered under the act as persons who may be liable for abusing high-risk adults with disabilities, as well as other persons who have responsibility for these adults, including workers in hospitals, nursing homes, or other similar care facilities. Abuse of high-risk adults with disabilities includes physical abuse, sexual abuse, neglect, and exploitation, including financial exploitation. Neglect includes failure to provide food, shelter, clothing, personal hygiene, and medical care; unreasonable confinement; and failure to protect the high-risk adult from abuse or from other hazards to their health or safety.

People who know of or suspect abuse or neglect may make a report of any known or suspected incident of abuse or neglect to the Illinois Department on Aging. Law enforcement officers in Illinois are required by law to assist high-risk adults in petitioning for an order of protection. The police also have the authority to enter premises or to make warrantless arrests in situations in which there is the probability of death or great bodily harm to a high-risk adult, or to prevent criminal activity. Health care workers must assist suspected victims of abuse by offering immediate information about services available in Illinois.

OTHER REMEDIES FOR ABUSE

Any person who has been abused may seek an order of protection. In addition, the abuse of some victims must be reported by designated mandatory reporters to agencies designed to address the abuse. There are other remedies for victims of abuse. Abusers are subject to arrest for the crimes they commit. Domestic battery, aggravated battery of a child or institutionalized mentally retarded person, aggravated battery of a senior citizen, and criminal neglect of an elderly or disabled person are specific crimes in Illinois. Victims may wish to work with prosecutors to have offenders tried on criminal charges. It is also possible under some circumstances to file a civil lawsuit against offenders for damages. Criminal hearings and civil lawsuits are discussed further in the Process of a Case and Criminal Law Chapters of this *Guidebook*.

People with any questions about abuse or about other aspects of family law, such as marriage or divorce, should contact the agency or organization that deals with their problem, or should seek the advice of an attorney.

RESOURCES

Illinois Coalition Against Domestic Violence, 730 Vine Street East, #109, Springfield, IL 62703, phone: (217) 789-2830. This organization offers the following free publications in English and Spanish: *Handbook for Domestic Violence Victims* and *Illinois Domestic Violence Act: Finally . . . Relief for Victims of the Hidden Crime*.

Illinois Department of Children and Family Services, Division of Child Protection, 406 Monroe Street East, Springfield, IL 62701, phone: (217) 785-1700, Chicago phone: (312) 814-6864. Contact this organization for information, to report child abuse and neglect, or to order the free brochure, *Care Enough to Call*.

Department of Public Aid, Division of Child Support Enforcement, Prescott E. Bloom Building, 201 South Grand Avenue East, Springfield, IL 62762, phone: (217) 524-4529.

Family Violence Prevention Fund, 383 Rhode Island Street, #304, San Francisco, CA 94103-5133, phone: (415) 252-8900.

Contact the Illinois Department of Public Health, Office of Vital Records, 605 Jefferson Street West, Springfield, IL 62702-5097, phone: (217) 782-6553, for birth, divorce, death, and marriage records.

Illinois Department on Aging, Division of Older American Services, 421 Capitol Avenue East, #100, Springfield, IL 62701-1789. Call for information about elder protective services at (800) 252-8966.

Illinois State Bar Association, Illinois Bar Center, Springfield, IL 62701-1779, phone: (217) 525-1760. Call or write for the free pamphlets, *Adoption; Advice to Newly Marrieds;* and *Domestic Relations*.

National Center on Women and Family Law, Inc., 799 Broadway, #402, New York, NY 10003, phone: (212) 674-8200. Call or write for publications such as *Child Support and You*, $5 publication; *Mediation and You*, $8 publication; *Pensions*, $3 publication.

National Clearinghouse on Marital and Date Rape, 2325 Oak Street, Berkeley, CA 94708, phone: (510) 524-1582.

National Council on Child Abuse and Family Violence, 1155 Connecticut Avenue NW, #300, Washington, D.C. 20036, phone: (202) 429-6695.

This chapter was reviewed and edited by Leading Illinois Attorney Edward I. Stein.

# Family Law Leading Illinois Attorneys

Illinois' Most Respected Legal Counsel As Selected By Their Peers.

The Leading Illinois Attorneys below were recommended by their peers in a statewide survey.

The Leading Illinois Attorneys listed below were nominated as exceptional by their peers in a statewide survey conducted by American Research Corporation (ARC). ARC asked several thousand licensed Illinois attorneys to name the lawyer to whom they would send a close friend or family member in need of legal assistance in specific areas of law. The attorneys below were nominated in the area of Family Law.

Because the survey results (all practice area results combined) represent less than three percent of Illinois' practicing attorneys, this list should not be construed as a complete list. Nevertheless, it is an excellent source of highly qualified and reputable Illinois attorneys.

For information on ARC's survey methodology, see page *xi*.
For the complete list of Leading Illinois Consumer Attorneys, see page *xii*.

The Leading Illinois Attorneys below are listed alphabetically in accordance with the geographic region in which their offices are located. Note that attorneys may handle clients from a broad geographic area; attorneys are not restricted to only serving clients residing within the cities in which their offices are located.

An attorney whose name appears in bold has included a biographical profile in this chapter.

Cook & Collar Counties

Allen, Gemma B. - Chicago
Arfa, Jack A. - Chicago
Ariano, Frank V. - Elgin
Arnold, Joel D. - Westmont
Azulay, J. Daniel - Chicago, page 181
Badesch, Robert T. - Chicago, page 181
Baizer, Robert S. - Highland Park
Ballard Bostick, Shelley - Chicago
Bayard, Forrest S. - Chicago, page 182
Beermann, Jon L. - Libertyville, page 182
Beermann, Miles N. - Chicago
Bell, Brigitte Schmidt - Chicago, page 183
Bennett, Margaret A. - Oak Brook, page 183
Berger, Michael J. - Chicago
Berman, Arthur M. - Chicago
Botti, Stephen R. - Oak Brook
Bourque, Starr - Wheaton
Brodsky, Joel A. - Chicago
Broecker, Howard W. - Geneva, page 184
Bush, Anna Markley - Barrington, page 184
Bush, John R. - Bensenville
Chapski, Robert A. - Elgin
Clark, William G., Jr. - Chicago
Cohen, Michael S. - Chicago
Cole, Melvin J. - Chicago
Culver, Richard W. - Schaumburg
DaRosa, Ronald A. - Wheaton
Davenport, Linda E. - Westmont
Davis, Muller - Chicago, page 185
Deitsch, Stephen M. - Wheaton
DiMaggio, Debra A. - Chicago
Dolci, Dominick P. - Oakbrook Terrace
Downs, Robert K. - Oak Park (Chicago), page 185
Drendel, Gilbert X., Jr. - Batavia

DuCanto, Joseph N. - Chicago, page 186
Eichner, Andrew D. - Chicago
Feinberg, Joy M. - Chicago
Feiwell, George S. - Chicago
Feldman, James H. - Chicago
Felice, Richard D. - Wheaton
Field, Harold G. - Wheaton
Fields, Jane F. - Chicago, page 186
Finkel, Leon I. - Chicago
Fischer, Bella - Lake Bluff
Flanigan, Wayne B. - Waukegan
Fleck, Charles J. - Chicago, page 187
Friedman, James J. - Rolling Meadows
Friedman, James T. - Chicago, page 187
Gitlin, H. Joseph - Woodstock
Glieberman, Herbert A. - Chicago, page 188
Glimco, Joseph P., III - Downers Grove, page 188
Gold, Nan M. - Skokie
Gordon, Stuart I. - Chicago
Grant, Burton F. - Chicago, page 189
Greenberg, Sharran R. - Highland Park, page 189
Grimbau, Rochelle - Chicago
Grund, David I. - Chicago, page 190
Gurewitz, Thomas M. - Waukegan
Haddad, Susan C. - Chicago
Hanno, Diana J. - Chicago
Hanrahan, Thomas P. - Chicago
Haskin, Lyle B. - Wheaton, page 190
Hirsch, John B. - Chicago
Hogan, Judy L. - Geneva
Hogan Morrison, Kathleen - Chicago
Hopkins, David. H. - Chicago, page 191
Johnson, Dorothy B. - Chicago

Family Law Leading Illinois Attorneys

Johnston, Jay J. - Waukegan
Jumes, Leon P. - Chicago
Kalcheim, Michael W. - Chicago, page 191
Kane, Larry R. - Chicago, page 192
Katz, Stephen H. - Lake Forest, page 192
King, John P. - Glen Ellyn
Kirsh, Sanford - Chicago
Konetski, James J. - Wheaton
Korstad, Dorothy C. - Wheaton
Kostelny, Marmarie J. - Elgin
Kralovec, Michael J. - Chicago
Kuhn, Daniel L. - Naperville
Lake, Steven R. - Chicago
Lengle, Philip J. - Chicago
Lessman, Sarah P. - Waukegan
Levin, Jerome S. - Skokie
Leving, Jeffery M. - Chicago
Levy, David H. Chicago, page 193
Lichter, Sally - Libertyville, page 193
Lifshitz, Richard A. - Chicago
Litwin, Stuart N. - Chicago
London, Howard A. - Chicago
Lonergan, Susan M. - St. Charles, page 194
Longwell, Marilyn F. - Chicago
Lunardi, Steven B. - Waukegan
MacRae, Roderick E. - Chicago, page 194
Malkin, Earle A. - Chicago, page 195
Marcus, Dorene - Chicago, page 195
Marinaccio, Lee A. - Oak Brook
Martin, Mary C. - Chicago
Mathein, Veronica B. - Chicago
McGann-Ryan, Maureen J. - Chicago
McJoynt, Timothy - Downers Grove
McKeown, Denis J. - Waukegan
McNish, Robert J., Jr. - Chicago
McWilliams, Clare - Palatine
Meyers, Ted A. - Elgin
Miller, Irving - Chicago
Miller, Robin - Wheaton
Mirabella, Joseph F., Jr. - Wheaton
Mirabelli, Enrico J. - Chicago, page 196
Monco, Walter J. - Chicago
Muller, Kurt A. - Chicago, page 196
Mulryan, Rosemary - Chicago
Murphy, Sandra R. - Chicago
Nadler, Floyd N. - Chicago
Nitikman, Franklin W. - Chicago
Nottage, Rosaire - Chicago
Oney, Claudia - Chicago, page 197
Parker, Julie - Chicago
Pasulka, David P. - Chicago

Pekala, Beverly A. - Chicago, page 197
Peskind, Steven N. - Aurora, page 198
Pritikin, James B. - Chicago
Puchalski, Donald E. - Chicago
Richter, Harold - Lansing, page 198
Rinella, Bernard B. - Chicago, page 199
Roberts, Keith E., Jr. - Wheaton
Robin, Neil A. - Chicago
Roseborough, Kathleen - Chicago
Rosenberg, Russell S. - Chicago
Rosenfeld, Howard H. - Chicago, page 199
Rosing, William G. - Waukegan
Rubens, James L. - Chicago, page 200
Ryan, Catherine M. - Chicago, page 200
Schaffner, Harry - Geneva, page 201
Schiller, Donald C. - Chicago, page 201
Schlesinger, Gary L. - Libertyville, page 202
Schneider, Gregg D. Chicago
Schwarz, Benedict, II - West Dundee, page 202
Scott, William J., Jr. - Wheaton
Shaw, Matthew G. - Aurora
Siegel, Carole - Chicago
Sigman, Helen - Chicago, page 203
Skelnik, Josette - Elgin
Skipper, Robert - Chicago
Sloan, Mel - Chicago
Smirl, Dale L. - Chicago
Solon, Joseph - Elmhurst
Somers, Kathryn M. - Chicago
Stein, Arnold - Chicago, page 203
Stein, David M. - Chicago
Stein, Edward I. - Northbrook, page 204
Steinke, Edward B. - St. Charles
Stogsdill, William J., Jr. - Wheaton, page 204
Strongin, Stuart J. - Chicago
Tatnall, Susan B. - Batavia
Tighe, Mary Beth S. - Park Ridge, page 205
Toback, Alan J. - Chicago
Trafelet, Janet - Chicago
Truemper, William J. - Aurora, page 205
Veon, Leslie L. - Chicago
Wasko, Steven E. - Park Ridge
Weiler, Rory T. - Batavia, page 206
Weinstein, Melvin A. - Chicago, page 206
White, Roger A. - Lake Bluff
Williamson, Carol A. - Round Lake
Wittenberg, Michael P. - Homewood
Wolf, Ilene M. - Arlington Heights
Yavitz, David B. - Chicago
Zavett, Errol - Chicago, page 207

Chapter 17: Family Law

Northwestern Illinois Including Rockford & Quad Cities

Abate, Alex M. - Rockford
Bruce, Joseph J. - Rockford
Bute, Daniel J. - Ottawa
Butera, Richard M. - Rockford
Cicero, Paul R. - Rockford
Cox, John W., Jr. - Galena
Gaziano, Mary J. - Rockford
Gorman, Mary P. - Rockford
Granneman, Faye M. - Rockford
Greenlee, Cheri N. - Rockford
Healy, Bernard, Jr. - Rockford
Jackman, Philip A. - Galena
Jensen, Philip F. - Galena, page 207
Kelly, Roger H. - Galena
Koonmen, Karl C. - Loves Park
Kreitlow, Margaret - Rockford
Kuleck, Edward J., Jr. - Ottawa
Luchetti, Thomas D. - Rockford
Marsh, C. Stephen - Rock Island
Martenson, David L. - Rockford
Meehan, Gerald J. - Rock Island
Mindrup, Nancy H. - Rockford
Morse, Keith S. - Rockford, page 208
Neppl, James L. - Rock Island
Rudy, Sharon R. - Rockford
Scovil, Douglas C. - Rock Island
Seigler, Darrell K. - Ottawa
Spelman, James C. - Rockford
Switzer, Peter S. - Rockford, page 208
Wham, Fred L., III - Rockford, page 209
Williams, Daniel T., Jr. - Rockford
Winstein, Arthur R. - Rock Island, page 209
Winstein, Stewart R. - Rock Island

Central Illinois

Barr, John - Decatur
Beckett, J. Steven - Urbana
Benassi, A. Lou - Peoria
Bernardi, John A. - Pekin
Bonjean, Robert V., Jr. - Jacksonville
Bower, Brian L. - Charleston
Campbell, Michael I. - Decatur
Casady-Trimble, Carolyn - Urbana
Corsentino, Anthony P. - Peoria, page 210
Coryell, James R. - Decatur
Elmore, James E. - Springfield
Erickson, Frederick P. - Decatur
Feldman, Howard W. - Springfield, page 210
Ferguson, Mark E. - Mattoon
Fombelle, Norman J. - Decatur
Fuller, Glenn O. - Decatur
Garst, Steven L. - Paris
Glenn, Ronda D. - Bloomington
Hammer, Don C. - Bloomington, page 211
Hasselberg, Michael R. - Peoria
Hirschfeld, John C. - Champaign
Holmes, Brent D. - Mattoon
Hopp, Richard W. - Decatur
Houchen, Vernon H. - Decatur
Johnson, James W. - Decatur
Jordan, Holly W. - Champaign
Keith, John R. - Springfield
Lerner, Arthur M. - Champaign
Lynch, David M. - Peoria, page 211
Marsh, Roger A. - Urbana
McCarthy, David H. - Peoria, page 212
Mellen, Thomas J., II - Danville
Metnick, Michael B. - Springfield, page 212
Murphy, G. Edward - Peoria
Nardulli, Steven - Springfield, page 213
Narmont, John S. - Springfield
O'Neal Johnson, Susan - Peoria
Ogar, Helen E. - Bloomington
Ores, Nicholas H. - Peoria, page 213
Osborne, Stephen M. - Springfield
Palmer, Charles L. - Champaign
Parker, Drew - Peoria, page 214
Phipps, John T. - Champaign
Pretnar, Alan - Taylor Springs
Prillaman, Terry S., Jr. - Urbana
Pusey, John R. - Peoria
Reid, William D. - Springfield
Resch, Marilyn B. - Effingham
Ryan, David J. - Danville
Ryan, Stephen R. - Mattoon
Scott, Gregory A. - Springfield
Scott, R. Stephen - Springfield
Sgro, Gregory P. - Springfield
Smith Anderson, Claudia - Danville
Straub, Marcia - Peoria
Sturm, Timothy - Springfield
Tinney, Sarah B. - Champaign
Underhill, Frederick H., Jr. - Danville
Weintraub, Alan I. - Bloomington
Winget, Walter W. - Peoria, page 214
Winter-Black, Janett S. - Mattoon
Zuckerman, Richard Wayne - Peoria, page 215

SOUTHERN ILLINOIS

Berkemann, Rosemary L. - Belleville
Blake, Edward J., Jr. - Belleville
Brown, Joseph R., Jr. - Edwardsville
Campbell, David A. - Mt. Vernon
Cannady, Thomas B. - Belleville
Crowder, Barbara - Edwardsville
Enloe, Douglas A. - Lawrenceville
Garrison, James T. - Marion
Gossage, Roza - Belleville, page 216
Harvey, Morris Lane - Fairfield, page 216
Heller, Edward J. - Murphysboro
Hunter, Eugenia C. - Carbondale
Katz, Julie K. - Belleville
Kurowski, John J. - Belleville (Swansea), page 217
Levine Levy, Elizabeth - Edwardsville
Levo, Bonnie - Collinsville
McGivern, Gerald - Alton

Mitchell, A. Ben - Mt. Vernon
Mott, Lorri - Belleville
Mudge, William A. - Edwardsville
Neubauer, Timothy R. - Mt. Vernon
O'Neill, Treva H. - Carbondale, page 217
Pike, Harold K., III - Centralia
Proctor, Janet C. - Carbondale, page 218
Reed, Gerald S. - Murphysboro
Slemer, Ronald R. - Edwardsville
Smoot, Carolyn B. - Marion
Stubblefield, Timothy C. - Belleville, page 218
Trone, D. Kent - Edwardsville
Verity, Duane P. - Marion
Wells, Robert E., Jr. - Belleville
Wilson, Susan P. - Belleville
Woodcock, George W. - Mt. Carmel

BIOGRAPHICAL PROFILES OF FAMILY LAW LEADING ILLINOIS ATTORNEYS

The Leading Illinois Attorneys profiled below were nominated as exceptional by their peers in a statewide survey conducted by American Research Corporation (ARC). ARC asked several thousand licensed Illinois attorneys to name the lawyer to whom they would send a close friend or family member in need of legal assistance in specific areas of law. The attorneys below were nominated in the area of Family Law.

Because the survey results (all practice area results combined) represent less than three percent of Illinois' practicing attorneys, this list should not be construed as a complete list. Nevertheless, it is an excellent source of highly qualified and reputable Illinois attorneys.

For information on ARC's survey methodology, see page *xi*.
For the complete list of Leading Illinois Consumer Attorneys, see page *xii*.
For the list of Leading Illinois Family Law Attorneys, see page 176.

The Leading Illinois Attorneys below are listed alphabetically in accordance with the geographic region in which their offices are located. Note that attorneys may handle clients from a broad geographic area; attorneys are not limited to only serving clients residing within the cities in which their offices are located.

The two-line attorney listings in this section are of attorneys who practice in this area but whose full biographical profiles appear in other sections of this book. A bullet "•" preceding a name indicates the attorney was nominated in this particular area of law.

For information on the format of the full biographical profiles, consult the "Using the Consumer Guidebook" section on page *xviii*.

The following abbreviations are used throughout these profiles:

App.	Appellate
Cir.	Circuit
Ct.	Court
Dist.	District
Sup.	Supreme
JD	Juris Doctor (Doctor of Law)
LLB	Legum Baccalaureus (Bachelor of Laws)
LLD	Legum Doctor (Doctor of Laws)
LLM	Legum Magister (Master of Laws)
ADR	Alternative Dispute Resolution
ABA	American Bar Association
ABOTA	American Board of Trial Advocates
ATLA	Association of Trial Lawyers of America
CBA	Chicago Bar Association
ISBA	Illinois State Bar Association
ITLA	Illinois Trial Lawyers Association
NBTA	National Board of Trial Advocacy

COOK & COLLAR COUNTIES

•J. DANIEL AZULAY: Mr. Azulay is President of Azulay & Azulay, P.C., concentrating in family and adoption law, and the interrelationship with immigration/naturalization matters, real estate, and trial practice. He has successfully represented clients in issues related to petitions for a dissolution of marriage, including alimony, property distributions, child support, child custody, visitation, pre- and antenuptial agreements, and paternity cases. He has practiced law in Illinois for more than 23 years and has had extensive experience in bringing cases to conclusion through settlement, mediation and/or trial. He also handles personal injury and immigration and naturalization. He has authored and assisted in several articles and publications, including "Motions Practice in Cook County," *The Judges' Journal,* 1973, and in the *Chicago Bar Record,* 1973, with Judge Nicholas J. Bua. He is the author of several legal articles published in the local press.
Education: JD 1973 with honors, Illinois Institute of Technology, Chicago-Kent; BA 1963, Roosevelt University.
Admitted: 1973 Illinois; 1974 U.S. Dist. Ct. (N. Dist. IL); 1976 U.S. Ct. App. (7th Cir.); 1979 U.S. Sup. Ct.
Employment History: President 1977-present, Azulay & Azulay, P.C.
Representative Clients: Mr. Azulay represents corporate and individual clients from the U.S. and abroad.
Professional Associations: American Assn. of Adoption Attorneys; American Arbitration Assn.; ABA; Assn. of Immigration and Nationality Lawyers; American Indicature Assn.; ATLA; Attorney's Title Guaranty Fund, Inc.; CBA; Commission of Law and Public Affairs; Decalogue Society of Lawyers; The Florida Bar; ISBA; International Assn. of Jewish Lawyers and Jurists.
Community Involvement: American Friends of KBY/Midwest Region (Founding Officer); Assn. for Torah Advancement (Officer); Bernard Horwich JCC; B'nai B'rith; Camp Moshava (Board Member); Commission on Law and Public Affairs, Chicago Region (Founding Officer); Hillel Torah Day School (past Officer); Ida Crown Jewish Academy (Officer); Jewish Sacred Society (Founding Member); Jewish United Fund of Chicago 1973-present (Social Welfare Committee); North Boundary Homeowners Assn.; Religious Zionist of Chicago (Officer); World Jewish Congress.
Firm: Azulay & Azulay, P.C., concentrates in several areas of law, including immigration, family law, real estate, trial work, and related areas. Clients include corporations and individuals located all over the world. The firm is in the forefront of providing family law and immigration legal services. It provides service in any immigration issue including family- and employment-related matters, court matters, temporary and permanent visas, deportation and exclusion, and naturalization and citizenship consular matters, for almost any person or under any circumstance, everywhere. *See complete firm profile in Appendix A. Mr. Azulay also practices Immigration Law.*

J. DANIEL AZULAY
Azulay & Azulay, P.C.
35 East Wacker Drive
Suite 3300
Chicago, IL 60601
Phone: (312) 832-9200
Fax: (312) 832-9212

•ROBERT T. BADESCH: Mr. Badesch practices family law, concentrating in all aspects of domestic relations, including custody, settlements, and the trial of contested matters in dissolution of marriage cases. He has lectured at various family law seminars sponsored by local bar associations and is involved in bar association activities.
Education: JD 1975, DePaul University; BA 1972, University of Illinois.
Admitted: 1975 Illinois; 1975 U.S. Dist. Ct. (N. Dist. IL); 1975 U.S. Ct. App. (7th Cir.).
Employment History: Associate 1988-present, Davis, Friedman, Zavett, Kane & MacRae; Associate 1985-88, Kirsh, Berman & Hoffenberg; Public Defender 1976-85, Public Defender's Office, Cook County.
Professional Associations: CBA; ISBA; Chicago Council of Lawyers (Board of Governors).
Community Involvement: Chicago Assn. for Retarded Citizens (Board of Directors).
Firm: Members of the firm practice family law exclusively. The legal experience of the firm's attorneys ranges from 35 years to just graduating from law school. The firm has been in existence for 50 years. The hallmark of the firm is to bring a high level of professional experience to difficult family law problems. *See complete firm profile in Appendix A.*

ROBERT T. BADESCH
Davis, Friedman, Zavett, Kane & MacRae
140 South Dearborn Street
Suite 1600
Chicago, IL 60603
Phone: (312) 782-2220
Fax: (312) 782-0464

Chapter 17: Family Law

FORREST S. BAYARD

Law Offices of Forrest S. Bayard
150 North Wacker Drive
Suite 2570
Chicago, IL 60606

Phone: (312) 236-3828
Fax: (312) 704-6746
E-mail: fsblaw@aol.com

Extensive Experience In:

- Divorce
- Custody
- Dispute Resolution

•**FORREST S. BAYARD:** Mr. Bayard has over 25 years' experience in divorce, custody, paternity, and related matters. He is committed to providing clients the possibility of resolving their divorces responsibly and amicably. He is a frequent speaker and has written on the subject of divorce, relationships, and transforming conflict into responsible solutions. He recently wrote *Divorce: 133 Ways to Diffuse the Battle—A New Approach.* This booklet provides new choices and possibilities for people engaged in the difficult journey of divorce—before, during and after. It supports their moving through issues with a new sense of purpose, clarity, and well-being. Mr. Bayard has extensive trial experience in a wide variety of legal areas. In the last 12 years, he has concentrated on developing new methods of resolving disputes in family law matters. Mr. Bayard is a trained mediator, an arbitrator for the Circuit Court of Cook County, a member of the Chicago Bar Association's Family Law Referral Panel, Adoption Law Referral Panel, and an approved Attorney for Children for the Circuit Court of Cook County. His bachelor's degree in mathematics and experience teaching college-level accounting allow him to resolve complex financial issues through negotiation, often avoiding lengthy trials concerning financial matters. He is deeply committed to children being cared for in all types of domestic relations proceedings. He has chaired committees in the Justice for Youth Program of the Chicago Bar Association, which is committed to children at risk in the Juvenile Court of Cook County. Mr. Bayard is a devoted father and has maintained an excellent relationship with his former wife in raising their primary school-aged son. In his free time, he is an avid motorcycle enthusiast, coin collector, amateur photographer, and Chicago Bulls fan. He has participated in and led self-development seminars.
Education: JD 1969, John Marshall Law School; BS 1966, Purdue University.
Admitted: 1969 Illinois; 1970 U.S. Dist. Ct. (N. Dist. IL).
Employment History: 1972-present, Law Offices of Forrest S. Bayard; 1969-71, Mullin and Devine.
Professional Associations: CBA [Matrimonial Law Committee; Alternative Dispute Resolution Committee; Adoption Law Committee; Justice for Youth Program Special Projects Committee (Chair 1992-94)]; ISBA (Family Law Section); ABA (Family Law Section).
Community Involvement: Landmark Education Corporation (Seminar Leader; Participant); Hunger Project 1985-present; Community Education Support Network; New Warrior Chicago, an organization supporting men's emotional development (Executive Board 1992-94). *Mr. Bayard also practices Alternative Dispute Resolution.*

JON L. BEERMANN

Jon L. Beermann & Associates, Ltd.
150 East Cook Avenue
Libertyville, IL 60048

Phone: (847) 680-7070
Fax: (847) 816-6122

Extensive Experience In:

- Custody & Visitation
- Support & Maintenance
- Contested Dissolutions

•**JON L. BEERMANN:** Mr. Beermann has concentrated almost exclusively in family law for the last 15 years. He has had extensive experience in family matters, including contested dissolution, custody, visitation, antenuptial agreements, support and maintenance, removal, and grandparent visitation. In addition to being an attorney, he is a Certified Public Accountant. He limits himself to the practice of law, utilizing his knowledge attained as a Certified Public Accountant to counsel clients on financial and tax planning matters when they are involved in dissolution of marriage cases. He has also lectured at family law seminars and has provided written articles on the topics that he has lectured on, including "Reviewable Maintenance" and "Gifts of Non-Marital Property to the Marital Estate."
Education: JD 1964, University of Chicago; BBA 1961 cum laude, University of Wisconsin.
Admitted: 1964 Illinois; 1969 U.S. Dist. Ct. (N. Dist. IL).
Employment History: Sole Practitioner 1966-present, Jon L. Beermann & Associates, Ltd.
Professional Associations: ABA; Lake County Bar Assn. (Family Law Committee); ISBA; CBA.
Community Involvement: Juvenile Diabetes Foundation (Fund Raiser).
Firm: The firm consists of Jon L. Beermann and two secretary/paralegals who try intensively to respond to the needs of the clients. In addition, another attorney who concentrates in family law shares offices with the firm, and on occasion, provides services for the firm's clients.

182 *Leading Illinois Attorneys Consumer Law Guidebook*

•**BRIGITTE SCHMIDT BELL:** Ms. Bell's interest in people and her work in mediation led her to family law, which is the main focus of her practice. She conducts mediations and represents people in mediations, focusing on neutrality or advocacy as may be appropriate in premarital agreements, divorce, custody matters, post-decree disputes, adoptions, and parental planning. She is often appointed as the guardian ad litem for children in disputed custody cases. Most of her cases are resolved without a trial because she helps clients and opposing counsel see the dispute as a set of financial and emotional issues to be resolved, rather than as a battle to be fought and won. Nevertheless, a small percentage of her cases involve significant pre-litigation and trial work. Her philosophy is that all clients are important, and their problems, no matter how inconsequential they appear to others, matter to her clients and are thus important to the cases at hand. Ms. Bell teaches mediation at Loyola Law School as an adjunct professor and speaks locally and nationally on issues in mediation and family law. She is a frequent speaker at seminars and a contributing writer in several publications.
Education: JD 1979, University of Chicago; Graduate Work 1979, University of Iowa; BA 1970 with high honors, Swarthmore College.
Admitted: 1979 Illinois; 1979 U.S. Dist. Ct. (N. Dist. IL); 1981 U.S. Ct. App. (7th Cir.); 1982 U.S. Tax Ct.
Employment History: Private Practice 1993-present, Brigitte Schmidt Bell, P.C.; Officer 1990-93, Pretzel & Stouffer, Chartered; Litigation Associate 1987-90, McDermott, Will & Emery; Litigation Associate 1979-82, 1985-87, Jenner & Block; Litigation Associate 1982-85, Butler, Rubin, Newcomer, Saltarelli & Boyd.
Professional Associations: ABA (Family Law Committee; Dispute Resolution Committee); CBA (Family Law Committee 1990-present; ADR Subcommittee 1993-present; Guardian Ad Litem Subcommittee 1993-present); Legal Assistance Foundation [Children's Rights Project Advisory Board 1985-90 (Chair 1985-86)]; Circuit Court of Cook County (Court Appointed Guardian Ad Litem Program 1990-present); American Academy of Family Mediators (Associate Member); Assn. of Family and Conciliation Courts 1990-present (Associate Member); Mediation Council of Illinois 1987-present (Board of Directors 1994-present).
Firm: The firm of Brigitte Schmidt Bell, P.C., was founded in 1993. Lynn A. Gaffigan, a trained mediator and former litigator in a large firm practice, joined the firm in 1995. Ms. Gaffigan shares the firm's objective to resolve cases in an efficient and cost-effective way by focusing on the needs of the parties and their children and encouraging mediation whenever possible. *Ms. Bell and Ms. Gaffigan also practice Alternative Dispute Resolution.*

BRIGITTE SCHMIDT BELL
Brigitte Schmidt Bell, P.C.
53 West Jackson Boulevard
Suite 702
Chicago, IL 60604

Phone: (312) 360-1124
Fax: (312) 360-1126

EDWIN J. BELZ - *Belz & McWilliams* - 4407 North Elston Avenue - Chicago, IL 60630 - Phone: (312) 282-9129, Fax: (312) 282-9811 - *See complete biographical profile in the Criminal Law: Felonies & White Collar Crime Chapter, page 111.*

•**MARGARET A. BENNETT:** Ms. Bennett practices family law and real estate law and was recently appointed as a Court Mediator. She is the recipient of several awards, including the Illinois State Bar Association Certificate of Appreciation, 1990; DuPage County Bar Association Certificate of Appreciation, 1989; and the President's Award from the Realtor Association of the Western Suburbs. She is the author of the "Comprehensive Law Office Real Estate System," *DuPage County Bar Brief,* October 1991, and *Attorney's Title Guaranty Fund, Inc., Newsletter,* Spring 1992; "The Allocation of Stock Options upon Dissolution of Marriage," *Illinois Family Law Report,* August 1996; "You Get What You Pay For," *REALTOR Association of the Western Suburbs Dispatch,* April 1995; "Penny Wise and Pound Foolish," *Illinois State Bar Association Real Property Newsletter,* July 1995; and "Real Estate for the Penny Wise," *Illinois State Bar Association Bar News,* September 15, 1995. Ms. Bennett was an instructor of real estate law at the American Institute for Paralegal Studies from 1992 to 1993.
Education: JD 1976, University of San Francisco and Loyola University of Chicago; AB 1972 cum laude, University of California-Berkeley.
Admitted: 1976 Illinois; 1977 U.S. Dist. Ct. (N. Dist. IL); 1983 U.S. Ct. App. (7th Cir.).
Representative Clients: McDonald's Corporation, Oak Brook, Illinois, 1982-present (real estate/legal matters); Stormwater Management Committee, DuPage County 1991-92 (land acquisition/real estate); DuPage County Fair and Exposition Authority 1991-95; DuPage Department of Transportation 1992-95 (right-of-way acquisitions).
Professional Associations: ISBA (General Assembly 1986-90, 1994-present); DuPage County Bar Assn. [Real Estate Law Committee (Chair 1994-95); Professional Responsibility Committee (Chair 1996-97); Matrimonial Committee (Vice Chair 1996-97)]; DuPage Assn. of Women Lawyers.
Community Involvement: Evangelical Health Foundation (Board of Sponsors 1988-92); Good Samaritan Hospital Development Counsel 1988-92; Next Generation Committee on Drug and Alcohol Abuse (Cochair 1990-93); DuPage County Blue Ribbon Committee on Disabilities.
Firm: Law Offices of Bennett & Bennett, Ltd. *Ms. Bennett also practices Real Estate Law and Alternative Dispute Resolution.*

MARGARET A. BENNETT
Law Offices of Bennett & Bennett, Ltd.
720 Enterprise Drive
Oak Brook, IL 60521

Phone: (630) 573-8800
Fax: (630) 573-9810

Extensive Experience In:

- Matrimonial Law
- Alternative Dispute Resolution
- Real Estate Law

Chapter 17: Family Law

HOWARD W. BROECKER
Howard W. Broecker & Associates, Ltd.
115 Campbell Street
Suite One
Geneva, IL 60134
Phone: (630) 232-1445
Fax: (630) 232-0575

Extensive Experience In:
- Divorce Mediation
- Divorce Litigation

•**HOWARD W. BROECKER:** Mr. Broecker's practice is concentrated in the areas of family law and family law mediation. He has lectured extensively in the area of family law for the Kane and DuPage County Bar Associations, Illinois State Bar Association, American Academy of Matrimonial Lawyers, and the Law Education Institute of Milwaukee, Wisconsin. Mr. Broecker has completed several courses on mediation, including a 40-hour program at the Center for Dispute Resolution in Boulder, Colorado. He is a faculty member of the Academy's Mediation Study Committee and has participated in the training of over 200 academy members. Mr. Broecker lectures and writes for the Illinois Institute for Continuing Legal Education and other publications. His articles include "Cross-Examination of a Business Valuation Expert Witness," *The Connecticut Family Law Journal*, Vol. 8, No. 4; "The Use of Financial Experts in Marital Litigation: The Attorney's Viewpoint and the Expert's Viewpoint," *American Journal of Family Law*, Fall 1987; "Mediation vs. Settlement Conference," *Chicago Daily Law Bulletin*, November 16, 1994; "The Automated Attorney: Your Law Office and Computers," *Law Education Institute*, January 1992; and "The Role of the Attorney in Mediation," *DuPage County Bar Journal*, Spring 1995.
Education: JD 1966, Illinois Institute of Technology, Chicago-Kent.
Admitted: 1966 Illinois.
Employment History: Panelist 1995-present, J•A•M•S/Endispute; Partner 1992-present, Johnson, Westra, Broecker, Whittaker & Newitt; Senior Vice President/Chief Operating Officer 1994-96, Judicial Resolutions Illinois, Inc.; 1982-92, Howard W. Broecker & Associates, Ltd.; 1966-82, Ehrlich, Bundesen & Broecker.
Professional Associations: American Academy of Matrimonial Lawyers [Fellow; Illinois Chapter (Vice President)]; American Academy [Mediation Study Committee (Faculty Member; Trainer)].
Community Involvement: Illinois Institute of Technology, Chicago-Kent College of Law [Alumni Assn. (past President); Partnership Program (Chair)]; Sunny Ridge Family Center (Board Member); Daystar University, Nairobi, Kenya (Board Member); Media Associates International (Board Member). *Mr. Broecker also practices Alternative Dispute Resolution.*

ANNA MARKLEY BUSH
Bush & Heise
18-3 East Dundee Road
Suite 210
Barrington, IL 60010
Phone: (847) 382-4560
Fax: (847) 382-0836

Extensive Experience In:
- Dissolution of Marriage
- Child Custody
- Prenuptial Agreements

•**ANNA MARKLEY BUSH:** Ms. Bush concentrates in family law, including prenuptial agreements, dissolution of marriage, paternity, adoption, and child custody. She has been in practice since 1977, and covers five counties, including Cook, Lake, Kane, McHenry, and DuPage. Ms. Bush is the author of "PMS: A Startling New Consideration in Matrimonial Cases," Parts I and II, *Northwest Suburban Bar Journal*, 1983; and "Motherhood and the Law," *Women's Bar Association of Illinois Journal*, 1987. She is also the subject of several articles written for *The Herald* and the *Chicago Tribune*. She appeared as a legal consultant in the television broadcasts of *Mothers Without Custody*, WBBM-TV, 1984-85; *Women Entrepreneurs*, Cox Cable, 1983; *Starting Your Own Business*, Warner-Amex Cable, 1982; and *Divorce Issues for Women*, Aurora Cable, 1989. Ms. Bush is also coauthor with Louise Schrank of *Divorce and the Family*, a video production produced by the Learning Seed Company, 1994.
Education: JD 1977, Valparaiso University; BA 1971 with honors, Valparaiso University.
Admitted: 1977 Illinois; 1977 U.S. Dist. Ct.; 1981 U.S. Sup. Ct.; 1982 U.S. Dist. Ct. (N. Dist. IL, Trial Bar).
Employment History: Senior Partner 1979-present, Bush & Heise; Adjunct Faculty Member 1980-present, Harper College; Village Trustee 1987-91, Village of Barrington; Law Associate 1977-79, Irwin & Associates; Law Clerk 1975-77, Stankiewiez & Associates; Intern 1974-75, Public Defender's Office, Indiana State Prison, Michigan City, Indiana.
Professional Associations: ISBA; Women's Bar Assn. of Illinois.
Community Involvement: Village of Barrington 1987-91 (Trustee; Plan Commission Member 1985-87, 1993-present); Barrington Area Business and Professional Women's Club (past President; past Director); Barrington United Methodist Church; Barrington Community Concert Band; Hough Street School Parent Teacher Organization (President 1994-present); Barrington Area Council on Aging (Vice President 1995-96).
Firm: Ms. Bush and her partner, Brian L. Heise, concentrate in estate planning, corporate law, and personal injury law, as well as family law. Both partners also practice real estate law, and do a substantial amount of public speaking. The firm focuses on individualized service.

•**MULLER DAVIS:** Mr. Davis practices family law, concentrating in all aspects of domestic relations and litigation. He has practiced family law exclusively for twenty-eight years, and previously was a general litigator for seven years. His publications include *The Illinois Practice of Family Law,* West Publishing Company; with Sherman C. Feinstein, *The Parental Couple in a Successful Divorce;* and various law articles. Mr. Davis is also a member of the Editorial Board of the *Equitable Distribution Journal* and lectures on family law and litigation topics.
Education: JD 1960, Harvard University; BA 1957 magna cum laude, Yale University.
Admitted: 1960 Illinois; 1961 U.S. Dist. Ct. (N. Dist. IL).
Employment History: Partner 1967-present, Davis, Friedman, Zavett, Kane & MacRae; Associate 1960-67, Jenner & Block.
Professional Associations: CBA [Civil Practice Committee (Chair 1981-82)]; ISBA (Family Law Section Council); ABA (Family Law Section); American Judicature Society; ATLA; American Academy of Matrimonial Lawyers; Law Club of Chicago; American Bar Foundation (Fellow).
Community Involvement: Legal Aid Society (Vice Chair); Infant Welfare Society of Chicago (Director; President 1978-82); Phillips Exeter Academy Class Capital Giving (Chair).
Firm: Members of the firm practice family law exclusively. The legal experience of the firm's attorneys ranges from 35 years to just graduating from law school. The firm has been in existence for 50 years. The hallmark of the firm is to bring a high level of professional experience to difficult family law problems. *See complete firm profile in Appendix A.*

MULLER DAVIS
Davis, Friedman, Zavett, Kane & MacRae
140 South Dearborn Street
Suite 1600
Chicago, IL 60603
Phone: (312) 782-2220
Fax: (312) 782-0464

•**ROBERT K. DOWNS:** Mr. Downs concentrates full-time in family law throughout the Chicago metropolitan area, with extensive trial and hearing experience. He is frequently court appointed attorney for the minor child and guardian ad litem in custody and visitation disputes. He is active in reform efforts for the Cook County Domestic Relations Courts. He served as a state representative in the Illinois House of Representatives, receiving the Ethel Parker and the Best Legislator awards from the Independent Voters of Illinois, as well as numerous other honors. He has been a frequent lecturer at Illinois State and Chicago Bar Associations seminars on topics including "Role of Attorney for the Minor Child," "Substitution of Judge," "Legislative Updates," and "Civil and Professionalism."
Education: JD 1965, Stetson University; BA 1957, Grinnell College.
Admitted: 1966 Illinois; 1965 Florida.
Employment History: Partner 1985-present, Downs & Downs, P.C.
Professional Associations: ISBA 1992-present [Family Law Section Council (Chair 1996-97); Legislative Relations Subcommittee (past Chair); Assembly 1992-present]; CBA [Matrimonial Law Committee (Vice Chair); Attorney for the Minor Child Subcommittee (Cochair); Legislation Subcommittee to Revise Proposed "Income Shares" Legislation (Chair); Court Liaison Committee; Domestic Relations Subcommittees, Circuit Court of Cook County]; ABA [National Pro Bono Service Award (Recipient 1995)]; Illinois Board of Managers (Fellow); American Academy of Matrimonial Lawyers [Divorce and Custody Mediation Service (President)]; West Suburban Bar Assn.; DuPage County Bar Assn.; Assn. of Family and Conciliation Courts; National Assn. of Counsel for Children; Mediation Council of Illinois.
Community Involvement: *Wednesday Journal, Inc.* [Board of Directors (Chair)]; Oak Park-River Forest Community Foundation (Board of Directors).
Firm: Downs & Downs, P.C., also has attorneys who handle general legal issues, including estate planning and real estate matters. *See complete firm profile in Appendix A. Mr. Downs also practices Adoption Law.*

ROBERT K. DOWNS
Downs & Downs, P.C.
1010 Lake Street
Suite 620
Oak Park (Chicago), IL 60301
Phone: (708) 848-0700
Fax: (708) 848-0029

Extensive Experience In:
• Family Law & Custody Litigation
• Adoption Law Litigation
• Child/Guardian Ad Litem Matters

Chapter 17: Family Law

JOSEPH N. DUCANTO

Schiller, DuCanto and Fleck
200 North LaSalle Street
Suite 2700
Chicago, IL 60601-1089

Phone: (312) 641-5560
Fax: (312) 641-6361

Extensive Experience In:

- Matrimonial Law
- Taxation
- Estate Planning, Trusts & Probate

•**JOSEPH N. DU CANTO:** Mr. DuCanto is recognized nationally as one of the foremost authorities on divorce, taxation, and finance, as well as on trusts and estate planning. A practicing divorce attorney for nearly 40 years, Mr. DuCanto is a prolific author. His articles include "Passing Your Wealth on to Others: How to Avoid Financial Pitfall," *USA Today*, March 1991; and "Federal Tax Law: Where You Divorce Does Make a Difference," 9 *Loyola University Law Journal* 397, 1978. He has contributed numerous other articles to professional journals and has published various study and practice aids used by lawyers and accountants. He is on the Board of Editors for several publications, including *Family Law Quarterly* and *Matrimonial Lawyer Strategist*. He has been a visiting lecturer on Family Law at Loyola University since 1968. *Town & Country* magazine cited Mr. DuCanto as one of the nation's best matrimonial lawyers, and he was one of nine Chicago matrimonial attorneys named in Naifeh and Smith's *Best Lawyers in America*.

Education: JD 1955, University of Illinois; BA 1952, Antioch College.

Admitted: 1955 Illinois; 1958 U.S. Tax Ct.; 1960 U.S. Sup. Ct.

Professional Associations: American Academy of Matrimonial Lawyers (past National President 1977-79); ISBA (Board of Governors 1983-89); CBA [Matrimonial Law Committee (Board of Managers 1976-78; Chair 1972)]; ABA [Family Law Section (Taxation Committee, Chair 1982-84)]; American College of Trust and Estate Counsel (1970-present).

Firm: The law firm of Schiller, DuCanto and Fleck is the largest matrimonial law firm in the United States. The firm's clients consist of sports figures, industrialists, entrepreneurs, political figures and other persons of note. The firm has offices in both Chicago and Lake Forest, Illinois. Of the seventeen Illinois family attorneys listed in *The Best Lawyers in America*, five are members of Schiller, DuCanto and Fleck. The firm's members include leaders in the American Bar Association, Illinois State Bar Association, and the Chicago Bar Association, including a former President of the Illinois State Bar Association and two former Chief Judges of the Domestic Relations Division of the Circuit Court of Cook County. *See complete firm profile in Appendix A.*

JANE F. FIELDS

Law Office of Jane F. Fields
Three First National Plaza
Suite 3970
70 West Madison Street
Chicago, IL 60602

Phone: (312) 263-6065
Fax: (312) 368-1361

Extensive Experience In:

- Custody
- Divorce
- Paternity

•**JANE F. FIELDS:** Ms. Fields is a sole practitioner who concentrates her practice in family law. Her practice encompasses every aspect of dissolution proceedings, child custody, and paternity proceedings. In 1983, she briefed and argued a paternity case before the Illinois Supreme Court, which was instrumental in the Illinois legislature restructuring the paternity statute in Illinois. Ms. Fields has written briefs and argued many cases before the Illinois Appellate Courts. She represents both men and women and has been both the court appointed attorney and guardian ad litem in many custody disputes. Ms. Fields' practice focuses on issues including custody, visitation, property allocation, child support, maintenance, domestic violence, the Hague Convention, paternity, and postjudgment modification and enforcement. In her representation of both parents and children, she has litigated numerous child custody disputes.

Education: JD 1980, Illinois Institute of Technology, Chicago-Kent; Graduate Certificate for Legal Research 1974, George Washington University; BA 1992, New York University.

Admitted: 1980 Illinois; 1981 U.S. Ct. App. (7th Cir.); 1982 U.S. Dist. Ct. (N. Dist. IL, Trial Bar).

Employment History: Sole Practitioner 1982-present, Law Office of Jane F. Fields; Of Counsel 1992-present, Schaps, Grotta and King; Partner 1981, Lapat, Saunders and Fields; Associate 1980, Miller, Forrest, Rodman & Huszagh.

Representative Clients: Men, women, and children in divorce and custody litigation.

Professional Associations: ABA; ISBA; CBA (Family Law Section 1981-present).

Community Involvement: Ms. Fields performs volunteer work for Shalva.

Firm: Ms. Fields counsels her clients and explains the law. She then presents her clients with realistic choices. She offers clients an overview of the legal procedures and fully explains what their expectations should be. She assists them in making decisions which will affect their futures and attempts to negotiate their cases amicably in an effort to minimize their costs and their exposure within the courtroom arena.

•**CHARLES J. FLECK:** Mr. Fleck practices primarily in all areas of family law. His early career consisted of years in the Illinois Attorney General's Office where he prosecuted tax violations and served in that office's General Litigation Division. In 1970, he was elected to the Illinois House of Representatives where he served on the Judiciary Committee for six years and sponsored numerous bills reforming Illinois divorce laws. In 1976, at the age of 36, he became a Judge of the Circuit Court of Cook County; and in 1979, he was appointed the youngest Chief Judge in Illinois history of the Domestic Relations Division of that court. In 1982, Mr. Fleck resigned his judgeship to become a partner in the law firm of Schiller, DuCanto and Fleck. Mr. Fleck has been recognized in *The Best Lawyers in America* and was listed by *Town & Country* magazine's "Guide to the Best Lawyers in America." Throughout his career, he has participated in seminars for continuing legal education programs, various bar associations, including the American Academy of Matrimonial Lawyers, and he has authored articles for various bar journals and law reviews.
Education: JD 1967, Valparaiso Law School; BA 1963, Northwestern University.
Admitted: 1967 Illinois; 1967 U.S. Dist. Ct. (N. Dist. IL).
Professional Associations: ABA [Family Law Section; Trial Techniques Committee (past Cochair); Courts Committee]; ISBA [Family Law Section; Bench/Bar Section (past Chair)]; CBA [Family Law Committee (past Board of Managers)]; Illinois Judges Assn.
Firm: The law firm of Schiller, DuCanto and Fleck is the largest matrimonial law firm in the United States. The firm's clients consist of sports figures, industrialists, entrepreneurs, political figures, and other persons of note. The firm has offices in both Chicago and Lake Forest, Illinois. Of the seventeen Illinois family attorneys listed in *The Best Lawyers in America,* five are members of Schiller, DuCanto and Fleck. The firm's members include leaders in the American Bar Association, Illinois State Bar Association, and the Chicago Bar Association, including a former President of the Illinois State Bar Association and two former Chief Judges of the Domestic Relations Division of the Circuit Court of Cook County. *See complete firm profile in Appendix A.*

CHARLES J. FLECK
Schiller, DuCanto and Fleck
200 North LaSalle Street
Suite 2700
Chicago, IL 60601-1089

Phone: (312) 641-5560
Fax: (312) 641-6361

•**JAMES T. FRIEDMAN:** Mr. Friedman has concentrated in the area of family law, including litigation, since 1961. He has participated as a speaker at family law seminars in 18 states and in Europe, and has published extensively on various family law subjects in local and national bar journals. He authored *The Divorce Handbook,* published by Random House, which is in its 13th year of publication. He has litigated extensively in business valuation and custody issues, and does appellate work as well.
Education: JD 1961, University of Michigan; BA 1958, University of Michigan.
Admitted: 1961 Illinois; 1961 U.S. Dist. Ct. (N. Dist. IL).
Employment History: Partner 1987-present, Davis, Friedman, Zavett, Kane & MacRae; Partner 1981-87, Schiff, Hardin & Waite; Sole Practitioner 1979-81, James T. Friedman, Ltd.; Partner 1961-81, Armstrong & Donnelly.
Representative Clients: The majority of Mr. Friedman's clients are business owners and professionals, or their spouses.
Professional Associations: CBA [Matrimonial Law Committee (Chair 1978)]; ISBA [Family Law Section Council (Chair 1981)]; ABA; American Academy of Matrimonial Lawyers (Governor; Vice President; Counsel; Treasurer 1984-85; President-elect 1986-87; President 1987-88).
Community Involvement: Mr. Friedman is a frequent speaker for community organizations and is a former board member of the Legal Assistance Foundation. He organized a lawyer pro bono legal assistance program for the Chicago Bar Association, which has operated for over 20 years. He participates in the American Academy of Matrimonial Lawyers' pro bono services program and is a board member of its foundation.
Firm: Davis, Friedman, Zavett, Kane & MacRae concentrates its practice in family law. Mr. Friedman uses a team approach in staffing each case with a paralegal and an associate who perform specific tasks appropriate to them to minimize cost and maximize efficiency. Each case is prepared as if trial is a possibility, but settlement is the preferred alternative in most cases. Client communication is emphasized at every level. *See complete firm profile in Appendix A.*

JAMES T. FRIEDMAN
Davis, Friedman, Zavett, Kane & MacRae
140 South Dearborn Street
Suite 1600
Chicago, IL 60603

Phone: (312) 782-2220
Fax: (312) 782-0464

Chapter 17: Family Law

Herbert A. Glieberman

Herbert A. Glieberman & Associates
19 South LaSalle Street
Suite 600
Chicago, IL 60603-3417

Phone: (312) 236-2879
Fax: (312) 236-3417

Extensive Experience In:

- Divorce Litigation
- All Family-Related Matters
- Prenuptial & Postnuptial Agreements

•**HERBERT A. GLIEBERMAN:** Mr. Glieberman has practiced family law exclusively for over 40 years. He represents clients in all issues arising in family law, including divorce, custody, alimony, child support, visitation, and paternity cases. Mr. Glieberman is the author of 22 articles, chapters, and books on family law, including *Confessions of a Divorce Lawyer; Four Weekends to an Ideal Marriage; Closed Marriage;* "Know Your Legal Rights," *Consumers Digest;* "Child Custody," *Illinois Family Law 2;* "Discovery Tactics in a Divorce Case" and "Trying a Divorce Case," *The Chicago Bar Record;* "No-Fault as Another Ground for Dissolution in Illinois," *Illinois Trial Lawyers Journal;* "Prenuptial Agreements," *Trial Magazine;* "Marriage—Divorce—Disaster," *Some Syndromes of Love;* and "Depositions and Divorce Actions," *The Practical Lawyer.* Mr. Glieberman has lectured at education seminars on family law for Chicago-Kent College of Law; Northwestern University Law School; Decalogue Society of Lawyers; American Bar Association; Illinois State Bar Association; Chicago Bar Association; American Academy of Matrimonial Lawyers; Association of Trial Lawyers of America; Illinois Trial Lawyers Association; North Carolina State Bar Association; Idaho State Bar Association; Northwest Suburban Bar Association; Illinois Certified Public Accountants Foundation; DuPage Estate Planning Council; Continuing Legal Education/Satellite Network, Inc.; and the International Law Institute, Washington, D.C. Mr. Glieberman is a consultant to the Illinois Institute for Continuing Legal Education in the area of family law, and was a consultant to *Law and Practice Alert,* a newsletter published by Professional Advancement Concepts, Springfield, Illinois. Mr. Glieberman is a frequent guest on radio and television programs across the country. He is the former host of *Ask the Lawyer* and *Law and Controversy,* two radio shows which aired in 38 states over NBC, and WMAQ in Chicago. Mr. Glieberman is listed in *Who's Who in the World; Who's Who in America; Who's Who in the Midwest; Who's Who in American Law; Who's Who in Finance and Industry; The Best Lawyers in America;* and *Million Dollar Lawyers.*

Education: JD 1953, Illinois Institute of Technology, Chicago-Kent.

Admitted: 1954 Illinois; 1987 Washington, D.C.

Employment History: Founder 1956-present, Herbert A. Glieberman & Associates; Associate 1954-56, Joseph H. and Norman Becker.

Professional Associations: American Academy of Matrimonial Lawyers (Charter Member); ABA (Matrimonial Law Section); ATLA [Family Law Litigation Section (past Chair)]; CBA (Matrimonial Law Committee); ISBA [Family Law Committee; Publicity Committee (past Chair); Matrimonial Law Committee]; ITLA [Matrimonial Law Section; Family Law Litigation Section (past Chair)].

Joseph P. Glimco III

Law Offices of Joseph P. Glimco III
6900 South Main Street
Suite 204
Downers Grove, IL 60515

Phone: (630) 852-3636
Fax: (630) 852-3880

•**JOSEPH P. GLIMCO III:** Mr. Glimco's practice involves all areas of family law, including divorce, custody, paternity, adoptions, child support, and domestic abuse. Mr. Glimco represents children's rights as a court appointed guardian ad litem. Mr. Glimco is a *Certified Family Law Attorney Mediator and is presently on the DuPage County Mediation List as an Approved Mediator for Judicial Appointments.

Education: JD 1985, Drake University; BA 1982 with honors, St. Ambrose College.

Admitted: 1985 Illinois.

Employment History: 1996-present, Law Offices of Joseph P. Glimco III; Partner 1993-96, Law Offices of Glimco & Olszowka; Attorney 1989-93, Law Office of William J. Stogsdill, Jr.; Attorney 1986-89, Law Offices of Botti, Marinaccio & DeLongis.

Representative Clients: Mr. Glimco represents clients who are in need of legal assistance in family law, divorce, custody, paternity, adoption, domestic abuse, child support, maintenance, and property distribution.

Professional Associations: DuPage County Mediation (Approved Attorney Mediator for Judicial Appointments); DuPage County Bar Assn.; ISBA.

Firm: The firm represents the rights of men, women, and children in all areas of family law. *Mr. Glimco also practices Alternative Dispute Resolution.*

*The Supreme Court of Illinois does not recognize certifications of specialties in the practice of law. A certificate, award or recognition is not a requirement to practice law in Illinois.

•**BURTON F. GRANT:** Mr. Grant is the President of Grant and Grant, a matrimonial law firm established in 1943. Grant and Grant is considered one of the oldest matrimonial law firms in the state of Illinois. Mr. Grant is a highly experienced matrimonial trial practitioner who has both lectured and written extensively on matrimonial law topics. He has been honored by various bar associations for his contributions to their continuing legal education programs, as well as by DePaul College of Law when he was invited to teach Family Law for several years. He has represented several prominent men and women and is responsible for higher court decisions that have helped shape Illinois matrimonial law. He practices with his wife, Joan, who is also recognized as a prominent attorney and bar association leader in the matrimonial law field.
Education: LLM Taxation 1965, John Marshall Law School; JD 1962, DePaul University; BA 1959, DePaul University.
Admitted: 1962 Illinois.
Professional Associations: American Academy of Matrimonial Lawyers (Fellow); ABA; ISBA; CBA; Lake County Bar Assn.; North Suburban Bar Assn. (Board of Managers); Northwest Suburban Bar Assn.; Decalogue Society of Lawyers.
Firm: Mr. Grant also has an office at Port Clinton Square, 600 Central Avenue, Suite 228, Highland Park, Illinois 60035 and an office at 707 Skokie Boulevard, Suite 600, Northbrook, Illinois 60062. Phone: (847) 291-4343. *See complete firm profile in Appendix A.*

BURTON F. GRANT

Grant and Grant
180 North LaSalle Street
Suite 2400
Chicago, IL 60601

Phone: (312) 641-3600
Fax: (312) 641-2723

Extensive Experience In:
• Divorce/Custody
• Marital Property Rights
• Adoption

•**SHARRAN R. GREENBERG:** Ms. Greenberg considers the heart of her law practice to be personal service. She has been concentrating in family law and real estate law since 1984, with some probate and small business consulting and litigation. She prides herself on being available to her clients on a twelve-hours-a-day, seven-days-a-week basis. Ms. Greenberg went through a four-year divorce, and is particularly sensitive to the management of the emotional issues that so frequently plague dissolution proceedings. She also considers the importance of the position of the children to the proceedings, as they relate to protracted divorce litigation.
Education: JD 1984, Illinois Institute of Technology, Chicago-Kent; MA 1965, Roosevelt University; BA 1961, Roosevelt University.
Admitted: 1984 Illinois.
Employment History: Sole Practitioner 1987-present; Associate 1984-87, Law Clerk 1982-84, Ralla, Klepak & Associates; Law Clerk 1983-84, Hollander & Hollander.
Representative Clients: Ms. Greenberg represents both men and women in contested and uncontested family law matters. She has considerable experience relating to divorces which involve children with physical and learning disabilities and the safeguards that need to be addressed regarding long-term care of those children.
Professional Associations: North Suburban Bar Assn. (Continuing Legal Education Committee 1995).
Community Involvement: Highland Park Community Development; Chicago Area Jewish Hospice (Board Member 1988-90; Hospice Volunteer 1988-90); Highland Park Historical Society.
Firm: Ms. Greenberg has been a sole practitioner since 1987. She offers her clients highly individualized and personalized service. She is available after business hours and on weekends. She works closely with an accountant and a financial planner in many transactions. *Ms. Greenberg also practices Real Estate Law.*

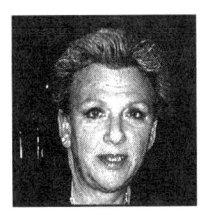

SHARRAN R. GREENBERG

Attorney at Law
205 Laurel Avenue
Highland Park, IL 60035-2617

Phone: (847) 433-5823
Fax: (847) 433-5883

Chapter 17: Family Law

DAVID I. GRUND

Grund & Starkopf, P.C.
One Illinois Center
111 East Wacker Drive
28th Floor
Chicago, IL 60601

Phone: (312) 616-6600
Fax: (312) 616-6606

Extensive Experience In:

• Financial Aspects
• Custody
• Complex Litigation

•**DAVID I. GRUND:** Mr. Grund practices exclusively in the area of family law, concentrating in all aspects of matrimonial litigation. He has successfully represented individuals in all issues arising from divorce proceedings, which involve, among other things, the valuation and disposition of substantial business interests, custody, maintenance, and other marital rights. Having an accounting background, Mr. Grund has earned a well-deserved reputation for his ability to have mastered all business-related issues in dissolution proceedings. He is known as a creative lawyer with a keen sense of the rules and the law governing the practice. He is committed to representing only the best interests of his clients. Mr. Grund is listed in *Who's Who in American Law*, 1994-95.
Education: JD 1973, DePaul University.
Admitted: 1973 Illinois; 1973 U.S. Dist. Ct. (N. Dist. IL, General Bar); 1973 U.S. Dist. Ct. (N. Dist. IL, Trial Bar); 1973 U.S. Ct. App. (7th Cir.); 1975 U.S. Tax Ct.
Employment History: Managing Partner 1985-present, Grund & Starkopf, P.C.; Private Practice 1972-85.
Representative Clients: Mr. Grund's clients are very successful, professional, social, and business people. His clients include television news anchors, CEOs of publicly traded companies, entrepreneurs, and other highly successful individuals, or their spouses.
Professional Associations: American Academy of Matrimonial Lawyers [Illinois Chapter 1987-present (Board of Governors); Admissions Committee (Chair 1991-94)]; ABA; ISBA (Family Law Section); CBA (Matrimonial Subcommittee); ITLA; Decalogue Society of Lawyers.
Community Involvement: Illinois Holocaust Foundation, Skokie (Board of Directors 1989-present); Standard Club, Chicago (Rules Subcommittee).
Firm: The firm of Grund & Starkopf, P.C., was formed in 1985. The firm's partners and associates have significant experience in such areas as valuation and disposition of business interests, custody, prenuptial agreements, appellate work and other significant matrimonial litigation. Mr. Grund is involved in the professional community through his active participation in bar activities, teaching, speaking, and writing for various publications.

LYLE B. HASKIN

Lyle B. Haskin & Associates
310 South County Farm Road
P.O. Box 31
Wheaton, IL 60189-0031

Phone: (630) 665-0800
Fax: (630) 665-1289

Extensive Experience In:

• Custody & Property Trials
• Appeals
• Alternative Dispute Resolution

•**LYLE B. HASKIN:** Mr. Haskin limits his practice primarily to family law. He was an adjunct professor at the National College of Chiropractic in Lombard, Illinois, 1985-90, and at the Law Education Institute in Milwaukee, Wisconsin. He is a frequent speaker at professional associations and organizations throughout Illinois, including "Legal Reporting Requirements in Sex Abuse Cases" for the Illinois Attorney General Seminar; "Civil Discovery in Illinois" and "Disclosure Pursuant to the Illinois Mental Health and Developmental Disabilities and Confidentiality Act" at the George Borovic Memorial Seminar for the DuPage County Bar Association. He is the author of "Proposed Standards in Determining Indigence in Criminal Cases," *Chicago-Kent Law Review*, 1971; "Issues Related to Abortion," *Chicago-Kent Law Review*, 1972; and "Issues Related to Proof of Computer Billing Records in Civil Litigation," *DuPage County Bar Association Journal*, 1987.
Education: JD 1972, Illinois Institute of Technology, Chicago-Kent; BA 1962, Northern Illinois University.
Admitted: 1972 Illinois; 1972 U.S. Dist. Ct. (N. Dist. IL).
Employment History: 1972-present, Lyle B. Haskin & Associates; Mediator 1986-present, Child Custody and Visitation Issues; College/Corporate Attorney 1985-90, National College of Chiropractic; Deputy Public Defender 1972-75, DuPage County.
Professional Associations: Academy of Family Mediators; ABA; Assn. of Family and Conciliation Courts; ATLA; DuPage County Bar Assn. (Family Law Committee); DuPage County Circuit Court (Committee on Custody and Visitation Conciliation 1985-93); Illinois Appellate Lawyers Assn.; ITLA; ISBA; National Assn. of Chiropractic Attorneys (past Member); National Assn. of College and University Attorneys (past Member). *Mr. Haskin also practices Alternative Dispute Resolution and Civil Appellate Law.*

•**JUDY L. HOGAN** - *Judy L. Hogan, P.C., Attorneys and Mediators* - 115 Cambell, Suite 100A - Geneva, IL 60134 - Phone: (630) 232-1886, Fax: (630) 232-1890 - *See complete biographical profile in the Alternative Dispute Resolution Chapter, page 46.*

•**DAVID H. HOPKINS:** In private practice since 1969, Mr. Hopkins has practiced family law since the mid-1970s, concentrating particularly in creative tax planning incident to divorce. He is a frequent lecturer and writer on divorce tax issues. In the early and mid-1980s, he chaired the American Bar Association's Domestic Relations Tax Simplification Task Force which spearheaded the overhaul of the divorce tax provisions of the Internal Revenue Code that led to the 1984 and 1986 Tax Reform Acts. He has also concentrated on reforms in other areas of family law, such as work including his Chairmanship of an inter-bar task force that met every six weeks for six years to rewrite the Illinois Domestic Violence Act, an effort that culminated in a totally revamped act being enacted in 1992. He was appointed in 1990 by the Illinois Supreme Court as a member of the Study Committee on Mediation of Child Custody, Support, and Visitation Disputes; and in 1994, to the Illinois Family Violence Coordinating Council. Mr. Hopkins is listed in *Town & Country* magazine's "Guide to the Best Lawyers in America."
Education: JD 1969, Columbia University; AB 1966, Duke University.
Admitted: 1969 Illinois; 1971 U.S. Tax Ct.
Employment History: Partner 1983-present, Schiller, DuCanto and Fleck; Associate/Income Partner/Capital Partner 1969-83, McDermott, Will & Emery.
Professional Associations: ABA [Domestic Relations Tax Simplification Task Force (Chair 1980-84); Tax Section (Domestic Relations Tax Problems Committee, Chair 1982-84); Family Law Section (Taxation Committee 1993-present)]; CBA [Board of Managers 1992-94; Domestic Relations Subcommittee (Chair); Circuit Court Liaison Committee 1993-present; Matrimonial Law Committee 1988-89]; ISBA [Family Law Section Council (Chair 1989-90); Joint ISBA/CBA Task Force on Illinois Domestic Violence Act (Chair 1986-92)]; American Academy of Matrimonial Lawyers (Fellow).
Firm: The law firm of Schiller, DuCanto and Fleck—in which Mr. Hopkins is one of the four equity partners—is the largest matrimonial law firm in the United States. The firm has offices in both Chicago and Lake Forest, Illinois. The firm's members include leaders in the American Bar Association, Illinois State Bar Association, and the Chicago Bar Association, including a former President of the Illinois State Bar Association and two former Chief Judges of the Domestic Relations Division of the Circuit Court of Cook County. *See complete firm profile in Appendix A.*

DAVID H. HOPKINS
Schiller, DuCanto and Fleck
200 North LaSalle Street
Suite 2700
Chicago, IL 60601-1089

Phone: (312) 641-5560
Fax: (312) 641-6361

Extensive Experience In:
• Tax Planning/Connection with Divorce
• Domestic Violence

•**MICHAEL W. KALCHEIM:** Mr. Kalcheim concentrates exclusively in family law, including contested custody matters, trials of financial issues, and complex family law litigation. He handles evaluation and disposition of marital estates where closely held corporations are part of the estate; analysis of tax ramifications and tax planning for maintenance and child support awards; evaluation and disposition of pensions; developments and trends in equitable distribution legislation; and prenuptial agreements. Mr. Kalcheim participates in various continuing legal education seminars and received a Certificate of Appreciation for Continuing Legal Education from the Chicago Bar Association. He has led other seminars on family law topics for the North Suburban Bar Association and other organizations. Mr. Kalcheim participated as a judge in the DePaul University College of Law Moot Court Competition. He is the author of various topical outlines, treatises and other written materials, including "Problems in Valuing Professional Goodwill in Divorce Proceedings," *Illinois Bar Journal*, Vol. 78, No. 2, 1990; "Illinois Moves Toward Reviewable (Maybe Permanent?) Maintenance," *Illinois Bar Journal*, Vol. 81, No. 12, 1993; "Illinois Is Following the National Trend Away from Limited Maintenance Awards," *Illinois Bar Journal*, December 1993; "Divorce ~~Death~~ and Taxes: Two Things Are Certain in Life," *Illinois Bar Journal* (accepted for publication in 1996); and a coauthor of "Professional Goodwill in Divorce After Zells," *Illinois Bar Journal*, Vol. 79, No. 12, 1991. He is also the author of the software program, *The DOM—Cash Flow Program*, 1987.
Education: JD 1967, DePaul University; BS 1965, University of Wisconsin.
Admitted: 1967 Illinois; 1967 U.S. Dist. Ct. (N. Dist. IL).
Employment History: Partner 1987-present, Kalcheim, Schatz & Berger; Partner 1984-87, Kalcheim & Schatz; Partner 1967-84, Kalcheim & Kalcheim.
Representative Clients: Mr. Kalcheim represents clients who need high-end financial tax planning. He also reviews and analyzes extensive interaction between closed corporations and individuals.
Professional Associations: ABA; ISBA (Family Law Section); CBA (Matrimonial Law Committee); American Academy of Matrimonial Lawyers [Illinois Chapter (past Vice President; past Board of Managers)]. *See complete firm profile in Appendix A. Mr. Kalcheim also practices Probate, Estate Planning & Trusts Law.*

MICHAEL W. KALCHEIM
Kalcheim, Schatz & Berger
161 North Clark
Suite 2800
Chicago, IL 60601

Phone: (312) 782-3456
Fax: (312) 782-8463

Chapter 17: Family Law

LARRY R. KANE

Davis, Friedman, Zavett, Kane & MacRae
140 South Dearborn Street
Suite 1600
Chicago, IL 60603

Phone: (312) 782-2220
Fax: (312) 782-0464

•**LARRY R. KANE:** Mr. Kane has concentrated his practice in all areas of family law since 1975, after ten years in a general litigation practice. The majority of his cases involve the negotiation or trial of complex issues, including income tax ramifications and business valuations. He has lectured on family law issues for the American Academy of Matrimonial Lawyers, the Illinois State Bar Association, the Chicago Bar Association, the Illinois Institute for Continuing Legal Education, and DePaul University Law School. He has chaired committees for several professional organizations and has been the principal draftsperson of matrimonial statutes, including an extensive revision of Illinois' maintenance and property division statutes.

Education: JD 1965, DePaul University; BS 1962, University of Illinois.
Admitted: 1965 Illinois; 1965 U.S. Dist. Ct. (N. Dist. IL.)
Employment History: Partner 1985-present, Davis, Friedman, Zavett, Kane & MacRae; Sole Practitioner or Named Partner in small law firm 1965-85.
Representative Clients: The majority of Mr. Kane's clients are executives, business owners or professionals, or the spouses of those individuals.
Professional Associations: American Academy of Matrimonial Lawyers 1980-present [National Section (Certified List Committee, Chair 1986-88; Forensic Resource Guide Committee, Chair 1995-present); Illinois Chapter (President 1986-87; Board of Managers 1980-present; Admissions Committee 1980-93)]; ISBA [Family Law Section Council 1985-89, 1990-94; *Family Law Newsletter* (Coeditor 1995-present)]; Lake County Bar Assn.; ABA; CBA [Matrimonial Law Committee 1972-present (Chair 1983-84); Judicial Evaluation Committee 1983-87; Civil Practice Committee 1976-81]; Cook County Circuit Court [Domestic Relations Management Advisory Committee; Executive Committee; Judicial Management Subcommittee (Chair)]. *See complete firm profile in Appendix A.*

STEPHEN H. KATZ

Schiller, DuCanto and Fleck
207 East Westminster Road
Suite 201
Lake Forest, IL 60045

Phone: (847) 615-8300
Fax: (847) 615-8284

•**STEPHEN H. KATZ:** Mr. Katz has practiced exclusively in family law since 1977. Out of law school, Mr. Katz joined the U.S. Army Judge Advocate General's Corps and practiced General Courts Martial litigation for four years. After the service, Mr. Katz began private practice in Lake County, Illinois, a suburban county just north of Chicago. In 1976, Mr. Katz began lecturing for the Illinois Institute for Continuing Legal Education, speaking on such topics as divorce taxation, child custody contests, and negotiating techniques. Mr. Katz has been a Fellow of the American Academy of Matrimonial Lawyers since 1977, and has lectured at academy seminars. Mr. Katz lectured on complex tax issues at the October 1994 Illinois Chapter seminar. Mr. Katz also has been active in the state and local bar associations. He has served as a delegate to the General Assembly of the Illinois State Bar Association. In addition, he has been the Chair of the Family Law Committee of the Lake County Bar Association, and has lectured frequently on divorce issues at the local bar level. Mr. Katz has been recognized in *The Best Lawyers in America* since its initial publication in 1983.

Education: JD 1966, University of Illinois; BA 1963, University of Illinois.
Admitted: 1966 Illinois; 1966 U.S. Dist. Ct. (N. Dist. IL).
Professional Associations: ABA (Family Law Section); ISBA (Family Law Section Council; Civil Litigation Section); Lake County Bar Assn. [Family Law Committee (past Chair)]; American Academy of Matrimonial Lawyers.
Firm: The law firm of Schiller, DuCanto and Fleck is the largest matrimonial law firm in the United States. The firm's clients consist of sports figures, industrialists, entrepreneurs, political figures and other persons of note. The firm has offices in both Chicago and Lake Forest, Illinois. Of the seventeen Illinois family attorneys listed in *The Best Lawyers in America,* five are members of Schiller, DuCanto and Fleck. The firm's members include leaders in the American Bar Association, Illinois State Bar Association, and the Chicago Bar Association, including a former President of the Illinois State Bar Association and two former Chief Judges of the Domestic Relations Division of the Circuit Court of Cook County. *See complete firm profile in Appendix A.*

•**DAVID H. LEVY:** Mr. Levy is an experienced trial attorney who, for the past 20 years, has devoted himself exclusively to the area of family law. He has been involved in the resolution of hundreds of divorce cases, ranging from simple defaults to complex financial matters. His experience includes a working knowledge of the psychological aspects of custody and visitation litigation. Mr. Levy has lectured extensively on both the national and state levels to various organizations, including the American Bar Association, American Academy of Matrimonial Lawyers, Illinois State Bar Association, and Chicago Bar Association. He has also appeared as a panelist on numerous television and radio shows concerning issues of family law. He is the author of the chapter, "Commingling, Transmutation, and Reimbursement," in the Illinois State Bar Association's *Family Law Handbook*.
Education: JD 1976, Illinois Institute of Technology, Chicago-Kent; BS 1973, Ohio University.
Admitted: 1976 Illinois.
Employment History: Partner 1987-present, Kalcheim, Schatz & Berger; Partner 1982-87, Feiwell, Galper, Lasky & Berger; Associate 1978-82, Feiwell, Galper, Lasky & Berger; Associate 1976-78, John B. Hirsh.
Professional Associations: American Academy of Matrimonial Lawyers [National Board of Governors 1995-present; Illinois Chapter (President 1994-95; Board of Managers 1988-present)]; ISBA [Family Law Section Council 1990-present (Chair 1995-96)]; ABA (Family Law Section 1980-present).
Community Involvement: Lincoln Park Conservation Assn. (Board of Directors); Lincoln Central Assn. (President); Northfield Village Caucus; Chicago Symphony Orchestra; Art Institute of Chicago; Steppenwolf Theatre; Kohl's Children's Museum; Child Abuse Prevention Services.
Firm: Kalcheim, Schatz & Berger limits its practice to family and matrimonial law, and is one of the largest firms of its kind in the country. The firm includes Fellows, Board Members, and the past President of the Illinois Chapter of the American Academy of Matrimonial Lawyers, as well as the present and recent Chairs of the Illinois State Bar Association's Family Law Section Council. Every member of the firm has published and/or lectured on family law issues. On both the trial and appellate levels, the firm's 15 attorneys handle cases involving substantial estates, valuation, tax, custody, and issues of paternity. Members of the firm are also proficient in drafting prenuptial and postnuptial agreements. Due to the growth of the firm, it has recently relocated to larger offices in downtown Chicago and opened an additional office in Lake Forest, Illinois. *See complete firm profile in Appendix A.*

DAVID H. LEVY
Kalcheim, Schatz & Berger
161 North Clark
Suite 2800
Chicago, IL 60601

Phone: (312) 782-3456
Fax: (312) 782-8463

Extensive Experience In:
• Identification/Division of Assets
• Custody & Visitation
• Maintenance & Child Support

•**SALLY LICHTER:** Ms. Lichter concentrates her practice in all aspects of family law. She provides litigation services in divorce, paternity, custody, support, and post-decree matters. She has successfully tried custody disputes and complex divorces involving privately owned business and multiple property holdings. Ms. Lichter is trained in mediation and may provide mediation services for custody and financial disputes. She is frequently appointed by Lake County judges to represent children in adoptions and complex custody disputes. Her philosophy is to provide her clients with complete information regarding the benefits of settlement or litigation and to help clients fully understand the effects of divorce on children. These concepts are intended to ease the trauma of divorce and prepare the client for a new life.
Education: JD 1985, DePaul University; BA 1982 with honors, DePaul University.
Admitted: 1985 Illinois; 1986 U.S. Dist. Ct. (N. Dist. IL).
Employment History: Partner 1990-present, Voegtle & Lichter; Associate 1990-91, Wildman, Harrold, Allen & Dixon; Associate 1986-90, Snyder, Clarke, Dalziel & Johnson.
Representative Clients: Ms. Lichter's clients are equally divided between men and women. This provides her with a broad exposure on issues concerning both husbands and wives.
Professional Associations: ISBA 1985-present; Lake County Assn. of Women Attorneys 1986-present (President 1992-94; Treasurer 1990-92); Lake County Bar Assn. (Family Law Committee 1989-present).
Community Involvement: Women's Business Exchange (past Vice President 1986-present); Libertyville/Mundelein/Vernon Hills Chamber of Commerce 1991-present; Northern Illinois Council Against Substance Abuse (Golf Committee 1993); Committee to Elect Charles F. Scott, Appellate Judge (Treasurer 1993-present); Committee to Re-elect Judges Drew, Geiger, Scott and Walter (Treasurer 1995-present).
Firm: Ms. Lichter and her partner, Clayton Voegtle, founded the firm in 1991. Ms. Lichter concentrates her practice in family law, and Mr. Voegtle provides assistance for clients in other family-related matters, including estate planning, real estate, and any cases which involve an appeal. Ms. Lichter also practices Real Estate Law.

SALLY LICHTER
Voegtle & Lichter
14047 West Petronella Drive
Suite 202A
Libertyville, IL 60048

Phone: (847) 918-9840
Fax: (847) 918-8247

Extensive Experience In:
• Custody & Visitation Disputes
• Financial Disputes
• Post-Decree Matters

Chapter 17: Family Law

SUSAN M. LONERGAN

Susan M. Lonergan
Attorney at Law, P.C.
1450 West Main Street
Suite C
P.O. Box 1416
St. Charles, IL 60174

Phone: (630) 513-8600
Fax: (630) 513-8602

Extensive Experience In:

- Custody
- Visitation
- Mediation

•**SUSAN M. LONERGAN:** Ms. Lonergan's practice is concentrated in family law and mediation. She is the Founder and Director of KIDS in a Divorcing Society, a mandated divorce education program, for the 16th Judicial Circuit. Her family law practice is focused on orders of protection, child custody, visitation, child support, removal, spousal support, division of property, adoption, domestic violence, paternity, guardianships, and termination of parental rights. She also practices personal injury law. She represents husbands, wives and children, serving as an attorney and/or guardian ad litem for the child. She is a *Certified Family Law Mediator and a mediator for the 16th Judicial Circuit and has served as an arbitrator for the St. Louis Better Business Bureau. She advocates conflict reduction as a vehicle to healthy post-divorce parenting and believes that emotional savings are as important as financial savings in dissolution of marriage proceedings. Ms. Lonergan has been featured on radio and television and has been the focus of articles in the *Chicago Tribune* and many local newspapers. She lectured at the First International Conference on Parent Education, and has published articles in several newsletters and the *Kane County Bar Briefs*. She is the recipient of the St. Charles Chamber of Commerce Image Award for 1992. Ms. Lonergan advises all clients on how to save fees and furnishes monthly service statements to clients. As a sole practitioner, she provides attentive and personalized service to her clients.

Education: JD 1983 with honors, Southern Illinois University; BS 1975, Southern Illinois University; *Mediation Certification 1991, Divorce Mediation Institute, Ann Arbor, Michigan.
Admitted: 1983 Illinois; 1984 U.S. Dist. Ct. (S. Dist. IL); 1991 U.S. Dist. Ct. (N. Dist. IL).
Employment History: 1983-present, Susan M. Lonergan, Attorney at Law, P.C.; Teacher/Coach 1975-79, Hoffman Estates High School.
Professional Associations: ISBA (Family Law Section); Kane County Bar Assn. [Family Law Committee; Mediation Subcommittee (Chair); Guardian Ad Litem Subcommittee; Bench/Bar Committee; Pro Active Discovery Committee]; Assn. of Family and Conciliation Courts.
Community Involvement: St. Charles Chamber of Commerce (Recipient of Image Award 1992); Women's Council; Zonta International; American Assn. of University Women [Public Policy Committee (Chair)]; St. Patrick's Catholic Church Parish (Council Member 1991-present; President 1992-present; Lector); Richmond and Davis Schools (Room Parent); Webster School (Scholastic Olympics Coach); Illinois Assn. of Legal Secretaries [Award of Excellence Competition (Election Judge)].
Firm: Ms. Lonergan shares office space with her husband, George E. Richeson, Attorney at Law and Certified Public Accountant, concentrating in business law and taxation. *Ms. Lonergan also practices Alternative Dispute Resolution and Adoption Law.*

*The Supreme Court of Illinois does not recognize certifications of specialties in the practice of law. A certificate, award or recognition is not a requirement to practice law in Illinois.

RODERICK E. MACRAE

Davis, Friedman, Zavett, Kane & MacRae
140 South Dearborn Street
Suite 1600
Chicago, IL 60603

Phone: (312) 782-2220
Fax: (312) 782-0464

•**RODERICK E. MAC RAE:** Mr. MacRae practices family law, concentrating in all aspects of domestic relations. He is a founding member of Davis, Friedman, Zavett, Kane & MacRae and is on the advisory committee of the *Illinois Family Law Reporter* and the *Illinois Divorce Digest*. He has, on occasion, been a speaker for the local bar association on matrimonial law issues.
Education: JD 1971, Vanderbilt University; BSFS 1968, Georgetown University.
Admitted: 1971 Illinois.
Employment History: Partner 1982-present, Davis, Friedman, Zavett, Kane & MacRae; Associate 1972-81, predecessor firms.
Professional Associations: CBA (Matrimonial Law Committee); ISBA (Family Law Section Council).
Firm: The law firm of Davis, Friedman, Zavett, Kane & MacRae practices in every aspect of domestic relations law, including trial and appellate court practice. The firm strives to amicably resolve the outstanding issues that arise in divorce action, but each member has the ability to be an aggressive litigator on behalf of his or her clients. *See complete firm profile in Appendix A.*

•**EARLE A. MALKIN:** Mr. Malkin is a sole practitioner who concentrates in family law and real estate litigation. He believes in divorce mediation, and advocates mediation over litigation. He has represented clients in many high-profile, celebrity family law cases. Mr. Malkin is the author of the chapter, "Negotiating Custody," Illinois Institute for Continuing Legal Education Handbook, *Child Custody Litigation;* "Extending the Umbrella," American Bar Association's *Family Advocate,* Fall 1990; "Insurance," Illinois State Bar Association's *Family Law Handbook,* 1994; as well as various articles on medical insurance and military pension benefits. Mr. Malkin wrote the legislative drafting of the Illinois Spousal Health Insurance Rights Act, the Child Support Judgment Act, and the Qualified Illinois Domestic Relations Order Pension Proposal. He is a frequent lecturer on family law and other topics at the Illinois Institute for Continuing Legal Education, the Chicago Bar Association, the Northwest Suburban Bar Association, and the Illinois State Bar Association. He has been a guest lecturer at DePaul College of Law on topics of pension and insurance considerations in matrimonial law. Mr. Malkin is listed in *Who's Who in American Law; Who's Who in the Midwest,* current and previous editions; and is listed in the appendix of *The Divorce Lawyers,* by Emily Couric, St. Martin's Press, 1993.
Admitted: 1956 Illinois; U.S. Dist. Ct. (N. Dist. IL); U.S. Ct. App. (7th Cir.); U.S. Sup. Ct.; U.S. Claims Ct.; U.S. Ct. App. (Military); U.S. Dist. Ct. (N. Dist. GA).
Employment History: Sole Practitioner 1982-present, Law Offices of Earle A. Malkin; Partner 1971-82, Lafontant, Wilkins & Ware; Colonel, U.S. Army Judge Advocate General's Corps, AUS-RET.
Professional Associations: Illinois Bar Foundation [Board of Directors; Fellows (Chair)]; ISBA [Assembly; Election (Teller 1994); Public Relations Committee (Chair); Legislation Committee; Family Law Section Council; Simplified Divorce Task Force]; American Academy of Matrimonial Lawyers [Illinois Chapter (Fellow; Board Member; Vice President)]; International Academy of Matrimonial Lawyers (Fellow); Illinois Attorney General's Women's Advisory Commission (Division of Women's Advocacy; Blue Ribbon Advisory Committee on Children 1991-94); Circuit Court of Cook County [Domestic Relations Division (Advisory Committee to the Presiding Judge)]; Women's Bar Assn. of Illinois; North Suburban Bar Assn. (President); Decalogue Society of Lawyers (Board Member); CBA [Matrimonial Law Committee (Chair); Military Law Committee (Chair)]; ISBA/CBA Domestic Violence Task Force. *Mr. Malkin also practices Alternative Dispute Resolution.*

EARLE A. MALKIN
Law Offices of Earle A. Malkin
33 North Dearborn Street
Suite 2300
Chicago, IL 60602

Phone: (312) 372-6150
Fax: (312) 236-4725

Extensive Experience In:
• Litigation
• Mediation

•**DORENE MARCUS:** Ms. Marcus practices family law. She is the author of "Valuation of Marital Property Rights," *Family Law Handbook,* Illinois Institute for Continuing Legal Education. She has lectured at seminars sponsored by the American Bar Association, Chicago Bar Association, Illinois Institute for Continuing Legal Education, and the American Academy of Matrimonial Lawyers.
Professional Associations: American Academy of Matrimonial Lawyers [Fellow; National Organization (Secretary); Illinois Chapter (President-elect)]; ABA [Family Law Section (Executive Council 1993-present); Long-Range Planning Committee (Chair); Publication Development Board]; CBA [Matrimonial Law Committee (past Chair); International Academy of Matrimonial Lawyers (Fellow); ISBA (Family Law Section); Women's Bar Assn. of Illinois (Family Law Section); Task Force of Child Support Enforcement (past Member).
Firm: Members of the firm practice family law exclusively. The legal experience of the firm's attorneys ranges from 35 years to just graduating from law school. The firm has been in existence for 50 years. The hallmark of the firm is to bring a high level of professional experience to difficult family law problems. *See complete firm profile in Appendix A.*

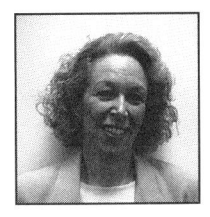

DORENE MARCUS
Davis, Friedman, Zavett, Kane & MacRae
140 South Dearborn Street
Suite 1600
Chicago, IL 60603

Phone: (312) 782-2220
Fax: (312) 782-0464

Chapter 17: Family Law

ENRICO J. MIRABELLI

Enrico J. Mirabelli & Associates
218 North Jefferson Street
Suite 101
Chicago, IL 60661

Phone: (312) 993-1500
Fax: (312) 993-1515

Extensive Experience In:

- Divorce Litigation
- Postjudgment Litigation
- Custody/Visitation Cases

•**ENRICO J. MIRABELLI:** Mr. Mirabelli concentrates in family law. He was twice a recipient of the Chicago Volunteer Legal Services Corporation Distinguished Service Award. He was awarded a Certificate of Appreciation from the Legal Assistance Foundation for his pro bono work on the "Baby Christopher" case, *In re: Adoptions of Indian Children,* 1995. In 1995, he received the John Marshall Law School Alumni Association, Distinguished Service Award. Mr. Mirabelli was published in *Family Law Section Council Newsletter* and is a coauthor of the amendment to Code of Civil Procedure, Sec. 5/2-401(e), which allows fictitious pleading. Mr. Mirabelli was the first attorney in Illinois to establish a cause of action for wrongful adoption in *Krueaer v. Leahy,* 89 L 18751 and third party liability for sexually transmitted diseases in *Doe v. Smith,* 91 L 16890. Copies of the complaints in each case have been reprinted in Callaghan's *Illinois Civil Practice Forms.* Mr. Mirabelli is a frequent author and speaker at seminars, including "Evidence—Its Uses and Abuses," ISBA Annual Meeting, June 1994; "Case Law Update," ISBA Seminar, December 1995 and June 1996; CBA, November 1994 and 1995; Will County Bar Association, February 1995; and "Custody in the '90s," ISBA Seminar, December 1993. He lectured at the American Bar Association Family Law Seminar, August 1995; "Fraud in the Nursery," Youth for Justice Seminar hosted by the CBA, June 1993; Judge Harold Sullivan's Panel Discussion on the Illinois Domestic Violence Act, February 1993; "Practical Aspects of Custody Cases," DePaul College of Law, February 1994 and John Marshall Law School, April 1995 and April 1996.

Education: JD 1981, John Marshall Law School, Chicago; BA 1978 magna cum laude, St. Mary's College, Winona, Minnesota.

Admitted: 1981 Illinois; 1981 U.S. Dist. Ct. (N. Dist. IL); 1986 U.S. Dist. Ct. (N. Dist. IL, Trial Bar); 1990 U.S. Ct. App. (7th Cir.).

Employment History: Principal, Enrico J. Mirabelli & Associates.

Professional Associations: ISBA (Board of Governors 1990-94; General Assembly 1986-94; Family Law Section Council); CBA; ABA; ITLA; Justinian Society of Lawyers (First Vice President); John Marshall Alumni Assn. 1986-present (President 1991).

Community Involvement: American Hearing Research Foundation (Board of Directors); National Republic Bank; Our Lady of Pompeii Shrine; Chicago Volunteer Legal Services Corporation (Advisory Board of Directors).

Firm: In addition to Mr. Mirabelli, the firm employs as associates: Philip J. Lengle, James M. Quigley, and Tracy M. Rizzo, and other staff personnel.

KURT A. MULLER

The Muller Firm, Ltd.
200 North Dearborn Street
Suite 4602
Chicago, IL 60601

Phone: (312) 855-9558
Fax: (312) 855-9362
Cable: MULLAW

Extensive Experience In:

- Visitation/Custody
- Prenuptial Agreements
- "Palimony"

•**KURT A. MULLER:** Mr. Muller concentrates his practice in hearings, trials, and appeals concerning divorce and family law, specifically child custody, support and visitation; property division (analysis of stock, option, commodity, real estate, insurance, pension, corporate, partnership and sole proprietorship holdings); spousal maintenance, post-decree enforcement and modification; domestic violence; paternity, adoption, "palimony," pre- and postnuptial agreements; and juvenile/family service matters. As Mr. Muller regularly receives national recognition, his involvement carries authority recognized by his peers and the judiciary. He is listed in *Who's Who in American Law; Who's Who in Practicing Attorneys; Who's Who in Emerging Leaders,* and *Who's Who in America.* Mr. Muller is a Family Law Commentator for *NBC News* and frequent family law informational source for *Time, Newsweek, USA Today, National Enquirer, Chicago Tribune, Chicago Sun Times, Chicago Magazine, Milwaukee Journal, Milwaukee Sentinel, A Current Affair,* and the *Oprah Winfrey Show.*

Admitted: 1986 Illinois; 1987 Arizona; 1989 Wisconsin; 1986 U.S. Dist. Ct. (N. Dist. IL, Trial Bar); 1989 U.S. Dist. Ct. (E. Dist. WI, Trial Bar).

Employment History: CEO/Attorney 1995, The Muller Firm, Ltd.; Partner 1992-95, Richter-Muller, P.C.; Sole Practitioner 1990-92, Law Offices of Kurt A. Muller; Associate 1987-90, Law Offices of Michael Harry Minton; Associate 1986-87, Gordon & Glickson, P.C.

Representative Clients: Although Mr. Muller focuses on high-profile family law matters, he recognizes that trouble has no socioeconomic boundaries. He is available to represent anyone with a legitimate problem which requires competent help. The initial retainer and hourly rate are individually tailored to the complexity of the matter and the particular client's ability to pay. Mr. Muller is also Special Counsel to the Investigative Group, Inc., an international agency specializing in complex factual investigations for major law firms and Fortune 500 corporations.

Professional Associations: The American Biographical Institute (Research Board of Advisors); ABA 1987-present; CBA 1987-present; Commodity Future Trading Commission (Associated Person); National Association of Securities Dealers (Registered Commodity Representative).

Community Involvement: Citizens for Justice Carl McCormick (Cochair); Citizens for Sheriff James O'Grady; Fullerton Cenacle (Board of Directors); Carl Sandburg Condominium (Board of Directors 1990).

Firm: The Muller Firm, Ltd., offers clients exclusive legal experience in divorce and family law along with over 15 consulting attorneys selected for their specific experience in legal areas tangential to the assessment and distribution of marital assets, including tax, corporate, real estate, securities, bankruptcy, immigration, employment and pension rights, collection, wills and trusts, personal injury, criminal, and intellectual property. *Mr. Muller also practices Arts, Entertainment & Intellectual Property Law and Alternative Dispute Resolution.*

CHERYL I. NIRO - *Partridge & Niro, P.C.; Associates in Dispute Resolution, Inc.* - 900 West Jackson Boulevard, Suite Five East - Chicago, IL 60607 - Phone: (312) 850-1906, Fax: (312) 850-1901 - *See complete biographical profile in the Alternative Dispute Resolution Chapter, page 47.*

•**CLAUDIA ONEY:** Ms. Oney practiced in the Cook County Domestic Relations Division for 17 years. She has handled many difficult and contentious custody cases and complex property divisions. She also has extensive trial experience in the "roller coaster" area of maintenance awards. Following an initial consultation, Ms. Oney believes it is her job to advise a client whether or not their case has merit, based on a complicated array of circumstances. She ensures that each client understands the law as it relates to his or her particular circumstances and she does not believe in making unrealistic promises. Since starting her own firm in 1978, most of her clients have been referrals from other clients. Ms. Oney utilizes a written retainer and her clients are thoroughly advised as to potential fees.
Education: JD 1978, DePaul University; BA 1968, University of Texas.
Admitted: 1978 Illinois; 1978 U.S. Ct. App. (7th Cir.); 1981 U.S. Dist. Ct. (N. Dist. IL, Trial Bar); 1983 U.S. Sup. Ct.
Employment History: 1978-present, Claudia Oney, P.C.
Professional Associations: ISBA; CBA; National Employment Lawyers' Assn.
Firm: Ms. Oney has recently invested in the latest computer hardware and software and has a connection to Lexis/Nexis; Lexis Counsel Connect; a direct internet connection; and a variety of CD-ROM materials, including the Illinois Annotated Statutes and Illinois Case Law, published by West Publishing Company. These extensive resources give Ms. Oney and her associates immediate access to constantly changing information databases, enabling them to serve clients efficiently and with accuracy. *Ms. Oney also practices Employment Law.*

CLAUDIA ONEY

Claudia Oney, P.C.
55 East Monroe Street
Suite 2920
Chicago, IL 60603

Phone: (312) 782-1900
Fax: (312) 782-1965

•**BEVERLY A. PEKALA:** Ms. Pekala concentrates her practice in the areas of litigation and family law. She has represented women and children in a number of highly publicized cases, including *Curran v. Bosze,* which drew nationwide attention as a case of first impression. Ms. Pekala's client was a single mother trying to protect her three-year-old twins from being forced to submit to bone marrow testing and transplant procedures desired by the children's father. Ms. Pekala successfully argued the *Curran* case twice at the trial court level and then before the Illinois Supreme Court which agreed to specially accept the case on an emergency basis. Through the *Curran* case and others, Ms. Pekala has garnered media attention, appearing on a variety of local news programs and national programs, including *Donahue, Good Morning America, The Today Show* and *CNN News.* In addition, she has been interviewed for various publications, and has been quoted in *USA Today, Time,* the *Chicago Tribune* and the *Chicago Sun Times.* From 1986 to 1991, Ms. Pekala served as an adjunct professor of law at Roosevelt University, teaching family law and corporate law. In addition, she has authored and coauthored publications, including a Family Law Survey in the *Loyola University Law Journal.* In January of 1994, Doubleday published Ms. Pekala's first book, *Don't Settle for Less: A Woman's Guide to Getting a Fair Divorce and Custody Settlement.*
Education: LLM Taxation 1986, John Marshall Law School; JD 1981, Illinois Institute of Technology, Chicago-Kent; BA 1979, DePaul University.
Admitted: 1982 Illinois.
Employment History: Principal 1994-present, The Law Offices of Beverly A. Pekala, P.C.; 1990-93, Robins, Kaplan, Miller & Ciresi; 1981-89, Grotefeld, Johnson & Pekala.
Professional Associations: Women's Bar Assn. of Illinois [Board of Directors; Matrimonial Law Committee (Cochair 1993-95)]; ABA; ISBA; CBA (Matrimonial Law Committee); Advocates Society.
Community Involvement: National Committee to Prevent Child Abuse (Chicago Board); pro bono attorney for various causes.

BEVERLY A. PEKALA

The Law Offices of
Beverly A. Pekala, P.C.
30 North LaSalle Street
43rd Floor
Chicago, IL 60602

Phone: (312) 251-0737
Fax: (312) 251-0733

Extensive Experience In:

• Women's Rights
• Children's Rights
• Custody

Chapter 17: Family Law

STEVEN N. PESKIND

Peskind & Peskind, Ltd.
Ten South River Street
Aurora, IL 60506

Phone: (630) 844-1263
Fax: (630) 844-0332

Extensive Experience In:

- Divorce Litigation
- Custody
- Property Division

•**STEVEN N. PESKIND:** Mr. Peskind concentrates his practice in divorce litigation at the trial and appellate court levels. Specifically, he represents parties in divorce litigation involving child custody, division of property, valuation and division of closely held companies, and related issues. Mr. Peskind focuses on providing a high level of service to his clients. He is an author and lecturer on divorce and family law topics. Mr. Peskind actively practices law in Kane and DuPage Counties, with offices located in Aurora and Wheaton. Formerly, he chaired the Kane County Bar Association Family Law Committee, and is currently the Assistant Editor of the American Bar Association family law litigation newsletter.

Education: JD 1985, DePaul University; BA 1982, Tulane University.
Admitted: 1985 Illinois; 1985 U.S. Dist. Ct. (N. Dist. IL).
Employment History: Partner 1990-present, Peskind & Peskind, Ltd.; Associate 1985-90, Law Offices of David P. Peskind.
Professional Associations: Kane County Bar Assn. [Secretary/Treasurer 1995-96; Family Law Committee (Chair 1993-95)]; ISBA (Assembly Member 1990-present).
Community Involvement: Mr. Peskind has sponsored the David P. Peskind Memorial Scholarship for graduating Northern Illinois University Law School students exemplifying excellence in family law studies. In 1989, he was the President of Breaking Free, a nonprofit agency, and was on the United Way Allocation Committee from 1987 to 1990.
Firm: The mission of Peskind & Peskind, Ltd., is to provide the highest quality legal services possible. The firm believes all of its clients deserve assertive and conscientious representation. In order to maintain the commitment to excellence, the firm believes that it is necessary to concentrate its practice in family law at the trial and appellate court levels. Further, through its advanced technological and computer resources, the firm can provide the advantages of a large firm, without sacrificing the personalized attention of a small firm.

HAROLD RICHTER

Law Offices of Harold Richter
18607 Torrence Avenue
Suite 2B
Lansing, IL 60438

Phone: (708) 862-2299
Fax: (708) 895-0220

•**HAROLD RICHTER:** With more than 40 years of experience, Harold Richter practices family law, concentrating in matrimonial law. His practice takes him to Cook, Will, and DuPage Counties in Illinois, and Lake County in Indiana. He successfully represents clients in all aspects of matrimonial law, including divorce, annulment, domestic abuse, antenuptial agreements, child custody and support, spousal maintenance and alimony, joint parenting agreements, property division, post-decree matters, paternity, visitation, and adoptions. Several times a year, Mr. Richter takes time away from his practice to serve as an arbitrator for the Circuit Court of Cook County. Mr. Richter also does some pro bono work with the Chicago Volunteer Legal Services Foundation and spends several days a year volunteering for the Chicago Bar Association, answering questions from people regarding divorce procedures in Illinois.

Education: JD 1952, Harvard University; BS 1948, University of Michigan.
Admitted: 1952 Illinois; 1953 Indiana; 1957 U.S. Ct. App. (7th Cir.); 1963 U.S. Sup. Ct.
Employment History: Mr. Richter has been a sole practitioner since 1994. Prior to that, he was a partner for 34 years with former Domestic Relations Judge, Samuel C. Maragos.
Representative Clients: Mr. Richter has clients from the states of Illinois and Indiana, as well as California, New York, Massachusetts, Oklahoma, Mississippi, and numerous other parts of the United States.
Professional Associations: American Academy of Matrimonial Lawyers (Fellow); CBA (Lawyer Referral Service); Decalogue Society of Lawyers; ABA (Senior Lawyers Division).
Firm: The Law Offices of Harold Richter is a law firm that focuses its energy in all areas of family law, including reconciliation, mediation, and counseling. Mr. Richter attempts to provide as amicable and equitable a settlement as possible for each of his clients, many of whom are in need of an attorney for the first time. He is available to his clients at all times to answer any questions or to manage any problems that may arise during this stressful period in their lives. The Law Offices of Harold Richter works along with its clients to ensure the most efficient management of each particular matter. Mr. Richter also has an office at 134 North LaSalle Street, Suite 2024, Chicago, Illinois 60601. Phone: (312) 759-2299.

•BERNARD B. RINELLA: Mr. Rinella has concentrated his practice exclusively in matrimonial law since 1961. A noted divorce litigator, he represents clients involved in high-profile and financially complex divorce cases, as well as clients whose cases involve general aspects of family law. He is a recognized authority on the drafting of premarital and postnuptial agreements. He is the coauthor of the Butterworth Publication, *Illinois Domestic Relations,* 1989, and is the Associate Editor of the Domestic Relations Section of *Law Notes* for the American Bar Association. He has lectured at seminars for several professional associations. Mr. Rinella has been selected for *The Best Lawyers in America* every year since 1982, and is listed in *Town & Country* magazine's "Guide to the Best Lawyers in America."
Education: JD 1961, DePaul University; BA 1958, University of Michigan.
Admitted: 1961 Illinois.
Employment History: Partner 1961-present, Rinella and Rinella, Ltd.
Professional Associations: American Academy of Matrimonial Lawyers 1965-present [Council 1986-87; Board of Governors 1982-83; Illinois Chapter (President 1982-84)]; CBA 1963-present [Matrimonial Law Committee (Chair 1980-81)]; ISBA [Family Law Section Council 1968-72 (Chair 1971); Economics of the Legal Profession Committee 1977-83]; ABA 1965-present [Family Law Committee; Divorce Laws and Procedures Subcommittee (Chair 1987); Parliamentarian Section 1988-90; *Law Notes* (Associate Editor 1967-75)]; Justinian Society of Lawyers 1968-present (President 1978).
Community Involvement: Child Welfare League of America, Inc. (Chicago Committee 1994-present); Allendale School [Community Board of Trustees 1984-90 (Chair); Development Committee (Chair 1992-present)]; Miami University (Parents Council 1991-present); Institute of Psychiatry Northwestern Memorial Hospital 1975-present [Advisory Board (Vice President 1983-present)]; University of Michigan Club of Chicago (President 1972-73); Union League Club of Chicago [Younger Members Group (Chair 1968-70)]; Union League Boys' Club (Trustee 1969-76); McGraw Foundation (Trustee 1970; President 1992-95); Children's Burn Awareness Program (Director 1994-present); Sunset Ridge Country Club (Director 1995-present).
Firm: Rinella and Rinella, Ltd., is the oldest matrimonial law firm in Illinois and is nationally recognized as one of the premier family law firms in the country. The firm's nine attorneys practice in all areas of matrimonial law, including legal separation, negotiating and drafting premarital and postnuptial agreements, judgment enforcement, child custody and support actions, domestic violence, appeals, paternity actions, and interstate support enforcement. The firm strives to provide quality and professional legal services at a reasonable fee. The firm has another office at 207 East Westminster Avenue, Lake Forest, Illinois 60045-1861. Phone: (847) 234-5486, Fax: (847) 234-6978.

BERNARD B. RINELLA
Rinella and Rinella, Ltd.
One North LaSalle Street
Suite 3400
Chicago, IL 60602

Phone: (312) 236-5454
Fax: (312) 236-6975

•HOWARD H. ROSENFELD: Mr. Rosenfeld is a member of the Advisory Panel of the *Illinois Trial Court Digest* and a member of the Liaison Committee to the Domestic Relations Division of the Circuit Court of Cook County, Illinois. He is a lecturer for the Illinois Institute for Continuing Legal Education, the Illinois Certified Public Accountants Society, and the American Academy of Matrimonial Lawyers. Mr. Rosenfeld is listed in several editions of *The Best Lawyers in America,* published by Woodward/White, including 1995-96, and in *Who's Who in American Law.*
Education: JD 1962, DePaul University; BA 1959, University of Illinois.
Admitted: 1962 Illinois; 1963 U.S. Dist. Ct. (N. Dist. IL).
Professional Associations: American Academy of Matrimonial Lawyers [Illinois Chapter (Vice President; past Board of Governors); Admission Commission; Samuel Berger Award Committee (Chair)]; CBA (Matrimonial Committee); ISBA; ATLA.
Firm: Rosenfeld, Rotenberg, Hafron & Shapiro.

HOWARD H. ROSENFELD
Rosenfeld, Rotenberg, Hafron & Shapiro
221 North LaSalle Street
Suite 1763
Chicago, IL 60601

Phone: (312) 372-6058
Fax: (312) 641-3139

Extensive Experience In:

• Support/Property Division
• Custody/Visitation
• Paternity

Chapter 17: Family Law

JAMES L. RUBENS

Davis, Friedman, Zavett, Kane & MacRae
140 South Dearborn Street
Suite 1600
Chicago, IL 60603

Phone: (312) 782-2220
Fax: (312) 782-0464

•**JAMES L. RUBENS:** Mr. Rubens practices family law, concentrating in all aspects of domestic relations. He has lectured on family law issues for the Illinois Institute for Continuing Legal Education, the Chicago Bar Association, including its Young Lawyers Section, and the Lorman Business Institute. He is the author of a chapter in a child custody litigation book published by the Illinois Institute for Continuing Legal Education. He is a past member of the Board of Governors for the Chicago Council of Lawyers and was Cochair of the State Judicial Evaluation Committee from 1989 through 1994.
Education: JD 1979, DePaul University; BS 1976, University of Illinois.
Admitted: 1979 Illinois; 1979 U.S. Dist. Ct. (N. Dist. IL).
Employment History: Partner/Associate 1986-present, Davis, Friedman, Zavett, Kane & MacRae; Associate 1986, Schiff, Hardin & Waite; Public Defender 1979-84, Public Defender's Office, Cook County.
Professional Associations: ISBA [*Family Law Newsletter* (Coeditor 1995)]; Chicago Council of Lawyers [Judicial Evaluation Committee 1989-94 (Cochair); Board of Governors (past Member)]; CBA.
Community Involvement: Young Men's Jewish Council (Board of Directors 1982). *See complete firm profile in Appendix A.*

CATHERINE M. RYAN

Ryan, Miller & Trafelet, P.C.
120 South Riverside Plaza
Suite 1150
Chicago, IL 60606-3910

Phone: (312) 207-1700
Fax: (312) 207-1332

•**CATHERINE M. RYAN:** Ms. Ryan practices law related to children, senior citizens and their families. Her primary area of practice is child welfare law, which includes both family law and juvenile delinquency law. Ms. Ryan has extensive courtroom experience, particularly in matters of adoption, child protection, child custody, visitation and support, parentage, and juvenile delinquency matters. She also works with senior citizens and their families regarding the legal aspects of health care decisions, guardianships, and financial protection. Ms. Ryan is the recipient of several awards, including an Award of Merit in 1974 from the Illinois State Bar Association; the Child Advocate Award in 1985 from the State of Illinois Department of Children and Family Services; an award in 1985 from the Maryville City of Youth; and the Catholic Lawyer of the Year Award in 1990 from the Catholic Lawyers Guild of Chicago. She is the author of several publications, including "Juvenile Court Jurisdiction: Intervention and Intrusion," *From Children to Citizens, Volume 11: The Role of the Juvenile Court,* 1987; and a coauthor of "Juvenile Law," 18 *Loyola University of Chicago Law Journal* 2, Winter 1986. She is a frequent lecturer on child welfare law, and health care and protection issues for seniors.
Education: JD 1972, Northwestern University; MBA 1979, DePaul University; BA 1969, Alverno College.
Admitted: 1972 Illinois; 1972 U.S. Dist. Ct. (N. Dist. IL); 1973 U.S. Ct. App. (7th Cir.).
Employment History: Shareholder 1985-present, Ryan, Miller & Trafelet, P.C.; Supervisor 1981-84, Juvenile Division, Cook County State's Attorney's Office; Coordinator 1975-84, Child Abuse Unit, Cook County State's Attorney's Office; Assistant State's Attorney 1973-84, Cook County State's Attorney's Office.
Professional Associations: CBA [Juvenile Law Committee (past Chair)]; ISBA.
Community Involvement: Citizens' Committee on the Juvenile Court (Chair); Maryville Academy (Board of Directors); Archdiocese of Chicago [Professional Fitness Review Board (Chair)]; City of Chicago 1989-95 [Board of Ethics (past Chair)]; Alvernia High School 1973-79 (past Board of Directors); Tau Home Health Care Agency, Inc. 1978-83 (past Board of Directors); Statewide Citizens' Committee on Child Abuse and Neglect 1985-88 [Illinois Department of Children and Family Services (past Advisor)]; Illinois Task Force on Gender Bias in the Courts 1988-89 (past Criminal Law Committee).
Firm: The firm of Ryan, Miller & Trafelet, P.C., is a four-person firm founded in 1985. The firm practices in various planning and litigation areas of family and criminal law. *Ms. Ryan also practices Criminal Law: DUI & Misdemeanors (Juveniles) and Elder Law.*

•**HARRY SCHAFFNER:** Mr. Schaffner concentrates his practice in complex family law cases. He has experience in trials, appeals, and negotiations of all family law matters. Representing both men and women, he has been involved in cases in Kane and DuPage Counties in Illinois. Mr. Schaffner is widely known as both tough and fair. He is skilled in court proceedings and negotiations. Many of his clients have been other attorneys, and most referrals come to him from other professionals. Mr. Schaffner was the recipient of the Austin Fleming Award in 1993 and the Distinguished Service Award in 1992. He is the author of *Don't Get Married Until You Read This Book,* Barrons, 1991.
Education: JD 1966, University of Illinois; BA 1964, University of Illinois.
Admitted: 1967 Illinois; 1967 U.S. Dist. Ct. (N. Dist. IL); 1987 U.S. Sup. Ct.
Employment History: 1969-present, Schaffner & Van Der Snick, P.C.
Representative Clients: Mr. Schaffner represents numerous professional and business people, and their spouses.
Professional Associations: American Academy of Matrimonial Lawyers 1975-present; ISBA [Family Law Section (Chair 1991-92); *Illinois Bar Journal* (Associate Editor 1992-95)].
Community Involvement: The Elgin Academy 1984-89 (Board Member); Lawyer Blood Bank Drive (Organizer); led lawyer CPR classes.
Firm: The firm has over 45 years of combined experience in Kane and DuPage Counties. The emphasis of the firm is on effective advocacy of family law clients. Hidden assets are often located and selfish behavior demonstrated. The firm declines to represent clients who do not pay child support and are not cooperative and reasonable.

HARRY SCHAFFNER
Schaffner & Van Der Snick, P.C.
115 Campbell Street
Geneva, IL 60134

Phone: (630) 232-8900
Fax: (630) 232-8908

•**DONALD C. SCHILLER:** A matrimonial attorney practicing for more than 20 years in family law, Mr. Schiller is a skilled litigator, frequent lecturer and writer, and bar association leader. He was very active in the Illinois General Assembly in the drafting and passage of major law reforms, including laws governing no-fault divorce. In 1988, Mr. Schiller was presented with the Distinguished Alumni Award from DePaul University. He is the author of "Alimony—Should Marital Misconduct Be a Factor?" *Alimony: New Strategies for a Pursuit and Defense,* American Bar Association, 1988; and "Fault Undercuts Equity," *Family Advocate,* American Bar Association. Mr. Schiller has been cited by *Town & Country* magazine, the *National Law Journal,* Crain's *Chicago Business,* and *The Best Lawyers in America* as one of the nation's top divorce lawyers. He is the subject of a chapter in the book, *The Divorce Lawyers,* by Emily Couric.
Education: JD 1966, DePaul University *(Law Review* 1965-66); 1960-63, Lake Forest College.
Admitted: 1966 Illinois; 1966 U.S Dist. Ct. (N. Dist. IL); 1972 U.S. Sup. Ct.
Professional Associations: ISBA [President 1987-88; Vice President 1984-87; Treasurer 1980-83; Board of Governors 1977-83; Family Law Section (Chair 1976-77)]; ABA [Board of Governors; Illinois State Delegate 1990-94; House of Delegates 1984-88; Family Law Section (Chair 1985-86); Divorce Law and Procedure Committee (Chair 1980-82); *Family Law Newsletter* (Editor-in-Chief 1977-79)]; CBA 1971-present [Matrimonial Law Committee (Chair 1976-77); Committee on Committees 1977-81; Candidates Evaluation Committee (Vice Chair 1978-80)]; ITLA [Family Law Section (Chair 1979-81)]; Illinois Institute for Continuing Legal Education (Faculty 1972-present; Board of Directors); American Academy of Matrimonial Lawyers [Vice President 1978-84; Illinois Chapter (Board of Managers 1973-84); Continuing Legal Education 1994-95 (National Chair)].
Firm: The law firm of Schiller, DuCanto and Fleck is the largest matrimonial law firm in the United States. The firm's clients consist of sports figures, industrialists, entrepreneurs, political figures and other persons of note. The firm has offices in both Chicago and Lake Forest, Illinois. Of the seventeen Illinois family attorneys listed in *The Best Lawyers in America,* five are members of Schiller, DuCanto and Fleck. The firm's members include leaders in the American Bar Association, Illinois State Bar Association, and the Chicago Bar Association, including a former President of the Illinois State Bar Association and two former Chief Judges of the Domestic Relations Division of the Circuit Court of Cook County. *See complete firm profile in Appendix A.*

DONALD C. SCHILLER
Schiller, DuCanto and Fleck
200 North LaSalle Street
Suite 2700
Chicago, IL 60601-1089

Phone: (312) 641-5560
Fax: (312) 641-6361

Chapter 17: Family Law

GARY L. SCHLESINGER
Law Office of Gary L. Schlesinger
1512 Artaius Parkway
Suite 300
P.O. Box 6229
Libertyville, IL 60048

Phone: (847) 680-4970
Fax: (847) 680-5459

Extensive Experience In:
- Contested Custody Cases

•**GARY L. SCHLESINGER:** Mr. Schlesinger limits his practice to family law, including custody, support, adoption, property, and juvenile abuse and neglect cases. He is often appointed as attorney by divorce judges to handle the representation of children in complex custody cases and is hired by psychologist groups to give in-house training on Illinois divorce law. Mr. Schlesinger has frequently testified before the Illinois legislature on various family law bills on behalf of the Illinois State Bar Association. He has presented annual divorce seminars for the Lake County Bar Association and the Illinois State Bar Association. Mr. Schlesinger has been involved with the Mundelein High School Adult Education Program on Illinois divorce law since 1990, and he also teaches for the Volunteer Lawyer Program for the Lake County Bar Association. He is a court appointed arbitrator for the 19th Judicial Circuit, Lake County, Illinois.
Education: JD 1970, Northwestern University; BS 1967, Loyola University of Chicago.
Admitted: 1971 Illinois; 1971 U.S. Dist. Ct. (N. Dist. IL).
Employment History: Principal 1986-present, Law Office of Gary L. Schlesinger; Partner 1976-86, Ray & Glick, Ltd.; Partner 1974-76, Overholser Flannery & Schlesinger; Director 1972-74, Legal Aid Office, Lake County, Illinois.
Professional Associations: ISBA (Assembly 1994-present; Family Law Section Council 1989-93); American Academy of Matrimonial Lawyers (Board Member 1994-present; Vice President 1993-94); Lake County Bar Assn. [Family Law Section (Chair 1982-84); Volunteer Lawyer Committee].
Community Involvement: Rotary Club, Libertyville, Illinois; Congregation Or Shalom (Vice President; Board of Trustees); Lake County Bar Assn. (Volunteer Lawyer Program).
Firm: As a sole practitioner, Mr. Schlesinger offers all of his clients individual service performed only by himself. No client will be shunted to an associate or other attorney for any legal work.
Mr. Schlesinger also practices Adoption Law.

BENEDICT SCHWARZ II
Law Offices of Benedict Schwarz II, Ltd.
303 West Main Street
West Dundee, IL 60118

Phone: (847) 428-7725
Fax: (847) 428-7750

Extensive Experience In:
- Divorce
- Custody Issues
- Mediation

•**BENEDICT SCHWARZ II:** Mr. Schwarz exclusively practices matrimonial and family law matters. He is a Court Approved Mediator for Kane and McHenry County Courts, with over 150 hours' experience. He helped initiate mediation in Kane County, and was invited by the presiding Judge of Family Division of McHenry County to aid in establishing court approved mediation. Since 1992, he has been the Commissioner of the Attorney Registration and Disciplinary Commission of the Supreme Court of Illinois. Mr. Schwarz's mediation training includes Divorce Mediation Basic Training, Mediation Institute of Atlanta, 1991; Advanced Training Workshop in Divorce Mediation, Divorce Mediation Institute, 1991; Mediating Parties Needing Special Consideration, 1993; coaching a mediation training class for Divorce Mediation Institute, 1994; basic techniques, advanced training, court-referred mediation, expanding horizons, Mediation Council of Illinois, 1994. Mr. Schwarz has lectured and taught courses on mediation for professional associations and schools throughout Illinois, including the Kane County Bar Association, DuPage County Bar Association, John Marshall Law School, Elgin Community College, and many others. He is the coauthor of "Negotiating Child Custody Issues," *Child Custody Litigation,* Illinois Institute for Continuing Legal Education.
Education: JD 1971, John Marshall Law School; BS 1964, University of Wisconsin-Madison.
Admitted: 1971 Illinois.
Employment History: Principal 1991-present, Law Offices of Benedict Schwarz II, Ltd.; Principal 1990-95, Law Firm of Schwarz and Ryan, Ltd.; Principal 1977-90, Schwarz, Golden, Golden and Ryan, Ltd.
Professional Associations: ISBA [Family Law Section Council; Child Support Subcommittee (Chair); Domestic Violence Task Force]; American Academy of Matrimonial Lawyers (Vice President 1995-96; Board of Directors 1978-present; Fellow 1978-present; ADR Committee); Kane County Bar Assn. [Family Law Committee (Chair 1991-93); Board of Directors 1993-94; Treasurer 1993-94; Legislative Committee (Chair 1994)]; Kane County State's Attorney's Task Force on Domestic Violence (Chair 1994-present); Kane County Batterers Task Force (Chair 1993-present; Founder); Lawyers Assistance Program (Board of Directors 1994-present); Academy Family of Mediators 1993-present.
Community Involvement: Northern Illinois University College of Law (Board of Visitors); Lutheran General Hospital (Intervention Training Program; Trained Intervenor April 1991).
Mr. Schwarz also practices Alternative Dispute Resolution.

•**HELEN SIGMAN:** Helen Sigman concentrates her practice in the areas of divorce, post-divorce, child custody, visitation, child support, grandparents rights, parentage, premarital agreements, domestic violence, adoption, guardianship, and juvenile court proceedings.
Education: JD 1980, Wayne State University; BA 1974, University of Michigan.
Admitted: 1980 Michigan; 1984 Illinois.
Employment History: Head of Firm 1989-present, Helen Sigman & Associates, Ltd.; Staff Attorney 1984-89, Legal Aid Bureau, United Charities, Family Law Division.
Representative Clients: Helen Sigman represents spouses, minor children, and other parties involved in divorce, child custody, visitation, support, and juvenile court proceedings. She represents adoptive parents seeking to adopt, and grandparents seeking custody and visitation orders.
Professional Associations: American Academy of Matrimonial Lawyers (Fellow); ISBA (Family Law Section); CBA (Matrimonial Law Committee); Women's Bar Assn. of Illinois [Matrimonial Law Committee (past Chair)].
Community Involvement: Chicago Volunteer Legal Services Foundation (Board of Directors); Pro Bono Advocates (Pro Bono Attorney); Legal Aid Bureau (Pro Bono Attorney); Cook County Legal Assistance Foundation (Pro Bono Attorney); Gads Hill Community Center (Board of Directors).
Firm: The firm was founded in 1989, and presently consists of two attorneys. The firm has a team approach which provides the client with better access to an attorney at all times. The firm practices exclusively in family law. The firm often refers matters to experienced mediators in appropriate cases to minimize expense and animosity between the parties.

HELEN SIGMAN

Helen Sigman & Associates, Ltd.
566 West Adams Street
Suite 501
Chicago, IL 60661-3627

Phone: (312) 258-8441
Fax: (312) 258-8017

Extensive Experience In:

• Divorce
• Adoption
• Orders of Protection

•**ARNOLD STEIN:** A seasoned and very successful litigator of financially complex divorce cases, Mr. Stein is recognized as a fine divorce lawyer and is listed in *The Best Lawyers in America*. He is a Phi Beta Kappa and James Scholar. He is the Chair of the Litigation Committee of the American Bar Association's Family Law Section, and has lectured extensively throughout the country on trial techniques and litigation strategy.
Education: JD 1974, Northwestern University (Phi Beta Kappa; Phi Alpha Theta; James Scholar); BS 1970, University of Illinois.
Admitted: 1975 Illinois.
Professional Associations: ABA; CBA; ISBA.
Firm: The law firm of Schiller, DuCanto and Fleck is the largest matrimonial law firm in the United States. The firm's clients consist of sports figures, industrialists, entrepreneurs, political figures and other persons of note. The firm has offices in both Chicago and Lake Forest, Illinois. Of the seventeen Illinois family attorneys listed in *The Best Lawyers in America,* five are members of Schiller, DuCanto and Fleck. The firm's members include leaders in the American Bar Association, Illinois State Bar Association, and the Chicago Bar Association, including a former President of the Illinois State Bar Association and two former Chief Judges of the Domestic Relations Division of the Circuit Court of Cook County. *See complete firm profile in Appendix A.*

ARNOLD STEIN

Schiller, DuCanto and Fleck
200 North LaSalle Street
Suite 2700
Chicago, IL 60601-1089

Phone: (312) 641-5560
Fax: (312) 641-6361

Chapter 17: Family Law

EDWARD I. STEIN

Edward I. Stein, Ltd.
707 Skokie Boulevard
Suite 600
Northbrook, IL 60062

Phone: (847) 291-4320
Fax: (847) 432-1132

Extensive Experience In:
- Divorce & Custody Trials
- Divorce-Related Business Evaluations
- Alimony & Child Support Arrearages

•**EDWARD I. STEIN:** Mr. Stein has been in private practice since 1971 in Lake and Cook Counties. His practice is limited to family law, including dissolution of marriage, legal separation, declaration of invalidity of marriage, custody and visitation disputes, tax and financial aspects of family law, premarital and postmarital agreements, contested trials and appeals, postdissolution litigation, predivorce planning, divorce mediation, paternity suits, adoption, and orders of protection. He has extensive experience in valuation and division issues regarding closely held companies, including partnerships, sole proprietorships, and privately held corporations. For 15 years, Mr. Stein authored the "Marital Settlement Agreements" chapter in the *Family Law Handbook* used by most Illinois lawyers. He was elected a Fellow of the American Academy of Matrimonial Lawyers in 1977. In 1978, he received an award for his significant contribution to the education of the bar from the Illinois Institute for Continuing Legal Education. He has published numerous articles in the field of family law, has been featured in the *National Law Journal, Money Magazine, Chicago Magazine,* Crain's *Chicago Business, The New York Times,* and many other publications. He founded the "Lawyers' Forum" column of the *Chicago Daily Law Bulletin,* where he headed a panel of 26 widely known lawyers. He has lectured extensively before the bar and the public, has been a featured guest speaker on many television and radio programs in the area of family law, and is listed in the national directory of *Who's Who in Executives and Professionals.*
Education: JD 1971, Illinois Institute of Technology, Chicago-Kent; BS 1967, Roosevelt University.
Admitted: 1971 Illinois; 1971 U.S. Dist. Ct. (IL); 1976 U.S. Sup. Ct.
Employment History: Founder 1974-present, Edward I. Stein, Ltd.
Professional Associations: ISBA; CBA; Lake County Bar Assn.
Community Involvement: Mr. Stein is an instructor at several adult continuing education programs in the area of divorce law.
Firm: Serving primarily the North Shore, the main office of Edward I. Stein, Ltd., is located in Northbrook, Cook County, with a satellite office in nearby Deerfield, Lake County. In order to serve the best interests of the client, consideration is given to the constructive settlement approach as well as the litigation process. Communication between attorney and client is afforded the highest priority so that the client is fully informed and can knowledgeably participate in the decision-making process.

WILLIAM J. STOGSDILL, JR.

Law Offices of
William J. Stogsdill, Jr., P.C.
1776 South Naperville Road
Building B
Suite 202
Wheaton, IL 60187

Phone: (630) 462-9500
Fax: (630) 690-5725

Extensive Experience In:
- Custody
- Division of Retirement Benefits

•**WILLIAM J. STOGSDILL, JR.:** Mr. Stogsdill practices family law exclusively, concentrating on custody and complicated property cases. He is a highly experienced trial attorney. Mr. Stogsdill is the recipient of the 1986 DuPage County Bar Association Outstanding Service Award for Pro Bono Legal Services. He is the author of "Division of Retirement Benefits in Domestic Relations Proceedings," Illinois State Bar Association's *Family Law Handbook,* 1995. He wrote several articles in the *DuPage County Lawyers' Bulletin,* including "Highlights of Procedure for Withholding of Income to Secure Payment of Support," Section 706.1, February 1982; "Allocations of Child Dependency Exemptions"; "Limitation of Factors Constituting a Substantial Change in Circumstances Justifying a Modification"; "The Uniform Child Custody Jurisdiction Act"; "Modification of Custody Judgments Under the Present Illinois Uniform Child Custody Jurisdiction Act"; and coauthored "Discharge in Bankruptcy of Hold Harmless Provisions, In Re the Marriage of Lytle," November 1988. Mr. Stogsdill has been a speaker for the DuPage County Bar Association, West Suburban Bar Association, College of DuPage, Illinois Institute for Continuing Legal Education, and the DuPage County Child Support Conference. Mr. Stogsdill was appointed to the Illinois State Bar Association Family Law Section Council from 1989 to 1997.
Education: JD 1974, John Marshall Law School; BBA 1971, Wisconsin State University-Whitewater.
Admitted: 1974 Illinois; 1974 U.S. Dist. Ct. (N. Dist. IL); 1980 U.S. Sup. Ct.
Employment History: 1984-present, Law Offices of William J. Stogsdill, Jr., P.C.; Appointed Special Assistant State's Attorney 1989, State's Attorney's Office, DuPage County; Partner 1976-84, Kowalczyk & Stogsdill, Ltd.; Assistant State's Attorney 1973-76, State's Attorney's Office, DuPage County.
Professional Associations: DuPage County Bar Assn. [Ad Hoc Rules Committee; Matrimonial Law Committee (Chair 1982-83, 1987-88, 1988-89; Cochair 1983-84); DuPage County Conciliation Program (Director/Advisor 1986-93)]; CBA; ISBA [Family Law Council Section (Appointed Member 1989-93, 1995-96); Subcommittee on Illinois Pensions (Chair 1991-92)]; ABA.
Firm: Mr. Stogsdill is the principal in the Law Offices of William J. Stogsdill, Jr., P.C., which employs five experienced family law attorneys.

•**MARY BETH S. TIGHE:** Ms. Tighe concentrates in all aspects of matrimonial law, including contested and uncontested divorces, antenuptial and premarital agreements, child custody, spousal maintenance, and post-decree matters. During her eight years of private practice, she has successfully represented a wide range of clients in divorce matters. In addition to handling matrimonial matters in Cook County, Ms. Tighe handles cases in Kane and DuPage Counties. Her practice also includes general practice matters, and she is an Administrative Hearing Officer for the State of Illinois Racing Board.
Education: JD 1983, John Marshall Law School; BS 1979, Michigan State University.
Admitted: 1983 Illinois; 1983 U.S. Dist. Ct. (N. Dist. IL).
Employment History: 1988-present, Mary Beth S. Tighe, Attorney at Law; 1984-87, Department of Law, City of Chicago; Assistant State's Attorney 1983-84, DuPage County State's Attorney's Office, Criminal Division.
Professional Associations: CBA; Northwest Suburban Bar Assn.
Community Involvement: Park Ridge Public Library (Board of Trustees); St. Paul of the Cross Home and School Board.
Firm: Ms. Tighe is a sole practitioner. She also has an office in DuPage County at 1415 West 22nd Street, Oak Brook, Illinois 60521.

MARY BETH S. TIGHE
Attorney at Law
824 North Busse Highway
Park Ridge, IL 60068
Phone: (847) 823-7771
Fax: (630) 574-1501

•**WILLIAM J. TRUEMPER:** Mr. Truemper has concentrated his practice in the area of family law for 18 years in the Illinois counties of DuPage, Kane, DeKalb, Kendall, and LaSalle. He provides experienced representation in the areas of divorce, custody, support, visitation, adoption, domestic violence, and other related areas. He represents attorneys, physicians, and other professional and business persons. He handles complex issues involving business and other asset valuation and provides tax advice to divorcing clients concerning property division and support issues. He is experienced in commercial and residential real estate transactions incident to property division, preparing prenuptial agreements for persons about to marry, and drafting wills and trusts for clients following divorce. He lectures to the Kane County Bar Association on family law matters and has been a speaker at meetings of divorced and single parent organizations on family law issues. He has received basic and advanced training in the mediation of family law issues and serves as guardian ad litem in custody and adoption matters to protect the best interests of children. He is licensed to practice in state and federal courts and is a member of the Federal Trial Bar.
Education: JD 1976, John Marshall Law School; BA 1973, Aurora University (Dean's List).
Admitted: 1977 Illinois; 1977 U.S. Dist. Ct. (N. Dist. IL); 1977 U.S. Dist. Ct. (N. Dist. IL, Trial Bar).
Employment History: Founding Partner 1978-present, Truemper, Hollingsworth, Wojtecki, Courtin & Titiner.
Professional Associations: Kane County Bar Assn.; ISBA (Family Law Section).
Community Involvement: Mr. Truemper has been a life-long resident of Aurora, Illinois. He provides legal advice to social organizations, including the Third Ward Social Club, Tiger Athletic Assn., Phoenix Club, and Aurora Kickers Club. He has received a commendation for providing free legal assistance to the elderly in his community.
Firm: The firm of Truemper, Hollingsworth, Wojtecki, Courtin & Titiner has six attorneys, one Of Counsel, and provides legal services for individuals, local government entities, businesses and business organizations in diverse areas of the law. The firm's representative clients include American Health Care Radiology Administrators; City of Aurora, Illinois; Greater Aurora Chamber of Commerce; Hollywood Casino-Aurora; Old Second National Bank of Aurora; and Aurora Firefighters Credit Union. *See complete firm profile in Appendix A. Mr. Truemper also practices Alternative Dispute Resolution and Adoption Law.*

WILLIAM J. TRUEMPER
Truemper, Hollingsworth, Wojtecki, Courtin & Titiner
1700 North Farnsworth Avenue
Suite 11
Aurora, IL 60505
Phone: (630) 820-8400
Fax: (630) 820-8582

Chapter 17: Family Law

RORY T. WEILER

Weiler & Noble, P.C.
335 North River Street
Suite 203
Batavia, IL 60510

Phone: (630) 879-3020
Fax: (630) 513-2929
E-mail: r.weiler@inil.com

Extensive Experience In:

- Divorce
- Child Custody
- Child Abuse & Neglect

•**RORY T. WEILER:** Mr. Weiler concentrates his practice in family law, with an emphasis on cases involving child custody, visitation, and child removal issues. His practice deals with all areas of family law, including divorce, paternity, legal separation, domestic abuse, and premarital (antenuptial) agreements. He was also involved as trial counsel in one of the first cases in Illinois dealing with grandparent visitation rights. His commitment to the protection and enhancement of children's rights in divorcing families led to his participation in an ad hoc committee which developed one of the first mandatory child awareness education programs in the country for divorcing parents. Mr. Weiler remains actively involved as an instructor in this program, KIDS in a Divorcing Society.
Education: JD 1979, John Marshall Law School (Staff Member, *Law Review*); BS 1975, Northern Illinois University.
Admitted: 1979 Illinois; 1979 U.S. Dist. Ct. (N. Dist. IL).
Employment History: Partner 1989-present, Weiler & Noble, P.C.; Partner 1982-89, Rory T. Weiler, P.C.; Associate 1979-82, Law Firm of Melvin E. Dunn, Ltd.
Representative Clients: Mr. Weiler represents individuals involved in or seeking a divorce, legal separation, or declaration of paternity, as well as individuals seeking or resisting child custody, support, visitation and/or removal, both before and after the original judgment. He has also served as legal counsel for DuKane Mental Health Clinics.
Professional Associations: Kane County Bar Assn. [Family Law Committee 1983-present (Vice Chair 1995-96); Courts Facilities Committee (Chair 1991-94)]; ISBA 1979-present.
Community Involvement: City of Batavia, Illinois (Alderman 1985-95; Legislative Committee 1989-95; Finance Committee 1991-95); Aurora Easter Seal Rehabilitation Center (Fund Raiser 1983-95); Batavia Easter Seal Telethon (Host 1990-95); Batavia Bulldog Booster Club 1987-95 (Vice President 1995); KIDS in a Divorcing Society (Instructor).
Firm: Weiler & Noble, P.C., was formed in 1989. The firm has over 30 years of combined experience in all areas of family law and children's issues. The firm represents clients in all aspects of divorce, custody, paternity, adoption, child abuse and neglect, and personal estate planning matters. The firm is active in the implementation of new programs to protect children, such as the Court Appointed Special Advocate (CASA) program. Both partners have lectured at bar and community forums and are dedicated to highly personalized representation of each client, with special attention to clients' personal needs and enhanced client communication. *See complete firm profile in Appendix A.*

MELVIN A. WEINSTEIN

Melvin A. Weinstein & Associates
134 North LaSalle Street
Suite 720
Chicago, IL 60602

Phone: (312) 263-2257
Fax: (312) 263-4942

•**MELVIN A. WEINSTEIN:** Mr. Weinstein practices primarily family law, concentrating in all aspects of matrimonial law. He has represented individual clients on issues arising out of divorce and legal separation proceedings, post-divorce litigation, spousal maintenance, child support, child custody and visitation, domestic and child abuse, antenuptial agreements, paternity and third party child custody proceedings, real estate, personal injury, and related trial work.
Education: JD 1952, DePaul University.
Admitted: 1951 Illinois; 1951 U.S. Dist. Ct. (N. Dist. IL).
Employment History: Founder 1956-present, Melvin A. Weinstein & Associates; 1954-56, Howard & Aronfeld.
Professional Associations: CBA (Matrimonial Committee); ISBA; ABA.
Community Involvement: Men's Club of K.J.S. (past President; Board of Directors).
Firm: As a result of the complexity of domestic relations practice, many issues arise involving business law, real estate, wills and probate, and criminal law matters. These additional areas of law have to be researched and handled in conjunction with the domestic relations issues, giving the firm broad experience of the law. In the 1960s, Mr. Weinstein tried over 400 zoning cases and the knowledge he acquired is highly beneficial to his clients. One of the firm's associates, Michael Simkin, is a former State's Attorney in Cook County and a supervisor in charge of a felony trial court and various supervisory positions (Narcotics Supervisor Courts and First Municipal District Courts Deputy Chief; Attorney, Legal Advisor and Chief Deputy in the Cook County Sheriff's Civil Division). *Mr. Weinstein also practices Personal Injury Law: General and Real Estate Law.*

Family Law Leading Illinois Attorneys

•**ERROL ZAVETT:** Mr. Zavett is a founding partner of Davis, Friedman, Zavett, Kane & MacRae. His practice is in all areas of family law, including premarital agreements, settlement and trial of dissolution of marriage cases, appeals, and related matters. He has lectured extensively on family law topics at continuing legal education seminars organized by the Chicago, Northwest Suburban, and Illinois State Bar Associations, the American Academy of Matrimonial Lawyers, the Women's Bar Association of Illinois, the South Carolina Trial Lawyers Association, the Kansas and Nevada State Bar Associations, the Illinois Institute for Continuing Legal Education, and others. He is on the Advisory Committee of the *Illinois Family Law Reporter* and the *Illinois Divorce Digest*. He served on the national committee which wrote *The Bounds of Advocacy, Standards of Conduct*, and the *Divorce Handbook*. He has written (or coauthored) articles or chapters on negotiations in family law cases, marital settlement agreements, and appeals from Illinois family law cases. He is listed in *The Best Lawyers in America*.
Education: JD 1963, University of Illinois; BA 1960, University of Iowa.
Admitted: 1964 Illinois; 1964 U.S. Dist. Ct. (N. Dist. IL).
Professional Associations: American Academy of Matrimonial Lawyers [Fellow; Illinois Chapter (President 1988-89; Board of Managers 1983-92)]; ISBA [Family Law Section (Chair 1985-86); *Family Law Newsletter* (Editor)]; CBA [Matrimonial Law Committee (Chair 1982-83)]; ITLA [Family Law Committee (Chair 1981-83)]; ABA [Family Law Section); Bounds of Advocacy Committee [past Member; Client Relations Committee (past Board of Managers)].
Community Involvement: West Suburban Temple Har Zion (President); Oak Park-River Forest Community Foundation (Vice President). *See complete firm profile in Appendix A.*

ERROL ZAVETT
Davis, Friedman, Zavett, Kane & MacRae
140 South Dearborn Street
Suite 1600
Chicago, IL 60603

Phone: (312) 782-2220
Fax: (312) 782-0464

NORTHWESTERN ILLINOIS
INCLUDING ROCKFORD & QUAD CITIES

•**PHILIP F. JENSEN:** Mr. Jensen is a partner in the firm of Hammer, Simon & Jensen, a firm with offices in Galena, Illinois, and Dubuque, Iowa. His practice involves all areas of family law, including divorce, custody, paternity, removal petitions, child support, and modification of judgments. In addition to his family law practice, he also represents a substantial number of small businesses, as well as being legal counsel for a municipality.
Education: JD 1984, University of Nebraska; BS 1981 with honors, Illinois State University.
Admitted: 1984 Illinois; 1988 Iowa; 1986 U.S. Dist. Ct. (N. Dist. IL).
Employment History: Partner/Associate 1988-present, Hammer, Simon & Jensen; Assistant State's Attorney 1985-88, Illinois State's Attorney's Office.
Professional Associations: ISBA; ATLA; Iowa State Bar Assn.; Jo Daviess County Bar Assn.; Dubuque County Bar Assn.; Christian Legal Society; Institute for Christian Conciliation.
Community Involvement: Jo Daviess County Chamber of Commerce (past Board Member); Sojourn House/Alcohol Rehabilitation Center (past Board Member); Tri-State Christian School (Board Member).
Firm: The firm of Hammer, Simon & Jensen was formed in 1989. The firm's partners and associates have substantial experience and concentrate in the areas of civil litigation, family law, small business representation, insurance defense, and municipal law. Representative clients include the City of Galena, Illinois; Interstate Power Company; St. Paul Fire and Marine Insurance; Traveler's Insurance; United Fire and Casualty; YMCA; and Apple Canyon Lake Property Owners' Association. *Mr. Jensen also practices Personal Injury Law: General and Small Business Law.*

PHILIP F. JENSEN
Hammer, Simon & Jensen
303 North Bench Street
P.O. Box 270
Galena, IL 61036

Phone: (815) 777-1101
Fax: (815) 777-9241

Extensive Experience In:
• Divorce Litigation
• Custody/Visitation
• Complex Property Settlements

17

July 1996   207

Chapter 17: Family Law

KEITH S. MORSE
Attorney at Law
810 East State Street
Suite 101
Rockford, IL 61104

Phone: (815) 967-5000
Fax: (815) 967-5002

Extensive Experience In:
- Divorce, Custody & Related Trials
- Domestic Violence & Spousal Abuse
- Paternity & Non-Support

•**KEITH S. MORSE:** Mr. Morse practices family law and is experienced in all types of cases involving matrimonial problems, paternity, divorce, legal separation, child custody and visitation. Mr. Morse has represented clients successfully in domestic abuse cases, and prepared and contested antenuptial agreements. His experience as a Special Assistant Attorney General in Illinois gives him a background in child/spousal support and paternity matters. He is a trained and experienced family law mediator and has extensive background in cases where the abuse of substances has been a factor in family problems. As an outgrowth of his experience with families with substance abuse problems, Mr. Morse has also represented treatment professionals and others in the substance abuse treatment community. He also assists clients in criminal matters that may arise from family and/or substance problems.
Education: JD 1964, Northwestern University; AB 1961, Northwestern University.
Admitted: 1965 Illinois; 1979 U.S. Dist. Ct. (N. Dist. IL).
Employment History: Attorney at Law 1995-96, Associated with East State Street Law Offices; Attorney at Law 1988-95, Associated with David North, Larry Ohlson & Timothy Condon; Partner 1979-88, Balsley, Morse & Smith; Special Assistant Attorney General 1976-79, Attorney General's Office, Illinois (paternity and non-support); Attorney at Law 1973-77; Associate Judge 1969-72, State of Illinois, 17th Judicial Circuit; Assistant State's Attorney 1966-79, State's Attorney's Office, Winnebago County.
Representative Clients: Mr. Morse represents primarily individuals in connection with his areas of emphasis. He serves as attorney for many professionals and executives in connection with legal needs in family law matters. He has served as attorney for the Alano Club of Rockford and many of its members and directors since 1985.
Professional Associations: Winnebago County Bar Assn. [Family Law Section 1966-present; Mediation Advisory Council 1994-present (Secretary 1995); Seely P. Forbes Memorial Award (Recipient 1995)]; ISBA 1979-present (Lawyer's Assistance Program).
Community Involvement: Rosecrance Health Network [Board of Directors (First Vice President 1993-96)]; AlCare of Rockford [Board of Directors 1984-93 (Chair 1993)].
Firm: Mr. Morse has recently associated with a group of five lawyers who offer a broad range of services to his clients. Included among his associates are attorneys whose practices emphasize bankruptcy law, small business law, juvenile law, personal injury law, and tax law and estate planning, as well as probate. *Mr. Morse also practices Criminal Law: DUI & Misdemeanors and Alternative Dispute Resolution.*

PETER B. NOLTE - *Attorney at Law* - 312 West State Street, Suite 1201 - Rockford, IL 61101 - Phone: (815) 965-2647, Fax: (815) 965-3820 - *See complete biographical profile in the Civil Appellate Law Chapter, page 85.*

PETER S. SWITZER
Barrick, Switzer, Long, Balsley & Van Evera
One Madison Street
Rockford, IL 61104

Phone: (815) 962-6611
Fax: (815) 962-0687

•**PETER S. SWITZER:** Mr. Switzer practices family law, civil trial law, and personal injury law. Previously, Mr. Switzer was an instructor in legal writing at the University of Wisconsin Law School, 1962-63. He has been an author and speaker on civil trial practice for the Illinois State Bar Association's Continuing Legal Education Section. He has been a speaker on "Civil Practice Before Trial" and on "Handling the Witness; Direct and Cross Examination," for Illinois Continuing Legal Education Section of the Bar. Mr. Switzer handles complex family law matters involving custody, and cases with substantial income and assets.
Education: LLB 1963, University of Wisconsin; BA 1960, Lawrence College.
Admitted: 1963 Illinois.
Professional Associations: Winnebago County Bar Assn. (Secretary 1968); ISBA; ITLA; ABA; Illinois Defense Counsel; Defense Research and Trial Lawyers Assn.
Firm: Barrick, Switzer, Long, Balsley & Van Evera was founded over 50 years ago. The firm's members practice a wide variety of law, including family law, insurance defense, banking, bankruptcy, commercial law, personal injury law, workers' compensation, estate planning, and municipal law. *Mr. Switzer also practices Alternative Dispute Resolution and Personal Injury Law: General.*

•**FRED L. WHAM III:** Mr. Wham has practiced family law for over 30 years. He represents clients in all issues arising in family law, including divorce, custody, spousal maintenance, child support, visitation, complex valuation issues, pensions and retirement plans, postdissolution matters, antenuptial agreements, and paternity cases. Mr. Wham also has extensive experience in corporate law, estate planning, trusts and probate, real estate, and general litigation.
Education: LLB 1962, University of Illinois; BS 1959, University of Illinois.
Admitted: 1964 Illinois; 1978 U.S. Dist. Ct. (N. Dist. IL).
Employment History: Private Practice 1965-present; Assistant State's Attorney 1964-65, State's Attorney's Office, Champaign County; 1962-64, United States Army.
Professional Associations: Winnebago County Bar Assn.; ISBA.
Community Involvement: Rockford School Board (past President); Rockford YMCA Y's Men's Club (past President); Rockford Kiwanis Club (past Director); Children's Development Center (Board of Directors).

FRED L. WHAM III
Attorney at Law
124 North Water Street
Suite 202
Rockford, IL 61107

Phone: (815) 964-6717
Fax: (815) 962-6153

Extensive Experience In:

• Divorce Litigation
• Custody
• Complex Valuation Issues

•**ARTHUR R. WINSTEIN:** Mr. Winstein concentrates his law practice in the area of family and domestic law, including custody, visitation, support, and property distribution. He has extensive trial experience in Rock Island, Henry, Whiteside, Mercer, Knox, and Henderson Counties. Mr. Winstein has successfully represented numerous men and women in obtaining custody of their children, expanded visitation privileges, and necessary child support actions. He has also defended non-custodial parents in support modification, removal petitions, and contempt charges. Mr. Winstein has successfully obtained large maintenance and alimony awards. He was awarded the Order of the Barrister from Washington University School of Law.
Education: JD 1988, Washington University (Order of the Barrister); BA 1985, University of Iowa.
Admitted: 1988 Illinois; 1988 U.S. Dist. Ct. (C. Dist. IL); 1988 U.S. Tax Ct.; 1989 U.S. Ct. App. (Fed. Cir.).
Employment History: Senior Partner/Associate 1990-present, Winstein, Kavensky & Wallace; Associate 1989-90, Wegner & Bretschneider, Washington, D.C.
Representative Clients: Mr. Winstein has represented bank presidents, doctors, school teachers, and factory workers, along with many homemakers. Winstein, Kavensky & Wallace represents both men and women in all matters, and continues to represent unions and members of the UAW, IBEW, and United Rubber Workers unions.
Professional Associations: Assn. for Matrimonial Lawyers of Rock Island (Secretary 1993-present); ABA; Rock Island County Bar Assn.
Community Involvement: Lion's Club; Elk's Club; Masonic Lodge; Shriner; Rotarian; Salvation Army (Board of Directors); American Cancer Society [Rock Island/Milan Chapter (Board of Directors)]; Putnam Musean (Advisory Group); Information and Referral of the Quad Cities Organization.
Firm: The firm of Winstein, Kavensky & Wallace has been in existence for over 50 years. The firm has represented thousands of persons seeking representation in various family law matters and criminal matters in an effort to obtain favorable conclusions. The firm also concentrates in the areas of workers' compensation, personal injury, labor law, and general civil litigation. *Mr. Winstein also practices Criminal Law: Felonies & White Collar Crime and Employment Law.*

ARTHUR R. WINSTEIN
Winstein, Kavensky & Wallace
224 18th Street
Fourth Floor
Rock Island, IL 61201

Phone: (309) 794-1515
Fax: (309) 794-9929
800: (800) 747-1527

Central Illinois

ANTHONY P. CORSENTINO

Anthony P. Corsentino, Ltd.
411 Hamilton Boulevard
Suite 1210
Peoria, IL 61602

Phone: (309) 676-1073
Fax: (309) 676-8475

Extensive Experience In:

- Custody
- Visitation
- Removal of Children from Illinois

•**ANTHONY P. CORSENTINO:** Mr. Corsentino's practice is limited exclusively to all areas of family law, including divorce, custody, visitation, support, property settlements, removal petitions, college expenses, paternity, and domestic violence defense. He has substantial experience in the "children's issues" of custody, visitation, and removal. He recognizes the high emotions and dynamics of these areas of law and believes his life experiences allow him to deal with these issues. Mr. Corsentino is a former Chicago Police Officer and First Lieutenant with the Military Police Corps. He earned a Bronze Star for Meritorious Service while serving his country in Vietnam. Mr. Corsentino has lectured on family law issues at seminars conducted by the Illinois State Bar Association and the Peoria County Bar Association. He is the author of an article relating to the issues of contempt, published in *The Legal Ease,* Peoria County Bar Association. Mr. Corsentino authored "Temporary Relief" in the Illinois State Bar Association's *Family Law Handbook.*
Education: JD 1967, DePaul University; BA 1964, DePaul University.
Admitted: 1967 Illinois; 1974 U.S. Dist. Ct. (C. Dist. IL).
Employment History: 1979-present, Anthony P. Corsentino, Ltd.; 1975-79, Law Offices of Sweat & Sweat; First Assistant State's Attorney 1973-75, Tazewell County; Assistant State's Attorney 1969-73, Cook County. Mr. Corsentino served as a Special Assistant State's Attorney 1982, Woodford County; and a Special Assistant State's Attorney 1983, Tazewell County.
Professional Associations: ISBA 1969-present (Family Law Section 1990-94); Peoria County Bar Assn. [Family Law Section (Chair 1993-94)].
Community Involvement: Peoria County Pro Bono Program (Volunteer).
Firm: Anthony P. Corsentino, Ltd., is a small firm which allows each client to receive individualized, personal attention. Along with Mr. Corsentino, the staff includes a paralegal and two secretaries. Mr. Corsentino arrives early each morning at 6:45 a.m. to start an 11-hour day. He promptly returns all telephone calls and treats each client with the utmost respect.

HOWARD W. FELDMAN

Feldman & Wasser
1307 South Seventh Street
P.O. Box 2418
Springfield, IL 62705

Phone: (217) 544-3403
Fax: (217) 544-1593

•**HOWARD W. FELDMAN:** Mr. Feldman has a general litigation practice with concentrations in family law, construction cases, and general civil litigation. He has handled many trials of large-asset marriage dissolution proceedings and custody/support matters and has tried numerous cases to verdict in both state and federal courts. Mr. Feldman is an arbitrator for the American Arbitration Association. He is the author of the chapters, "Illinois Court of Claims" and "Civil Service Commission," for the Illinois Institute for Continuing Legal Education's Handbook, *Illinois Administrative Law.*
Education: JD 1973, Indiana University; BS 1968, Purdue University.
Admitted: 1973 Illinois; 1975 U.S. Dist. Ct. (C. Dist. IL); 1976 U.S. Ct. App. (7th Cir.); 1977 U.S. Sup. Ct.
Employment History: 1987-present, Feldman & Wasser; 1982-87, Solo Practice; General Counsel 1979-82, Illinois Capital Development Board; 1973-74 Assistant Illinois Attorney General, Attorney General's Office, Illinois.
Representative Clients: Merril Contractors; Williams Brothers Construction; Evan Lloyd & Associates Arch.; Stanley Grainick/Associates Architects.
Professional Associations: Abraham Lincoln Inn of Court 1994-present; Sangamon County Bar Assn. 1973-present; ISBA [Assembly; Administrative Law Section Council (Chair)]; ABA (Construction Law Committee 1973-present; Family Law Section).
Community Involvement: Springfield Jewish Federation (Board Member; President); Rees Carillon Society (Board Member); Springfield Jewish Community Relation Council (Chair); Springfield Board of Jewish Education (President).
Firm: Feldman & Wasser was founded in 1987 by Howard Feldman and Stanley Wasser for the general practice of law. The firm represents a diverse group of clients, from those charged with federal crimes to the preparation of corporate documents. The firm has a broad range of experience. The six lawyers in the firm concentrate in different areas of law, including family law, estate and probate law, construction litigation, criminal and civil trials and appeals, employment law, real estate and municipal law. *See complete firm profile in Appendix A. Mr. Feldman also practices Criminal Law: Felonies & White Collar Crime and Small Business Law.*

GREGG N. GRIMSLEY - *Carter & Grimsley* - 1500 Commerce Bank Building - Peoria, IL 61602 - Phone: (309) 673-3517, Fax: (309) 673-3318 - *See complete biographical profile in the Bankruptcy Law Chapter, page 74.*

•**DON C. HAMMER:** Mr. Hammer focuses a substantial portion of his practice on family law, involving issues of divorce, paternity, prenuptial planning, and adoptions. He also provides mediation services, including mediation of custody and visitation disputes, and mediation of financial issues. Mr. Hammer is an adjunct professor at Illinois State University.
Education: JD 1975 magna cum laude, John Marshall Law School; BA 1967, Ohio State University.
Admitted: 1975 Illinois; 1976 Washington, D.C.; 1975 U.S. Dist. Ct. (N. Dist. IL); 1978 U.S. Dist. Ct. (C. Dist. IL).
Employment History: Partner 1978-present, Hayes, Hammer, Miles, Cox & Ginzkey; Staff Attorney 1976-78, Board of Governors, Federal Reserve System; Judicial Clerk 1975, Justice Howard Ryan, Supreme Court of Illinois.
Professional Associations: Robert C. Underwood Inn of Court (Director 1995-present); McLean County Bar Assn. (Director 1993-95); Mediation Council of Illinois (President 1993-95); McLean County Divorce Mediators (Chair 1991-present); ISBA 1975-present.
Community Involvement: MARC Foundation 1985-92 (Board of Directors; President 1989-91).
Firm: The firm offers a full range of civil and business services to clients, including estate planning, tax, real estate, incorporations, partnerships, personal injury litigation, and civil litigation. *See complete firm profile in Appendix A. Mr. Hammer also practices Alternative Dispute Resolution and Adoption Law.*

DON C. HAMMER
Hayes, Hammer, Miles, Cox & Ginzkey
202 North Center Street
PO Box 3067
Bloomington, IL 61702-3067
Phone: (309) 828-7331
Fax: (309) 827-7423

Extensive Experience In:
• Property Division
• Adoption
• Mediation

MARY LEE LEAHY - *Leahy Law Offices* - 308 East Canedy Street - Springfield, IL 62703 - Phone: (217) 522-4411, Fax: (217) 522-7119 - *See complete biographical profile in the Employment Law Chapter, page 149.*

•**DAVID M. LYNCH:** Mr. Lynch practices primarily family law, including marriage dissolutions, legal separations, custody disputes, tax and financial aspects of family law, prenuptial agreements, and related areas. He was a mediator and author for the National Business Institute, Inc., family law litigation in Illinois class, "'Winning' for Your Client." Mr. Lynch was a member of the United States Army, 1969-71.
Education: JD 1974, University of Illinois; BA 1969, Monmouth College.
Admitted: 1974 Illinois; 1974 U.S. Dist. Ct. (C. Dist. IL).
Professional Associations: Peoria County Bar Assn. [President; Domestic Relations Committee (Chair 1981-84; 1986-88); Board of Directors (At Large Member 1983-86)]; ISBA [Young Lawyers Division 1978-81; Family Law Committee (Associate Member 1985-86)]; ITLA; ATLA; ABA.
Community Involvement: Campaigns for State Senator Prescott E. Bloom (Chair 1978-86); Campaign for State Representative Mary Lou Summner (Chair); Peoria County Republican Party Committee (Central Committee 1984-88).
Firm: Lynch & Bloom, P.C., primarily practices family law and related matters. Approximately 15 percent of the firm's time is spent in personal injury work. The firm does prepare wills and other similar matters for clients involved in dissolution. *Mr. Lynch also practices Personal Injury Law: General and Adoption Law.*

DAVID M. LYNCH
Lynch & Bloom, P.C.
411 Hamilton Boulevard
Suite 1300
Peoria, IL 61602
Phone: (309) 673-7415
Fax: (309) 673-3189

Extensive Experience In:
• Custody
• Property Divisions
• Maintenance Requests

David H. McCarthy

Attorney at Law
1820 First Financial Plaza
Peoria, IL 61602

Phone: (309) 674-4508
Fax: (309) 674-4546

Extensive Experience In:

- Custody
- Maintenance
- Property Division

•**DAVID H. MC CARTHY:** Mr. McCarthy has been in private practice in the Peoria area since 1973. He has concentrated his practice in family law, trying hundreds of cases concerning custody, visitation, maintenance, and related issues. He has been appointed Special Prosecutor by Peoria County on three occasions. He has presented lectures to the Peoria County Bar Association and other professional associations. Mr. McCarthy represents numerous physicians and attorneys, as well as their spouses, in family law litigation. In addition, he handles issues related to valuation and distribution of businesses.

Education: JD 1973, St. Louis University; BS 1967, Illinois State University.
Admitted: 1973 Illinois; 1977 U.S. Dist. Ct. (C. Dist. IL).
Employment History: Sole Practitioner 1980-present; 1976-80, Kelly & McCarthy; 1973-76, Kelly & Baner.
Representative Clients: Ninety percent of the cases Mr. McCarthy handles are family law cases. He also represents four Burger King restaurants in the Danville area, and Welch Systems. Many of Mr. McCarthy's clients are corporate clients.
Professional Associations: ISBA (Family Law Section); Peoria County Bar Assn.
Community Involvement: Friends of Glen Oak Zoo for ten years (Board of Directors); Peoria Soccer Club for ten years [Board of Directors; Officer; Boys Travel Team (Coach)]; Woodruff High School, Peoria (Varsity Boys Soccer Coach 1995).
Firm: Mr. McCarthy works personally with all clients and is assisted by his secretary of ten years. *Mr. McCarthy also practices Adoption Law and Real Estate Law.*

Michael B. Metnick

Metnick, Wise, Cherry & Frazier
Number One West Old State Capital Plaza
Myers Building
Suite 200
Springfield, IL 62701

Phone: (217) 753-4242
Fax: (217) 753-4642
800: (800) 500-4242

Extensive Experience In:

- Dissolution
- Custody
- Maintenance Issues

•**MICHAEL B. METNICK:** Mr. Metnick has represented individuals in a range of matrimonial-related cases, with an emphasis on professional and other high-income marital dissolutions. In addition to lecturing on family law matters to the Illinois Institute for Continuing Legal Education and the Illinois Trial Lawyers Association, he has extensive appellate and trial court experience. Through utilization of the most up-to-date research techniques and highly qualified paralegal and support staffs, the law firm of Metnick, Wise, Cherry & Frazier is well equipped to handle the most complex matrimonial law cases. During his career, Mr. Metnick has represented both husbands and wives in dissolution and custody proceedings. In recent years, Mr. Metnick's law firm has, through appellate court decisions, made significant contributions in the areas of maintenance termination, *In re: Marriage of Herrin;* removal, *In re: Marriage of Eaton;* child support, *In re: Marriage of McCormick;* contribution to nonmarital property, *In re: Marriage of Werries;* injury awards, *In re: Marriage of Murphy;* and custody, *In re: Marriage of Manuele.* Although Mr. Metnick is a well-respected trial attorney, he initially seeks to resolve matrimonial law cases through traditional methods of negotiation, mediation, and settlement.

Education: JD 1975, John Marshall Law School; BA 1970, University of Oklahoma.
Admitted: 1975 Illinois; 1975 U.S. Ct. App. (7th Cir.); 1975 U.S. Dist. Ct. (C. Dist. IL).
Professional Associations: ISBA; ATLA; ITLA; NACDL; Lincoln-Douglas Inn of Courts.
Firm: Metnick, Wise, Cherry & Frazier represents clients in civil and criminal cases in state and federal courts. The firm's practice includes personal injury and malpractice cases; civil appeals and other civil actions; dissolution and custody matters; criminal felonies; misdemeanors, reckless homicide, murder, DUIs and other traffic offenses; financial cases; and employment law. The firm litigates in state and federal courts and argues criminal appeals in the U.S. and Illinois Supreme Courts. *Mr. Metnick also practices Criminal Law: Felonies & White Collar Crime and Personal Injury Law: General.*

•**STEVEN NARDULLI:** Mr. Nardulli restricts his practice to the representation of individuals involved in family-related litigation. He has substantial trial and appellate experience, primarily in complex financial litigation and contested child custody matters. He is frequently consulted by Illinois state legislators with regard to legislation that affects the Illinois Marriage and Dissolution of Marriage Act. He is also active as a lecturer in the area of continuing legal education, speaking at seminars conducted by organizations such as the Illinois State Bar Association, the Illinois Institute for Continuing Legal Education, and the University of Illinois in Springfield.
Education: JD 1975, Illinois Institute of Technology, Chicago-Kent; BA 1972, Knox College (Phi Beta Kappa).
Admitted: 1975 Illinois; 1976 U.S. Dist. Ct. (N. Dist. IL); 1976 U.S. Ct. App. (7th Cir.); 1981 U.S. Dist. Ct. (C. Dist. IL).
Employment History: Partner 1981-present, Stratton and Nardulli.
Representative Clients: Mr. Nardulli exclusively represents clients who need assistance in family law matters.
Community Involvement: Springfield Lutheran High School Assn. (Chair); Springfield YMCA [Board of Directors; Youth Committee (Chair)]; Trinity Lutheran School [Board of Christian Day School (Chair)]; Rape Information and Counseling Service (Board of Directors); Sangamon County Alternate Dispute Resolution Council.
Firm: Stratton and Nardulli is a 15-lawyer firm which serves individuals, small businesses, and trade associations with a high caliber of legal representation. It is best known for its representation of individuals in the area of family law and its representation of highly regulated entities before various government agencies. *Mr. Nardulli also practices Adoption Law.*

STEVEN NARDULLI
Stratton and Nardulli
725 South Fourth Street
Springfield, IL 62703
Phone: (217) 528-2183
Fax: (217) 528-1874

•**NICHOLAS H. ORES:** Mr. Ores' practice focuses on all aspects of family law, criminal law, and civil trial practice. His extensive family law practice involves dissolution, postdissolution matters, custody, support, visitation, spousal maintenance, property division, paternity, removal of child from state, and related matters. Mr. Ores is involved in cases with small businesses and matters of complex financial issues. This includes valuation and divisions of closely held family businesses. Mr. Ores also handles cases involving serious criminal matters, both state and federal. He actively practices in the central Illinois area, including the counties of Peoria, Tazewell, Fulton, Knox, Marshall, Woodford, and McLean.
Education: JD 1983 summa cum laude, Southern University of Illinois; BS 1979, Colorado State University.
Admitted: 1984 Illinois; 1983 Missouri; 1983 U.S. Dist. Ct. (E. Dist. MI); 1983 U.S. Dist. Ct. (W. Dist. MI); 1984 U.S. Dist. Ct. (S. Dist. IL); 1988 U.S. Dist. Ct. (C. Dist. IL).
Employment History: Owner 1988-present, Nicholas H. Ores, Attorney at Law; Partner 1987-88, Reynolds, Ores & Associates; Associate 1986-87, Lakin & Herndon; Associate 1983-86, Thompson & Mitchell, St. Louis, Missouri.
Representative Clients: Mr. Ores limits his practice to family law and criminal law matters. He practices a substantial amount of criminal law at the federal and state levels.
Professional Associations: ISBA 1984-present; Peoria County Bar Assn. 1987-present; Missouri Bar Assn. 1983-present; St. Louis Bar Assn. 1983-87.
Community Involvement: Catholic Men's Club; Homeowner's Assn.
Mr. Ores also practices Criminal Law: Felonies & White Collar Crime and Criminal Law: DUI & Misdemeanors.

NICHOLAS H. ORES
Attorney at Law
1720 First Financial Plaza
Peoria, IL 61602
Phone: (309) 674-5297
Fax: (309) 674-5299

Chapter 17: Family Law

Drew Parker

Parker & Halliday
414 Hamilton Boulevard
Suite 300
Peoria, IL 61602

Phone: (309) 673-0069
Fax: (309) 673-8791

Extensive Experience In:

• Custody
• Removal Petitions
• Property Divisions

•**DREW PARKER:** Mr. Parker has an almost exclusively litigation-oriented practice, and engages in all aspects of matrimonial law, including divorce, custody, visitation, and support. Due to his background as a former Peoria County prosecutor and Cook County Assistant Public Defender, he also practices plaintiffs' personal injury and criminal defense. Both of these former positions provided him with considerable courtroom experience. A frequent speaker on custody issues, Mr. Parker is an enthusiastic advocate of joint custody in appropriate cases. He is an annual member of the Divorce Law Committee of the Peoria County Bar Association, is a member of the Illinois State Bar Association, and is a Master of the Bench in the Clarence Darrow Inns of Court in Peoria.
Education: JD 1976, Illinois Institute of Technology, Chicago-Kent (Bar and Gavel Society); BA 1973, University of Illinois.
Admitted: 1976 Illinois; 1978 U.S. Dist. Ct. (C. Dist. IL); 1983 U.S. Ct. App. (7th Cir.).
Employment History: Private Practice 1978-present, Parker & Halliday; Assistant State's Attorney 1977-78, Peoria County State's Attorney's Office; Assistant Public Defender 1976-77, Cook County Public Defender's Office.
Representative Clients: Mr. Parker represents many professionals and business owners in divorce litigation.
Professional Associations: Peoria County Bar Assn. 1977-present [Divorce Law Committee 1985-present; Criminal Law Committee (Chair 1992-93)]; ISBA 1978-present; Clarence Darrow Inns of Court (Master of the Bench 1992-present).
Firm: Drew Parker and Ronald E. Halliday began practicing together in early 1980. By combining their trial experience from prior positions, they have created an extensive litigation practice over the years. The firm concentrates in all areas of family and matrimonial law together with a significant personal injury practice and criminal defense practice. Both attorneys with the firm have handled an extensive number of custody issues, as well as divorces involving property divisions totaling millions of dollars. In other areas, both lawyers have handled many wrongful death cases and a number of murder cases. *Mr. Parker also practices Criminal Law: Felonies & White Collar Crime and Personal Injury Law: General.*

Walter W. Winget

Winget & Kane
Commerce Bank Building
416 Main Street
Suite 807
Peoria, IL 61602

Phone: (309) 674-2310
Fax: (309) 674-9722

Extensive Experience In:

• Complex Property Settlements
• Contested Custody
• Trial of Complex Cases

•**WALTER W. WINGET:** Mr. Winget practices family, business, corporate, and real estate law. He is *Certified as a Civil Trial Advocate by the National Board of Trial Advocacy. In family law, he represents clients in the areas of dissolution of marriage; property settlements, especially in cases involving complex and substantial assets; child support; maintenance and defense against maintenance; child custody and visitation; and other related family law issues. Mr. Winget has had substantial experience in cases involving physicians, attorneys, and business people. He believes that while settlement of cases should always be attempted in family law matters, the willingness and ability to try cases successfully in court is essential to settlements that are in the best interest of a client's economic health. He and his office pride themselves on the prompt return of client telephone calls and the prompt setting of appointments. Mr. Winget is a frequent lecturer on family law topics.
Education: JD 1961, University of Michigan (Senior Judge, Moot Court Competition); AB 1958 with honors, Princeton University; Woodrow Wilson School of Public and International Affairs.
Admitted: 1962 Illinois; 1971 U.S. Sup. Ct.
Employment History: Partner 1969-present, Winget & Kane; Associate 1961-64, Edwards & Angell, Providence, Rhode Island; Summer Associate 1959-60, Shearman & Sterling & Wright, New York, New York.
Professional Associations: ITLA [Family Law Committee (past Chair)]; Peoria County Bar Assn. [President 1991-92; Continuing Legal Education Program (Founder)].
Community Involvement: Peoria County Pro Bono Program (Volunteer); Better Business Bureau of Central Illinois, Inc. [Board of Directors (past Chair)]. *Mr. Winget also practices Small Business Law and Real Estate Law.*

*The Supreme Court of Illinois does not recognize certifications of specialties in the practice of law. A certificate, award or recognition is not a requirement to practice law in Illinois.

•**RICHARD WAYNE ZUCKERMAN:** Mr. Zuckerman has 20 years of trial and appellate court experience. He concentrates in all areas of family law, including pre- and post-divorce matters, paternity, child custody and support, visitation and removal, and adoption. Mr. Zuckerman has presented seminars for the Peoria County Bar Association, Illinois State Bar Association, and the Illinois Institute for Continuing Legal Education. He is the author of "Enforcement of Child Support," ISBA's *Family Law Handbook,* 1994; "Child Support and Your Driver's License," March 1996, and "Illinois Supreme Court Limits Modifiability of Maintenance," December 1990, *Family Law Newsletter.* He practices throughout central Illinois.

Education: JD 1976, John Marshall Law School; BS 1973, Bradley University.

Admitted: 1976 Illinois; 1977 U.S. Dist. Ct. (C. Dist. IL); 1977 U.S. Ct. App. (7th Cir.).

Employment History: 1994-present, Law Offices of Richard W. Zuckerman; Of Counsel 1980-94, Goldfine and Bowles, P.C.; Staff Attorney/Senior Staff Attorney 1977-80, Prairie State Legal Services, Inc.; Law Clerk 1975-76, Davis, Jones and Baer.

Professional Associations: American Academy of Matrimonial Lawyers (Fellow); Abraham Lincoln Inns of Court (Master); ABA (Alimony, Maintenance and Child Support Committee 1993-95; Federal Legislation and Procedures Committee 1993-95; Custody Committee 1993-95); ISBA [Assembly 1984-90, 1995-present; Family Law Section Council 1988-92, 1993-present (Secretary 1996-97); Legislation Committee 1995-present; Delivery of Legal Services Committee 1993-present; Supreme Court Rules Committee 1994-96; Reduction of Costs, Delays and Involvement 1983-84; Alternative Form of Dispute Resolution 1981-83 (Chair 1982-83); Arbitration of Disputes 1981-82]; Peoria County Bar Assn. [Board of Directors at Large 1993-95, 1996-present; Family Law Committee 1982-92, 1994-present (Chair 1992-94)]; Attorney Registration and Disciplinary Commission (Inquiry Panel 1993-present).

Community Involvement: Moss-Bradley Residential Assn. (Board; past President); West Bluff Council (twice past President); West Bluff Neighborhood Housing Services (past President); Peoria Art Guild (Board; twice past President).

Firm: Having practiced law for 20 years, 16 of those years in private practice, Mr. Zuckerman concentrates 95 percent of his time in family law matters, including all aspects of matrimonial law. Through the American Academy of Matrimonial Lawyers and the Illinois State Bar Association, Mr. Zuckerman has developed an extensive network of Illinois attorneys for national referrals, research and assistance. Complex and unusual litigation, including multi-state litigation, is a regular component of his practice. He offers compassionate, understanding, personal representation to all of his clients. *Mr. Zuckerman also practices Adoption Law and Bankruptcy Law.*

RICHARD WAYNE ZUCKERMAN

Law Offices of Richard W. Zuckerman
124 SW Adams
Suite 520
Peoria, IL 61602

Phone: (309) 637-3732
Fax: (309) 637-5788

Extensive Experience In:

• Child Custody
• Paternity
• Property Matters

Chapter 17: Family Law

SOUTHERN ILLINOIS

ROZA GOSSAGE

Roza Gossage, P.C.
525 West Main Street
Suite 130
Belleville, IL 62220

Phone: (618) 277-6800
Fax: (618) 277-6820

Extensive Experience In:

- Matrimonial Law
- Custody/Visitation
- Employment Discharge

•**ROZA GOSSAGE:** Ms. Gossage is an experienced trial attorney who now devotes her practice to all areas of matrimonial law and probate. Her practice includes extensive experience in marriage dissolutions, legal separations, custody disputes, and financial aspects of family law, prenuptial agreements, and related areas. Ms. Gossage was recognized by the *Chicago Tribune* for her work as an Assistant State's Attorney in Cook County, and President Reagan recognized Ms. Gossage for her work in prosecuting welfare cheaters in her role as Assistant State's Attorney in St. Clair County. Her background as a prosecutor, her personal experiences as a child of survivors of the Holocaust, and her extensive matrimonial law experience have prepared her to be a strong advocate for persons ranging from business executives with large assets to single parents with custody and support concerns. Ms. Gossage combines the toughness she gained in her years as a prosecutor with her compassion gained from her own personal experiences to advocate for clients and to provide qualified representation for all of her clients. She has undertaken representation of clients in sexual harassment and employment disputes.
Education: JD 1971, DePaul University; BA 1968, University of Illinois.
Admitted: 1971 Illinois; 1972 Florida; 1981 Missouri; 1971 U.S. Dist. Ct. (N. Dist. IL); 1972 U.S. Ct. App. (7th Cir.); 1978 U.S. Dist. Ct. (E. Dist. IL).
Employment History: Sole Practitioner 1978-present, Roza Gossage, P.C.; Clerk 1971-72, Federal Judge Julius Hoffman; Assistant State's Attorney 1972-74, State's Attorney's Office, Cook County; Assistant State's Attorney 1974, State's Attorney's Office, St. Clair County; Legal Advisor 1978-80, Public Aid Commission to Rewrite Public Aid Code.
Professional Associations: St. Clair County Bar Assn. 1990-present; ISBA 1990-present; The Missouri Bar; The Florida Bar; Women Lawyers Assn. of Greater St. Louis 1990-present.
Community Involvement: Washington University School of Law, St. Louis, Missouri [Moot Court (Judge)]; Women Lawyers Assn. of Greater St. Louis (Mentor Program).
Firm: Ms. Gossage is joined by an experienced legal assistant and an administrative assistant who treat clients as individuals, not as files. Her entire office prides itself on providing personalized, responsive service. Phone calls are promptly returned and clients are always kept fully apprised of their cases. The entire office is especially proud of how many previous clients, and even previous clients' ex-spouses, refer cases to the Gossage law office. The office is conveniently located in Belleville, with ample free parking right outside the office. *Ms. Gossage also practices Adoption Law and Employment Law.*

MORRIS LANE HARVEY

Law Offices of Morris Lane Harvey
215 SE Third Street
Suite 100
P.O. Box 820
Fairfield, IL 62837

Phone: (618) 842-5117
Fax: (618) 842-5773

•**MORRIS LANE HARVEY:** Mr. Harvey's practice is limited to civil litigation, with an emphasis in family law, including divorce, custody, spousal and child abuse, adoption and postjudgment matters. In addition, he regularly handles personal injury matters, including product liability, oil and gas, and construction litigation.
Education: JD 1974, University of Kentucky; BS 1972, Murray State University.
Admitted: 1975 Illinois; 1979 U.S. Dist. Ct. (S. Dist. IL); 1995 U.S. Ct. App. (7th Cir.).
Employment History: Owner 1985-present, Law Offices of Morris Lane Harvey; Partner 1977-85, Feiger, Quindry, Molt & Harvey and successor firms; Associate 1975-77, Hanagan and Dousman.
Representative Clients: Venturi Group; Republic Oil Company; People's National Bank.
Professional Associations: ISBA (Family Law Section; Practice and Procedure Section); ITLA; ATLA; American Judicature Society; ABA.
Community Involvement: Woodmen of the World (State President 1985-87; National Fraternal Committee 1987-89; National Legislative Committee 1989-93; National Judicial Committee 1993-present); Rotary Club; Paul Harris Fellow.
Firm: The Law Offices of Morris Lane Harvey seeks to provide capable legal representation for its clients. In addition, it is the goal of the firm to provide support services and acquaint its clients with support resources available in the community to assist them with the problems faced during the difficult process of the family breakup. The firm facilitates counseling of parents and children in an effort to minimize the stress occasioned by this process. It is the philosophy of the firm that to be successful, the attorney must assist not only in obtaining a favorable result from the legal system, but also in providing a basis for his or her clients to rebuild their lives. *Mr. Harvey also practices Personal Injury Law: General and Civil Appellate Law.*

•JOHN J. KUROWSKI: Mr. Kurowski is an experienced lawyer who has practiced in all areas of family and matrimonial law for 18 years, with substantial experience in complicated, sophisticated, and high-profile cases. Mr. Kurowski has lobbied and testified before four Illinois state legislative committees on family law, from 1989 to the present. He is a frequent lecturer for the Illinois State Bar Association's family law programs, the Illinois Institute for Continuing Legal Education, the People's Law School, and other private groups. He is the author of several publications, including the 1988, 1989, 1993, and 1995 editions of the parentage chapter in the *Family Law Handbook*, Illinois Institute for Continuing Legal Education; "The Establishment of Child Support in Illinois," a chapter in the ISBA's *Family Law Handbook*, 1995; as well as several articles in the ISBA's *Family Law Section Council Newsletter*. Mr. Kurowski was selected as the Illinois State Bar Association representative for the Illinois General Assembly Child Support Advisory Committee, 1990-91, which was empowered to review compliance with the federal mandate on Illinois' child support guidelines statutes. He received a special merit award in 1991 for his work on this committee from the Family Law Section Council Chairman.
Education: JD 1978, St. Louis University (*Law Journal*); BA 1975 cum laude, Loyola University of Chicago.
Admitted: 1978 Illinois; 1993 Missouri; 1978 U.S. Dist. Ct. (S. Dist. IL); 1981 U.S. Ct. App. (7th Cir.); 1987 U.S. Dist. Ct. (C. Dist. IL); 1991 U.S. Dist. Ct. (S. Dist. IN); 1993 U.S. Dist. Ct. (E. Dist. MO).
Employment History: Founder/Managing Partner 1983-present, The Kurowski Law Firm, P.C., and its predecessor law firms.
Professional Associations: ISBA [Family Law Section Council 1983-95 (Chair 1993-94; Secretary 1992-93); Standing Committee on Legislation 1988-95; Assembly 1982-84; Illinois General Assembly Child Support Advisory Committee (Representative 1990-91)]; East St. Louis Bar Assn. (President 1990-91); St. Clair County Bar Assn. (Director 1988-90); American Academy of Matrimonial Lawyers (Fellow).
Firm: At The Kurowski Law Firm, P.C., the emphasis of its attorneys' practice is service. Each client is assigned a paralegal who assists with certain tasks, creating efficiency and savings on legal fees. The firm is on the cutting-edge of technology, using the latest state-of-the-art software for preparing valuations, client budgets, and calculating support payments. Each attorney with the firm is required to be computer literate. The publications, lectures, academy memberships, and legislative work in this firm are all current. Developments and resources in the family law area are at the firm's disposal, which maximizes the opportunity for favorable results for its clients.

JOHN J. KUROWSKI
The Kurowski Law Firm, P.C.
12 Park Place Professional Centre
Belleville (Swansea), IL 62226

Phone: (618) 277-5500
Fax: (618) 277-6334

•TREVA H. O'NEILL: Ms. O'Neill devotes 75 percent of her practice to family law, including dissolution of marriage, custody, post-divorce issues, paternity issues, and adoption. Ms. O'Neill has extensive experience in contested custody trials, international custody jurisdiction, interstate custody issues, dissolutions of marriage involving professional practices, small businesses, family farm partnerships, retirement and pension issues, military benefits, and contested issues of spousal support. She also practices labor law, primarily representing public employers in labor relations issues, including practice before the Illinois Labor Relations Board, negotiating with unions, arbitrators, and in general negotiations. Ms. O'Neill has written several published articles on family law, including "Survey of Family Law," *Southern Illinois Law Journal*, Volume II, Spring 1987, and "Negotiating and Drafting a Premarital Agreement," Illinois State Bar Association's *Family Law Handbook*, 1995. She has also lectured at numerous workshops on family law.
Education: JD 1981 magna cum laude, Southern Illinois University-Carbondale (Outstanding Woman Law Student 1981; International Law Moot Court Team 1981; Client Counseling Team 1981); MSW 1967, University of Denver; BA 1964, Hardin-Simmons University.
Admitted: 1981 Illinois.
Employment History: Partner 1982-present, law firm currently known as O'Neill & Proctor; Staff Attorney 1985-88, Southern Illinois University-Carbondale Legal Clinic; Adjunct Professor 1989, Pre-Trial Advocacy, Southern Illinois University School of Law.
Professional Associations: ISBA (Family Law Section Council 1987-93); Jackson County Bar Assn. (President 1993-94; Vice President 1992-93; Secretary 1991-92; Treasurer 1990-91); ABA 1983-present [Family Law Section 1993-present (Alimony and Spousal Support Committee; Juvenile Law and Needs of Children Committee)].
Community Involvement: Carbondale Community High School [Athletic Booster Club 1987-93 (Chair 1990-91)].
Firm: O'Neill & Proctor is a small law office in which all are geared to providing personal and individualized services to clients. The counseling and family development backgrounds of the two partners allow for strong support of individuals and families in crisis. *Ms. O'Neill also practices Adoption Law.*

TREVA H. O'NEILL
O'Neill & Proctor
818 West Main Street
P.O. Box 878
Carbondale, IL 62903-0878

Phone: (618) 457-3561
Fax: (618) 549-5267
E-mail: oneill@intrnet.net

Extensive Experience In:

• Public Employer Labor Relations

Chapter 17: Family Law

Janet C. Proctor
O'Neill & Proctor
818 West Main Street
P.O. Box 878
Carbondale, IL 62901

Phone: (618) 457-3561
Fax: (618) 549-5267

•**JANET C. PROCTOR:** Ms. Proctor's extensive background in social services adds a unique perspective to her family and elder law practice. She frequently lectures at conferences, including Advocating for Victims of Abuse, 1993, co-sponsored by the Illinois Attorney General and the Illinois Coalition Against Domestic Violence; the Southern Illinois Women's Health Conference at John A. Logan College in Carterville; and the Elder Rights Conference held in Chicago each summer, with sessions including The People's Court: Guardianship and Older Adults; Determining Capacity for Decision Making; Legal Tools to Assist Victims of Abuse; and Investigating Financial Exploitation. She is a contributor to the Illinois State Bar Association's publication, *Set Your Sights on Senior Rights: A Fact Book for Older Illinoisans,* 1995. As coordinator of the Alternative Dispute Resolution Clinic of Southern Illinois University School of Law, Ms. Proctor worked with the Mediation Association of Southern Illinois to begin the court affiliated mediation program in the First Circuit. She is a trained family mediator and teaches mediation.
Education: JD 1992 summa cum laude, Southern Illinois University-Carbondale (Order of Barristers; Phi Delta Phi Balfour Foundation Scholarship; Phi Kappa Phi Scholastic Frat); MS 1971, Simmons College, Boston, Massachusetts; BA 1968 magna cum laude, Austin College, Sherman, Texas.
Admitted: 1992 Illinois.
Employment History: Partner 1993-present, O'Neill & Proctor; Adjunct Professor 1992-93, 1995-present, Southern Illinois University-Carbondale; Associate/Trainer/Developer 1989-present, Illinois Department on Aging (Elder Rights Division).
Representative Clients: Ms. Proctor represents a variety of clients in family law cases, including corporation executives; administrators and faculty of Southern Illinois University; and low income clients through the Land of Lincoln Legal Services Foundation Private Attorney Involvement Program. She handles dissolution, custody, adoption, and juvenile matters.
Professional Associations: ABA 1989-present; ISBA 1989-present (Family Law Section); Jackson Community Bar Assn. 1992-present (Treasurer 1995-present); National Guardianship Assn. 1994-present; Academy of Family Mediators 1992-present; National Academy of Elder Law Attorneys 1993-present.
Community Involvement: Illinois Department on Aging (Elder Rights Advisory Council 1993-present); Southern Illinois Regional Family Law Project (Volunteer Attorney 1993-present).
Firm: The partners of O'Neill & Proctor come from social work backgrounds and work to assist the client and family holistically. Referrals are made for counseling, work re-entry programs, victim's advocates of police and the State's Attorney's Office, and other services which may be helpful to a family coping with transition. *Ms. Proctor also practices Elder Law.*

MIKE REED - *Law Office of Mike Reed* - 423 South Poplar Street - Centralia, IL 62801 - Phone: (618) 533-0122, Fax: (618) 533-7541, 800: (800) 693-4471 - *See complete biographical profile in the Bankruptcy Law Chapter, page 76.*

Timothy C. Stubblefield
Nelson, Bement, Stubblefield & Levenhagen, P.C.
420 North High Street
P.O. Box Y
Belleville, IL 62222

Phone: (618) 277-4000
(618) 277-8260
Fax: (618) 277-1136

•**TIMOTHY C. STUBBLEFIELD:** Mr. Stubblefield practices primarily in areas of law which involve litigation, specifically family law, workers' compensation, and personal injury. He has successfully represented clients in all areas of family law, including divorce, maintenance and support, child support, visitation, grandparent visitation, child custody, and child abuse cases. He has also successfully represented disabled children and adults in matters concerning employment, education, and guardianships.
Education: JD 1983, St. Louis University (Phipps Scholar; Vice President, Moot Court Board); BA 1980, Northwestern University.
Admitted: 1983 Illinois.
Employment History: Partner 1989-present, Nelson, Bement, Stubblefield & Levenhagen, P.C.; Partner 1983-89, Hillsbrand & Stubblefield, P.C.
Representative Clients: The firm concentrates in the representation of individual clients, as opposed to businesses or corporations.
Professional Associations: Monroe County Bar Assn. (President 1993; Vice President 1992); Attorney General's Advisory Committee for Disabled Adults 1985-89; St. Clair County Bar Assn. 1983-present; ISBA 1983-present.
Community Involvement: Epilepsy Assn. of Southern Illinois (Board of Directors 1986-94; President 1988-91; Vice President 1987).
Firm: Nelson, Bement, Stubblefield & Levenhagen, P.C., is a litigation-oriented law firm. The majority of the firm's clients are individuals, as opposed to businesses or corporations. The firm provides a full range of legal services in family law, wills and estates, workers' compensation, and personal injury cases. *See complete firm profile in Appendix A. Mr. Stubblefield also practices Civil Appellate Law, Personal Injury Law: General and Workers' Compensation Law.*

CHAPTER 18

IMMIGRATION LAW

For centuries, people from around the world have been coming to the United States. They come to work, get an education, escape oppression, start a new life, do business, visit friends, or sightsee. Over the years, the United States has seen tremendous diversity in the countries immigrants come from and their reasons for coming here. In response to the incredible demand for permission to enter this country, the federal government has established a complex set of laws that determines who may enter this country and for what reasons. This chapter discusses legal immigration and travel to the United States.

UNITED STATES CITIZENSHIP

United States citizens have a right to travel to and live in the United States and enjoy the fullest protection of United States laws. People who are not citizens of the United States usually must have a visa to enter and may not enjoy the protection of all United States laws.

A person can become a United States citizen either through birth or through a process known as naturalization. A person can be a United States citizen from birth either by being born here, or by being born in a foreign country but having a parent who is a citizen of the United States. Anyone born in the United States has automatic citizenship, regardless of the parents' citizenship, and even if both parents are living in this country illegally at the time of the child's birth. The only exception is that children born to foreign diplomats in the United States do not get automatic citizenship. Anyone not born a citizen must be naturalized to become a citizen. Occasionally, a group of people is naturalized by treaty or by act of Congress. Usually, a person goes through the process individually.

ALIENS, IMMIGRANTS, NONIMMIGRANTS AND RESIDENTS

An alien is a citizen of any country other than the United States. A person who comes here to stay permanently is called an immigrant. Someone who intends to return to his or her country of origin is called a nonimmigrant, even if he or she intends to stay for a substantial period of time. For example, a student might stay in the United States many years to complete an education and still be considered a nonimmigrant. The distinction between immigrant and nonimmigrant is crucial. Permission to enter as a nonimmigrant often is easier to get than permission to enter as an immigrant, so some people are tempted to claim they intend to return to their home country in order to enter this country. The Immigration and Naturalization Service (INS) is aware of this temptation and often will deny a nonimmigrant visa application to anyone suspected of wanting to remain permanently. Also, being granted a nonimmigrant visa sometimes can make it more difficult to get an immigrant visa later. A permanent resident is an alien who has been given permission to live permanently in the United States.

In a dispute with the INS over an applicant's true intent, the applicant always bears the burden of proving intent to remain here temporarily. For some people, this burden is nearly impossible to overcome. For example, the spouse of a permanent resident normally must wait over two years for available immigrant visas. If he or she claims to want to visit only temporarily, he or she must overcome the presumption that a married person would want to remain permanently with his or her spouse.

THE VISA SYSTEM

A visa is a stamp in a person's passport that gives him or her conditional approval to enter the United States. Most matters involving visas are handled by the INS. Most aliens apply for visas from a consulate or embassy of the United States in the alien's home country.

Citizens of some countries, primarily European countries and Japan, may enter the United States for up to 90 days without a visa. To be eligible, citizens of these countries must show the INS that they have a return ticket home

Chapter 18: Immigration Law

and that they intend to engage in a type of business or tourist activity that would be allowed under a "B Visa," described below. Canadian citizens generally do not need visas to enter temporarily. In some instances, they must obtain INS approval in advance if they are coming here to work.

Congress establishes a complex set of quotas that limits the number of visas that can be granted for most types of visas. Whether an applicant receives a visa depends on the type of visa requested, the applicant's reason for traveling to the United States, and the applicant's country of origin. Probably the most important element to obtaining a visa successfully is knowing for which visa category to apply. For certain categories of visas and certain countries of origin, an applicant can wait many years before he or she even will be considered for a visa. Sometimes the wait would be much shorter if the applicant applied for a different type of visa. Unfortunately, once an applicant applies for one type of visa, it can be difficult to change the application to another class of visa. For this reason, it is wise to consult an immigration attorney before applying for any kind of visa.

NONIMMIGRANT VISAS

There are different kinds of nonimmigrant visas, identified by the letters A–R, available for persons who do not intend to remain in the United States permanently. All nonimmigrant visas are based on what the applicant intends to do in this country. Following is a list of the visa categories:

- A Visas: for diplomats and their families.
- B Visas: for aliens coming to this country to do business but not for employment or labor for hire; B Visas are commonly used by aliens coming to do business research, engage in litigation, or negotiate contracts; B-2 Visas, the most common nonimmigrant visas, allow aliens to enter the country temporarily to engage in tourism, visit with friends or relatives, or to receive medical treatment.
- C Visas: for entrance into the United States only for immediate and continuous transit through the country to a third country.
- D Visas: for crew members of foreign vessels or airplanes.
- E Visas: for traders and investors covered by commercial treaties between the United States and foreign countries, as well as spouses and children of E Visa holders.
- F Visas: for students in full-time academic programs, from the elementary school level up to the post-graduate level, as well as spouses and children of F Visa holders; F Visa holders are allowed to be employed for fewer than 20 hours a week, mainly at certain on-campus jobs typically done by students.
- G Visas: for representatives, officers, and employees of foreign countries to international organizations.
- H Visas: for workers needed by United States employers to fill temporary openings; H-1B Visas commonly are held by aliens with highly specialized knowledge working in professional jobs.
- I Visas: for media representatives and their families.
- J Visas: designed to bring foreigners here to participate in exchange programs designated by the United States Information Agency.
- K Visas: to allow an alien engaged to a United States citizen to enter to marry the citizen, as well as for any minor children of the alien.
- L Visas: for intracompany employee transfers (e.g., for employees of multinational corporations).
- M Visas: for students in vocational or nonacademic study programs.
- N Visas: for relatives of certain international organization employees here on G Visas.
- O Visas: for artists, entertainers, athletes, scientists, and certain business professionals with extraordinary abilities in their fields, and persons needed to accompany and assist them.
- P Visas: for performing artists, entertainers and athletes; similar to O Visas, but easier to get and intended more for group entertainers or athletes who come here for a specific performance or tour.
- Q Visas: for participants in international cultural exchanges.
- R Visas: for religious workers and their families.

IMMIGRANT VISAS

An applicant who intends to stay in this country permanently generally is admitted either on the basis of employment or family connections. The main exception is for political asylum seekers.

Employment-Based Immigration

An alien can receive permission to immigrate to this country on the basis of his or her employment. There are five categories of employment, known as preferences, through which aliens can be permitted to immigrate:

First Preference: Individuals of extraordinary ability, outstanding professors or researchers, and multinational executives.

Second Preference: Professionals with advanced degrees and aliens with exceptional abilities in science, art, or business. (Note: "Exceptional ability" is a different standard than "extraordinary ability" required for a first preference.)

Third Preference: Skilled workers, professionals, and other workers for which there is a shortage of workers in the United States.

Fourth Preference: Certain special workers, such as religious workers.

Fifth Preference: Investors creating employment for workers in the United States; the investment must be substantial (i.e., between $500,000 and $1,000,000).

Family-Based Immigration

An alien can get a visa as an immediate relative of a United States citizen if he or she is a child, spouse, or parent of the citizen. In addition, there are four family-based immigrant visa categories:

First Preference: Unmarried children of United States citizens.
Second Preference: Spouses and unmarried children of lawful permanent residents.
Third Preference: Married children of United States citizens.
Fourth Preference: Siblings of adult United States citizens.

Each preference is allotted a total number of visas. Generally speaking, the higher the applicant's preference, the shorter the wait to get a visa.

Special Classes of Immigrants

Some groups of immigrants receive special treatment and fall outside the preference system described above.

Diversity immigrants are immigrants from countries deemed under-represented in the pool of applicants for visas throughout the years. Under a new program implemented by the INS in 1995, a certain number of visas will be granted to applicants from low-admission countries and who have a high school education or two years of training or experience in a particular occupation.

Refugees and asylees also receive special treatment. A person is a refugee if he or she is outside the United States, is fleeing or has fled his or her country, and has a well-founded fear that if returned to the home country, he or she will be persecuted because of race, religion, nationality, membership in a particular social group, or political opinion. An asylee is an alien already in the United States who, like a refugee, has a well-founded fear of persecution if returned to his or her home country. The President and Congress decide each year the total number of refugees and asylees to accept into the country. Occasionally, Congress grants immigrant visas allotted for individuals from specific countries according to political factors. Recent programs have included China, Hong Kong, and Tibet.

ENTRY AND EXCLUSION

A visa only gives conditional approval to enter the country. Once an alien arrives in the United States with a visa, he or she must apply for entry from INS officials at the point of entry. For most aliens, this is a mere formality, but the INS can exclude persons with valid visas for a variety of reasons, including communicable diseases, physical or mental disorders that pose a threat to others, drug addiction, or criminal history. Involvement in espionage or terrorist activity against the United States government or its people is grounds for exclusion. The Secretary of State also has broad discretion to bar entry of anyone whose presence would have an adverse effect on the foreign policy of the United States. Sometimes waivers are available for aliens who otherwise would be denied entry for certain reasons. For example, the child of a United States citizen may be granted a waiver to enter to receive treatment for drug addiction.

GETTING A GREEN CARD AND BECOMING A NATURALIZED CITIZEN

Becoming a permanent resident is the first step that an alien must take to become a naturalized American citizen. People with permission to live in the United States permanently are issued "green cards" that allow them to work with few restrictions. A permanent resident can apply to become a naturalized citizen after five years, or three years if married to a United States citizen.

The INS is diligent in investigating marriages between United States citizens and aliens to ensure that aliens do not become permanent residents through sham marriages. Immigration law specifies that an alien seeking permanent residence based on a marriage to a United States citizen of less than two years first is granted conditional permanent resident status. After two years, the husband and wife must apply to the INS to remove this conditional status.

DEPORTATION

Deportation is the expulsion of an alien who entered the United States illegally, or entered legally but has done something to become deportable. With few exceptions, any violation of the conditions of a visa, no matter how minor, is grounds for deportation to a person's country of origin. Conviction for any crime but the most minor is also grounds for deportation. Deportation can delay an alien whose long-term goal is to live permanently in this country. After being deported, aliens are forbidden to re-enter the country for five years. Aliens deported for aggravated felonies, such as drug smuggling, are barred from re-entry for 20 years or may be barred permanently. The delay in returning to the United States may be even greater for aliens from countries with long waiting lists. Returning home under a deportation order may result in the embassy's refusal to entrust the individual with another temporary visa.

There are a number of remedies to deportation, especially if the deportable person has lived in the United States for a long time, building a life that demonstrates good moral character. Even if the deportable individual has not been here long, there may be certain waivers or defenses to deportation. Among the most common is asking the court for "voluntary departure," which allows the individual to depart the United States on his or her own. In any case, anyone facing deportation should seek the advice of counsel well in advance of a deportation hearing.

RESOURCES

Amnesty International, Refugee Office, 500 Sansome Street, #615, San Francisco, CA 94111, phone: (415) 291-0601.

Exodus World Service, P.O. Box 7000, West Chicago, IL 60185, phone: (312) 733-8433, provides assistance and advocacy for refugees.

Immigration and Naturalization Service, Chicago District, Ten Jackson Boulevard West, Chicago, IL 60604. Call (312) 353-7334 for information in English or Spanish; call (800) 870-FORM (3676) for forms.

Lawyers Committee for Human Rights, 330 Seventh Avenue, Tenth Floor, New York, NY 10001, phone: (212) 629-6170, can provide information on refugee protection.

Immigration Law Leading Illinois Attorneys

The Leading Illinois Attorneys listed below were nominated as exceptional by their peers in a statewide survey conducted by American Research Corporation (ARC). ARC asked several thousand licensed Illinois attorneys to name the lawyer to whom they would send a close friend or family member in need of legal assistance in specific areas of law. The attorneys below were nominated in the area of Immigration Law.

Because the survey results (all practice area results combined) represent less than three percent of Illinois' practicing attorneys, this list should not be construed as a complete list. Nevertheless, it is an excellent source of highly qualified and reputable Illinois attorneys.

For information on ARC's survey methodology, see page *xi*.
For the complete list of Leading Illinois Consumer Attorneys, see page *vii*.

The Leading Illinois Attorneys below are listed alphabetically in accordance with the geographic region in which their offices are located. Note that attorneys may handle clients from a broad geographic area; attorneys are not restricted to only serving clients residing within the cities in which their offices are located.

An attorney whose name appears in bold has included a biographical profile in this chapter.

LEADING ILLINOIS ATTORNEYS

Illinois' Most Respected Legal Counsel As Selected By Their Peers.

The Leading Illinois Attorneys below were recommended by their peers in a statewide survey.

Cook & Collar Counties

Ahlgren, Robert D. - Chicago
Anvaripour, Mark - Chicago
Asonye, Uche O. - Chicago, page 226
Azulay, J. Daniel - Chicago
Azulay, Y. Judd - Chicago, page 227
Bass, Renee F. - Chicago
Bensinger, Ethan - Chicago
Berg, Royal F. - Chicago
Blumenfeld, Barry E. - Chicago
Carpenter, Robert T. - Chicago
Carper, Nancy - Chicago
Carroll, Jane S. - Chicago
Clifford, Robert A. - Chicago
Cooper, Scott F. - Chicago
Davidson, Mark S. - Chicago
Donenfeld, J. Douglas - Chicago
Fawell, Jeffrey B. - Wheaton
Feiertag, Terry Yale - Chicago
Fortino, Susan R. - Chicago
Fox, Leon - Chicago
Gaber, Kathleen M. - Chicago
Geman, Kenneth Y. - Chicago
Gzesh, Susan R. - Chicago
Hallagan, James E. - Chicago
Hanus, Richard - Chicago
Kagan, Linda S. - Chicago
Kempster, Donald - Chicago
Kim, Ben H. - Chicago
Kinnally, Patrick - Aurora
Krengel, Ellen D. - Chicago
Kriezelman, Jeffrey A. - Chicago
Lasko, William E., II - Chicago
McCormick, Margaret H. - Chicago
Morgen, Perry - Chicago
Owens, John E., Jr. - Park Ridge
Provenzano, William J. - Libertyville
Puchalski, Donald E. - Chicago
Puchalski, Richard J. - Chicago
Resnick, Kalman D. - Chicago
Rubman, David - Chicago
Scott, Lisa - Chicago
Siebert, William Newell - Chicago, page 227
Smirl, Dale L. - Chicago
Tapia-Ruano, Carlina - Chicago
Thomas, Mark Jacob - Chicago
Zulkie, Paul L. - Chicago

Northwestern Illinois Including Rockford & Quad Cities

Sullivan, Donald P. - Rockford
Williams, Michael A. - Rock Island

CENTRAL ILLINOIS

Burkhardt, Craig S. - Springfield
Feldman, Lynne R. - Champaign
Lied, Michael R. - Peoria

Biographical Profiles of Immigration Law Leading Illinois Attorneys

The Leading Illinois Attorneys profiled below were nominated as exceptional by their peers in a statewide survey conducted by American Research Corporation (ARC). ARC asked several thousand licensed Illinois attorneys to name the lawyer to whom they would send a close friend or family member in need of legal assistance in specific areas of law. The attorneys below were nominated in the area of Immigration Law.

Because the survey results (all practice area results combined) represent less than three percent of Illinois' practicing attorneys, this list should not be construed as a complete list. Nevertheless, it is an excellent source of highly qualified and reputable Illinois attorneys.

For information on ARC's survey methodology, see page *xi*.
For the complete list of Leading Illinois Consumer Attorneys, see page *xii*.
For the list of Leading Illinois Immigration Law Attorneys, see page 223.

The Leading Illinois Attorneys below are listed alphabetically in accordance with the geographic region in which their offices are located. Note that attorneys may handle clients from a broad geographic area; attorneys are not limited to only serving clients residing within the cities in which their offices are located.

The two-line attorney listings in this section are of attorneys who practice in this area but whose full biographical profiles appear in other sections of this book. A bullet "•" preceding a name indicates the attorney was nominated in this particular area of law.

For information on the format of the full biographical profiles, consult the "Using the Consumer Guidebook" section on page *xviii*.

The following abbreviations are used throughout these profiles:

App.	Appellate
Cir.	Circuit
Ct.	Court
Dist.	District
Sup.	Supreme
JD	Juris Doctor (Doctor of Law)
LLB	Legum Baccalaureus (Bachelor of Laws)
LLD	Legum Doctor (Doctor of Laws)
LLM	Legum Magister (Master of Laws)
ADR	Alternative Dispute Resolution
ABA	American Bar Association
ABOTA	American Board of Trial Advocates
ATLA	Association of Trial Lawyers of America
CBA	Chicago Bar Association
ISBA	Illinois State Bar Association
ITLA	Illinois Trial Lawyers Association
NBTA	National Board of Trial Advocacy

Chapter 18: Immigration Law

Cook & Collar Counties

UCHE O. ASONYE

Asonye & Associates
203 North LaSalle Street
Suite 2100
Chicago, IL 60601

Phone: (312) 558-1792
Fax: (312) 558-1787

Extensive Experience In:

- Representing Health Care Institutions
- H Visas/Permanent Residency
- J-1 Visa Waivers

•**UCHE O. ASONYE:** Mr. Asonye practices all aspects of immigration law, including H Visas, L Visas, E Visas, permanent residency, and labor certification. His clients include health care facilities and professionals who seek representation for H Visa petitions, J-1 Visa Waiver applications, and permanent residency petitions. He also counsels immigrants on U.S. tax matters.
Education: JD 1992, Loyola University; Certified Public Accountant 1987, Illinois; BSC 1985 with honors, DePaul University.
Admitted: 1992 Illinois; 1992 U.S. Dist. Ct. (N. Dist. IL); 1995 U.S. Tax Ct.
Employment History: 1994-present, Asonye & Associates; 1992-93, Lindner, Speers & Reuland, P.C.; Summer Associate 1991, Baker & McKenzie; Tax/Computer Consultant 1986-91, Arthur Anderson & Co.
Representative Clients: Mr. Asonye's immigration clients include health care institutions, physicians, individuals, as well as clients seeking professional visas, employment visas, H Visas, L Visas, permanent residency, and J-1 Visa Waivers.
Professional Associations: ABA; National Employment Lawyers Assn.; CBA; Cook County Bar Assn.; ATLA.
Community Involvement: Campus Green Assn. (Board of Directors 1993-95). In addition, Mr. Asonye accepts pro bono cases on a regular basis.
Firm: Asonye & Associates is dedicated to providing competent and individualized legal services. The firm represents individuals and small companies in filing visa petitions such as H-1 Visas, L-1 Visas, E Visas, J-1 Visa Waivers, and permanent residency based on employment. *Mr. Asonye also practices Employment Law and Tax Law.*

J. DANIEL AZULAY - *Azulay & Azulay, P.C.* - 35 East Wacker Drive, Suite 3300 - Chicago, IL 60601 - Phone: (312) 832-9200, Fax: (312) 832-9212 - *See complete biographical profile in the Family Law Chapter, page 181.*

•**Y. JUDD AZULAY:** Mr. Azulay is Vice President of the law firm of Azulay & Azulay, P.C. His area of concentration is immigration and naturalization law, including family and employment petitions, asylum, deportation, exclusion, waivers, citizenship, and litigation matters before the INS and all courts. Mr. Azulay has been assisting individuals belonging to many different nationalities and corporations in obtaining both permanent and temporary visas to both work and live in the U.S. In addition, he assists asylum seekers in remaining in the U.S. and obtaining employment authorization. He has also developed a solid reputation for assisting clients in obtaining alternatives to deportation. He has traveled to foreign consulates worldwide to assist clients in obtaining both permanent and temporary visas to the U.S. Mr. Azulay has been active in the American Jewish Congress. He has been cited frequently in different publications for his unending legal support for pro bono work. Mr. Azulay provides immigration information to many not-for-profit organizations. He is a recipient of the Chicago Volunteer Legal Services Distinguished Service Award.
Education: JD 1973, Cumberland School of Law, Samford University; MS 1970, University of Alabama; BA 1967, University of Miami.
Admitted: 1973 Illinois; 1973 U.S. Dist. Ct. (N. Dist. IL); 1974 U.S. Ct. App. (7th Cir.); 1974 U.S. Sup. Ct.; 1974 U.S. Ct. (Fed. Cir.).
Employment History: Vice President 1977-present, Azulay & Azulay, P.C.; Group Counsel 1975-76, American Hospital Supply Co., Evanston; 1974-75, Abbott Laboratories, North Chicago; Associate 1973-74, Alter, Weiss, Whitesel & Laff.
Representative Clients: Mr. Azulay represents hospitals, nursing homes, corporate and individual clients.
Professional Associations: American Immigration Lawyers Assn.; ABA; Chicago Patent Law Assn.; ISBA.
Community Involvement: Ida Crown Academy, Chicago (Financial Vice President); Hillel Torah Day School, Skokie (Board Officer); Or Torah Congregation, Skokie (Board Officer).
Firm: Azulay & Azulay, P.C., concentrates in several areas of law, including immigration, family law, real estate, trial work, and related areas. Clients include corporations and individuals located all over the world. The firm provides clients with the best possible legal advice and representation in the most expeditious manner. The firm is in the forefront of providing immigration legal services. It is prepared to enter and provide service in any immigration issue, including family- and employment-related matters, court matters, temporary and permanent visas, deportation and exclusion, naturalization and citizenship, and consular matters, for almost any person or under any circumstance, everywhere. *See complete firm profile in Appendix A.*

Y. JUDD AZULAY
Azulay & Azulay, P.C.
One East Wacker Drive
Suite 2700
Chicago, IL 60601

Phone: (312) 832-9200
Fax: (312) 832-9212

Extensive Experience In:
• Immigration Matters
• Trademarks

•**WILLIAM NEWELL SIEBERT:** Mr. Siebert has concentrated in immigration law since 1969, with an emphasis in representing health care professionals, hospitals, medical schools, physician recruiters and related health care providers. He is active as a speaker and author of immigration law topics as they relate to the needs of the health care industry.
Education: JD 1969, University of Detroit; BA 1966, Michigan State University.
Admitted: 1969 Illinois; 1971 Florida.
Employment History: 1971-present, William Newell Siebert & Associates; Associate Attorney 1969-71, Peterson & Beck.
Representative Clients: Mr. Siebert represents primarily health care related associations, groups, corporations and partnerships.
Professional Associations: ISBA; The Florida Bar; CBA; ABA; American Immigration Lawyers Assn. (Chicago Chapter; Miami Chapter).
Firm: William Newell Siebert & Associates provides legal advice and service on immigration matters relating to the health care industry on a nationwide basis. Communication is primarily conducted telephonically. E-mail, fax, and related electronic computerized communication is also a normal part of the practice.

WILLIAM NEWELL SIEBERT
William Newell Siebert & Associates
307 North Michigan Avenue
Suite 924
Chicago, IL 60601

Phone: (312) 329-0646
Fax: (312) 553-4419
E-mail: 73344.462@compuserve.com

PERSONAL INJURY LAW: GENERAL

Personal injuries, as their name implies, are injuries to individual persons. Crimes are wrongful acts against society. The government punishes those who commit crimes with criminal penalties. For personal injuries, the government does not punish the wrongdoer but gives the victim the right to pursue a private, civil lawsuit, called a tort action, against the wrongdoer. Some wrongful acts are both crimes and torts, and can subject the wrongdoer to both criminal penalties and tort remedies. This chapter outlines the actions that lead to most personal injury lawsuits, including general accidents and injuries, use of defective products, and injuries occurring to workers on the job. The Personal Injury Law: Transportation Chapter deals with actions that result from transportation-related accidents. The Personal Injury Law: Medical & Professional Malpractice Chapter discusses medical and legal negligence.

GENERAL CONCEPTS OF TORT LAW

Tort laws are based on the premise that when someone does something to harm another person physically, mentally, or financially, the person harmed ought to be compensated for the loss. Tort lawsuits are governed by a set of rules that are different from the rules that govern criminal lawsuits.

DEGREE OF FAULT NEEDED TO RECOVER

There are three kinds of torts—negligence, intentional misconduct, and strict liability. Each requires the plaintiff to show a different degree of fault to recover from the defendant.

Negligence

A person is negligent if he or she fails to act as a reasonable person would act in a similar situation. Examples of negligence include inattentive driving that causes an automobile accident, or a store owner failing to repair a defective escalator that causes a fall. If a reasonable person would have driven attentively, or if a reasonable store owner would have fixed the unsafe escalator, the person who drove inattentively or failed to make repairs could be found negligent by a judge or jury. Negligent behavior is almost never criminal.

Intentional Misconduct

Intentional misconduct occurs when someone, acting deliberately, does something that hurts another person or damages that person's property. The law does not require that a person intended to cause the injury he or she actually inflicted, only that he or she acted deliberately or with complete indifference toward a person's own safety or the safety of others. For example, a driver of an automobile may intend only to scare a pedestrian by swerving toward the pedestrian, but if the driver hits the pedestrian, the driver commits intentional misconduct. Intentional misconduct can be more difficult to prove than negligence, but often a plaintiff can recover greater damages if he or she can show the defendant acted intentionally. Intentional misconduct is often criminal behavior also. Examples of intentional misconduct include assault and battery.

Strict Liability

In some situations, a plaintiff can recover for injuries received even if the defendant uses utmost care. In these situations, a defendant is said to be strictly, or absolutely, liable for any damages resulting from his or her actions. The principle behind strict liability is that some activities are necessary but so dangerous that even a reasonable person cannot make them completely safe. As a social policy, defendants are permitted to engage in certain activities but are held strictly liable for any injury resulting from the activity. Strict liability claims most commonly result from extremely dangerous activities such as blasting, excavating or demolishing a building, or from defective products.

Comparative Fault

Tort law attempts to compensate victims if their injuries are caused by another person. When one person clearly causes all of another person's injury, blame is easy to place. In many other cases, however, the victim's actions help cause the injury or make it worse than it would otherwise be. For instance, a negligent driver might injure a pedestrian who is negligently walking in the street instead of on a sidewalk, where a prudent pedestrian normally walks. A person injured by a defective chain saw may have suffered more severe injuries by negligently failing to wear safety goggles while using the chain saw. In these cases, a judge or jury must calculate how much each party is at fault. Each state has its own rules for calculating damages that can be recovered when a victim is at least partially to blame for his or her own injury.

Illinois has a comparative fault rule. Under the comparative fault rule, a judge reduces the amount of any damage award by the percent that the victim's own actions contributed to his or her injuries. For example, if a jury finds that a plaintiff suffered $100,000 in damages, but was 30 percent at fault, the judge reduces the damage award by 30 percent to $70,000. The reduction may be made only up to 50 percent. If the victim is more than 50 percent at fault, he or she collects nothing.

VICARIOUS LIABILITY

There are several ways a person can be held liable for the actions of another person. This is known as vicarious liability. For example, a parent might be held responsible for damage caused by his or her child if the parent knows that the child is likely to injure someone, the parent has the ability to control the child, and the parent negligently fails to exercise any control over the child. The owner of a vehicle can be held responsible for accidents caused when another person drives the vehicle if the owner negligently entrusts the vehicle to the other driver. The most common form of vicarious liability is called *respondeat superior*. Under respondeat superior, an employer is responsible for torts committed by employees within the scope of their employment. A business owner is not usually responsible for acts committed by independent contractors. For example, if a pedestrian is struck and injured by a person driving to a party, the victim has a claim against the driver. If the pedestrian is hit by a person driving a delivery van for his or her employer, then respondeat superior gives the pedestrian claims against both the driver and the employer. As a practical matter, personal injury plaintiffs often focus their recovery efforts on the employers because employers usually have more money or better insurance.

BURDEN OF PROOF

The burden of proof in a civil lawsuit is less strict than the proof required in a criminal case. In a criminal case, the state must prove a person's guilt beyond a reasonable doubt. The state is required to meet this high standard because a defendant's liberty, and possibly even life, are at stake. The plaintiff in a personal injury lawsuit need only show that it is more probable than not that an injury was caused by the defendant's actions. If the jury finds that the evidence even slightly favors the injured party, then it must find for the plaintiff. The personal injury plaintiff need only meet this lower standard because the defendant's life and liberty are not at stake.

DEFENSES

Sometimes people are allowed, or privileged, to commit acts that otherwise constitute assault or battery, and not be liable for damages. If one acts in defense of self, others, or one's land, the use of force can be justified. Illinois has a "Good Samaritan" law that states that a civilian has no duty to provide aid to an injured person; however, once a person voluntarily assists someone, he or she becomes liable for any injury that results from the failure to exercise due care. Law enforcement officials and firefighters have a defense to liability if they injure someone while providing good-faith emergency care. For example, if a firefighter responds to a call, and in trying to help the victim accidentally worsens the victim's injury, the firefighter has a defense to charges of assault and battery.

DAMAGES

The damages a victim may collect depend on the type of tort alleged. For torts to the body, a plaintiff can collect lost wages, diminished earning capacity, costs of medical care, pain, and suffering. For torts to property, a plaintiff can recover diminished value of the property, replacement costs, or cost of repair.

In a lawsuit alleging intentional misconduct, the plaintiff often may be able to recover punitive damages in addition to any awards for injuries, pain, and suffering. Punitive damages, designed to punish people or organizations for unlawful acts, are usually very large sums of money. Until recently, there were few limits to punitive damages. Although federal and state legislatures have recently passed laws capping punitive damages in certain types of cases, it can still be to the plaintiff's advantage to convince a jury that injuries were the result of an intentional act and not mere negligence.

A wrongful death lawsuit is a lawsuit filed by the surviving relatives of a person. For example, under Illinois law, any dependent heirs, such as sons or daughters, of a person killed by a defective product can sue the manufacturer for loss of that person's future income. Surviving relatives cannot, however, sue a manufacturer to collect damages for the pain and suffering of a person wrongfully killed by a manufacturer's defective product.

However, the estate of the deceased person can sue to collect money needed to pay any bills for medical treatment received by the person before he or she died.

A surviving spouse can sue for damages to recover for loss of advice, comfort, assistance, and protection. Illinois recognizes a viable fetus as a "person." Therefore, any personal injury action that can be brought by one who was born can also be brought on behalf of an unborn, viable fetus.

Suing the Government

There was a time when citizens could not sue the government for torts committed by government employees. The federal and state governments enjoyed complete immunity from tort lawsuits. This immunity has been partially waived, but there are limits on tort actions against the government. Although the federal and most state governments now permit suits for personal injuries suffered because of the negligence of a government employee or as a result of a dangerous condition on government property, there are limits on how much can be collected and when a suit must be initiated. Typically, the State of Illinois may only be sued in the court of claims for actions of breach of contract with the state, tort by an agent of the state, and tort by an escaped inmate.

AREAS OF PERSONAL INJURY PRACTICE

Lawyers practicing general personal injury law generally fall into one of three practice areas: product liability, general accidents and injuries, and workers' compensation.

Product Liability

Injuries resulting from defective products are the basis of some personal injury lawsuits. Product liability lawsuits frequently receive attention in the media. Stories of people recovering damages for faulty breast implants, exploding gas tanks, or flammable children's clothing all make headlines. Because a faulty product line can injure many people, product liability lawsuits are sometimes brought as class action lawsuits in which many injured people—the class—bring one united lawsuit against the manufacturer, share legal costs, and split any award.

Product liability claims usually rely on one of three theories: strict liability, negligence, or breach of warranty. Each of these has its standards and potential damages. Often a single injury leads a plaintiff to bring claims under all three theories against the manufacturer. For example, a person injured when a microwave oven explodes might allege that the oven's manufacturer breached a warranty, negligently manufactured the oven, and that the oven was so dangerous that its manufacturer should be held strictly liable for all injuries it caused.

Strict Product Liability

Strict liability makes the manufacturer of a product liable to someone injured while using the product if the product was unreasonably dangerous. This theory focuses on the product itself. In Illinois, a person alleging strict product liability must show that

- The product was in a defective condition, so that it was unreasonably dangerous even if used for its intended purpose
- The defect existed when the product left the manufacturer's control
- The defect caused the plaintiff's injury

For example, if a chair had a defective leg that made it unsafe to sit on, the leg was defective when the chair left the manufacturer, and that weak leg caused injury to a person who fell after sitting in the chair, the manufacturer may be strictly liable for damages.

Negligent Design or Manufacture

Manufacturers can be sued for negligence. If a manufacturer negligently designs or manufactures a product, the manufacturer is liable to those hurt by the product. Unlike strict liability theory, which focuses on the product, negligence claims focus on the manufacturer's actions in designing and manufacturing the product. As in all negligence cases, the manufacturer can be found liable if a judge or jury finds that the manufacturer failed to exercise the degree of care that a reasonable manufacturer would exercise in manufacturing the product or that the product was not manufactured according to the manufacturer's own specifications.

Under this theory, the manufacturer of the faulty chair might be liable if the company did not conduct reasonable inspections to ensure that products were checked for defects before being sold to consumers. It is important to note that the manufacturer is not negligent merely for failing to produce a perfectly safe product. Illinois courts use a reasonable care balancing test that asks jurors to balance the likelihood and seriousness of harm against the feasibility and burden of possible precautions that might have avoided the harm. For example, manufacturers might not be required to install a safety feature if doing so would make the product prohibitively expensive or impossible to use. In these cases, the manufacturer has a duty to warn users of the product of the risks associated with its use so that users can protect themselves. This is why ladders, for example, have so many warnings on them. No ladder can be made perfectly safe, so manufacturers warn consumers of their dangers.

Some of the most convincing evidence of negligence is evidence of the actions of other manufacturers of similar products. If a manufacturer fails to take precautions or to provide warnings that are standard in the industry, there is a strong likelihood a jury will find that the manufacturer was negligent.

Breach of Warranty

Manufacturers can also be liable for product injuries caused by a breach of warranty. Breach of warranty lawsuits may involve the Uniform Commercial Code (UCC), which is a bundle of statutes adopted in Illinois and other states to govern many commercial transactions. Under the UCC, a product must be fit for its intended purpose. If a consumer buys a product and is hurt while using it for a purpose for which it is clearly intended, the manufacturer can be liable. A product must also be fit for a particular purpose for which the seller knows the buyer is purchasing the item. A manufacturer also may make additional warranties to the consumer. The breach of any of these warranties can make the manufacturer liable to consumers hurt by the product. In some situations, a manufacturer is allowed to disclaim some of these warranties, so a plaintiff must check to determine which of the warranties apply.

GENERAL ACCIDENTS AND INJURIES

A broad variety of accidents and injuries may lead to personal injury lawsuits. Some of the most common are discussed in this chapter. Libel and slander are discussed in the Arts, Entertainment & Intellectual Property Law Chapter.

ASSAULT AND BATTERY

Many people believe that assault and battery are one action. They are actually two closely related but distinct actions. Assault is the attempt or threat to inflict injury on another person when coupled with the apparent ability to carry out the attempt or threat. Assault does not require actual physical contact. For example, if someone threatens to strike a neighbor and appears capable of carrying out the threat, the person making the threat may be liable for assault even though he or she never touches the neighbor. Battery is similar to assault but requires actual unwelcome physical contact. The physical contact need not be so strong as to injure the other person. For example, a person can commit battery by touching another person in an unwelcome sexual manner.

ILLEGAL CONFINEMENT

Illegal confinement, also known as false imprisonment, is confinement by force, threats of force, or physical barriers when one has no right to do so. Unlike in other states, Illinois merchants are not permitted to make a person suspected of shoplifting wait against his or her wishes for the police to arrive. If the merchant keeps the suspect longer than is reasonable or necessary under the circumstances (beyond the person's wishes), the merchant may be liable for illegal confinement.

LANDOWNER LIABILITY

There are several ways a landowner may be liable to someone injured on the landowner's property. Business owners and homeowners may be sued if they do something wrong that causes others to be injured on their property. A business owner sometimes is sued for injuries caused by people committing crimes on his or her property if the business owner did not take appropriate measures to ensure the safety of customers. An example of this type of case occurs when a person is attacked in a parking lot and then sues the lot's owner for failing to provide security measures that could have prevented the attack.

In general, a landowner is not liable for the injuries of a trespasser; however, the landowner must take reasonable care to protect the people he or she knows come on the property for legitimate purposes, such as letter carriers. A landowner may be responsible to children injured on his or her property if there is something on the property—like a swimming pool—that is dangerous, the children are likely to exercise less care than adults, and the landowner fails to exercise sufficient care to prevent injury to a reasonable child. Other states place a greater liability on landowners in this scenario through what is commonly called the "attractive nuisance doctrine." Illinois does not recognize the attractive nuisance theory.

Workers' Compensation

Illinois' workers' compensation system compensates workers for injuries occurring in the workplace. Without a workers' compensation system, workers injured on the job would have to prove that their employers' negligence led to the injury. Because the system does not require proving negligence, a worker injured on the job has a better chance of being compensated than if he or she is injured in some other way and has to file a civil lawsuit. Instead of filing suit, a worker notifies her employer of the injury and the employer then contacts its insurance carrier, which handles payment of any medical bill and other claims made by the employee. All employers subject to the Illinois Workers' Compensation Act must either carry workers' compensation insurance or demonstrate they have the financial resources to cover any reasonably anticipated claims.

The trade-off for this relatively easy route to compensation is a limit to the amount of money that can be awarded for a work-related injury. With few exceptions, employers or their insurers are only required to pay for medical expenses, permanent injuries, and/or lost wages. An employer cannot be made to pay for emotional distress such as pain and suffering.

Often a worker contacts an attorney because the employer or its insurance carrier refuses to pay a workers' compensation claim, maintaining that either the injury was not work-related or that the benefits demanded exceed those justified for the injury. Sometimes a dispute arises after an employer stops making workers' compensation payments. When disputes arise, a worker has a variety of options, including an administrative conference, small claims court, or—as a final option—a hearing before a workers' compensation judge.

The most common way to resolve disputes is through a semi-formal administrative conference, subject to rules established by the Illinois Department of Labor and Industry. At the conference, a department representative acts as an informal mediator and referee who decides what kind of evidence may be considered by those attending. Typically, the employer, an investigator from the insurance company if the employer is not self-insured, the department representative, the injured employee, and the employee's attorney attend the conference. The goal of a conference is to reach a voluntary resolution to the dispute. If the parties cannot resolve their dispute, the department representative issues a judgment that everyone is obligated to follow. Such a judgment can be appealed to the department by anyone involved in the conference.

Going to small claims court is another way to resolve disputes over a workers' compensation claim. Both the employer and employee, however, must agree to turn over the dispute to a conciliation court, and the amount of the dispute cannot exceed $5,000. Either party can decide whether to be represented by an attorney in such a proceeding.

Finally, a dispute over a workers' compensation claim can be taken to a special workers' compensation court, where a judge will formally hear evidence about the injury and will resolve the dispute in a written decision that both sides must follow. Anyone disagreeing with the decision has a right to appeal it to the Illinois Workers' Compensation Court of Appeals and, if still unsatisfied, to the Illinois Supreme Court.

RESOURCES

Contact the Illinois Industrial Commission, 100 Randolph Street West, Eighth Floor, Room 200, Chicago, IL 60601, phone: (312) 814-6611, for information on workers' compensation.

The Products Liability Resource Manual: An Attorney's Guide to Analyzing Issues, Developing Strategies, and Winning Cases, James T. O'Reilly and Nancy C. Cody, American Bar Association General Practice Section, Chicago, IL, 1993.

Personal Injury Law: General Leading Illinois Attorneys

The Leading Illinois Attorneys listed below were nominated as exceptional by their peers in a statewide survey conducted by American Research Corporation (ARC). ARC asked several thousand licensed Illinois attorneys to name the lawyer to whom they would send a close friend or family member in need of legal assistance in specific areas of law. The attorneys below were nominated in the area of Personal Injury Law: General.

Because the survey results (all practice area results combined) represent less than three percent of Illinois' practicing attorneys, this list should not be construed as a complete list. Nevertheless, it is an excellent source of highly qualified and reputable Illinois attorneys.

For information on ARC's survey methodology, see page *xi*.
For the complete list of Leading Illinois Consumer Attorneys, see page *xii*.

The Leading Illinois Attorneys below are listed alphabetically in accordance with the geographic region in which their offices are located. Note that attorneys may handle clients from a broad geographic area; attorneys are not restricted to only serving clients residing within the cities in which their offices are located.

An attorney whose name appears in bold has included a biographical profile in this chapter.

LEADING ILLINOIS ATTORNEYS

Illinois' Most Respected Legal Counsel As Selected By Their Peers.

The Leading Illinois Attorneys below were recommended by their peers in a statewide survey.

Cook & Collar Counties

Avgeris, George N. - Hinsdale, page 238
Baizer, Robert S. - Highland Park
Barder, Fredrick B. - Chicago
Baum, David M. - Chicago
Block, Michael D. - Joliet
Bloom, Marvin - Chicago
Bobb, Patricia C. - Chicago
Boyle, Charles A. - Chicago, page 238
Brill, Aaron P. - Chicago
Bristol, Douglas - Chicago
Buege, Robert M. - Waukegan
Burke, John M. - Chicago
Burke, William J. - Chicago
Carpenter, Robert T. - Chicago
Clancy, Thomas A. - Chicago
Clancy, Wendell W. - St. Charles
Clifford, Robert A. - Chicago
Cobb, Ronald W., Jr. - Chicago
Cogan, Michael P. - Chicago
Coladarci, Peter R. - Chicago
Collins, George B. - Chicago
Conway, Kevin J. - Chicago
Cooney, Robert J., Jr. - Chicago
Corboy, Philip H. - Chicago
Corboy, Philip Harnett, Jr. - Chicago
Crowe, Brian L. - Chicago
Curcio, Joseph R. - Chicago
Davidson, Keith L. - Chicago
Decker, David A. - Waukegan
Demetrio, Michael K. - Chicago
Demetrio, Thomas A. - Chicago
Demos, James T. - Chicago
DeSanto, James J. - Libertyville, page 239
Dicker, Steven M. - Chicago
Durkin, Kevin P. - Chicago, page 239
Elsener, George M. - Chicago
Enright, Karen A. - Chicago
Episcope, Paul B. - Chicago
Epstein, Edna S. - Chicago
Epstein, James R. - Chicago
Esrig, Jerry A. - Chicago
Farina, James L. - Chicago
Farrow, Mark R. - Naperville
Flaherty, Patrick M. - Aurora
Fleisher, Richard S. - Chicago
Foote, Robert M. - Aurora, page 240
Ford, Christopher - Chicago
Frost, Michael J. - Chicago
Gabric, Ralph A. - Wheaton
Gibson, Scott B. - Waukegan, page 240
Gifford, Geoffrey L. - Chicago
Gilbert, Howard E. - Skokie
Glenn, Robert J. - Chicago
Glink, Martin - Arlington Heights
Goldberg, Barry D. - Chicago
Goldberg, Jeffrey M. - Chicago
Good, Neil H. - Palatine
Goodman, Bruce D. - Chicago
Gorey, John J. - North Riverside
Gray, Jonathan K. - Chicago
Greenberg, Steven A. - Chicago
Haddon, James T. - Chicago
Harte, William J. - Chicago, page 241
Healy, Martin J., Jr. - Chicago, page 241
Heller, Stephen J. - Chicago
Hilfman, Louis - Chicago

July 1996 233

Chapter 19: Personal Injury Law: General

Hofeld, Albert F. - Chicago
hooks, william h. - Chicago
Hoscheit, John J. - St. Charles
Hurley, Christopher T. - Chicago
Hyman, Lawrence H. - Chicago
Ialongo, A. Mark - Chicago
Indomenico, Sal - Chicago
Jeep, Markham M. - Waukegan
Jones, Robert E. - Wheaton
Kadison, Steven J. - Chicago
Kaiser, Daniel J. - Bensenville
Karr, Robert W. - Chicago
Kelly, John P. - Wheaton
Kimnach, Richard A. - Chicago
Kincaid, John B. - Wheaton
Kleinmuntz, Ira M. - Chicago
Knippen, James H. - Wheaton
Kohen, Bruce M. - Chicago, page 242
Kostelny, Marmarie J. - Elgin
Kralovec, John B. - Chicago
Kramer, Jack L. - Chicago
Kremin, David K. - Chicago, page 243
Krentz, Paul G. - Aurora
Kroll, Jeffrey J. - Chicago
Kuhlman, Richard S. - Chicago
Laks, Perry M. - Chicago
Lamont, John M. - Aurora
Lane, Fred - Chicago, page 243
Lane, Stephen I. - Chicago, page 244
Lansky, Marvin S. - Chicago
Latherow, Jerry A. - Chicago, page 244
Lavin, Terrence J. - Chicago
Leahy, Tom - Chicago
Lee, Thomas J. - Chicago
Leopold, Valerie A. - Chicago
Levin, Steven M. - Chicago
Levy, Steven B. - Naperville, page 245
Lindner, George P. - Aurora
Linn, Craig M. - Waukegan
Loggans, Susan E. - Chicago
Mahoney, Patrick E. - Chicago
Mahoney, Terence J. - Chicago
Miller, Kenneth C. - Chicago
Miroballi, Joseph J. - Chicago
Mirza, Jerome - Chicago
Monico, Michael D. - Chicago
Motherway, Nicholas J. - Chicago
Mullen, Michael T. - Chicago
Munday, John J. - Chicago
Murphy, William C. - Aurora
Nathan, Thomas J. - Chicago

O'Brien, Timothy M. - Chicago
Ozmon, Laird M. - Joliet
Ozmon, Nat P. - Chicago, page 246
Panter, Michael R. - Chicago
Passen, Stephen M. - Chicago
Patterson, Robert B. - Chicago, page 246
Pavalon, Eugene - Chicago
Pfaff, Bruce R. - Chicago
Phillips, John G. - Chicago
Postilion, Michael H. - Chicago
Power, Joseph A., Jr. - Chicago
Prendergast, Richard J. - Chicago
Presbrey, Kim E. - Aurora
Rapoport, David E. - Rosemont
Reuland, Timothy J. - Aurora, page 247
Rice, T. Patrick - Wheaton
Rodin, Curt N. - Chicago, page 247
Rogers, Larry R., Sr. - Chicago
Ross, Gilbert J. - Chicago
Rumsey, Richard L. - Chicago
Russo, Richard D. - Wheaton
Saltzberg, Gerald B. - Chicago
Salvi, Patrick A. - Waukegan
Salzetta, Paul L. - Chicago
Scanlan, Edmund J. - Chicago, page 248
Schaffner, Harry - Geneva
Schaffner, Howard S. - Chicago
Schroeder, Carl F. - Wheaton
Schwartz, Allen N. - Chicago
Schwarz, Benedict, II - West Dundee
Shancer, Jeffrey M. - Chicago, page 248
Shovlain, Peter T. - Waukegan
Skipper, Robert - Chicago
Smith, Todd A. - Chicago
Speers, Robert L. - Aurora, page 249
Spinak, Michael D. - Chicago
Stelle, Lori J. - Chicago
Stone, Jeffrey E. - Chicago
Sussman, Jeffrey B. - Chicago
Tallis, Jeffrey J. - Chicago
Taradash, Randall M. - McHenry
Thompson, Charles F., Jr. - Aurora
Touhy, Timothy J. - Chicago
Tyrrell, Thomas J. - Chicago
Wadington, Robert N. - Chicago, page 249
Walsh, Edward J., Jr. - Wheaton
Williams, Jeffrey - Chicago
Winkler, Charles R. - North Riverside
Wittenberg, David M. - Chicago
Zaideman, Robert J. - Chicago
Zazove, Neal C. - Chicago

Northwestern Illinois Including Rockford & Quad Cities

Alexander, Peter - Rockford
Barrett, Gregory E. - Rockford
Bertrand, Louis L. - Peru
Boreen, John M. - Rockford
Braud, Walter D. - Rock Island
Brooks, Jack L. - Rock Island
Cacciatore, William T. - Rockford
Clark, Robert H. - Rockford
Cox, John W., Jr. - Galena
Donohue, James L. - Rockford
Ferracuti, Peter F. - Ottawa
Fox, Dennis R. - Moline

Fredrickson, Robert A. - Rockford, page 250
Greenwald, Thomas E. - Rockford
Haldeman, Richard R. - Rockford
Hartsock, Allan - Rock Island
Kavensky, Craig L. - Rock Island, page 250
Kavensky, Harrison - Rock Island
Kelly, Roger H. - Galena
Lefstein, Stuart R. - Rock Island
Lousberg, Peter H. - Rock Island
Luchetti, Thomas D. - Rockford
Maher, Edward M. - Rockford
Martenson, David L. - Rockford

Personal Injury Law: General Leading Illinois Attorneys

Meehan, Gerald J. - Rock Island
Morrissey, Joseph A. - Rockford
Noe, Robert J. - Moline
Ohlander, Jan H. - Rockford, page 251
Perrecone, Frank A. - Rockford
Raccuglia, Anthony C. - Peru
Reese, Randall K. - Rockford
Ruud, Glenn F. - Rock Island
Scovil, Douglas C. - Rock Island

Seigler, Darrell K. - Ottawa
Sullivan, Peter T. - Rockford
Switzer, Peter S. - Rockford
Turner, Harold L. - Rockford
VanHooreweghe, Francis R. - Moline
Warner, Michael J. - Rock Island
Westensee, John H. - Rock Island
Williams, Daniel T., Jr. - Rockford

Central Illinois

Ansel, Marc J. - Champaign
Beckett, J. Steven - Urbana
Beeman, Bruce A. - Springfield
Benassi, A. Lou - Peoria
Benassi, Patricia C. - Peoria
Blan, Kenneth W., Jr. - Danville, page 252
Bowles, James E. - Peoria
Brown, Robert E. - Charleston
Bruno, Thomas A. - Urbana
Clark, Gary L. - Peoria
Cusack, Daniel P. - Peoria
Delano, Charles H., III - Springfield
Devens, Charles J. - Danville
Dorris, David V. - Bloomington
Dukes, Carroll W. - Danville
Eberspacher, David Y. - Mattoon
Faber, William C., Jr. - Decatur
Ferguson, Mark E. - Mattoon
Fombelle, Norman J. - Decatur
Frederick, Jeffrey D. - Urbana
Gadau, John E. - Champaign
Geiler, Lorna K. - Champaign
Geisler, Gary F. - Decatur
Hagen, Henry C. - Springfield
Hagle, James J. - Urbana
Hamm, Ronald L. - Peoria
Hasselberg, Michael R. - Peoria
Hefner, M. John, Jr. - Mattoon
Heller, Harlan - Mattoon
Holley, Grady E. - Springfield
Holmes, Brent D. - Mattoon
Janssen, Jay H. - Peoria
Johnson, Evan H. - Decatur
Kelly, Timothy - Bloomington
Kingery, Arthur - Peoria

Kirchner, Robert G. - Champaign
Kreckman, Alfred H., Jr. - Paris
Lipton, Mark D. - Champaign
Londrigan, Thomas F. - Springfield
Maher, Jerelyn D. - Peoria
Manion, Paul T. - Danville
McCarthy, Kitty M. - Decatur
McElvain, Mike - Bloomington
Mellen, Thomas J., II - Danville
Metnick, Michael B. - Springfield, page 253
Meyer, Michael J. - Effingham
Nessler, Frederic W. - Springfield, page 253
Nicoara, John P. - Peoria, page 254
Novak, Anthony E. - Urbana
O'Brien, Daniel R. - Peoria
Osborne, Stephen M. - Springfield
Owen, Robert M. - Decatur
Palmer, Charles L. - Champaign
Panichi, William T. - Springfield
Parker, Drew - Peoria
Phebus, Joseph W. - Urbana
Randle, Craig A. - Springfield
Rawles, Edward H. - Champaign, page 255
Robertson, John W. - Galesburg
Robeson, J. Jay - Springfield
Rose, Raymond - Peoria
Ryan, Michael D. - Mattoon
Ryan, Stephen R. - Mattoon
Slevin, John A. - Peoria, page 255
Smith, S. Craig - Paris
Stephens, G. Douglas - Peoria
Stine, Robert E. - Springfield, page 256
Sturm, Timothy - Springfield
Tulin, Ronald - Charleston
Willoughby, Stephen O. - Decatur

July 1996

Southern Illinois

Bartholomew, Joseph - Belleville
Bonifield, Jerald J. - Belleville
Brandon, Wm. Kent - Carbondale
Brown, Joseph R., Jr. - Edwardsville
Callis, Lance - Granite City
Calvo, Larry A. - Granite City
Cannady, Thomas B. - Belleville
Carey, Jack - Belleville
Carlson, Jon G. - Edwardsville
Carr, Rex - East St. Louis, page 257
Cates, Judy L. - Belleville
Chapman, Morris B. - Granite City
Coffel, Ron D. - Benton
Constance, Michael B. - Belleville
Cook, Bruce N. - Belleville
Cueto, Amiel - Belleville
Douglas, Robert L. - Robinson
Elliott, Ivan A., Jr. - Carmi
Enloe, Douglas A. - Lawrenceville
Habiger, Richard J. - Carbondale
Hanagan, Michael J. - Mt. Vernon
Hanagan, Steven F. - Mt. Vernon
Hanagan, William D. - Mt. Vernon
Hassakis, Mark D. - Mt. Vernon, page 257
Heiligenstein, C. E. - Belleville
Howerton, Robert H. - Marion
Hughes, R. Courtney - Carbondale
Keefe, Thomas Q., Jr. - Belleville
Lakin, L. Thomas - Wood River
Lambert, Richard G. - Marion
Mitchell, A. Ben - Mt. Vernon
Mitchell, Sam C. - West Frankfort
Murphy, G. Patrick - Marion
Peel, Gary E. - Edwardsville
Prince, Mark D. - Carbondale
Reagan, Michael J. - Belleville
Shevlin, Gregory L. - Belleville
Tillery, Stephen M. - Belleville
Veltman, R. Edward - Centralia
Weilmuenster, J. Michael - Belleville
Womick, John - Carbondale, page 258
Woodcock, George W. - Mt. Carmel

Biographical Profiles of Personal Injury Law: General Leading Illinois Attorneys

The Leading Illinois Attorneys profiled below were nominated as exceptional by their peers in a statewide survey conducted by American Research Corporation (ARC). ARC asked several thousand licensed Illinois attorneys to name the lawyer to whom they would send a close friend or family member in need of legal assistance in specific areas of law. The attorneys below were nominated in the area of Personal Injury Law: General.

Because the survey results (all practice area results combined) represent less than three percent of Illinois' practicing attorneys, this list should not be construed as a complete list. Nevertheless, it is an excellent source of highly qualified and reputable Illinois attorneys.

For information on ARC's survey methodology, see page *xi*.
For the complete list of Leading Illinois Consumer Attorneys, see page *xii*.
For the list of Leading Illinois Personal Injury Law: General Attorneys, see page 233.

The Leading Illinois Attorneys below are listed alphabetically in accordance with the geographic region in which their offices are located. Note that attorneys may handle clients from a broad geographic area; attorneys are not limited to only serving clients residing within the cities in which their offices are located.

The two-line attorney listings in this section are of attorneys who practice in this area but whose full biographical profiles appear in other sections of this book. A bullet "•" preceding a name indicates the attorney was nominated in this particular area of law.

For information on the format of the full biographical profiles, consult the "Using the Consumer Guidebook" section on page *xviii*.

The following abbreviations are used throughout these profiles:

App.	Appellate
Cir.	Circuit
Ct.	Court
Dist.	District
Sup.	Supreme
JD	Juris Doctor (Doctor of Law)
LLB	Legum Baccalaureus (Bachelor of Laws)
LLD	Legum Doctor (Doctor of Laws)
LLM	Legum Magister (Master of Laws)
ADR	Alternative Dispute Resolution
ABA	American Bar Association
ABOTA	American Board of Trial Advocates
ATLA	Association of Trial Lawyers of America
CBA	Chicago Bar Association
ISBA	Illinois State Bar Association
ITLA	Illinois Trial Lawyers Association
NBTA	National Board of Trial Advocacy

Chapter 19: Personal Injury Law: General

Cook & Collar Counties

George N. Avgeris

George N. Avgeris, Chartered
Attorney at Law
29 East First Street
Hinsdale, IL 60521

Phone: (630) 654-4161
Fax: (630) 654-9661

•**GEORGE N. AVGERIS:** Mr. Avgeris practices law solely in cases involving personal injury and wrongful death, including automobile accidents, general negligence, construction negligence, medical negligence, products liability, and workers' compensation. Many of his cases are substantial and complex. Mr. Avgeris has handled cases of first impression, including the first wrongful death recovery for the suicide of a prisoner confined to jail, and he defeated the motorcycle helmet defense law for a motorcyclist who was not wearing a helmet. He has been an author and lecturer for the Melvin M. Belli Society, Illinois State Bar Association, DuPage County Bar Association, *The Brief* and the *Chicago Daily Law Bulletin* with regard to substantive law, evidentiary law, and trial demonstrations.
Education: JD 1964, University of Illinois; BA 1961, North Central College.
Admitted: 1964 Illinois.
Employment History: 1969-present, George N. Avgeris, Chartered.
Professional Associations: ATLA; ITLA; ISBA; CBA; DuPage County Bar Assn.
Firm: George N. Avgeris, Chartered, limits its practice to personal injury and wrongful death cases. The firm considers it a privilege to represent its clients and to do its best to competently represent them, for the clients are the lifeblood of any law firm. *Mr. Avgeris also practices Personal Injury Law: Medical & Professional Malpractice.*

ARNOLD BERNSTEIN - *Attorney at Law* - 121 South Wilke, Suite 101 - Arlington Heights, IL 60005 - Phone: (847) 394-4017, Fax: (847) 797-9090 - *See complete biographical profile in the Personal Injury Law: Medical & Professional Malpractice Chapter, page 266.*

•**MARVIN BLOOM** - *Marvin Bloom & Associates* - 53 West Jackson, Suite 1430 - Chicago, IL 60604 - Phone: (312) 641-1044, Fax: (312) 554-8780 - *See complete biographical profile in the Criminal Law: Felonies & White Collar Crime Chapter, page 111.*

Charles A. "Pat" Boyle

Charles A. Boyle & Associates, Ltd.
29 South LaSalle Street
Suite 345
Chicago, IL 60603

Phone: (312) 346-4944
Fax: (312) 368-1061
E-mail: jlbarr@gnn.com
joetybor@getonline.com

•**CHARLES A. "PAT" BOYLE:** Celebrating 30 years in law, Charles A. "Pat" Boyle focuses on product liability, personal injury, medical malpractice, and class action suits, often representing the underdog. He has obtained many substantial verdicts, including *Peterson v. Goodyear*, in which a failed tire caused a Ford Bronco to roll over, rendering the client a quadriplegic. One of his memorable cases uncovered foot-dragging by the City of Chicago and the State to install median guard rails on the scenic drive along Lake Michigan. In the 17 years prior to Mr. Boyle's suit, an average of five persons annually lost their lives on the stretch of highway. Another David v. Goliath case involved General Motors. Mr. Boyle was lead counsel in a national class action suit accusing the manufacturer of surreptitiously switching Chevrolet engines into Oldsmobile autos without disclosing the substitute to consumers. He was liaison counsel in the substantial settlement of the GM 200 THM Transmission case. Mr. Boyle has been trying civil and criminal cases since 1967, first as an Assistant U.S. Attorney in Chicago. He tried *Simmons v. U.S.*, the landmark photographic line-up identification case, on remand from the U.S. Supreme Court; defended government agencies under the Federal Tort Claims Act; and prosecuted criminal tax evasion cases. After leaving the U.S. Attorney's Office, he successfully defended Gregory White on charges of murder during an aborted airline hi-jacking. He also overturned a formidable Tax Court decision involving a physician and a non-profit medical clinic in *Kenner v. U.S.*; and was the trial counsel and appellate architect of the landmark Securities Churning Case, *Fey v. Walston*. In his private practice over the past 25 years, Mr. Boyle has kept on the cutting-edge of technology. He is adept at fashioning successful trial teams with mock jurors, jury consultants, nationally recognized experts, corporate whistleblowers, and the latest in computer enhanced visual aids to ensure that his clients receive personalized attention and the best representation.
Education: JD 1966, Loyola University; BA 1964, Loyola University.
Admitted: 1966 Illinois; 1985 Wisconsin; 1967 U.S. Dist. Ct. (N. Dist. IL); 1968 U.S. Ct. App. (7th Cir.); 1982 U.S. Dist. Ct. (E. Dist. WI).
Employment History: 1970-present, Charles A. Boyle & Associates, Ltd.; Assistant U.S. Attorney 1967-69, Northern District of Illinois, Chicago.
Professional Associations: ISBA; CBA; ATLA; ABA.
Community Involvement: Illinois Action for Children; Franciscan Outreach; Misericordia.
Firm: In addition to Mr. Boyle, the firm consists of Jennifer L. Barron, Associate; David J. Gubbins, Of Counsel; and Joseph R. Tybor, Of Counsel.

Personal Injury Law: General Leading Illinois Attorneys

DAVID E. CAMIC - *Camic, Johnson, Wilson & Bloom, P.C.* - 546 West Galena Boulevard - Aurora, IL 60506 - Phone: (630) 859-0135, Fax: (630) 859-1910, 800: (800) 750-0135 - *See complete biographical profiles in the Criminal Law: Felonies & White Collar Crime Chapter, page 112 and Criminal Law: DUI & Misdemeanors Chapter, page 96.*

•**THOMAS A. CLANCY** - *Clancy & Stevens* - Barrister Hall, Suite 220 - 29 South LaSalle Street - Chicago, IL 60603-1501 - Phone: (312) 782-2800, Fax: (312) 782-2852 - *See complete biographical profile in the Personal Injury Law: Medical & Professional Malpractice Chapter, page 267.*

•**ROBERT A. CLIFFORD** - *Clifford Law Offices* - 120 North LaSalle Street, 31st Floor - Chicago, IL 60602 - Phone: (312) 899-9090, Fax: (312) 251-1160 - *See complete biographical profile in the Personal Injury Law: Transportation Chapter, page 280.*

•**JAMES J. DE SANTO:** Mr. DeSanto concentrates his trial and appellate practice in the areas of personal injury and commercial litigation. He has successfully represented injured persons and their families in such matters as road and highway accidents, railroad crossing injuries, boating incidents, dangerous premises, and defective product litigation. He and his associates have effectively represented victims of medical negligence, legal malpractice, and commercial/banking malfeasance.
Education: JD 1969, DePaul University; BA 1965, University of Illinois.
Admitted: 1969 Illinois; 1969 U.S. Dist. Ct. (N. Dist. IL); 1973 U.S. Ct. App. (7th Cir.); 1975 U.S. Sup. Ct.
Employment History: Principal 1991-present, Law Offices of James J. DeSanto, P.C.; Senior Partner 1985-91, DeSanto & Bonamarte, P.C.; Senior Partner 1980-85, DeSanto & Goshgarian; Partner 1975-80, Rawles, Katz, DeSanto & Goshgarian; Associate 1972-75, Finn, Geiger & Rafferty; Assistant State's Attorney 1969-72, State's Attorney's Office, Lake County, Illinois.
Professional Associations: Lake County Bar Assn. (President 1993-94); ISBA [Tort Law Section Council (Chair 1991-92); Assembly Finance and Budget Committee (Chair 1988-89); Mutual Insurance Company (Director 1990-present); *Tort Trends* (Editor 1988-91); Civil Practice Section Council 1981-85]; ITLA; ATLA; CBA; Jefferson Inns of Court; Illinois Bar Foundation (Fellow).
Community Involvement: Village of Libertyville (Trustee 1991-93); Rotary Club of Libertyville (President 1990-91); Waukegan Rotary Club (Secretary 1980); Easter Seal Society, Lake County Chapter.
Firm: At the Law Offices of James J. DeSanto, P.C., clients receive the personal attention of attorneys and staff necessary to keep them properly informed throughout all stages of the litigation process. Mr. DeSanto has over 25 years of litigation experience in the trial courts of Lake County, Illinois. He continues to keep current and to serve the community through writing in professional journals, and by speaking at engagements for bar associations in matters relating to the law of trial procedure and evidence. *Mr. DeSanto also practices Personal Injury Law: Medical & Professional Malpractice and Personal Injury Law: Transportation.*

JAMES J. DESANTO
Law Offices of James J. DeSanto, P.C.
339 North Milwaukee Avenue
Libertyville, IL 60048

Phone: (847) 816-8100
Fax: (847) 816-8126

Extensive Experience In:
• Auto (Accidents & Injuries)
• Products Liability
• Medical Malpractice

•**KEVIN P. DURKIN:** As an attorney practicing for over 15 years, Mr. Durkin adds depth and experience to the trials and cases for which he is responsible. He has achieved numerous large jury verdicts and settlements in state and federal courts. Mr. Durkin handles a variety of personal injury and wrongful death cases, with a concentration in aviation, truck accident, FELA, and medical malpractice cases. Mr. Durkin has been an adjunct faculty member at DePaul University College of Law, teaching a course in trial advocacy for nearly ten years.
Education: Trial Instructor 1989, National Institute of Trial Advocacy; JD 1980, DePaul University; BS 1977, University of Illinois.
Admitted: 1980 Illinois; 1980 U.S. Dist. Ct. (N. Dist. IL); 1984 U.S. Dist. Ct. (C. Dist. IL).
Employment History: Partner 1995-present, Clifford Law Offices; Partner 1994-95, Corboy Demetrio Clifford; Associate 1988-94, Robert A. Clifford & Associates; Assistant State's Attorney 1980-88, Cook County State's Attorney's Office, Chicago.
Representative Clients: Mr. Durkin represents victims and families of victims in complex personal injury and wrongful death cases, particularly against railroad companies, truck lines, and airlines.
Professional Associations: CBA [Tort Law Committee 1988-91; Judicial Evaluation Committee 1988-present (Chair 1994-95; Vice Chair 1993-94)]; ABA (Aviation Law Committee 1990-present; Litigation Section 1990-present); ITLA (Legislative Committee 1993; Board of Advocates 1993-present); ATLA 1988-present; ISBA (Tort Law Committee 1989-present; Civil Practice and Procedure Committee 1989-present).
Community Involvement: Mr. Durkin has frequently lectured on trial advocacy and trial techniques before student and professional groups throughout the legal community. *See complete firm profile in Appendix A. Mr. Durkin also practices Personal Injury Law: Medical & Professional Malpractice and Personal Injury Law: Transportation.*

KEVIN P. DURKIN
Clifford Law Offices
120 North LaSalle Street
31st Floor
Chicago, IL 60602

Phone: (312) 899-9090
Fax: (312) 251-1160
800: (800) 899-0410
E-mail:
102554,2453@compuserve.com

Extensive Experience In:
• Railroad & Truck Accident Cases
• Aviation
• Medical Malpractice

Chapter 19: Personal Injury Law: General

DENNIS R. FAVARO - *Thill, Kolodz & Favaro, Ltd.* - 835 Sterling Avenue, Suite 100 - Palatine, IL 60067 - Phone: (847) 934-0060, Fax: (847) 934-6899 - *See complete biographical profile in the Employment Law Chapter, page 143.*

ROBERT M. FOOTE
Murphy, Hupp, Foote, Mielke and Kinnally
Eight East Galena Boulevard
Suite 202
P.O. Box 5030
Aurora, IL 60507
Phone: (630) 844-0056
Fax: (630) 844-1905

•**ROBERT M. FOOTE:** Mr. Foote has practiced law in Kane County, Illinois, all of his professional life. Upon graduation from law school, Mr. Foote concentrated his career in trial work. He has a successful verdict record and obtained the first verdict in a commercial case for "predatory pricing," against Browning-Ferris Industries. He has been involved in a broad scope of business damage trials, as well as injunctive work related to labor problems, municipalities, covenants, minority shareholders rights, and environmental issues. In 1982, he was elected to attend the National Institute for Trial Advocacy, and elected to the Advisory Board for the Illinois Head Injury Association.
Education: JD 1979, University of Wisconsin; BA 1976, Harvard University.
Admitted: 1979 Illinois; 1986 Wisconsin; 1980 U.S. Dist. Ct. (N. Dist. IL, General Bar); 1984 U.S. Dist. Ct. (N. Dist. IL, Trial Bar).
Employment History: 1979-present, Murphy, Hupp, Foote, Mielke and Kinnally; Past Special Prosecutor, Kane County State's Attorney's Office.
Representative Clients: Kane County Sheriff; Hollywood Casino; Association of Professional Police Officers Union; County of Kane.
Professional Associations: ATLA; ITLA (Board of Advocates); Kane County Bar Assn. (past Director); DuPage County Bar Assn.; Kendall County Bar Assn.; Illinois Head Injury Assn. (Advisory Board).
Firm: Murphy, Hupp, Foote, Mielke and Kinnally was founded in 1983. The firm of nine lawyers concentrates in civil litigation both for injured persons and companies that have been financially injured by unfair business practices. Mr. Foote and his partners have over 100 years of combined experience in civil trial work. *See complete firm profile in Appendix A.*

SCOTT B. GIBSON
Law Offices of Scott B. Gibson, Ltd.
415 West Washington Street
Suite 103
Waukegan, IL 60085
Phone: (847) 263-5100
Fax: (847) 249-7588

Extensive Experience In:
• General Personal Injury
• Medical Malpractice
• Products Liability

•**SCOTT B. GIBSON:** Mr. Gibson concentrates his practice in personal injury law. He is the author of "Negligent and Intentional Infliction of Emotional Distress—Supreme Court Abolishes Physical Impact Rule," 27 *Tort Trends* 9, Autumn 1991; and "When Is a Plaintiff Barred from Pursuing a Claim for Common-Law Damages Against a Physician Due to the Workers' Compensation Act?" 28 *Tort Trends* 6, June 1993. Mr. Gibson is a frequent lecturer on personal injury law and insurance topics at seminars for local bar associations.
Education: JD 1982, DePaul University; BA 1979, University of Illinois.
Admitted: 1982 Illinois; 1982 U.S. Dist. Ct. (N. Dist. IL, General Bar); 1988 U.S. Dist. Ct. (N. Dist. IL, Trial Bar); 1989 U.S. Claims Ct. (Washington, D.C.).
Employment History: 1993-present, Law Offices of Scott B. Gibson, Ltd.; 1992-93, Goshgarian and Gibson; 1987-92, Decker & Linn, Ltd.; Felony Trial Attorney 1983-87, Lake County Illinois State's Attorney's Office.
Professional Associations: ISBA [Elected Assembly Member 1989-94; Tort Section 1989-93 (Subcommittee on Liens and Statutory Disbursements, Chair 1991-93; Subcommittee on Legislative Affairs)]; ITLA 1987-present (New Membership Committee 1988-present); Lake County Bar Assn. 1987-present (Legal/Medical Committee 1994-present; Civil Trial Committee 1989-present); American Inns of Court 1989-present; CBA 1991-present (Tort Practice Committee 1993-94); ATLA (Professional Negligence Section 1994-present); Illinois Bar Foundation 1993-present; Lake County Trial Lawyers' Assn.
Community Involvement: Lake County Child Advocacy Center (Treasurer; Founding Board Member 1987-89); Lake County Volunteer Legal Program Alumni Assn. 1987-present; Lake County State's Attorney's Alumni Assn. (Vice President 1987-present); University of Dubuque (Pre-Law Committee 1992-present). *Mr. Gibson also practices Personal Injury Law: Medical & Professional Malpractice and Workers' Compensation Law.*

•**HOWARD E. GILBERT** - *Howard E. Gilbert & Associates, Ltd.* - 5420 Old Orchard Road, Suite A205 - Skokie, IL 60077 - Phone: (847) 966-6600, Fax: (847) 966-6638 - *See complete biographical profile in the Small Business Law Chapter, page 307.*

•**JEFFREY M. GOLDBERG** - *Jeffrey M. Goldberg & Associates, Ltd.* - 20 North Clark Street, Suite 3100 - Chicago, IL 60602 - Phone: (312) 236-4146, Fax: (312) 236-5913 - *See complete biographical profile in the Personal Injury Law: Medical & Professional Malpractice Chapter, page 268.*

•**BRUCE D. GOODMAN** - *Steinberg, Polacek & Goodman* - 309 West Washington Street, Suite 500 - Chicago, IL 60606 - Phone: (312) 782-1386, Fax: (312) 782-6739 - *See complete biographical profile in the Personal Injury Law: Medical & Professional Malpractice Chapter, page 268.*

Personal Injury Law: General Leading Illinois Attorneys

•**WILLIAM J. HARTE:** Mr. Harte practices in all fields of litigation. He is the author of numerous articles in legal periodicals and handbooks on various areas of trial and appellate litigation. He is a former Associate Editor of *The Trial Lawyers Guide,* a quarterly legal periodical, and a former Case Editor of the *Notre Dame Lawyer,* a quarterly periodical of the Notre Dame Law School. Mr. Harte has lectured on trial and appellate practice at various law schools.
Education: JD 1959, Notre Dame; BA 1954, Quincy College.
Admitted: 1959 Illinois; 1971 U.S. Sup. Ct.
Employment History: Sole Principal 1960-present, William J. Harte, Ltd.
Representative Clients: While Mr. Harte represents individuals and corporations from all sectors of society on an ad hoc trial and appellate basis, he has an ongoing engagement with Amgen, Inc., a Fortune 500 biogenetic firm.
Professional Associations: American College of Trial Lawyers (Fellow 1976); International Academy of Trial Lawyers (Fellow 1977); ABOTA (Fellow 1977); American Academy of Appellate Lawyers (Fellow 1991); Appellate Lawyers Assn. of Illinois (past President 1972); ITLA (past President 1975); ABA; ISBA; CBA (past Board of Managers); Federal Bar Assn.; ATLA; Society of Trial Lawyers; The Legal Club of Chicago.
Community Involvement: Police and Fire Commission 1970-83, Oak Park, Illinois.
Firm: William J. Harte, Ltd., has seven associates and six attorneys "of counsel" to the firm. *Mr. Harte also practices Criminal Law: Felonies & White Collar Crime and Civil Appellate Law.*

WILLIAM J. HARTE
William J. Harte, Ltd.
111 West Washington Street
Suite 1100
Chicago, IL 60602

Phone: (312) 726-5015
Fax: (312) 641-2455

Extensive Experience In:
• Trial Litigation
• Appellate Litigation

ROBERT J. HAUSER - *Sullivan, Smith, Hauser & Noonan, Ltd.* - 25 North County Street - Waukegan, IL 60085-4342 - Phone: (847) 244-0111, Fax: (847) 244-0513 - *See complete biographical profile in the Criminal Law: Felonies & White Collar Crime Chapter, page 113.*

•**MARTIN J. HEALY, JR.:** Mr. Healy only represents plaintiffs in personal injury cases. He is *Certified as a Civil Trial Advocate by the National Board of Trial Advocacy and was recently elected Vice President of the Illinois Trial Lawyers Association (ITLA). Over the years, Mr. Healy has won many large verdicts for seriously injured plaintiffs, in cases involving brain damage, paralysis, amputation, and hearing and vision loss. He has tried medical malpractice, products liability, construction, railroad and municipal, and many other types of injury cases. A recent medical malpractice verdict was listed as one of the significant verdicts in the country in 1995 by the *National Law Journal.* Mr. Healy has written and lectured on various legal subjects for ITLA, ISBA, CBA, ATLA, and Illinois Institute for Continuing Education.
Education: JD 1968, Loyola University (Associate Editor, *Law Review;* Academic Scholarship); BA 1965, University of Notre Dame (Dean's List).
Admitted: 1968 Illinois; 1968 U.S. Dist. Ct. (N. Dist. IL, Trial Bar); 1968 U.S. Ct. App. (7th Cir.); 1977 U.S. Sup. Ct.
Employment History: Law Clerk, Supreme Court of Illinois; Counsel, Illinois House of Representatives; Associate, James Dooley Associates; First Assistant Corporation Counsel, Corporation Counsel Office, City of Chicago.
Representative Clients: Mr. Healy represents clients in cases involving personal injury, wrongful death, products liability, medical malpractice, transportation (railroad, trucking and aviation) and construction injury.
Professional Associations: ITLA (Third Vice President 1995-96); ISBA [Tort Law Section Council (Secretary 1995-96)]; ATLA [Truck Underride Litigation Group (Chair 1993-present)]; CBA [Tort Litigation Committee (Chair 1988)]; National Board of Trial Advocacy (Diplomate 1990-present); Illinois Supreme Court Commission on Jury Instructions 1982-present.
Community Involvement: Irish Fellowship Club of Chicago (President; Chair); Queen of All Saints School (Executive Committee); St. Patrick's Day Parade Committee (Director); Sauganash Community Organization (Director); Irish American Heritage Library Fundraising Committee (Chair).
Firm: Martin J. Healy, Jr. & Associates is a dynamic, aggressive firm consisting of seven attorneys: Martin J. Healy, Jr., Daniel B. Malone, J.T. Terence Geoghegan (also previously licensed to practice in Ireland), John P. Scanlon, Dave P. Huber, James G. McCarthy and Jonathan D. Woods. The firm often receives exceptionally favorable results in difficult and complex cases involving personal injury, wrongful death, products liability, medical malpractice, transportation and construction injuries. *See complete firm profile in Appendix A. Mr. Healy also practices Personal Injury Law: Medical & Professional Malpractice and Personal Injury Law: Transportation.*

*The Supreme Court of Illinois does not recognize certifications of specialties in the practice of law. A certificate, award or recognition is not a requirement to practice law in Illinois.

MARTIN J. HEALY, JR.
Martin J. Healy, Jr. & Associates
111 West Washington Street
Suite 1425
Chicago, IL 60602

Phone: (312) 977-0100
Fax: (312) 977-0795
800: (800) 922-4500

Extensive Experience In:
• Medical Malpractice
• Products Liability
• Transportation

Chapter 19: Personal Injury Law: General

KEITH A. HEBEISEN - *Clifford Law Offices* - 120 North LaSalle Street, 31st Floor - Chicago, IL 60602 - Phone: (312) 899-9090, Fax: (312) 251-1160 - *See complete biographical profile in the Personal Injury Law: Medical & Professional Malpractice Chapter, page 269.*

•**WILLIAM H. HOOKS** - *Hooks Law Offices, P.C.* - Three First National Plaza, 52nd Floor - 70 West Madison Street, Suite 5200 - Chicago, IL 60602 - Phone: (312) 553-5252, Fax: (312) 553-1510 - *See complete biographical profile in the Criminal Law: Felonies & White Collar Crime Chapter, page 114.*

•**MARKHAM M. JEEP** - *Markham M. Jeep, P.C.* - 450 North Green Bay Road - Waukegan, IL 60085 - Phone: (847) 360-3300, Fax: (847) 360-3303 - *See complete biographical profile in the Workers' Compensation Law Chapter, page 341.*

GARY V. JOHNSON - *Camic, Johnson, Wilson & Bloom, P.C.* - 546 West Galena Boulevard - Aurora, IL 60506 - Phone: (630) 859-0135, Fax: (630) 859-1910, 800: (800) 750-0135 - *See complete biographical profiles in the Criminal Law: Felonies & White Collar Crime Chapter, page 114 and Criminal Law: DUI & Misdemeanors Chapter, page 97.*

ROGER J. KELLY - *Law Offices of Roger J. Kelly* - 53 West Jackson Boulevard, Suite 1252 - Chicago, IL 60604 - Phone: (312) 663-3699, Fax: (312) 663-3689 - *See complete biographical profiles in the Real Estate Law Chapter, page 296 and Employment Law Chapter, page 145.*

RICHARD A. KIMNACH - *Anesi, Ozmon & Rodin, Ltd.* - 161 North Clark Street, Suite 2100 - Chicago, IL 60601 - Phone: (312) 372-3822, Fax: (312) 372-3833, 800: (800) 458-3822 within IL - *See complete biographical profile in the Workers' Compensation Law Chapter, page 341.*

BRUCE M. KOHEN
Anesi, Ozmon & Rodin, Ltd.
161 North Clark Street
Suite 2100
Chicago, IL 60601

Phone: (312) 372-3822
Fax: (312) 372-3833
800: (800) 458-3822 within IL

•**BRUCE M. KOHEN:** Mr. Kohen is an experienced and seasoned trial attorney who has dedicated his legal career to the representation of victims of serious and catastrophic personal injuries. He concentrates his practice in the fields of personal injury, products liability, medical malpractice, wrongful death, and construction-related injuries. Mr. Kohen has successfully obtained substantial records/verdicts and settlements on behalf of his clients. He is a sought-after lecturer who frequently speaks before the Illinois Trial Lawyers Association, the Chicago Bar Association, and at local area law schools. He is the author of numerous articles and publications in the area of tort litigation. He is extremely active in, and one of the leaders of, trial lawyer associations, serving on the Board of Managers of the Illinois Trial Lawyers Association and the Board of Governors of the Association of Trial Lawyers of America. Mr. Kohen is also one of the lead lawyers in the litigation challenging the constitutionality of Illinois' new Tort Reform Act. He is the Chair of the Legislative Committee of the Illinois Trial Lawyers Association, fighting to preserve laws that protect Illinois consumers and victims.
Education: JD 1979, Illinois Institute of Technology, Chicago-Kent; BS 1976, University of Illinois.
Admitted: 1979 Illinois; 1979 U.S. Dist. Ct. (N. Dist. IL); 1980 U.S. Ct. App. (7th Cir.); 1983 U.S. Sup. Ct.; 1995 U.S. Dist. Ct. (C. Dist. IL).
Employment History: Partner/Associate 1979-present, law firm currently known as Anesi, Ozmon & Rodin, Ltd.
Representative Clients: Mr. Kohen represents victims and their families who have suffered serious personal injuries as a result of the negligence of others. These include construction injuries, product liability, medical malpractice, wrongful death, and personal injury actions.
Professional Associations: ITLA 1979-present [Board of Advocates 1990-92; Board of Managers 1992-present; Legislative Committee (Chair 1993-present); Publications Committee (Chair 1995-present)]; ATLA [Sustaining Member 1980-present; State Delegate 1993-96; Board of Governors 1996-present; Roscoe Pound Foundation (Fellow 1996-present)]; CBA 1979-present; ISBA 1979-present (Elected Assemblyman 1994-present); ABA 1980-present; Decalogue Society of Lawyers 1980-present.
Firm: Anesi, Ozmon & Rodin, Ltd., with 28 attorneys and a staff of over 100, is the largest law firm in Illinois concentrating its practice in the representation of injury victims. The firm is committed to vigorously representing its clients in the areas of personal injury litigation, workers' compensation, and Social Security practice. *See complete firm profile in Appendix A. Mr. Kohen also practices Personal Injury Law: Medical & Professional Malpractice and Personal Injury Law: Transportation.*

STEVEN S. KOUKIOS - *Koukios & Associates* - 1480 Northwest Highway, Suite 203 - Park Ridge, IL 60068 - Phone: (847) 299-4440, Fax: (847) 299-4468 - *See complete biographical profile in the Bankruptcy Law Chapter, page 72.*

•**DAVID K. KREMIN:** Mr. Kremin and his cases have been recognized nationally by *ABC Prime Time Live, CNN, The Wall Street Journal,* as well as *Common Ground* and most Chicago TV and radio news programs and newspapers. An attorney for more than a decade, Mr. Kremin has earned the respect and admiration of his clients, colleagues, and of medical professionals. He is one of the limited number of attorneys on the Chicago Bar Association Panel who is referred sophisticated personal injury claims by the Chicago Bar Association. Mr. Kremin is an arbitrator for Circuit Court of Cook County Mandatory Arbitration and has been appointed Judge Advocate. Mr. Kremin is known to take and win cases other attorneys have shied away from, including those against municipalities and major corporations. He has been an instructor at Roosevelt University and is certified by the United States Coast Guard Auxiliary. Mr. Kremin is listed in *Who's Who in American Law; Who's Who in Executives and Professionals;* and is on the Million Dollar Plus List of *Chicago Lawyers* magazine.
Education: JD with highest honors, Illinois Institute of Technology, Chicago-Kent; Commenced MBA, University of Illinois; BA, University of Illinois (Dean's List); Continuing Education, University of Chicago.
Admitted: 1983 Illinois; 1983 U.S. Dist. Ct. (N. Dist. IL).
Professional Associations: CBA; ATLA; ITLA; Decalogue Society; ISBA; National Lawyers Assn. [Torts Division (Chair)].
Firm: David K. Kremin & Associates, P.C., practices in all aspects of tort litigation, including automobile accidents, premises liability, product liability, fire and casualty cases, medical malpractice, dram shop, and workers' compensation. The firm represents those with catastrophic injuries, providing services that often highlight the need for change. The firm believes that although lawsuits are generally filed on behalf of one person, they really help everyone by setting precedents that can foster change and prevent the same injury from happening to others. David K. Kremin & Associates has cases pending and clients throughout the United States, and has recovered large compensation awards for injured clients.

DAVID K. KREMIN

David K. Kremin & Associates
A Professional Corporation
77 West Washington Street
Suite 1720
Chicago, IL 60602

Phone: (312) 456-9000
Fax: (312) 456-9900
800: (800) 275-2529

Extensive Experience In:

- 911 & Paramedic Negligence
- All Vehicle Injuries

•**FRED LANE:** Mr. Lane is a former Assistant State's Attorney for Cook County (Trial Division) and is a partner in the Chicago law firm of Lane & Lane. He is a dynamic contributor to the community and a dedicated professional in the legal field. Mr. Lane is a nationally recognized lecturer and author in the fields of trial technique and litigation. He was the Director of the Trial Technique Institute which he donated to the Illinois State Bar Association. Weekly, he teaches at the Trial Technique Institute located in the ISBA Chicago regional office. In 1987, Mr. Lane was the first recipient of the prestigious American ORT (Organization for Rehabilitation Training) Federation's Jurisprudence Award, which was created to honor individuals who have made outstanding contributions in the realm of public service. He currently serves ORT as First Vice President and Director of its Executive Board. He is the author of three multi-volume sets of law books: *Lane-Goldstein Trial Technique; Lane Medical Litigation Guide;* and *Lane-Goldstein Litigation Forms.* He is also the Editor of the *Medical Trial Technique Quarterly.*
Education: JD 1950, Loyola University.
Admitted: 1950 Illinois; U.S. Sup. Ct.
Professional Associations: ITLA (past President); ABOTA [Diplomate; Illinois Chapter (past President)]; ISBA (past President); American Bar Foundation (Fellow); International Academy of Trial Lawyers (Fellow); Chicago Bar Foundation (Fellow); ATLA; CBA; Society of Trial Lawyers; Decalogue Society of Lawyers (past President).
Community Involvement: Parent Teachers Association (past President); B'nai B'rith [Maccabee Lodge (past President)]; Attorney General's Office [Lawyers Advisory Council (Disabled Persons Division)]. Whether working with inner-city youth, programs for the disabled, hospitals and other institutions for children, or seniors and other disadvantaged people, Mr. Lane always has found, and continues to find, time to service the community. He regularly teaches and performs magic for charitable organizations. *See complete firm profile in Appendix A. Mr. Lane also practices Alternative Dispute Resolution as a mediator.*

FRED LANE

Lane & Lane
33 North Dearborn Street
Suite 2300
Chicago, IL 60602

Phone: (312) 332-1400
Fax: (312) 899-8003

Extensive Experience In:

- Personal Injury
- Malpractice/Products Liability
- Mediator-Alternative Dispute Resolution

STEPHEN I. LANE

Lane & Lane
33 North Dearborn Street
Suite 2300
Chicago, IL 60602

Phone: (312) 332-1400
Fax: (312) 899-8003

Extensive Experience In:

- Personal Injury
- Products Liability
- Malpractice Cases

•**STEPHEN I. LANE:** Mr. Lane is a partner with the Chicago personal injury litigation firm of Lane & Lane. He has extensive civil litigation experience and has lectured and authored for the Illinois Institute for Continuing Legal Education, Lawyers' Post-Graduate Clinics, Illinois State Bar Association, Chicago Bar Association, Illinois Trial Lawyers Association, Northwest Suburban Bar Association, American Association of Legal Nurse Consultants, and other community and professional associations in the areas of civil litigation, trial practice, personal injury, and tort practice. Mr. Lane is the author of the Respondents in Discovery Statute, and has testified for the ISBA before the state legislature in support of ISBA legislative programs.

Education: JD 1978, Illinois Institute of Technology, Chicago-Kent; BA 1975, University of Illinois-Urbana.

Admitted: 1978 Illinois.

Professional Associations: ISBA [Board of Governors; Secretary; Assembly; Tort Law Section Council; Special Committee on Professionalism; Task Force on Professionalism; Committee to Study the ISBA Lawyer Referral Service; Special Committee to Review ISBA Mock Trial Programs 1989-90; Amicus Curiae Study Committee; Assembly Budget and Audits Legislation Committee; Scope Committee; Correlation Committee; Special Committee to Review the Clients Security Fund; Standing Committee on Community Involvement (Chair)]; ITLA; ATLA; CBA [Civil Practice Committee; Hospital and Health Care Committee; Medico-Legal Relations Committee; Sports Law Committee; Trial Techniques Committee; Tort Litigation Committee; Circuit Court Committee; Entertainment and Judicial Evaluation Committee; Subcommittee to Investigate the Use of Mail, Fax and Teleconferencing in the Courts (Chair)]; ABA; American Assn. of Legal Nurse Consultants; Decalogue Society of Lawyers; Bohemian Lawyers' Assn. of Chicago; Justinian Society; DuPage County Bar Assn.; Kane County Bar Assn.; Northwest Suburban Bar Assn.; Lake County Bar Assn.; Law of the American College of Legal Medicine (Associate); Illinois Bar Foundation (Board of Directors).

Community Involvement: ISBA [Committee on Community Involvement (Chair)]. *See complete firm profile in Appendix A. Mr. Lane also practices Personal Injury Law: Medical & Professional Malpractice and Personal Injury Law: Transportation.*

JERRY A. LATHEROW

Law Office of Jerry A. Latherow
77 West Washington Street
Suite 1900
Chicago, IL 60602

Phone: (312) 372-0052
Fax: (312) 372-8043

•**JERRY A. LATHEROW:** Mr. Latherow practices exclusively in plaintiffs' personal injury and wrongful death litigation, including medical malpractice, products liability, Structural Work Act, and automobile collision-related cases. He has received numerous substantial recoveries by jury verdict and settlement on behalf of his clients. Mr. Latherow's litigation experience started as a Cook County Assistant State's Attorney. After only eighteen months of various work, including misdemeanor trials, he was assigned to the highly visible Repeat Offender Courts, where he went to jury verdict nearly once per month over a period of more than two years. The trials in this area were all in the categories of armed robbery, rape, attempted murder, and murder. Some of the murder trials were death penalty cases. Upon leaving the State's Attorney's Office, he joined the law firm of Philip H. Corboy & Associates (now known as Corboy & Demetrio) in 1982, where he was the trial attorney in various personal injury and wrongful death trials. He left that firm after three years in order to establish his own office. He lectures frequently on personal injury and wrongful death litigation and general trial work. He has lectured to law students at Loyola University of Chicago School of Law, and to practicing attorneys at numerous litigation seminars conducted by the Illinois Institute for Continuing Legal Education, the Chicago Bar Association, and the Illinois Trial Lawyers Association. He was honored by Loyola University of Chicago School of Law with the St. Robert Bellarmine Award for distinguished service to the law profession.

Education: JD 1976, Loyola University of Chicago (President, Student Bar Assn.; Leadership and Service Award); BS 1973, Illinois State University.

Admitted: 1976 Illinois; 1976 U.S. Dist. Ct. (N. Dist. IL).

Employment History: Principal 1985-present, Law Office of Jerry A. Latherow; Associate 1982-85, Corboy & Demetrio; Assistant State's Attorney 1976-82, Cook County State's Attorney's Office.

Professional Associations: ISBA (Assembly 1980-86, 1990-92; PAC Committee 1994-present; Treasurer 1996-present); ITLA (Board of Managers 1990-present); ATLA 1982-present; CBA (Judicial Evaluation Committee).

Firm: Mr. Latherow is a principal of the Law Office of Jerry A. Latherow. His firm practices exclusively in plaintiffs' personal injury and wrongful death litigation, including medical malpractice, products liability, Structural Work Act, and automobile collision-related cases. *Mr. Latherow also practices Personal Injury Law: Transportation and Personal Injury Law: Medical & Professional Malpractice.*

Personal Injury Law: General Leading Illinois Attorneys

•STEVEN B. LEVY: Mr. Levy practices exclusively in the areas of bodily injury and wrongful death claims. He negotiates settlements and litigates trials of bodily injury and wrongful death claims of all kinds and complexity, including automobile accidents. Mr. Levy has written for the Illinois Institute for Continuing Legal Education and for other professional publications. He has lectured for the Illinois State CPA Society and other professional organizations. In June of 1996, Mr. Levy received the DuPage County Bar Association's 20th Annual Lawyer of the Year award in recognition and appreciation of his distinguished leadership and meritorious services.
Education: JD 1978, Illinois Institute of Technology, Chicago-Kent; BA 1975, University of Illinois-Urbana.
Admitted: 1979 Illinois; 1980 Florida; 1979 U.S. Dist. Ct. (N. Dist. IL); 1979 U.S. Ct. App. (7th Cir.); 1980 U.S. Dist. Ct. (S. Dist. FL; M. Dist. FL); 1980 U.S. Ct. App. (10th Cir.; 11th Cir.); 1993 U.S. Sup. Ct.
Employment History: 1979-present, Steven B. Levy, Ltd.
Representative Clients: Injured persons seeking reasonable compensation for legitimate injuries.
Professional Associations: Illinois Supreme Court Committee on Professional Responsibility (Appointed by Illinois Supreme Court 1996-98); DuPage County Bar [*Journal* (Editor-in-Chief 1995 97)]; ISBA [*Journal* (Editorial Board 1996-97); Continuing Legal Education (Standing Committee 1994)]; American Inns of Court [DuPage County Chapter (Founding Member 1994)].
Community Involvement: Mr. Levy is active in numerous charitable organizations.
Firm: The firm's practice is devoted to providing personal attention and professional advocacy for individuals and their families who have been injured or who have suffered wrongful death due to the carelessness of others. The firm strives to do its best in all ways for each and every client because members of the firm believe that word-of-mouth referrals based on client satisfaction is, and always will be, the best advertisement of a professional's success. References are available upon request. The firm welcomes the opportunity to be of service to the readers of this *Guidebook*.

STEVEN B. LEVY

Steven B. Levy, Ltd.
40 Shuman Boulevard
Suite 151
Naperville, IL 60563

Phone: (630) 416-6300
Fax: (630) 416-6564
800: (800) 742-8892
E-mail: sblevyltd@aol.com

Extensive Experience In:

• Vehicle Collision Injuries
• Unsafe Property Injuries
• Defective Product/Service Injuries

•GEORGE P. LINDNER - *Lindner, Speers & Reuland, P.C.* - 54 West Downer Place - P.O. Box 5055 - Aurora, IL 60507 - Phone: (630) 892-8109, Fax: (630) 892-8151 - *See complete biographical profile in the Personal Injury Law: Medical & Professional Malpractice Chapter, page 270.*

•JOSEPH J. MIROBALLI - *Anesi, Ozmon & Rodin, Ltd.* - 161 North Clark Street, Suite 2100 - Chicago, IL 60601 - Phone: (312) 372-3822, Fax: (312) 372-3833, 800: (800) 458-3822 within IL - *See complete biographical profile in the Personal Injury Law: Medical & Professional Malpractice Chapter, page 270.*

Chapter 19: Personal Injury Law: General

NAT P. OZMON

Anesi, Ozmon & Rodin, Ltd.
161 North Clark Street
Suite 2100
Chicago, IL 60601

Phone: (312) 372-3822
Fax: (312) 372-3833
800: (800) 458-3822 within IL

•**NAT P. OZMON:** Mr. Ozmon has practiced law for over 40 years. His entire practice has been in trials and appeals within the field of personal injury and wrongful death, with a particular emphasis on tort litigation, which is growing from the construction industry and products liability fields. He is *Certified by the American Board of Trial Advocates; a Diplomate of the American Board of Professional Liability Attorneys; a Fellow and Founder of the Roscoe Pound Foundation, Trial Lawyers for Public Justice, and Institute for Injury Reduction. He is a past President of the Illinois Trial Lawyers Association. For 35 years, Mr. Ozmon has lectured and contributed numerous articles to legal publications. He has taught or served on boards for the National Institute for Trial Advocacy, Court Practice Institute, Illinois College of Advocacy, Loyola University Law School, and Illinois Institute for Continuing Legal Education. He received an award from ATLA for his efforts to protect citizens from injury by reason of defective products; Illinois Institute for Continuing Legal Education for Extraordinary Contributions to Legal Education; Circuit Court of Cook County for his contributions towards the study of case flow problems; and Harvard Law School Study of Naifeh and Smith, resulting in his biography being listed in *The Best Lawyers in America*. Recently, he received the Leonard Ring Lifetime Achievement Award for his commitment to victims' rights and trial by jury.

Education: JD 1954, Northwestern University (Order of the Coif; First in Class Rank); 1948-50, New York University.

Admitted: 1954 Illinois; 1954 U.S. Dist. Ct. (N. Dist. IL); 1964 U.S. Ct. App. (7th Cir.); 1973 U.S. Sup. Ct.

Employment History: Senior Member 1978-94, the law firm currently known as Anesi, Ozmon & Rodin, Ltd.

Representative Clients: Mr. Ozmon represents plaintiffs who have suffered severe injuries and/or death as a result of a violation of the tort law.

Professional Associations: ITLA (President 1970-71; Board of Managers 1958-present); ATLA (Board of Governors 1973-75); CBA (Board of Managers 1974-76); ISBA [Tort Council Committee (Chair 1968-69); LAWPAC Committee (Trustee 1982-85)]; Illinois Institute for Continuing Legal Education (Board of Directors 1981-84); Appellate Lawyers Assn. (Board of Directors 1972-74); Society of Trial Lawyers (Board of Directors 1977-78).

Community Involvement: Board of Education, District 50 (President 1967-72); Northwestern University School of Law (Visiting Committee 1993-present).

Firm: *See complete firm profile in Appendix A. Mr. Ozmon also practices Personal Injury Law: Medical & Professional Malpractice and Personal Injury Law: Transportation.*

*The Supreme Court of Illinois does not recognize certifications of specialties in the practice of law. A certificate, award or recognition is not a requirement to practice law in Illinois.

ROBERT B. PATTERSON

Law Offices of Robert B. Patterson, Ltd.
221 North LaSalle Street
Suite 1050
Chicago, IL 60601

Phone: (312) 236-0995
Fax: (312) 984-5791

Extensive Experience In:

• Medical Negligence
• Products Liability
• Transportation—Trucking

•**ROBERT B. PATTERSON:** Representing only injured people, Mr. Patterson has devoted 25 years to providing fair compensation to victims of wrongful conduct by other persons and corporations. Mr. Patterson exclusively practices as a trial lawyer, handling numerous cases involving motor vehicles, transportation issues, medical malpractice, products liability and fraud. His cases include the Laurie Dann shooting, Sears ratchet wrench fraud, and Red Cross distribution of AIDS-contaminated blood. Mr. Patterson is a *Certified Civil Trial Advocate by the National Board of Trial Advocacy, and is listed in *Who's Who in American Law, Who's Who in the World,* and the *Bar Register of Preeminent Lawyers*. Mr. Patterson has written many professional articles and chapters for legal education manuals and has lectured frequently at continuing legal education programs and for medical organizations.

Education: JD 1971 cum laude, Northwestern University; BA 1968 with distinction, Pennsylvania State University (Phi Beta Kappa; Omicron Delta Kappa).

Admitted: 1971 Illinois; 1971 U.S. Dist. Ct. (N. Dist. IL); 1973 U.S. Ct. App. (7th Cir.); 1978 U.S. Sup. Ct.; 1980 U.S. Ct. App. (8th Cir.).

Employment History: Partner/President 1993-present, Law Offices of Robert B. Patterson, Ltd.; Partner/Vice President 1982-93, Drumke & Patterson, Ltd.; Associate 1971-82, Law Offices of Louis G. Davidson & Associates, Ltd.

Professional Associations: CBA 1971-present [Life Fellow; Medical Legal Relations Committee 1975-83 (Secretary 1975-77; Vice Chair 1977-78; Chair 1978-79); Federal Civil Practice Committee 1973-87 (Secretary 1979-80; Vice Chair 1980-81; Chair 1981-82); Civil Procedure Committee 1973-87; Executive Committee 1977-86 (Vice Chair 1978-79; Chair 1979-80, 1984-85); Candidates Evaluation Committee 1977-81]; ISBA (Fellow; Standing Committee on ARDC 1995-96; J. Editorial Board 1995-96); ABA; ITLA; ATLA; Appellate Lawyers Assn.

Community Involvement: Penn State Club of Greater Chicago 1968-present (Board of Directors 1972-80; President 1975-77); scouting and youth activity leader.

Firm: The professional philosophy of the Law Offices of Robert B. Patterson, Ltd., is to remain a small firm devoted to providing high quality, personally handled civil litigation services to redress injury inflicted on people, usually by large corporations. *Mr. Patterson also practices Personal Injury Law: Medical & Professional Malpractice and Personal Injury Law: Transportation.*

*The Supreme Court of Illinois does not recognize certifications of specialties in the practice of law. A certificate, award or recognition is not a requirement to practice law in Illinois.

Personal Injury Law: General Leading Illinois Attorneys

•**KIM E. PRESBREY** - *Presbrey and Associates, P.C.* - 821 West Galena Boulevard - Aurora, IL 60506 - Phone: (630) 264-7300, Fax: (630) 897-8637, 800: (800) 552-8622 - *See complete biographical profile in the Workers' Compensation Law Chapter, page 342.*

•**DAVID E. RAPOPORT** - *Rapoport & Kupets Law Offices* - O'Hare International Center - 10275 West Higgins Road, Suite 370 - Rosemont, IL 60018 - Phone: (847) 803-9880, Fax: (847) 803-9881, 800: (800) 545-6437 - *See complete biographical profile in the Personal Injury Law: Transportation Chapter, page 281.*

•**TIMOTHY J. REULAND:** Mr. Reuland concentrates his practice in the trial of civil lawsuits. He represents individuals who have been injured by defective products, the negligence of professionals, or in accidents. In addition, he represents individuals, businesses, and corporations in disputes arising out of commercial transactions, employment controversies, contracts, rezoning matters, condemnation proceedings, and claims for civil damages. He has over 20 years' experience in civil trials, including numerous bench trials and jury trials.
Education: JD 1973 cum laude, Northwestern University; BA 1970 cum laude, Loyola University.
Admitted: 1973 Illinois; 1973 U.S. Dist. Ct. (N. Dist. IL).
Employment History: Principal 1979-present, Lindner, Speers & Reuland, P.C.; Associate/Partner 1973-79, Reid, Ochsenschlager, Murphy & Hupp.
Representative Clients: Mr. Reuland represents various corporations, businesses, and individuals, frequently by way of referrals from other attorneys.
Professional Associations: ITLA 1973-present (Board of Managers 1990-96); Kane County Bar Assn. 1973-present (Board of Managers 1994-present); ISBA 1973-present; ABA 1973-present; ATLA 1973-present; CBA 1979-present.
Community Involvement: Marmion Academy (Board of Trustees); Hesed House, Inc.; Fox Knoll, Mercy Retirement Community; Holy Angels Church; Greater Aurora Area Chamber of Commerce (past Board Member; past Officer).
Firm: Since its inception in 1979, Lindner, Speers & Reuland, P.C., has concentrated its practice in civil litigation, including plaintiffs' personal injury, wrongful death cases, commercial litigation, and insurance defense. Members of the firm, including Mr. Reuland, have written for various legal publications and lectured to professional associations. The firm strives to represent its clients aggressively and efficiently. *See complete firm profile in Appendix A.*

TIMOTHY J. REULAND
Lindner, Speers & Reuland, P.C.
54 West Downer Place
P.O. Box 5055
Aurora, IL 60507
Phone: (630) 892-8109
Fax: (630) 892-8151

Extensive Experience In:
• Personal Injury
• Commercial Litigation

•**CURT N. RODIN:** Mr. Rodin concentrates in representing victims of serious injuries involving products liability, wrongful death, medical malpractice, and construction accidents. He is a frequent lecturer for the Illinois Trial Lawyers Association, Chicago Bar Association, and Illinois State Bar Association on topics including trial tactics, demonstrative evidence, substantive tort law, ethical considerations in personal injury practice, and constitutional law. He has been *Board Certified by the National Board of Trial Advocacy as a Civil Trial Specialist since 1983. He is listed in *The Best Lawyers in America* and has published numerous articles in the fields of civil trial practice and tort law. He has obtained substantial verdicts and settlements in Illinois for clients who have been catastrophically injured as a result of the fault of others, and was recognized by the *National Law Journal* in 1994 as one of 13 achievers in the law throughout the country.
Education: JD 1975, Loyola University; BA 1972 with high honors, University of Illinois.
Admitted: 1975 Illinois; 1976 U.S. Dist. Ct. (N. Dist. IL); 1979 U.S. Ct. App. (7th Cir.); 1979 U.S. Sup. Ct.
Employment History: Partner/Associate 1975-present, law firm currently known as Anesi, Ozmon & Rodin, Ltd.
Professional Associations: ITLA 1975-present (Board of Managers 1986-present; Third Vice President 1991-92; Second Vice President 1992-93; President-elect 1993-94; President 1994-95; Sustaining Member); ATLA 1976-present; Roscoe Pound Foundation (Fellow 1991-present); CBA 1975-present; ISBA 1975-present; ABA 1975-present; Appellate Lawyers Assn. of Illinois 1981-present.
Representative Clients: Mr. Rodin's clients are persons who have been seriously injured in construction accidents, victims of medical negligence, persons injured by defective products or in automobile or motorcycle accidents. He also represents the families of persons who have been wrongfully killed through the fault of others, and persons who have sustained catastrophic spinal cord and head injuries.
Firm: Anesi, Ozmon & Rodin, Ltd., with 28 attorneys and a staff of over 100, is the largest law firm in Illinois concentrating its practice in the representation of injury victims. The firm is committed to vigorously representing its clients in the areas of personal injury litigation, workers' compensation, and Social Security practice. *See complete firm profile in Appendix A. Mr. Rodin also practices Personal Injury Law: Medical & Professional Malpractice and Personal Injury Law: Transportation.*

    *The Supreme Court of Illinois does not recognize certifications of specialties in the practice of law. A certificate, award or recognition is not a requirement to practice law in Illinois.

CURT N. RODIN
Anesi, Ozmon & Rodin, Ltd.
161 North Clark Street
Suite 2100
Chicago, IL 60601
Phone: (312) 372-3822
Fax: (312) 372-3833
800: (800) 458-3822 within IL

July 1996

Chapter 19: Personal Injury Law: General

EDMUND J. SCANLAN
Law Offices of Edmund J. Scanlan, Ltd.
134 North LaSalle Street
Suite 220
Chicago, IL 60602

Phone: (312) 372-0020
Fax: (312) 372-1211

•**EDMUND J. SCANLAN:** Mr. Scanlan has practiced exclusively in the area of personal injury since 1976. He has represented injured parties and victims of automobile accidents, construction accidents, medical malpractice, products liability, premises liability, civil rights, airline and railroad accidents, sexual abuse, sexual and racial discrimination, as well as legal malpractice. Mr. Scanlan is a very active jury trial lawyer and has lectured on numerous occasions for the Illinois Trial Lawyers Association on trial practice. Mr. Scanlan is on the Board of Advocates of the Illinois Trial Lawyers Association, Chicago Bar Association, and Illinois State Bar Association. Mr. Scanlan is the host of *Law Talk,* which is aired by Chicago Cable Access. *Law Talk* is a call-in television program dealing with legal issues affecting consumers, particularly focusing on difficulties dealing with malpractice, products liability, work injuries, and civil litigation in general.

Education: JD 1976, DePaul University; BA 1971, University of Notre Dame.
Admitted: 1976 Illinois; 1976 U.S. Dist. Ct. (N. Dist. IL); 1977 U.S. Ct. App. (7th Cir.); 1989 U.S. Sup. Ct.
Employment History: Sole Owner 1988-present, Law Offices of Edmund J. Scanlan, Ltd.; Partner 1981-88, Scanlan & Hartigan, Ltd.; Attorney 1976-81, Garbutt & Jacobson.
Representative Clients: Mr. Scanlan represents clients who have been injured in automobile accidents, construction accidents, medical malpractice, products liability, premises liability, airline and railroad accidents, civil rights, sexual abuse, and sexual and racial discrimination, as well as legal malpractice.
Professional Associations: ITLA (Board of Advocates 1993-present); CBA (Civil Litigation Committee 1991-94); ISBA (Civil Litigation Committee 1990-95); ATLA 1990-present; West Suburban Bar Assn.
Community Involvement: Sierra Club; Audubon Society.
Firm: Mr. Scanlan, with 20 years' jury trial experience, heads a law firm that brings an individual approach to many of its high-profile cases. Numerous clients that the firm has represented through the years have been subjects of radio, television, and newspaper articles. The firm's philosophy is to provide clients with personalized attention, while always preparing their cases for success in the courtroom. *Mr. Scanlan also practices Personal Injury Law: Transportation and Personal Injury Law: Medical & Professional Malpractice.*

JEFFREY M. SHANCER
Law Offices of Jeffrey M. Shancer
Three First National Plaza
Suite 3750
Chicago, IL 60602

Phone: (312) 558-5167
Fax: (312) 558-7767

Extensive Experience In:

- Construction Accidents
- Vehicular Accidents
- Medical Malpractice

•**JEFFREY M. SHANCER:** Mr. Shancer has become one of the Chicago-area's leading personal injury attorneys through his intelligent, aggressive, and creative representation of injury victims in Cook, Lake, DuPage, and Will Counties. In 1993, Mr. Shancer defeated the world's largest manufacturer of epoxy products, attaining a verdict far exceeding expectations of the court, his client, and opposing counsel. Keeping abreast of every change on the ever-changing landscape of Illinois trial law, Mr. Shancer has consistently obtained outstanding results on behalf of his seriously injured clients.

Education: JD 1986, DePaul University; BA 1983, University of Illinois-Urbana; 1979-81, University of Chicago.
Admitted: 1986 Illinois; 1986 U.S. Dist. Ct. (N. Dist. IL).
Employment History: Owner 1994-present, Law Offices of Jeffrey M. Shancer; Associate 1992-93, Goldberg, Weisman & Cairo; Associate 1989-92, Williams & Montgomery; Associate 1986-89, Anesi, Ozmon & Rodin.
Representative Clients: Mr. Shancer represents construction workers (ironworkers, carpenters, laborers, plumbers, pipefitters, millwrights, electricians), victims of defective products, injured pedestrians, passengers and drivers in vehicular accidents, medical malpractice victims, injured railroad workers, and aircraft crash victims.
Professional Associations: ITLA 1986-present (Legislative Committee; Publications Committee); ABA 1986-present; CBA 1986-present.
Firm: The Law Offices of Jeffrey M. Shancer strives to provide its clients with the highest degree of personalized service available. Through aggressive investigation and representation, Jeffrey M. Shancer has become regarded as one of the top names in personal injury trial law in the Chicago area. *Mr. Shancer also practices Workers' Compensation Law and Personal Injury Law: Medical & Professional Malpractice.*

•**ROBERT L. SPEERS:** Mr. Speers has over 23 years of experience in civil trials, with numerous cases tried to verdict. His jury trials have included cases involving personal injury, products liability, premises liability, defamation, dram shop, fire loss, and cases under the Structural Work Act and the Animal Control Act. The cases tried to verdict have involved wrongful death, paralysis, brain injury, and amputation. He also has represented clients at arbitration hearings and has been asked to be an arbitrator on many occasions by other members of the Trial Bar. He has spoken at seminars presented by the Kane County Bar Association on matters relating to civil litigation.
Education: JD 1972, University of Illinois; BS 1967, Iowa State University.
Admitted: 1972 Illinois; 1972 U.S. Dist. Ct. (N. Dist. IL).
Employment History: 1979-present, Lindner, Speers & Reuland, P.C.; 1972-79, Reid, Ochsenschlager, Murphy & Hupp.
Representative Clients: Mr. Speers has represented many injured individuals, along with clients referred to him by Farmers Insurance Group of Companies.
Professional Associations: Kane County Bar Assn. (President 1988-89); ISBA; ITLA; ATLA.
Community Involvement: Aurora YMCA 1978-83 (Board of Directors).
Firm: The firm was founded in 1979 by George Lindner, Robert Speers and Timothy Reuland. The firm has concentrated its practice in civil litigation since its inception. The firm handles cases involving plaintiffs' personal injury and wrongful death, commercial litigation, and insurance defense. The firm has consistently been among the leaders in cases tried to verdict in the state of Illinois. *See complete firm profile in Appendix A.*

ROBERT L. SPEERS
Lindner, Speers & Reuland, P.C.
54 West Downer Place
P.O. Box 5055
Aurora, IL 60507
Phone: (630) 892-8109
Fax: (630) 892-8151

•**ROBERT N. WADINGTON:** Mr. Wadington's educational background includes both a master's degree in business administration as well as his law degree. His entire legal career has involved the representation of injured persons. Mr. Wadington has published numerous articles in various journals, including the *Kane County Bar Journal* and the *Illinois Trial Lawyers Association Journal.* He is deeply involved in community and charitable activities in his hometown of St. Charles, Illinois, having served as a member of the St. Charles Planning Commission and on various boards of directors. He is currently a member of the Alumni Board of Directors of the John Marshall Law School. He was elected in 1992 as a Full Advocate Member of the prestigious American Board of Trial Advocates. He has had great success in obtaining both settlements and verdicts in a wide variety of personal injury matters and has unique experience in each.
Education: JD 1986, John Marshall Law School; MBA 1983, Indiana University; BS 1979, Indiana University.
Admitted: 1986 Illinois; 1986 U.S. Dist. Ct. (N. Dist. IL); 1986 U.S. Sup. Ct.; 1995 U.S. Dist. Ct. (W. Dist. WI).
Employment History: Owner 1993-present, Robert N. Wadington & Associates; Associate 1986-93, Cooney and Conway.
Representative Clients: Mr. Wadington limits his practice exclusively to the representation of injured persons.
Professional Associations: ABOTA (Advocate); ITLA (Amicus Curiae Committee; Membership Committee); ISBA; CBA; ATLA; Kane County Bar Assn.
Community Involvement: Northwestern Hospital Auxiliary (Board of Directors); Big Brothers/Big Sisters Fund Raising Committee; City of St. Charles Planning Commission; St. Charles Congregational Church (Board of Trustees).
Firm: Mr. Wadington purposely keeps the number of cases he accepts to an acceptable level, thus ensuring that each client receives the care and attention that he or she deserves. Each client understands that he or she will not be treated as "just another case," but with the respect that the defendants and their insurers will never render unless forced to. Mr. Wadington, and each lawyer employed by him, has extensive trial experience. They are willing to do whatever is necessary to achieve a successful result for each client. *Mr. Wadington also practices Personal Injury Law: Medical & Professional Malpractice and Workers' Compensation Law.*

ROBERT N. WADINGTON
Robert N. Wadington & Associates
111 West Washington Street
Suite 1460
Chicago, IL 60602
Phone: (312) 629-2706
Fax: (312) 629-8022

Extensive Experience In:
• Product Liability

MELVIN A. WEINSTEIN - *Melvin A. Weinstein & Associates* - 134 North LaSalle Street, Suite 720 - Chicago, IL 60602 - Phone: (312) 263-2257, Fax: (312) 263-4942 - *See complete biographical profile in the Family Law Chapter, page 206.*

Chapter 19: Personal Injury Law: General

NORTHWESTERN ILLINOIS
INCLUDING ROCKFORD & QUAD CITIES

ROBERT A. FREDRICKSON
Reno, Zahm, Folgate, Lindberg & Powell
1415 East State Street
Suite 900
Rockford, IL 61104
Phone: (815) 987-4050
Fax: (815) 987-4092

•**ROBERT A. FREDRICKSON:** Mr. Fredrickson has 25 years of experience as a trial lawyer handling cases in state and federal courts. He handles all areas of civil litigation, with the major concentration in personal injury, wrongful death, and product liability. As a litigator, Mr. Fredrickson has represented a wide variety of clients and covered a broad range of civil litigation issues in courts in Illinois, Wisconsin, and surrounding states. Additionally, he is often selected as an arbitrator and mediator for private proceedings, and is a *Certified Arbitrator for the American Arbitration Association and a Court Appointed Mediator for the 17th Judicial Circuit, Major Case Mediation Program. Mr. Fredrickson obtains favorable verdicts and settlements for his clients by taking a practical approach to litigation based on a thorough knowledge of the law, an insightful understanding of the litigation process, and his extensive experience.
Education: JD 1971 with honors, University of Wisconsin-Madison; BBA 1967 with honors, University of Wisconsin-Madison.
Admitted: 1971 Illinois; 1971 Wisconsin; 1971 U.S. Dist. Ct. (N. Dist. IL, General Bar, Trial Bar); 1971 U.S. Dist. Ct. (W. Dist. WI); 1983 U.S. Sup. Ct.
Employment History: Partner 1974-present, Associate 1971-74, Reno, Zahm, Folgate, Lindberg & Powell.
Professional Associations: ATLA; ITLA; ISBA; State Bar of Wisconsin; American Arbitration Assn.; Winnebago County Bar Assn.
Community Involvement: University of Wisconsin [Alumni Club of Northern Illinois (Charter Member; Director)]; Rockford Rotary Club.
Firm: Reno, Zahm, Folgate, Lindberg & Powell has served clients throughout Illinois and Wisconsin since 1923. The firm provides clients with established experience in all phases of trial law, business law, real estate law, employment law, and tax law, as well as other areas of law. The firm has successfully tried a wide variety of cases, including all types of injury cases as well as complex business disputes. As a local firm comprised of attorneys with a strong commitment to its community, Reno, Zahm, Folgate, Lindberg & Powell serves its clients at the highest standard of legal representation. *See complete firm profile in Appendix A. Mr. Fredrickson also practices Personal Injury Law: Transportation and Alternative Dispute Resolution.*

*The Supreme Court of Illinois does not recognize certifications of specialties in the practice of law. A certificate, award or recognition is not a requirement to practice law in Illinois.

PHILIP F. JENSEN - *Hammer, Simon & Jensen* - 303 North Bench Street - P.O. Box 270 - Galena, IL 61036 - Phone: (815) 777-1101, Fax: (815) 777-9241 - *See complete biographical profiles in the Family Law Chapter, page 207 and Small Business Law Chapter, page 308.*

CRAIG L. KAVENSKY
Winstein, Kavensky & Wallace
224 18th Street
Fourth Floor
Rock Island, IL 61201

Phone: (309) 794-1515
Fax: (309) 794-9929

Extensive Experience In:
• Products Liability

•**CRAIG L. KAVENSKY:** Mr. Kavensky limits his practice exclusively to representing victims of personal injury, products liability, wrongful death, and work-related injuries. He has successfully represented numerous parties in claims arising out of auto collisions, including victims who have suffered serious, permanent injuries as well as fatal injuries. He has also represented thousands of persons in claims against their employers under the Workers' Compensation Act. In 1995, he successfully represented an injured worker through the appellate court process in a case which established new law in Illinois in the area of calculation of average weekly wage.
Education: JD 1982 with high honors, Illinois Institute of Technology, Chicago-Kent; BS 1979 with high honors, University of Illinois.
Admitted: 1982 Illinois; 1982 U.S. Dist. Ct. (C. Dist. IL).
Employment History: Managing Partner 1982-present, Winstein, Kavensky & Wallace.
Representative Clients: All of Mr. Kavensky's clients are individuals who have been injured in accidents. The firm of Winstein, Kavensky & Wallace also represents unions and members of unions, including the UAW, IBEW, and United Rubber Workers.
Professional Associations: ATLA 1982-present; ITLA 1982-present; ABA 1982-present; Rock Island County Bar Assn. 1982-present.
Firm: The firm of Winstein, Kavensky & Wallace has been in existence for over 50 years. The firm has represented thousands of injured persons in an effort to obtain fair compensation in claims arising out of personal injury, workers' compensation, and wrongful death. The firm also concentrates in the areas of criminal law, family law, labor law, and general civil litigation. *Mr. Kavensky also practices Workers' Compensation and Personal Injury Law: Medical & Professional Malpractice.*

•**JAN H. OHLANDER:** Mr. Ohlander has a civil practice concentrated in state and federal trials, including personal injury, wrongful death, product liability, construction accidents, automobile and road hazards, transportation and electrocution. As a civil trial lawyer, he represents injured parties and families in a wide variety of cases throughout Illinois and Wisconsin, and has obtained substantial verdicts and settlements for his clients. In addition to injury claims, Mr. Ohlander represents employers and employees in claims arising out of termination of employment, reduction in force, and conditions of employment. He serves as a Mediator for the 17th Judicial Circuit Major Case Mediation Program.
Education: JD 1979, Marquette University (*Law Review*); BS 1976, University of Illinois.
Admitted: 1979 Illinois; 1979 Wisconsin; 1979 U.S. Dist. Ct. (N. Dist. IL, General Bar, Trial Bar); 1979 U.S. Dist. Ct. (E. Dist. WI; W. Dist. WI); 1988 U.S. Ct. App. (7th Cir.); 1990 U.S. Sup. Ct.
Employment History: Partner 1982-present, Associate 1979-82, Reno, Zahm, Folgate, Lindberg & Powell.
Professional Associations: ATLA; ITLA; ISBA; State Bar of Wisconsin; Winnebago County Bar Assn.
Community Involvement: Rockford Area Crime Stoppers (Board of Directors); Rockford Ducks Unlimited (Director; past Chair).
Firm: Reno, Zahm, Folgate, Lindberg & Powell has served clients throughout Illinois and Wisconsin since 1923. The firm provides clients with established experience in all phases of trial law, business law, real estate law, employment law, and tax law, as well as other areas of law. The firm has successfully tried a very wide variety of cases including all types of injury cases as well as complex business disputes. As a local firm comprised of attorneys with a strong commitment to its community, Reno, Zahm, Folgate, Lindberg & Powell serves its clients at the highest standard of legal representation. *See complete firm profile in Appendix A. Mr. Ohlander also practices Employment Law, Personal Injury Law: Transportation and Workers' Compensation Law.*

JAN H. OHLANDER
Reno, Zahm, Folgate, Lindberg & Powell
1415 East State Street
Suite 900
Rockford, IL 61104
Phone: (815) 987-4050
Fax: (815) 987-4092

R. CRAIG SAHLSTROM - *Attorney and Counsellor at Law* - One Court Place, Suite 301 - Rockford, IL 61101 - Phone: (815) 964-4601, Fax: (815) 964-3292 - *See complete biographical profile in the Criminal Law: Felonies & White Collar Crime Chapter, page 116.*

•**PETER S. SWITZER** - *Barrick, Switzer, Long, Balsley & Van Evera* - One Madison Street - Rockford, IL 61104 - Phone: (815) 962-6611, Fax: (815) 962-0687 - *See complete biographical profile in the Family Law Chapter, page 208.*

Central Illinois

KENNITH W. BLAN, JR.

Blan Law Offices
712 West Fairchild
P.O. Box 1995
Danville, IL 61834

Phone: (217) 443-5400
Fax: (217) 443-5155

Extensive Experience In:

- Roll-Over & Air Bags
- Failure to Diagnose Cancer
- Birth Trauma

•**KENNITH W. BLAN, JR.:** Mr. Blan concentrates his practice in personal injury law, including medical malpractice, product liability, and workers' compensation. He has participated on the Illinois Trial Lawyers Association "Friend of the Court" appellate briefing committee, and is also recognized by frequent referrals from professional colleagues of legal malpractice and insurance coverage cases. Mr. Blan accepts cases throughout east-central Illinois. He is a founding member of the Civil Justice Foundation, and has been listed in *Who's Who in American Law* each year since its first publication.

Education: JD 1971, University of Illinois; BS 1968, University of Illinois.

Admitted: 1972 Illinois; 1973 U.S. Dist. Ct. (C. Dist. IL); 1975 U.S. Ct. App. (7th Cir.); 1978 U.S. Sup. Ct.

Employment History: Sole Practitioner 1976-present; Associate 1972-76, Graham, Meyer, Young, Welch & Maton.

Representative Clients: Mr. Blan limits his representation to injured individuals and their families.

Professional Associations: ITLA (Board of Advocates 1994-present); ATLA (Sustaining Member); ABA (Litigation Section); ISBA (Civil Practice Section; Workers' Compensation Section); Christian Legal Society.

Community Involvement: The Gideons International; Christian Businessmen's Committee, U.S.A.; Aircraft Owners & Pilots Assn.; University of Illinois Alumni Assn. (Life Member); Christian Churches/Churches of Christ.

Firm: Mr. Blan is a sole practitioner committed to a hands-on approach with each of his clients. His support staff is well trained and qualified, and the firm believes in the value and importance of clear communication among attorney, staff, and client. Mr. Blan recognizes that each case presents a unique opportunity for service, that each client has special needs, and that a client's priorities warrant the firm's utmost respect and consideration. This firm culture is inculcated from the first meeting with a new client, and guides every case, from start to finish. *Mr. Blan also practices Personal Injury Law: Medical & Professional Malpractice and Workers' Compensation Law.*

•**GARY L. CLARK** - *The Law Offices of Frederic W. Nessler and Associates* - 433 Hamilton Boulevard - First Financial Plaza, Suite Two - Peoria, IL 61602 - Phone: (309) 673-6404, Fax: (309) 674-6407 - *See complete biographical profile in the Personal Injury Law: Medical & Professional Malpractice Chapter, page 272.*

GREGG N. GRIMSLEY - *Carter & Grimsley* - 1500 Commerce Bank Building - Peoria, IL 61602 - Phone: (309) 673-3517, Fax: (309) 673-3318 - *See complete biographical profile in the Bankruptcy Law Chapter, page 74.*

DAVID M. LYNCH - *Lynch & Bloom, P.C.* - 411 Hamilton Boulevard, Suite 1300 - Peoria, IL 61602 - Phone: (309) 673-7415, Fax: (309) 673-3189 - *See complete biographical profile in the Family Law Chapter, page 211.*

Personal Injury Law: General Leading Illinois Attorneys

•**MICHAEL B. METNICK:** During the past 20 years, Mr. Metnick has developed trial skills to handle all personal injury and professional malpractice cases. Mr. Metnick has been successful in obtaining sizable verdicts and settlements in personal injury, automobile, workers' compensation, wrongful death, medical malpractice, and police misconduct cases. His statewide practice involves representing plaintiffs in cases from Chicago to Carbondale, in both state and federal courts. Mr. Metnick's skilled trial techniques have made him a popular speaker at legal education seminars sponsored by the Illinois Trial Lawyers Association, Illinois Institute for Continuing Legal Education, Illinois Attorneys for Criminal Justice, and the Illinois State Bar Association. His law practice is devoted to providing representation to individuals who need professional legal counsel.
Education: JD 1975, John Marshall Law School; BA 1970, University of Oklahoma.
Admitted: 1975 Illinois; 1975 U.S. Ct. App. (7th Cir.); 1975 U.S. Dist. Ct. (C. Dist. IL).
Professional Associations: ISBA; ATLA; ITLA; NACDL; Lincoln-Douglas Inn of Courts.
Firm: Metnick, Wise, Cherry & Frazier represents clients in civil and criminal cases in state and federal courts. The firm's practice includes personal injury and malpractice cases; civil appeals and other civil actions; dissolution and custody matters; criminal felonies; misdemeanors, reckless homicide, murder, DUIs and other traffic offenses; financial cases; and employment law. The firm litigates in state and federal courts and argues criminal appeals in the U.S. and Illinois Supreme Courts. *Mr. Metnick also practices Criminal Law: Felonies & White Collar Crime, Family Law, Personal Injury Law: Medical & Professional Malpractice and Workers' Compensation Law.*

MICHAEL B. METNICK

Metnick, Wise, Cherry & Frazier
Number One West Old State Capital Plaza
Myers Building
Suite 200
Springfield, IL 62701

Phone: (217) 753-4242
Fax: (217) 753-4642
800: (800) 500-4242

Extensive Experience In:

• Automobile Accidents
• Medical Negligence
• Workers' Compensation

•**FREDERIC W. NESSLER:** Mr. Nessler practices plaintiffs' personal injury law, including handling wrongful death, product liability, workers' compensation, and medical malpractice cases. He concentrates his efforts in serious and catastrophic injuries and has handled many such cases resulting in significant financial recovery. Mr. Nessler has lectured, and continues to lecture, on personal injury and workers' compensation law and related topics. Mr. Nessler is a life-long resident of central Illinois. He has an extensive agricultural background which affords him the ability and experience to handle a variety of farm-related cases. He and his family also manage diverse farming interests including land, cattle, swine and grain. Mr. Nessler served as a legislative assistant to the late Congressman Edward Madigan, U.S. Congress, Washington, D.C. He has served on the Tort Section Council of the Illinois State Bar Association and has been active with the Illinois Trial Lawyers Association in efforts to protect victims' rights.
Education: JD 1977 cum laude, Illinois Institute of Technology, Chicago-Kent; BA 1974, University of Illinois (past Vice President, Sachem Honorary Society; past Vice President, Omnicron Delta Kappa Honorary Society; Gamma Sigma Delta, Honor Society of Agriculture).
Admitted: 1977 Illinois; 1990 Colorado.
Professional Associations: ATLA; ITLA (Legislation Committee; Medical Negligence Committee; Product Liability Committee); ISBA [Tort Section Council (past Member)]; ABA; Sangamon County Bar Assn.; Logan County Bar Assn. (past President).
Community Involvement: Calvary Temple Christian Center (Board Member); United Cerebral Palsy Foundation (Contributing Sponsor); Calvary Academy [Athletic Steering Committee (Chair)]; Illinois Maine Anjou Assn. (Board Member; past President).
Firm: Mr. Nessler started his law practice in 1977 in Lincoln, Illinois. Today, he maintains seven office locations throughout central Illinois. He and his associates are available to consult on injury and wrongful death cases, and they handle those cases on a contingency fee basis. Mr. Nessler also has offices at 305 Decatur Street, Lincoln, Illinois 62656; Two First Financial Plaza, Peoria, Illinois 61602; 352 Millikin Court, Decatur, Illinois 62523; 237 East Front Street, Bloomington, Illinois 61701; and 202 West Green Street, Urbana, Illinois 61801. *See complete firm profile in Appendix A. Mr. Nessler also practices Workers' Compensation Law and Personal Injury Law: Medical & Professional Malpractice.*

FREDERIC W. NESSLER

The Law Offices of
Frederic W. Nessler and Associates
800 Myers Building
Springfield, IL 62701

Phone: (217) 753-5533
Fax: (217) 753-4631
800: (800) 727-8010

Extensive Experience In:

• Automobile Accidents
• Medical Malpractice
• Insurance Issues

JOHN P. NICOARA

Nicoara & Steagall
416 Main Street
Suite 815
Peoria, IL 61602

Phone: (309) 674-6085
Fax: (309) 674-6032
E-mail: Compuserve 70754, 3140

Extensive Experience In:

- Trucking & Railroad Accident Cases
- Medical Malpractice
- Products Liability

•**JOHN P. NICOARA:** Mr. Nicoara concentrates his practice in the area of motor vehicle, products liability, professional malpractice, insurance, and general negligence law. After his graduation from the University of Michigan, he served for two years in the U.S. Army Test and Evaluation Command's Legal Division. He graduated from the University of Illinois College of Law in 1975, where he was the Notes and Comments Editor of the *University of Illinois Law Review*. He gained extensive jury trial experience as an Assistant State's Attorney for three years in Woodford County. Since 1978, he has devoted himself exclusively to tort litigation and insurance coverage disputes, representing both plaintiffs and defendants in jury and bench trials in federal and state courts throughout central Illinois. Among his most notable victories is the case of *Knighton v. Southwest Motor Freight, Inc.*, believed to be one of the largest personal injury jury verdicts in Peoria's federal court. Mr. Nicoara is a frequent lecturer at continuing legal education programs in Illinois, and his annual Tort Case Law Update is referred to by judges and practitioners alike for its concise compilation of Illinois Appellate and Supreme Court opinions. In addition to serving as an advocate on behalf of his clients, Mr. Nicoara is frequently sought out as a neutral arbitrator to help resolve disputes between claimants and insurance companies in uninsured and underinsured motorist cases and other alternative dispute resolution contexts.

Education: JD 1975, University of Illinois (Notes and Comments Editor 1974-75, *Law Review*); AB 1970, University of Michigan.

Admitted: 1975 Illinois; 1976 U.S. Dist. Ct. (C. Dist. IL); 1982 U.S. Ct. App. (7th Cir.); 1984 U.S. Sup. Ct.

Employment History: Partner 1980-present, Nicoara & Steagall; Partner 1976-80, Baner & Nicoara; First Assistant State's Attorney 1975-78, Woodford County, Illinois.

Professional Associations: Peoria County Bar Assn. (Board of Directors 1982-present; President-elect 1995-96; President 1996-97); Abraham Lincoln Inn of Court 1988-present (Master/Executive Committee Member); Civil Justice Reform Act (Advisory Board 1995-present); Woodford County Bar Assn.; ABA 1980-present; ISBA 1976-present; ITLA 1978-present; Illinois Defense Counsel; Defense Research Institute 1976-present.

Community Involvement: Friends of Glen Oak Zoo; Western Avenue Greenway Project; Glen Oak Neighborhood Assn.

Firm: Mr. Nicoara practices law with Richard L. Steagall under the firm name of Nicoara & Steagall. The firm also provides representation in the area of employment and civil rights discrimination. *Mr. Nicoara also practices Personal Injury Law: Medical & Professional Malpractice and Alternative Dispute Resolution.*

•**DREW PARKER** - *Parker & Halliday* - 414 Hamilton Boulevard, Suite 300 - Peoria, IL 61602 - Phone: (309) 673-0069, Fax: (309) 673-8791 - *See complete biographical profile in the Family Law Chapter, page 214.*

•**EDWARD H. RAWLES:** Mr. Rawles practices primarily civil litigation in both state and federal courts, concentrating on personal injury matters. He handles all types of negligence actions, including professional and medical negligence as well as product liability cases. Mr. Rawles is the only attorney in Champaign County who is *Board Certified as a Civil Trial Advocate by the National Board of Trial Advocacy, Washington, D.C. He obtained that certification in 1982. Mr. Rawles is the coauthor of "Deposing the Medical Witness," *Lawyers Guide to Medical Proof,* Matthew Bender, 1982, and has been listed in *Who's Who in American Law* since 1985.
Education: JD 1970 summa cum laude, Illinois Institute of Technology, Chicago-Kent (Kent Society of Honor Men; *Law Review* 1968-70); BA 1967, University of Illinois.
Admitted: 1970 Illinois; 1984 Colorado; 1970 U.S. Dist. Ct. (C. Dist. IL); 1974 U.S. Ct. App. (7th Cir.); 1974 U.S. Sup. Ct.; 1992 U.S. Claims Ct.
Employment History: President 1995-present, Rawles, O'Byrne, Stanko & Kepley, P.C.; President 1990-95, Reno, O'Byrne & Kepley, P.C.; Partner 1973-90, Reno, O'Byrne & Kepley; Associate 1970-73, Reno, O'Byrne & Kepley.
Representative Clients: University of Illinois (Board of Trustees); Covenant Medical Center; Bank One of Champaign; Pekin Insurance Company.
Professional Associations: ISBA; Colorado State Bar Assn.; ABA (Special Committee on Insurance Company Taxation 1985-86); ATLA (Sustaining Member); ITLA (Civil Practice Committee 1982-present); NBTA (Diplomate 1982-present); American Arbitration Assn. (Panel of Arbitrators); Champaign County Bar Assn.; Bar Assn. of the Seventh Federal Circuit; Illinois Bar Foundation (Charter Fellow).
Community Involvement: Rotary Club of Champaign, Illinois (West Chapter); University of Illinois [Student Legal Services (Advisory Board 1979-present)].
Firm: Originally formed in 1931 by Donald M. Reno, Sr., the firm, early on, established a reputation for excellence in litigation matters from the local, state and federal courts in central Illinois through, and including, matters before the U.S. Supreme Court. The firm is willing to consider difficult, complex, and unpopular cases that other firms may be unwilling or unable to undertake. The size and staff of the firm enable Rawles, O'Byrne, Stanko & Kepley, P.C., to bring a high level of experience and competence over a broad range of legal matters directly to a client's case. *See complete firm profile in Appendix A. Mr. Rawles also practices Personal Injury Law: Medical & Professional Malpractice and Employment Law.*

*The Supreme Court of Illinois does not recognize certifications of specialties in the practice of law. A certificate, award or recognition is not a requirement to practice law in Illinois.

EDWARD H. RAWLES
Rawles, O'Byrne, Stanko & Kepley, P.C.
501 West Church Street
Champaign, IL 61820

Phone: (217) 352-7661
Fax: (217) 352-2169
E-mail: ehrawles@prairienet.org

Extensive Experience In:
• Professional/Medical Negligence
• Products Liability
• Vehicular Cases

•**JOHN A. SLEVIN:** Mr. Slevin concentrates in civil trials and workers' compensation law. He has handled many jury trials involving personal injury; products liability, including asbestos litigation; medical and legal malpractice; and commercial litigation, including tortious interference with business contracts, RICO, and job discrimination. He has appeared and argued numerous cases in Illinois Appellate Court, the Illinois Supreme Court, and the Seventh Circuit Court of Appeals. He is a *Certified Civil Trial Advocate by the National Board of Trial Advocacy, which requires specified trial experience, written proof of competency in civil trial work, and successfully passing a written exam. He has lectured on civil trial matters in seminars conducted by the Peoria County Bar Association, and is Chair of the Paralegal Advisory Committee for Illinois Central College. He is listed in *Who's Who in American Law.*
Education: JD 1960, University of Notre Dame (*Law Review*); PhB 1957 cum laude, University of Notre Dame.
Admitted: 1960 Illinois; 1962 U.S. Dist. Ct. (C. Dist. IL); 1966 U.S. Ct. App. (7th Cir.); 1967 U.S. Dist. Ct. (N. Dist. IL); 1967 U.S. Dist. Ct. (S. Dist. IL).
Employment History: Partner 1966-present, Vonachen, Lawless, Trager & Slevin; Sole Practitioner 1964-65; Partner 1963, Koos & Slevin; Associate 1960-62, Hershey & Bliss.
Representative Clients: Mr. Slevin represents clients who need legal help in personal injury law, workers' compensation, asbestos claims, and medical and legal malpractice.
Professional Associations: Abraham Lincoln Inns of Court (Master; Board of Directors); ATLA (Sustaining Member); ITLA; Peoria County Bar Assn. [Courts and Procedures Committee (Chair)].
Community Involvement: University of Notre Dame [Alumni Assn. (Board of Directors 1983-86); Notre Dame Club of Peoria (Man of the Year Award 1982)]; Peoria Cursillo (Board of Directors 1991-95); Visiting Nurses Assn. (Board of Directors 1978-84; President 1983-84); St. Brendan's Society (Irish Cultural); Knights of Columbus; Multiple Sclerosis Society (Board of Directors 1964-70); United Way (past Special Gifts Volunteer).
Firm: Mr. Slevin is a partner in the law firm of Vonachen, Lawless, Trager & Slevin and is Chair of the Litigation Group. The firm consists of 13 attorneys who concentrate in various areas of practice, handling matters including domestic relations, child custody, criminal, bankruptcy, partnerships, corporations, wills and trusts, and real estate. This wide variety of experience allows the firm to offer full service to individuals and businesses. *Mr. Slevin also practices Personal Injury Law: Medical & Professional Malpractice and Workers' Compensation Law.*

*The Supreme Court of Illinois does not recognize certifications of specialties in the practice of law. A certificate, award or recognition is not a requirement to practice law in Illinois.

JOHN A. SLEVIN
Vonachen, Lawless, Trager & Slevin
456 Fulton Street
Suite 425
Peoria, IL 61602

Phone: (309) 676-8986
Fax: (309) 676-4130

Chapter 19: Personal Injury Law: General

GLENN A. STANKO - *Rawles, O'Byrne, Stanko & Kepley, P.C.* - 501 West Church Street - P.O. Box 800 - Champaign, IL 61824 - Phone: (217) 352-7661, Fax: (217) 352-2169 - *See complete biographical profile in the Employment Law Chapter, page 149.*

ROBERT E. STINE

Stine, Wolter & Greer
426 South Fifth Street
Springfield, IL 62701

Phone: (217) 744-1000
Fax: (217) 744-1444
E-mail: robert.stine@accessil.com

Extensive Experience In:
- Auto Accidents
- Wrongful Death
- Health Care Law

•**ROBERT E. STINE:** Mr. Stine concentrates in personal injury law, with an emphasis in vehicle collision and insurance cases. He has authored a legal column in the *Illinois Chiropractic Journal* since 1980, and is a frequent lecturer to physician groups and others. His lectures have included "The Auto Accident Patient," "The Medical Witness," "Medical Record Keeping," and other medico-legal topics. Mr. Stine brings a unique perspective to his clients' cases, having been involved in the drafting of the Medical Practice Act and other Illinois health care laws. He was a Special Assistant Attorney General for 12 years, as well as a hearing officer.
Education: JD 1968, University of Iowa; BS 1964, Eastern Illinois University.
Admitted: 1968 Illinois; 1968 Iowa; 1968 U.S. Dist. Ct. (S. Dist. IL); 1972 U.S. Ct. App. (8th Cir.).
Employment History: Partner 1977-present, Stine, Wolter & Greer and its predecessors; Associate 1971-77, Drach, Terrell & Deffenbaugh; City Attorney 1969-71, City of Burlington, Iowa; Staff Attorney 1968-69, Illinois Legislative Reference Bureau.
Representative Clients: Illinois Chiropractic Society; National College of Chiropractic; Interstate Bakeries Corporation; Illinois Assn. of Osteopathic Physicians and Surgeons; Divernon Township; Curran-Gardner Water District; Two Fire Protection Districts.
Professional Associations: ISBA 1968-present; Sangamon County Bar Assn. 1968-present.
Community Involvement: Juvenile Diabetes Foundation [Springfield Chapter (Officer)]; Lincolnland Depression Era Glass Club; Springfield Model Railroad Club; Various church committee offices held over the years.
Firm: Stine, Wolter & Greer offers a wide scope of services. The firm's members concentrate in various areas of law. The firm emphasizes first-person contact with its clients throughout the period of representation. The office is centrally located near the state government complex and the courts. *See complete firm profile in Appendix A.*

ROBERT C. STRODEL - *Law Offices of Robert C. Strodel, Ltd.* - 927 Commerce Bank Building - Peoria, IL 61602 - Phone: (309) 676-4500, Fax: (309) 676-4566 - *See complete biographical profile in the Personal Injury Law: Medical & Professional Malpractice Chapter, page 273.*

SOUTHERN ILLINOIS

•**LANCE CALLIS** - *Callis, Papa, Jensen, Jackstadt & Halloran, P.C.* - 1326 Niedringhaus Avenue - Granite City, IL 62040 - Phone: (618) 452-1323, Fax: (618) 452-8024 - *See complete biographical profile in the Personal Injury Law: Transportation Chapter, page 282.*

•**JON G. CARLSON** - *Carlson Wendler & Sanderson, P.C.* - 90 Edwardsville Professional Park - P.O. Box 527 - Edwardsville, IL 62025 - Phone: (618) 656-0066, Fax: (618) 656-0009, 800: (800) 527-3352 within IL, (800) 338-3352 outside IL - *See complete biographical profile in the Personal Injury Law: Transportation Chapter, page 283.*

Personal Injury Law: General Leading Illinois Attorneys

•**REX CARR:** Mr. Carr practices personal injury, medical malpractice, products liability, and class action litigation. He has obtained numerous large verdicts in a wide range of injury cases including products liability, medical malpractice, libel, business litigation, toxic torts, vehicular accidents and cases under the Federal Employer's Liability Act. He has participated in a large number of trial advocacy seminars as a lecturer, including trial lawyers' associations, the University of Illinois and the St. Louis University Colleges of Law. Mr. Carr has been listed in *The Best Lawyers in America* since 1987.
Education: JD 1949, University of Illinois (Phi Alpha Delta); BA 1948, University of Illinois.
Admitted: 1950 Illinois; 1984 Missouri; 1950 U.S. Dist. Ct. (S. Dist. IL); 1955 U.S. Dist. Ct. (C. Dist. IL); 1970 U.S. Ct. App. (7th Cir.); 1973 U.S. Ct. App. (8th Cir.); 1975 U.S. Sup. Ct.; 1975 U.S. Ct. App. (D.C.); 1995 U.S. Dist. Ct. (E. Dist. MI).
Employment History: Partner 1950-present, Carr, Korein, Tillery, Kunin, Montroy & Glass.
Professional Associations: Inner Circle of Advocates 1975-present (President 1987-89); ABOTA; ITLA (Board of Governors); ATLA; ABA.
Firm: Carr, Korein, Tillery, Kunin, Montroy & Glass consists of 19 lawyers who practice primarily personal injury law, with particular emphasis on class actions, medical malpractice, FELA, Maritime and Jones Act, products liability, and business torts. *See complete firm profile in Appendix A. Mr. Carr also practices Personal Injury Law: Transportation, Personal Injury Law: Medical & Professional Malpractice and Workers' Compensation Law.*

REX CARR
Carr, Korein, Tillery, Kunin, Montroy & Glass
412 Missouri Avenue
East St. Louis, IL 62201

Phone: (618) 274-0434
Fax: (618) 274-8369
800: (800) 333 5297

Extensive Experience In:

• Product Liability

MARK GLASS - *Carr, Korein, Tillery, Kunin, Montroy & Glass* - 412 Missouri Avenue - East St. Louis, IL 62201 - Phone: (618) 274-0434, Fax: (618) 274-8369, 800: (800) 333-5297 - *See complete biographical profile in the Workers' Compensation Law Chapter, page 345.*

MORRIS LANE HARVEY - *Law Offices of Morris Lane Harvey* - 215 SE Third Street, Suite 100 - P.O. Box 820 - Fairfield, IL 62837 - Phone: (618) 842-5117, Fax: (618) 842-5773 - *See complete biographical profile in the Family Law Chapter, page 216.*

•**MARK D. HASSAKIS:** Mr. Hassakis practices personal injury law and workers' compensation law. He has also served on the Advisory Board of James Publishing Company for problems involving tort matters.
Education: JD 1976, St. Louis University; BA 1973, Northwestern University.
Admitted: 1976 Illinois; 1977 U.S. Dist. Ct. (S. Dist. IL); 1986 U.S. Ct. App. (7th Cir.); 1995 U.S. Sup. Ct.
Employment History: Principal 1976-present, Hassakis & Hassakis, P.C.
Representative Clients: Mr. Hassakis represents individuals, workers and consumers in the areas of personal injury and workers' compensation, professional malpractice and general tort damages and injuries.
Professional Associations: Jefferson County Bar Assn. 1976-present (President 1980); ISBA (Assembly Member 1978-84, 1988-94; Membership and Bar Activities Committee 1994-present; Committee on Delivery of Legal Services 1980-86); Illinois Bar Foundation (Board Member 1990-present); ABA; ITLA; ATLA.
Community Involvement: Mt. Vernon Downtown Development Corporation; Jefferson County Historical Society; Mt. Vernon West Rotary Club (President 1984-94); Mt. Vernon Bright and Beautiful (Board Member); Saints Constantine and Helen Greek Orthodox Church (Audit Committee 1993-96); Mt. Vernon Township High School (Board Member 1976-85).
Firm: Hassakis & Hassakis, P.C., has provided legal services to individual clients throughout southern Illinois for over 45 years. It has established a tradition of aggressively representing the individual in his or her claim against an employer, insurance company or other entity. The firm has established a niche in representing injured parties in premises liability claims and serious injury and wrongful death suits involving truck and motorcycle collisions, as well as construction negligence suits. The firm is composed of lawyers who recognize the needs of the client and who treat each client with the highest respect. The firm's members try to never forget that people are important. *Mr. Hassakis also practices Workers' Compensation Law and Personal Injury Law: Medical & Professional Malpractice.*

MARK D. HASSAKIS
Hassakis & Hassakis, P.C.
Boston Building
206 South Ninth Street
Suite 201
P.O. Box 706
Mt. Vernon, IL 62864

Phone: (618) 244-5335
Fax: (618) 244-5330
800: (800) 553-3125*

Extensive Experience In:

• Premises Liability
• Truck & Motorcycle Cases
• Construction Site Claims

*800 number is only available in area codes 618 and 217.

Chapter 19: Personal Injury Law: General

SANDOR KOREIN - *Carr, Korein, Tillery, Kunin, Montroy & Glass* - 412 Missouri Avenue - East St. Louis, IL 62201 - Phone: (618) 274-0434, Fax: (618) 274-8369 - *See complete biographical profile in the Personal Injury Law: Transportation Chapter, page 284.*

GERALD L. MONTROY - *Carr, Korein, Tillery, Kunin, Montroy & Glass* - 412 Missouri Avenue - East St. Louis, IL 62201 - Phone: (618) 397-9191, Fax: (618) 274-8369, 800: (800) 333-5297 - *See complete biographical profile in the Personal Injury Law: Medical & Professional Malpractice Chapter, page 274.*

ROBERT C. NELSON - *Nelson, Bement, Stubblefield & Levenhagen, P.C.* - 420 North High Street - P.O. Box Y - Belleville, IL 62222 - Phone: (618) 277-4000, Fax: (618) 277-1136 - *See complete biographical profile in the Workers' Compensation Law Chapter, page 346.*

TIMOTHY C. STUBBLEFIELD - *Nelson, Bement, Stubblefield & Levenhagen, P.C.* - 420 North High Street - P.O. Box Y - Belleville, IL 62222 - Phone: (618) 277-4000 or (618) 277-8260, Fax: (618) 277-1136 - *See complete biographical profiles in the Civil Appellate Law Chapter, page 87 and Family Law Chapter, page 218.*

•STEPHEN M. TILLERY - *Carr, Korein, Tillery, Kunin, Montroy & Glass* - 5520 West Main Street - Belleville, IL 62223 - Phone: (618) 277-1180, Fax: (618) 277-9804 - *See complete biographical profile in the Personal Injury Law: Transportation Chapter, page 284.*

JOHN WOMICK
Womick & Associates, Chartered
1100 West Main Street
Carbondale, IL 62901

Phone: (618) 529-2440
Fax: (618) 457-2680
800: (800) 598-2440

•JOHN WOMICK: Mr. Womick has practiced primarily in the area of general personal injury law for the past 18 years, with an emphasis in medical malpractice, product liability, Jones Act, and workers' compensation cases. He has repeatedly acquired substantial verdicts in the southern Illinois area in these types of cases.

Education: JD 1971, University of Illinois; BA 1968, University of Illinois.

Admitted: 1971 Illinois; 1972 U.S. Dist. Ct. (S. Dist. IL); 1976 U.S. Dist. Ct. (N. Dist. IL); 1980 U.S. Sup. Ct.; 1984 U.S. Ct. App. (7th Cir.); 1989 U.S. Ct. App. (6th Cir.); 1994 U.S. Dist. Ct. (C. Dist. IL).

Employment History: 1971-present, Womick & Associates, Chartered; City Attorney 1972-79, City of Carbondale.

Representative Clients: Mr. Womick represents primarily individuals who have been injured. He has no insurance companies as clients.

Professional Associations: ATLA 1989-present; ITLA 1983-present (Board of Directors); ISBA 1971-present.

Community Involvement: Mr. Womick is a member of Our Savior Lutheran Church.

Firm: In addition to John Womick, Charles Cavaness and Julie Dudenbostel are employed by the firm. The emphasis of the firm is on general personal injury practice and workers' compensation law. *Mr. Womick also practices Personal Injury Law: Medical & Professional Malpractice, Personal Injury Law: Transportation, and Workers' Compensation Law.*

CHAPTER 20

PERSONAL INJURY LAW: MEDICAL & PROFESSIONAL MALPRACTICE

For injuries caused by the negligence of a medical professional or lawyer, the government generally does not punish the wrongdoer but gives the victim the right to pursue a private, civil lawsuit, called a tort action, against the wrongdoer. This chapter outlines the actions that lead to most professional malpractice lawsuits. General accidents and injuries and injuries occurring to workers on the job are discussed in the Personal Injury Law: General Chapter. The Personal Injury Law: Transportation Chapter deals with actions that result from transportation-related accidents.

PROFESSIONAL MALPRACTICE

A malpractice lawsuit can be brought against any kind of professional, including psychologists, clergy, accountants, financial advisors, doctors, and lawyers. Two common types of professional malpractice claims are those against doctors and lawyers.

LEGAL MALPRACTICE

There is no precise definition of legal malpractice. Generally speaking, a lawyer commits legal malpractice when he or she fails to provide quality legal services to a client. Bad conduct that is not unique to lawyers may lead to a lawsuit, but it does not constitute legal malpractice. For instance, a lawyer who misses deadlines, inadequately prepares for a trial, or represents both sides in a dispute without informing both parties, commits legal malpractice. A lawyer who steals funds from, assaults, or defrauds a client, has committed a crime but probably has not committed legal malpractice. Many of the steps discussed in the How to Hire an Attorney Chapter may help a consumer avoid malpractice disputes.

ELEMENTS OF LEGAL MALPRACTICE

A legal malpractice lawsuit generally has four elements: duty, breach, injury, and proximate causation. A judge or jury examines all four elements in a legal malpractice trial, and if any element is missing, the plaintiff cannot recover.

Duty

The duty a lawyer owes his or her client has two components. The lawyer must exercise the legal skill that a competent attorney would exercise, and must meet all of his or her fiduciary obligations to the client. Fiduciary obligations include a duty of undivided loyalty to the client's interests and confidentiality. No lawyer is expected to know the law so well that he or she can give perfect answers to obscure legal questions. Lawyers are expected to know how to research issues and to recognize their limits when they reach an unsettled or unclear area of law.

Breach

A lawyer commits a breach if he or she fails to do his or her duty. Breach is frequently the toughest element to prove in a legal malpractice lawsuit, because a lawyer can make mistakes and still not commit a breach. Law is an inexact science. Even competent lawyers frequently disagree on the best course of action in a particular legal matter. Sometimes, the strategy chosen is a combination of knowledge about the law and how the lawyer thinks a judge or jury will react to the facts of a case. A client may be able to show that another lawyer would have pursued a different strategy, and still the client may be unable to show that the first lawyer committed a breach.

Injury

A plaintiff must show that he or she was injured by the lawyer's breach of duty. For example, a lawyer might miss a deadline, but if he or she is subsequently granted an extension, the client is not injured. If missing the deadline bars the plaintiff's claim, however, he or she has been injured. A lawyer might forget to assert a claim, but if the claim would have been denied anyway, the client has not been injured. Usually a plaintiff only recovers direct economic losses, such as the money needed to pay another attorney to re-do legal work, any fees or penalties paid, or any interest income lost because of an attorney's malpractice. It is difficult, although not impossible, to recover for speculative losses, that is, for what might have happened if a different lawyer had been hired, emotional losses, or legal expenses incurred in hiring a new lawyer to sue the previous lawyer.

Proximate Cause

Finally, the client must show that the breach was the proximate cause of the plaintiff's injury. Proximate cause is a thorny legal concept that essentially asks whether the breach was sufficiently responsible for the injury so that the lawyer should be held responsible. Proximate cause is easiest to prove if a lawyer misses a deadline or gives advice that is clearly wrong. In these cases, the client usually can show exactly what would have happened had the lawyer met the deadline or given correct advice. Proximate cause is more difficult to show in cases in which a lawyer pursues a course of action in trial that works to the client's disadvantage. In this case, the client has to show what the judge or jury would have done had the lawyer chosen another strategy. This can be difficult to show. The client needs to prove, to the judge or jury's satisfaction, what another lawyer would have done, and how the jury in the underlying case would have reacted to that strategy. The first lawyer might argue successfully that even if a different strategy had been pursued, the outcome of the case would have been the same.

Attorneys who try legal malpractice cases have had increasing success recently with new theories of liability for legal malpractice. One trend focuses on attorney investments and financial dealings. Courts have found that a lawyer breached a fiduciary duty to a client by failing to reveal stock ownership in an opposing corporate party, or by using insider information learned about the client to make profits in the stock market. Another growing trend is for the court to allow claims brought against lawyers by persons other than clients. For example, the beneficiaries under a client's will might bring a legal malpractice action against a lawyer who incorrectly drafted a deceased client's will if the beneficiaries are dissatisfied with their share of the estate. Depositors in a failed savings and loan company might sue lawyers who gave advice to the savings and loan.

MEDICAL MALPRACTICE

Medical malpractice includes many forms of liability-producing conduct that occur in rendering medical services. Medical malpractice does not apply solely to medical doctors. Psychiatrists, dentists, nurses, and hospitals can be sued for medical malpractice. Wrongful conduct that is not unique to doctors or other health care professionals may give rise to a legal action, but does not meet the definition of medical malpractice. For example, a patient might bring a breach of contract claim against a doctor who fails to provide services agreed upon in a contract, or a patient might bring fraud charges against a doctor for misrepresenting his or her expertise. These are not medical malpractice claims.

ELEMENTS OF MEDICAL MALPRACTICE

A medical malpractice lawsuit—like a legal malpractice action—generally has four elements: duty, breach, injury, and proximate causation. A judge or jury examines all four elements in a medical malpractice trial, and if any element is missing, the plaintiff cannot recover.

Duty

A doctor who has agreed to treat a patient has a duty to that patient to use at least the same level of care that any other reasonably competent doctor would use to treat a condition under the same circumstances. One problem in determining duty is that the average juror or judge may not be able to determine what a doctor should have done in a particular instance. Medical malpractice lawsuits require expert testimony from another doctor as to the standard of care that should have been given. The plaintiff needs an affidavit from a medical expert when starting a lawsuit.

There are many complex questions in deciding what testimony to allow. In every case, the judge must decide whether a doctor's actions are to be judged against all other doctors or only against doctors specializing in a particular type of practice. Some judges may allow evidence of what other doctors in the same region would have done, while some judges allow testimony about what doctors in other parts of the country would have done. Success in a medical malpractice case frequently depends on how a judge answers these questions.

Breach

A person breaches a duty when he or she fails to use the same level of care another reasonably competent professional would exercise in the same circumstances. Breach is frequently the toughest point to prove in a medical malpractice lawsuit, because competent doctors frequently disagree on the best course of action in a particular medical matter. Like law, medicine is an inexact science. A client may show that another doctor would have taken a different course of action and still be unable to show the first doctor committed a breach. The plaintiff must prove the level of care a reasonably competent professional would have exercised and show that the defendant's actions fell short of that level.

Injury

Injury is usually not difficult to prove in medical malpractice actions. A patient who dies or suffers a permanent disability or chronic pain obviously has been injured. Often, it is the doctor who has most trouble disproving this element because it can be difficult to prove that a patient who claims to be injured is not. Many legitimate injuries, such as whiplash, have few quantifiable manifestations even though they cause their sufferers to feel pain. An injury need not be permanent to be compensable.

Proximate Cause

Finally, proximate causation can be difficult for a patient to prove because a bad result does not necessarily equal malpractice. Even with excellent treatment, a patient might not recover totally from the condition for which he or she seeks treatment. A doctor accused of malpractice might be able to show that even had a different treatment been followed, the patient would have suffered identical injuries.

THIRD-PARTY LAWSUITS

Third persons can sometimes bring medical malpractice lawsuits against doctors. For example, a person who gets an infectious disease from a friend might sue the friend's doctor for inadequately treating the disease. A person injured in an automobile accident might bring a medical malpractice lawsuit against the driver's doctor if the doctor medicated the patient without telling the patient not to operate a vehicle while under the effect of the medication.

CONSENT FORMS

Consent forms required by most doctors and hospitals typically include warnings that patients must assume all the risks of any surgical procedures. By signing one of these forms, a patient does not give up all rights to sue if things go wrong. Such an agreement may not be valid if a doctor does not fully inform the patient of risks associated with a particular procedure. Even a valid consent form is no protection for a doctor who either performs surgery that goes beyond the consent given or who fails to perform a procedure according to well-accepted medical standards.

RESOURCES

Illinois Attorney General's Office, 500 South Second Street, Springfield, IL 62706, phone: (217) 782-1090 or 100 West Randolph Street, Chicago, IL 60601, phone: (312) 814-3000.

Illinois State Bar Association, Illinois Bar Center, 424 South Second Street, Springfield, IL 62701, phone: (217) 525-1760.

Personal Injury Law: Medical & Professional Malpractice Leading Illinois Attorneys

Illinois' Most Respected Legal Counsel As Selected By Their Peers.

The Leading Illinois Attorneys below were recommended by their peers in a statewide survey.

The Leading Illinois Attorneys listed below were nominated as exceptional by their peers in a statewide survey conducted by American Research Corporation (ARC). ARC asked several thousand licensed Illinois attorneys to name the lawyer to whom they would send a close friend or family member in need of legal assistance in specific areas of law. The attorneys below were nominated in the area of Personal Injury Law: Medical & Professional Malpractice.

Because the survey results (all practice area results combined) represent less than three percent of Illinois' practicing attorneys, this list should not be construed as a complete list. Nevertheless, it is an excellent source of highly qualified and reputable Illinois attorneys.

For information on ARC's survey methodology, see page *xi*.
For the complete list of Leading Illinois Consumer Attorneys, see page *xii*.

The Leading Illinois Attorneys below are listed alphabetically in accordance with the geographic region in which their offices are located. Note that attorneys may handle clients from a broad geographic area; attorneys are not restricted to only serving clients residing within the cities in which their offices are located.

An attorney whose name appears in bold has included a biographical profile in this chapter.

Cook & Collar Counties

Avgeris, George N. - Hinsdale
Baum, David M. - Chicago
Benjamin, Fred I. - Chicago
Berdelle, Richard L., Jr. - Chicago
Bernstein, Arnold - Arlington Heights, page 266
Bobb, Patricia C. - Chicago
Boyle, Charles A. - Chicago
Bravos, Zachary M. - Wheaton
Burke, Dennis J. - Chicago
Burke, John M. - Chicago
Burke, William J. - Chicago
Canel, James H. - Chicago
Cirignani, Thomas R. - Chicago, page 266
Clancy, Thomas A. - Chicago, page 267
Clifford, Robert A. - Chicago
Coladarci, Peter R. - Chicago
Conway, Kevin J. - Chicago
Cooney, Robert J., Jr. - Chicago
Corboy, Philip H. - Chicago
Corboy, Philip Harnett, Jr. - Chicago
Crowe, Brian L. - Chicago
Curcio, Joseph R. - Chicago
Davidson, Keith L. - Chicago
De Jong, David J. - Chicago
Decker, David A. - Waukegan
Demetrio, Michael K. - Chicago
Demetrio, Thomas A. - Chicago
Demos, James T. - Chicago
Denny, Steven A. - Chicago
Dentino, Michael P. - Chicago
DeSanto, James J. - Libertyville
Duffy, John M. - Chicago

Durkin, Kevin P. - Chicago
Ekl, Terry A. - Clarendon Hills
Enright, Karen A. - Chicago
Episcope, Paul B. - Chicago
Erb, John C. - Chicago
Esrig, Jerry A. - Chicago
Farina, James L. - Chicago
Foote, Robert M. - Aurora
Ford, Christopher - Chicago
Frost, Michael J. - Chicago
Galliani, William R. - Chicago
Gifford, Geoffrey L. - Chicago
Goldberg, Barry D. - Chicago
Goldberg, Jeffrey M. - Chicago, page 268
Goldstein, Louis S. - Chicago
Goodman, Bruce D. - Chicago, page 268
Gorey, John J. - North Riverside
Harte, William J. - Chicago
Healy, Martin J., Jr. - Chicago
Hebeisen, Keith A. - Chicago, page 269
Hofeld, Albert F. - Chicago
Hoscheit, John J. - St. Charles
Hurley, Christopher T. - Chicago
Indomenico, Sal - Chicago
Jones, Robert E. - Wheaton
Kaiser, Daniel J. - Bensenville
Karahalios, James N. - Chicago
Karchmar, Larry - Chicago
Karr, Robert W. - Chicago
Kelly, E. Michael - Chicago
Kleinmuntz, Ira M. - Chicago
Knippen, James H. - Wheaton

Kominsky, Robert - Chicago
Kramer, Jack L. - Chicago
Kremin, David K. - Chicago
Lamont, John M. - Aurora
Lane, Fred - Chicago
Lane, Stephen I. - Chicago
Latherow, Jerry A. - Chicago
Lavin, Terrence J. - Chicago
Leahy, Tom - Chicago
Leopold, Valerie A. - Chicago
Levin, Steven M. - Chicago
Lindner, George P. - Aurora, page 270
Loggans, Susan E. - Chicago
Mahoney, Patrick E. - Chicago
Marino, Frank C. - Chicago
Miroballi, Joseph J. - Chicago, page 270
Mirza, Jerome - Chicago
Moran, Terence J. - Chicago
Motherway, Nicholas J. - Chicago
Mullen, John C. - Chicago
Mullen, Michael T. - Chicago
Munday, John J. - Chicago
Nathan, Thomas J. - Chicago
Ozmon, Laird M. - Joliet
Ozmon, Nat P. - Chicago
Patterson, Robert B. - Chicago
Pavalon, Eugene - Chicago
Pavich, Robert J. - Chicago
Pfaff, Bruce R. - Chicago
Phillips, John G. - Chicago
Phillips, Stephen D. - Chicago
Postilion, Michael H. - Chicago
Power, Joseph A., Jr. - Chicago
Reuland, Timothy J. - Aurora
Robbins, Elliott H. - Chicago
Rogers, Larry R., Sr. - Chicago
Rogich, Richard B. - Chicago
Salvi, Albert J. - Waukegan
Salvi, Patrick A. - Waukegan
Scanlan, Edmund J. - Chicago
Schaffner, Howard S. - Chicago
Schwartz, Allen N. - Chicago
Schwartz, John B. - Chicago
Slutsky, Mark G. - Chicago
Smith, Todd A. - Chicago
Speers, Robert L. - Aurora
Sussman, Jeffrey B. - Chicago
Thompson, Charles F., Jr. - Aurora
Touhy, Timothy J. - Chicago
Walsh, Edward J., Jr. - Wheaton
Winkler, Charles R. - North Riverside
Zaideman, Robert J. - Chicago

NORTHWESTERN ILLINOIS INCLUDING ROCKFORD & QUAD CITIES

Alexander, Peter - Rockford
Barrett, Gregory E. - Rockford
Bertrand, Louis L. - Peru
Boreen, John M. - Rockford
Brooks, Jack L. - Rock Island
Cacciatore, William T. - Rockford
Donohue, James L. - Rockford
Fieweger, Peter C. - Rock Island
Haldeman, Richard R. - Rockford
Kavensky, Craig L. - Rock Island
Lefstein, Stuart R. - Rock Island
Lousberg, Peter H. - Rock Island
Perrecone, Frank A. - Rockford
Raccuglia, Anthony C. - Peru
Sparkman, James D. - Rockford
Switzer, Peter S. - Rockford
Turner, Harold L. - Rockford
VanHooreweghe, Francis R. - Moline
Warner, Michael J. - Rock Island

CENTRAL ILLINOIS

Auler, Robert I. - Urbana
Beeman, Bruce A. - Springfield
Blan, Kenneth W., Jr. - Danville
Bowles, James E. - Peoria
Brady, Gerald, Jr. - Peoria
Bruno, Thomas A. - Urbana
Clark, Gary L. - Peoria, page 272
Delano, Charles H., III - Springfield
Dorris, David V. - Bloomington
Durree, Edward D. - Peoria
Eberspacher, David Y. - Mattoon
Faber, William C., Jr. - Decatur
Gadau, John E. - Champaign
Hagen, Henry C. - Springfield
Hagle, James J. - Urbana
Halliday, Ronald E. - Peoria
Hefner, M. John, Jr. - Mattoon
Heller, Harlan - Mattoon
Holley, Grady E. - Springfield
Joy, Richard M. - Champaign
Kelly, Timothy - Bloomington
Kreckman, Alfred H., Jr. - Paris
Londrigan, Thomas F. - Springfield
Maher, Jerelyn D. - Peoria
Manion, Paul T. - Danville
McElvain, Mike - Bloomington
Mellen, Thomas J., II - Danville
Nicoara, John P. - Peoria
Osborne, Stephen M. - Springfield
Owen, Robert M. - Decatur
Phebus, Joseph W. - Urbana
Randle, Craig A. - Springfield
Rose, Raymond - Peoria
Slevin, John A. - Peoria
Strodel, Robert C. - Peoria, page 273
West, Richard T. - Champaign
Willoughby, Stephen O. - Decatur

Chapter 20: Personal Injury Law: Medical & Professional Malpractice

SOUTHERN ILLINOIS

Bonifield, Jerald J. - Belleville
Callis, Lance - Granite City
Carr, Rex - East St. Louis, page 274
Chapman, Morris B. - Granite City
Cook, Bruce N. - Belleville
Cueto, Amiel - Belleville
Douglas, Robert L. - Robinson
Hughes, R. Courtney - Carbondale
Keefe, Thomas Q., Jr. - Belleville
Korein, Sandor - East St. Louis
Lockwood, Brocton D. - Marion

Mendillo, James R. - Belleville
Montroy, Gerald L. - East St. Louis, page 274
Murphy, G. Patrick - Marion
Nowak, Michael K. - Belleville
Peel, Gary E. - Edwardsville
Prince, Mark D. - Carbondale
Reagan, Michael J. - Belleville
Ripplinger, George R. - Belleville
Tillery, Stephen M. - Belleville
Weilmuenster, J. Michael - Belleville

Biographical Profiles of Personal Injury Law: Medical & Professional Malpractice Leading Illinois Attorneys

The Leading Illinois Attorneys profiled below were nominated as exceptional by their peers in a statewide survey conducted by American Research Corporation (ARC). ARC asked several thousand licensed Illinois attorneys to name the lawyer to whom they would send a close friend or family member in need of legal assistance in specific areas of law. The attorneys below were nominated in the area of Personal Injury Law: Medical & Professional Malpractice.

Because the survey results (all practice area results combined) represent less than three percent of Illinois' practicing attorneys, this list should not be construed as a complete list. Nevertheless, it is an excellent source of highly qualified and reputable Illinois attorneys.

For information on ARC's survey methodology, see page *xi*.
For the complete list of Leading Illinois Consumer Attorneys, see page *xii*.
For the list of Leading Illinois Personal Injury Law: Medical & Professional Malpractice Attorneys, see page 262.

The Leading Illinois Attorneys below are listed alphabetically in accordance with the geographic region in which their offices are located. Note that attorneys may handle clients from a broad geographic area; attorneys are not limited to only serving clients residing within the cities in which their offices are located.

The two-line attorney listings in this section are of attorneys who practice in this area but whose full biographical profiles appear in other sections of this book. A bullet "•" preceding a name indicates the attorney was nominated in this particular area of law.

For information on the format of the full biographical profiles, consult the "Using the Consumer Guidebook" section on page *xviii*.

The following abbreviations are used throughout these profiles:

App.	Appellate
Cir.	Circuit
Ct.	Court
Dist.	District
Sup.	Supreme
JD	Juris Doctor (Doctor of Law)
LLB	Legum Baccalaureus (Bachelor of Laws)
LLD	Legum Doctor (Doctor of Laws)
LLM	Legum Magister (Master of Laws)
ADR	Alternative Dispute Resolution
ABA	American Bar Association
ABOTA	American Board of Trial Advocates
ATLA	Association of Trial Lawyers of America
CBA	Chicago Bar Association
ISBA	Illinois State Bar Association
ITLA	Illinois Trial Lawyers Association
NBTA	National Board of Trial Advocacy

Chapter 20: Personal Injury Law: Medical & Professional Malpractice

Cook & Collar Counties

•**GEORGE N. AVGERIS** - *George N. Avgeris, Chartered, Attorney at Law* - 29 East First Street - Hinsdale, IL 60521
Phone: (630) 654-4161, Fax: (630) 654-9661 - *See complete biographical profile in the Personal Injury Law: General Chapter, page 238.*

ARNOLD BERNSTEIN
Attorney at Law
121 South Wilke
Suite 101
Arlington Heights, IL 60005

Phone: (847) 394-4017
Fax: (847) 797-9090

Extensive Experience In:

• Medical Malpractice Litigation

•**ARNOLD BERNSTEIN:** Mr. Bernstein practices medical malpractice and personal injury litigation, including the trial of sophisticated litigation matters. He has represented individuals with severe brain injuries, undiagnosed cancer, and other similar issues. He maintains an appellate practice that is currently involved in medical malpractice matters. In addition to his law education, he is a Certified Public Accountant.
Education: JD 1977, John Marshall Law School; BS 1972, Northern Illinois University; CPA Certificate 1986, State of Illinois.
Admitted: 1977 Illinois; 1979 U.S. Dist. Ct. (N. Dist. IL).
Employment History: Sole Practitioner 1982-present; Partner 1979-82, Karatosic and Bernstein.
Representative Clients: Mr. Bernstein represents plaintiffs in personal injury matters.
Professional Associations: ITLA (Medical Malpractice Committee 1993).
Firm: The firm is involved in representing people who have been wronged by the negligent acts of medical professionals. Mr. Bernstein advocates his clients' positions and strives to obtain optimal benefits on behalf of his clients and to assure that persons seriously injured are justly compensated. The firm maintains access to medical/legal software that allows for the creation of demonstrative aids for purposes of settlement and trial. *Mr. Bernstein also practices Personal Injury Law: General.*

THOMAS R. CIRIGNANI
Thomas R. Cirignani & Associates
200 West Madison Avenue
Suite 3660
Chicago, IL 60606

Phone: (312) 346-8700
Fax: (312) 346-5180

Extensive Experience In:

• Medical Negligence
• Birth Injuries
• Wrongful Death

•**THOMAS R. CIRIGNANI:** Mr. Cirignani is a nationally known trial lawyer who primarily practices personal injury litigation, with a concentration in the area of medical negligence. He has successfully represented individuals and families across the country in complex litigation for injuries suffered through the negligence of physicians, hospitals, nurses, and other health care providers. He has gained recognition for his skills in cross-examination of medical experts, and is frequently a requested guest speaker. Mr. Cirignani has successfully litigated cases in all areas of medicine, including catastrophic birth injuries, misdiagnosis of cancer and other diseases, surgical errors, and anesthesia errors. He is a speaker on medical malpractice at seminars for the Illinois Trial Lawyers Association and has also been a guest lecturer at a local teaching hospital. He is also a contributing member of the Illinois State Bar Association and the New York Trial Lawyers Association. Mr. Cirignani is the coauthor of the chapter on cancer for an Illinois Institute for Continuing Legal Education publication. He is a member of the Million Dollar Advocates Forum.
Education: JD 1978, John Marshall Law School; BA 1973, University of Illinois.
Admitted: 1978 Illinois; 1978 U.S. Dist. Ct. (N. Dist. IL).
Representative Clients: Mr. Cirignani represents individuals and families who have sustained a devastating loss through a personal injury or an act of medical negligence. References are available upon request.
Professional Associations: ABA; ATLA; ITLA; CBA; ISBA.
Firm: The firm of Thomas R. Cirignani & Associates limits its practice to representing individuals and families who have suffered a loss through a personal injury or an act of medical negligence. The five-lawyer firm is recognized for its concentration and experience in matters involving medical negligence. One of the lawyers at Thomas R. Cirignani & Associates is also a dual board certified physician, while another lawyer is board certified in respiratory care.

•**THOMAS A. CLANCY:** Mr. Clancy practices primarily in the areas of personal injury, wrongful death, medical malpractice, and products liability. As President of the Illinois State Bar Association, and in other elected and appointed positions, Mr. Clancy has worked to make the legal profession responsive to the community.
Education: JD 1973, Indiana University; BA 1969, Loyola University; 1967-68, Rome Center of Liberal Arts, Rome, Italy.
Admitted: 1974 Illinois; 1973 Indiana; 1974 Florida.
Employment History: Partner 1994-present, Clancy & Stevens; Partner 1986-74, Law Offices of Thomas A. Clancy; Partner 1978-86, Mullen & Clancy; Associate 1974-78, John C. Mullen & Associates.
Professional Associations: ISBA [President 1991-92; Mutual Insurance Company (President 1993-94)]; ABA (House of Delegates 1989-92); CBA; ITLA (Board of Managers 1977-present); ATLA; Illinois Bar Foundation (Director 1996-present); American Bar Foundation (Fellow).
Community Involvement: Special Supreme Court Committee on the Administration of Justice 1991-93; Coordinated Advice and Referral Program for Legal Services [Board of Directors (President 1996-present)]; Illinois U.S. Senate Judicial Nominations Committee 1993-present; Chicago Crime Commission.
Firm: Clancy & Stevens is a small firm dedicated to providing personalized legal service to its clients. In addition to Mr. Clancy, Jeanine Stevens is a well-respected attorney in the personal injury field. She received her JD from DePaul University. Together, Mr. Clancy and Ms. Stevens bring to the community extensive experience in representing injured persons. *Mr. Clancy also practices Personal Injury Law: General, Personal Injury Law: Transportation and Personal Injury Law: Products Liability.*

THOMAS A. CLANCY
Clancy & Stevens
Barrister Hall
Suite 220
29 South LaSalle Street
Chicago, IL 60603-1501

Phone: (312) 782-2800
Fax: (312) 782-2852

Extensive Experience In:
• Products Liability

•**ROBERT A. CLIFFORD** - *Clifford Law Offices* - 120 North LaSalle Street, 31st Floor - Chicago, IL 60602 - Phone: (312) 899-9090, Fax: (312) 251-1160 - *See complete biographical profile in the Personal Injury Law: Transportation Chapter, page 280.*

•**JAMES J. DE SANTO** - *Law Offices of James J. DeSanto, P.C.* - 339 North Milwaukee Avenue - Libertyville, IL 60048 - Phone: (847) 816-8100, Fax: (847) 816-8126 - *See complete biographical profile in the Personal Injury Law: General Chapter, page 239.*

•**KEVIN P. DURKIN** - *Clifford Law Offices* - 120 North LaSalle Street, 31st Floor - Chicago, IL 60602 - Phone: (312) 899-9090, Fax: (312) 251-1160 - *See complete biographical profile in the Personal Injury Law: General Chapter, page 239.*

SCOTT B. GIBSON - *Law Offices of Scott B. Gibson, Ltd.* - 415 West Washington Street, Suite 103 - Waukegan, IL 60085 - Phone: (847) 263-5100, Fax: (847) 249-7588 - *See complete biographical profile in the Personal Injury Law: General Chapter, page 240.*

Chapter 20: Personal Injury Law: Medical & Professional Malpractice

JEFFREY M. GOLDBERG

Jeffrey M. Goldberg & Associates, Ltd.
20 North Clark Street
Suite 3100
Chicago, IL 60602

Phone: (312) 236-4146
Fax: (312) 236-5913

Extensive Experience In:

- Birth Injury Litigation
- Medical Malpractice
- Product Liability

•**JEFFREY M. GOLDBERG:** Mr. Goldberg has concentrated his practice in the representation of individuals who have been seriously injured or who have died as a result of medical malpractice, product design defects, aviation or transportation accidents, and other similar issues. He has represented multiple individuals with severe brain injuries, spinal cord injuries, and other severe permanent injuries. He is the senior member of his firm which practices primarily in this area. In addition to individual representation, he has been involved in class action lawsuits on behalf of multiple tort victims in birth control device situations and similar matters. He is the current Secretary of the Illinois Trial Lawyers Association and has served on its Executive Board for many years. A frequent speaker at continuing legal education seminars in Illinois, he has published multiple articles, and the lead chapter in the *Medical Malpractice Handbook,* published by the Illinois Institute for Continuing Legal Education. He strives to obtain optimal benefits on behalf of his clients, and to assure that persons seriously injured need never again worry about financial concerns as a result of their injuries. In addition to his law education, he has a background in mechanical engineering and is also a pilot.
Education: JD 1974, John Marshall Law School (Associate Editor, *Law Review*); BS 1970, Bradley University.
Admitted: 1974 Illinois; 1974 U.S. Dist. Ct. (N. Dist. IL); 1988 U.S. Ct. App. (7th Cir.); 1990 U.S. Sup. Ct.
Employment History: 1974-present, Jeffrey M. Goldberg & Associates, Ltd.
Professional Associations: ITLA (Treasurer 1994; Secretary 1995; Board of Directors 1985-present); CBA [Tort Litigation Section (Chair 1978; Vice Chair 1977; Judicial Evaluation Committee 1978-85)]; ATLA (Birth Trauma Litigation Section; Aviation Section); Lawyers Pilots Bar Assn.; Legal Clinic for the Disabled (Board of Directors); Organization for Rehabilitation and Training (Board of Directors).
Firm: The firm is structured to maximize recoveries for clients. It is composed of experienced attorneys who have diverse backgrounds in the representation of seriously injured individuals. The firm maintains its own audio/visual department for the creation of demonstrative aids for purposes of settlement and trial. The firm has access to multiple national computer banks which it utilizes for state-of-the-art research. The firm also has on its full-time staff two nurses and a Board Certified physician for review and analysis of medical records to ensure appropriate interpretation. *Mr. Goldberg also practices Personal Injury Law: General and Personal Injury Law: Transportation.*

BRUCE D. GOODMAN

Steinberg, Polacek & Goodman
309 West Washington Street
Suite 500
Chicago, IL 60606

Phone: (312) 782-1386
Fax: (312) 782-6739

Extensive Experience In:

- Medical Malpractice
- Personal Injury Law: General
- Transportation

•**BRUCE D. GOODMAN:** Mr. Goodman practices in the areas of personal injury, products liability, and medical malpractice. He represents children and adults in cases against physicians, hospitals, nursing homes and other health care providers. He has handled a wide variety of drug and product liability claims, including L-tryptophan and Copper 7 litigation. He also represents clients in product liability, construction, aviation, and automobile cases. Mr. Goodman is a frequent lecturer on trial techniques and advocacy for several professional organizations in Illinois. He is the author of *Trying the Soft Tissue Injury Case in Illinois.*
Education: JD 1974, DePaul University; BA 1971, University of Illinois.
Admitted: 1974 Illinois; U.S. Ct. App. (7th Cir.); U.S. Dist. Ct. (N. Dist. IL); U.S. Claims Ct.
Employment History: Principal, Steinberg, Polacek & Goodman.
Professional Associations: CBA; ISBA; ABA; ATLA; ITLA (Medical Negligence Committee; Product Liability Committee).
Firm: Mr. Goodman's firm was founded in 1931 as Steinberg & Polacek, making it one of the oldest plaintiffs' law firms in Illinois. Mr. Goodman has been with the firm since he was admitted to the Illinois Bar in 1974, and has been its principal since 1980. The firm has four lawyers, all of whom concentrate on representing clients in significant injury and death cases. Mr. Goodman and his firm have obtained record-setting verdicts, and in cases before the Illinois Appellate Supreme Court, have established important precedents to benefit the victims of negligence. *Mr. Goodman also practices Personal Injury Law: General and Personal Injury Law: Transportation.*

ROBERT J. HAUSER - *Sullivan, Smith, Hauser & Noonan, Ltd.* - 25 North County Street - Waukegan, IL 60085-4342 - Phone: (847) 244-0111, Fax: (847) 244-0513 - *See complete biographical profile in the Criminal Law: Felonies & White Collar Crime Chapter, page 113.*

•**MARTIN J. HEALY, JR.** - *Martin J. Healy, Jr. & Associates* - 111 West Washington Street, Suite 1425 - Chicago, IL 60602 - Phone: (312) 977-0100, Fax: (312) 977-0795, 800: (800) 922-4500 - *See complete biographical profile in the Personal Injury Law: General Chapter, page 241.*

•**KEITH A. HEBEISEN:** Since becoming an attorney, trained over 13 years ago in law school under the tutelage of Robert Clifford, Mr. Hebeisen has obtained numerous large settlements and verdicts on behalf of clients in Illinois and other states. He represents clients in all types of personal injury and wrongful death cases, with particular interest in medical malpractice, product liability, and motor vehicle accident cases. Mr. Hebeisen has been an adjunct professor of law in Medical Malpractice Law at DePaul University College of Law and is the author of several publications, including *Proving Fault and Defending Auto Accident Cases—How to Handle Particular Types of Collision Cases,* Illinois Institute for Continuing Legal Education, Chicago, 1990; "Products Liability: In-Depth Study of Litigation Involving Products," *Jury Instructions/Pleadings/Summary Judgment, ISBA Law Education Series,* 1992. He edited the Illinois Trial Lawyers Association's *ITLA Medical Malpractice Trial Notebook* in 1992, 1993, 1994, and 1995, and was a contributing author in 1989. Mr. Hebeisen has planned and moderated numerous continuing legal education programs, including the ITLA Medical Malpractice Seminar, Chicago, 1994. He has presented numerous lectures at seminars for professional associations, including "Trial Demonstration—Closing Arguments," 13th Annual Defense Tactics Seminar Program, Chicago, 1995; "Economic Loss," ITLA Shotgun Seminar, Chicago, 1993; "Handling the Defendant's Expert," ITLA Point/Counterpoint Seminar, Chicago, 1994; and "Anesthesiology Malpractice Cases," ITLA Medical Malpractice Seminar, Chicago, 1994.
Education: JD 1983 with honor, DePaul University; BA 1976, University of Illinois.
Admitted: 1983 Illinois; 1983 U.S. Dist. Ct. (N. Dist. IL); 1987 U.S. Dist. Ct. (N. Dist. IL, Trial Bar); 1987 U.S. Dist. Ct. (N. Dist. IL); 1990 U.S. Dist. Ct. (E. Dist. WI); 1990 U.S. Dist. Ct. (W. Dist. MI); 1992 U.S. Ct. App. (6th Cir.); 1994 U.S. Sup. Ct.
Employment History: Partner 1995-present, Clifford Law Offices; Partner 1994-95, Corboy Demetrio Clifford; Associate 1984-94, Robert A. Clifford & Associates; Associate 1983-84, Albert F. Hofeld, Ltd.
Representative Clients: Mr. Hebeisen represents clients in all types of personal injury and wrongful death cases, with particular interest in medical malpractice, product liability, and motor vehicle accident cases.
Professional Associations: ITLA [Membership Committee (Cochair 1995); Elected Board of Managers 1989-present; Seminar Planning Committee (Chair 1990-91); Medical Negligence Committee 1989-present; Executive Committee 1995-96]; ISBA [*Illinois Bar Journal* (Standing Committee; Editorial Board 1995-96)]. *See complete firm profile in Appendix A. Mr. Hebeisen also practices Personal Injury Law: General and Personal Injury Law: Transportation.*

KEITH A. HEBEISEN
Clifford Law Offices
120 North LaSalle Street
31st Floor
Chicago, IL 60602
Phone: (312) 899-9090
Fax: (312) 251-1160
E-mail:
102554,2453@compuserve.com

Extensive Experience In:
• Motor Vehicle Accidents
• Products Liability
• Wrongful Death/Medical Malpractice

WILLIAM H. HOOKS - *Hooks Law Offices, P.C.* - Three First National Plaza, 52nd Floor - 70 West Madison Street, Suite 5200 - Chicago, IL 60602 - Phone: (312) 553-5252, Fax: (312) 553-1510 - *See complete biographical profile in the Criminal Law: Felonies & White Collar Crime Chapter, page 114.*

MARKHAM M. JEEP - *Markham M. Jeep, P.C.* - 450 North Green Bay Road - Waukegan, IL 60085 - Phone: (847) 360-3300, Fax: (847) 360-3303 - *See complete biographical profile in the Workers' Compensation Law Chapter, page 341.*

BRUCE M. KOHEN - *Anesi, Ozmon & Rodin, Ltd.* - 161 North Clark Street, Suite 2100 - Chicago, IL 60601 - Phone: (312) 372-3822, Fax: (312) 372-3833, 800: (800) 458-3822 within IL - *See complete biographical profile in the Personal Injury Law: General Chapter, page 242.*

•**STEPHEN I. LANE** - *Lane & Lane* - 33 North Dearborn Street, Suite 2300 - Chicago, IL 60602 - Phone: (312) 332-1400, Fax: (312) 899-8003 - *See complete biographical profile in the Personal Injury Law: General Chapter, page 244.*

•**JERRY A. LATHEROW** - *Law Office of Jerry A. Latherow* - 77 West Washington Street, Suite 1900 - Chicago, IL 60602 - Phone: (312) 372-0052, Fax: (312) 372-8043 - *See complete biographical profile in the Personal Injury Law: General Chapter, page 244.*

Chapter 20: Personal Injury Law: Medical & Professional Malpractice

GEORGE P. LINDNER

Lindner, Speers & Reuland, P.C.
54 West Downer Place
P.O. Box 5055
Aurora, IL 60507

Phone: (630) 892-8109
Fax: (630) 892-8151

Extensive Experience In:

• Civil Trials
• Medical Negligence Work

•**GEORGE P. LINDNER:** Mr. Lindner practices only plaintiffs' work, concentrating primarily in the area of medical/health care provider negligence. He also handles all forms of personal injury actions arising out of defective products, railroad negligence, automobile collisions, excessive force by law enforcement officials, and sexual harassment cases. Mr. Lindner tried his first jury case six weeks after receiving his law license and has tried numerous jury cases since that time. Mr. Lindner has spoken extensively at county and state seminars sponsored by the Illinois State Bar Association and by the Illinois Trial Lawyers Association.
Education: LLB 1965, University of Colorado; BA 1962, University of Colorado.
Admitted: 1965 Illinois; 1984 U.S. Dist. Ct. (N. Dist. IL); 1985 U.S. Ct. App. (7th Cir.).
Employment History: 1979-present, Lindner, Speers & Reuland, P.C.; 1965-79, Reid, Ochsenschlager, Murphy & Hupp.
Representative Clients: Mr. Lindner represents people who have been injured by the negligence of doctors and health care providers. He also represents people who have been injured by defective products, negligent drivers, negligent railroads, and abusive law enforcement officials.
Professional Associations: ISBA (Vice Chair 1995-96; Law Pac); Kane County Bar Assn. [Medical/Legal Committee 1993-95 (Chair)]; ITLA (Board of Managers 1985-present); ATLA 1965-present.
Community Involvement: YMCA (past Board Member); Kane County Bar Assn. (Pro Bono Program).
Firm: The firm was founded in 1979 by George Lindner, Robert Speers and Timothy Reuland. The firm has concentrated its practice in civil litigation since its inception. The firm handles cases which primarily involve injuries suffered by persons as a result of other people's negligence. The firm has consistently been among the leaders in the volume of cases tried to verdict in the state of Illinois.
See complete firm profile in Appendix A. Mr. Lindner also practices Personal Injury Law: General.

JOSEPH J. MIROBALLI

Anesi, Ozmon & Rodin, Ltd.
161 North Clark Street
Suite 2100
Chicago, IL 60601

Phone: (312) 372-3822
Fax: (312) 372-3833
800: (800) 458-3822 within IL

•**JOSEPH J. MIROBALLI:** Mr. Miroballi has been practicing almost exclusively in the exciting and challenging areas of medical malpractice and products liability for 16 years. He has handled medical malpractice cases involving almost every area of medicine. Mr. Miroballi has tried numerous cases involving hospital, physician and nursing home negligence in Cook County as well as many other counties in the state of Illinois. His clients have obtained substantial awards against many of the well-known medical institutions. In addition to being requested to speak to the legal community on the subject of medical malpractice, Mr. Miroballi has been invited as a guest lecturer to the medical profession and the insurance industry on subjects of medicine and the law, and products liability. He appeared as a guest panel speaker on CLTV in Chicago. In 1995, he and his partners visited many local unions throughout Illinois, talking about the recent changes in the laws which affect them and their rights as workers, consumers and patients. Mr. Miroballi has written and published numerous articles on various topics of law, particularly medical malpractice, including for the last five years, two chapters in *The Medical Malpractice Notebook,* which is published annually by the Illinois Trial Lawyers Association and the *Illinois Bar Journal.* He has also written and published articles for the medical profession on medical malpractice prevention, including for the World Medical Communications Organization and the National Medical Legal Information Network.
Education: JD 1979, John Marshall Law School; BA 1975, Northern Illinois University.
Admitted: 1979 Illinois; 1979 U.S. Dist. Ct. (N. Dist. IL).
Employment History: 1984-present, Anesi, Ozmon & Rodin, Ltd.; 1979-84, Albert F. Hofeld, Ltd.
Professional Associations: Justinian Society of Lawyers 1992-present; ATLA 1982-present; ITLA 1980-present; CBA 1981-present; ISBA 1979-present; ABA 1979-present; Federal Bar Assn. 1979-present.
Firm: Anesi, Ozmon & Rodin, Ltd., with 28 attorneys and a staff of over 100, is the largest law firm in Illinois concentrating its practice in the representation of injury victims. The firm is committed to vigorously representing its clients in the areas of personal injury litigation, workers' compensation, and Social Security practice. *See complete firm profile in Appendix A. Mr. Miroballi also practices Personal Injury Law: General and Personal Injury Law: Transportation.*

•**NAT P. OZMON** - *Anesi, Ozmon & Rodin, Ltd.* - 161 North Clark Street, Suite 2100 - Chicago, IL 60601 - Phone: (312) 372-3822, Fax: (312) 372-3833, 800: (800) 458-3822 within IL - *See complete biographical profile in the Personal Injury Law: General Chapter, page 246.*

•**ROBERT B. PATTERSON** - *Law Offices of Robert B. Patterson, Ltd.* - 221 North LaSalle Street, Suite 1050 - Chicago, IL 60601 - Phone: (312) 236-0995, Fax: (312) 984-5791 - *See complete biographical profile in the Personal Injury Law: General Chapter, page 246.*

DAVID E. RAPOPORT - *Rapoport & Kupets Law Offices* - O'Hare International Center - 10275 West Higgins Road, Suite 370 - Rosemont, IL 60018 - Phone: (847) 803-9880, Fax: (847) 803-9881, 800: (800) 545-6437 - *See complete biographical profile in the Personal Injury Law: Transportation Chapter, page 281.*

Personal Injury Law: Medical & Professional Malpractice Leading Illinois Attorneys

CURT N. RODIN - *Anesi, Ozmon & Rodin, Ltd.* - 161 North Clark Street, Suite 2100 - Chicago, IL 60601 - Phone: (312) 372-3822, Fax: (312) 372-3833, 800: (800) 458-3822 within IL - *See complete biographical profile in the Personal Injury Law: General Chapter, page 247.*

•**EDMUND J. SCANLAN** - *Law Offices of Edmund J. Scanlan, Ltd.* - 134 North LaSalle Street, Suite 220 - Chicago, IL 60602 - Phone: (312) 372-0020, Fax: (312) 372-1211 - *See complete biographical profile in the Personal Injury Law: General Chapter, page 248.*

JEFFREY M. SHANCER - *Law Offices of Jeffrey M. Shancer* - Three First National Plaza, Suite 3750 - Chicago, IL 60602 - Phone: (312) 558-5167, Fax: (312) 558-7767 - *See complete biographical profile in the Personal Injury Law: General Chapter, page 248.*

ROBERT N. WADINGTON - *Robert N. Wadington & Associates* - 111 West Washington Street, Suite 1460 - Chicago, IL 60602 - Phone: (312) 629-2706, Fax: (312) 629-8022 - *See complete biographical profile in the Personal Injury Law: General Chapter, page 249.*

NORTHWESTERN ILLINOIS
INCLUDING ROCKFORD & QUAD CITIES

•**CRAIG L. KAVENSKY** - *Winstein, Kavensky & Wallace* - 224 18th Street, Fourth Floor - Rock Island, IL 61201 - Phone: (309) 794-1515, Fax: (309) 794-9929 - *See complete biographical profiles in the Personal Injury Law: General Chapter, page 250 and Workers' Compensation Law Chapter, page 344.*

CENTRAL ILLINOIS

•**KENNITH W. BLAN, JR.** - *Blan Law Offices* - 712 West Fairchild - P.O. Box 1995 - Danville, IL 61834 - Phone: (217) 443-5400, Fax: (217) 443-5155 - *See complete biographical profile in the Personal Injury Law: General Chapter, page 252.*

Chapter 20: Personal Injury Law: Medical & Professional Malpractice

GARY L. CLARK

The Law Offices of
Frederic W. Nessler and Associates
433 Hamilton Boulevard
First Financial Plaza
Suite Two
Peoria, IL 61602

Phone: (309) 673-6404
Fax: (309) 674-6407

Extensive Experience In:

• Products Liability

•**GARY L. CLARK:** Mr. Clark is a private practitioner concentrating in personal injury litigation of all kinds. He has successfully handled cases in the fields of automobile negligence, products liability, premises liability and medical malpractice, resulting in significant recovery. Mr. Clark is the past Chair of the Tort Section Council of the Illinois State Bar Association. He is a *Certified Civil Trial Advocate by the National Board of Trial Advocacy. Mr. Clark is a frequent lecturer on tort law and civil litigation for the Peoria County Bar Association, the Illinois State Bar Association, the Illinois Trial Lawyers Association, and the Illinois Institute for Continuing Legal Education.

Education: LLB 1963, University of Illinois; BA 1960, St. Ambrose College (Delta Epsilon Sigma; Phi Delta Phi).

Admitted: 1963 Illinois; 1963 U.S. Dist. Ct. (S. Dist. Il.)

Employment History: Private Practice 1964-present.

Professional Associations: Peoria County Bar Assn.; ISBA [Assemblyman 1980-86, 1987-present; Tort Section Council 1980-86 (Vice Chair 1981-82; Chair 1982-83); Finance Committee 1982-83]; ATLA; ITLA; Society of Trial Lawyers of Illinois.

Firm: The firm also has offices at 305 Decatur Street, Lincoln, Illinois 62656; Two First Financial Plaza, Peoria, Illinois 61602; 352 Millikin Court, Decatur, Illinois 62523; 237 East Front Street, Bloomington, Illinois 61701; and 202 West Green Street, Urbana, Illinois 61801. *See complete firm profile in Appendix A. Mr. Clark also practices Personal Injury Law: General and Workers' Compensation Law.*

*The Supreme Court of Illinois does not recognize certifications of specialties in the practice of law. A certificate, award or recognition is not a requirement to practice law in Illinois.

MICHAEL B. METNICK - *Metnick, Wise, Cherry & Frazier* - Number One West Old State Capital Plaza - Myers Building, Suite 200 - Springfield, IL 62701 - Phone: (217) 753-4242, Fax: (217) 753-4642, 800: (800) 500-4242 - *See complete biographical profiles in the Personal Injury Law: General Chapter, page 253, Criminal Law: Felonies & White Collar Crime Chapter, page 117 and Family Law Chapter, page 212.*

FREDERIC W. NESSLER - *The Law Offices of Frederic W. Nessler and Associates* - 800 Myers Building - Springfield, IL 62701 - Phone: (217) 753-5533, Fax: (217) 753-4631 - *See complete biographical profile in the Personal Injury Law: General Chapter, page 253.*

•**JOHN P. NICOARA** - *Nicoara & Steagall* - 416 Main Street, Suite 815 - Peoria, IL 61602 - Phone: (309) 674-6085, Fax: (309) 674-6032 - *See complete biographical profile in the Personal Injury Law: General Chapter, page 254.*

EDWARD H. RAWLES - *Rawles, O'Byrne, Stanko & Kepley, P.C.* - 501 West Church Street - Champaign, IL 61820 - Phone: (217) 352-7661, Fax: (217) 352-2169 - *See complete biographical profile in the Personal Injury Law: General Chapter, page 255.*

•**JOHN A. SLEVIN** - *Vonachen, Lawless, Trager & Slevin* - 456 Fulton Street, Suite 425 - Peoria, IL 61602 - Phone: (309) 676-8986, Fax: (309) 676-4130 - *See complete biographical profile in the Personal Injury Law: General Chapter, page 255.*

ROBERT E. STINE - *Stine, Wolter & Greer* - 426 South Fifth Street - Springfield, IL 62701 - Phone: (217) 744-1000, Fax: (217) 744-1444 - *See complete biographical profile in the Personal Injury Law: General Chapter, page 256.*

•**ROBERT C. STRODEL:** Mr. Strodel is a *Board Certified Civil Trial Specialist by the National Board of Trial Advocacy, and specializes in personal injury litigation. He is both a general practitioner and a trial lawyer, and acts as prosecutor and defense counsel in criminal and civil litigation. He served two years active duty as a Special Agent, U.S. Army Counterintelligence Corps, and seven years in the Army Reserves. During active duty, he was cited for instruction in criminal law and investigation subjects by the U.S. Army CounterIntelligence School, Ft. Holabird, Maryland. Mr. Strodel has written numerous articles and books, is a frequent lecturer for educational and professional organizations, and has been an instructor in Business Law at Bradley University. He has received the Illinois State Bar Association's Lincoln Award for legal writing. In 1983, Mr. Strodel was appointed by President Reagan to the Presidential Commission for the German-American Tricentennial. In 1984, Mr. Strodel was decorated by the West German Government with the Officer's Cross of the Order of Merit for contributions to German-American relations. He is listed in the *Bar Register of Preeminent Lawyers; Who's Who in America; Who's Who in American Law; Who's Who in Society;* and Oxford's *Who's Who.*

Education: JD 1955, University of Michigan; BS 1952, Northwestern University.

Admitted: 1955 Illinois; U.S. Sup. Ct.; U.S. Ct. App. (7th Cir.); U.S. Dist. Ct. (N. Dist. IL; C. Dist. IL).

Professional Associations: ATLA [Board of Governors 1987-present; Tort Section (Vice Chair)]; ITLA (Board of Managers 1984-present); ISBA [Public Relations Committee (Secretary); Civil Practice and Procedure Council]; ABA; Illinois Bar Foundation (Charter Fellow); National Civil Justice Foundation (Founding Sponsor); American Board of Professional Liability Attorneys (Diplomate); American Board of Forensic Examiners (Diplomate); Peoria County Bar Assn.; National College of Advocacy 1989-present (Faculty Member).

Community Involvement: Selected Outstanding Young Man in Peoria, 1963; Peoria Jaycees (Vice President; past Board of Directors); City of Peoria [Campaign Ethics Board (Mayor's Appointee); Chair 1975); Commission on Human Relations (Mayor's Appointee)]; Peoria Cancer Crusade (General Chair); Peoria-Tazewell Counties Easter Seal Campaign (General Chair); Peoria Crippled Children's Center (Board of Directors); Peoria Cancer Society (Board of Directors); Peoria Symphony Orchestra (Board of Directors); Peoria Lakeview Center for the Arts and Sciences [Advance Gifts (Chair)]; Peoria Civic Ballet (President); Explorer Scout Legal Post (Founder; First Advisor; Program Lecturer); People's Law School, Peoria (Founder; Programmer); St. Paul's Episcopal Cathedral [Governing Body (Elected Member)]. *Mr. Strodel also practices Personal Injury Law: General and Criminal Law: Felonies & White Collar Crime.*

*The Supreme Court of Illinois does not recognize certifications of specialties in the practice of law. A certificate, award or recognition is not a requirement to practice law in Illinois.

ROBERT C. STRODEL
Law Offices of Robert C. Strodel, Ltd.
927 Commerce Bank Building
Peoria, IL 61602

Phone: (309) 676-4500
Fax: (309) 676-4566

Extensive Experience In:
• Professional Malpractice
• Medical Products
• Product Liability

SOUTHERN ILLINOIS

JON G. CARLSON - *Carlson Wendler & Sanderson, P.C.* - 90 Edwardsville Professional Park - P.O. Box 527 - Edwardsville, IL 62025 - Phone: (618) 656-0066, Fax: (618) 656-0009, 800: (800) 527-3352 within IL, (800) 338-3352 outside IL - *See complete biographical profile in the Personal Injury Law: Transportation Chapter, page 283.*

Chapter 20: Personal Injury Law: Medical & Professional Malpractice

REX CARR

Carr, Korein, Tillery, Kunin,
Montroy & Glass
412 Missouri Avenue
East St. Louis, IL 62201

Phone: (618) 274-0434
Fax: (618) 274-8369
800: (800) 333-5297

Extensive Experience In:

• Product Liability

•**REX CARR:** Mr. Carr practices personal injury, medical malpractice, products liability, and class action litigation. He has obtained numerous large verdicts in a wide range of injury cases including products liability, medical malpractice, libel, business litigation, toxic torts, vehicular accidents and cases under the Federal Employer's Liability Act. He has participated in a large number of trial advocacy seminars as a lecturer, including trial lawyers' associations, the University of Illinois and the St. Louis University Colleges of Law. Mr. Carr has been listed in *The Best Lawyers in America* since 1987.
Education: JD 1949, University of Illinois (Phi Alpha Delta); BA 1948, University of Illinois.
Admitted: 1950 Illinois; 1984 Missouri; 1950 U.S. Dist. Ct. (S. Dist. IL); 1955 U.S. Dist. Ct. (C. Dist. IL.); 1970 U.S. Ct. App. (7th Cir.); 1973 U.S. Ct. App. (8th Cir.); 1975 U.S. Sup. Ct.; 1975 U.S. Ct. App. (D.C.); 1995 U.S. Dist. Ct. (E. Dist. MI).
Employment History: Partner 1950-present, Carr, Korein, Tillery, Kunin, Montroy & Glass.
Professional Associations: Inner Circle of Advocates 1975-present (President 1987-89); ABOTA; ITLA (Board of Governors); ATLA; ABA.
Firm: Carr, Korein, Tillery, Kunin, Montroy & Glass consists of 19 lawyers who practice primarily personal injury law, with particular emphasis on class actions, medical malpractice, FELA, Maritime and Jones Act, products liability, and business torts. *See complete firm profile in Appendix A. Mr. Carr also practices Personal Injury Law: Transportation, Personal Injury Law: General and Workers' Compensation Law.*

MARK D. HASSAKIS - *Hassakis & Hassakis, P.C.* - Boston Building - 206 South Ninth Street, Suite 201 - P.O. Box 706 - Mt. Vernon, IL 62864 - Phone: (618) 244-5335, Fax: (618) 244-5330, 800: (800) 553-3125 (only available in area codes 618 and 217) - *See complete biographical profile in the Personal Injury Law: General Chapter, page 257.*

•**SANDOR KOREIN** - *Carr, Korein, Tillery, Kunin, Montroy & Glass* - 412 Missouri Avenue - East St. Louis, IL 62201 - Phone: (618) 274-0434, Fax: (618) 274-8369 - *See complete biographical profile in the Personal Injury Law: Transportation Chapter, page 284.*

GERALD L. MONTROY

Carr, Korein, Tillery, Kunin,
Montroy & Glass
412 Missouri Avenue
East St. Louis, IL 62201

Phone: (618) 397-9191
Fax: (618) 274-8369
800: (800) 333-5297

Extensive Experience In:

• Product Liability

•**GERALD L. MONTROY:** Mr. Montroy has been concentrating his practice in medical and hospital negligence since 1978. He is a frequent lecturer and author on medical negligence. His lectures include a seminar titled "Supreme Court Rule 215" for the Illinois Trial Lawyers Association in 1985.
Education: JD 1973, University of Illinois; STB 1965, Immaculate Conception College; MA 1963, Immaculate Conception Seminary; BA 1961, Immaculate Conception College.
Admitted: 1973 Illinois; 1984 Missouri; 1974 U.S. Dist. Ct. (S. Dist. IL).
Employment History: Partner 1981-present, Associate 1974-80, Carr, Korein, Tillery, Kunin, Montroy & Glass.
Representative Clients: Mr. Montroy represents persons injured as a result of medical or hospital negligence.
Professional Associations: ATLA 1974-present; ITLA 1974-present [Board of Managers 1985-present; Executive Committee; Medical Negligence Committee (Cochair 1990-present)]; Missouri Assn. of Trial Attorneys 1984-present.
Firm: Carr, Korein, Tillery, Kunin, Montroy & Glass consists of 19 lawyers who practice primarily personal injury, with particular emphasis on class actions, medical malpractice, FELA, Maritime and Jones Act, products liability, and business torts. The attorneys in the firm have the skills and experience necessary to handle any third party issues arising from on-the-job injuries initially covered by workers' compensation, including retaliatory and discriminatory discharge, or violations of the Americans with Disabilities Act. The firm's additional offices in Belleville, Illinois, and St. Louis, Missouri, also provide enhanced access to its services for victims of occupational accidents and diseases. *See complete firm profile in Appendix A. Mr. Montroy also practices Personal Injury Law: General.*

•**STEPHEN M. TILLERY** - *Carr, Korein, Tillery, Kunin, Montroy & Glass* - 5520 West Main Street - Belleville, IL 62223 - Phone: (618) 277-1180, Fax: (618) 277-9804 - *See complete biographical profile in the Personal Injury Law: Transportation Chapter, page 284.*

JOHN WOMICK - *Womick & Associates, Chartered* - 1100 West Main Street - Carbondale, IL 62901 - Phone: (618) 529-2440, Fax: (618) 457-2680, 800: (800) 598-2440 - *See complete biographical profile in the Personal Injury Law: General Chapter, page 258.*

CHAPTER 21

PERSONAL INJURY LAW: TRANSPORTATION

Though accidents can occur virtually anywhere and under any circumstances, some of the more serious and costly accidents occur while people are involved in transportation-related activities. This chapter provides a brief overview of the laws and issues regarding automobile, maritime, railroad, and aviation accidents. It should be stressed that tort litigation involving transportation-related activities can be extremely complicated. Retaining an inexperienced lawyer may result in a plaintiff losing a lawsuit or not receiving the recovery that he or she deserves. It is important that plaintiffs choose attorneys with appropriate levels of experience and familiarity with the subject matter of the lawsuit.

AUTOMOBILE ACCIDENTS

> **AUTO ACCIDENT CHECKLIST**
>
> If you are in an accident, particularly if someone is injured or there is a great deal of property damage, try to collect the following information from the other driver(s) involved in the accident:
> - Name and address
> - License plate number
> - Make, model, and year of car
> - Driver's license number
> - Whether it appears the driver(s) had been drinking
> - Any verbal statements made by other driver(s) as to the cause of the accident
> - Names and addresses of passengers in other car(s)
>
> Before moving any of the vehicle(s) involved in the accident, attempt to note:
> - Position of your vehicle
> - Position of any other vehicles
> - Location of any tire marks, blood, broken glass, etc., on the road or side of the road
> - Location of point of impact in relation to the center of the road
> - Road conditions
> - Traffic conditions
> - Weather conditions
>
> While the accident is still fresh in your memory, write down:
> - Date and time of accident
> - Location of accident
> - Speed of your car just before the accident
> - Direction of your car and other car(s) involved in the accident
> - Indications that the other driver(s) had been drinking
> - Whether either car was turning
> - Whether the car turning had its turn signal on
> - If the accident occurred at night, whether the lights of the vehicle(s) were on
> - Any other pertinent facts

Like any state, Illinois has its share of serious automobile accidents. Illinois requires its residents to carry minimum vehicle liability insurance for their vehicles. The purpose of the requirement is to ensure coverage for motorists involved in accidents with uninsured drivers. Each person in an accident files a claim with his or her own insurance company asking for reimbursement for any medical bills resulting from the accident and for any economic losses such as lost wages. The minimum insurance requirements are $40,000 for injury or death of more than one person in an accident, $20,000 for injury or death of one person in an accident, and $15,000 for damage to the property of another person. Illinois' mandatory insurance provides insurance to cover motorists who have an accident with an uninsured or underinsured motorist. The Illinois Safety Responsibility Law requires at-fault uninsured motorists to pay for the damages they cause or face license plate and driver's license suspensions. Inquiries about the Safety Responsibility Law may be made to the Illinois Department of Transportation.

A lawsuit for a motor vehicle accident in Illinois requires proving fault. If a jury awards damages as a result of such a lawsuit, the law requires that the damage award to the injured motorist be reduced by any amount of money already received under the insurance benefit system.

MARITIME PERSONAL INJURY

Recreational boaters, cruise ship passengers, sailors on commercial ships, longshore and harbor workers, and off-shore oil employees may at some point in time become injured and require the services of an attorney. When choosing an attorney regarding a maritime matter, it is very important to choose someone experienced in maritime law. The law governing maritime issues is a complicated jumble of federal statutes, United States Supreme Court decisions, and centuries-old common law. A general practitioner unfamiliar with the dips and turns of maritime law may have difficulty properly representing a client.

RAILROAD ACCIDENTS

The October 1995 deaths of seven high school students in Fox River, Illinois, whose school bus was hit by a commuter train at a railroad crossing, is a reminder that railroad accidents remain an all-too-frequent occurrence. By law, railroad carriers have a duty to maintain the reasonable safety of their tracks, particularly around railroad crossings. Railroad carriers can be held liable if an accident occurs where there are defective or an insufficient number of warning lights and signs. Additionally, railroad engineers and crews have a duty to keep a lookout for potential problems and to sound the train's horn when approaching potentially dangerous areas. Persons crossing or near railroad tracks also have a duty to act reasonably. Remember that Illinois recognizes the doctrine of comparative negligence. If a person is partially responsible for an accident, any damage award he or she receives can be reduced by the extent to which he or she was responsible.

Railroad employees who are hurt on the job are entitled to recover damages from their employer under the Federal Employer's Liability Act (FELA). FELA is like a workers' compensation program for railroad employees. FELA enables railroad employees to recover for any injury "resulting in whole or in part from the negligence of any of the officers, agents, or employees of [the railroad], or by reason of any defect or insufficiency, due to its negligence, in its cars, engines, appliances, machinery, tracks, roadbeds, works, boats, wharves or other equipment." Recovery under FELA is the exclusive remedy for railroad employees injured on the job.

AVIATION ACCIDENTS

While commercial aircraft remain the safest means of long-distance travel, accidents do happen, and the litigation that follows an airline crash is notoriously complicated. Plaintiff lawyers in airline cases face a variety of difficult issues. For example: What law (federal or state) should be used? Where is the best forum for the trial? Should lawsuits be brought individually or as a class action? Who should be sued as a defendant (aircraft manufacturer; aircraft operator or owner; airport operator, manufacturer or corporate officers; component-parts manufacturers)? What is the best theory of recovery (strict liability, negligence, breach of warranty, statutory)? What is the best method of proving damages? How should evidence of the crash be preserved? It is obvious, therefore, that when choosing an attorney to represent your interests after an airline accident, it is best to choose someone with experience in airline tort litigation.

RESOURCES

Illinois Department of Transportation, Accident Records Section, 3215 Executive Park Drive, Springfield, IL 62794, phone: (217) 782-4516.

Contact the Illinois State Bar Association, Illinois Bar Center, 424 South Second Street, Springfield, IL 62701, phone: (217) 525-1760, for information or to order free pamphlets such as *Auto Accidents*.

Office of the Secretary of State, Mandatory Insurance Division, 429 Howlett Building, Springfield, IL 62756, phone: (217) 524-4946.

United States Department of Transportation, Federal Aviation Administration, 800 Independence Avenue SW, Washington, D.C. 20591, phone: (202) 267-3111; Federal Railroad Administration, 400 Seventh Street SW, #8206, Washington, D.C. 20590, phone: (202) 366-0710; Maritime Administration, 400 Seventh Street SW, #8206, Washington, D.C. 20590, phone: (202) 366-5823; National Highway Traffic Safety Administration, 400 Seventh Street SW, Washington, D.C. 20590, phone: (202) 366-9550.

Personal Injury Law: Transportation
Leading Illinois Attorneys

The Leading Illinois Attorneys listed below were nominated as exceptional by their peers in a statewide survey conducted by American Research Corporation (ARC). ARC asked several thousand licensed Illinois attorneys to name the lawyer to whom they would send a close friend or family member in need of legal assistance in specific areas of law. The attorneys below were nominated in the area of Personal Injury Law: Transportation.

Because the survey results (all practice area results combined) represent less than three percent of Illinois' practicing attorneys, this list should not be construed as a complete list. Nevertheless, it is an excellent source of highly qualified and reputable Illinois attorneys.

For information on ARC's survey methodology, see page *xi*.
For the complete list of Leading Illinois Consumer Attorneys, see page *xii*.

The Leading Illinois Attorneys below are listed alphabetically in accordance with the geographic region in which their offices are located. Note that attorneys may handle clients from a broad geographic area; attorneys are not restricted to only serving clients residing within the cities in which their offices are located.

An attorney whose name appears in bold has included a biographical profile in this chapter.

LEADING ILLINOIS ATTORNEYS

Illinois' Most Respected Legal Counsel As Selected By Their Peers.

The Leading Illinois Attorneys below were recommended by their peers in a statewide survey.

Cook & Collar Counties

Baizer, Robert S. - Highland Park
Baum, David M. - Chicago
Bingle, Robert J. - Chicago
Broida, Ronald J. - Naperville
Burke, John M. - Chicago
Clifford, Robert A. - Chicago, page 280
Conway, Kevin J. - Chicago
Corboy, Philip H. - Chicago
Corboy, Philip Harnett, Jr. - Chicago
Decker, David A. - Waukegan
Decker, Thomas D. - Chicago
Demetrio, Thomas A. - Chicago
Demos, James T. - Chicago
Dicker, Steven M. - Chicago
Farina, James L. - Chicago
Foote, Robert M. - Aurora
Frost, Michael J. - Chicago
Galliani, William R. - Chicago
Gifford, Geoffrey L. - Chicago
Kaiser, Daniel J. - Bensenville
Knippen, James H. - Wheaton
Kuhlman, Richard S. - Chicago
Lamont, John M. - Aurora
Lane, Fred - Chicago
Lane, Stephen I. - Chicago
Latherow, Jerry A. - Chicago
Leopold, Valerie A. - Chicago
Lindner, George P. - Aurora
Lowrey, John J. - Chicago
Marino, Frank C. - Chicago
Marszalek, John E. - Chicago
Miller, Kenneth C. - Chicago
Mirza, Jerome - Chicago
Murphy, William C. - Aurora
Nathan, Thomas J. - Chicago
Nolan, Donald J. - Chicago
Pavalon, Eugene - Chicago
Power, Joseph A., Jr. - Chicago
Rapoport, David E. - Rosemont, page 281
Reuland, Timothy J. - Aurora
Rogers, Larry R., Sr. - Chicago
Russo, Richard D. - Wheaton
Salvi, Patrick A. - Waukegan
Scanlan, Edmund J. - Chicago
Schaffner, Howard S. - Chicago
Schwartz, Allen N. - Chicago
Slutsky, Mark G. - Chicago
Smith, Todd A. - Chicago
Spinak, Michael D. - Chicago
Sussman, Jeffrey B. - Chicago
Thompson, Charles F., Jr. - Aurora
Touhy, Timothy J. - Chicago
Zaideman, Robert J. - Chicago

Northwestern Illinois Including Rockford & Quad Cities

Ferracuti, Peter F. - Ottawa
Fisher, John W. - Peru
Rapoport, David E. - Rosemont, page 281
Warner, Michael J. - Rock Island

Central Illinois

Bowles, James E. - Peoria
Brady, Gerald, Jr. - Peoria
Dorris, David V. - Bloomington
Dukes, Carroll W. - Danville
Durree, Edward D. - Peoria
Halliday, Ronald E. - Peoria
Hefner, M. John, Jr. - Mattoon
Heller, Harlan - Mattoon
Londrigan, Thomas F. - Springfield
Maher, Jerelyn D. - Peoria
Nicoara, John P. - Peoria
Phebus, Joseph W. - Urbana
Rapoport, David E. - Rosemont, page 281
Rose, Raymond - Peoria
Stine, Robert E. - Springfield
Taylor, John C. - Champaign
Willoughby, Stephen O. - Decatur

Southern Illinois

Callis, Lance - Granite City, page 282
Carlson, Jon G. - Edwardsville, page 283
Carr, Rex - East St. Louis
Cates, Judy L. - Belleville
Cook, Bruce N. - Belleville
Cueto, Amiel - Belleville
Glass, Mark - East St. Louis
Hughes, R. Courtney - Carbondale
Keefe, Thomas Q., Jr. - Belleville
Korein, Sandor - East St. Louis, page 284
Lakin, L. Thomas - Wood River
Mitchell, Sam C. - West Frankfort
Murphy, G. Patrick - Marion
Prince, Mark D. - Carbondale
Rapoport, David E. - Rosemont, page 281
Reagan, Michael J. - Belleville
Tillery, Stephen M. - Belleville, page 284
Wham, James B. - Centralia
Womick, John - Carbondale
Woodcock, George W. - Mt. Carmel

Biographical Profiles of Personal Injury Law: Transportation Leading Illinois Attorneys

The Leading Illinois Attorneys profiled below were nominated as exceptional by their peers in a statewide survey conducted by American Research Corporation (ARC). ARC asked several thousand licensed Illinois attorneys to name the lawyer to whom they would send a close friend or family member in need of legal assistance in specific areas of law. The attorneys below were nominated in the area of Personal Injury Law: Transportation.

Because the survey results (all practice area results combined) represent less than three percent of Illinois' practicing attorneys, this list should not be construed as a complete list. Nevertheless, it is an excellent source of highly qualified and reputable Illinois attorneys.

For information on ARC's survey methodology, see page *xi*.
For the complete list of Leading Illinois Consumer Attorneys, see page *xii*.
For the list of Leading Illinois Personal Injury Law: Transportation Attorneys, see page 277.

The Leading Illinois Attorneys below are listed alphabetically in accordance with the geographic region in which their offices are located. Note that attorneys may handle clients from a broad geographic area; attorneys are not limited to only serving clients residing within the cities in which their offices are located.

The two-line attorney listings in this section are of attorneys who practice in this area but whose full biographical profiles appear in other sections of this book. A bullet "•" preceding a name indicates the attorney was nominated in this particular area of law.

For information on the format of the full biographical profiles, consult the "Using the Consumer Guidebook" section on page *xviii*.

The following abbreviations are used throughout these profiles:

App.	Appellate
Cir.	Circuit
Ct.	Court
Dist.	District
Sup.	Supreme
JD	Juris Doctor (Doctor of Law)
LLB	Legum Baccalaureus (Bachelor of Laws)
LLD	Legum Doctor (Doctor of Laws)
LLM	Legum Magister (Master of Laws)
ADR	Alternative Dispute Resolution
ABA	American Bar Association
ABOTA	American Board of Trial Advocates
ATLA	Association of Trial Lawyers of America
CBA	Chicago Bar Association
ISBA	Illinois State Bar Association
ITLA	Illinois Trial Lawyers Association
NBTA	National Board of Trial Advocacy

Chapter 21: Personal Injury Law: Transportation

Cook & Collar Counties

THOMAS A. CLANCY - *Clancy & Stevens* - Barrister Hall, Suite 220 - 29 South LaSalle Street - Chicago, IL 60603-1501 - Phone: (312) 782-2800, Fax: (312) 782-2852 - *See complete biographical profile in the Personal Injury Law: Medical & Professional Malpractice Chapter, page 267.*

ROBERT A. CLIFFORD

Clifford Law Offices
120 North LaSalle Street
31st Floor
Chicago, IL 60602

Phone: (312) 899-9090
Fax: (312) 251-1160
800: (800) 899-0410
E-mail:
102554,2453@compuserve.com

Extensive Experience In:

- Transportation Liability
- Medical Negligence
- Products Liability

•**ROBERT A. CLIFFORD:** Mr. Clifford was selected one of the nation's top ten litigators of 1993 by the *National Law Journal*. He was voted by his peers to appear in the prestigious *Best Lawyers in America*. Mr. Clifford regularly handles complex personal injury and wrongful death cases, routinely receiving large verdicts and settlements. Mr. Clifford is a columnist for the respected *Chicago Lawyer* publication and is frequently asked to lecture for various legal organizations throughout the country. He was Cochair of the American Bar Association's Litigation Section for its 1995 annual meeting.
Education: JD 1976, DePaul University (Research and Development Editor, *Law Review*); BSC 1973, DePaul University.
Admitted: 1976 Illinois; 1976 U.S. Dist. Ct. (N. Dist. IL); 1981 U.S. Sup. Ct.; 1981 U.S. Dist. Ct. (E. Dist. WI); 1993 U.S. Dist. Ct. (C. Dist. IL).
Employment History: Principal Partner 1995-present, Clifford Law Offices; Principal Partner 1994-95, Corboy Demetrio Clifford; Principal Partner 1984-94, Robert A. Clifford & Associates; Associate 1976-84, Corboy & Demetrio.
Representative Clients: Mr. Clifford represents victims and families of victims who have suffered aviation wrongful death and personal injury, medical negligence, products liability, automobile and railroad personal injury and wrongful death, as well as complex commercial law cases. He currently represents Rachel Barton, internationally acclaimed violinist who was severly injured in a train accident, as well as dozens of passengers hurt or killed in airline crashes around the world.
Professional Associations: International Academy of Trial Lawyers 1994-present; American College of Trial Lawyers 1994-present; ABA [Litigation Section (Annual Convention Cochair 1995)]; Chicago Inns of Court (President 1994-95); ITLA (President 1990); CBA (Board of Managers 1993).
Community Involvement: DePaul University (Board of Trustees); Roscoe Pound Foundation; Isaac Ray Center; Mercy Hospital and Medical Center, Chicago (Board of Advisors); Judge James A. Gerovlis Educational Foundation (Advisory Board).
Firm: Mr. Clifford recently endowed his alma mater, DePaul University College of Law, with a grant to form the first Chair in Tort Law and Social Policy. Mr. Clifford was instrumental in forming the first organization in Illinois whose members have been victimized by wrongful conduct. He is a champion of consumer rights and frequently speaks out or writes on these issues, and has been called "The People's Voice," by *The Chicago Tribune. See complete firm profile in Appendix A. Mr. Clifford also practices Personal Injury Law: General and Personal Injury Law: Medical & Professional Malpractice.*

JAMES J. DE SANTO - *Law Offices of James J. DeSanto, P.C.* - 339 North Milwaukee Avenue - Libertyville, IL 60048 - Phone: (847) 816-8100, Fax: (847) 816-8126 - *See complete biographical profile in the Personal Injury Law: General Chapter, page 239.*

KEVIN P. DURKIN - *Clifford Law Offices* - 120 North LaSalle Street, 31st Floor - Chicago, IL 60602 - Phone: (312) 899-9090, Fax: (312) 251-1160 - *See complete biographical profile in the Personal Injury Law: General Chapter, page 239.*

JEFFREY M. GOLDBERG - *Jeffrey M. Goldberg & Associates, Ltd.* - 20 North Clark Street, Suite 3100 - Chicago, IL 60602 - Phone: (312) 236-4146, Fax: (312) 236-5913 - *See complete biographical profile in the Personal Injury Law: Medical & Professional Malpractice Chapter, page 268.*

BRUCE D. GOODMAN - *Steinberg, Polacek & Goodman* - 309 West Washington Street, Suite 500 - Chicago, IL 60606 - Phone: (312) 782-1386, Fax: (312) 782-6739 - *See complete biographical profile in the Personal Injury Law: Medical & Professional Malpractice Chapter, page 268.*

Personal Injury Law: Transportation Leading Illinois Attorneys

MARTIN J. HEALY, JR. - *Martin J. Healy, Jr. & Associates* - 111 West Washington Street, Suite 1425 - Chicago, IL 60602 - Phone: (312) 977-0100, Fax: (312) 977-0795, 800: (800) 922-4500 - *See complete biographical profile in the Personal Injury Law: General Chapter, page 241.*

KEITH A. HEBEISEN - *Clifford Law Offices* - 120 North LaSalle Street, 31st Floor - Chicago, IL 60602 - Phone: (312) 899-9090, Fax: (312) 251-1160 - *See complete biographical profile in the Personal Injury Law: Medical & Professional Malpractice Chapter, page 269.*

BRUCE M. KOHEN - *Anesi, Ozmon & Rodin, Ltd.* - 161 North Clark Street, Suite 2100 - Chicago, IL 60601 - Phone: (312) 372-3822, Fax: (312) 372-3833, 800: (800) 458-3822 within IL - *See complete biographical profile in the Personal Injury Law: General Chapter, page 242.*

•STEPHEN I. LANE - *Lane & Lane* - 33 North Dearborn Street, Suite 2300 - Chicago, IL 60602 - Phone: (312) 332-1400, Fax: (312) 899-8003 - *See complete biographical profile in the Personal Injury Law: General Chapter, page 244.*

•JERRY A. LATHEROW - *Law Office of Jerry A. Latherow* - 77 West Washington Street, Suite 1900 - Chicago, IL 60602 - Phone: (312) 372-0052, Fax: (312) 372-8043 - *See complete biographical profile in the Personal Injury Law: General Chapter, page 244.*

JOSEPH J. MIROBALLI - *Anesi, Ozmon & Rodin, Ltd.* - 161 North Clark Street, Suite 2100 - Chicago, IL 60601 - Phone: (312) 372-3822, Fax: (312) 372-3833, 800: (800) 458-3822 within IL - *See complete biographical profile in the Personal Injury Law: Medical & Professional Malpractice Chapter, page 270.*

NAT P. OZMON - *Anesi, Ozmon & Rodin, Ltd.* - 161 North Clark Street, Suite 2100 - Chicago, IL 60601 - Phone: (312) 372-3822, Fax: (312) 372-3833, 800: (800) 458-3822 within IL - *See complete biographical profile in the Personal Injury Law: General Chapter, page 246.*

ROBERT B. PATTERSON - *Law Offices of Robert B. Patterson, Ltd.* - 221 North LaSalle Street, Suite 1050 - Chicago, IL 60601 - Phone: (312) 236-0995, Fax: (312) 984-5791 - *See complete biographical profile in the Personal Injury Law: General Chapter, page 246.*

•DAVID E. RAPOPORT: Mr. Rapoport is the State Coordinator for the National Board of Trial Advocacy and a Certified Arbitrator who has concentrated in personal injury law since 1981. He limits his practice to representing clients who have suffered serious personal injuries, and the families of victims who have been killed as a result of someone else's negligence. Mr. Rapoport's trial techniques are published in *Accident Cases,* and he wrote the chapter, "Trial and Evidentiary Considerations in Wrongful Death Actions," *Illinois Wrongful Death Actions.* He is frequently interviewed for newspapers, radio, and television, and is a frequent lecturer at ITT-Kent College of Law, at the Illinois Institute for Continuing Legal Education, and at various labor union functions. He is listed in *Who's Who Worldwide, Who's Who in American Law* and *Who's Who in the Midwest.*
Education: JD 1981 with highest honors, Illinois Institute of Technology, Chicago-Kent; Certificate in Trial Advocacy 1983, Lawyer's Post Graduate Institute; BS 1978, Northern Illinois University (Dean's List).
Admitted: 1981 Illinois; 1994 Wisconsin; 1981 U.S. Dist. Ct. (N. Dist. IL); 1981 U.S. Ct. App. (7th Cir.); 1989 U.S. Dist. Ct. (C. Dist. IL); 1992 U.S. Dist. Ct. (S. Dist. IL).
Employment History: Trial Attorney/Partner 1995, Rapoport & Kupets Law Offices; Trial Attorney/Partner 1990-95, Baizer & Rapoport; Senior Trial Attorney 1981-90, Katz, Friedman, Schur & Eagle.
Representative Clients: Mr. Rapoport represents victims of negligence, including victims of mass disasters, people seriously injured, and the families of people wrongfully killed. Mr. Rapoport either has represented, or is currently representing, the interests of passengers or crew members injured or killed in most of the recent air disasters which have taken place in the U.S. He has successfully represented injured parties in every type of personal injury case including medical malpractice, product liability, vehicular collisions, train, plane and boat crashes, and premises liability. In addition to representing clients near his office, Mr. Rapoport accepts appropriate cases throughout Illinois.
Professional Associations: ATLA 1981-present; ITLA 1981-present (Sustaining Member 1992-present); ABA 1983-present; NBTA 1991-present (Illinois State Coordinator; Diplomate; Civil Trial Advocacy Section); ISBA 1981-present; Cook County Bar Assn. 1981-present; Lake County Bar Assn. 1991-present; Roscoe Pound Foundation 1993-present; Trial Lawyers for Public Justice 1993-present [Illinois Chapter 1995 (Founding Member)]; Lawyers Pilots Bar Assn. 1994-present.
Firm: The firm has four attorneys, two paralegals, researchers, secretaries, and close relationships with investigators, physicians, pilots, engineers, and other technical consultants. The firm also has an office at 77 West Washington Street, Chicago, Illinois 60602. Phone: (312) 368-0801; (800) 545-6437. *Mr. Rapoport also practices Personal Injury Law: General and Personal Injury Law: Medical & Professional Malpractice.*

DAVID E. RAPOPORT

Rapoport & Kupets Law Offices
O'Hare International Center
10275 West Higgins Road
Suite 370
Rosemont, IL 60018

Phone: (847) 803-9880
Fax: (847) 803-9881
800: (800) 545-6437

Extensive Experience In:

• Air Disasters/Train Crashes
• Bus/Vehicular Crashes
• Product Liability

Chapter 21: Personal Injury Law: Transportation

CURT N. RODIN - *Anesi, Ozmon & Rodin, Ltd.* - 161 North Clark Street, Suite 2100 - Chicago, IL 60601 - Phone: (312) 372-3822, Fax: (312) 372-3833, 800: (800) 458-3822 within IL - *See complete biographical profile in the Personal Injury Law: General Chapter, page 247.*

•**EDMUND J. SCANLAN** - *Law Offices of Edmund J. Scanlan, Ltd.* - 134 North LaSalle Street, Suite 220 - Chicago, IL 60602 - Phone: (312) 372-0020, Fax: (312) 372-1211 - *See complete biographical profile in the Personal Injury Law: General Chapter, page 248.*

Northwestern Illinois
Including Rockford & Quad Cities

ROBERT A. FREDRICKSON - *Reno, Zahm, Folgate, Lindberg & Powell* - 1415 East State Street, Suite 900 - Rockford, IL 61104 - Phone: (815) 987-4050, Fax: (815) 987-4092 - *See complete biographical profile in the Personal Injury Law: General Chapter, page 250.*

JAN H. OHLANDER - *Reno, Zahm, Folgate, Lindberg & Powell* - 1415 East State Street, Suite 900 - Rockford, IL 61104 - Phone: (815) 987-4050, Fax: (815) 987-4092 - *See complete biographical profile in the Personal Injury Law: General Chapter, page 251.*

Southern Illinois

•**LANCE CALLIS:** Mr. Callis is a widely recognized trial lawyer who concentrates in serious personal injuries. He is Designated Counsel for the United Transportation Union. Mr. Callis worked in the steel rail industry and as an investigator concerning plaintiffs' railroad cases while going to college and law school. He is uniquely qualified to handle all personal injury cases, and in particular, anything dealing with the railroads. He has successfully handled, and brought to trial, all types of railroad cases, including crossing cases, passengers cases, and in particular, employee injuries or death cases, both in federal and state courts. He has vigorously defended employees' rights to legal representation and is experienced in all phases of the Federal Employer's Liability Act. Mr. Callis frequently lectures in the area of trial practice.
Education: JD 1959, St. Louis University; BS 1956, St. Louis University.
Admitted: 1959 Illinois; 1959 Missouri; 1968 U.S. Sup. Ct.; 1980 U.S. Dist. Ct. (E. Dist. MI); 1986 U.S. Ct. App. (7th Cir.); 1986 U.S. Dist. Ct. (C. Dist. IL; S. Dist. IL).
Employment History: Senior Partner 1991-present, Callis, Papa, Jensen, Jackstadt & Halloran, P.C.
Representative Clients: Mr. Callis is the Designated Counsel for the United Transportation Union and is the Counsel for the Democratic Party of Madison County, Illinois.
Professional Associations: Madison County Bar Assn. (President 1976-77); Tri-City Bar Assn. (President 1954-64); ISBA; ABA; The Missouri Bar; ITLA; The Fellows; Illinois Bar Foundation.
Community Involvement: Veteran of Foreign Wars; The Elks; The DuBourg Society, St. Louis University.
Firm: Callis, Papa, Jensen, Jackstadt & Halloran, P.C., provides representation to individuals in all aspects of personal injury matters, including workers' compensation, pensions, medical payments, insurance questions, disability pensions, and estates. The firm's experience traverses the entire spectrum of the injured plaintiff and his or her family's needs. The firm has been in practice in Granite City for over 35 years and also has an office in St. Louis, Missouri. *Mr. Callis also practices Personal Injury Law: General and Workers' Compensation Law.*

LANCE CALLIS
Callis, Papa, Jensen,
Jackstadt & Halloran, P.C.
1326 Niedringhaus Avenue
Granite City, IL 62040

Phone: (618) 452-1323
Fax: (618) 452-8024

•**JON G. CARLSON:** Mr. Carlson has been active in all forms of personal injury and wrongful death cases, including railroad and truck accident litigation, products liability, and medical malpractice. A large number of Mr. Carlson's cases come from referrals by other lawyers. He has represented many injured railroad employees as well as members of other crafts. Mr. Carlson has received numerous large verdicts in injury cases and has assisted other lawyers in handling complex cases.
Education: JD 1967, University of Illinois; BA 1965, University of Illinois.
Admitted: 1967 Illinois; 1990 Missouri; 1968 U.S. Dist. Ct. (S. Dist. IL); 1983 U.S. Ct. App. (8th Cir.); 1991 U.S. Ct. App. (7th Cir.); 1993 U.S. Sup. Ct.; 1994 U.S. Dist. Ct. (C. Dist. IL).
Representative Clients: Mr. Carlson represents members of railroad unions and other labor unions.
Professional Associations: ITLA (President 1987-88); Missouri Assn. of Trial Attorneys; ATLA; ISBA; The Missouri Bar.
Firm: In addition to the firm of Carlson Wendler & Sanderson, the Missouri firm of Abele, Carlson & Sanderson has the resources and background to retain the top expert witnesses in the country to assist with litigation. Both firms also have a full-time investigator on staff. *Mr. Carlson also practices Personal Injury Law: General and Personal Injury Law: Medical & Professional Malpractice.*

JON G. CARLSON
Carlson Wendler & Sanderson, P.C.
90 Edwardsville Professional Park
P.O. Box 527
Edwardsville, IL 62025

Phone: (618) 656-0066
Fax: (618) 656-0009
800: (800) 527-3352 within IL
(800) 338-3352 outside IL

Extensive Experience In:

• FELA
• Products Liability

•**REX CARR** - *Carr, Korein, Tillery, Kunin, Montroy & Glass* - 412 Missouri Avenue - East St. Louis, IL 62201 - Phone: (618) 274-0434, Fax: (618) 274-8369, 800: (800) 333-5297 - *See complete biographical profiles in the Personal Injury Law: Medical & Professional Malpractice Chapter, page 274 and Personal Injury Law: General Chapter, page 257.*

•**MARK GLASS** - *Carr, Korein, Tillery, Kunin, Montroy & Glass* - 412 Missouri Avenue - East St. Louis, IL 62201 - Phone: (618) 274-0434, Fax: (618) 274-8369, 800: (800) 333-5297 - *See complete biographical profile in the Workers' Compensation Law Chapter, page 345.*

Chapter 21: Personal Injury Law: Transportation

SANDOR KOREIN

Carr, Korein, Tillery, Kunin, Montroy & Glass
412 Missouri Avenue
East St. Louis, IL 62201

Phone: (618) 274-0434
Fax: (618) 274-8369

•**SANDOR KOREIN:** Mr. Korein handles general plaintiff personal injury cases, particularly employees, on the Jones Act and in other maritime-related injury cases, as well as FELA, products liability, and legal and medical malpractice. He is the past President of the St. Louis-Southern Illinois Chapter of the American Board of Trial Advocates. Mr. Korein is a frequent lecturer at continuing legal education programs for trial practice at Washington University, the Illinois State Bar Association, and Tulane University. He is the author of articles on maritime injury law for the *St. Louis Bar Association Journal*.

Education: LLB 1956, Washington University, St. Louis University.

Admitted: 1956 Illinois; 1957 Missouri; 1958 U.S. Dist. Ct. (S. Dist. IL); 1991 U.S. Sup. Ct.

Employment History: Partner 1960-present, Carr, Korein, Tillery, Kunin, Montroy & Glass.

Representative Clients: Mr. Korein primarily represents clients that have sustained various types of injuries.

Professional Associations: ABA 1956-present; ISBA 1957-present; Bar Assn. of Metropolitan St. Louis 1956-present; The Missouri Bar 1956-present.

Community Involvement: Belleville Grade School District (School Board); America-Israel Public Affairs Board (Executive Committee); St. Louisians for Better Government.

Firm: Carr, Korein, Tillery, Kunin, Montroy & Glass consists of 19 lawyers, including several personal injury trial attorneys. The attorneys in the firm have the skills and experience necessary to handle any third party issues arising from on-the-job injuries initially covered by workers' compensation, including retaliatory and discriminatory discharge, or violations of the Americans with Disabilities Act. The firm's additional offices in Belleville, Illinois, and St. Louis, Missouri, also provide enhanced access to its services for victims of occupational accidents and diseases. *See complete firm profile in Appendix A. Mr. Korein also practices Personal Injury Law: General and Personal Injury Law: Medical & Professional Malpractice.*

STEPHEN M. TILLERY

Carr, Korein, Tillery, Kunin, Montroy & Glass
5520 West Main Street
Belleville, IL 62223

Phone: (618) 277-1180
Fax: (618) 277-9804

•**STEPHEN M. TILLERY:** In nearly 20 years of practice, Mr. Tillery has handled major civil cases in the areas of general negligence, product liability, medical malpractice, and the Federal Employer's Liability Act. Many of his clients have received substantial verdicts and settlements. He has successfully represented injured plaintiffs in complex litigation against major domestic and foreign manufacturing companies (e.g., General Electric, Ford Motor, Chrysler, Mitsubishi, Howell Electric) as well as most major railroad transportation companies. Mr. Tillery's success in litigation makes him a frequently requested lecturer for legal education seminars on trial practice and litigation. For over ten years, he served as an adjunct professor of law and co-director of the Advanced Trial Advocacy Program at St. Louis University School of Law. Mr. Tillery has authored numerous articles and books. He is the coauthor of *Protecting Litigation Rights* for the Illinois Institute for Continuing Legal Education; and *Illinois Personal Injury Complaints,* West Publishing Company, 1994.

Education: JD 1976 magna cum laude, St. Louis University (Order of Woolsack); BA 1972 magna cum laude, Illinois College (Phi Beta Kappa).

Admitted: 1976 Illinois; 1990 Missouri; 1978 U.S. Dist. Ct. (S. Dist. IL); 1982 U.S. Ct. App. (7th Cir.); 1988 U.S Sup. Ct.

Employment History: Partner 1988-present, Carr, Korein, Tillery, Kunin, Montroy & Glass; Partner 1979-88, Kassly, Bone, Becker, Dix, Tillery & Young; Law Clerk 1976-77, Honorable George Moran, Fifth District Court of Appeals, Illinois.

Representative Clients: Mr. Tillery is Designated Counsel for the United Transportation Union. He has represented plaintiffs who have suffered severe personal injuries and/or death from defective products, industrial accidents, railroad on-duty accidents, medical malpractice, and vehicular accidents.

Professional Associations: ITLA [Board of Managers 1987-present; Amicus Curiae Committee 1983-present; Civil Practice Committee (Chair 1992-present); Publications Committee 1992-present]; ISBA (Civil Practice and Procedure Section Council 1981-85; Tort Law Section Council 1988-89); ABA; Missouri Assn. of Trial Attorneys; St. Louis Metropolitan Bar Assn.; ATLA; St. Clair County Bar Assn.

Firm: The firm of Carr, Korein, Tillery, Kunin, Montroy & Glass, and its predecessor firms, has represented plaintiff clients throughout the midwestern United States for over 40 years. The firm of 19 lawyers has distinguished itself by providing quality representation for injured clients and through its experience in handling large and complex claims and issues. *See complete firm profile in Appendix A. Mr. Tillery also practices Personal Injury Law: Medical & Professional Malpractice and Personal Injury Law: General.*

•**JOHN WOMICK** - *Womick & Associates, Chartered* - 1100 West Main Street - Carbondale, IL 62901 - Phone: (618) 529-2440, Fax: (618) 457-2680, 800: (800) 598-2440 - *See complete biographical profile in the Personal Injury Law: General Chapter, page 258.*

CHAPTER 22

REAL ESTATE LAW

Real estate law involves rights in the ownership and possession of land and buildings attached to land. Real estate law often is referred to as the law of real property to distinguish it from the law of personal property, which includes all other property. A stumbling block for many consumers entering the real estate market is the number of unfamiliar terms frequently used by real estate professionals. Because real estate is one of the oldest areas of the law, it uses many old terms and concepts, but many rights and responsibilities regarding real estate have evolved and been updated as society has changed.

This chapter summarizes some of the real estate concepts and terms one involved in real estate is likely to encounter, the process one goes through to buy or sell a house, and the rights and responsibilities of landlords and tenants.

ENCUMBRANCE

An encumbrance is a legal interest in property held by someone other than the owner of the property. An encumbrance is not an ownership interest in real property, but it creates some kind of obligation for the owner. An encumbrance attaches to the property, not the property owner, so the property may be bought and sold even though there is an encumbrance attached.

EASEMENT

An easement is the right to use another person's land for a particular purpose. There are many forms of easements. Public utility companies frequently have utility easements that permit them to run gas, water, or electrical lines through the property of others. The owner of property near a lake might buy from the owner of lake shore property an easement to cross his or her property to access the lake. A person who owns property that is land-locked may receive an easement from an adjacent land owner to have access in and out of the property. This is called a right of way.

DEED RESTRICTION

Deed restrictions may also be known as covenants, conditions, or restrictions. Deed restrictions, which usually are included in the seller's deed to the buyer, generally are imposed to maintain certain standards. Restrictions may limit the color one may paint a house, the kind of trees one may plant, or the size of home one may build on the property.

LIEN

A lien is a charge against property that provides security for a debt or obligation of the property owner. The lien holder does not own the property. Some liens are voluntary, such as when an owner of property takes out a mortgage. Other liens may be imposed. For example, a lien may be imposed on property for nonpayment of taxes. One of the most common liens is the mechanic's lien. A mechanic's lien arises when someone furnishes labor or materials to improve a piece of property. A worker or supplier who is not paid may file a notice of lien with the county recorder and the property owner and collect the amount owed from a subsequent sale of the property.

ASSESSMENT

An assessment is a value placed on real property by a local taxing authority for the purpose of levying taxes. Real estate taxes are calculated by multiplying the assessed value of a piece of property by the tax rate. Most properties are reassessed periodically, and a property's assessed value may not be the same as its actual market value. A special assessment is a tax levied on a piece of property to pay for improvements that benefit the particular property, such as streets, sidewalks, and street lighting. Special assessments are liens on the property until they are paid.

REAL ESTATE OWNERSHIP

Typically, ownership of real estate includes the following rights:

- To sell
- To use the property as security for loans (encumber)
- To improve the land or buildings on the land
- To use and possess the property

Property can be owned by one or more persons. The two common ways in which parties co-own a piece of property are joint tenancy and tenancy in common.

Joint Tenancy

Although joint tenancy is a popular way for a husband and wife to own property, there is no requirement that joint tenants be married or that there only be two joint tenants. Owners in joint tenancy have a right to sell, encumber, and possess the entire property. When one joint tenant dies, the remaining joint tenants automatically take the deceased joint tenant's share of the property by right of survivorship. The surviving joint tenants are required to file a death certificate and an affidavit with the county recorder. Joint tenancy allows the surviving joint tenants to avoid probate, transfer and death taxes.

Tenants in Common

Tenants in common, like joint tenants, share the right to possess, sell, and encumber the property. Unlike joint tenants, however, tenants in common do not have a right of survivorship. Upon the death of one tenant in common, his or her ownership interest passes to his or her heirs as part of the estate.

Advantages and Disadvantages of Co-Ownership

Although there are advantages to co-owning property, there are drawbacks as well. If co-owners cannot agree on use, sale, or possession of a piece of property, they may have to go to court to resolve the matter in a partition action. In a partition action a joint tenant or tenant in common asks the court to split the property in a fair and just manner. Real property may be difficult to divide and partial interests may be difficult to sell, so a court will usually order that the property be sold and proceeds from the sale distributed to the co-owners in relation to their interests.

RESIDENTIAL REAL ESTATE

The most common consumer real estate transaction involves the sale of a home. Unlike years past, today a home buyer has a variety of options in deciding the type of dwelling to buy. Single family houses are still the most common selections for home buyers. Single family homes provide the maximum amount of privacy and freedom to their owners, but they may also be the most expensive option and require the most upkeep.

Condominiums and townhouses may be an option for some purchasers. Both give their owners many of the advantages of home ownership, such as tax deductibility of mortgage interest, without some of the responsibilities some people consider to be disadvantages, such as lawn care and exterior upkeep. Residents usually pay association fees to cover maintenance.

A homestead is not a particular type of dwelling; instead, it is a tax classification that can dramatically lower what a homeowner pays in real estate taxes. People who live in the property they own are taxed at a much lower rate than if they rent out that property to others. If a person buys property that currently is rental property, he or she must fill out an application to change the property's tax status; otherwise, the person could end up paying non-homestead taxes for the first year of ownership.

Title

Title to real estate is the ownership of the property. Title may refer to the actual ownership or to the documentary evidence of that ownership. Title is what gives the owner the right to the property. In order to sell a piece of property, all title matters must be cleared. Usually, this is accomplished through a title search. A title search is a diligent search of all records relating to a piece of property to determine whether the owner is authorized to sell the property and whether there are any claims against it. If any defects in title are discovered during the title search, the seller usually has time to cure the defect.

Often people have title insurance to protect them against any hidden defects in the title. There are two types of title insurance. One type protects the lender's interest in the property and the other protects the homeowner's interest.

DEEDS

A deed is a written instrument that transfers the title of property from one person to another. There are many different types of deeds. Generally, in Illinois, title is transferred by a general warranty deed. A general warranty deed provides the greatest protection to the purchaser because the seller pledges or warrants that he or she legally owns the property and that there are no outstanding liens, mortgages, or other encumbrances against it. A warranty deed is also a guarantee of title, which means that the seller may be held liable for damages if the buyer discovers that the title is defective. A warranty deed is no substitute for title insurance, however, because a warranty from a seller who later dies or goes bankrupt may have little value.

Another type of deed used is a quitclaim deed. A quitclaim deed relinquishes whatever interest, if any, the seller may have in the property to the buyer. A quitclaim deed gives the buyer the least protection of any deed. If the seller is the sole owner of the property, the quitclaim deed is enough to transfer title, but the buyer takes a risk by accepting a quitclaim deed because it offers the buyer no guarantee that the title is valid. Quitclaim deeds customarily are used during the property settlement phase of a marriage dissolution.

RECORDING

In Illinois, real estate owners and parties with real estate interests are required to file with the county all documents affecting their interest in property in order to give public notice of the interest. Since 1992, Illinois titles are transferred under the abstract system. Abstract records go back hundreds of years and an abstract of title is a record of all the entries for that property.

BUYING OR SELLING A HOME

Because Illinois has many programs to help people buy a home, home ownership is a possibility for people at all income levels. Buying a home may be both rewarding and stressful. Every home purchase involves a number of complex legal issues, unfamiliar terminology, and lots of paperwork. Knowing how the process works may reduce much of the headache.

REAL ESTATE AGENTS

One of the first decisions for someone interested in buying or selling a home is whether to use the services of a real estate agent. Real estate agents are hired to help buyers and sellers meet to complete the sale of a house. Home buyers and sellers may choose to work with an agent exclusively or non-exclusively.

A person who decides to work with an agent will sign several contracts to clarify the relationship between the consumer and the agent. These contracts may include provisions regarding dual agency. This term refers to the arrangement in which an agent represents both the buyer and the seller of the house. It may be difficult for one agent to represent both a buyer and a seller fairly. When the agent finds a buyer for a house that the agency has listed, the agent's dual loyalties become apparent. The seller wants the highest price possible while the buyer wants to pay the lowest price. The contracts state what the agent may share with the other party and which information must remain confidential.

SELLER DISCLOSURES

In Illinois, the Residential Real Property Disclosure Act requires that when a seller signs the standard purchase agreement, he or she must attach a disclosure document. This document must disclose to the buyer any material defects, which are known hazards or problems with the structure or the heating, plumbing, mechanical, or electrical system. Just because problems are listed on this statement does not mean that the seller must repair the problems, but the buyer may request either repair or a price break because of the problem. In some communities, the seller also is required to complete an inspection report. In that case, an inspector checks the house for defects and these defects are listed in the report.

HOME WARRANTIES

Whenever a builder sells a home in Illinois, the home comes with an implied warranty of habitability. This means that the builder guarantees that there are no major problems with the home, even problems that may not be apparent right away. The buyer has a reasonable amount of time to discover any major problems covered under the warranty. For example, if it rains every day for a month and the roof does not leak, everyone may assume the roof is sound. If the roof begins leaking during a rainy period a year later, it is probably too late to claim the house was sold with a defective roof. The buyer had a reasonable amount of time to discover the defect. The leaky roof would not be covered under the implied warranty of habitability.

Illinois law also provides that any residential unit sold by installment contract is voidable unless there is attached to the contract information about dwelling code compliance. The seller may attach either a certificate of compliance, or may include an express written warranty that the home has not been the subject of any dwelling code violations in the past ten years. If there have been violations, the seller must attach a copy of every notice of violation.

Home buyers should be aware of state laws dealing with removal of lead-based paint from a home. The Lead Poisoning Prevention Act requires owners to remove, replace, or secure and permanently cover walls covered in lead-based paint. Owners must take care of lead problems after receiving notice from the Department of Public Health. Failure to comply with the act may subject the owner to criminal misdemeanor charges.

Foreclosure

Nobody in the process of buying a house wants to think about the possibility of falling behind in house payments to the extent that the bank or mortgage company will foreclose on the loan and claim possession of the house. Nevertheless, it is wise for a consumer to understand why a lender forecloses on a piece of property, so the consumer can minimize the possibility of losing a house.

Up to a point, a lender will typically work with a homeowner who falls behind in making payments because the lender does not want to go through the hassle and expense of foreclosing on a property. Homeowners should communicate with their lenders if there are financial difficulties present that make paying the mortgage difficult. It can take months for a lender to begin a foreclosure, and more months before it is completed, so usually there is time to get the money needed to assure a lender that there will not be a default. After a lender begins the foreclosure process, there is a period of time called a redemption period during which a homeowner can stop the foreclosure by making all delinquent mortgage payments plus the lender's court costs and attorney fees.

In Illinois, a lender may accept the deed to the property instead of foreclosing. The property owner loses the property, but if he or she truly has no other way to avoid foreclosure, offering the deed as a way to satisfy the debt can prevent his or her credit rating from being severely damaged by a foreclosure. However, because lenders generally want cash and not real estate, there is no guarantee that a lender will accept a deed offered in lieu of foreclosure.

A notice of foreclosure must state the name of the person whose property is subject to foreclosure, the court, the case number, the name of the person who holds the title to the property, a legal description of the property, and the mortgage identification information. It must be signed by the foreclosing party or the party's attorney.

LANDLORD–TENANT

Under Illinois law, whenever the owner (landlord) of a house, apartment, room, or any other living space agrees to let someone else (tenant) use the space for a fee, the two parties enter into a legally binding rental contract. General contract principles are discussed in the Contract Law Chapter. Rental contracts are a special class of contracts that are governed by many unique rules. This section discusses the laws applicable to rental contracts.

Leases

The terms of any rental agreement are stated in the lease. A lease can be an oral agreement or a written document. There are two general types of leases: the periodic lease and the lease for a definite term. A periodic lease continues for a specific time period and is automatically renewed at the end of the period for an indefinite time, without a specific end date. For example, parties may agree on a month-to-month lease without specifying how many months the renter will stay. The lease continues until one party terminates it. Most periodic leases will state the rules for notice: how much time each party has to give notice of termination, and the form the notice must take. If the periodic lease does not specify when or how notice is to be given, the parties must follow state law. Illinois law requires that a party to a year-to-year lease give 60 days' notice, a party to a week-to-week lease give one week's notice, and a party to any other periodic lease give 30 days' notice. All notices must be written.

A term lease is a rental agreement specifying a definite time period. For example, a lease for one year is a term lease. Term leases are almost always written. If the parties to the lease do not state when and what kind of notice is required, the lease automatically ends on the last day of the time period.

Security Deposits

A landlord has the right to insist that a renter pay a security deposit before moving in. The security deposit—also called a penalty deposit—is used to pay for any damage beyond ordinary wear and tear that the tenant might do to the rental property, or to satisfy any debts between the tenant and landlord. The deposit cannot be used by the renter to pay rent. There is no limit to how much the landlord may require for a security deposit. The landlord may increase the security deposit at any time during a periodic lease if the tenant is given proper notice, which generally is one rental period plus one day. If the lease is a term lease, no changes may be made to the deposit until the lease comes up for renewal or the parties agree otherwise.

At the end of the tenancy, the landlord must return the deposit to the renter. If the landlord rents to 25 or more tenants, the landlord must pay five percent interest on the security deposit. The landlord is allowed to keep some or all of the deposit if there have been damages or if the tenant does not give timely written notice of termination. If the tenant has paid a penalty deposit, the landlord may keep only the amount necessary to repair damages. The landlord may keep the entire amount of a security deposit, even if the actual damages are not that high. Within 30 days of the termination of the lease, if the landlord plans to keep the deposit, he or she must provide the former tenant with an itemized statement of the damages the tenant caused. In any case, the landlord has 45 days to return the deposit to the tenant.

REPAIRS

Owners of rental property are required to keep the property in reasonable repair. This requirement cannot be waived by the parties, but the tenant may agree to make repairs or perform maintenance if the arrangement is in writing and the tenant receives compensation in return. For example, a renter might agree to make routine plumbing repairs in return for a reduction in rent or payment from the owner. If the parties have not agreed the tenant will do repairs, repairs remain the responsibility of the landlord. If something needs repair, the tenant, by law, must notify the landlord and give the landlord a reasonable opportunity to make the repairs or have them made. If the owner refuses to make repairs, the renter has several options.

Call an Inspector

The renter may call local fire, health, housing, or energy inspectors to investigate whether there is a code violation in the unit. If the tenant believes there is a lead-based paint problem, he or she should call the Department of Public Health. If an inspector finds a code violation, the inspector has authority to summon the owner to appear in court. Often, an inspector's report of a code violation is enough to convince a landlord to correct problems. Calling an inspector is a necessary first step to several of the other options described in the following sections. The law provides protection for a renter if the owner attempts to evict the renter in retaliation for calling an inspector. Under the Lead Poisoning Prevention Act, a landlord is prevented from retaliating against a renter with an elevated blood lead level.

Withhold Rent

If there is a serious problem in a unit, the renter may withhold rent. Under extreme circumstances, the tenant may withhold rent and claim constructive eviction. This means that the rental unit has become uninhabitable because of the problem; in effect, the landlord has evicted the tenant by failing to make the unit livable. Before withholding rent, the renter should notify the owner, in writing, of the needed repairs and give the owner an opportunity to make repairs. If the landlord does not make repairs, the tenant should notify local inspectors, as described above, and get a written copy of the inspector's report. If repairs still are not made, the tenant should notify the landlord, in writing, that all or part of the rent will be withheld until repairs are made.

If the tenant is claiming constructive eviction, he or she must prepare to leave the rental property within a reasonable time after withholding rent. The tenant cannot stay in the apartment or house without paying rent and claim it is not livable. Illinois recognizes the failure to remedy certain problems as a breach of the warranty of habitability. The tenant would have the right to claim constructive eviction under any of the following circumstances:

- No heat
- No water or no hot water
- Electricity, gas, or any other utility shut off
- Flooding
- Leaking or damaged pipes or other plumbing fixtures
- Landlord changed or plugged locks
- Pests
- Lead-based paint hazard
- Fire damage

Withholding rent is a drastic step that should only be taken if the tenant has a strong case against the landlord.

Criminal or Civil Action

Under Illinois law, a landlord may be charged with criminal housing management for extreme failure to comply with the implied warranty of habitability. Criminal housing management is recklessly or intentionally permitting the physical condition of residential real property to be or remain in a condition that endangers a person's health or safety. A person who feels his or her landlord should be charged with criminal housing management may contact the attorney general's office and request the landlord be prosecuted for this crime.

A tenant who has suffered damages by a landlord's gross failure to remedy problems may bring a lawsuit or civil action against the landlord for damages. Usually, damages are limited to the actual amount of money the renter has lost by the landlord's negligence or breach of contract, such as the cost of replacing personal property damaged by chronically leaking pipes. Sometimes, however, renters can recover lost wages, medical costs, or even payment for emotional damages. A tenant who believes he or she has a case against a landlord should contact an attorney for guidance.

EVICTION

Under no circumstances may a landlord forcibly remove a tenant from rental property. In order to get a tenant out of a rental unit, the landlord must bring a lawsuit against the tenant. Legitimate grounds for bringing a suit include nonpayment of rent, breach of a lease, or refusal to leave a unit after the tenancy expires. (The Illinois Retaliatory Eviction Act prohibits a landlord from evicting a tenant for complaining to any governmental authority, such as a housing inspector.)

The landlord first must give the renter written notice of the eviction, which must state the reason he or she plans to start eviction proceedings. The tenant has five days to pay all rent owing, if nonpayment of rent is the reason for eviction. If the reason for eviction is a violation of the lease, the landlord is required to give the tenant ten days' notice. The landlord then must file a complaint in court against the tenant. At the hearing, each side has an opportunity to present its side of the story, through witnesses, with the assistance of counsel, and by presenting evidence. The tenant has a right to a trial by jury. The judge will deliver an opinion. The judge may order the tenant to move immediately, but usually gives the tenant two weeks to vacate. If the judge decides the tenant has no legal reason for refusing to leave the property, the judge may order the sheriff to force the tenant out. If the sheriff has to perform the eviction, the tenant's property may be stored on-site or in a warehouse.

TENANT RIGHTS

Tenants enjoy a number of rights, even if those rights are not specified in the rental contract. The tenant has a right to quiet enjoyment of the premises, which means that the landlord may not interfere illegally or unreasonably in the tenant's life, just because the landlord owns the property. Renters have the right to use the rented premises in any way, as long as it is legal.

Privacy

Generally, a landlord may enter a tenant's unit only with the tenant's consent, except in an emergency. After a tenant has given notice of termination, a landlord has the right to enter the unit to show it to prospective renters. A landlord also may enter for a "reasonable business purpose," such as maintenance, only after giving the tenant reasonable notice. If a landlord fails to get permission or give notice, the landlord is trespassing and may be sued. The tenant whose privacy rights have been violated may recover damages.

Access

Tenants have a right of access to the property they rent. It is illegal for a landlord to lock a tenant out of his or her unit without a court order. A tenant who is unlawfully locked out may petition the court to get back in. The court has authority to order law enforcement officers to help the tenant regain access. If the court finds that the landlord knew or should have known that the lockout was illegal, it may order the landlord to pay damages.

Sublease

Subleasing is having someone else take over a tenant's rights and obligations under a lease before the original lease expires. The tenant has a right to sublet a unit if the lease does not prohibit doing so. If the new tenant does not pay rent, damages the unit, leaves before the lease expires, or breaches another condition of the lease, the landlord may hold the original tenant responsible. The original tenant then may sue the new tenant for those costs.

UTILITIES

Generally landlords who rent property are responsible for paying the utility bills. A landlord and a tenant may agree in the lease that the tenant will obtain his or her own account with the utility companies, as long as the tenant is responsible only for utilities in his or her unit. It is unlawful for landlords to request or require that tenants pay utility bills for common areas or other units. If a landlord fails to pay a utility bill for which he or she is responsible, a tenant may pay the bill and deduct the payment from his or her rent.

UTILITY SUSPENSION

Landlords who are responsible for paying for the provision of utilities are forbidden under Illinois law from shutting off utilities, except in emergencies or for repairs. A tenant whose electricity, water, or heat are terminated because the landlord has failed to pay the bills has several options. The tenant may stop paying rent, as noted above. The tenant may recover 100 percent of the rent paid for any period during which he or she did not have utility service, and each tenant in the landlord's building may recover up to $300 in damages. Utility companies must abide by certain guidelines prior to shutting off service. In the case of rented property, utility companies must give tenants ten days' notice prior to terminating service, and the exact date service will be terminated must be provided.

COLD WEATHER UTILITY RULE

Illinois has a state policy that no residence should be denied essential utility service during the winter due to a failure or inability of the consumer to pay the utility bill. This law dictates that residents and people working for utility companies will work together in a fair manner and that they will act in good faith to resolve any problems with paying for or providing utility service in the winter.

DISCRIMINATION IN HOUSING

Federal and Illinois laws prohibit home sellers and landlords from discriminating on the basis of age, ancestry, citizenship, color, creed, disability, marital status, national origin, race, religion, reliance on public assistance, sex, or unfavorable military discharge. The law prohibits discrimination against families with children under the age of 18. Some areas have local laws that provide additional protection from discrimination. For example, Chicago has a city ordinance forbidding discrimination on the basis of sexual orientation.

The following are some examples of prohibited actions by landlords, owners, or real estate agents:

- Failing to rent to people of a particular race
- Using restrictive covenants to prohibit people of a particular ethnic origin from living in a development
- Charging a blind tenant more money for keeping a guide dog (unless the dog actually causes damage to the property)
- Failing to design housing that is accessible to people with disabilities

Depending on the nature of the violation, federal or state agencies are responsible for enforcing non-discrimination laws. The Illinois Human Rights Act, for instance, is enforced by the Illinois Department of Human Rights.

RESOURCES

Illinois Attorney General, 500 Second Street South, Springfield, IL 62706, phone: (217) 782-1090, TDD: (217) 785-2771 or Illinois Attorney General, 100 Randolph Street West, Chicago, IL 60601, phone: (312) 814-3000, TDD: (312) 814-3374, toll-free: (800) 252-8666. Call or write for information or to order the free publication, *Landlord & Tenant*.

Illinois Department of Human Rights, 222 College South, #101, Springfield, IL 62706, phone: (217) 785-5100, TDD: (217) 785-5125 or 100 Randolph Street West, #10-100, Chicago, IL 60601, phone: (312) 814-6200, TDD: (312) 263-1579.

Illinois Department of Public Health, 535 Jefferson Street West, Springfield, IL 62761, phone: (217) 782-4977.

Illinois Housing Development Authority, 401 Michigan Avenue North, #900, Chicago, IL 60611-4205, phone: (312) 836-5200 or (800) 942-8439, TDD: (312) 836-5222. Call for information or to order the free booklets, *Bridging the Gap . . .* and *Illinois First-Time Homebuyer Program*.

Illinois State Bar Association, 424 South Second Street, Springfield, IL 62701-1779, phone: (217) 525-1760. Call to order the free pamphlet, *Landlord-Tenant*.

Chapter 22: Real Estate Law

REAL ESTATE LAW LEADING ILLINOIS ATTORNEYS

LEADING ILLINOIS ATTORNEYS

Illinois' Most Respected Legal Counsel As Selected By Their Peers.

The Leading Illinois Attorneys below were recommended by their peers in a statewide survey.

The Leading Illinois Attorneys listed below were nominated as exceptional by their peers in a statewide survey conducted by American Research Corporation (ARC). ARC asked several thousand licensed Illinois attorneys to name the lawyer to whom they would send a close friend or family member in need of legal assistance in specific areas of law. The attorneys below were nominated in the area of Real Estate Law.

Because the survey results (all practice area results combined) represent less than three percent of Illinois' practicing attorneys, this list should not be construed as a complete list. Nevertheless, it is an excellent source of highly qualified and reputable Illinois attorneys.

For information on ARC's survey methodology, see page *xi*.
For the complete list of Leading Illinois Consumer Attorneys, see page *xii*.

The Leading Illinois Attorneys below are listed alphabetically in accordance with the geographic region in which their offices are located. Note that attorneys may handle clients from a broad geographic area; attorneys are not restricted to only serving clients residing within the cities in which their offices are located.

An attorney whose name appears in bold has included a biographical profile in this chapter.

COOK & COLLAR COUNTIES

Aiello, Chris J. - Villa Park
Alschuler, Benjamin P. - Aurora
Amari, Leonard F. - Chicago
Applehans, Stephen G. - Waukegan
Bazos, Peter C. - Elgin
Bennett, Margaret A. - Oak Brook
Berman, Edward A. - Chicago
Bers, Alan B. - Chicago
Block, Michael D. - Joliet
Carlson, Ray M. - Mundelein
Carter, Andrew M. - Wheaton
Churchill, William A. - Grayslake
Clark, William G., Jr. - Chicago
Cobb, Ronald W., Jr. - Chicago
Collander, Dan M. - Naperville
Day, Scott M. - Naperville
Dean, Kenneth A. - Chicago
Donatelli, Mark R. - Hinsdale
Ehrenreich, Richard F. - Northfield
Esposito, Kathleen C. - Elmhurst
Ferri, Richard H. - Chicago
Flanagan, Leo M., Jr. - Elgin
Fleming, Michael W. - Elmhurst
Flynn, James R. - Hinsdale
Foran, Thomas A. - Chicago
Fox, Leon - Chicago
Frandsen, Roger K. - Elgin
Goggin, Michael J. - Oak Park
Grach, Brian S. - Waukegan

Graham, William M. - Libertyville
Greenberg, Sharran R. - Highland Park, page 296
Grimbau, Rochelle - Chicago
Guerard, Richard M. - Wheaton
Hodes, Scott D. - Chicago
Hodge, Gerald K. - Aurora
Hunt, Thomas C. - Bensenville
Hupp, Robert B. - Aurora
Jacobs, Alan - Chicago
Jumes, Leon P. - Chicago
Kahn, Donald W. - Libertyville
Kelly, Roger J. - Chicago, page 296
Kilberg, Howard E. - Chicago
Knorr, Alfred L. - Glenview
Kuhn, Richard W. - Naperville
Leff, Sherwin H. - Chicago
Levine, Harold I. - Chicago
Levine, Samuel H. - Chicago
Loveless, R. Craig - Wheaton
Lyman, William D. - Oak Brook
Magee, James T. - Round Lake
Malato, Stephen A. - Chicago
Manetti, Mark D. - Oak Brook
Marks, Kenneth E. - Downers Grove
McJoynt, Timothy - Downers Grove
Meyers, Ted A. - Elgin
Miselman, Michael D. - Chicago
Moltz, Marshall J. - Chicago
Motel, Robert - Lincolnwood

Pietsch, Leigh R. - Wheaton
Powell, W. Thomas - Wheaton
Primack, Ronald N. - Lansing
Schiever, Carey J. - Libertyville
Schirmer, Robin L. - Oak Park
Schneider, Gregg D. - Chicago
Scott, Daniel P. - Northbrook
Smythe, Terry J. - Waukegan

Stein, Steven G. - Chicago
Strange, Jeffrey - Wilmette
Talbot, Earl A. - Chicago
Thayer, Steven J. - Chicago
Wilcox, Barbara L. - Chicago
Wolf-Friestedt, Betsy J. - Libertyville
York, Mary M. - Chicago

Northwestern Illinois Including Rockford & Quad Cities

Alexander, Peter - Rockford
Blade, Thomas A. - Moline
Breen, Thomas M. - Addison
Cox, John W., Jr. - Galena
Ecklund, Gary L. - Rockford
Edwards, Frank R. - Rock Island
Galvin, Frank J. - Rock Island
Gehlbach, Gary - Dixon
Horberg, Kurt J. - Cambridge
Huntoon, H. Karl - Moline
Hyzer, Keith - Rockford
Hyzer, Nancy - Rockford

Jackman, Philip A. - Galena
Koenig, Philip E. - Rock Island
Lambert, J. Laird - Rockford, page 297
Phares, William T. - East Moline
Ross-Shannon, Bruce - Rockford
Roth, Robert R. - Galena
Savaiano, Anthony A. - Loves Park
Spelman, James C. - Rockford
VanHooreweghe, Francis R. - Moline
Wham, Fred L., III - Rockford
Zimmerman, Steven P. - Rockford

Central Illinois

Ansel, Marc J. - Champaign
Austin, William W. - Effingham
Barr, John - Decatur
Bennett, Jim A. - Mattoon
Bochenek, Stephen J. - Springfield
Booth, Edward - Decatur
Braden, Glenn A. - Neoga
Brady, John C. - Peoria
Brittingham, Francis M. - Danville
Cole, Paul R. - Champaign
Coletta, Robert J. - Peoria
Connor, William C. - Peoria
Erwin, Sam - Champaign
Flynn, Leonard T. - Champaign
Garst, Steven L. - Paris
Giganti, Francis J. - Springfield
Gilfillan, Joseph P. - Peoria
Glenn, Ralph D. - Mattoon
Grosso, J. Michael - Bloomington
Hall, Charles C. - Danville
Hall, Robert C. - Peoria
Hasselberg, Eric E. - Peoria
Haughey, Roger E. - Champaign
Heavner, Richard L. - Decatur
Holley, Grady E. - Springfield
Holmes, Brent D. - Mattoon
Holzgrafe, Roger E. - Peoria
Hopp, Richard W. - Decatur
Hunt, Mark B., Jr. - Mattoon
Jones, Larry B. - Paris
Joy, Richard M. - Champaign

Kelly, James D. - Springfield
Knox, E. Phillips - Urbana
Kouri, Stephen A. - Peoria
Kramer, Henry E. - Charleston
Kreckman, Alfred H., Jr. - Paris
Kuppler, Karl B. - Peoria
Laukitis, Richard V. - Chillicothe
Lawless, J. Martin - Peoria
Lestikow, James M. - Springfield
Lierman, Joseph H. - Champaign
Lietz, Gary R. - Champaign
Marsh, Roger A. - Urbana
Mellen, Thomas J., II - Danville
Moore, Daniel M., Jr. - Decatur
Mooty, Brian D. - Peoria
Narmont, John S. - Springfield
Phebus, Joseph W. - Urbana
Presney, Paul E., Jr. - Springfield
Radley, David B. - Peoria
Sgro, Gregory P. - Springfield
Shawler, Omer T. - Marshall
Sheehan, Patrick J. - Springfield
Silkwood, Larry R. - Urbana
Solls, Joseph J. - Peoria
Taylor, John C. - Champaign
Thomas, Lott H. - Champaign
Tietz, Christopher M. - Decatur
Washkuhn, Wilson C. - Peoria
Wilson, Michael J. - Bloomington
Wolff, Dale F. - Effingham

Southern Illinois

Benedick, Thomas F. - O'Fallon
Black, Terry R. - Mt. Vernon
Boie, Wesley L. - Anna
Bone, Maurice E. - Belleville
Cannady, Thomas B. - Belleville
Douglas, Robert L. - Robinson
Drone, R. Michael - Carmi
Duke, Patrick L. - Flora
Flanigan, Frank L. - Edwardsville
Frankland, David K. - Albion
Hawkins, Robert J. - Fairfield
Hedin, Craig R. - Mt. Vernon
Heller, Edward J. - Murphysboro
Hunter, Eugenia C. - Carbondale
LeChien, Thomas A. - Belleville
McCarthy, Edward T. - Edwardsville
Metzger, Donald L. - Edwardsville
Murphy, G. Patrick - Marion
Neubauer, Terry J. - Fairview Heights
Rouhandeh, Mary Lou - Carbondale
Sterling, Harry J. - Fairview Heights
Weihl, Donald E. - Belleville

BIOGRAPHICAL PROFILES OF REAL ESTATE LAW LEADING ILLINOIS ATTORNEYS

The Leading Illinois Attorneys profiled below were nominated as exceptional by their peers in a statewide survey conducted by American Research Corporation (ARC). ARC asked several thousand licensed Illinois attorneys to name the lawyer to whom they would send a close friend or family member in need of legal assistance in specific areas of law. The attorneys below were nominated in the area of Real Estate Law.

Because the survey results (all practice area results combined) represent less than three percent of Illinois' practicing attorneys, this list should not be construed as a complete list. Nevertheless, it is an excellent source of highly qualified and reputable Illinois attorneys.

For information on ARC's survey methodology, see page *xi*.
For the complete list of Leading Illinois Consumer Attorneys, see page *xii*.
For the list of Leading Illinois Real Estate Law Attorneys, see page 292.

The Leading Illinois Attorneys below are listed alphabetically in accordance with the geographic region in which their offices are located. Note that attorneys may handle clients from a broad geographic area; attorneys are not limited to only serving clients residing within the cities in which their offices are located.

The two-line attorney listings in this section are of attorneys who practice in this area but whose full biographical profiles appear in other sections of this book. A bullet "•" preceding a name indicates the attorney was nominated in this particular area of law.

For information on the format of the full biographical profiles, consult the "Using the Consumer Guidebook" section on page *xviii*.

The following abbreviations are used throughout these profiles:

App.	Appellate
Cir.	Circuit
Ct.	Court
Dist.	District
Sup.	Supreme
JD	Juris Doctor (Doctor of Law)
LLB	Legum Baccalaureus (Bachelor of Laws)
LLD	Legum Doctor (Doctor of Laws)
LLM	Legum Magister (Master of Laws)
ADR	Alternative Dispute Resolution
ABA	American Bar Association
ABOTA	American Board of Trial Advocates
ATLA	Association of Trial Lawyers of America
CBA	Chicago Bar Association
ISBA	Illinois State Bar Association
ITLA	Illinois Trial Lawyers Association
NBTA	National Board of Trial Advocacy

Chapter 22: Real Estate Law

Cook & Collar Counties

•**MARGARET A. BENNETT** - *Law Offices of Bennett & Bennett, Ltd.* - 720 Enterprise Drive - Oak Brook, IL 60521 - Phone: (630) 573-8800, Fax: (630) 573-9810 - *See complete biographical profile in the Family Law Chapter, page 183.*

JOHN S. BIALLAS - *Attorney at Law* - 2020 West Dean Street, Unit F - St. Charles, IL 60174 - Phone: (630) 513-7878, Fax: (630) 513-7880 - *See complete biographical profile in the Bankruptcy Law Chapter, page 71.*

HOWARD E. GILBERT - *Howard E. Gilbert & Associates, Ltd.* - 5420 Old Orchard Road, Suite A205 - Skokie, IL 60077 - Phone: (847) 966-6600, Fax: (847) 966-6638 - *See complete biographical profile in the Small Business Law Chapter, page 307.*

SHARRAN R. GREENBERG
Attorney at Law
205 Laurel Avenue
Highland Park, IL 60035-2617

Phone: (847) 433-5823
Fax: (847) 433-5883

•**SHARRAN R. GREENBERG:** Ms. Greenberg considers the heart of her law practice to be personal service. She has been concentrating in family law and real estate law since 1984, with some probate and small business consulting and litigation. She prides herself on being available to her clients on a twelve-hours-a-day, seven-days-a-week basis.
Education: JD 1984, Illinois Institute of Technology, Chicago-Kent; MA 1965, Roosevelt University; BA 1961, Roosevelt University.
Admitted: 1984 Illinois.
Employment History: Sole Practitioner 1987-present; Associate 1984-87, Law Clerk 1982-84, Ralla, Klepak & Associates; Law Clerk 1983-84, Hollander & Hollander; Licensed Real Estate Sales Associate 1977-80, Kenneth Friend Realty.
Representative Clients: Ms. Greenberg represents individual buyers and sellers of residential, commercial and vacant properties. She consults with some of the largest real estate firms on the North Shore.
Professional Associations: North Suburban Bar Assn. (Continuing Legal Education Committee 1995).
Community Involvement: Highland Park Community Development; Chicago Area Jewish Hospice (Board Member 1988-90; Hospice Volunteer 1988-90); Highland Park Historical Society.
Firm: Ms. Greenberg has been a sole practitioner since 1987. She offers her clients highly individualized and personalized service. She is available after business hours and on weekends. She works closely with an accountant and a financial planner in many transactions. *Ms. Greenberg also practices Family Law.*

ROGER J. KELLY
Law Offices of Roger J. Kelly
53 West Jackson Boulevard
Suite 1252
Chicago, IL 60604

Phone: (312) 663-3699
Fax: (312) 663-3689

Extensive Experience In:

• Real Estate Closings/Litigation
• Foreclosures/Evictions/Condemnations
• Environmental Issues/Zoning Issues

•**ROGER J. KELLY:** Mr. Kelly's practice focuses on the legal problems and issues of individuals and their families. He has extensive experience representing sellers, buyers, lenders, and developers in both residential and commercial transactions. Mr. Kelly also handles real property litigation such as boundary disputes, quiet title actions, mortgage foreclosures, partition actions, and evictions. To complement his real estate practice, Mr. Kelly also provides legal advice in the areas of employment discrimination, personal injury litigation, and estate planning.
Education: JD 1983, Loyola University; BA 1977, University of Notre Dame.
Admitted: 1983 Illinois; 1984 U.S. Dist. Ct. (N. Dist. IL, General Bar); 1984 U.S. Dist. Ct. (N. Dist. IL, Trial Bar); 1989 U.S. Ct. App. (7th Cir.).
Employment History: Principal 1994-present, Law Offices of Roger J. Kelly; Partner 1991-94, O'Connor & Kelly, P.C.; Associate 1985-91, Zukowski, Rogers and Flood; Lecturer 1983-85, Loyola University of Chicago Law School.
Representative Clients: Town & Country Homes; DHK Development, Inc.; First Bank Systems, Inc.; Firstar Bank.
Professional Associations: CBA (Labor and Employment Law Committee; Real Estate Committee); ISBA (Real Property Section; Employment Law Section; Trial Section); Loyola University of Chicago (Board of Governors 1990-93); Federal Trial Bar.
Community Involvement: Children's Memorial Hospital (Volunteer); St. Josaphat's Grammar School (Youth Sports Coach); Misericordia and Maryville Academy (Volunteer). *Mr. Kelly also practices Employment Law and Personal Injury Law: General.*

296 *Leading Illinois Attorneys Consumer Law Guidebook*

STEVEN S. KOUKIOS - *Koukios & Associates* - 1480 Northwest Highway, Suite 203 - Park Ridge, IL 60068 - Phone: (847) 299-4440, Fax: (847) 299-4468 - *See complete biographical profile in the Bankruptcy Law Chapter, page 72.*

SALLY LICHTER - *Voegtle & Lichter* - 14047 West Petronella Drive, Suite 202A - Libertyville, IL 60048 - Phone: (847) 918-9840, Fax: (847) 918-8247 - *See complete biographical profile in the Family Law Chapter, page 193.*

ERICA CROHN MINCHELLA - *Minchella & Porter, Ltd.* - 19 South LaSalle Street, Suite 1500 - Chicago, IL 60603-1403 - Phone: (312) 759-1700, Fax: (312) 759-8813 - *See complete biographical profile in the Bankruptcy Law Chapter, page 72.*

EDWARD E. REDA, JR. - *Reda, Ltd.* - 8501 West Higgins, Suite 440 - Chicago, IL 60631 - Phone: (312) 399-1122, Fax: (312) 399-1144 - *See complete biographical profile in the Estate Planning, Wills & Trusts Law Chapter, page 162.*

•**CAREY J. SCHIEVER** - *Carey J. Schiever, Ltd.* - 1512 Artaius Parkway, Suite 300 - Libertyville, IL 60048-5231 - Phone: (847) 680-1123, Fax: (847) 680-1124 - *See complete biographical profile in the Estate Planning, Wills & Trusts Law Chapter, page 163.*

MELVIN A. WEINSTEIN - *Melvin A. Weinstein & Associates* - 134 North LaSalle Street, Suite 720 - Chicago, IL 60602 - Phone: (312) 263-2257, Fax: (312) 263-4942 - *See complete biographical profile in the Family Law Chapter, page 206.*

ARIEL WEISSBERG - *Weissberg and Associates, Ltd.* - 401 South LaSalle Street, Suite 403 - Chicago, IL 60605 - Phone: (312) 663-0004, Fax: (312) 663-1514 - *See complete biographical profile in the Bankruptcy Law Chapter, page 73.*

NORTHWESTERN ILLINOIS
INCLUDING ROCKFORD & QUAD CITIES

JAMIE J. SWENSON CASSEL - *Reno, Zahm, Folgate, Lindberg & Powell* - 1415 East State Street, Suite 900 - Rockford, IL 61104 - Phone: (815) 987-4050, Fax: (815) 987-4092 - *See complete biographical profile in the Bankruptcy Law Chapter, page 73.*

•**J. LAIRD LAMBERT:** Mr. Lambert has practiced law in Rockford, Illinois, since 1981. Although most of the matters he handles for his clients are in the areas of real estate, elder law, and estate planning through the use of wills and trusts, he does accept cases of other types, particularly for existing clients or those referred by existing clients. Mr. Lambert is a frequent speaker at seminars and before small groups.
Education: JD 1981, John Marshall Law School; BA 1973, Washington University, St. Louis, Missouri.
Admitted: 1981 Illinois.
Employment History: Sole Practitioner 1994-present; Partner 1981-94, Crosby & Lambert.
Professional Associations: ISBA; Winnebago County Bar Assn.
Community Involvement: Barbara Olson Center of Hope (Board of Directors); Shelter Care Ministries (Board of Directors); Rockford Film Project (Board of Directors); Emmanuel Episcopal Church (Vestry Member; Choir Member); Downtown Rockford Rotary Club. *Mr. Lambert also practices Estate Planning, Wills & Trusts Law and Elder Law.*

J. LAIRD LAMBERT
Attorney at Law
910 Second Avenue
Suite 300
Rockford, IL 61104

Phone: (815) 969-8800
Fax: (815) 969-8821

KENNETH F. RITZ - *Ritz, Willette & Hampilos* - 728 North Court Street - Rockford, IL 61103 - Phone: (815) 968-1807, Fax: (815) 961-1917 - *See complete biographical profile in the Bankruptcy Law Chapter, page 74.*

Chapter 22: Real Estate Law

•**FRED L. WHAM III** - *Attorney at Law* - 124 North Water Street, Suite 202 - Rockford, IL 61107 - Phone: (815) 964-6717, Fax: (815) 962-6153 - *See complete biographical profile in the Family Law Chapter, page 209.*

CENTRAL ILLINOIS

A. CLAY COX - *Hayes, Hammer, Miles, Cox & Ginzkey* - 202 North Center Street - P.O. Box 3067 - Bloomington, IL 61702-3067 - Phone: (309) 828-7331, Fax: (309) 827-7423 - *See complete biographical profile in the Tax Law Chapter, page 330.*

DANIEL J. GREER - *Stine, Wolter & Greer* - 426 South Fifth Street - Springfield, IL 62701 - Phone: (217) 744-1000, Fax: (217) 744-1444 - *See complete biographical profile in the Estate Planning, Wills & Trusts Law Chapter, page 165.*

DAVID H. MC CARTHY - *Attorney at Law* - 1820 First Financial Plaza - Peoria, IL 61602 - Phone: (309) 674-4508, Fax: (309) 674-4546 - *See complete biographical profile in the Family Law Chapter, page 212.*

STEPHEN K. SHEFFLER - *Pelini & Sheffler* - 501 West Church Street - P.O. Box 1486 - Champaign, IL 61820 - Phone: (217) 359-6242, Fax: (217) 359-6271 - *See complete biographical profile in the Bankruptcy Law Chapter, page 75.*

WALTER W. WINGET - *Winget & Kane* - Commerce Bank Building - 416 Main Street, Suite 807 - Peoria, IL 61602 - Phone: (309) 674-2310, Fax: (309) 674-9722 - *See complete biographical profile in the Family Law Chapter, page 214.*

SOUTHERN ILLINOIS

MIKE REED - *Law Office of Mike Reed* - 423 South Poplar Street - Centralia, IL 62801 - Phone: (618) 533-0122, Fax: (618) 533-7541 - *See complete biographical profile in the Bankruptcy Law Chapter, page 76.*

DONALD C. RIKLI - *Attorney at Law* - 914 Broadway - Highland, IL 62249-1897 - Phone: (618) 654-2364, Fax: (618) 654-4752, 800: (800) 24-RIKLI (247-4554) - *See complete biographical profile in the Estate Planning, Wills & Trusts Law Chapter, page 166.*

TERRELL "TERRY" LEE SHARP - *Law Office of Terry Sharp, P.C.* - 1115 Harrison Street - P.O. Box 906 - Mt. Vernon, IL 62864 - Phone: (618) 242-0246, Fax: (618) 242-1170, 800: (800) 769-7000 - *See complete biographical profile in the Bankruptcy Law Chapter, page 76.*

CHAPTER 23

SMALL BUSINESS LAW

There are several ways to organize a business, and the option selected depends on various factors. The option chosen by a small family-owned and operated venture may not be the same choice of a company with several owners and many employees. Each option has benefits and drawbacks. The option selected by a business may change over time as the business' needs, identity, size, budget, and liabilities change. A person may start out as a sole proprietor but decide years later to incorporate. Before a person or persons decide what option would best meet their needs, an attorney experienced in business matters should be consulted.

The *Leading Illinois Attorneys Business Law Guidebook* contains information on issues of concern to businesspersons as well as listings of Leading Illinois Business Attorneys.

The following is a brief summary of the common forms of business organization. At the end of the chapter, issues that may affect all forms of business will be outlined, including registering an assumed name and obtaining tax identification numbers and licenses.

SOLE PROPRIETORSHIP

A sole proprietorship is the simplest form of business organization. One person owns, manages, and controls the business. A sole proprietorship may have employees, but only the owner is in charge of the business. The owner receives the business profits and losses. This person is also responsible for any debts the business may incur. Income, expenses, and losses are reported on the business owner's individual tax return.

A sole proprietorship is relatively easy to organize. The business owner must acquire the appropriate licenses, if any, and tax identification numbers, and must register the business name. There are no specific state filing requirements for this business option.

The benefits of the sole proprietorship include having complete control over the business, ease of the initial set-up, and having business profits taxed at the individual taxpayer rate, which is lower than the rate charged to corporations.

The drawbacks to sole proprietorship include the owner being personally responsible for debts and liabilities of the business. For example, if a business owner has debts that are not being paid, the creditors can reach the personal assets of the business owner, such as a personal checking account. A business owner may obtain insurance to minimize this drawback. Other drawbacks include lack of continuity—when the business owner dies, the business ceases to exist—and the fact that a sole proprietor is not able to deduct benefits like health, dental, and life insurance on his or her income tax return as business expenses.

PARTNERSHIP

A partnership is a business owned by two or more parties. In Illinois, it is possible to form three types of partnerships: general, limited, and limited liability.

GENERAL PARTNERSHIP

A general partnership occurs when two or more persons own, manage, and control a business. Persons in a general partnership share the rights, duties, and responsibilities. Partnerships may also have employees; however, only the partners have control of the business activities.

A partnership has more issues to address than a sole proprietorship. Aside from obtaining the appropriate licenses and tax numbers and registering the business name, partners must agree on the treatment of business profits, expenses, losses, and other business concerns. Typically, there is a written agreement between the partners to address these issues. A general partnership in Illinois need not be registered with the state, and there are no formal requirements for its formation. However, state law governs the conduct, liabilities, and dissolution of a partnership, as well as the relationship between and liabilities of the partners.

The benefits of a general partnership include the owners' control of the business. However, unlike the sole proprietor who has exclusive control, partners share control and responsibilities. Partners have the advantage of more than one resource for finances, ideas, and sharing the work load. The formation of a general partnership can be less complicated than other business formats, such as limited partnerships and corporations. Finally, profits from the partnership are included on the partners' individual tax returns and taxed at the individual taxpayer rate, which is lower than the rate charged to corporations.

The drawbacks to a general partnership include the partners' personal responsibility for the debts and liabilities of the partnership. A partner can be liable for debts incurred by other partners in furtherance of the business. As in a sole proprietorship, a partnership may obtain insurance to minimize this drawback. Business partners are treated like sole proprietors with regard to deducting benefits provided to themselves. Benefits like health, dental, and life insurance may generally not be deducted on partners' income tax returns as business expenses.

In a general partnership, the business generally dissolves upon the death, retirement or withdrawal of a partner, unless there is an express agreement to continue the business under such circumstances. If the business is continued, the former partner, or the former partner's legal representative, is entitled to the value of the former partner's interest, or the profits attributable to the use of the former partner's right in the property. By law, if a partnership interest is assigned to another person, that person is only entitled to the partner's profits from the business. That person may not participate in the management or operation of the partnership unless all the partners agree. These legal requirements may be modified by a partnership agreement. A partnership agreement may detail how a partnership interest may be sold, transferred, or handled upon the death of a partner. Addressing potential issues in an agreement may be one way to prevent disputes from occurring.

LIMITED PARTNERSHIP

A limited partnership is similar in many respects to a general partnership. However, in a limited partnership, there are two types of partners—general and limited. Illinois law requires that a limited partnership have one or more general partners and one or more limited partners. The principal difference between a general and limited partner is that the limited partner can limit his or her personal liability for partnership debts to the amount he or she invests in the partnership. The limited partner, in exchange for the reduction in liability, does not control or manage the business. The general partner controls and manages the business and is personally liable for partnership debts.

Because limited partnerships must meet specific Illinois statutory requirements, they can be more complicated to establish. A limited partnership must apply for a certificate of limited partnership from the Illinois Secretary of State, and this certification must be renewed every two years. A limited partnership must maintain certain records, and must follow specific requirements for registering the business name. A limited partnership is not permitted to engage in the businesses of insurance, banking, or operating a railroad.

The benefits of a limited partnership depend on whether one is a general or limited partner. The general partner enjoys control and management responsibilities. The limited partner receives limited personal liability. Profits for both types of partners are included on the partners' individual tax returns and taxed at the individual taxpayer rate, which is lower than the rate charged to corporations.

The drawbacks to a limited partnership also depend on whether one is a general or limited partner. A general partner is personally responsible for the business debts while the limited partner is only liable for debts up to the amount he or she has invested in the partnership. The limited partner does not participate in the management or control of the business. Business partners are treated like sole proprietors with regard to deducting benefits provided to themselves. Benefits like health, dental, and life insurance may generally not be deducted on partners' income tax returns as business expenses.

Unlike a sole proprietorship or general partnership, when a limited partnership wishes to dissolve, it must file a certificate of cancellation with the Illinois Secretary of State in order to cancel its certificate of limited partnership. As mentioned previously, there are laws that apply to limited partnerships specifically that make this format more time-consuming and complex.

A limited partnership can continue after the death or departure of a partner. The departing partner (or his or her beneficiaries) may be entitled to the fair market value of the partnership interest. The beneficiaries also may have the option of becoming limited partners. A partner's interest in a limited partnership may be assigned. However, the party receiving the assignment is only entitled to the profits that the assigning partner would have received. The partners may agree that the person receiving the assignment become a limited partner. This legal requirement may be modified by a partnership agreement. A partnership agreement may detail the conditions of how a partnership interest may be sold, transferred, or handled upon the departure or death of a partner.

LIMITED LIABILITY PARTNERSHIP

Since 1994, businesses in Illinois have had the option of filing as limited liability partnerships. A partner in a registered limited liability partnership is not liable for the debts or liabilities of the partnership arising from the negligence or wrongful acts of another partner, an employee, or agent of the partnership. However, each partner is always liable for that partner's own negligence or wrongful acts, and remains liable for the debts and liabilities of the partnership that arise from other causes, such as debts owed on business loans.

A limited liability partnership must register with the Illinois Secretary of State by filing an application and paying a fee. The registration must be renewed annually. There are also restrictions on the name such a partnership may use. In all other respects, the limited liability partnership is the same as a general partnership.

CORPORATION

The creation of a corporation is the creation of an artificial person. For legal and tax purposes, a corporation is a separate entity from its owners. A corporation can make purchases, enter into contracts, pay taxes, and sue and be sued.

Corporations must be established in compliance with the requirements set forth in Illinois law. Shareholders are the owners of a corporation. Management and control of the corporation are the responsibility of the board of directors, who may or may not be the shareholders. Income, expenses, and losses of the business are filed on the corporation's tax returns.

There are many requirements for a business to become incorporated. A discussion of the incorporation requirements may be found in the *Leading Illinois Attorneys Business Law Guidebook*.

The benefits of a corporation include protecting the shareholders from business debts and responsibilities in most cases. Unlike the business options previously discussed, a corporation's creditors may not seek to collect debts from the owners of the corporation. However, owners of a new corporation may be required by financial institutions to give personal financial assurances in order to receive funding. There is continuity of a corporate business regardless of individual shareholder status. Even if several shareholders sell their shares in a business or a principal stockholder dies, the existence of the corporation is not affected. Also, a corporation may sell stock or shares in its business to raise capital. Corporations may have several types of stocks or shares available, such as voting shares and nonvoting shares.

The drawbacks of a corporation include double taxation. The corporation files its own tax returns and pays taxes on its profits before paying dividends to the shareholders. When the shareholders receive the dividends, these profits are included on the individual shareholders' tax returns and taxed.

SUBCHAPTER S CORPORATION

A Subchapter S corporation derives its name from a section of the Internal Revenue Code. Under Subchapter S in the Internal Revenue Code, a corporation that meets certain requirements may be treated as a corporation for liability purposes but treated as a partnership for taxation purposes. Shareholders of an S corporation receive limited liability protection, and their profits from the business are included on their individual income tax returns. Illinois has similar tax treatment for such corporations.

The requirements of an S corporation include

- No more than 35 shareholders
- Shareholders must be natural persons (not corporations or partnerships)
- Shareholders cannot be nonresident aliens
- One class of stock

After a business has incorporated, all shareholders must consent to Subchapter S treatment. The election to be treated as an S corporation must be filed with the Internal Revenue Service in a timely manner.

NONPROFIT CORPORATION

In order to be considered nonprofit, a corporation must have been formed for a purpose other than the financial benefit of its shareholders. Also, a nonprofit corporation cannot pay any dividends or other financial rewards to its shareholders. There are specific Illinois laws for nonprofit corporations. To receive tax-exempt status, an organization must first incorporate as a nonprofit corporation. After incorporation, applications for tax-exempt status must be filed with the Internal Revenue Service and the Illinois Department of Revenue. In order for contributions to the organization to be tax deductible, other requirements must be met. Certain charitable organizations must register with the Division of Charitable Trust and Solicitations.

FRANCHISE

A franchise is a method of selling and distributing goods and services. Franchises are available for many types of ventures. A franchise, unlike the options previously discussed, is not a form of business organization. A franchise is an arrangement between at least two parties, in which one party pays the other a fee for the right to engage in a particular business venture. Franchises are regulated by the Federal Trade Commission and the Franchise Division of the Illinois Attorney General. Franchises are discussed further in the *Leading Illinois Attorneys Business Law Guidebook*.

GENERAL BUSINESS ISSUES

As previously mentioned, there are a number of issues that impact businesses, whether they be sole proprietorships or corporations. The following will summarize the most common of these issues.

NAME REGISTRATION
Illinois law states that any business doing business in Illinois under a name other than the full name of the business owner must register the assumed name in the office of the county clerk of each county in which the company conducts business. A business owner must complete an application for a certificate of assumed name, and submit the proper fee. Notice of filing the certificate must be published in a newspaper in the county where application is made, once a week for three consecutive weeks. After the owner submits proof of publication to the county clerk, the name is registered and is valid indefinitely without renewal. In Illinois, more than one business owner is permitted to operate under the same assumed name. Requirements for corporations and limited partnerships are different and can be found in the *Leading Illinois Attorneys Business Law Guidebook*.

TAX IDENTIFICATION NUMBERS
A business in Illinois must obtain a federal employer identification number. This identification number is the equivalent of a Social Security number for individuals. While sole proprietors without employees generally use their Social Security numbers, other businesses file Form SS-4 with the Internal Revenue Service.

A business with employees must also register with the Illinois Department of Labor for an unemployment compensation number.

A business that sells retail goods or services must obtain a retailer's occupation tax number. A business that sells at wholesale must obtain a resale certificate number. Both types of numbers are obtained through the Sales Tax Division of the Illinois Department of Revenue.

LICENSES
Businesses operating in Illinois may also have to obtain federal, state, or local licenses. A businessperson must determine which licenses and permits are required before beginning his or her venture. A good place to start is the First Stop Business Information Center in Springfield, a comprehensive referral service that compiles permitting, licensing, and other regulatory requirements applicable to businesses.

RESOURCES

Contact the First Stop Business Information Center, 620 Adams Street East, Springfield, IL 62701, phone: (217) 785-8019, for the free handbook and start-up kit, *Starting a Business in Illinois*.

Contact the Illinois Secretary of State, Department of Business Services, Howlett Building, Third Floor, Springfield, IL 62756, phone: (217) 782-6961 or 17 North State Street, Chicago, IL 60602, phone: (312) 793-3380, to order the free booklets, *A Guide for Organizing Domestic Corporations* and *A Guide for Organizing Not-For-Profit Corporations*.

Illinois Department of Revenue, 101 West Jefferson, Springfield, IL 62708, toll-free: (800) 732-8866 or 100 West Randolph, Chicago, IL 60601, phone: (312) 814-5258.

Illinois Department of Labor, Division of Unemployment Insurance, 910 South Michigan Avenue, 11th Floor, Chicago, IL 60605, toll-free: (800) 247-4984. Call for the free packet, *New Employer's Packet*.

Internal Revenue Service, Forms Services, 230 South Dearborn, Chicago, IL 60609, toll-free: (800) 829-3676.

Service Corps of Retired Executives (SCORE), 500 West Madison Street, #1250, Chicago, IL 60661, phone: (312) 353-7724.

Small Business Development Center, 620 Adams Street East, Springfield, IL 62701, phone: (217) 785-6310.

Small Business Assistance–Springfield, 511 West Capitol Avenue, Springfield, IL 62701, phone: (217) 492-4416.

Small Business Assistance–Chicago, 500 West Madison, #1250, Chicago, IL, phone: (312) 353-4528.

How to Form a Nonprofit Corporation by Volunteer Lawyers for the Arts is available from Nolo Press by sending $39.95 plus $5.00 shipping and handling to VLA, Publications, One 53rd Street East, New York, NY 10022.

The Partnership Book: How to Write a Partnership Agreement by Volunteer Lawyers for the Arts is available from Nolo Press by sending $24.95 plus $4.00 shipping and handling to VLA, Publications, One 53rd Street East, New York, NY 10022.

Small Business Law Leading Illinois Attorneys

Illinois' Most Respected Legal Counsel As Selected By Their Peers.

The Leading Illinois Attorneys below were recommended by their peers in a statewide survey.

The Leading Illinois Attorneys listed below were nominated as exceptional by their peers in a statewide survey conducted by American Research Corporation (ARC). ARC asked several thousand licensed Illinois attorneys to name the lawyer to whom they would send a close friend or family member in need of legal assistance in specific areas of law. The attorneys below were nominated in the area of Small Business Law.

Because the survey results (all practice area results combined) represent less than three percent of Illinois' practicing attorneys, this list should not be construed as a complete list. Nevertheless, it is an excellent source of highly qualified and reputable Illinois attorneys.

For information on ARC's survey methodology, see page *xi*.
For the complete list of Leading Illinois Consumer Attorneys, see page *xii*.

The Leading Illinois Attorneys below are listed alphabetically in accordance with the geographic region in which their offices are located. Note that attorneys may handle clients from a broad geographic area; attorneys are not restricted to only serving clients residing within the cities in which their offices are located.

An attorney whose name appears in bold has included a biographical profile in this chapter.

Cook & Collar Counties

Adams Murphy, Jennifer - Chicago
Alschuler, Benjamin P. - Aurora
Bazos, Peter C. - Elgin
Berk, Keith H. - Chicago
Bers, Alan B. - Chicago
Boylan, William E. - Wheaton
Brezina, David C. - Chicago
Brown, Kenneth H. - Highland Park
Chamberlin, Darcy J. - Oak Brook
Colombik, Richard M. - Schaumburg
Dean, Kenneth A. - Chicago
DeFranco, Leonard S. - Oak Brook
Dickson, Fred H. - Aurora
Donatelli, Mark R. - Hinsdale
Duffy, John M. - Chicago
Einstein, Jean M. - Chicago
Farrell, John E. - Chicago
Friedberg, Michael R. - Chicago
Gilbert, Howard E. - Skokie, page 307
Gordon, Mark L. - Chicago
Grach, Brian S. - Waukegan
Graham, William M. - Libertyville
Hardy, Ralph C., Jr. - Elgin
Hodge, Gerald K. - Aurora
Horwood, Richard M. - Chicago
Hoscheit, John J. - St. Charles
Hunt, Thomas C. - Bensenville
Hupp, Robert B. - Aurora
Jumes, Leon P. - Chicago

Kaergard, Kenneth L. - St. Charles
Kuhn, Richard W. - Naperville
Leff, Sherwin H. - Chicago
Manetti, Mark D. - Oak Brook
McHugh, Timothy - Elmhurst
McParland, James E. - Chicago
Mendelson, Michael S. - Chicago
Neville, Ronald F. - Chicago
Palmieri, Vincent L. - Libertyville
Pawlan, Mitchell D. - Northbrook
Polisky, Joel S. - Chicago
Poulos, Michael D. - Evanston
Primack, Ronald N. - Lansing
Reed, Daniel A. - Aurora
Rolewick, David F. - Wheaton
Rosenberg, Steven J. - Chicago
Rotman, Michael H. - Chicago
Schanlaber, William C. - Aurora
Schiever, Carey J. - Libertyville
Schiller, Richard D. - Oswego
Stein, Steven G. - Chicago
Strange, Jeffrey - Wilmette
Streit, Thomas J. - Aurora
Thayer, Steven J. - Chicago
Wagner, Irvin J. - Chicago
Weissberg, Ariel - Chicago
Wexler, Leon C. - Chicago
Wilcox, Barbara L. - Chicago
Zazove, Neal C. - Chicago

Northwestern Illinois Including Rockford & Quad Cities

Balch, Bruce L. - Rock Island
Balsley, William L. - Loves Park
Churchill, Daniel - Moline
Cicero, Paul R. - Rockford
Cox, John W., Jr. - Galena
Galvin, Frank J. - Rock Island
Greenwald, Thomas E. - Rockford
Horberg, Kurt J. - Cambridge
Huntoon, H. Karl - Moline
Jackman, Philip A. - Galena
Jensen, Philip F. - Galena, page 308
Keeling, James W. - Rockford
Lambert, J. Laird - Rockford
Natale, Bernard J. - Rockford
Nepple, James A. - Rock Island
Oliver, Robert J. - Rockford
Petro, Nerino J., Jr. - Loves Park
Roth, Robert R. - Galena
Sahlstrom, R. Craig - Rockford
Slover, John A., Jr. - Moline
Stojan, Clark J. - Rock Island
Winkler, Karl F. - Rockford

Central Illinois

Austin, William W. - Effingham
Barr, John - Decatur
Bennett, Jim A. - Mattoon
Brady, John C. - Peoria
Coletta, Robert J. - Peoria
Cusack, Daniel P. - Peoria
Dwyer, Edward W. - Springfield
Erwin, Sam - Champaign
Flynn, Leonard T. - Champaign
Frisse, David M. - Paris
Goldstein, William M. - Urbana
GreenLeaf, John L., Jr. - Decatur
Grimsley, Gregg N. - Peoria
Hall, Robert C. - Peoria
Heavner, Richard L. - Decatur
Hodge, Katherine D. - Springfield
Holzgrafe, Roger E. - Peoria
Houchen, Vernon H. - Decatur
Jones, Lance T. - Springfield
Kouri, Stephen A. - Peoria
Kramer, Henry E. - Charleston
Kuppler, Karl B. - Peoria
Laukitis, Richard V. - Chillicothe
Lestikow, James M. - Springfield
Lietz, Gary R. - Champaign
Manion, Paul T. - Danville
Marsh, Roger A. - Urbana
McNeely, Charles - Jacksonville
Meachum, Clyde - Danville
Narmont, John S. - Springfield
Potter, James R. - Springfield
Silkwood, Larry R. - Urbana
Stumpe, Karen M. - Peoria
Sutkowski, Edward F. - Peoria
Swartz, John L. - Springfield
Tagge, Stephen A. - Springfield
Tietz, Christopher M. - Decatur
Turner, Mercer - Bloomington
Washkuhn, Wilson C. - Peoria
Webber, Carl M. - Urbana

Southern Illinois

Applegate, Steven D. - Carbondale
Blake, Edward J., Jr. - Belleville
Boyne, Kevin M. - Belleville
Cunningham, Roscoe D. - Lawrenceville
Garrison, James T. - Marion
Hawkins, Robert J. - Fairfield
Hedin, Craig R. - Mt. Vernon
Hendricks, Scott P. - Carbondale
Jennings, Robert L. - Belleville
LeChien, Thomas A. - Belleville
Mager, T. Richard - Carbondale
Mathis, Patrick B. - Belleville
McCarthy, Edward T. - Edwardsville
Mitchell, A. Ben - Mt. Vernon
Reed, Michael E. - Centralia
Terlizzi, Eric L. - Salem
Van Winkle, Theodore - McLeansboro
Vieira, Michelle - Marion
Weihl, Donald E. - Belleville
Welch, Kay A. - Belleville
Wham, James B. - Centralia
Whittington, Rebecca A. - Carbondale

Biographical Profiles of Small Business Law Leading Illinois Attorneys

The Leading Illinois Attorneys profiled below were nominated as exceptional by their peers in a statewide survey conducted by American Research Corporation (ARC). ARC asked several thousand licensed Illinois attorneys to name the lawyer to whom they would send a close friend or family member in need of legal assistance in specific areas of law. The attorneys below were nominated in the area of Small Business Law.

Because the survey results (all practice area results combined) represent less than three percent of Illinois' practicing attorneys, this list should not be construed as a complete list. Nevertheless, it is an excellent source of highly qualified and reputable Illinois attorneys.

For information on ARC's survey methodology, see page *xi*.
For the complete list of Leading Illinois Consumer Attorneys, see page *xii*.
For the list of Leading Illinois Small Business Law Attorneys, see page 304.

The Leading Illinois Attorneys below are listed alphabetically in accordance with the geographic region in which their offices are located. Note that attorneys may handle clients from a broad geographic area; attorneys are not limited to only serving clients residing within the cities in which their offices are located.

The two-line attorney listings in this section are of attorneys who practice in this area but whose full biographical profiles appear in other sections of this book. A bullet "•" preceding a name indicates the attorney was nominated in this particular area of law.

For information on the format of the full biographical profiles, consult the "Using the Consumer Guidebook" section on page *xviii*.

The following abbreviations are used throughout these profiles:

App.	Appellate
Cir.	Circuit
Ct.	Court
Dist.	District
Sup.	Supreme
JD	Juris Doctor (Doctor of Law)
LLB	Legum Baccalaureus (Bachelor of Laws)
LLD	Legum Doctor (Doctor of Laws)
LLM	Legum Magister (Master of Laws)
ADR	Alternative Dispute Resolution
ABA	American Bar Association
ABOTA	American Board of Trial Advocates
ATLA	Association of Trial Lawyers of America
CBA	Chicago Bar Association
ISBA	Illinois State Bar Association
ITLA	Illinois Trial Lawyers Association
NBTA	National Board of Trial Advocacy

COOK & COLLAR COUNTIES

JOHN S. BIALLAS - *Attorney at Law* - 2020 West Dean Street, Unit F - St. Charles, IL 60174 - Phone: (630) 513-7878, Fax: (630) 513-7880 - *See complete biographical profile in the Bankruptcy Law Chapter, page 71.*

•**DARCY J. CHAMBERLIN** - *Attorney at Law* - 1211 West 22nd Street, Suite 1006 - Oak Brook, IL 60521 - Phone: (630) 447-2478, Fax: (630) 572-1432 - *See complete biographical profile in the Estate Planning, Wills & Trusts Law Chapter, page 160.*

PATRICIA A. FELCH - *ARTSLaw Offices of Patricia A. Felch, P.C.* - Three First National Plaza, Suite 3600 - 70 West Madison - Chicago, IL 60602 - Phone: (312) 236-0404, Fax: (312) 236-0403 - *See complete biographical profile in the Arts, Entertainment & Intellectual Property Law Chapter, page 60.*

•**HOWARD E. GILBERT:** Mr. Gilbert has a no-nonsense, hands-on practice, drawing upon years of experience in both law and business. He provides practical legal consultation on a cost-conscious basis and believes it is necessary to deal with the entire client, as opposed to narrowly specializing. Mr. Gilbert is listed in *Who's Who Worldwide.*
Education: JD 1972, DePaul University; BS 1969, University of Illinois.
Admitted: 1972 Illinois; 1993 Florida; 1972 U.S. Dist. Ct. (N. Dist. IL); 1973 U.S. Tax Ct.; 1974 U.S. Ct. App. (7th Cir.); 1979 U.S. Sup. Ct.
Employment History: 1986-present, Howard E. Gilbert & Associates, Ltd.; 1982-85, Gilbert, Shapiro & Richman; 1975-82, Herman, Tannebaum, Levine & Gilbert; 1974-75, Panter, Nelson & Bernfield; 1972-74, Altheimer & Gray.
Representative Clients: Illinois Tool Works, Inc.; Safety Kleen Oil Recovery Co.; Arthur Gallagher & Co.; Snap-On Tools, Inc.; Main Insurance Company; State Farm Insurance Co.; Taylor Management Co., Inc; H & R Industries, Inc.; National Hospital and Healthcare, Inc.; Illinois Health Reform Coalition. Mr. Gilbert handles numerous closely held corporate and family businesses, estate planning issues, real estate, litigation, and personal injury matters.
Professional Associations: North Suburban Bar Assn.; ITLA; ATLA; CBA; ISBA; ABA; Circuit Court of Cook County, Illinois (Trial Arbitrator 1995).
Community Involvement: Misericordia (Family Fest Sponsor; Candy Days); Reef Point Yacht Club (past Vice Commodore); Ellenwood Landing Dockominium Assn. (Acting President); Chicago Yacht Club; Aircraft Owners and Pilots Assn.; Attorney Disciplinary and Registration Commission (Standing Committee); Northshore Congregation Israel (Choir).
Firm: Howard E. Gilbert & Associates, Ltd., is an old-fashioned, hands-on firm. It provides many types of legal services for long-time clients through experienced attorneys and personnel. Within the firm, there are attorneys who concentrate in tax law, estate planning, litigation, real estate, personal injury, and general practice. *Mr. Gilbert also practices Personal Injury Law: General, Estate Planning, Wills & Trusts Law and Real Estate Law.*

HOWARD E. GILBERT
Howard E. Gilbert & Associates, Ltd.
5420 Old Orchard Road
Suite A205
Skokie, IL 60077
Phone: (847) 966-6600
Fax: (847) 966-6638
E-mail: justiceb.aol.com

Extensive Experience In:
• Business Litigation
• Large Arbitration Disputes
• Insurance Coverage & Acquisitions

ROBERT E. MC KENZIE - *McKenzie & McKenzie, P.C.* - 5450 North Cumberland Avenue, Suite 120 - Chicago, IL 60656 - Phone: (312) 714-8040, Fax: (312) 714-8055 - *See complete biographical profile in the Tax Law Chapter, page 329.*

ERICA CROHN MINCHELLA - *Minchella & Porter, Ltd.* - 19 South LaSalle Street, Suite 1500 - Chicago, IL 60603-1403 - Phone: (312) 759-1700, Fax: (312) 759-8813 - *See complete biographical profile in the Bankruptcy Law Chapter, page 72.*

EDWARD E. REDA, JR. - *Reda, Ltd.* - 8501 West Higgins, Suite 440 - Chicago, IL 60631 - Phone: (312) 399-1122, Fax: (312) 399-1144 - *See complete biographical profile in the Estate Planning, Wills & Trusts Law Chapter, page 162.*

•**DAVID F. ROLEWICK** - *Rolewick & Gutzke, P.C.* - 1776 South Naperville Road, Suite 104A - Wheaton, IL 60187 - Phone: (630) 653-1577, Fax: (630) 653-1579 - *See complete biographical profile in the Estate Planning, Wills & Trusts Law Chapter, page 162.*

Chapter 23: Small Business Law

•**CAREY J. SCHIEVER** - *Carey J. Schiever, Ltd.* - 1512 Artaius Parkway, Suite 300 - Libertyville, IL 60048-5231 - Phone: (847) 680-1123, Fax: (847) 680-1124 - *See complete biographical profile in the Estate Planning, Wills & Trusts Law Chapter, page 163.*

EDWARD I. STEIN - *Edward I. Stein, Ltd.* - 707 Skokie Boulevard, Suite 600 - Northbrook, IL 60062 - Phone: (847) 291-4320, Fax: (847) 432-1132 - *See complete biographical profile in the Family Law Chapter, page 204.*

RORY T. WEILER - *Weiler & Noble, P.C.* - 335 North River Street, Suite 203 - Batavia, IL 60510 - Phone: (630) 879-3020, Fax: (630) 513-2929 - *See complete biographical profile in the Family Law Chapter, page 206.*

•**ARIEL WEISSBERG** - *Weissberg and Associates, Ltd.* - 401 South LaSalle Street, Suite 403 - Chicago, IL 60605 - Phone: (312) 663-0004, Fax: (312) 663-1514 - *See complete biographical profile in the Bankruptcy Law Chapter, page 73.*

Northwestern Illinois
Including Rockford & Quad Cities

JAMIE J. SWENSON CASSEL - *Reno, Zahm, Folgate, Lindberg & Powell* - 1415 East State Street, Suite 900 - Rockford, IL 61104 - Phone: (815) 987-4050, Fax: (815) 987-4092 - *See complete biographical profile in the Bankruptcy Law Chapter, page 73.*

PHILIP F. JENSEN
Hammer, Simon & Jensen
303 North Bench Street
P.O. Box 270
Galena, IL 61036
Phone: (815) 777-1101
Fax: (815) 777-9241

Extensive Experience In:
• Business Litigation
• Small Business Incorporation
• Real Estate Leasing & Acquisitions

•**PHILIP F. JENSEN:** Mr. Jensen is a partner in the firm of Hammer, Simon & Jensen, a law firm with offices in Galena, Illinois, and Dubuque, Iowa. In addition to his role as legal counsel for a municipality, he represents a substantial number of small businesses and non-profit corporations. His practice also includes family law and civil litigation.
Education: JD 1984, University of Nebraska; BS 1981 with honors, Illinois State University.
Admitted: 1984 Illinois; 1988 Iowa; 1986 U.S. Dist. Ct. (N. Dist. IL).
Employment History: Partner/Associate 1988-present, Hammer, Simon & Jensen; Assistant State's Attorney 1985-88, Illinois State's Attorney's Office.
Professional Associations: ISBA; ATLA; Iowa State Bar Assn.; Jo Daviess County Bar Assn.; Dubuque County Bar Assn.; Christian Legal Society; Institute for Christian Conciliation.
Community Involvement: Jo Daviess County Chamber of Commerce (past Board Member); Sojourn House/Alcohol Rehabilitation Center (past Board Member); Tri-State Christian School (Board Member).
Firm: The firm of Hammer, Simon & Jensen was formed in 1989. The firm's partners and associates have substantial experience and concentrate in the areas of civil litigation, family law, small business representation, insurance defense, and municipal law. Representative clients include the City of Galena, Illinois; Interstate Power Company; St. Paul Fire and Marine Insurance; Traveler's Insurance; United Fire and Casualty; YMCA; and Apple Canyon Lake Property Owners' Association. *Mr. Jensen also practices Family Law and Personal Injury Law: General.*

KENNETH F. RITZ - *Ritz, Willette & Hampilos* - 728 North Court Street - Rockford, IL 61103 - Phone: (815) 968-1807, Fax: (815) 961-1917 - *See complete biographical profile in the Bankruptcy Law Chapter, page 74.*

•**R. CRAIG SAHLSTROM** - *Attorney and Counsellor at Law* - One Court Place, Suite 301 - Rockford, IL 61101 - Phone: (815) 964-4601, Fax: (815) 964-3292 - *See complete biographical profile in the Criminal Law: Felonies & White Collar Crime Chapter, page 116.*

CENTRAL ILLINOIS

HOWARD W. FELDMAN - *Feldman & Wasser* - 1307 South Seventh Street - P.O. Box 2418 - Springfield, IL 62705 - Phone: (217) 544-3403, Fax: (217) 544-1593 - *See complete biographical profile in the Family Law Chapter, page 210.*

•LANCE T. JONES - *Reid & Jones Law Offices* - 2041 West Iles, Suite A - Springfield, IL 62704 - Phone: (217) 546-1001, Fax: (217) 546-1771 - *See complete biographical profile in the Employment Law Chapter, page 148.*

WILLIAM A. PEITHMANN - *Peithmann Law Office* - 111 South Main Street - P.O. Box 228 - Farmer City, IL 61842 - Phone: (309) 928-3390 - *See complete biographical profile in the Estate Planning, Wills & Trusts Law Chapter, page 165.*

WALTER W. WINGET - *Winget & Kane* - Commerce Bank Building - 416 Main Street, Suite 807 - Peoria, IL 61602 - Phone: (309) 674-2310, Fax: (309) 674-9722 - *See complete biographical profile in the Family Law Chapter, page 214.*

CHAPTER 24

SOCIAL SECURITY LAW

Millions of people in the United States rely on some form of financial assistance from the government. People with disabilities are eligible for such assistance, as are people in lower income brackets. As workers age, they begin to reap the benefits of years in the work force, receiving the retirement assistance commonly referred to as "Social Security." This chapter describes the federal Social Security Act and the major programs created thereunder. Other issues of interest to senior citizens are addressed in the Elder Law Chapter.

THE SOCIAL SECURITY ACT

Congress passed the Social Security Act in 1935 to create a very broad social safety net for all United States workers and their families. Originally intended to provide financial support for elderly workers who could no longer perform gainful labor, Social Security has expanded to include workers with disabilities, dependents of persons qualified to receive Social Security, and survivors (widows, widowers, or children) of someone who died but had become legally eligible to receive Social Security. Thus, depending on a person's circumstances, he or she may be eligible for Social Security benefits at any age.

The public benefit programs started by the Social Security Act and its amendments are financed generally by taxes levied on workers. Employers automatically deduct a portion of each worker's paycheck and match that amount with money from their business or organization. As of 1995, 7.65 percent of the employee's gross salary goes to Social Security. This deduction is usually labeled "FICA" for the Federal Insurance Contributions Act, which authorizes the payroll tax. A person's employer also is required to contribute 7.65 percent of the employee's gross salary to Social Security. Self-employed workers are responsible for paying the entire amount themselves. If a person is self-employed, he or she pays 15.3 percent of his or her taxable income to Social Security, but half of that is deductible from federal income tax as a business expense.

Of the money received from Social Security payroll taxes, the largest portion goes to pay retirement benefits; smaller portions pay disability benefits and Medicare. As of 1995, there were approximately 141 million people paying into Social Security.

The three largest programs within the Social Security Act are Retirement, Survivors, and Disability Health Insurance (RSDHI); Supplemental Security Income (SSI); and Medicaid. RSDHI is the name of the federal government's benefits program for workers and retirees, and itself contains three separate programs to cover retirement, disability, and health insurance (Medicare).

These three programs are extremely complex. Although detailed descriptions are beyond the space limitations of this chapter, a general familiarity with them is helpful for understanding one's entitlements.

BENEFITS FOR RETIREES

Retirement and Survivors Insurance

Despite the fact that Retirement and Survivors Insurance (RSI) is only one branch of RSDHI, which in turn is only one branch of the Social Security Act, when most people refer to "Social Security" they actually mean RSI. Payments from RSI are the Social Security checks that millions of Americans receive each month. RSI was not intended to be a person's sole source of income, but to supplement other income sources such as pensions, insurance, savings, and investments. However, for many, RSI is their only source of income.

A worker gains RSI coverage by performing covered employment for a certain amount of time. The term "covered employment" means most types of work, including full- or part-time wage or salaried work, self-employment, farm work, membership in the United States Armed Services, employment in private nonprofit organizations, most domestic work, and most federal, state, and local government employment. The only major exceptions are railroad employees separately covered by the Railroad Retirement System, federal workers hired before 1984, and certain religious workers. The rules of eligibility and benefit amount are quite complex and provide limited coverage for spouses, children, and survivors.

Generally, a person begins receiving RSI benefits at age 65; however, a worker has the option of initiating benefits at age 62. All benefits are based on what is called the primary insurance amount (PIA): the amount a worker is entitled to if he or she retires exactly at age 65. The amount of the monthly check varies depending on how much the worker made each year. The higher his or her pay, the higher the benefits, up to a maximum dollar amount. A person who initiates benefits at age 62 receives a reduced monthly amount equal to a percentage of his or her PIA. This is a permanent reduction that amounts to approximately seven percent of the PIA for each year a person receives benefits before age 65. Postponing the receipt of benefits until after age 65 can entitle a worker to receive higher monthly amounts. Cost-of-living increases are built into the system so that the monthly amount automatically increases each year as the national cost of living rises.

Family members receive benefits based on the worker's retirement benefits. The spouse of an eligible worker draws spousal benefits on the worker's account—usually one-half of the worker's PIA—if the spouse is at least 62 years old or cares for a child eligible for child's benefits on the worker's account. Other bases for family eligibility are

- Spousal benefits for a divorced spouse if he or she was married to the insured worker for at least ten continuous years and has not remarried
- Full benefits for a surviving widow or widower of a fully insured worker from age 65
- A one-time death benefit (currently $255) for surviving relatives of fully insured workers who apply within two years of the worker's death
- Benefits for the child or grandchild of an insured worker if he or she was dependent on the worker when benefits began, is unmarried, and
    - Is 18 years old or younger
    - Is 19 years old or younger but enrolled as a full-time elementary or secondary school student, or
    - Is older than 18 years but became disabled before reaching age 22

As a general rule, an eligible individual must apply for RSI benefits in order to receive them. Failure to apply for benefits as soon as one is entitled to them can forfeit earned benefits.

Railroad Retirement System

The Railroad Retirement System is a federal income insurance program specifically for workers in the railroad industry. Originally, this system was independent of the Social Security Administration, but in 1974, the two programs' provisions were integrated. The integration was not entirely smooth, however, which has led to complex and confusing rules that are often the source of errors in awarding benefits.

Most of the rules for Railroad Retirement closely parallel those for RSI. A retired railroad worker is eligible for monthly benefits if he or she worked for a railroad employer for at least ten years before reaching age 65. As with RSI, a worker can opt to retire earlier, at age 62, but will receive reduced benefits. Anyone with fewer than ten years' employment in the railroad industry is ineligible for railroad benefits, but the years of railroad employment can be added to years of non-railroad employment for purposes of calculating RSI benefits.

Some railroad workers who retired before January 1, 1975, are entitled to draw both full RSI benefits and full Railroad Retirement benefits. Most other workers, however, have their RSI benefits reduced by the amount of the Railroad Retirement benefits.

DISABILITY BENEFITS

The federal government has two disability benefit programs administered by the Social Security Administration for qualified applicants: RSDHI Disability Insurance and Supplemental Security Income (SSI). These two programs are similar and are governed by many of the same rules. An individual who qualifies for one program occasionally can receive benefits from both programs simultaneously.

Both RSDHI and SSI programs define disability as "inability to engage in any substantial gainful activity by reason of any medically determined physical or mental impairment which can be expected to last for a continuous period of not less than 12 months." The physical or mental disability must be "of such severity" that an applicant not only is unable to do the work he or she did previously, but is unable to engage in any kind of gainful work.

The applicant for either RSDHI disability or SSI has the burden of proving by medical evidence that he or she is disabled or blind. Most applicants must wait five full months before their benefits begin. Each applicant's case is reviewed periodically to determine whether his or her condition has improved to the point that he or she is able to resume working.

RSDHI Disability Insurance

RSDHI Disability Insurance provides benefits for workers with substantial work histories in covered employment who are unable to continue work because they became disabled before reaching age 25. The term "covered employment" includes most types of work. The disabled worker and his or her dependents usually are eligible for RSDHI disability benefits. In some cases, disabled survivors of an insured worker can receive benefits.

Supplemental Security Income

SSI is a nationwide income maintenance program designed to help persons with limited income and assets who are elderly, blind, or disabled. Although SSI is administered by the Social Security Administration, it is not funded by Social Security taxes. Unlike Social Security, SSI is based on need. A person's work record is not relevant in determining eligibility for SSI. Thus, a disabled person under age 65 who has not worked a sufficient amount of time to qualify for RSDHI disability may be eligible to receive SSI disability benefits.

To receive SSI, a person must be 65 years of age or older, be blind or disabled, and have financial need. The formula for determining SSI eligibility and benefits takes into account both income level and assets. When calculating a person's income, the government includes earnings, Social Security benefits, payments from pensions, any non-cash items like food, clothing, or shelter, and items that the individual may own. Some things, however, are exempt from consideration, such as

- A person's home (regardless of its value)
- Household goods and personal property (worth less than $2,000)
- One car (worth less than $4,500)
- Income tax refunds
- The value of food stamps
- A portion of monthly earnings

A person qualifying on the basis of blindness or disability must be referred to vocational rehabilitation services. If the disability is related to alcohol or drug dependency, the applicant may be required to enroll in an appropriate treatment program or risk losing eligibility. Residence in a public institution, such as a prison or certain hospitals, disqualifies an applicant. If a person receives SSI, he or she also may be eligible for other benefits such as food stamps and Medicaid, discussed below.

When the federal government created SSI, it replaced many state-administered welfare programs for the elderly, blind, and disabled. The State of Illinois chose to continue its own program to supplement SSI benefits. This program is known as State Supplemental Payments (SSP). SSP provides additional assistance to qualified elderly, blind, and disabled persons, including those whose income levels are above the SSI standards. The purpose of SSP is to help very poor Illinois residents who are unable to work but whose needs are not met by other federal or state programs.

MEDICARE

Medicare—also called Medical Assistance in Illinois—is a federal program administered by the Social Security Administration designed to cover some basic medical and health care costs of eligible individuals over age 65, as well as many people with disabilities. Medicare has become an enormous federal program, providing billions of dollars in coverage every year.

Medicare should not be confused with Medicaid. Medicaid is a program administered by the Social Security Administration to pay doctor and hospital bills of people with limited income and assets. Medicare benefits are available to qualified individuals regardless of financial need. Because Medicare is closely linked to RSI, Disability Insurance, and Railroad Disability benefits, a basic understanding of the eligibility requirements and application procedures for those programs is helpful for an understanding of Medicare.

Medicare Parts A and B

Medicare has two basic divisions, called Part A and Part B. Medicare Part A, commonly known as Hospital Insurance, covers medically necessary hospital and related health care. Included in Part A are costs for such expenses as inpatient hospital care necessitated by acute illness, skilled nursing home care, certified hospice care for the terminally ill, inpatient psychiatric care, and care in the home by a certified home health care provider. People qualify for Hospital Insurance when they turn 65 or if they are covered by Social Security or Railroad Retirement benefits.

Medicare Part B, commonly known as Medical Insurance, is a voluntary health insurance program designed to cover some of the costs not covered by Medicare Part A, such as outpatient hospital services, outpatient physical therapy, speech pathology services, necessary ambulance service, and medical equipment. Unlike Part A, which is paid for out of Social Security taxes and is free to anyone who qualifies, Part B is an optional program that carries a monthly premium of under $50.

The federal government contracts with private insurance companies to handle routine claims processing, payment, and other functions under Parts A and B. Medicare recipients have the right to choose how they will receive hospital, doctor, and other health care services covered by Medicare. One option is the traditional fee-for-service system. Under this system, the recipient visits a hospital or doctor of his or her choice and pays a fee for any services provided. Medicare will pay a percentage of that fee, but the recipient is responsible for certain deductible and coinsurance payments. Most people covered by a fee-for-service Medicare plan also have private insurance (commonly called Medigap) to supplement their Medicare coverage.

Another option is to use a health maintenance organization (HMO). HMOs offer a wide range of health care services in exchange for a fixed premium paid in advance. Medicare recipients enrolled in an HMO rarely require additional Medigap insurance because the HMO plan itself supplements Medicare. One drawback of an HMO, however, is that health care services can only be provided by a member of the HMO's health care network. Medicare recipients lose the freedom to consult any health care provider of their choice.

Costs Not Covered by Medicare

Medicare never was intended to provide comprehensive coverage for all medical needs of America's elderly population, but rather, was intended to supplement private resources. Many health services are not covered by Medicare. For example, Medicare does not pay for

- Custodial care provided by someone without medical training and intended to help the patient with his or her daily living needs, such as help with bathing, walking, or exercising
- Dentures or routine dental care
- Eyeglasses, hearing aids, and examinations to prescribe or fit them
- Nursing home care (except skilled nursing care)
- Prescription drugs
- Routine physical checkups and related tests (except for some screening procedures, such as Pap smears and mammograms)
- Most immunization shots
- Services outside the United States
- Personal comfort items

MEDICAID

Medicaid should not be confused with Medicare. Despite their similar names, the two programs are different. While Medicare is funded and administered entirely by the federal government to provide health care to elderly persons and people with disabilities, Medicaid is a cooperative program funded partly by the federal government and partly by the individual states. The federal government's role in Medicaid is quite limited. It pays a percentage of the cost of each state's health care program for indigent people and ensures that every state's program complies with various federal requirements. The amount of money a state receives from the federal government is called the Federal Financial Participation (FFP). Each state's FFP is determined by a formula based on the state's per capita income and the amount of medical services the state chooses to provide to needy people within the state. Many people qualify for Medicaid, Medicare, and other forms of assistance that often are administered in an overlapping or cooperative fashion.

Each state has wide latitude to decide how Medicaid operates within the state. In Illinois, Medicaid is administered by the Illinois Department of Public Aid. To receive Medicaid, a person must have assets with a low value and very low income, as determined by a complex formula. In Illinois, a person generally cannot have more than $3,000 in assets or more than $591 in income per month, although there is a complex formula applied that considers the applicant's unique situation. There are several assets the formula does not count. Assets not counted include

- Homestead
- Automobile necessary for employment or otherwise to produce income, to receive health care, or essential for transporting a person with disabilities
- Income-producing property
- Household goods and personal effects

Certain other unavailable assets are not counted, such as jointly held real estate if the other joint owner refuses to sell, and property tied up in probate.

Chapter 24: Social Security Law

A person can reduce his or her assets to the point that he or she qualifies for Medicaid. As long as transfers are compensated, it is legal to restructure one's assets and income with the intent of qualifying for Medicaid. For example, it is permissible for a person to invest all of his or her available cash in a larger homestead or to expand a business in order to reduce his or her counted assets below $3,000. It is not permissible simply to give the available cash to family members or friends.

A person whose income is above Medicaid limits might be able to qualify for Medicaid under a spend-down provision. The spend-down is equal to the amount a person's income is over Medicaid limits. Medicaid occasionally agrees to cover the amount that a person's medical bills exceed a patient's spend-down.

Restructuring assets to qualify for Medicaid can be an especially attractive option for senior citizens, even if they already qualify for Medicare. Medicaid coverage is better for persons living in nursing homes because Medicaid pays for a wider variety of nursing care services and for a longer period of time than does Medicare. Lawyers who specialize in Medicaid have experience in advising clients how to restructure their assets and income to qualify for Medicaid.

OTHER STATE ASSISTANCE

In addition to SSP, described above, the Illinois Comprehensive Health Insurance Plan is a state program offering additional financial assistance to Illinois residents. This program was intended as an alternative to traditional health insurance. It benefits Illinois residents who are refused health insurance by private health insurance companies, or who can obtain insurance but only at an excessive rate. The Comprehensive Health Insurance Plan provides coverage for medically necessary treatment, such as hospital services.

In Illinois, two additional programs help older people and people with disabilities pay for their Medicare coverage. In order to be eligible for these programs, an individual must have assets of no more than $4,000 and must live in Illinois. The Qualified Medicare Beneficiary Program (QMB) assists those who have Part A Hospital Insurance and whose income is at 100 percent or less than the federal poverty level. The Specified Low-Income Medicare Beneficiary Program (SLMB) covers Part B Medical Insurance for individuals with incomes between 100 percent and 110 percent of the poverty level. These programs are run by the Illinois Department of Public Aid.

APPLYING FOR BENEFITS

To apply for Social Security benefits, a person should visit his or her local Social Security Office and fill out an application. By calling the Social Security Administration's toll-free number (see below), a person can obtain the address of the closest office and set up an appointment with a Social Security representative. For retirement benefits, it is advisable to begin the application process several months before a person wants to start receiving benefits. A person who becomes disabled should apply for benefits immediately; usually, benefits do not begin until the sixth month of the disability. Anyone applying for benefits should take the following to the office:

- Social Security card or number
- Birth certificate
- Tax information, such as his or her most recent W-2 form or tax return
- Information about his or her home, such as a real estate title
- Income and ownership information, such as payroll slips, bank books, insurance policies, and vehicle registration
- Marriage certificate, spouse's birth certificate and spouse's Social Security number (if spouse is applying for benefits)
- Children's birth certificates and Social Security numbers (if applying for children's benefits)
- Military discharge papers

All documents must be originals or certified copies. If a person does not have all of the necessary documents, the Social Security Administration offers assistance in locating the missing information.

RIGHT TO APPEAL

Filling out an application does not automatically entitle a person to benefits. A person may be denied benefits because his or her application is incomplete, or because he or she does not qualify due to age, disability status, or for some other reason. The Social Security Administration notifies people that their benefits have been denied by sending notice by letter. If a person disagrees with a decision of the Social Security Administration regarding benefits, he or she has the right to appeal and to be represented by an attorney.

There are three steps to the administrative appeals process. The first step is reconsideration. An administration representative (someone other than the person who made the original decision) reconsiders the matter and issues an opinion. If, on reconsideration, the decision is negative again, the second step is a hearing before an administrative law judge. At this stage, the claimant has the right to subpoena and cross-examine witnesses, present evidence, and read relevant files. After listening to both sides, the administrative law judge issues a decision. In most cases, this will end the matter, but if the decision is negative and the claimant wishes to press his or her claim, the third and final step is the Appeals Council. If the Appeals Council decides to review the case (its jurisdiction is discretionary), it conducts a "paper" review of the entire matter. This means it issues a decision based on the files accumulated in the two previous steps. There is no additional opportunity to testify, although the appellant may submit additional documentation if necessary.

It is important to know that there are time limits in which to make an appeal. If a person is interested in appealing a decision regarding benefits, he or she should not delay in contacting the nearest Social Security Administration Office.

RESOURCES

The Social Security Administration operates a toll-free, 24-hour telephone service to provide information on Social Security and related government benefit programs, including estimates of retirement benefits. Most questions about Social Security should be addressed to the Social Security Administration. To reach a service representative, call (800) 772-1213 between the hours of 7:00 a.m. and 7:00 p.m. on business days.

The Social Security Administration also publishes a number of booklets, forms, and pamphlets designed to explain different types of government benefits, all of which are available free of charge. They include the following:

Disability (Publication No. 05-10029)
Medicare (Publication No. 05-10043)
Retirement (Publication No. 05-10035)
SSI Supplemental Security Income (Publication No. 05-11000)
Survivors (Publication No. 05-10084)
The Appeals Process (Publication No. 05-10041)
Understanding Social Security (Publication No. 05-10024)
You May Be Able to Get SSI (Publication No. 05-11069)

These and other publications are available at any local Social Security Office or by calling the toll-free telephone number above.

For on-line information, visit the Social Security Administration's World Wide Web Site: http://www.ssa.go.

The Illinois Department of Public Aid, Division of Medical Programs, Prescott E. Bloom Building, 201 South Grand Avenue East, Springfield, IL 62763, phone: (217) 782-2570, toll-free: (800) 252-8635, also provides information about Medicaid, Medicare, SSI, and SSP.

Chapter 24: Social Security Law

SOCIAL SECURITY LAW LEADING ILLINOIS ATTORNEYS

Illinois' Most Respected Legal Counsel As Selected By Their Peers.

The Leading Illinois Attorneys below were recommended by their peers in a statewide survey.

The Leading Illinois Attorneys listed below were nominated as exceptional by their peers in a statewide survey conducted by American Research Corporation (ARC). ARC asked several thousand licensed Illinois attorneys to name the lawyer to whom they would send a close friend or family member in need of legal assistance in specific areas of law. The attorneys below were nominated in the area of Social Security Law.

Because the survey results (all practice area results combined) represent less than three percent of Illinois' practicing attorneys, this list should not be construed as a complete list. Nevertheless, it is an excellent source of highly qualified and reputable Illinois attorneys.

For information on ARC's survey methodology, see page *xi*.
For the complete list of Leading Illinois Consumer Attorneys, see page *xii*.

The Leading Illinois Attorneys below are listed alphabetically in accordance with the geographic region in which their offices are located. Note that attorneys may handle clients from a broad geographic area; attorneys are not restricted to only serving clients residing within the cities in which their offices are located.

An attorney whose name appears in bold has included a biographical profile in this chapter.

COOK & COLLAR COUNTIES

Kraus, Grace M. - Elmhurst

NORTHWESTERN ILLINOIS INCLUDING ROCKFORD & QUAD CITIES

Beu, William R. - Rockford

CENTRAL ILLINOIS

Casady-Trimble, Carolyn - Urbana
Henry, Thomas M. - Peoria
Sutterfield, David W. - Effingham, page 318

BIOGRAPHICAL PROFILES OF SOCIAL SECURITY LAW LEADING ILLINOIS ATTORNEYS

The Leading Illinois Attorneys profiled below were nominated as exceptional by their peers in a statewide survey conducted by American Research Corporation (ARC). ARC asked several thousand licensed Illinois attorneys to name the lawyer to whom they would send a close friend or family member in need of legal assistance in specific areas of law. The attorneys below were nominated in the area of Social Security Law.

Because the survey results (all practice area results combined) represent less than three percent of Illinois' practicing attorneys, this list should not be construed as a complete list. Nevertheless, it is an excellent source of highly qualified and reputable Illinois attorneys.

For information on ARC's survey methodology, see page *xi*.
For the complete list of Leading Illinois Consumer Attorneys, see page *xii*.
For the list of Leading Illinois Social Security Law Attorneys, see page 316.

The Leading Illinois Attorneys below are listed alphabetically in accordance with the geographic region in which their offices are located. Note that attorneys may handle clients from a broad geographic area; attorneys are not limited to only serving clients residing within the cities in which their offices are located.

The two-line attorney listings in this section are of attorneys who practice in this area but whose full biographical profiles appear in other sections of this book. A bullet "•" preceding a name indicates the attorney was nominated in this particular area of law.

For information on the format of the full biographical profiles, consult the "Using the Consumer Guidebook" section on page *xviii*.

The following abbreviations are used throughout these profiles:

App.	Appellate
Cir.	Circuit
Ct.	Court
Dist.	District
Sup.	Supreme
JD	Juris Doctor (Doctor of Law)
LLB	Legum Baccalaureus (Bachelor of Laws)
LLD	Legum Doctor (Doctor of Laws)
LLM	Legum Magister (Master of Laws)
ADR	Alternative Dispute Resolution
ABA	American Bar Association
ABOTA	American Board of Trial Advocates
ATLA	Association of Trial Lawyers of America
CBA	Chicago Bar Association
ISBA	Illinois State Bar Association
ITLA	Illinois Trial Lawyers Association
NBTA	National Board of Trial Advocacy

Chapter 24: Social Security Law

COOK & COLLAR COUNTIES

RICHARD A. KIMNACH - *Anesi, Ozmon & Rodin, Ltd.* - 161 North Clark Street, Suite 2100 - Chicago, IL 60601 - Phone: (312) 372-3822, Fax: (312) 372-3833, 800: (800) 458-3822 within IL - *See complete biographical profile in the Workers' Compensation Law Chapter, page 341.*

CENTRAL ILLINOIS

J. MICHAEL MATHIS - *The Mathis Law Firm* - 7707 Knoxville Avenue, Suite 105 - Peoria, IL 61614 - Phone: (309) 692-2600, Fax: (309) 692-2633, 800: (800) 2-MATHIS - *See complete biographical profile in the Elder Law Chapter, page 130.*

DAVID W. SUTTERFIELD
Sutterfield & Johnson, P.C.
208 South Second Street
P.O. Box 836
Effingham, IL 62401

Phone: (217) 342-3100
Fax: (217) 347-8723

•**DAVID W. SUTTERFIELD:** Mr. Sutterfield concentrates in Social Security Law and elder law. He regularly appears before the Office of Hearings and Appeals in Evansville, Peoria, St. Louis, Chicago, Oak Brook, and Indianapolis. Referrals come from former clients, attorneys, disability insurance companies, doctors, and the National Organization of Social Security Claimants Representatives. Since 1980, Mr. Sutterfield has been a Title III B Legal Service Provider under the Federal Older Americans Act. He has extensive experience in medical assistance planning, and has lectured to seventeen different county bar associations and four different judicial circuits. He has presented numerous lectures on nursing home rights before the public and Alzheimer support groups. Mr. Sutterfield handles living wills, health care powers of attorney, medicare, social security, consumer rights, and litigation involving nursing home neglect and abuse. *Modern Maturity* magazine has written an article on the legal services Mr. Sutterfield provides to members of the Illinois Retired Teachers Association. *The Boston Herald* featured an Illinois appellate case in which Mr. Sutterfield asserted that a bank's duty, as guardian, is to know and properly apply for Medical Assistance for long-term nursing home care.
Education: JD 1980, University of Illinois; BA 1977 cum laude, North Central College.
Admitted: 1980 Illinois; 1982 U.S. Dist. Ct. (S. Dist. IL); 1983 U.S. Dist. Ct. (C. Dist. IL).
Employment History: President/Owner 1986-present, Sutterfield & Johnson, P.C.; President 1986-present, Staff Attorney 1982-86, Senior Citizens Legal Services, Inc.; Staff Attorney 1980-82, Land of Lincoln Legal Assistance Foundation.
Representative Clients: Illinois Retired Teachers Assn.; Retired Teachers Assn. of Chicago; Midland Area Agency on Aging; Project Life Area Agency on Aging; Project Nursing Home Ombudsman Program; Victims of Nursing Home Abuse/Neglect; Social Security Disability Claimants.
Professional Associations: Effingham County Bar Assn. 1980-present (President 1996); ISBA 1980-present; ATLA (Nursing Home Litigation Section 1990-present); ITLA 1990-present; National Organization of Social Security Claimants Representatives 1986-present; Rotary International 1996.
Community Involvement: ARC Community Support Systems [Board Member 1993-present (President 1995-present)]; Little League Baseball Coach; Rollerblade Hockey Coach; United Methodist Church (Board of Trustees). *Mr. Sutterfield also practices Elder Law.*

SOUTHERN ILLINOIS

ROBERT C. NELSON - *Nelson, Bement, Stubblefield & Levenhagen, P.C.* - 420 North High Street - P.O. Box Y - Belleville, IL 62222 - Phone: (618) 277-4000, Fax: (618) 277-1136 - *See complete biographical profile in the Workers' Compensation Law Chapter, page 346.*

CHAPTER 25

TAX LAW

UNDERSTANDING TAX LAW

There is a saying that the only two sure things in life are death and taxes. Tax laws affect all people and touch most areas of life, so it would be helpful if tax laws were simple, clear, and easy to understand. Unfortunately, the tax system that exists has none of these characteristics. Many tax laws are unclear from the time they are written. Often, writing tax legislation involves so much compromise and redrafting that by the time a tax bill becomes law, even its author and sponsors do not fully understand what they have created. Other tax laws might be perfectly clear as written, but it may be difficult to know how to apply the law to a particular taxpayer. Finally, different courts in different jurisdictions can apply the same law to similar fact situations and reach completely different interpretations, each interpretation valid in that particular jurisdiction. Tax collectors have an important task because they collect taxes and help ensure that everyone pays his or her fair share. One of the most effective ways to encourage people to pay their fair share of taxes is to give them the impression that cheating will be noticed and punished. Simply put, the system would not work if the threat of a possible audit did not hang over every tax return submitted.

Given the complexity of tax law, this chapter cannot describe all aspects of tax law. Instead, this chapter explains how consumers can manage tax disputes with the federal or state government.

Avoidance Versus Evasion

There simply are not enough resources for the government to calculate everyone's taxes or to audit every return filed. The tax collection system assumes that most taxpayers will be honest when reporting their income and calculating their tax obligations. The government has many ways of checking the accuracy of information the taxpayer provides. Employers provide the IRS with information on how much employees earn and financial institutions report the interest income their investors and depositors receive. Still, there is a tension built into the system. Taxpayers want to pay as little tax as legally possible but tax collectors want to ensure that taxpayers pay as much as they are legally obligated to pay. The terms "tax evasion" and "tax avoidance" are frequently used interchangeably to describe this tension, but the terms have different meanings.

To avoid taxes is to use legal means to limit one's tax liability. It is perfectly acceptable for a taxpayer to try to avoid taxes. Federal and state tax codes describe many ways a taxpayer can lower his or her tax burden. There are many ways to structure income to pay a minimum of taxes. There is nothing illegal in taking advantage of loopholes or shelters to avoid paying taxes. Tax evasion is using illegal means to get around paying one's taxes. It is illegal to evade paying legitimately owed taxes. Most taxpayers are tax avoiders. It is the job of tax collectors to find the tax evaders.

Federal Tax Disputes

The Internal Revenue Service (IRS) is the arm of the federal government charged with collecting federal income taxes. For most consumers, the federal income tax is the largest federal tax paid. The federal government collects taxes on a variety of different items including telephone calls, airplane tickets, cigarettes, and imported goods, but most consumers never challenge these taxes. For this reason, this section focuses on disputes with the IRS over the federal income tax.

IRS Audit

Pity the poor IRS agent. It is a safe bet that no one looks forward to being audited. Even if a taxpayer does nothing wrong, an audit, also called an examination by the IRS, can be confusing, frustrating, disruptive, and time consuming. IRS employees know their task is not a popular one, and they do not try to aggravate taxpayers on purpose. They, too, struggle with a huge bureaucracy and must make do with outdated computers and a complex tax code with many gray areas of law.

The IRS audits approximately three million returns annually. About two million of those taxpayers end up paying more taxes to the IRS. Getting an audit letter from the IRS is not an indication that the IRS believes the taxpayer is a cheater; it usually means that there is some irregularity in the return or that the taxpayer has been selected for a random audit. The taxpayer usually winds up paying Uncle Sam more money.

Who Is Audited

The IRS has three primary methods of selecting which returns to audit. The first method is random selection. By choosing to audit some returns at random, the IRS promotes better voluntary compliance with the tax code. Because every return has a chance of being selected for an audit, taxpayers are more likely to be honest. Relatively few of the returns selected this way contain significant errors, but the IRS uses the results of the random audits to measure compliance with the law and to update and improve the overall tax collection system.

The second method is a computerized process whereby the IRS separates out returns that it believes may contain errors or be fraudulent. The computer program is fine-tuned each year based on the experience IRS gains from applying the tax code. Most of the returns selected this way have some unusual characteristic that raises a red flag for auditors. For example, if the IRS determines that many taxpayers claiming very large deductions for entertainment expenses are trying to defraud the government, the computer can be programmed to separate out returns with unusually large entertainment deductions. If the IRS learns from its random audits that many people misunderstand a particular application of the tax code, the computer can be programmed to separate out all returns relying on that application.

An important point to know about this second method of selecting returns is that it is completely impersonal—any return raising a particular red flag is tagged by the computer. Thus, if a taxpayer has an unusual circumstance that gives him or her an unusually large, yet legitimate deduction, the computer will select the return for audit every year. IRS auditors try to avoid repeat examinations for the same issue. Thus, if the IRS examined a taxpayer's return for the same issue in either of the previous two years and found in favor of the taxpayer, the taxpayer should call this to the attention of the IRS. Often in these cases, the audit is terminated without further investigation.

The third method for selecting returns for audit compares information provided by the taxpayer with information from other sources. For example, if someone reports less income on his or her return than is reported on the W-2 form provided by the taxpayer's employer, the IRS can seek to clarify the discrepancy.

Audit Process

The audit process begins as soon as the taxpayer receives a letter from the IRS stating that his or her return has been selected for further examination. The audit may be done entirely by mail if the IRS has only a few questions, or it may be at an IRS office or at the taxpayer's home or business if the IRS has more substantial questions. The taxpayer can request that the audit interview be transferred to another IRS district if a different location is more convenient for the taxpayer.

Time Limits

Under normal circumstances, the IRS cannot audit tax returns filed more than three years ago. For example, the deadline for the IRS to audit a 1995 tax return, filed at the latest on April 15, 1996, is April 15, 1999. Under certain circumstances, the three-year limit is extended. The IRS can demand records as far back as six years if an audit reveals that the amount of income the taxpayer failed to report on his or her latest return exceeds by 25 percent or more the income reported. Also, the IRS has no time limit if the taxpayer fails to file a return or if it determines that the taxpayer deliberately filed a false or fraudulent return.

Records

IRS auditors almost always want to see financial records that relate to the return they are examining. This raises a commonly asked question: How long does a taxpayer need to keep records relating to income tax filings? The answer is generally three-and-a-half years because after that time, the IRS typically cannot audit the taxpayer. A taxpayer should keep financial documents longer than three-and-a-half years if they might affect any future returns. Thus, a person should keep records of any stocks purchased until they are sold, because only then can profit or loss be determined and reported on the next income tax return.

Taxpayer Rights in an IRS Audit

Some taxpayers claim they are made to feel like criminals in IRS audits. In fact, the audit procedure differs significantly from a criminal proceeding and may provide fewer procedural safeguards for the taxpayer. Unlike a criminal trial in which a defendant is presumed innocent until proven guilty, in an IRS audit the taxpayer must prove to the IRS's satisfaction that the information on a return is correct and legal. For example, if the IRS questions a deduction for business-related travel expenses, the IRS does not have to show that the travel was entirely for pleasure or that the taxpayer never traveled during the year of the return. The burden is on the taxpayer to show that he or she really did incur the amount of travel expenses claimed. If he or she cannot document the expenses, the IRS can disallow the deduction without offering any evidence at all.

A person has the right to ask the IRS to cancel a penalty if he or she can show his or her actions were the result of bad advice from the IRS. Thus, if someone pays less tax than owed, and the IRS discovers and penalizes the taxpayer for it, the taxpayer might have the fine canceled if he or she reasonably followed IRS advice in calculating taxes.

The first step in proving that bad advice from the IRS caused a mistake is to document what an IRS employee said in person, over the telephone, or by letter. It is important to write down any tax advice received over the telephone or in person, and to note the time, the date and the name of the IRS employee giving the advice. The second step is to show that reliance on that advice was reasonable. Just because someone says what the taxpayer wants to hear is not sufficient reason for the taxpayer to rely on that information; reliance must be reasonable. Determining reasonableness is tricky, but the taxpayer should be aware that if a piece of advice seems too good to be true, it may not be true. If a reasonable person would seek a second opinion, then the taxpayer should also seek another opinion. Although the IRS may cancel a penalty for relying on bad advice, it is not obligated to cancel the interest accumulated on any additional tax the taxpayer may owe.

The taxpayer need answer only the questions that the auditor asks. The taxpayer should not commit perjury, but he or she need not make the auditor's job easier by volunteering damaging information. If the taxpayer is instructed by the IRS to make documents available during an audit, it is best to have all these documents available for inspection in an organized and logical manner. In an audit conducted at home or at a place of business, called a field audit by the IRS, the taxpayer need not give the auditor access to a copying machine or allow the auditor to take original documents back to IRS offices. The taxpayer should, however, make copies of the documents that the auditor specifically requests and make a note of which documents the auditor gets copies of. If an audit is by mail, the taxpayer should send to the IRS only copies of those items specifically requested. Documentation should always be sent to the IRS via certified mail with a return receipt requested.

Many taxpayers are concerned about the privacy of information they provide on a tax return or in an audit. The government is obligated to respect the confidentiality of information a taxpayer provides in the tax collection process, and anyone who prepares a return or represents the taxpayer is also obligated to respect the client's privacy. In limited circumstances, the IRS is allowed to share some taxpayer information with state tax agencies, the Department of Justice, or other federal agencies. During an audit or at any time the IRS asks for information, the taxpayer has the right to know why the agency wants the information, how the information will be used, and what may happen if the taxpayer chooses not to give the information.

The taxpayer has the right to take someone along to an IRS audit interview. This could be an attorney, a certified public accountant, the person who filled out the tax forms, or an enrolled agent. Another person may represent the taxpayer in his or her absence during an audit interview, as long as the taxpayer files with the IRS a power of attorney form or a similar document.

The taxpayer has the right to tape record the audit interview. To do so, the taxpayer must inform the IRS in writing of the intention to tape the interview at least ten days in advance, and must supply the tape recorder. If the IRS decides to tape record an interview, it must inform the taxpayer at least ten days in advance. The taxpayer has a right to a copy of the IRS tape, but must pay for the copying expenses.

If at any point in the audit process the taxpayer feels that the proceeding is not going well, he or she always has three options. First, the taxpayer can agree with the IRS, pay additional taxes, and vow to be more careful when filing future tax returns. Second, the taxpayer can ask the IRS for a notice of deficiency and take the case to a federal tax court. Third, the taxpayer can pay the disputed amount, file a claim for a refund, and then take the case to the federal district court, the federal tax court, or the federal claims court.

Result of an Audit

A minority of taxpayers who are audited receive from the IRS a no-change report, a letter stating that the IRS accepts an audited return without changes. Only about 30 percent of the people audited get a no-change letter. In even rarer situations, the IRS owes the taxpayer money after an audit. However, in most cases, the IRS determines that the taxpayer owes more money.

If the taxpayer owes more money, the IRS sends the taxpayer a 30-day letter and a copy of the audit report outlining the additional taxes owed. If the taxpayer agrees to the changes detailed in the audit report, he or she can sign the enclosed form and send it back within 30 days to the IRS with a check. If the taxpayer sends a signed form back without a check, the IRS sends the taxpayer a bill, which must be paid within ten days. Either way, the taxpayer pays interest on the extra tax, calculated from the due date of the audited return to the billing date.

Another option outlined in the 30-day letter is the IRS's internal appeals process, which can be initiated by submitting, within 30 days, a written protest to the IRS requesting a conference with an appeals officer. If the amount of the additional tax is less than $2,500, the protest does not need to be in written form.

If the taxpayer ignores the 30-day letter, the IRS sends a notice of deficiency, sometimes called a 90-day letter, because it notifies the taxpayer that he or she has 90 days to either settle the matter with the IRS or to file suit in one of three federal courts.

Appealing an Audit

If a taxpayer disputes the results of an audit, he or she can appeal the auditor's decision to a regional IRS appeals office or directly to a federal court. Appealing within the IRS is relatively straightforward and generally less expensive and time consuming than going to court. If taxpayers go to federal court and win there, they can sometimes recover from the IRS some or all of their administrative and litigation costs, but only if they first use the IRS appeals process.

Appealing Within the IRS

A taxpayer can start the IRS appeals process by requesting a conference through the IRS's local district director. The district director then arranges a meeting with one of the IRS's appeals officers, located in most major cities. The request for an appeals conference should state the exact elements in the auditor's report with which the taxpayer disagrees, the elements of tax law that support the taxpayer's case, and any facts that support the taxpayer's position.

As in any dealings with the IRS, the taxpayer can be represented or advised by an attorney during the appeals conference and can bring along witnesses to support statements of facts. These conferences are informal, and they represent a last chance to resolve a dispute before going to court. There is no guarantee what will happen, but quite often the IRS officers make some concessions at this point in order to avoid going to court.

Going to Court

If a taxpayer decides that the IRS's decision is unfair, unjust, or unreasonable, he or she can take the dispute to one of three federal courts, all of which operate independently of the IRS. Deciding whether to file suit in tax court, claims court, or district court depends on a number of legal and personal factors. Each court is guided by the previous cases that it has decided. As a result, a taxpayer's odds of success may be better in one court than in another. Most cases, no matter which court first hears them, can ultimately be appealed to the U.S. Supreme Court. The only exception to this rule is for cases heard under the small tax case procedure in tax court.

A taxpayer may go to any one of three courts without first going through the IRS appeals process, but quite often a tax court judge will not hear a case unless it has been considered for settlement by a regional IRS appeals office. If a taxpayer goes to tax court without first going through the IRS appeals process and loses his or her court case, the tax court judge may fine the taxpayer up to $5,000 if he or she determines that the lawsuit was a tactic to delay paying the IRS or that the suit was otherwise frivolous. In all three courts, the taxpayer has the burden of proving that the IRS is wrong. In other words, the court assumes that the IRS correctly interpreted the tax laws as they apply to a case, and the taxpayer does not win unless he or she convinces the court otherwise.

U.S. Tax Court: Tax court hears only tax cases. In order to go to tax court, a taxpayer need not pay the disputed tax amount first, unlike the other two courts where he or she must pay the disputed amount before filing suit. In tax court, the taxpayer does not have a right to trial by jury, so cases are heard by a judge who is experienced in tax law, rather than by a group of peers who might be swayed by emotion. If a taxpayer wants to take a case to tax court, he or she must file suit within 90 days after the IRS mails a notice of deficiency to the taxpayer's last known address. In general, tax court rules are less strict than those used in the other two courts.

If a dispute with the IRS is for an amount under $10,000, the taxpayer can go through the tax court's small tax case procedure, which is generally quicker and even less formal than the court's standard procedure. However, the decision of a judge who hears cases under the small tax case procedure is final, so if a taxpayer chooses this procedure, he or she loses the right to appeal the court's decision. Because the taxpayer does not need to be represented by an attorney in this procedure, it may be a good option in a dispute regarding smaller dollar amounts in which any money won would be wiped out to pay attorney fees.

Finally, a taxpayer should be aware of what is often called the "tax court trap," which describes the ability of the IRS to impose even more fines based on any new information that it discovers about the taxpayer during a tax court proceeding.

Tax court is the most popular route for taxpayers, in large part because it does not require that the disputed tax be paid first. But tax court can also be a very unsuccessful route. IRS statistics show that only about five percent of the taxpayers who bring their cases in tax court win. The taxpayer success rate in the other two courts, however, is only marginally better at about 11 percent.

U.S. District Court: Of the three courts that hear taxpayer disputes with the IRS, only in federal district court is there a right to a trial by jury. To bring suit in district court, the taxpayer must first pay the disputed tax to the IRS and then claim a refund for that amount by filing the proper form with the IRS. If the IRS denies the refund request, the taxpayer can sue the IRS in district court. The taxpayer can sue for any amount of refund in district court, no matter how small. However, because the taxpayer is usually represented by an attorney in district court, going to district court may make sense only for larger monetary disputes.

If the IRS does not make a decision on a refund claim in six months, the taxpayer can file suit in district court. The taxpayer has up to two years after the IRS rejects a refund claim in which to file suit in district court.

U.S. Claims Court: The federal claims court follows the same rules as the district court regarding filing lawsuits for refunds from the IRS. A taxpayer must first pay the disputed amount and then file a lawsuit in claims court for a refund of that amount. There is no minimum limit to the amount of a refund claim that can be litigated in claims court. However, the taxpayer cannot file suit in claims court if the claim is for a refund of a penalty relating to tax shelter abuse. Also, a taxpayer cannot file suit in claims court to recover a penalty assessed by the IRS for fraudulently preparing someone else's tax return.

ILLINOIS TAX DISPUTES

The State of Illinois assesses taxes for income, sales, excise, motor fuel, property and gambling. Illinois offers free tax help during the tax season (January through April 15). For information about the nearest one-stop shop available to you, call or write to Taxpayer Information, Illinois Department of Revenue, P.O. Box 19001, Springfield, IL 62794-9001, toll-free phone: (800) 356-6302.

The state relies less on income taxes for revenue than does the federal government. Illinois' income tax is far less elaborate than the federal government's and there are fewer disputes over it. When the state does audit a taxpayer's state income tax return, the procedure is much like the procedure used in IRS income tax audits. An Illinois taxpayer who is audited may question the audit through an informal conference, followed by an administrative hearing and final review by the Illinois Board of Appeals. If you have questions regarding the specific process of an Illinois audit and appeal, contact the Board of Appeals, Illinois Department of Revenue, 100 West Randolph Street, Chicago, IL 60601-3274, phone: (312) 814-3004.

Property taxes, which are levied, collected and spent locally, are discussed in the Real Estate Chapter. The Illinois Department of Revenue has no direct involvement in the appeal process of assessed value of property, upon which the property tax is based.

The rights that Illinois taxpayers have against the Department of Revenue closely parallel the rights against the IRS. For example, the taxpayer has a right to have an attorney, accountant, or other person represent him or her at any meetings, and the taxpayer has a right to record meetings. The department must provide taxpayers with written information on their rights when they deal with the department. Illinois taxpayers have a right to sue the department. If a taxpayer wins, he or she may be able to collect damages if a court finds that the department knowingly or recklessly disregarded a state law or knowingly or recklessly failed to release a lien.

RESOURCES

The Internal Revenue Service, Kansas City, MO 64999, phone: (800) 829-3676, has free tax publications available.

Call the Internal Revenue Service, phone: (708) 435-1040, (312) 435-1040, toll-free: (800) 829-1040, TDD: (800) 829-4059, for free tax help information.

How to Cope with the IRS, Randy Bruce Blaustein, Retirement Living Publishing Co., New York, NY, 1991.

Keys to Surviving a Tax Audit, D. Larry Crumbley and Jack P. Friedman, Barron's, New York, NY, 1991.

Tax Procedure and Tax Fraud in a Nutshell, Patricia T. Morgan, West Publishing Co., St. Paul, MN, 1990.

Contact the Illinois Department of Revenue, P.O. Box 19468, Springfield, IL 62794-9468, phone: (217) 782-3336, toll-free: (800) 732-8866, TDD: (800) 544-2304, for information and free bulletins.

TAX LAW LEADING ILLINOIS ATTORNEYS

The Leading Illinois Attorneys listed below were nominated as exceptional by their peers in a statewide survey conducted by American Research Corporation (ARC). ARC asked several thousand licensed Illinois attorneys to name the lawyer to whom they would send a close friend or family member in need of legal assistance in specific areas of law. The attorneys below were nominated in the area of Tax Law.

Because the survey results (all practice area results combined) represent less than three percent of Illinois' practicing attorneys, this list should not be construed as a complete list. Nevertheless, it is an excellent source of highly qualified and reputable Illinois attorneys.

For information on ARC's survey methodology, see page *xi*.
For the complete list of Leading Illinois Consumer Attorneys, see page *xii*.

The Leading Illinois Attorneys below are listed alphabetically in accordance with the geographic region in which their offices are located. Note that attorneys may handle clients from a broad geographic area; attorneys are not restricted to only serving clients residing within the cities in which their offices are located.

An attorney whose name appears in bold has included a biographical profile in this chapter.

Illinois' Most Respected Legal Counsel As Selected By Their Peers.

The Leading Illinois Attorneys below were recommended by their peers in a statewide survey.

COOK & COLLAR COUNTIES

Alschuler, Benjamin P. - Aurora
Amari, Leonard F. - Chicago
Arnold, Joel D. - Westmont
Asonye, Uche O. - Chicago
Berg, Gershon S. - Skokie
Biallas, John S. - St. Charles
Boylan, William E. - Wheaton
Cohen, Aaron - Chicago
Colombik, Richard M. - Schaumburg, page 328
DeFranco, Leonard S. - Oak Brook
Dickson, Fred H. - Aurora
Dobben, Brian L. - Chicago
Dobosz, Glen T. - Elgin
Donatelli, Mark R. - Hinsdale
Drendel, Gilbert X., Jr. - Batavia
Farrell, John E. - Chicago
Gensburg, Lane M. - Chicago
Glassberg, Donald A. - Chicago
Grach, Brian S. - Waukegan
Harris, Steven M. - Chicago
Hem, Ronald M. - Aurora
Hodge, Gerald K. - Aurora
Hoogendoorn, Case - Chicago
Horwood, Richard M. - Chicago
Jiganti, John J. - Chicago
Knorr, Alfred L. - Glenview

Kuhn, Richard W. - Naperville
Martin, Royal B. - Chicago
Marutzky, William F. - Chicago
McHugh, Timothy - Elmhurst
McKenzie, Robert E. - Chicago, page 329
Moore, John G. - Chicago
Morrison, John J. - Chicago, page 329
Palmieri, Vincent L. - Libertyville
Pawlan, Mitchell D. - Northbrook
Polisky, Joel S. - Chicago
Provenza, James C. - Glenview
Reed, Daniel A. - Aurora
Rolewick, David F. - Wheaton
Rosenberg, Herbert B. - Chicago
Ruddy, C. John - Aurora
Schanlaber, William C. - Aurora
Schlack, David A. - Chicago
Segal, Alan F. - Chicago
Siegal, Barry P. - Chicago
Sinars, Theodore A. - Chicago
Soskin, Rollin J. - Skokie
Statland, Donald A. - Chicago
Stone, Howard L. - Chicago
Sugar, Richard A. - Chicago
Tully, Thomas M. - Chicago
von Mandel, Michael J. - Chicago

Northwestern Illinois Including Rockford & Quad Cities

Balch, Bruce L. - Rock Island
Churchill, Daniel - Moline
Howard, William J. - Rockford
Johnson, Raymond E. - Rockford
Maggio, Frank P. - Rockford
Nepple, James A. - Rock Island
Oliver, Robert J. - Rockford
Slover, John A., Jr. - Moline
Stojan, Clark J. - Rock Island

Central Illinois

Barr, John - Decatur
Bellatti, Robert M. - Springfield
Burton, R. Nicholas - Decatur
Cox, A. Clay - Bloomington, page 330
Flynn, Leonard T. - Champaign
Graham, Hugh J., III - Springfield
Grebe, James R. - Peoria
Heller, J. Brian - Washington
Higgs, David L. - Peoria
Horn, Jerold I. - Peoria
Kuppler, Karl B. - Peoria
Lestikow, James M. - Springfield

Mescher, Gregory A. - Peoria
O'Day, Daniel G. - Peoria
Saint, Gale W. - Bloomington
Scott, Gregory A. - Springfield
Sheehan, Patrick J. - Springfield
Smith, Timothy O. - Danville
Stumpe, Karen M. - Peoria
Sutkowski, Edward F. - Peoria
Tepper, Michael - Urbana
Turner, Mercer - Bloomington
Washkuhn, Wilson C. - Peoria

Southern Illinois

Blake, Edward J., Jr. - Belleville
Broom, William L., III - Carbondale
Brown, W. Campbell - West Frankfort
Elliott, Ivan A., Jr. - Carmi
Farrell, John A. - Godfrey
Guymon, David E. - Belleville
Hawkins, Robert J. - Fairfield
Hendricks, Scott P. - Carbondale
Jacknewitz, Dennis J. - Belleville

Johnson, Don E. - Pinckneyville
Marifian, George E. - Belleville
Mathis, Patrick B. - Belleville
McCarthy, Edward T. - Edwardsville
Mottaz, Steven N. - Alton
Richter, Kevin J. - Belleville
Vassen, John J. - Belleville
Vieira, Michelle - Marion
Wolf, Thomas J., Jr. - Harrisburg

Biographical Profiles of Tax Law Leading Illinois Attorneys

The Leading Illinois Attorneys profiled below were nominated as exceptional by their peers in a statewide survey conducted by American Research Corporation (ARC). ARC asked several thousand licensed Illinois attorneys to name the lawyer to whom they would send a close friend or family member in need of legal assistance in specific areas of law. The attorneys below were nominated in the area of Tax Law.

Because the survey results (all practice area results combined) represent less than three percent of Illinois' practicing attorneys, this list should not be construed as a complete list. Nevertheless, it is an excellent source of highly qualified and reputable Illinois attorneys.

For information on ARC's survey methodology, see page *xi*.
For the complete list of Leading Illinois Consumer Attorneys, see page *xii*.
For the list of Leading Illinois Tax Law Attorneys, see page 325.

The Leading Illinois Attorneys below are listed alphabetically in accordance with the geographic region in which their offices are located. Note that attorneys may handle clients from a broad geographic area; attorneys are not limited to only serving clients residing within the cities in which their offices are located.

The two-line attorney listings in this section are of attorneys who practice in this area but whose full biographical profiles appear in other sections of this book. A bullet "•" preceding a name indicates the attorney was nominated in this particular area of law.

For information on the format of the full biographical profiles, consult the "Using the Consumer Guidebook" section on page *xviii*.

The following abbreviations are used throughout these profiles:

App.	Appellate
Cir.	Circuit
Ct.	Court
Dist.	District
Sup.	Supreme
JD	Juris Doctor (Doctor of Law)
LLB	Legum Baccalaureus (Bachelor of Laws)
LLD	Legum Doctor (Doctor of Laws)
LLM	Legum Magister (Master of Laws)
ADR	Alternative Dispute Resolution
ABA	American Bar Association
ABOTA	American Board of Trial Advocates
ATLA	Association of Trial Lawyers of America
CBA	Chicago Bar Association
ISBA	Illinois State Bar Association
ITLA	Illinois Trial Lawyers Association
NBTA	National Board of Trial Advocacy

Cook & Collar Counties

•**UCHE O. ASONYE** - *Asonye & Associates* - 203 North LaSalle Street, Suite 2100 - Chicago, IL 60601 - Phone: (312) 558-1792, Fax: (312) 558-1787 - *See complete biographical profiles in the Employment Law Chapter, page 142 and Immigration Law Chapter, page 226.*

RICHARD M. COLOMBIK
Richard M. Colombik & Associates, P.C.
1111 Plaza Drive
Suite 430
Schaumburg, IL 60173

Phone: (847) 619-5700
Fax: (847) 619-0971
E-mail: rcolom29@starnetinc.com
Web: http://www.colombik.com

•**RICHARD M. COLOMBIK:** Mr. Colombik is a tax, business, asset protection, and estate planning attorney. He has been the liaison to the District Director of the Internal Revenue Service for the Illinois State Bar Association since 1990. He previously chaired the Illinois State Bar Association's Federal Taxation Section Council, the Northwest Suburban Bar Association's Estate, Probate and Tax Section Council, and was the Vice Chair of the American Bar Association's Taxation Subcommittee of the General Practice Council. Mr. Colombik is a member of the Offshore Institute, relative to implementation of offshore and domestic asset protection planning. He has recently authored a book, *Business Entity Selection Within Illinois,* published by the Illinois Institute for Continuing Legal Education. From his initial background as one of the members on the private tax staff of one of the world's wealthiest families, Mr. Colombik's extensive tax experience was expanded by his additional education through law school. He later became a Tax Manager at Touche, Ross & Company, currently Deloitte & Touche. Mr. Colombik entered private practice and has been operating his own law firm since 1982. Its current size is ten people. Mr. Colombik has published approximately 100 articles on taxation, estate planning, business planning, and asset protection planning. He has appeared on television, radio, newspapers and magazines, relative to taxation, corporate and business planning, and asset protection planning. He is a sought-after lecturer by many local, regional, and state bar associations and corporations. He has been recognized by various associations for his contributions and support through his publications and dedication.

Education: JD 1980 cum laude, John Marshall Law School; CPA 1977, University of Illinois; BS 1975, University of Colorado (Dean's List).

Employment History: 1982-present, Richard M. Colombik & Associates, P.C.; 1980-82, Touche, Ross & Co. (now Deloitte & Touche); Tax Manager 1977-78, Henry Crown and Company (Illinois).

Professional Associations: Northwest Suburban Bar Assn. [Vice President 1996; Probate, Estate Planning and Tax Committee (Chair 1989-90)]; ISBA [Federal Taxation Section Council 1990-94 (Chair 1993-94); Business Advice and Financial Planning Section Council 1990; Trusts and Estates Section Council 1995-96]; American Assn. of Attorney CPAs (Vice President 1992-96); North Suburban Bar Assn. (Governor 1991-94); ABA [Taxation Committee (Vice Chair); Section of General Practice Committee 1995]; North Shore Estate Planning Council 1990; Northwest Estate Planning Council 1992-96.

•**ROYAL B. MARTIN** - *Martin, Brown & Sullivan, Ltd.* - 321 South Plymouth Court, Tenth Floor - Chicago, IL 60604 - Phone: (312) 360-5000, Fax: (312) 360-5026 - *See complete biographical profile in the Criminal Law: Felonies & White Collar Crime Chapter, page 115.*

•**ROBERT E. MC KENZIE:** Mr. McKenzie has lectured extensively on the subject of taxation. He has presented courses before thousands of CPAs, attorneys and enrolled agents nationwide. Prior to entering private practice, Mr. McKenzie was employed by the Internal Revenue Service, Collection Division, in Chicago, Illinois, from 1972 to 1978. During that time, he worked as a Revenue Officer, a Classroom and OJT Instructor of Revenue Officers, and as an Advisory Revenue Officer in the Chicago Special Staff. Since entering private practice, he has dedicated a major portion of his time to the representation of individuals and companies before the IRS in Illinois and other states. Mr. McKenzie is past Chair of the Employment Tax Committee of the American Bar Association Section on Taxation, and Chair of the Chicago Bar Association Federal Tax Committee. He is also a member of the Chicago District Director's Liaison Committee. Mr. McKenzie is the author of *Representation Before the Collection Division of the IRS* and coauthor of *Representing the Audited Taxpayer Before the IRS.*
Education: JD 1979 with high honors, Illinois Institute of Technology, Chicago-Kent; BA 1970, Michigan State University.
Admitted: 1979 Illinois; 1979 U.S. Dist. Ct. (N. Dist. IL); 1979 U.S. Tax Ct.; 1980 U.S. Ct. App. (7th Cir.); 1983 U.S. Sup. Ct.; 1983 U.S. Dist. Ct. (N. Dist. IL, Trial Bar); 1991 U.S. Claims Ct.
Employment History: Partner 1979-present, McKenzie & McKenzie, P.C.; Law Clerk 1979, Illinois Attorney General's Office; Revenue Officer 1972-78, Internal Revenue Service.
Representative Clients: Mr. McKenzie represents companies and individuals who owe taxes to the Internal Revenue Service or state tax agencies; and companies and individuals who are audited by the Internal Revenue Service or state tax agencies.
Professional Associations: CBA [Federal Taxation Committee (Chair 1996-present)]; ABA [Tax Section (Employment Tax Committee, Chair 1992-94)]; Federal Bar Assn. (Tax Committee); Clark Boardman Callaghan's Tax Advisory Board 1992-present; Cook County Courts Arbitrations Panel 1990-present; American Tax Policy Institute (Life Member 1993-present).
Community Involvement: Chicago Tax Law Assistant Project 1995-present; National Political Convention (Delegate 1980).
Firm: McKenzie & McKenzie, P.C., aggressively represents individuals and companies in tax disputes. The firm acts as an advocate to reduce tax liabilities, negotiate compromises, and to protect clients' rights when they are confronted by the IRS. The firm provides representation from the first IRS contact, through the U.S. District Court, the U.S. Tax Court, and the U.S. Court of Appeals. *Mr. McKenzie also practices Bankruptcy Law and Small Business Law.*

ROBERT E. MCKENZIE
McKenzie & McKenzie, P.C.
5450 North Cumberland Avenue
Suite 120
Chicago, IL 60656

Phone: (312) 714-8040
Fax: (312) 714-8055
E-mail: mckenziere@aol.com

Extensive Experience In:

• Tax Litigation
• Bankruptcy
• State Tax Disputes

•**JOHN J. MORRISON:** Mr. Morrison practices federal and state taxation law, with an emphasis on civil and criminal tax investigations, disputes and litigation with the Internal Revenue Service, the United States Attorney's Offices, the Illinois Department of Revenue, and the Illinois Attorney General. He has been an expert witness in U.S. District Court and Illinois administrative proceedings. He is the coauthor of "Jeopardy and Termination Assessments and Jeopardy Levies," "Offers in Compromise," and "Tax Court from the IRS Perspective," *Federal Civil Tax Practice,* Illinois Institute for Continuing Legal Education. Mr. Morrison is a frequent lecturer for the Federal Bar Association, the Chicago Bar Association, the American Bar Association, and other professional organizations. He received a Special Achievement Award from the Deputy Chief Counsel of the IRS, August 1984.
Education: JD 1978 with honors, DePaul University; MS 1973, University of Illinois-Chicago; BS 1971 with high honors, University of Illinois-Chicago.
Admitted: 1978 Illinois; 1978 U.S. Tax Ct.; 1978 U.S. Dist. Ct. (N. Dist. IL, General Bar); 1982 U.S. Ct. App. (7th Cir.); 1983 U.S. Dist. Ct. (N. Dist. IL, Trial Bar); 1985 U.S. Sup. Ct.; 1985 U.S. Claims Ct.; 1988 U.S. Dist. Ct. (E. Dist. WI); 1993 U.S. Dist. Ct. (E. Dist. MI).
Employment History: Principal 1984-present, Law Office of John J. Morrison, Ltd.; Senior Attorney 1978-84, Office of Chief Counsel, U.S. Department of Treasury, Internal Revenue Service, Chicago, Illinois; Senior Engineer 1976-78, International Telephone and Telegraph Corp., Des Plaines, Illinois; Staff Engineer 1972-76, G.T.E. Automatic Electric Laboratories, Inc., Northlake, Illinois.
Professional Associations: ABA; CBA [Federal Taxation Committee; Procedure and Administration Division (Chair/Vice Chair 1986-88)]; ISBA; Federal Bar Assn. [Chicago Chapter (Board of Directors 1989-present)]; IRS (District Directors Liaison Committee 1988-present). *Mr. Morrison also practices Estate Planning, Wills & Trusts Law and Criminal Law: Felonies & White Collar Crime.*

JOHN J. MORRISON
Law Office of John J. Morrison, Ltd.
135 South LaSalle Street
Suite 3600
Chicago, IL 60603

Phone: (312) 641-3484
Fax: (312) 641-0727
E-mail: jjmtaxatty@aol.com

Extensive Experience In:

• Criminal & Civil Tax Investigations
• Federal & State Tax Litigation
• IRS Appeals

KERRY R. PECK - *Kerry R. Peck & Associates* - 105 West Adams Street, 31st Floor - Chicago, IL 60603 - Phone: (312) 201-0900, Fax: (312) 201-0803 - *See complete biographical profile in the Estate Planning, Wills & Trusts Law Chapter, page 161.*

•**JAMES C. PROVENZA** - *James C. Provenza, P.C.* - 1701 East Lake Avenue, Suite 407 - Glenview, IL 60025 - Phone: (847) 729-3939, Fax: (847) 657-6801 - *See complete biographical profile in the Estate Planning, Wills & Trusts Law Chapter, page 161.*

Chapter 25: Tax Law

JOHN H. REDFIELD - *Attorney at Law* - 5420 Old Orchard Road, #A-205 - Skokie, IL 60077 - Phone: (847) 966-9920, Fax: (847) 966-6638 - *See complete biographical profile in the Bankruptcy Law Chapter, page 72.*

•**DAVID F. ROLEWICK** - *Rolewick & Gutzke, P.C.* - 1776 South Naperville Road, Suite 104A - Wheaton, IL 60187 - Phone: (630) 653-1577, Fax: (630) 653-1579 - *See complete biographical profile in the Estate Planning, Wills & Trusts Law Chapter, page 162.*

EDWARD I. STEIN - *Edward I. Stein, Ltd.* - 707 Skokie Boulevard, Suite 600 - Northbrook, IL 60062 - Phone: (847) 291-4320, Fax: (847) 432-1132 - *See complete biographical profile in the Family Law Chapter, page 204.*

CENTRAL ILLINOIS

A. CLAY COX

Hayes, Hammer, Miles, Cox & Ginzkey
202 North Center Street
P.O. Box 3067
Bloomington, IL 61702-3067

Phone: (309) 828-7331
Fax: (309) 827-7423

Extensive Experience In:

- Bankruptcy
- Employee Benefits
- Probate

•**A. CLAY COX:** Mr. Cox practices business and commerical law, including federal and state income and estate tax, estate and business planning, corporate, partnership and limited liability companies, and bankruptcy. He is a frequent speaker for the Illinois State Bar Association and the Illinois Institute for Continuing Legal Education in programs on employee benefits, estate planning, and tax. Mr. Cox is the author of "Employee Benefits and Bankruptcy," *Employee Benefits Handbook,* Illinois Institute for Continuing Legal Education.
Education: JD 1979, University of Illinois; BS/BA 1976 magna cum laude, University of Missouri.
Admitted: 1979 Illinois; 1979 U.S. Dist. Ct. (C. Dist. IL); 1982 U.S. Tax Ct.; 1985 U.S. Ct. App. (7th Cir.).
Employment History: Partner 1987-present, Hayes, Hammer, Miles, Cox & Ginzkey; Associate 1982-87, Hayes, Scheider, Hammer & Miles; Associate 1979-82, Sorling, Northrup, Hanna, Cullen & Cochran.
Representative Clients: Bloomington Radiology; All-Brite Signs; Bloomington Broadcasting Corporation; Beer Nuts, Inc.
Professional Associations: ISBA [Employee Benefits Council (Chair 1986-87)]; Illinois Society of Certified Public Accountants.
Community Involvement: McLean County Art Assn. (Chair 1987-88); Youth Soccer Coach 1989-92; Bloomington/Normal YMCA [Swim Team (Official 1993-present); Volunteer of the Year 1996].
Firm: The firm offers a full range of civil and business services to clients, including estate planning, tax, real estate, incorporations, partnerships, personal injury litigation, and civil litigation. *See complete firm profile in Appendix A. Mr. Cox also practices Estate Planning, Wills & Trusts Law and Real Estate Law.*

DANIEL J. GREER - *Stine, Wolter & Greer* - 426 South Fifth Street - Springfield, IL 62701 - Phone: (217) 744-1000, Fax: (217) 744-1444 - *See complete biographical profile in the Estate Planning, Wills & Trusts Law Chapter, page 165.*

WILLIAM A. PEITHMANN - *Peithmann Law Office* - 111 South Main Street - P.O. Box 228 - Farmer City, IL 61842 - Phone: (309) 928-3390 - *See complete biographical profile in the Estate Planning, Wills & Trusts Law Chapter, page 165.*

CHAPTER
26

WORKERS' COMPENSATION LAW

Each year thousands of Illinois employees suffer work-related injuries. Like many other states, Illinois has a workers' compensation system to compensate employees for accidental injuries occurring in the workplace. All employers subject to the Illinois Workers' Compensation Act must either carry workers' compensation insurance or demonstrate that they are self-insured and have the financial resources to cover any reasonably anticipated claims. Employees may obtain information about coverage from their employers or from the Illinois Industrial Commission. Workers' compensation law is complicated and its regulations and procedures frequently change. A worker with questions concerning workers' compensation should consult an attorney, particularly after suffering an injury. This chapter provides an outline of Illinois' workers' compensation program. Other employment issues, including discrimination against persons with disabilities, are discussed in the Employment Law Chapter.

WORKERS' COMPENSATION: THE BASICS

Workers' compensation is a state program that requires employers to have insurance policies covering employees for work-related injuries. When an employee is accidentally injured on the job, the employer or the insurance company pays for medical care and lost wages due to the injury, regardless of fault. No part of the premium or benefits can be charged to employees.

The notion of employers paying for employee work-related injuries originated in Germany during the latter half of the 19th century. Among the chief proponents of a German workers' compensation program was Bertha von Krupp of the famed German manufacturer, Krupp Works. Krupp had long believed that taking care of workers was in the best interest of business and in 1884, successfully persuaded Chancellor Otto von Bismark to support workers' compensation for all of Germany.

Workers' compensation came to the United States in about 1910, when New York and Massachusetts adopted programs. Illinois adopted its workers' compensation program in 1911. This program is administered by the Illinois Industrial Commission.

The advent of workers' compensation relieved injured employees from having to sue their employers to collect any sort of damages. Before workers' compensation, an employee had to prove that the employer had negligently failed to provide a safe work environment. This was often difficult and resulted in many injured workers going without compensation. Under workers' compensation, however, employees usually collect benefits regardless of fault. That is, even if an employee is responsible for his or her own accidental injury, the employee is covered by workers' compensation under most circumstances, as long as the injury occurred on the job. The main restriction to the program is that in most cases, workers' compensation benefits are the only form of remedy for workplace injuries. After receiving benefits, an injured employee may not sue his or her employer for further compensation.

WHO IS COVERED

Employers
Illinois has a two-tiered system for providing workers' compensation coverage. Certain employers are required to have coverage under the Workers' Compensation Act. This group includes all government and school agencies, as well as those who employ domestic workers in their homes at least 40 hours per week for 13 or more weeks per year. It also includes businesses that are declared to be extrahazardous. Under the law, the following businesses are extrahazardous:

- Most manufacturing, construction and development companies
- Food and beverage providers

- Beauty shops
- Mining industries

Certain small businesses may elect not to be covered, even if they fall generally into one of the statutory categories.

Employers who are not automatically required to carry coverage under the Workers' Compensation Act may elect to do so voluntarily, or they may elect to be self-insured. In 1988, Illinois passed legislation that encourages businesses to apply for self-insurer status. Selection of one option does not, however, preclude an employer from changing to the other status at a later date. Regardless of the option selected, every employer must post notices in the workplace that provide employees with the name, business address, and telephone number of the person, service company, or insurance company to contact for information regarding the coverage.

Employees at Work

Only employees are eligible for workers' compensation benefits. Broadly defined, an employee is anyone under oral or written appointment or contract for hire, working on a full- or part-time basis. This definition encompasses even aliens who are unlawfully employed, minors, and prisoners on work-release programs. Not included in this definition, however, are domestic workers in private homes (except those indicated above), volunteers in nongovernmental entities, professional athletes, casual laborers, real estate brokers and sales representatives who work exclusively on commission, and independent contractors or anyone who is not subject to the control and direction of the employer.

An employee's injury must arise "out of and in the course of employment" to be covered by workers' compensation. Basically, this means that the injury has to occur while the employee is involved in some activity directly related to his or her job. For example, an employee injured at the job site while performing tasks at the direction of the employer is covered. An employee who is injured on a business trip is covered as long as the employee is engaged in employment duties. Workers' compensation coverage even extends to an emergency situation in which an employee leaves work intending to save life or property. Under Illinois law, however, an employee is not covered during volunteer work-related or work-sponsored recreational events (such as sporting events, picnics, or parties) unless the employee was assigned or ordered by his or her supervisor to participate. An employee is not covered while traveling to or from the place of employment, unless the employer asks the employee to perform a special duty on the way. Employees injured during work breaks when no work is being performed also may not be covered, depending on the circumstances.

NATURE OF INJURY

Workers' compensation benefits primarily cover accidental injuries. Accidental injuries are those that happen unexpectedly, without design or plan. This includes many repetitive stress injuries such as carpal-tunnel syndrome, as well as heart attacks, strokes, or other physical problems caused by work. In addition to accidental injuries, an employee also may recover if a pre-existing physical condition is made worse by his or her work. Workers' compensation does not cover injuries caused by intentional acts of assault or aggression by an employer or a fellow employee. For those types of injuries, an employee would seek compensation in the civil courts.

AVAILABLE BENEFITS

Workers' compensation entitles an employee to all reasonable and necessary medical care related to the injury, to payments for lost wages, and to rehabilitation and training. Under the Illinois Workers' Compensation Act an injured employee may be eligible for some or all of the following benefits:

- Medical services, including all reasonable expenses for necessary care and treatment, which may include first aid, visits to an approved health care provider, surgery, hospital care, dental or orthodontic treatment, prescription drugs, and medical supplies ordered by an approved physician
- Temporary total disability payments that provide the employee with up to two-thirds of his or her weekly wage for the time the worker is unable to work. (No compensation is payable, however, for loss of wages during the first three working days after the injury unless the employee is unable to work for 14 or more days after the date of the injury.)
- Permanent total disability or disfigurement payments (up to two-thirds of the worker's salary at the time of the injury) for employees who are totally disabled, scarred, or otherwise disfigured, and unable to work again
- Death benefits for burial expenses and benefits to dependents of the deceased employee in the case of fatal work-related injuries

An employer usually cannot be made to pay for emotional distress, pain, suffering, or loss of companionship, affection, or sexual relations. Workers' compensation benefit payments are not considered income and are therefore not subject to state or federal tax.

THE EMPLOYER'S RESPONSIBILITIES

With the few exceptions described above, all Illinois employers must cover their employers with workers' compensation insurance. The cost of premiums for compensation insurance is determined by factors such as the number of employees a business has, how safe the record of the workplace proves to be, and how much employees are paid.

The trade-off for an employee's relatively simple route to compensation is a limit to the amount of money that can be awarded for a work-related injury. Employers who maintain workers' compensation insurance programs to cover on-the-job injuries are immune from liability unless they act intentionally to cause injury. Coverage under the act does not, however, limit a person from seeking compensation for injuries from a third party whose negligence may have contributed to the injury or death of the worker.

Employers are prohibited from harassing, discharging, or threatening any employee for asserting a valid claim for workers' compensation benefits. It is illegal for an employer to refuse to hire or rehire an individual because he or she exercised his or her rights under the Workers' Compensation Act. It is also unlawful for an employer to refuse to hire or rehire an employee who has a disabling condition from a prior injury. However, if an employee suffers an injury that is made worse because of a condition existing prior to the time of hiring, the employer is protected from some liability under the Illinois Second Injury Law. The purpose of this law is to encourage employers to hire people who may have disabilities from a previous injury.

REPORTING AN INJURY AND COLLECTING BENEFITS

If an employee is injured on the job, he or she must notify the employer as soon as possible, but no later than 45 days after the date of the injury, the date when the effects of the injury first become apparent, or the date when a medical expert first discovers the injury. If the injury is from exposure to radiological material or equipment, the worker must give notice within 90 days of learning or suspecting that he or she has received an excessive dose. If the injury is related to an occupational disease, the employee must notify the employer as soon as practicable after he or she becomes aware of the disease. Failure to meet the notice requirements may threaten the employee's right to benefits. Notice may be verbal or written, and must include the approximate date and place of the accident, if known. It is recommended that, to avoid delay in processing claims, the notice also include the name, address, and telephone number of the injured employee, along with a brief description of the accident, injury, or illness. An employee gives notice by informing his or her supervisor of the injury. Notice to a fellow employee who is not a member of management is not sufficient. In cases in which the employer reasonably should have known that the injury occurred, the employer is said to have "constructive notice." Because of the potential for overreaching by an employer, Illinois law has declared that any contract or agreement made between the employer and the employee within seven days of an injury, concerning compensation or liability for the injury, is presumed to be fraudulent.

After receiving actual or constructive notice of the injury, an employer must promptly notify its insurance carrier or the administrator responsible for its workers' compensation program. If the injury or illness keeps the employee off of work for more than three days, the employer must do one of the following: (1) start to pay the employee temporary total disability; (2) notify the employee in writing of the additional information needed to begin making payments; or (3) provide the employee with a written explanation of why benefits are being denied. The employer also must file an Employer's First Report of Injury or Illness Form with the Illinois Industrial Commission for all injuries resulting in loss of work of three days or more. These reports must be filed between the 15th and the 25th of each month. If a death has occurred, the employer must notify the Industrial Commission in writing within 48 hours of the death. The employer also must notify each injured employee of his or her right to rehabilitation services, of the locations of available public rehabilitation centers, and of any other services known to the employer. The Illinois Industrial Commission also provides employees with benefits information.

PAYMENT OF BENEFITS

The employer or insurance carrier is obligated to provide necessary medical treatment. Treatment that is "medically necessary" is any medical treatment that assists the employee in recovering or helps to improve the employee's condition. Usually, this treatment ranges from diagnostic procedures to physical therapy, and may include psychiatric counseling, chiropractic care, plastic surgery, medicine, prostheses and other medical supplies, travel expenses (for travel to obtain medical treatment), and attendant or custodial care.

An employee may select his or her own treating doctor or hospital, and should notify the employer of this selection. The employer is responsible for the costs of all first aid and emergency services, two treating physicians, surgeons or hospitals of the employee's choice, and additional care provided through referrals. After this initial treatment phase, the employee must obtain approval from the employer before seeking treatment from additional physicians or at other hospitals. If the employee is treated by non-approved providers, the employer is not required to pay.

The employer may require a person receiving benefits under the Workers' Compensation Act to submit to a medical examination by a physician selected and paid by the employer. This exam may be required to determine the nature, extent, and possible duration of the injury and the disability compensation amounts. The employee may also be required to submit to examination by medical experts selected and paid by the employer. Refusal to submit to required examinations, or attempts to unnecessarily obstruct the exams, may result in the temporary suspension of benefit payments. Suspended payments cannot later be recovered.

WHEN AN EMPLOYER OR CARRIER REFUSES BENEFITS

Under some circumstances, employers may refuse to pay workers' compensation benefits. An employer may refuse to pay a workers' compensation claim because he or she believes the injury was not work-related or the benefits demanded exceed those justified for the injury. Benefits also may be jeopardized if an employee fails to follow safety rules and consequently suffers injury.

When a dispute arises, two options exist to settle it. One option is to file a claim with the Illinois Industrial Commission. The Industrial Commission will appoint an arbitrator, who will conduct a hearing and issue a decision. Either party may appeal the decision to the Industrial Commission, which will review the case and may hear arguments. For employees of the State of Illinois, the decisions of the Industrial Commission are final. In all other cases, parties may appeal Industrial Commission decisions to the Illinois Circuit Court. Further appeals may be taken to the Industrial Division of the Illinois Appellate Court and, in some case, to the Illinois Supreme Court.

The second option for resolving disputes is through voluntary arbitration. This option is available when the only disputed issues involve total temporary disability, permanent partial disability, or medical expenses. Parties who submit their case to an arbitrator waive their right to review by the Industrial Commission. The arbitrator's decision is final as to the factual issues in dispute, but questions of law may be appealed to the Illinois Circuit Court.

RESOURCES

The Illinois Industrial Commission oversees administration of workers' compensation for Illinois. The commission is located in the James R. Thompson Center, 100 Randolph Street West, Chicago, IL 60601, phone: (312) 814-6611. The commission publishes the free *Handbook on Workers' Compensation and Occupational Diseases*. Illinois established the Commissions Review Board to review complaints about commissioners and arbitrators. This board is chaired by the chair of the Industrial Commission. Information about the board is available from the Illinois Industrial Commission.

Workers' Compensation Law Leading Illinois Attorneys

The Leading Illinois Attorneys listed below were nominated as exceptional by their peers in a statewide survey conducted by American Research Corporation (ARC). ARC asked several thousand licensed Illinois attorneys to name the lawyer to whom they would send a close friend or family member in need of legal assistance in specific areas of law. The attorneys below were nominated in the area of Workers' Compensation Law.

Because the survey results (all practice area results combined) represent less than three percent of Illinois' practicing attorneys, this list should not be construed as a complete list. Nevertheless, it is an excellent source of highly qualified and reputable Illinois attorneys.

For information on ARC's survey methodology, see page *xi*.
For the complete list of Leading Illinois Consumer Attorneys, see page *xii*.

The Leading Illinois Attorneys below are listed alphabetically in accordance with the geographic region in which their offices are located. Note that attorneys may handle clients from a broad geographic area; attorneys are not restricted to only serving clients residing within the cities in which their offices are located.

An attorney whose name appears in bold has included a biographical profile in this chapter.

LEADING ILLINOIS ATTORNEYS

Illinois' Most Respected Legal Counsel As Selected By Their Peers.

The Leading Illinois Attorneys below were recommended by their peers in a statewide survey.

Cook & Collar Counties

Aiello, Chris J. - Villa Park
Aleksy, Richard E. - Chicago
Alschuler, Benjamin P. - Aurora
Alt, Leo F. - Chicago
Baime, Stephen G. - Chicago
Barder, Fredrick B. - Chicago
Barr, Richard J., Jr. - Chicago
Bass, Richard I. - Chicago
Bell, Joel M. - Chicago
Block, Michael D. - Joliet
Blum, Alan A. - Northbrook
Blumenfeld, Barry E. - Chicago
Bogusz, Richard P., Sr. - Chicago
Bongiorno, Salvatore J. - Chicago
Bowman, John T. - Chicago, page 339
Brill, Aaron P. - Chicago
Capron, Daniel F. - Chicago
Castaneda, John J. - Chicago
Cobb, Ronald W., Jr. - Chicago
Coladarci, Peter R. - Chicago
Cooney, Robert J., Jr. - Chicago
Corti, Peter D. - Chicago
Cronin, John J. - Chicago
Cronin, Thomas G. - Chicago
Cullen, George J. - Chicago, page 339
DeCarlo, Vito D. - Chicago
Denny, Steven A. - Chicago
Dentino, Michael P. - Chicago
Dicker, Steven M. - Chicago
Eagle, Warren E. - Chicago
Esposito, Paul V. - Chicago
Flaherty, Patrick M. - Aurora
Gabric, Ralph A. - Wheaton
Gaines, George L. - Chicago
Galliani, William R. - Chicago
Garcia, Martha A. - Chicago
Given, Kenneth R. - Chicago
Glink, Martin - Arlington Heights
Goldberg, Jeffrey M. - Chicago
Goldstein, Bernard - Chicago
Gore, Kenneth B. - Chicago
Guth, Glenn J. - Chicago
Hannigan, Richard D. - Mundelein, page 340
Haskins, Charles G., Jr. - Chicago, page 340
Hetherington, W. Joseph - Chicago
Hoscheit, John J. - St. Charles
Jeep, Markham M. - Waukegan, page 341
Jutila, Gerald D. - Waukegan
Kaplan, James L. - Chicago
Kimnach, Richard A. - Chicago, page 341
Knight, Anne S. - Chicago
Kominsky, Robert - Chicago
Koutsky, Kenneth F. - Chicago
Kralovec, Michael J. - Chicago
Kremin, David K. - Chicago
Lakernick, Harriette - Chicago
Laks, Perry M. - Chicago
Leahy, W. Daniel - Chicago
Lewis, Kenneth S. - Chicago
Linn, Craig M. - Waukegan
Loats, J. Timothy - Aurora, page 342
Marszalek, James J. - Chicago
Masur, W. Mark - Aurora
Melber, Michael D. - Chicago
Mielke, Craig S. - Aurora
Millon, Kevin H. - Wheaton
Murray, James E. - Chicago
Newquist, Elaine T. - Chicago

Ory, Christine - Wheaton
Page, Robin A. - Oak Brook
Patke, Marshall P. - Lake Forest
Peters, Kenneth D. - Chicago
Presbrey, Kim E. - Aurora, page 342
Robbins, Elliott H. - Chicago
Rodin, Curt N. - Chicago
Ross, Gilbert J. - Chicago
Rubin, Arnold G. - Chicago, page 343
Schiff, Matthew B. - Chicago
Schur, Jerome - Chicago
Shancer, Jeffrey M. - Chicago
Shapiro, Jay M. - Chicago
Sherman, Barbara - Chicago
Shovlain, Peter T. - Waukegan
Sostrin, Ellis M. - Chicago
Stein, Steven G. - Chicago
Stelle, Lori J. - Chicago
Strom, Neal B. - Chicago
Szesny, Henry C. - Chicago
Taradash, Randall M. - McHenry
Tenzer, Steven J. - Chicago
Tyrrell, Ross - Chicago
Wishnick, Neal K. - Chicago
Wittenberg, David M. - Chicago
Woodruff, Casey - Chicago

NORTHWESTERN ILLINOIS INCLUDING ROCKFORD & QUAD CITIES

Alexander, Peter - Rockford
Black, James F. - Rockford
Boreen, John M. - Rockford
Ferracuti, Peter F. - Ottawa
Finnegan, Frank R. - Rockford
Frischmeyer, Linda E. - Rock Island
Gesmer, James A. - Rockford
Gesmer, Jason N. - Rockford
Hannigan, Richard D. - Mundelein
Hartsock, Allan - Rock Island
Kavensky, Craig L. - Rock Island, page 344
Kavensky, Harrison - Rock Island
Morrissey, Joseph A. - Rockford
Nash, Thomas - Rockford
Neighbour, Hubbard B. - Moline
Nelson, Steven L. - Rock Island
Raccuglia, Anthony C. - Peru
Raymond, E. James - Addison
Reese, Randall K. - Rockford
Ruud, Glenn F. - Rock Island
Savaiano, Anthony A. - Loves Park
Sparkman, James D. - Rockford
Sullivan, Peter T. - Rockford
Truitt, John R. - Rockford
Tuite, Gregory E. - Rockford
VanHooreweghe, Francis R. - Moline
Westensee, John H. - Rock Island
White, Francine B. - Rockford
Williams, Daniel T., Jr. - Rockford

CENTRAL ILLINOIS

Benassi, A. Lou - Peoria
Berg, Steven W. - Springfield
Blan, Kenneth W., Jr. - Danville
Bowles, James E. - Peoria
Brown, Robert E. - Charleston
Bryan, George G. - Urbana
Bucklin, Bradford C. - Springfield
Delano, Charles H., III - Springfield
Devens, Charles J. - Danville
Durree, Edward D. - Peoria
Faber, William C., Jr. - Decatur
Ferguson, Mark E. - Mattoon
Frederick, Jeffrey D. - Urbana
Geiler, Lorna K. - Champaign
Halliday, Ronald E. - Peoria
Hamm, Ronald L. - Peoria
Heiple, Jeremy H. - Peoria
Holley, Grady E. - Springfield
Janssen, Jay H. - Peoria
Joy, Richard M. - Champaign
Kingery, Arthur - Peoria
LaMarca, William - Springfield
Lierman, Joseph H. - Champaign
Little, Thomas E. - Decatur
Logan, Michael J. - Springfield
Maher, Jerelyn D. - Peoria
Martin, John F. - Danville
McCarthy, D. Douglas - Decatur
McCarthy, Kitty M. - Decatur
McCarthy, Robert W. - Decatur
McElvain, Mike - Bloomington
McIntyre, Robert J. - Springfield
Moos, Patrick T. - Peoria
Narmont, John S. - Springfield
Nicoara, John P. - Peoria
Novak, Anthony E. - Urbana
O'Brien, Daniel R. - Peoria
Pryor, William A. - Springfield
Robeson, J. Jay - Springfield
Robinson, Jon D. - Decatur
Ryan, Michael D. - Mattoon
Ryan, Roger E. - Springfield
Selin, Paul E. - Champaign
Slevin, John A. - Peoria
Smith, S. Craig - Paris
Stephens, G. Douglas - Peoria
Swee, Jean A. - Bloomington
Taylor, John C. - Champaign
Tulin, Ronald - Charleston
Waters, M. Michael - Peoria
Williams, Robert E. - Bloomington
Willoughby, Stephen O. - Decatur

SOUTHERN ILLINOIS

Badgley, Brad L. - Belleville
Bonifield, Jerald J. - Belleville
Boyne, Kevin M. - Belleville
Brown, Joseph R., Jr. - Edwardsville
Calvo, Larry A. - Granite City
Cannady, Thomas B. - Belleville
Cates, Judy L. - Belleville
Coffel, Ron D. - Benton
Crosby, Thomas F., III - Marion
Glass, Mark - East St. Louis, page 345
Hanagan, Steven F. - Mt. Vernon
Hanagan, William D. - Mt. Vernon
Heiligenstein, C. E. - Belleville
Hughes, R. Courtney - Carbondale
Keefe, Thomas Q., Jr - Belleville
Kibler, Keith W. - Marion
Lakin, L. Thomas - Wood River
Lambert, Richard G. - Marion
Mendenhall, Douglas R. - Alton
Mitchell, A. Ben - Mt. Vernon
Nelson, Robert C. - Belleville, page 346
Nowak, Michael K. - Belleville
Prince, Mark D. - Carbondale
Rich, Thomas C. - Fairview Heights
Samuelson, Joseph L. - Belleville
Shevlin, Gregory L. - Belleville
Veltman, R. Edward - Centralia
Weilmuenster, J. Michael - Belleville
Womick, John - Carbondale
Woodcock, George W. - Mt. Carmel

Biographical Profiles of Workers' Compensation Law Leading Illinois Attorneys

The Leading Illinois Attorneys profiled below were nominated as exceptional by their peers in a statewide survey conducted by American Research Corporation (ARC). ARC asked several thousand licensed Illinois attorneys to name the lawyer to whom they would send a close friend or family member in need of legal assistance in specific areas of law. The attorneys below were nominated in the area of Workers' Compensation Law.

Because the survey results (all practice area results combined) represent less than three percent of Illinois' practicing attorneys, this list should not be construed as a complete list. Nevertheless, it is an excellent source of highly qualified and reputable Illinois attorneys.

For information on ARC's survey methodology, see page *xi*.
For the complete list of Leading Illinois Consumer Attorneys, see page *xii*.
For the list of Leading Illinois Workers' Compensation Law Attorneys, see page 335.

The Leading Illinois Attorneys below are listed alphabetically in accordance with the geographic region in which their offices are located. Note that attorneys may handle clients from a broad geographic area; attorneys are not limited to only serving clients residing within the cities in which their offices are located.

The two-line attorney listings in this section are of attorneys who practice in this area but whose full biographical profiles appear in other sections of this book. A bullet "•" preceding a name indicates the attorney was nominated in this particular area of law.

For information on the format of the full biographical profiles, consult the "Using the Consumer Guidebook" section on page *xviii*.

The following abbreviations are used throughout these profiles:

App.	Appellate
Cir.	Circuit
Ct.	Court
Dist.	District
Sup.	Supreme
JD	Juris Doctor (Doctor of Law)
LLB	Legum Baccalaureus (Bachelor of Laws)
LLD	Legum Doctor (Doctor of Laws)
LLM	Legum Magister (Master of Laws)
ADR	Alternative Dispute Resolution
ABA	American Bar Association
ABOTA	American Board of Trial Advocates
ATLA	Association of Trial Lawyers of America
CBA	Chicago Bar Association
ISBA	Illinois State Bar Association
ITLA	Illinois Trial Lawyers Association
NBTA	National Board of Trial Advocacy

COOK & COLLAR COUNTIES

•JOHN T. BOWMAN: Mr. Bowman's practice is focused in the area of workers' compensation, representing employees who have sustained work-related injuries. He has handled a wide variety of cases involving occupational disease and post-traumatic stress disorders. Other cases involve assessment of physical disabilities and loss of earnings. Mr. Bowman is listed in *Who's Who in the Midwest*, 1994-95.
Education: JD 1976, Southern Illinois University; BS 1969, Syracuse University.
Admitted: 1976 Illinois; 1976 U.S. Dist. Ct. (N. Dist. IL).
Employment History: Partner 1992-present, Bowman & Corday, Ltd.; Partner 1984-92, Murges, Bowman & Corday, Ltd.; Partner 1980-84, Murges & Bowman; Associate 1976-80, Law Offices of George J. Murges.
Representative Clients: Bowman & Corday, Ltd., represents individuals who have sustained work-related injuries. Client references are available upon request.
Professional Associations: Illinois Workers' Compensation Lawyers Assn.; ITLA; ATLA; ISBA; CBA.
Community Involvement: SS Cyril & Methodius Church; Willows Academy for Girls (Fathers' Club). Mr. Bowman is a frequent contributor to the Misericordia Home and the Evans Scholarship program.
Firm: Bowman & Corday, Ltd., was formed in January 1992, to represent individuals who have sustained work-related injuries in Cook County, including Chicago, and the collar counties of Will, DuPage, Kane, Lake, and McHenry. The firm has 35 years of combined experience representing the injured worker before the Illinois Industrial Commission, and on appeal to the Circuit, Appellate and Supreme Courts. A substantial number of clients are referred from other law firms. *See complete firm profile in Appendix A.*

JOHN T. BOWMAN
Bowman & Corday, Ltd.
20 North Clark Street
Suite 500
Chicago, IL 60602
Phone: (312) 606-9675
Fax: (312) 606-9887

•GEORGE J. CULLEN: Mr. Cullen concentrates in workers' compensation law, representing petitioners. In addition to being an attorney with over 36 years' experience in workers' compensation and personal injury law, Mr. Cullen represents several clients as a consultant on legislative matters in both Springfield and Chicago.
Education: JD 1959, Loyola University; BS 1957, Loyola University.
Admitted: 1960 Illinois; 1960 U.S. Dist. Ct. (N. Dist. IL).
Employment History: Partner 1976-present, Cullen, Haskins, Nicholson & Menchetti, P.C.; 1960-75, George J. Cullen & Associates.
Professional Associations: City of Chicago [Chicago Planning Commission (Chair 1980-82); Zoning Board of Appeals 1982-87]; ITLA [Workers' Compensation Section (Chair)]; CBA [Workers' Compensation Section (Chair)]; Illinois Industrial Commission [Advisory Committee (Chair)]; Illinois State Federation of Labor (Workers' Compensation Advisory Attorney); Illinois House of Representatives (Workers' Compensation Consultant, Democrats).
Firm: Cullen, Haskins, Nicholson & Menchetti, P.C., offers over 75 years of combined legal experience together with personal attention. The client is always personally and professionally assisted directly by the attorney assigned to his or her case, or by the attorney's assistant. The office is computer-efficient and client case information is always at the attorneys' fingertips. Having this information so readily available helps the firm to represent each client with maximum efficiency. The firm is always dedicated to assisting each client comfortably through the legal process. The goal of Cullen, Haskins, Nicholson & Menchetti, P.C., is to obtain the best results possible for each individual client. *See complete firm profile in Appendix A.*

GEORGE J. CULLEN
Cullen, Haskins, Nicholson & Menchetti, P.C.
35 East Wacker Drive
Suite 1760
Chicago, IL 60601
Phone: (312) 332-2545
Fax: (312) 332-4543

Extensive Experience In:
• Personal Injury
• Legislative Consulting

SCOTT B. GIBSON - *Law Offices of Scott B. Gibson, Ltd.* - 415 West Washington Street, Suite 103 - Waukegan, IL 60085 - Phone: (847) 263-5100, Fax: (847) 249-7588 - *See complete biographical profile in the Personal Injury Law: General Chapter, page 240.*

Chapter 26: Workers' Compensation Law

RICHARD D. HANNIGAN

Richard D. Hannigan, Ltd.
505 East Hawley Street
Suite 240
Mundelein, IL 60060

Phone: (847) 949-1070
Fax: (847) 949-1084

•**RICHARD D. HANNIGAN:** Mr. Hannigan has practiced workers' compensation law for the past 23 years. For the past 20 years, he has exclusively limited his practice to the area of workers' compensation, representing insurance companies and employees from 1973 to 1991, and now limits his practice to serving the injured worker. Mr. Hannigan has lectured and published articles on workers' compensation for the Illinois State Bar Association, the National Business Institute, and the Lake County Bar Association. Having successfully represented workers' compensation clients in the Supreme and Appellate Courts of the State of Illinois, Mr. Hannigan possesses the technical knowledge of guiding a case through the maze known as "Workers' Compensation." His knowledge of the law in the workers' compensation field contributes to his clients' ability to obtain the best possible results at the Illinois Industrial Commission.

Education: JD 1973, John Marshall Law School (Illinois Appellate Defender Program); BS 1970, University of Dayton.

Admitted: 1973 Illinois; 1975 Arizona; 1973 U.S. Dist. Ct. (N. Dist. IL).

Employment History: 1991-present, Richard D. Hannigan, Ltd.; 1973-91, Law Offices of Anthony V. Fanone.

Professional Associations: ISBA (Council Section 1992-96); Workers' Compensation Lawyers Assn. (President 1992; Vice President 1991; Secretary 1989-90; Board Member 1984-88, 1993-95); Lake County Bar Assn. [Workers' Compensation Section (Chair 1988, 1991)].

Firm: Mr. Hannigan and his associate practice law exclusively representing injured workers in Lake, McHenry, Cook, and Kane Counties. His staff and paralegal have over 25 years' experience in handling the injured worker's case. Having represented insurance companies gives Mr. Hannigan unique insight into what the insurance company is doing to the injured worker and how to fight for that worker's rights. The first consultation is free. Fees range from $100.00 for a statutory loss to 20 percent of amounts recovered for all other workers' compensation claims.

CHARLES G. HASKINS, JR.

Cullen, Haskins, Nicholson & Menchetti, P.C.
35 East Wacker Drive
Suite 1760
Chicago, IL 60601

Phone: (312) 332-2545
Fax: (312) 332-4543

•**CHARLES G. HASKINS, JR.:** Mr. Haskins emphasizes his practice in workers' compensation law, handling all aspects from trial through appeals to the Illinois Supreme Court. He has successfully represented injured workers, seeking all remedies available under the Illinois Workers' Compensation and Occupational Diseases Acts. Ancillary to the representation of claimants before the Industrial Commission, Mr. Haskins has successfully handled claims before the Social Security Office of Hearings and Appeals as well as obtained pensions for police officers under the Illinois Pension Code. He is a frequent lecturer and is Coeditor of the Illinois Trial Lawyers Association's *Workers' Compensation Case Notebook*. Mr. Haskins is the subject of biographical record in Marquis' *Who's Who in American Law*, 9th ed. 1996/1997, and is listed in *The Best Lawyers in America*.

Education: JD 1976 with distinction, John Marshall Law School; BA 1972, University of Illinois-Urbana.

Admitted: 1976 Illinois; 1976 U.S. Dist. Ct. (N. Dist. IL).

Employment History: Shareholder 1989-present, Cullen, Haskins, Nicholson & Menchetti, P.C.; Shareholder/Associate 1976-89, George J. Cullen & Associates, Ltd.

Representative Clients: Mr. Haskins limits his practice to representing injured claimants. His client base includes a broad spectrum of construction, manufacturing and service employees.

Professional Associations: ITLA [Board of Managers 1988-present; Workers' Compensation Committee 1980-present (Cochair 1991-present); Annual Seminar Committee (Cochair 1992-present)]; Workers' Compensation Lawyers Assn. (Officer 1986-89; President 1989; Board of Managers 1990-present); CBA 1976-present [Industrial Commission (Chair 1987-88)].

Firm: The firm of Cullen, Haskins, Nicholson & Menchetti, P.C., was founded by George J. Cullen in 1963, and restructured in its current form in 1989. The firm has over 75 years' combined experience representing injured workers in all matters related to the Illinois Workers' Compensation and Occupational Diseases Acts. The firm's members have long been active leaders in the various bar association committees devoted to workers' compensation issues. *See complete firm profile in Appendix A.*

•MARKHAM M. JEEP: Mr. Jeep practices almost exclusively in personal injury law, with a concentration in Illinois workers' compensation claims. He handles substantial construction litigation claims, motor vehicle collision matters, medical negligence, and premise liability matters. Mr. Jeep is a frequent lecturer on trial practice and workers' compensation law.
Education: JD 1979, Loyola University; MA 1976, Northern Illinois University; BA 1974 cum laude, Northern Illinois University.
Admitted: 1979 Illinois; 1979 U.S. Dist. Ct. (N. Dist. IL); 1982 U.S. Ct. App. (7th Cir.).
Employment History: 1991-present, Markham M. Jeep, P.C.; Partner 1986-91, Hermann & Jeep; Associate 1981-86, Charles M. May, Ltd.; Associate 1979-81, May, Decker & Associates.
Representative Clients: Mr. Jeep represents working men and women. He recently resolved a major medical negligence claim on behalf of a child born with cerebral palsy, and another matter against a podiatrist responsible for crippling a client in an unnecessary surgery.
Professional Associations: ITLA 1979-present.
Community Involvement: Waukegan Senior Housing Corporation (past President); Gurnee School District 56 (President).
Firm: Markham M. Jeep, P.C., vigorously and unswervingly represents the rights and interests of the victims of injuries against corporate and insurance greed. The firm tries several cases each month in the Illinois Industrial Commission and has an active practice in the circuit court. The firm presently has major cases pending in the federal court. *Mr. Jeep also practices Personal Injury Law: General and Personal Injury Law: Medical & Professional Malpractice.*

MARKHAM M. JEEP
Markham M. Jeep, P.C.
450 North Green Bay Road
Waukegan, IL 60085

Phone: (847) 360-3300
Fax: (847) 360-3303

•RICHARD A. KIMNACH: Mr. Kimnach devotes his practice to representing injured workers. He primarily practices before the Illinois Industrial Commission and the courts that review workers' compensation claims. The claims he has handled range from mundane sprains and strains to fatal or career-ending injuries. He has represented workers suffering from catastrophic injuries arising from amputations, paralysis and/or brain damage. He has successfully presented claims involving atypical injuries, including heart attacks and the sequelae of repetitive trauma. In prosecuting such claims, Mr. Kimnach has appeared from time to time before arbitrators throughout most of northern Illinois. He also has appeared before both panels of reviewing commissioners. As a corollary to this practice, Mr. Kimnach has represented his severely injured clients in their pursuit of Social Security disability benefits. In doing so, he has appeared before a variety of Administrative Law Judges in several venues in northern Illinois and northwestern Indiana. In addition to these professional activities, undertaken on behalf of individual clients, Mr. Kimnach has written numerous briefs *amicus curiae* for the Illinois Trial Lawyers Association. He has generally done so when the outcome of a case on appeal could have a substantial impact upon other victims of personal injury. Mr. Kimnach has often addressed business and bar associations as a guest speaker, offering insight into the rights and responsibilities that attend work-related injuries.
Education: JD 1980, Loyola University; BA 1975, University of Illinois.
Admitted: 1980 Illinois; 1980 U.S. Dist. Ct. (N. Dist. IL).
Employment History: 1980-present, Anesi, Ozmon & Rodin, Ltd.
Representative Clients: Mr. Kimnach has represented numerous injured employees. The majority are union workers and, of them, most are in the construction trades. Among those tradeworkers are ironworkers, carpenters, sheet metal workers, plumbers, pipefitters, laborers, brick masons, cement masons, and electricians.
Professional Associations: ISBA 1980-present; ITLA 1980-present (Amicus Curiae Committee; Workers' Compensation Committee); CBA 1980-present (Workers' Compensation Committee); ATLA 1980-present; Workers' Compensation Lawyers Assn. 1980-present.
Community Involvement: United States Naval Institute (Associate Member).
Firm: Anesi, Ozmon & Rodin, Ltd., with 28 attorneys and a staff of over 100, is the largest law firm in Illinois concentrating its practice in the representation of injury victims. The firm is committed to vigorously representing its clients in the areas of personal injury litigation, workers' compensation, and Social Security practice. *See complete firm profile in Appendix A. Mr. Kimnach also practices Personal Injury Law: General and Social Security Law.*

RICHARD A. KIMNACH
Anesi, Ozmon & Rodin, Ltd.
161 North Clark Street
Suite 2100
Chicago, IL 60601

Phone: (312) 372-3822
Fax: (312) 372-3833
800: (800) 458-3822 within IL

Chapter 26: Workers' Compensation Law

J. TIMOTHY LOATS

Law Offices of J. Timothy Loats
330 North Broadway
Aurora, IL 60505

Phone: (630) 898-4200
Fax: (630) 897-9058
E-mail: aulw@aol.com

Extensive Experience In:

- Repetitive Traumas
- Casino/Riverboat Injuries
- Contested Claims

•**J. TIMOTHY LOATS:** Mr. Loats has been exclusively involved in workers' compensation practice for 17 years. He is the author of *Labor and Employment Law for Supervisors,* Aurora University, 1990, and "The Injured Employee," *The Complete Lawyer,* ABA Press, Winter 1996. He has been an instructor in employment law at Aurora University since 1985, and at Waubonsee Community College since 1992. He is listed in *Who's Who in America; Who's Who in American Law;* and *Who's Who in Emerging Leaders of America.*

Education: JD 1978, Notre Dame (National Moot Court Team; National Mock Trial Team; Kappa Delta Pi); BA 1975 summa cum laude, George Williams College.

Admitted: 1978 Illinois; 1978 U.S. Dist. Ct. (N. Dist. IL, General Bar, Trial Bar).

Employment History: Sole Practitioner 1995-present, Law Offices of J. Timothy Loats; Instructor 1985-present, Aurora University; Instructor 1992-present, Waubonsee Community College; Full Partner/Managing Partner 1990-94, Alschuler, Funkey, Loats & Pilmer, P.C.; Arbitrator 1989-present, 18th Judicial Circuit, DuPage, Illinois; Founder/Owner 1981-90, Fox Valley Legal Clinic; Associate 1979-81, Scheele, Serkland & Boyle, Ltd.; Associate 1978-79, Graney & Gerstein, P.C.

Representative Clients: Mr. Loats represents clients exclusively in the area of work-related injuries.

Professional Associations: ISBA 1978-present [Young Lawyers' Division (Economic Section, Chair 1986-87)]; ABA 1978-present [Workers' Compensation Committee (Vice Chair 1994-95); General Practice Section 1990-present]; Kane County Bar Assn. 1981-present [Labor and Employment Law Committee 1989-present; Workers' Compensation Committee (Chair 1992-93, 1994-95)]; DuPage County Bar Assn. 1981-present (Civil Practice Committee; Employment Law Committee); Illinois Workers' Compensation Lawyers Assn. 1979-present; American Judicature Society.

Community Involvement: Fox Valley Villages Rotary Club (Charter Member; President 1988-89); Fox Valley Villages Community Assn. (Founding President 1981-82; Vice President 1986-87); Aurora Interfaith Food Pantry (Board of Directors); Family Counseling Service (Board of Directors); Big Brothers/Big Sisters of Southern Kane and Kendall Counties (Chair); Mutual Ground, Inc. (Board of Directors); Cities in Schools Aurora 2000, Inc. (Founding President 1993-94); United Way of Aurora (Vice President 1995-96; President 1996-97).

Firm: As a solo practitioner, all clients meet and have telephone calls directly with Mr. Loats. He returns all phone calls within two hours. Mr. Loats represents his clients in all hearings; no associates or partners handle cases for him. His office is fully computerized. Normally, all forms will be prepared for signing during the first meeting. All fees are paid by the employer.

KIM E. PRESBREY

Presbrey and Associates, P.C.
821 West Galena Boulevard
Aurora, IL 60506

Phone: (630) 264-7300
Fax: (630) 897-8637
800: (800) 552-8622

•**KIM E. PRESBREY:** Mr. Presbrey practices primarily in the area of employment law, concentrating in workers' compensation. He has lectured extensively on numerous workers' compensation issues, including temporary total disability benefits, permanent partial disability benefits, death benefits, wage differential, settlement contract preparation, and the prosecution of defense claims. Additionally, he has handled employment issues at the federal and state levels, including temporary restraining orders and other collective bargaining issues.

Education: JD 1976, Vanderbilt University; BA 1973, Northwestern University.

Admitted: 1977 Illinois.

Employment History: Private Practice 1977-present.

Representative Clients: United Auto Workers; International Assn. of Machinists; United Steel Workers; Kane County and Illinois Compensation Trust.

Professional Associations: ITLA (Board of Managers 1992-present); Illinois Workers' Compensation Lawyers Assn. (Board of Managers 1991-95); Kane County Bar Assn. [Workers' Compensation Section (Founder 1980)]; ISBA (Counsel Section 1989-present).

Community Involvement: Aurora Boys Baseball (Sponsor); Illinois Future, Inc., a charitable organization for funding of scholarships for children of disabled/deceased workers (Founder).

Firm: The firm was originally founded in 1948 for the purpose of representing clients in labor-related matters, concentrating in workers' compensation. Since 1977, the firm has also represented unions in general labor-related matters. Presbrey and Associates, P.C., also handles employment discrimination cases, including matters involving the ADA and human rights. The firm also handles personal injury, divorce, real estate and criminal defense. Presbrey and Associates, P.C., also defends select clients in matters regarding workers' compensation. *Mr. Presbrey also practices Employment Law and Personal Injury Law: General.*

•**ARNOLD G. RUBIN:** Mr. Rubin concentrates his practice in workers' compensation law. He has presented several cases before the Illinois Supreme Court and Illinois Appellate Courts involving various issues in workers' compensation law. The reported cases include the following: *Phillips Products Co., Inc. v. Industrial Commission,* 446 N.E.2d 234 (Illinois Supreme Court, 1983); *Domagalski v. Industrial Commission,* 454 N.E.2d 295 (Illinois Supreme Court, 1983); *Forest City Steel Erectors v. Industrial Commission,* 636 N.E.2d 969 (First District, Illinois Appellate Court, Industrial Commission Division, 1994); *Lakeside Architectural Metals v. Industrial Commission,* 642 N.E.2d 796 (Second District, Illinois Appellate Court, 1994). Mr. Rubin is the author of numerous articles for various publications, including "Sunship Decision Sinks Federal Exclusivity Doctrine in Longshoremen's and Harbor Workers' Claims," *Illinois State Bar Journal,* 69:11, 1981; "An Evaluation of Vocational Rehabilitation Under the Illinois Workers' Compensation Act," *Illinois Trial Lawyers Journal,* Spring/Summer 1983; "Recent Developments in Vocational Rehabilitation," *Illinois Trial Lawyers Journal,* Fall/Winter 1987; "Third Party Cases and Subrogation," National Business Institute Seminar, April 1994; "Petitioner's Rights Under Section 8(d)1 of the Act," Chapter 12, *Workers' Compensation Notebook,* Illinois Trial Lawyers Association, 1995; "An Overview of Industrial Vocational Rehabilitation Statutes and Approaches," (coauthor), *Illinois State Bar Journal,* 74;7, 1986; Chapter 10, "Vocational Rehabilitation/Physical Rehabilitation," (coauthor), *Workers' Compensation Notebook,* Illinois Trial Lawyers Association, 1995. He has lectured for the Chicago Bar Association, Illinois Institute for Continuing Legal Education, Illinois Trial Lawyers Association and the Illinois State Bar Association on various topics involving workers' compensation law.
Education: JD 1978, Illinois Institute of Technology, Chicago-Kent; BA 1975, Northwestern University.
Admitted: 1978 Illinois.
Employment History: 1994-present, Law Offices of Arnold G. Rubin, Ltd.; Attorney 1978-94, Partner 1984-94, Anesi, Ozmon & Lewin, Ltd.
Professional Associations: Workers' Compensation Lawyers Assn. (Board of Directors 1994-present; President 1993); ITLA [Board of Managers 1992-present; Workers' Compensation Committee (Cochair 1987-present)]; CBA [Industrial Commission Committee (Chair 1989-90)].

ARNOLD G. RUBIN
Law Offices of Arnold G. Rubin, Ltd.
100 West Monroe
Suite 1605
Chicago, IL 60603
Phone: (312) 899-0022
Fax: (312) 899-8141

•**JEFFREY M. SHANCER** - *Law Offices of Jeffrey M. Shancer* - Three First National Plaza, Suite 3750 - Chicago, IL 60602 - Phone: (312) 558-5167, Fax: (312) 558-7767 - *See complete biographical profile in the Personal Injury Law: General Chapter, page 248.*

ROBERT N. WADINGTON - *Robert N. Wadington & Associates* - 111 West Washington Street, Suite 1460 - Chicago, IL 60602 - Phone: (312) 629-2706, Fax: (312) 629-8022 - *See complete biographical profile in the Personal Injury Law: General Chapter, page 249.*

Chapter 26: Workers' Compensation Law

NORTHWESTERN ILLINOIS
INCLUDING ROCKFORD & QUAD CITIES

CRAIG L. KAVENSKY
Winstein, Kavensky & Wallace
224 18th Street
Fourth Floor
Rock Island, IL 61201

Phone: (309) 794-1515
Fax: (309) 794-9929

Extensive Experience In:
- Products Liability

•**CRAIG L. KAVENSKY:** Mr. Kavensky limits his practice exclusively to representing victims of personal injury, Mr. Kavensky limits his practice exclusively to representing victims of personal injury, products liability, wrongful death, and work-related injuries. He has successfully represented numerous parties in claims arising out of auto collisions, including victims who have suffered serious, permanent injuries as well as fatal injuries. He has also represented thousands of persons in claims against their employers under the Workers' Compensation Act. In 1995, he successfully represented an injured worker through the appellate court process in a case which established new law in Illinois in the area of calculation of average weekly wage.

Education: JD 1982 with high honors, Illinois Institute of Technology, Chicago-Kent; BS 1979 with high honors, University of Illinois.

Admitted: 1982 Illinois; 1982 U.S. Dist. Ct. (C. Dist. IL).

Employment History: Managing Partner 1982-present, Winstein, Kavensky & Wallace.

Representative Clients: All of Mr. Kavensky's clients are individuals who have been injured in accidents. The firm of Winstein, Kavensky & Wallace also represents unions and members of unions, including the UAW, IBEW, and United Rubber Workers.

Professional Associations: ATLA 1982-present; ITLA 1982-present; ABA 1982-present; Rock Island County Bar Assn. 1982-present.

Firm: The firm of Winstein, Kavensky & Wallace has been in existence for over 50 years. The firm has represented thousands of injured persons in an effort to obtain fair compensation in claims arising out of personal injury, workers' compensation, and wrongful death. The firm also concentrates in the areas of criminal law, family law, labor law, and general civil litigation. *Mr. Kavensky also practices Personal Injury Law: General and Personal Injury Law: Medical & Professional Malpractice.*

JAN H. OHLANDER - *Reno, Zahm, Folgate, Lindberg & Powell* - 1415 East State Street, Suite 900 - Rockford, IL 61104 - Phone: (815) 987-4050, Fax: (815) 987-4092 - *See complete biographical profile in the Personal Injury Law: General Chapter, page 251.*

CENTRAL ILLINOIS

•**KENNITH W. BLAN, JR.** - *Blan Law Offices* - 712 West Fairchild - P.O. Box 1995 - Danville, IL 61834 - Phone: (217) 443-5400, Fax: (217) 443-5155 - *See complete biographical profile in the Personal Injury Law: General Chapter, page 252.*

GARY L. CLARK - *The Law Offices of Frederic W. Nessler and Associates* - 433 Hamilton Boulevard - First Financial Plaza, Suite Two - Peoria, IL 61602 - Phone: (309) 673-6404, Fax: (309) 674-6407 - *See complete biographical profile in the Personal Injury Law: Medical & Professional Malpractice Chapter, page 272.*

MICHAEL B. METNICK - *Metnick, Wise, Cherry & Frazier* - Number One West Old State Capital Plaza - Myers Building, Suite 200 - Springfield, IL 62701 - Phone: (217) 753-4242, Fax: (217) 753-4642 - *See complete biographical profiles in the Personal Injury Law: General Chapter, page 253, Criminal Law: Felonies & White Collar Crime Chapter, page 117 and Family Law Chapter, page 212.*

FREDERIC W. NESSLER - *The Law Offices of Frederic W. Nessler and Associates* - 800 Myers Building - Springfield, IL 62701 - Phone: (217) 753-5533, Fax: (217) 753-4631, 800: (800) 727-8010 - *See complete biographical profile in the Personal Injury Law: General Chapter, page 253.*

•**JOHN A. SLEVIN** - *Vonachen, Lawless, Trager & Slevin* - 456 Fulton Street, Suite 425 - Peoria, IL 61602 - Phone: (309) 676-8986, Fax: (309) 676-4130 - *See complete biographical profile in the Personal Injury Law: General Chapter, page 255.*

ROBERT E. STINE - *Stine, Wolter & Greer* - 426 South Fifth Street - Springfield, IL 62701 - Phone: (217) 744-1000, Fax: (217) 744-1444 - *See complete biographical profile in the Personal Injury Law: General Chapter, page 256.*

SOUTHERN ILLINOIS

LANCE CALLIS - *Callis, Papa, Jensen, Jackstadt & Halloran, P.C.* - 1326 Niedringhaus Avenue - Granite City, IL 62040 - Phone: (618) 452-1323, Fax: (618) 452-8024 - *See complete biographical profile in the Personal Injury Law: Transportation Chapter, page 282.*

REX CARR - *Carr, Korein, Tillery, Kunin, Montroy & Glass* - 412 Missouri Avenue - East St. Louis, IL 62201 - Phone: (618) 274-0434, Fax: (618) 274-8369, 800: (800) 333-5297 - *See complete biographical profiles in the Personal Injury Law: Medical & Professional Malpractice Chapter, page 274 and Personal Injury Law: General Chapter, page 257.*

•**MARK GLASS:** After 12 years of personal injury and civil trials, Mr. Glass has spent the past decade primarily on Illinois workers' compensation cases. Representing injured Illinois workers now constitutes virtually his entire practice. He is supported by another attorney and paralegal to give clients thorough and efficient representation. Mr. Glass has participated in statewide workers' compensation committees and has worked with unions to fight for legislation protecting the rights of injured workers in Illinois. He has lectured before professional groups and conducts seminars on workers' compensation.
Education: JD 1974, St. Louis University (Law Day Honors); BA 1969, University of Illinois (Dean's List; James Scholar).
Admitted: 1974 Illinois; 1980 Missouri; 1974 U.S. Dist. Ct. (S. Dist. IL); 1975 U.S. Ct. App. (7th Cir.).
Employment History: Partner/Associate 1974-present, Carr, Korein, Tillery, Kunin, Montroy & Glass.
Representative Clients: Mr. Glass represents injured Illinois workers.
Professional Associations: ITLA 1987-present (Workers' Compensation Committee); ISBA 1974-present (Workers' Compensation Section 1990-92); ATLA 1974-present; St. Clair County Bar Assn. 1974-present; Missouri Assn. of Trial Attorneys 1990-present; American Arbitration Assn. (Panel of Arbitrators 1980-present).
Community Involvement: American Civil Liberties Union; Life Crisis Services (Suicide Hotline Volunteer).
Firm: Carr, Korein, Tillery, Kunin, Montroy & Glass consists of 19 lawyers, including several personal injury trial attorneys. The attorneys in the firm have the skills and experience necessary to handle any third party issues arising from on-the-job injuries initially covered by workers' compensation, including retaliatory and discriminatory discharge, or violations of the Americans with Disabilities Act. The firm's additional offices in Belleville, Illinois, and St. Louis, Missouri, also provide enhanced access to its services for victims of occupational accidents and diseases. *See complete firm profile in Appendix A. Mr. Glass also practices Personal Injury Law: General and Personal Injury Law: Transportation.*

MARK GLASS
Carr, Korein, Tillery, Kunin, Montroy & Glass
412 Missouri Avenue
East St. Louis, IL 62201

Phone: (618) 274-0434
Fax: (618) 274-8369
800: (800) 333-5297

Extensive Experience In:

• Wage Differential Analysis
• Vocational Rehabilitation Benefits
• Orthopedic/Neurological Causation Issues

MARK D. HASSAKIS - *Hassakis & Hassakis, P.C.* - Boston Building - 206 South Ninth Street, Suite 201 - P.O. Box 706 - Mt. Vernon, IL 62864 - Phone: (618) 244-5335, Fax: (618) 244-5330, 800: (800) 553-3125 (only available in area codes 618 and 217) - *See complete biographical profile in the Personal Injury Law: General Chapter, page 257.*

Robert C. Nelson

Nelson, Bement, Stubblefield & Levenhagen, P.C.
420 North High Street
P.O. Box Y
Belleville, IL 62222

Phone: (618) 277-4000
Fax: (618) 277-1136

Extensive Experience In:

- Personal Injury General
- Construction Accidents
- Social Security Disability

•**ROBERT C. NELSON:** Mr. Nelson limits his practice to representing injured persons. Since 1973, he has practiced in Belleville, Illinois, concentrating his practice in personal injury and workers' compensation claims. He works closely with various unions, including the Laborers' International Local 44, the United Paper Workers' International Union Local 1215, and the Illinois Education Association. He has published various articles on workers' compensation, and lectured at seminars for the Illinois Trial Lawyers Association, Illinois State Bar Association, and the National Business Institute. His articles and presentations include "Computation of Average Weekly Wage," *Workers' Compensation Handbook,* Illinois Trial Lawyers Association; "Current Issues in Workers' Compensation Law," 1994; "Did You Know These Cases Could Be Compensable?" (heart attack, repetitive trauma, recreational activities, assault, parking lot injuries), ITLA; "Initial Consideration in Accepting a Claimant's Case," ISBA; "Evidence in Trial Practice in Illinois—Update Review of Workers' Compensation and Illinois Structural Workers' Act"; and many talks given to various unions in southern Illinois.

Education: JD 1973, University of Illinois; BA 1970, University of Illinois.

Admitted: 1973 Illinois; 1975 U.S. Ct. App. (7th Cir.).

Employment History: Senior Partner 1980-present, Nelson, Bement, Stubblefield & Levenhagen, P.C.

Professional Associations: St. Clair County Bar Assn.; ISBA; ITLA; ATLA; Workers' Compensation Lawyers Assn.

Community Involvement: Mr. Nelson has been active in a variety of community service organizations. He has enjoyed coaching recreational and select soccer teams for two of his four children. He has been the lay leader of his church. He is politically active as the Precinct Committeeman.

Firm: Nelson, Bement, Stubblefield & Levenhagen, P.C., practices in a certified historical structure approximately five blocks from the courthouse in Belleville, Illinois. The firm is professionally active with state and local bar associations, including publishing in the *ISBA Journal* and testifying before the state legislature. Each attorney is a member of the Illinois Trial Lawyers Association. While a relatively young firm, the attorneys have considerable litigation experience. The staff is particularly talented and resourceful. Nearly the entire professional staff has worked with the attorneys on a long-term basis, some as long as 20 years. Most of the staff members belong to the St. Clair County Legal Professionals Association. The firm sponsors many community activities such as Walk for Cystic Fibrosis, 10K runs, and a great variety of soccer and baseball teams. *See complete firm profile in Appendix A. Mr. Nelson also practices Personal Injury Law: General and Social Security Law.*

TIMOTHY C. STUBBLEFIELD - *Nelson, Bement, Stubblefield & Levenhagen, P.C.* - 420 North High Street - P.O. Box Y - Belleville, IL 62222 - Phone: (618) 277-4000 or (618) 277-8260, Fax: (618) 277-1136 - *See complete biographical profiles in the Civil Appellate Law Chapter, page 87 and Family Law Chapter, page 218.*

•**JOHN WOMICK** - *Womick & Associates, Chartered* - 1100 West Main Street - Carbondale, IL 62901 - Phone: (618) 529-2440, Fax: (618) 457-2680, 800: (800) 598-2440 - *See complete biographical profile in the Personal Injury Law: General Chapter, page 258.*

APPENDIX A

PROFILED ATTORNEYS & LAW FIRMS BY REGION

The following index is intended to enable quick identification of profiled Leading Illinois Attorneys and law firms by location. In the lists below, the area of practice in which each attorney is profiled appears following the city. An attorney whose name appears in bold is a member of a firm which chose to support this *Guidebook* by publishing a firm profile in this section.

Note: Within a firm profile, a bullet "•" preceding an attorney's name indicates that the attorney has an individual biographical profile elsewhere in this book.

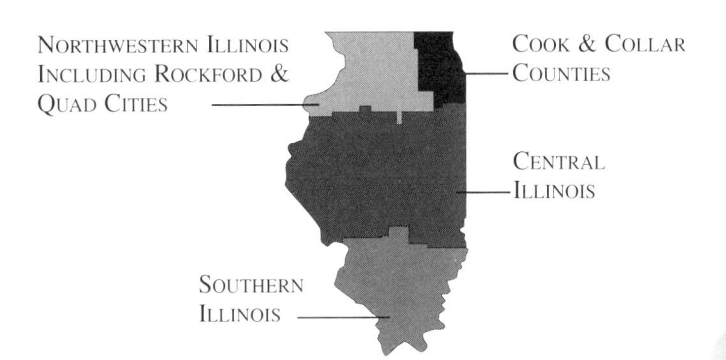

NORTHWESTERN ILLINOIS INCLUDING ROCKFORD & QUAD CITIES

COOK & COLLAR COUNTIES

CENTRAL ILLINOIS

SOUTHERN ILLINOIS

COOK & COLLAR COUNTIES

Ackerman, Allan A. - *Allan A. Ackerman, P.C.* - Chicago - Criminal Law: Felonies & White Collar Crime
Aimen, Julie B. - *Attorney at Law* - Chicago - Criminal Law: Felonies & White Collar Crime
Asonye, Uche O. - *Asonye & Associates* - Chicago - Employment Law, Immigration Law
Avgeris, George N. - *George N. Avgeris, Chartered, Attorney at Law* - Hinsdale - Personal Injury Law: General
Azulay, J. Daniel - *Azulay & Azulay, P.C.* - Chicago - Family Law – firm profile, page 352
Azulay, Y. Judd - *Azulay & Azulay, P.C.* - Chicago - Immigration Law – firm profile, page 352
Badesch, Robert T. - *Davis, Friedman, Zavett, Kane & MacRae* - Chicago - Family Law – firm profile, page 354
Bayard, Forrest S. - *Law Offices of Forrest S. Bayard* - Chicago - Family Law
Beermann, Jon L. - *Jon L. Beermann & Associates, Ltd.* - Libertyville - Family Law
Bell, Brigitte Schmidt - *Brigitte Schmidt Bell, P.C.* - Chicago - Family Law, Alternative Dispute Resolution
Belz, Edwin J. - *Belz & McWilliams* - Chicago - Criminal Law: Felonies & White Collar Crime
Bennett, Margaret A. - *Law Offices of Bennett & Bennett, Ltd.* - Oak Brook - Family Law
Berman, Peter J. - *Peter J. Berman, Ltd.* - Chicago - Alternative Dispute Resolution
Bernstein, Arnold - *Attorney at Law* - Arlington Heights - Personal Injury Law: Medical & Professional Malpractice
Biallas, John S. - *Attorney at Law* - St. Charles - Bankruptcy Law
Bloom, Marvin - *Marvin Bloom & Associates* - Chicago - Criminal Law: Felonies & White Collar Crime
Bowman, John T. - *Bowman & Corday, Ltd.* - Chicago - Workers' Compensation Law – firm profile, page 352
Boyle, Charles A. - *Charles A. Boyle & Associates, Ltd.* - Chicago - Personal Injury Law: General
Brezina, David C. - *Lee, Mann, Smith, McWilliams, Sweeny & Ohlson* - Chicago - Arts, Entertainment & Intellectual Property Law
Broecker, Howard W. - *Howard W. Broecker & Associates, Ltd.* - Geneva - Family Law; *J•A•M•S/Endispute* - Chicago - Alternative Dispute Resolution – firm profile, page 356
Bush, Anna Markley - *Bush & Heise* - Barrington - Family Law
Camic, David E. - *Camic, Johnson, Wilson & Bloom, P.C.* - Aurora - Criminal Law: Felonies & White Collar Crime – firm profile, page 353
Chamberlin, Darcy J. - *Attorney at Law* - Oak Brook - Estate Planning, Wills & Trusts Law
Cirignani, Thomas R. - *Thomas R. Cirignani & Associates* - Chicago - Personal Injury Law: Medical & Professional Malpractice
Clancy, Thomas A. - *Clancy & Stevens* - Chicago - Personal Injury Law: Medical & Professional Malpractice
Clifford, Robert A. - *Clifford Law Offices* - Chicago - Personal Injury Law: Transportation – firm profile, page 353
Colombik, Richard M. - *Richard M. Colombik & Associates, P.C.* - Schaumburg - Tax Law, Estate Planning, Wills & Trusts Law
Cullen, George J. - *Cullen, Haskins, Nicholson & Menchetti, P.C.* - Chicago - Workers' Compensation Law – firm profile, page 354

Appendix A: Profiled Attorneys & Law Firms by Region

Davis, Muller - *Davis, Friedman, Zavett, Kane & MacRae* - Chicago - **Family Law – firm profile, page 354**
DeSanto, James J. - *Law Offices of James J. DeSanto, P.C.* - Libertyville - Personal Injury Law: General
Downs, Robert K. - *Downs & Downs, P.C.* - Oak Park (Chicago) - **Family Law, Adoption Law – firm profile, page 355**
DuCanto, Joseph N. - *Schiller, DuCanto and Fleck* - Chicago - **Family Law – firm profile, page 361**
Durkin, Kevin P. - *Clifford Law Offices* - Chicago - **Personal Injury Law: General – firm profile, page 353**
Dutton, Janna S. - *Monahan & Cohen* - Chicago - Elder Law
Ecker, Lori D. - *Kahan & Ecker* - Chicago - **Employment Law – firm profile, page 357**
Favaro, Dennis R. - *Thill, Kolodz & Favaro, Ltd.* - Palatine - Employment Law
Felch, Patricia A. - *ARTSLaw Offices of Patricia A. Felch, P.C.* - Chicago - Arts, Entertainment & Intellectual Property Law
Fields, Jane F. - *Law Office of Jane F. Fields* - Chicago - Family Law
Fleck, Charles J. - *Schiller, DuCanto and Fleck* - Chicago - **Family Law – firm profile, page 361**
Foote, Robert M. - *Murphy, Hupp, Foote, Mielke and Kinnally* - Aurora - **Personal Injury Law: General – firm profile, page 360**
Frankel, Scott J. - *Frankel & Cohen, Attorneys at Law* - Chicago - **Employment Law, Criminal Law: Felonies & White Collar Crime – firm profile, page 355**
Friedman, James T. - *Davis, Friedman, Zavett, Kane & MacRae* - Chicago - **Family Law – firm profile, page 354**
Friedman, Linda D. - *Leng Stowell Friedman & Vernon* - Chicago - **Employment Law – firm profile, page 358**
Gibson, Scott B. - *Law Offices of Scott B. Gibson, Ltd.* - Waukegan - Personal Injury Law: General
Gilbert, Howard E. - *Howard E. Gilbert & Associates, Ltd.* - Skokie - Small Business Law
Glieberman, Herbert A. - *Herbert A. Glieberman & Associates* - Chicago - Family Law
Glimco, Joseph P., III - *Law Offices of Joseph P. Glimco III* - Downers Grove - Family Law
Goldberg, Jeffrey M. - *Jeffrey M. Goldberg & Associates, Ltd.* - Chicago - Personal Injury Law: Medical & Professional Malpractice
Goodman, Bruce D. - *Steinberg, Polacek & Goodman* - Chicago - Personal Injury Law: Medical & Professional Malpractice
Grant, Burton F. - *Grant and Grant* - Chicago - **Family Law – firm profile, page 356**
Greenberg, Sharran R. - *Attorney at Law* - Highland Park - Family Law, Real Estate Law
Grund, David I. - *Grund & Starkopf, P.C.* - Chicago - Family Law
Hannigan, Richard D. - *Richard D. Hannigan, Ltd.* - Mundelein - Workers' Compensation Law
Harte, William J. - *William J. Harte, Ltd.* - Chicago - Personal Injury Law: General
Haskin, Lyle B. - *Lyle B. Haskin & Associates* - Wheaton - Family Law
Haskins, Charles G., Jr. - *Cullen, Haskins, Nicholson & Menchetti, P.C.* - Chicago - **Workers' Compensation Law – firm profile, page 354**
Hauser, Robert J. - *Sullivan, Smith, Hauser & Noonan, Ltd.* - Waukegan - Criminal Law: Felonies & White Collar Crime
Healy, Martin J., Jr. - *Martin J. Healy, Jr. & Associates* - Chicago - **Personal Injury Law: General – firm profile, page 360**
Hebeisen, Keith A. - *Clifford Law Offices* - Chicago - **Personal Injury Law: Medical & Professional Malpractice – firm profile, page 353**
Hogan, Judy L. - *Judy L. Hogan, P.C., Attorneys and Mediators* - Geneva - Alternative Dispute Resolution
hooks, william h. - *Hooks Law Offices, P.C.* - Chicago - Criminal Law: Felonies & White Collar Crime
Hopkins, David H. - *Schiller, DuCanto and Fleck* - Chicago - **Family Law – firm profile, page 361**
Jeep, Markham M. - *Markham M. Jeep, P.C.* - Waukegan - Workers' Compensation Law
Johnson, Gary V. - *Camic, Johnson, Wilson & Bloom, P.C.* - Aurora - **Criminal Law: Felonies & White Collar Crime – firm profile, page 353**
Kahan, Penny Nathan - *Kahan & Ecker* - Chicago - **Employment Law – firm profile, page 357**
Kalcheim, Michael W. - *Kalcheim, Schatz & Berger* - Chicago - **Family Law – firm profile, page 357**
Kane, Larry R. - *Davis, Friedman, Zavett, Kane & MacRae* - Chicago - **Family Law – firm profile, page 354**
Kaplan, Melvin J. - *Melvin J. Kaplan & Associates* - Chicago - Bankruptcy Law
Katz, Stephen H. - *Schiller, DuCanto and Fleck* - Lake Forest - **Family Law – firm profile, page 361**
Kelly, Roger J. - *Law Offices of Roger J. Kelly* - Chicago - Real Estate Law, Employment Law
Kimnach, Richard A. - *Anesi, Ozmon & Rodin, Ltd.* - Chicago - **Workers' Compensation Law – firm profile, page 351**
Kohen, Bruce M. - *Anesi, Ozmon & Rodin, Ltd.* - Chicago - **Personal Injury Law: General – firm profile, page 351**
Koukios, Steven S. - *Koukios & Associates* - Park Ridge - Bankruptcy Law
Kremin, David K. - *David K. Kremin & Associates, A Professional Corporation* - Chicago - Personal Injury Law: General
Lane, Fred - *Lane & Lane* - Chicago - **Personal Injury Law: General – firm profile, page 358**
Lane, Stephen I. - *Lane & Lane* - Chicago - **Personal Injury Law: General – firm profile, page 358**
Latherow, Jerry A. - *Law Office of Jerry A. Latherow* - Chicago - Personal Injury Law: General
Levy, David H. - *Kalcheim, Schatz & Berger* - Chicago - **Family Law – firm profile, page 357**
Levy, Steven B. - *Steven B. Levy, Ltd.* - Naperville - Personal Injury Law: General
Lichter, Sally - *Voegtle & Lichter* - Libertyville - Family Law
Lindner, George P. - *Lindner, Speers & Reuland, P.C.* - Aurora - **Personal Injury Law: Medical & Professional Malpractice – firm profile, page 359**
Loats, J. Timothy - *Law Offices of J. Timothy Loats* - Aurora - Workers' Compensation Law
Lonergan, Susan M. - *Susan M. Lonergan, Attorney at Law, P.C.* - St. Charles - Family Law
MacRae, Roderick E. - *Davis, Friedman, Zavett, Kane & MacRae* - Chicago - **Family Law – firm profile, page 354**
Malkin, Earle A. - *Law Offices of Earle A. Malkin* - Chicago - Family Law
Marcus, Dorene - *Davis, Friedman, Zavett, Kane & MacRae* - Chicago - **Family Law – firm profile, page 354**
Martin, Royal B. - *Martin, Brown & Sullivan, Ltd.* - Chicago - **Criminal Law: Felonies & White Collar Crime – firm profile, page 359**
McKenzie, Robert E. - *McKenzie & McKenzie, P.C.* - Chicago - Tax Law
Minchella, Erica Crohn - *Minchella & Porter, Ltd.* - Chicago - Bankruptcy Law
Mirabelli, Enrico J. - *Enrico J. Mirabelli & Associates* - Chicago - Family Law

Miroballi, Joseph J. - *Anesi, Ozmon & Rodin, Ltd.* - **Chicago - Personal Injury Law: Medical & Professional Malpractice – firm profile, page 351**
Morrison, John J. - *Law Office of John J. Morrison, Ltd.* - Chicago - Tax Law
Muller, Kurt A. - *The Muller Firm, Ltd.* - Chicago - Family Law
Niro, Cheryl I. - *Partridge & Niro, P.C.; Associates in Dispute Resolution, Inc.* - Chicago - Alternative Dispute Resolution
Oney, Claudia - *Claudia Oney, P.C.* - Chicago - Employment Law, Family Law
Ozmon, Nat P. - *Anesi, Ozmon & Rodin, Ltd.* - **Chicago - Personal Injury Law: General – firm profile, page 351**
Patterson, Robert B. - *Law Offices of Robert B. Patterson, Ltd.* - Chicago - Personal Injury Law: General
Peck, Kerry R. - *Kerry R. Peck & Associates* - Chicago - Estate Planning, Wills & Trusts Law
Pekala, Beverly A. - *The Law Offices of Beverly A. Pekala, P.C.* - Chicago - Family Law
Peskind, Steven N. - *Peskind & Peskind, Ltd.* - Aurora - Family Law
Presbrey, Kim E. - *Presbrey and Associates, P.C.* - Aurora - Workers' Compensation Law
Provenza, James C. - *James C. Provenza, P.C.* - Glenview - Estate Planning, Wills & Trusts Law
Rapoport, David E. - *Rapoport & Kupets Law Offices* - Rosemont - Personal Injury Law: Transportation
Reda, Edward E., Jr. - *Reda, Ltd.* - Chicago - Estate Planning, Wills & Trusts Law
Redfield, John H. - *Attorney at Law* - Skokie - Bankruptcy Law
Reuland, Timothy J. - *Lindner, Speers & Reuland, P.C.* - **Aurora - Personal Injury Law: General – firm profile, page 359**
Richter, Harold - *Law Offices of Harold Richter* - Lansing - Family Law
Rinella, Bernard B. - *Rinella and Rinella, Ltd.* - Chicago - Family Law
Rodin, Curt N. - *Anesi, Ozmon & Rodin, Ltd.* - **Chicago - Personal Injury Law: General – firm profile, page 351**
Rolewick, David F. - *Rolewick & Gutzke, P.C.* - **Wheaton - Estate Planning, Wills & Trusts Law – firm profile, page 361**
Rosenfeld, Howard H. - *Rosenfeld, Rotenberg, Hafron & Shapiro* - Chicago - Family Law
Ross, Jay B. - *Jay B. Ross and Associates, P.C.* - Chicago - Arts, Entertainment & Intellectual Property Law
Rubens, James L. - *Davis, Friedman, Zavett, Kane & MacRae* - **Chicago - Family Law – firm profile, page 354**
Rubin, Arnold G. - *Law Offices of Arnold G. Rubin, Ltd.* - Chicago - Workers' Compensation Law
Ryan, Catherine M. - *Ryan, Miller & Trafelet, P.C.* - Chicago - Family Law
Scanlan, Edmund J. - *Law Offices of Edmund J. Scanlan, Ltd.* - Chicago - Personal Injury Law: General
Schaffner, Harry - *Schaffner & Van Der Snick, P.C.* - Geneva - Family Law
Schiever, Carey J. - *Carey J. Schiever, Ltd.* - Libertyville - Estate Planning, Wills & Trusts Law
Schiller, Donald C. - *Schiller, DuCanto and Fleck* - **Chicago - Family Law – firm profile, page 361**
Schlesinger, Gary L. - *Law Office of Gary L. Schlesinger* - Libertyville - Family Law
Schwarz, Benedict, II - *Law Offices of Benedict Schwarz II, Ltd.* - West Dundee - Family Law
Shancer, Jeffrey M. - *Law Offices of Jeffrey M. Shancer* - Chicago - Personal Injury Law: General
Siebert, William Newell - *William Newell Siebert & Associates* - Chicago - Immigration Law
Sigman, Helen - *Helen Sigman & Associates, Ltd.* - Chicago - Family Law
Smith, Robert S., Jr. - *Law Offices of Robert S. Smith, Jr.* - Deerfield - Estate Planning, Wills & Trusts Law
Speers, Robert L. - *Lindner, Speers & Reuland, P.C.* - **Aurora - Personal Injury Law: General – firm profile, page 359**
Stein, Arnold - *Schiller, DuCanto and Fleck* - **Chicago - Family Law – firm profile, page 361**
Stein, Edward I. - *Edward I. Stein, Ltd.* - Northbrook - Family Law
Stogsdill, William J., Jr. - *Law Offices of William J. Stogsdill, Jr., P.C.* - Wheaton - Family Law
Stone, Jed - *Law Offices of Jed Stone, Ltd.* - Chicago - Criminal Law: Felonies & White Collar Crime
Stowell, Mary - *Leng Stowell Friedman & Vernon* - **Chicago - Employment Law – firm profile, page 358**
Tighe, Mary Beth S. - *Attorney at Law* - Park Ridge - Family Law
Tobin, Craig D. - *Craig D. Tobin & Associates* - Chicago - Criminal Law: Felonies & White Collar Crime
Trevino, Fern Niehuss - *Law Office of Fern N. Trevino* - Chicago - Employment Law
Truemper, William J. - *Truemper, Hollingsworth, Wojtecki, Courtin & Titiner* - **Aurora - Family Law – firm profile, page 362**
VanDemark, Ruth E. - *Law Offices of Ruth E. VanDemark* - Chicago - Civil Appellate Law
Wadington, Robert N. - *Robert N. Wadington & Associates* - Chicago - Personal Injury Law: General
Wasserman, Laurie J. - *Law Offices of Laurie J. Wasserman* - Skokie - Employment Law
Weiler, Rory T. - *Weiler & Noble, P.C.* - **Batavia - Family Law – firm profile, page 362**
Weinstein, Melvin A. - *Melvin A. Weinstein & Associates* - Chicago - Family Law
Weissberg, Ariel - *Weissberg and Associates, Ltd.* - Chicago - Bankruptcy Law
Wimmer, John R. - *The Law Offices of John R. Wimmer* - Downers Grove - Alternative Dispute Resolution, Civil Appellate Law
Zavett, Errol - *Davis, Friedman, Zavett, Kane & MacRae* - **Chicago - Family Law – firm profile, page 354**

NORTHWESTERN ILLINOIS INCLUDING ROCKFORD & QUAD CITIES

Cassel, Jamie J. Swenson - *Reno, Zahm, Folgate, Lindberg & Powell* - **Rockford - Bankruptcy Law – firm profile, page 363**
Fredrickson, Robert A. - *Reno, Zahm, Folgate, Lindberg & Powell* - **Rockford - Personal Injury Law: General – firm profile, page 363**
Jensen, Philip F. - *Hammer, Simon & Jensen* - Galena - Family Law, Small Business Law
Kavensky, Craig L. - *Winstein, Kavensky & Wallace* - Rock Island - Personal Injury Law: General, Workers' Compensation Law
Koenig, Philip E. - *Katz, McHard, Balch, Lefstein & Fieweger, P.C.* - Rock Island - Estate Planning, Wills & Trusts Law
Lambert, J. Laird - *Attorney at Law* - Rockford - Real Estate Law
Morse, Keith S. - *Attorney at Law* - Rockford - Family Law
Nolte, Peter B. - *Attorney at Law* - Rockford - Civil Appellate Law
Ohlander, Jan H. - *Reno, Zahm, Folgate, Lindberg & Powell* - **Rockford - Personal Injury Law: General – firm profile, page 363**
Rapoport, David E. - *Rapoport & Kupets Law Offices* - Rosemont - Personal Injury Law: Transportation

Appendix A: Profiled Attorneys & Law Firms by Region

CENTRAL ILLINOIS

Blan, Kennith W., Jr. - *Blan Law Offices* - Danville - Personal Injury Law: General
Clark, Gary L. - *The Law Offices of Frederic W. Nessler and Associates* **- Peoria - Personal Injury Law: Medical & Professional Malpractice – firm profile, page 366**
Corsentino, Anthony P. - *Anthony P. Corsentino, Ltd.* - Peoria - Family Law
Cox, A. Clay - *Hayes, Hammer, Miles, Cox & Ginzkey* **- Bloomington - Tax Law – firm profile, page 364**
Feldman, Howard W. - *Feldman & Wasser* **- Springfield - Family Law – firm profile, page 364**
Greer, Daniel J. - *Stine, Wolter & Greer* **- Springfield - Estate Planning, Wills & Trusts Law – firm profile, page 365**
Grimsley, Gregg N. - *Carter & Grimsley* - Peoria - Bankruptcy Law
Hammer, Don C. - *Hayes, Hammer, Miles, Cox & Ginzkey* **- Bloomington - Family Law – firm profile, page 364**
Jones, Lance T. - *Reid & Jones Law Offices* - Springfield - Employment Law
Leahy, Mary Lee - *Leahy Law Offices* - Springfield - Employment Law
Lynch, David M. - *Lynch & Bloom, P.C.* - Peoria - Family Law
Mathis, J. Michael - *The Mathis Law Firm* - Peoria - Elder Law
McCarthy, David H. - *Attorney at Law* - Peoria - Family Law
Metnick, Michael B. - *Metnick, Wise, Cherry & Frazier* - Springfield - Criminal Law: Felonies & White Collar Crime, Family Law, Personal Injury Law: General
Nardulli, Steven - *Stratton and Nardulli* - Springfield - Family Law
Nessler, Frederic W. - *The Law Offices of Frederic W. Nessler and Associates* **- Springfield - Personal Injury Law: General – firm profile, page 366**
Nicoara, John P. - *Nicoara & Steagall* - Peoria - Personal Injury Law: General
Ores, Nicholas H. - *Attorney at Law* - Peoria - Family Law
Parker, Drew - *Parker & Halliday* - Peoria - Family Law
Peithmann, William A. - *Peithmann Law Office* - Farmer City - Estate Planning, Wills & Trusts Law
Rapoport, David E. - *Rapoport & Kupets Law Offices* - Rosemont - Personal Injury Law: Transportation
Rawles, Edward H. - *Rawles, O'Byrne, Stanko & Kepley, P.C.* **- Champaign - Personal Injury Law: General – firm profile, page 365**
Saint, Gale W. - *Saint & Carmichael, P.C.* - Bloomington - Estate Planning, Wills & Trusts Law
Sheffler, Stephen K. - *Pelini & Sheffler* - Champaign - Bankruptcy Law
Slevin, John A. - *Vonachen, Lawless, Trager & Slevin* - Peoria - Personal Injury Law: General
Stanko, Glenn A. - *Rawles, O'Byrne, Stanko & Kepley, P.C.* **- Champaign - Employment Law – firm profile, page 365**
Stine, Robert E. - *Stine, Wolter & Greer* **- Springfield - Personal Injury Law: General – firm profile, page 365**
Strodel, Robert C. - *Law Offices of Robert C. Strodel, Ltd.* - Peoria - Personal Injury Law: Medical & Professional Malpractice
Sutterfield, David W. - *Sutterfield & Johnson, P.C.* - Effingham - Social Security Law
Wasser, Stanley N. - *Feldman & Wasser* **- Springfield - Employment Law – firm profile, page 364**
Winget, Walter W. - *Winget & Kane* - Peoria - Family Law
Zuckerman, Richard Wayne - *Law Offices of Richard W. Zuckerman* - Peoria - Family Law

SOUTHERN ILLINOIS

Callis, Lance - *Callis, Papa, Jensen, Jackstadt & Halloran, P.C.* - Granite City - Personal Injury Law: Transportation
Carlson, Jon G. - *Carlson Wendler & Sanderson, P.C.* - Edwardsville - Personal Injury Law: Transportation
Carr, Rex - *Carr, Korein, Tillery, Kunin, Montroy & Glass* **- East St. Louis - Personal Injury Law: Medical & Professional Malpractice, Personal Injury Law: General – firm profile, page 366**
Glass, Mark - *Carr, Korein, Tillery, Kunin, Montroy & Glass* **- East St. Louis - Workers' Compensation Law – firm profile, page 366**
Gossage, Roza - *Roza Gossage, P.C.* - Belleville - Family Law
Harvey, Morris Lane - *Law Offices of Morris Lane Harvey* - Fairfield - Family Law
Hassakis, Mark D. - *Hassakis & Hassakis, P.C.* - Mt. Vernon - Personal Injury Law: General
Kionka, Edward J. - *Professor of Law* - Carbondale - Civil Appellate Law
Korein, Sandor - *Carr, Korein, Tillery, Kunin, Montroy & Glass* **- East St. Louis - Personal Injury Law: Transportation – firm profile, page 366**
Kurowski, John J. - *The Kurowski Law Firm, P.C.* - Belleville (Swansea) - Family Law
Montroy, Gerald L. - *Carr, Korein, Tillery, Kunin, Montroy & Glass* **- East St. Louis - Personal Injury Law: Medical & Professional Malpractice – firm profile, page 366**
Mueller, William A. - *The Bankruptcy Center* - Belleville - Bankruptcy Law
Nelson, Robert C. - *Nelson, Bement, Stubblefield & Levenhagen, P.C.* **- Belleville - Workers' Compensation Law – firm profile, page 367**
O'Neill, Treva H. - *O'Neill & Proctor* - Carbondale - Family Law
Proctor, Janet C. - *O'Neill & Proctor* - Carbondale - Family Law
Rapoport, David E. - *Rapoport & Kupets Law Offices* - Rosemont - Personal Injury Law: Transportation
Reed, Mike - *Law Office of Mike Reed* - Centralia - Bankruptcy Law
Rikli, Donald C. - *Attorney at Law* - Highland - Estate Planning, Wills & Trusts Law
Sharp, Terrell Lee - *Law Office of Terry Sharp, P.C.* - Mt. Vernon - Bankruptcy Law
Stubblefield, Timothy C. - *Nelson, Bement, Stubblefield & Levenhagen, P.C.* **- Belleville - Civil Appellate Law, Family Law – firm profile, page 367**
Tillery, Stephen M. - *Carr, Korein, Tillery, Kunin, Montroy & Glass* **- Belleville - Personal Injury Law: Transportation – firm profile, page 366**
Womick, John - *Womick & Associates, Chartered* - Carbondale - Personal Injury Law: General

Cook & Collar Counties

ANESI, OZMON & RODIN, LTD.

161 North Clark Street, Suite 2100, Chicago, IL 60601 - Phone: (312) 372-3822, Fax: (312) 372-3833, 800: (800) 458-3822 within IL

Founded over 50 years ago, Anesi, Ozmon & Rodin, Ltd., is the largest law firm in Illinois which concentrates its practice in the areas of plaintiffs' personal injury litigation and workers' compensation law. With 28 attorneys and a support staff of over 100, the firm provides both the ability and resources to achieve the best results for its clients.

The partners of Anesi, Ozmon & Rodin, Ltd., are leaders of the Trial Bar. Two have been President of the Illinois Trial Lawyers Association. Two are listed in the publication, *The Best Lawyers in America*. They have achieved substantial verdicts in jurisdictions throughout Illinois in the areas of construction injuries, medical malpractice, product liability, automobile negligence, and wrongful death. Their reputation for trial competence has resulted in numerous large settlements in cases involving devastating injuries resulting in spinal cord injury, brain damage, or death.

The firm's overriding goal is to provide superb representation and personal attention to each client. While vigorous in the pursuit of its clients' rights, the firm is mindful of its responsibility to the bar and the public to act in a professional and competent manner in all dealings.

All of the firm's senior attorneys regularly lecture at various bar association seminars on the areas of trial practice, tort law, professional responsibility, and constitutional law.

Each of the firm's attorneys has devoted substantial time and effort to the preservation of the civil justice system and workers' compensation remedies in order to preserve and improve the rights of present and future clients. This effort is reflected in the firm filing the lead case challenging the constitutionality of the Illinois Tort Reform Statute. This massive undertaking, which required the exclusive effort of two partners, three associates, and numerous clerks and paralegals, exemplifies the commitment that Anesi, Ozmon & Rodin has to the right to a fair jury trial and the continued ability for injured victims to hold accountable those responsible under the law.

AZULAY & AZULAY, P.C.

One East Wacker Drive, Suite 2700, Chicago, IL 60601 - Phone: (312) 832-9200, Fax: (312) 832-9212

Stephen D. Berman, Y. Judd Azulay, Pai-Pai Cheng, J. Daniel Azulay, Bonita B. Hwang, Robert R. Gard

Azulay & Azulay, P.C., has been in business for almost 20 years. Founding members •**J. Daniel Azulay,** President, and •**Y. Judd Azulay,** Vice President, have built solid reputations working together in developing and guiding the firm.

The firm is in the forefront of providing family law and immigration legal services. It represents clients in all venues, including the U.S. Immigration and Naturalization Service; U.S. Department of Justice; U.S. Department of Labor; and U.S. Consulates. Frequently, the firm's attorneys travel abroad on behalf of clients to assist in consular processing of visa matters.

The firm provides legal services and assistance in

- Family and employment-based immigrant visa processing
- Non-immigrant visa petitions, including employment-related and corporate transfer petitions
- Naturalization and citizenship
- Alien employment certification
- Deportation issues and defense
- Immigration-related litigation
- Employer sanctions defense
- Domestic relations and adoption

Stephen D. Berman concentrates in immigration and naturalization law and family law, with particular emphasis in related litigation.

Robert R. Gard concentrates his practice in immigration law. He has been Chair of the Greater Chicago Chapter of the American Immigration Lawyers Association and a member of its National Board of Directors.

Bonita B. Hwang concentrates in immigration and naturalization law and family law. She is a member of the American Bar Association and Korean Bar Association.

Pai-Pai Cheng, Of Counsel, practices exclusively business immigration matters. She is a past President of the Chinese American Bar Association and Education Chair of the Greater Chicago Chapter of the American Immigration Lawyers Association. She was a founding member of the Chinese-American Voters Coalition, among her other community involvements.

Azulay & Azulay, P.C., maintains a leadership role through its membership and participation in various professional, community, and ethnic social boards and committees. The firm gives to the community by regularly leading and participating in pro bono programs; its members are proud of their service record to those who require the services of a private attorney.

BOWMAN & CORDAY, LTD.

20 North Clark Street, Suite 500, Chicago, IL 60602 - Phone: (312) 606-9675, Fax: (312) 606-9887

Bowman & Corday, Ltd., is a law firm dedicated exclusively to the representation of clients who have been injured on the job. John T. Bowman and Lane Allan Corday have more than 35 years' combined experience in representing clients before the Illinois Industrial Commission. Although the firm is located in Chicago, Mr. Bowman and Mr. Corday also represent clients who have been injured in Will, DuPage, Kane, McHenry and Lake Counties.

•**John T. Bowman** is a graduate of Syracuse University and the Southern Illinois University School of Law. He served in the United States Air Force from 1966 to 1973. He is a member of the Illinois Trial Lawyers Association, American Trial Lawyers Association, and Workers' Compensation Lawyers Association, as well as numerous other state and local bar associations.

Lane Allan Corday graduated from the University of Illinois and the University of Illinois College of Law. He has been practicing before the Illinois Industrial Commission since 1980. He is a member of the Illinois Trial Lawyers Association, American Trial Lawyers Association, Workers' Compensation Lawyers Association, and state and local bar associations.

Bowman & Corday, Ltd., takes great pride in the personal attention it gives to each client. The firm has developed a substantial number of referral attorneys who rely on the firm's experience in the area of workers' compensation.

CAMIC, JOHNSON, WILSON & BLOOM, P.C.

546 West Galena Boulevard, Aurora, IL 60506 - Phone: (630) 859-0135, Fax: (630) 859-1910, 800: (800) 750-0135

Camic, Johnson, Wilson & Bloom, P.C., has evolved from a partnership that began in 1987. The firm emphasizes trial practice in state and federal courts in Illinois and sister states. The firm includes three partners, three associates, and Mr. Bloom, who is Of Counsel to the firm. Three members of the firm primarily practice criminal law. All three, •**Mr. Camic**, •**Mr. Johnson** and •**Mr. Bloom**, practice primarily criminal trial law and all three have been selected by their peers as Leading Illinois Attorneys.

The firm also includes members who practice family law and debtor/creditor law. Included among the corporate clients are several large credit unions which have been represented by the firm for several years. The partners of the firm regularly act as co-trial counsel with several leading personal injury attorneys. The firm maintains an extensive appellate and post-conviction practice, which has included several appellate court reversals and trial court orders of new trials where the firm has filed appearances to take over cases from other lawyers following convictions.

The firm's criminal trial partners have represented clients in complex and high-profile cases. The firm's clients have included policemen, priests, school officials, gang leaders, multiple murders, lawyers, and judges.

The partners bring extensive experience to the firm. Mr. Johnson was the elected State's Attorney of Kane County, Mr. Camic was a police officer for several years, and Mr. Bloom has been on the faculty of The John Marshall Law School, teaching trial practice to lawyers.

The firm's trial partners have lectured on criminal law at seminars and programs for various bar associations, community groups, and agencies. Members have published articles and comments in several legal publications. The firm maintains an extensive electronic library and maintains close contact with experts in medicine, forensics and the sciences.

The law firm of Camic, Johnson, Wilson & Bloom, P.C., maintains high standards for itself. The firm believes that when a client retains one of its attorneys, the client retains all of the attorneys in the firm, and the entire firm is committed to that client. The firm believes that it is not only the client who is on trial, but the firm's reputation.

See Mr. Camic's and Mr. Johnson's profiles in the Criminal Law: Felonies & White Collar Crime and Criminal Law: DUI & Misdemeanors Chapters. See Mr. Bloom's profile in the Criminal Law: Felonies & White Collar Crime Chapter. Mr. Camic and Mr. Dixon of this firm reviewed and edited the two Criminal Law Chapters of this Guidebook.

CLIFFORD LAW OFFICES

120 North LaSalle Street, 31st Floor, Chicago, IL 60602 - Phone: (312) 899-9090, Fax: (312) 251-1160, 800: (800) 899-0410

Clifford Law Offices regularly handles complex damage cases, including claims for wrongful death and personal injury arising out of aviation, product liability, railroad, and medical malpractice claims.

•**Robert Clifford**, Founder of the firm, routinely receives substantial verdicts and settlements in these cases. He was named one of the Top Ten Litigators by the *National Law Journal*. Mr. Clifford was voted by his peers to be included in the latest edition of *The Best Lawyers in America*. He is past President of the Illinois Trial Lawyers Association and was Cochair of the American Bar Association's Litigation Section for the 1995 Annual Meeting. Mr. Clifford was inducted into the American College of Trial Lawyers and the International Academy of Trial Lawyers. As a graduate of DePaul University School of Law, Mr. Clifford founded the School of Law's Tort Law and Social Policy Committee. This committee annually sponsors seminars on issues important to the legal community.

•**Keith Hebeisen** and •**Kevin Durkin**, also partners in the firm, have vast experience in personal injury and wrongful death litigation. Mr. Hebeisen, trained under the tutelage of Robert Clifford, represents clients in all types of personal injury and wrongful death cases, with particular interest in medical malpractice, product liability, and motor vehicle accident cases. Mr. Durkin, also an adjunct professor at DePaul University, concentrates in aviation, railroad litigation, and products liability.

Robert A. Clifford

Keith A. Hebeisen

Kevin P. Durkin

The firm employs 12 associates experienced in the following areas of law:

- Plaintiffs' personal injury litigation
- Aviation litigation
- Medical and professional negligence
- FELA
- Products liability
- Premises liability
- Construction accidents
- Wrongful death law
- Vehicular accident law
- Railroad litigation

The attorneys have a depth of experience that has made a mark in Illinois and around the country. The staff is dedicated; many have been with Robert Clifford since he founded the firm in his name in 1984. With the latest, state-of-the-art computer technology, Clifford Law Offices represents the cutting-edge of sophisticated resources both in the courtroom and behind the scenes.

CULLEN, HASKINS, NICHOLSON & MENCHETTI, P.C.

35 East Wacker Drive, Suite 1760, Chicago, IL 60601 - Phone: (312) 332-2545, Fax: (312) 332-4543

Cullen, Haskins, Nicholson & Menchetti, P.C., offers over 75 years of combined legal experience together with personal attention. The office is computer-efficient and client case information is always at the attorneys' fingertips.

Cullen, Haskins, Nicholson & Menchetti, P.C., is dedicated to assisting each client through the legal process as comfortably as possible. The goal of the firm is to obtain the best results possible for each individual client.

•**George J. Cullen** has over 34 years' experience in workers' compensation and personal injury law. He represents several clients as a consultant on legislative matters in both Springfield and Chicago. He was Chair of the Chicago Plan Commission and was a member of the Zoning Board of Appeals of the City of Chicago. He served on the Board of Managers of the ITLA and has either chaired or served on several committees for the ITLA, CBA, and ISBA.

•**Charles G. Haskins, Jr.,** concentrates his practice in workers' compensation, handling cases from trial through the Illinois Supreme Court. He is the Editor of the Illinois Trial Lawyers Association's *Workers' Compensation Handbook*, the former Chair of the Industrial Commission Section of the CBA, and the past President of the Illinois Workers' Compensation Lawyers Association. He currently serves on the Board of Managers of the ITLA, and is the Chair of the Workers' Compensation Committee. He is a frequent lecturer on workers' compensation.

Patrick B. Nicholson practices workers' compensation law, personal injury law, and in the areas of corporate, real estate, and probate law. He is the author of the chapter, "Total Permanent Disability," in the Illinois Trial Lawyers Association's *Workers' Compensation Handbook*.

David B. Menchetti practices workers' compensation law and is a former staff counsel to the Illinois State Senate President, where he concentrated in legislation dealing with insurance, pensions, and license activities. He served as attorney to the Illinois State Senate President and Senate Minority Leader advising on, and drafting reforms to, the Workers' Compensation Act. He is the author of the chapter, "Penalties," in the Illinois Trial Lawyers Association's *Workers' Compensation Handbook*.

Susan O. Pigott practices workers' compensation law. She is the Program Coordinator of the Hospice Legal Assistance Program of the Young Lawyers Section of the CBA.

Gerald A. Granada practices workers' compensation law. While in law school, Mr. Granada worked at the Illinois Industrial Commission as an extern and was also a Mediator with the Center for Conflict Resolution.

DAVIS, FRIEDMAN, ZAVETT, KANE & MACRAE

140 South Dearborn Street, Suite 1600, Chicago, IL 60603 - Phone: (312) 782-2220, Fax: (312) 782-0464

All 13 of the lawyers in the law firm of Davis, Friedman, Zavett, Kane & MacRae practice only family law.

The firm was created in 1985 by the merger of three firms, one of which was founded in 1945.

One of the partners has authored a book about divorce for lay audiences that sold well for over 10 years (Friedman, *The Divorce Handbook*, Random House, 1982, 1984), another has written a widely praised book on Illinois family law practice for lawyers (Davis, *The Illinois Practice of Family Law*, Random House, 1995), and several partners have written articles for the Illinois Institute for Continuing Legal Education (e.g., Zavett, Kane, Rubens and Marcus), among other publications.

Lawyers in the firm frequently lecture before other lawyers in Chicago and around the country on family law topics. Lawyers in the firm have led organized bar groups in their field, including serving as President of the American Academy of Matrimonial Lawyers; President of the Illinois Chapter of the American Academy of Matrimonial Lawyers (two); Chair of the Chicago Bar Association Matrimonial Law Committee (four); Chair of the Illinois State Bar Association Family Law Section Council (two); and others. The partners have addressed family law seminars (usually sponsored by state bar associations) in many states, including, for example, Colorado, Florida, Kansas, Missouri, Nevada, Oklahoma, Pennsylvania, and South Carolina.

DOWNS & DOWNS, P.C.

1010 Lake Street, Suite 620, Oak Park (Chicago), IL 60301 - Phone: (708) 848-0700, Fax: (708) 848-0029

Robert K. Downs   Barbara A. Downs   Kirsten C. Olson

Partners in law and life, Bob and Barbara Downs bring to their family law firm all the necessary ingredients for success: experience, hard work, and the joy of doing something they love. The firm's early reform-oriented practice (including a stint in the Illinois legislature for Mr. Downs) provides the depth of experience for their client-centered firm of the '90s. Downs & Downs, P.C., concentrates in family law, including divorce, adoption and custody matters, and related issues of estate planning, probate, and real estate. The firm utilizes innovative video and computerization techniques to keep services, costs, and results effective.

•**Robert K. Downs** (JD 1965, Stetson University) is Chair of the Illinois State Bar Association Family Law Section Council, Vice Chair of the Chicago Bar Association Matrimonial Law Committee, and on the Board of Managers of the Illinois Chapter of the American Academy of Matrimonial Lawyers. In 1995, he received the American Bar Association Family Law Section's Pro Bono Award.

Barbara A. Downs (LLM 1989, JD 1984, DePaul University) handles family law issues of financial and property discovery. She also heads the firm's estate planning, probate, and real estate departments.

Kirsten C. Olson, Associate (JD 1994, Chicago Kent Law School), practices family law exclusively. A former aide to Senator Paul Simon, Ms. Olson was recently elected to the Assembly of the Illinois State Bar Association.

The firm's services cover the range from simple family law matters to high-profile custody or property cases. The firm has represented clients as diverse as international corporations, multi-million dollar social services agencies, and television personalities. What counts to this firm is top client service and effective representation.

Downs & Downs, P.C., serves the Chicago area from its offices in centrally located suburban Oak Park. Their client service area includes Cook, DuPage, and Lake Counties.

FRANKEL & COHEN, ATTORNEYS AT LAW

77 West Washington Street, Suite 1711, Chicago, IL 60602 - Phone: (312) 759-9600, Fax: (312) 759-9603

Frankel & Cohen is a civil and criminal litigation firm focusing its practice in the areas of employment litigation, criminal defense, and civil litigation.

Within the labor and employment practice area, Frankel & Cohen advises and represents clients in all labor and employment-related matters, including employment discrimination, retaliatory and wrongful discharge, sexual harassment, breach of contract, and arbitration hearings.

Within the area of criminal defense, the firm advises and represents clients in all criminal-related matters, including both federal and state criminal matters, at trial on appeal, and in post-conviction proceedings.

Within the general civil litigation practice area, Frankel & Cohen advises and represents clients in all types of civil litigation, including contract, tort, and statutory-related causes of action.

Robert R. Cohen: After graduating from the University of Chicago Law School in 1986, Mr. Cohen became associated with the law firm of Mayer, Brown & Platt, where he practiced general commercial civil litigation. In September 1987, Mr. Cohen left that firm to become a Clinical Lecturer in Law at the University of Chicago Law School. There, Mr. Cohen taught Litigation Methods and worked in the Edwin F. Mandel Legal Aid Clinic, where he concentrated in the area of employment law litigation.

Mr. Cohen is currently a part-time Administrative Hearing Officer for both the City of Chicago's Commission on Human Relations and the Cook County Commission on Human Rights. Mr. Cohen served as Chair of the Chicago Bar Association Committee on Civil Rights, 1994-96.

•**Scott J. Frankel:** Mr. Frankel received his JD from Ohio State University College of Law, graduating with honors in 1985. Mr. Frankel served as Editor-in-Chief of the Ohio State *Law Journal*. He also received the Becker Memorial Award for Leadership and Scholarship, and the Rightmire Memorial Award for Leadership and Scholarship. After graduating from law school, Mr. Frankel clerked for Judge David S. Porter in the United States District Court for the Southern District of Ohio from 1985 to 1987. Thereafter, from September 1987 until January 1989, Mr. Frankel was associated with the law firm of Mayer, Brown & Platt, where he practiced general civil litigation.

In 1989, Mr. Frankel joined the Cook County Public Defender's Office, where he represented clients charged with misdemeanors and felonies. Mr. Frankel's experience at the Public Defender's Office and in private practice includes litigating numerous bench and jury trials. *See Mr. Frankel's complete biographical profiles in the Employment Law and Criminal Law: Felonies & White Collar Crime Chapters.*

Grant and Grant

180 North LaSalle Street, Suite 2400, Chicago, IL 60601 - Phone: (312) 641-3600, Fax: (312) 641-2723

Joan C. Grant *Burton F. Grant*

Grant and Grant, a boutique matrimonial law firm, consists of partners •**Burton F. Grant** and **Joan C. Grant.** A unique husband and wife team, both are distinguished practitioners of family law whose approach to domestic relations litigation is based upon personal service to their clientele, team strategy, and strong litigation skills.

The firm concentrates in complex divorce litigation; contested child custody; removal and visitation matters; property, support, maintenance and parentage litigation; pre- and postmarital agreements; and valuation and division of pensions, property, and business interests.

Mr. Grant is well respected for his exceptional trial practice skills, strong tax law background, motion practice strategy, and appellate court experience. Mrs. Grant is known as a strong negotiator and advocate for the client. The firm has offices in Chicago, Northbrook, and Highland Park, Illinois.

•**Burton Grant,** with over 33 years' experience and a master's degree in tax law, is a Fellow of the American Academy of Matrimonial Lawyers and a former instructor of family law at DePaul College of Law. Mr. Grant has lectured for the Chicago Bar Association, American Academy of Matrimonial Lawyers, Illinois Institute for Continuing Legal Education, and Loyola Law School, and is the author of *Motion Practice Before Trial* for the Illinois Institute for Continuing Legal Education, a DePaul *Law Review* article, and numerous family law articles.

Joan Grant joined her husband's practice 16 years ago and has distinguished herself as a bar leader and officer. Mrs. Grant served on the Board of Managers and as Chair of the Matrimonial Law Committee of the Chicago Bar Association. She is on the Family Law Section Council of the Illinois State Bar Association, lectures for both bar associations, and has represented them on Chicago television. She authored the college education chapter of the Illinois State Bar Association's *Family Law Handbook* and is coauthor of the National Business Institute's *Family Law Litigation in Illinois*. Mrs. Grant is frequently appointed as guardian ad litem for children in custody disputes.

The Grants are at the forefront of changes in family law as a result of their appellate practice, their legislative proposals, their utilization of computer technology research, including computer generated tax and support analyses, and are dedicated to retaining their niche as a dynamic personal service firm well positioned to bring experience and knowledge to clients confronted with complicated family law matters.

J•A•M•S/Endispute

Three First National Plaza, Suite 200, Chicago, IL 60602 - Phone: (312) 739-0200, Fax: (312) 739-0617

The aftermath of disagreement in American society is becoming all too familiar: negotiations have failed, a lawyer is consulted, and a lawsuit is filed. Years later, on the eve of trial, the case is settled—after thousands of dollars have been invested in legal fees and other costs. But many individuals, companies, and their attorneys have found a better way: Alternative Dispute Resolution (ADR). And they're resolving disputes earlier, rather than later, with J•A•M•S/Endispute, an Illinois-based provider of Alternative Dispute Resolution services.

In response to spiraling litigation costs and an over-loaded legal system, the past decade has seen a growing number of professional individuals and organizations offering Alternative Dispute Resolution (ADR) services. These organizations offer a forum for quicker, less costly resolution of civil disputes outside our crowded courtrooms.

J•A•M•S/Endispute was formed in 1994, with the merger of three of the nation's oldest ADR providers: Bates Edwards Group, Endispute, Inc., and Judicial Arbitration & Mediation Services, Inc. (J•A•M•S).

By pooling the resources and talents of these three ADR providers, J•A•M•S/Endispute now offers clients the most complete range of ADR services available in the country. The organization employs more than 350 ADR practitioners, including former and retired judges as well as attorneys and other professional mediators and arbitrators.

J•A•M•S/Endispute offers an unparalleled combination of ADR personnel, services, and facilities:

- Highly trained, experienced ADR professionals
- Private conference facilities specifically designed to support and enhance the resolution process in a supportive, neutral environment
- A comprehensive range of ADR formats from simple two-party to complex, multi-party mediations, arbitrations, and private trials
- A unique ADR education and training program offered in conjunction with the Institute for Dispute Resolution at Pepperdine University School of Law
- Neutral fact finding to aid both parties in employment disputes
- The Environmental Dispute Forum, designed to meet the complex challenges of environmental disputes
- Consulting and systems designed to help businesses integrate ADR practices into their procedures
- Divorce mediation with experienced family law mediators/practitioners

J•A•M•S/Endispute's business is conflict—its resolution, management and prevention. Conflict is inevitable, and often fosters innovation and efficiency. But uncontrolled conflict wastes time and money.

For 15 years, J•A•M•S/Endispute has provided practical, workable solutions to the problems that conflict imposes on corporations, government and individuals.

KAHAN & ECKER
180 North LaSalle Street, Suite 2323, Chicago IL 60601 - Phone: (312) 855-1660, Fax: (312) 855-1431

Penny Nathan Kahan   Lori D. Ecker

Kahan & Ecker is an employment law firm. The firm offers consultation and legal services for individual employees on a wide variety of employment issues. The firm is committed to providing the highest quality legal representation to its clients.

The firm's goal is to resolve employment disputes amicably, without resorting to litigation. Frequently, Kahan & Ecker is successful in negotiating salary continuation agreements and other forms of separation packages. For cases in which a fair result cannot be achieved prior to initiating a lawsuit, Kahan & Ecker is successful and skilled in litigation.

The firm has successfully negotiated settlements with, and litigated against, virtually all of the larger law firms representing management in the Chicago area, and many national labor law firms whose clients have included numerous Fortune 500 companies.

Perhaps the most significant indication of the firm's skill and reputation is the fact that the majority of Kahan & Ecker's referrals come from past clients, defense attorneys, and employer representatives.

KALCHEIM, SCHATZ & BERGER
161 North Clark, Suite 2800, Chicago, IL 60601 - Phone: (312) 782-3456, Fax: (312) 782-8463

Kalcheim, Schatz & Berger limits its practice to family and matrimonial law and is one of the largest firms of its kind in the country.

The firm includes Fellows, Board Members, and the past President of the Illinois Chapter of the American Academy of Matrimonial Lawyers as well as the current and past Chairs of the Illinois State Bar Association Family Law Section Council. Every member of the firm has published or lectured on family law issues.

On both the trial and appellate levels, the firm's 15 attorneys handle cases involving substantial estates, valuation, tax, custody, and issues of paternity. Members of the firm are also proficient in drafting prenuptial and post-nuptial agreements.

The growth of the firm has necessitated a relocation to larger offices in downtown Chicago and the opening of an additional office in Lake County.

Lane & Lane

33 North Dearborn Street, Suite 2300, Chicago, IL 60602 - Phone: (312) 332-1400, Fax: (312) 899-8003

Lane & Lane is an experienced plaintiffs' personal injury and tort firm, handling serious personal injury cases resulting from medical and other professional malpractice, automobile, trucking, railroad, airline, boating, motorcycle and other vehicular accidents, product defects, and construction and workplace accidents throughout the United States.

The firm works with highly qualified and specialized medical, employment and scientific experts to ensure that its clients receive the finest presentation and prosecution of their cases. The cases the firm handles are often the only chance for clients to obtain fair compensation for the injuries and damages they have suffered.

The firm consists of •**Fred Lane**, •**Stephen I. Lane, Scott D. Lane** and **Joseph M. Dooley, III**. Each member has extensive civil litigation experience and has lectured and authored on civil litigation, trial practice, and personal injury practice for the Illinois Institute for Continuing Legal Education, Illinois State Bar Association, Chicago Bar Association, Illinois Trial Lawyers Association, and other groups.

The partners are active leaders in organized bar association activities, and include a past President of the Illinois Trial Lawyers Association, Illinois State Bar Association, and Decalogue Society of Lawyers, a Diplomate and past President of the American Board of Trial Advocates (Illinois), a member of the Illinois State Bar Association Board of Governors and Assembly, a Fellow of the American Bar Foundation, International Academy of Trial Lawyers, Chicago Bar Foundation, American Trial Lawyers Association, Chicago Bar Association, and Society of Trial Lawyers, and various board directorships, committee memberships, and chaired positions among bar and community organizations. All of the firm's partners are Associates in Law of the American College of Legal Medicine.

Fred Lane, Stephen I. Lane, and Scott D. Lane have authored and edited three law textbooks: *Lane-Goldstein Trial Technique*, *Lane Medical Litigation Guide* and *Lane-Goldstein Litigation Forms*. Fred Lane is Editor of the *Medical Trial Technique Quarterly*.

Leng Stowell Friedman & Vernon

321 South Plymouth Court, 14th Floor, Chicago, IL 60604 - Phone: (312) 431-0888, Fax: (312) 431-0228

Leng Stowell Friedman & Vernon is a litigation firm with a national practice, whose partners have a breadth of experience in both civil and criminal matters. The firm's partners include two former Assistant U.S. Attorneys, a former federal law clerk, and a former managing partner of a major Chicago law firm.

Since its inception, the firm has been involved in many significant matters, including

- Successful jury trials and/or significant settlements on cases challenging sexual harassment and discrimination, glass ceiling, unequal pay, racial discrimination, age discrimination, religion and national origin discrimination, disability and other civil rights violations, employment claims, and related state torts

- Certification as class counsel in complex civil rights cases

- Putative class counsel in cases involving claims of systemic discrimination in the securities industry and challenges to mandatory arbitration

- Summary judgment awarded to three clients who were mandatorily retired at age 63 pursuant to a City of Chicago Municipal Ordinance; judgment was sustained on appeal with resulting judgments entered for 24 other firefighters and police officers who were retired under the policy

- Successful defense of the president of a corporation who was acquitted after a jury trial in a federal criminal prosecution

- Successful defense on both a national and regional basis of product liability litigation against major equipment manufacturers

The firm's partners have significant experience in a wide range of matters, including employment discrimination, civil rights, product liability, white collar criminal law, commodities regulation, antitrust and trade regulation, unfair competition, employment covenants, and personal injury.

LINDNER, SPEERS & REULAND, P.C.
54 West Downer Place, P.O. Box 5055, Aurora, IL 60507 - Phone: (630) 892-8109, Fax: (630) 892-8151

Lindner, Speers & Reuland, P.C., was formed by George P. Lindner, Robert L. Speers and Timothy J. Reuland in 1979. The firm has concentrated its practice in civil litigation since its inception. The members of the firm have always striven to provide quality, aggressive and efficient representation for clients involved in litigation. The firm has consistently been among the leaders in cases tried to verdict. The firm handles a wide variety of personal injury and wrongful death cases for both plaintiffs and defendants and a variety of commercial litigation for both plaintiffs and defendants.

•**George P. Lindner** (JD 1965, University of Colorado) concentrates his practice in the representation of plaintiffs in personal injury and wrongful death litigation. He is a member of the Board of Directors of the Illinois Trial Lawyers Association and is also a member of the Association of Trial Lawyers of America.

•**Robert L. Speers** (JD 1972, University of Illinois) also concentrates his practice in civil litigation, representing both plaintiffs and defendants. He is a member of the Illinois Trial Lawyers Association and the Association of Trial Lawyers of America. Mr. Speers is also a past President of the Kane County Bar Association.

•**Timothy J. Reuland** (JD 1973, Northwestern University) devotes his time to handling plaintiffs' personal injury, wrongful death litigation and commercial litigation for both plaintiffs and defendants. Mr. Reuland is a member of the Illinois Trial Lawyers Association and the Association of Trial Lawyers of America, and has served on the Board of Directors of the Illinois Trial Lawyers Association and the Kane County Bar Association.

The firm's associates are **John Felton** (JD 1990, Illinois Institute of Technology, Chicago-Kent), **Sandra Petras Bruckner** (JD 1986, Northern Illinois University), and **Heather L. Outland** (JD 1994, Illinois Institute of Technology, Chicago-Kent).

George P. Lindner

Robert L. Speers

Timothy J. Reuland

MARTIN, BROWN & SULLIVAN, LTD.
321 South Plymouth Court, Tenth Floor, Chicago, IL 60604 - Phone: (312) 360-5000, Fax: (312) 360-5026

Martin, Brown & Sullivan, Ltd., emphasizes white collar criminal defense, business litigation and advice, and the representation of taxpayers in controversies of all kinds involving the IRS.

In white collar criminal defense, not only does the firm have proven capabilities in representing companies or executives already facing charges, it also provides counsel and crisis communication during governmental investigations to avoid or minimize formal actions. The firm's trial lawyers are particularly skilled in handling high-profile white collar defense matters, including those involving the Departments of Justice, Defense and Agriculture, and the Internal Revenue Service.

The firm's business dispute practice represents plaintiffs and defendants across a wide spectrum of commercial disputes, including contract disagreements, banking and financial industry controversies, partnerships and shareholder litigation, consumer fraud, and debtor-creditor litigation.

To corporations, individuals, partnerships, and estates, the firm provides civil tax controversy representation by trial lawyers with an exceptional breadth and depth of tax controversy experience.

The firm's transactional practice involves representing individuals and business entities at all stages of business operations, such as the formation of business entities, acquisition of assets, negotiations with financial institutions, contract negotiations, and the preparation of shareholders' agreements.

•**Royal B. Martin:** *See Mr. Martin's complete biographical profile in the Criminal Law: Felonies & White Collar Crime Chapter.*

Steven S. Brown: After service with the Offices of Regional Counsel and District Counsel of the IRS in Chicago, Mr. Brown entered private practice in 1979. He concentrates in federal tax litigation and federal tax administrative practice.

William G. Sullivan: During his tenure with the Office of the Attorney General of Illinois, Mr. Sullivan held a variety of posts, including Chief of the General Law Division, of the Consumer Protection Division, and of the Toxic Waste Strike Force. In private practice, Mr. Sullivan focuses on commercial disputes.

Leigh D. Roadman: A Certified Public Accountant as well as a lawyer, Mr. Roadman concentrates on white collar criminal defense and federal civil tax controversies. His prior experience includes practice with the Chicago office of the accounting firm, Price Waterhouse.

Daniel T. Hartnett: Before entering private practice, Mr. Hartnett served as a trial attorney with the Tax Division of the U.S. Department of Justice, where he tried criminal and civil tax cases in the U.S. District Courts. Mr. Hartnett's areas of practice include white collar criminal defense and civil tax controversies.

The firm's associates are **Michael D. Cotton, Robert S. Grabemann,** and **William K. Kane.**

Martin J. Healy, Jr. & Associates

111 West Washington Street, Suite 1425, Chicago, IL 60602 - Phone: (312) 977-0100, Fax: (312) 977-0795, 800: (800) 922-4500

Martin J. Healy, Jr. & Associates is a dynamic, aggressive firm consisting of seven attorneys: •**Martin J. Healy, Jr., Daniel B. Malone, J.T. Terence Geoghegan** (also previously licensed to practice in Ireland), **John P. Scanlon, Dave P. Huber, James G. McCarthy,** and **Jonathan D. Woods.**

The firm often receives exceptionally favorable results in difficult and complex cases involving personal injury, wrongful death, products liability, medical malpractice, transportation, and construction injuries.

Top row: John P. Scanlon, Daniel B. Malone, James G. McCarthy, J.T. Terence Geoghegan
Bottom row: Jonathan D. Woods, Martin J. Healy, Jr., Dave P. Huber

Murphy, Hupp, Foote, Mielke and Kinnally

Eight East Galena Boulevard, Suite 202, P.O. Box 5030, Aurora, IL 60507 - Phone: (630) 844-0056, Fax: (630) 844-1905

The firm of Murphy, Hupp, Foote, Mielke and Kinnally has over 100 years of combined experience representing persons who have been injured on the job, in auto accidents, by defective products, and also in cases of more complex liability situations. The firm's ability to move cases forward and push ahead for speedy trials results in attaining earlier trial dates and in having insurance companies settle cases promptly and fairly.

William C. Murphy has a broad range of tort injury experience. He was responsible for the elimination of sovereign immunity in Illinois. He undertook the first cases in the "asbestos crisis" and outlined how the industry would manage claims totaling over 100 billion dollars.

Robert B. Hupp has extensive experience in the commercial banking, corporate, real estate, estate planning, and tax fields. He was Chair of the Kane County Bar Association's Probate Section for many years.

•**Robert M. Foote** has concentrated in litigation since 1979. He has been involved in a broad scope of business damage trials as well as injunctive work related to labor problems, municipalities, covenants, minority shareholder's rights, and environmental issues.

Craig S. Mielke concentrates in workers' compensation and all facets of injury and commercial litigation. He also has substantial experience with insurance coverage litigation, including asbestos and environmental claims. Mr. Mielke represents defendants, as well as plaintiffs, in injury and insurance litigation.

Patrick M. Kinnally was an attorney and teacher for the Immigration and Naturalization Service prior to entering private practice. Mr. Kinnally practices in the areas of tort, commercial and general litigation, as well as immigration and environmental law.

Paul G. Krentz concentrates in personal injury cases and condemnation cases.

Joseph C. Loran concentrates in civil trial work, including personal injury and corporate litigation.

Gerald K. Hodge concentrates in estate planning, corporate planning, real estate, and probate.

Timothy D. O'Neil was employed as a prosecutor for the Kane County State's Attorney's Office prior to joining the firm. He hardened his trial skills prosecuting drug lords and gang members on behalf of the citizens of Kane County. He now concentrates in civil litigation and personal injury.

ROLEWICK & GUTZKE, P.C.
1776 South Naperville Road, Suite 104A, Wheaton, IL 60187 - Phone: (630) 653-1577, Fax: (630) 653-1579

John Dirk Gutzke   David F. Rolewick

Rolewick & Gutzke, P.C., was founded by David Rolewick in 1978, when he departed from a Wheaton insurance defense law firm where he had worked for four years as the head of the general practice department. He established a general practice firm, which he then incorporated in 1981 as a professional service corporation. The company has grown since that time from a one-man law office to a diversified firm consisting of seven full-time attorneys and a staff of qualified paralegals and secretaries.

The firm regularly handles matters in DuPage, Cook, Kane, Will, Kendall, and McHenry Counties, and it represents individuals and businesses throughout the state of Illinois.

Whether the situation is simple or complicated, matters are handled with a dedication to detail, with courteous and prompt attention, and with a level of skill and expertise hard to surpass. Any matter which cannot be handled with the degree of knowledge and experience necessary to accomplish the client's objective and be cost effective to both the client and the firm will be referred to some other law office in the Chicagoland area that has the qualifications needed to do the best job possible. The firm works diligently in its pursuit of outstanding legal talent, whether it be in-house or in its referral network.

Although the types of matters handled by the firm are too diverse to list fully, they fall into the following categories: estate planning, business planning and organization, elder law, business litigation, trusts, employment matters, commercial and residential real estate, construction litigation, banking, probate, estates, professional standards and misconduct, and personal injury.

•**David F. Rolewick:** *See complete biographical profile in the Estate Planning, Wills & Trusts Law Chapter.*

John Dirk Gutzke: Mr. Gutzke graduated from the University of Illinois College of Law in 1984, and has been employed by the firm since that time. He became a principal of the firm in 1991. He has lived in the Chicago area most of his life and presently resides in Downers Grove with his family. He is a member of the ISBA (Trusts and Estate Section Council) and the DuPage County Bar Association and DuPage County Estate Planning Council. His areas of concentration include commercial and residential real estate transactions, estate planning and probate, business planning and organization, and elder law.

SCHILLER, DUCANTO AND FLECK
200 North LaSalle Street, Suite 2700, Chicago, IL 60601-1089 - Phone: (312) 641-5560, Fax: (312) 641-6361

Schiller, DuCanto and Fleck, with 23 attorneys and offices in Chicago and Lake Forest, Illinois, is the country's largest matrimonial law firm and focuses on upper bracket cases. Clients and their spouses include corporate executives of Fortune 500 and Forbes 400 companies, entrepreneurs, professionals, academics, movie stars, sports figures, astronauts, prominent politicians, and celebrities.

The firm began in 1980, when Donald Schiller and Joseph DuCanto merged their practices. Two years later Charles Fleck, former Presiding Judge of the Cook County Domestic Relations Division, joined the firm. Arnold Stein and David Hopkins became senior partners in 1990.

Five of the sixteen Illinois matrimonial lawyers recognized in *The Best Lawyers in America* are partners of Schiller, DuCanto and Fleck, with firm members named in "The Nation's Top Forty Divorce Lawyers," *The National Law Journal*. The emphasis of the firm is on quality representation and sensitivity to the needs of the client.

Schiller, DuCanto and Fleck attorneys are not only accomplished trial attorneys, but on staff are Certified Public Accountants and financial planners concentrating in complex financial cases, financial discovery and analysis, federal taxation, estate and financial planning, retirement benefits, custody, mediation, negotiation, and appeals. Many of the firm's cases involve complex financial matters. The firm has played a major role in shaping Illinois divorce and federal tax law through the litigation of precedent-setting cases and the legislative process.

In 1995, Benjamin S. Mackoff, then the Presiding Judge of the Cook County Domestic Relations Division, left the bench to become the firm's Director of Mediation Services. Schiller, DuCanto and Fleck recognizes the need for mediation in some cases as an alternative method of dispute resolution. The firm's mediators use their legal skills to help identify issues and areas of agreement or disagreement.

Firm members include

•**Joseph N. DuCanto,** •**Donald C. Schiller,** •**Charles J. Fleck, David H. Hopkins,** •**Arnold B. Stein, Benjamin S. Mackoff, Burton S. Hochberg,** •**Stephen H. Katz, Carlton R. Marcyan, Sarane C. Siewerth, Timothy M. Daw, Ilene Beth Goldstein, Todd R. Warren, Anita M. Bolanos, Andrea Muchin, David A. King, Karen Pinkert-Lieb, Daniel R. Stefani, Sharon Warning, Melinda C. Rogers,** and **Harold G. Field.**

Of Counsel to the firm are

Sidney S. Schiller and **David Linn.**

The firm also has offices at 207 East Westminster Avenue, Suite 300, Lake Forest, Illinois 60043-1837 - Phone: (847) 615-8300, Fax: (847) 615-8284 and 300 South County Farm Road, Suite A, Wheaton, Illinois 60187 - Phone: (630) 665-5800, Fax: (630) 665-6082.

Truemper, Hollingsworth, Wojtecki, Courtin & Titiner

1700 North Farnsworth Avenue, Suite 11, Aurora, IL 60505 - Phone: (630) 820-8400, Fax: (630) 820-8582

Truemper, Hollingsworth, Wojtecki, Courtin & Titiner is a firm dedicated to the principle that all clients, regardless of wealth or legal problems, deserve professional and thorough legal representation. The firm's practice areas include a wide spectrum of legal services for both companies and individuals. The firm's success has earned it an excellent reputation in the community for providing quality legal services.

Since its inception on May 1, 1979, Truemper, Hollingsworth, Wojtecki, Courtin & Titiner has developed substantial experience in the areas of family law, estate planning and probate. The firm's litigation experience includes personal injury, workers' compensation, real estate, criminal law, and commercial law, including creditor issues. The law firm has maintained its excellent reputation by encouraging its attorneys to concentrate their practices in specific areas. This has resulted in each of the firm's attorneys gaining extensive experience in his respective area of practice.

The principals of the law firm include the following:

•**William J. Truemper,** one of the founding partners of the firm, concentrates his practice in family law and its related issues. *See complete biographical profile in the Family Law Chapter.*

Dewey G. Hollingsworth, also one of the founding partners of the firm, practices primarily in the areas of workers' compensation, probate and estate planning, and commercial law.

Leonard J. Wojtecki, the third founding partner, is a former Cook County State's Attorney and current Kendall County Public Defender. He concentrates his practice primarily in the areas of criminal law and plaintiffs' personal injury litigation.

Scott Courtin, formerly a partner in a large firm, and a litigation attorney for the City of Aurora, joined the firm in 1988. His practice is focused on personal injury, civil rights, and commercial litigation.

Steven D. Titiner, licensed in 1987, joined the firm in 1994. His practice focuses on commercial law, concentrating in creditors' rights, commercial and residential real estate transactions, and probate and estate planning.

Representative business clients include: American Healthcare Radiology Administrators; City of Aurora; Greater Aurora Chamber of Commerce; Hollywood Casino-Aurora, Inc.; Old Second National Bank of Aurora; and Aurora Firefighters Credit Union.

Weiler & Noble, P.C.

335 North River Street, Suite 203, Batavia, IL 60510 - Phone: (630) 879-3020, Fax: (630) 513-2929

Weiler & Noble, P.C., was formed in 1989. The partners have over 30 years of combined experience in all areas of family law and children's issues and in general civil litigation. The firm represents clients in all aspects of divorce, custody, paternity, adoption, child abuse and neglect, and personal estate planning matters. In addition, matters in all areas of civil litigation from trial through the appellate process are handled by the firm.

•**Rory T. Weiler** started the firm in 1982, concentrating his practice in the family law field, with an emphasis on cases involving child custody, visitation, and child removal issues. His practice deals with all areas of family law, including divorce, paternity, domestic abuse, and postjudgment custody and visitation disputes. His commitment to the protection and enhancement of children's rights in divorcing families led to his participation in an ad hoc committee which developed one of the first mandatory child awareness education programs in the country for divorcing parents. He remains an instructor in this program, KIDS in a Divorcing Society.

John S. Noble joined Mr. Weiler in the practice in 1989, following his affiliation with a firm involved in business and commercial litigation. He is currently on the Board of Directors of Court Appointed Special Advocates (CASA), a local program which provides representation free of charge to children involved in juvenile court proceedings, such as proceedings to terminate parental rights. He has participated in numerous juvenile court proceedings and is actively involved in a variety of civil litigation, personal estate planning, annexation, zoning, and other commercial real estate matters.

Patrick J. Keane joined the firm as an associate in March of 1995 to handle residential real estate, estate planning, business, and corporate matters. He received an MBA from DePaul University, Chicago, in 1988, and his JD from the John Marshall Law School in 1993.

Both Rory T. Weiler and John S. Noble have lectured at bar and community forums and are dedicated to highly personalized representation of each client, with special attention to each client's personal needs and enhanced client communication. The firm chooses to tailor its services to the specific needs of the individual client, and to keep the client actively involved in and aware of all aspects of their handling of the matter at hand, including strategy and economic decisions.

NORTHWESTERN ILLINOIS
INCLUDING ROCKFORD & QUAD CITIES

RENO, ZAHM, FOLGATE, LINDBERG & POWELL
1415 East State Street, Suite 900, Rockford, IL 61104 - Phone: (815) 987-4050, Fax: (815) 987-4092

A commitment to the highest standard of legal representation and a determined effort to obtain practical results have sustained Reno, Zahm, Folgate, Lindberg & Powell since 1923. A corresponding commitment to its community has allowed the firm to grow and develop areas of practice to best serve the needs of its clients throughout northern Illinois and southern Wisconsin.

Through the years, the firm has expanded into virtually all practice areas to meet the diverse needs of its business and individual clients, thereby adding to the broad technical base of its lawyers.

The firm practices primarily in the following areas:

- Corporate law/business counseling
- Employee benefits
- State and federal trials
- Estate and trusts
- Bankruptcy and secured transactions
- Employment law
- Real estate
- Acquisitions and mergers
- Environmental matters
- Insurance
- Tax
- Mediation and dispute resolution

The firm's partners include:

Wesley E. Lindberg (LLB 1959, U of IL) practices primarily in business, real estate development, and construction-related areas.

R. Jerome Pfister (JD 1961 high honors, U of IL) practices primarily in corporate law/business counseling, tax, estate planning, and environmental law.

•**Robert A. Fredrickson** (JD 1971 with honors, U of WI) has a state and federal trial practice including personal injury, commercial, and corporate matters.

Jack D. Ward (JD 1978 cum laude, BYU) practices primarily in business, real estate, estate planning, bankruptcy, and commercial litigation.

•**Jan H. Ohlander** (JD 1979, Marquette U) has a state and federal trial practice including mediation and dispute resolution.

James D. Zeglis (JD 1980 cum laude, IN U) has a business practice with an emphasis in labor law, real estate, and family law matters.

John H. Young (JD 1985 with honors, Drake U) has a litigation practice emphasizing insurance matters, workers' compensation, and employment matters.

•**Jamie J. Swenson Cassel** (JD 1986, U of WY) has a business and corporate practice including transactions, real estate, business and commercial trials, and bankruptcy.

Craig P. Thomas (JD 1989, U of IL) has a general corporate and business practice with an emphasis in labor, employment, and employee benefits.

Central Illinois

FELDMAN & WASSER

1307 South Seventh Street, P.O. Box 2418, Springfield, IL 62705 - Phone: (217) 544-3403, Fax: (217) 544-1593

In 1982, after nine years of service to state government, **Howard W. Feldman** entered the private practice of law. In January 1987, **Stanley N. Wasser** left state government after 12 years of service, and the firm of Feldman & Wasser was founded.

Feldman & Wasser provides to businesses, individuals, and not-for-profit organizations a full range of legal services, including

- Corporation and partnership formation and maintenance
- Contracts and documents for the sale and financing of all kinds of goods and services, buildings and businesses
- Engineering and construction matters, including lien, bond, delay, and warranty claims
- Divorce, adoption, child support, and custody
- Wills, powers of attorney, probate, estate administration, and guardianship
- Traffic, DUI, and driver's licenses
- Criminal misdemeanors and felonies, state and federal
- Government regulations, including licenses, permits, investigations, and penalty proceedings
- Employment and discrimination

The firm's members include

•**Howard W. Feldman:** *See complete biographical profile in the Family Law Chapter.*

•**Stanley N. Wasser:** *See complete biographical profile in the Employment Law Chapter.*

Carl R. Draper (JD 1981, University of Illinois) is admitted to practice in all Illinois state and federal courts and the U.S. Tax Court. He is a member of the Illinois State Bar Association (Mineral Law Section Council 1988-89) and Sangamon County Bar Association. Mr. Draper is a former Assistant Attorney General and Counsel to Governor of Illinois James R. Thompson.

Fredric Benson (JD 1972, University of Illinois) is admitted to practice in all Illinois state and federal courts and the U.S. Court of Appeals. He is a member of the American Bar Association, Illinois State Bar Association, and Sangamon County Bar Association. Mr. Benson is a former Assistant Attorney General and former Corporation Counsel for the City of Springfield.

J. Randall Cox (JD 1991, Southern Illinois University School of Law) is admitted to practice in all Illinois state and federal courts and the U.S. Court of Appeals. He is a member of the Illinois State Bar Association. Mr. Cox has been with the firm since 1991.

Bradley R. Bucher (JD 1992, California Western School of Law; MBA 1989, Marshall University) is admitted to practice in all state and federal courts of Illinois and California. He is a member of the American Bar Association, Illinois State Bar Association, Sangamon County Bar Association, and the San Diego County Bar Association. Mr. Bucher was with two California law firms prior to joining Feldman & Wasser in 1996.

HAYES, HAMMER, MILES, COX & GINZKEY

202 North Center Street, P.O. Box 3067, Bloomington, IL 61702-3067 - Phone: (309) 828-7331, Fax: (309) 827-7423

Hayes, Hammer, Miles, Cox & Ginzkey is a law firm originally founded by Merrick C. Hayes in 1976. Currently, the firm has six attorneys providing a wide range of services ranging from commercial, corporate and tax law to family law and personal injury plaintiffs and defense work.

The partners in the firm include

Merrick C. Hayes, who represents clients in the areas of estate planning, tax, corporate and business law.

•**Don C. Hammer,** who represents clients in family law, adoption, real estate, commercial litigation, mediation and alternative dispute resolution.

Frank Miles, whose practice emphasizes all areas of real estate law, including zoning, land use, and municipal law.

•**A. Clay Cox,** who works in all areas of commercial law, emphasizing estate planning, tax and corporate law, and also serves on the panel of Chapter 7 Bankruptcy Trustees.

James P. Ginzkey, who emphasizes litigation, representing both plaintiffs and defendants in personal injury matters and commercial litigation.

The firm focuses on prompt, professional legal services for small- to medium-sized businesses and for individuals with substantial assets.

RAWLES, O'BYRNE, STANKO & KEPLEY, P.C.
501 West Church Street, Champaign, IL 61820 - Phone: (217) 352-7661, Fax: (217) 352-2169

Rawles, O'Byrne, Stanko & Kepley, P.C., has earned the trust and respect of clients and the legal community through sound judgment, sincere concern, and seasoned insight.

Founded in 1931 by Donald M. Reno, Sr., the firm handles personal injury, civil litigation, criminal defense, estate and business planning, probate, real estate, hospital law, insurance defense, malpractice, criminal law, taxation, domestic relations, employment law, bankruptcy, and general counseling. It is a full-service firm staffed by professionals experienced in a broad range of legal issues.

•**Edward H. Rawles** (JD 1970 summa cum laude, IIT, Chicago-Kent) concentrates in civil litigation, personal injury and federal practice. *See complete biographical profile in the Personal Injury Law: General Chapter.*

J. Michael O'Byrne (JD 1949, U of IL) is Chair of the Board of Directors for the firm. He concentrates in general counseling, corporate and taxation law, estate planning, business litigation, real estate law, and appellate matters.

Stephen M. O'Byrne (JD 1975, U of IL) concentrates in health law, business law, and general counseling. His business practice includes counseling on issues involving the formation, operation, and management of proprietorships, partnerships, corporations, and other business entities.

•**Glenn A. Stanko** (JD 1976, U of IL) concentrates in plaintiffs' personal injury suits, employment law, employment discrimination cases, and criminal defense. He litigates a wide range of issues, including contract disputes, environmental cases, civil rights claims, and family matters. He also practices real estate, contracts and leases, and basic estate matters. *See complete biographical profile in the Employment Law Chapter.*

Brett A. Kepley (JD 1986, N IL U) concentrates in insurance law and insurance defense litigation. He practices in the areas of workers' compensation, bankruptcy law, real estate and commercial litigation, as well as traffic law.

Timothy S. Jefferson (JD 1986, U of MI-Columbia) concentrates in probate law, estate planning, taxation, corporate law, and real estate law. He also has experience in employee benefits, corporate taxation, and environmental law.

Karen B. Judd (CLA) performs legal assistant functions in civil litigation, criminal defense, family law, corporate law, estate administration, and federal taxation.

Rose M. Lanter (CLA) performs legal assistant functions in civil litigation, criminal defense, family law, real estate, and estate administration.

Sharon L. Van Grinsven (Controller) is responsible for the financial operations of the firm, including client billing, accounts receivable, accounts payable, general ledger, financial statements, management reports, group insurance administration, and trust account administration.

STINE, WOLTER & GREER
426 South Fifth Street, Springfield, IL 62701 - Phone: (217) 744-1000, Fax: (217) 744-1444

The partners of Stine, Wolter & Greer have extensive experience in the following areas:

- Legislative and administrative law
- Personal injury and workers' compensation law
- Probate and estate planning
- Professional malpractice
- Health care law
- Personal taxation

•**Robert E. Stine,** who has been selected as a Leading Illinois Attorney, is a graduate of the University of Iowa Law School and was admitted to the Illinois and Iowa Bars in 1968. He is a member of the Sangamon County and Illinois State Bar Associations and practices primarily in the areas of legislative, governmental, health care, and personal injury law. *See complete biographical profile in the Personal Injury Law: General Chapter.*

Randall A. Wolter was admitted to the Illinois Bar in 1974. A graduate of the University of Illinois School of Law and the University of Chicago Graduate School of Business, he concentrates in personal injury law, workers' compensation, commercial litigation, and professional malpractice. Mr. Wolter has handled numerous cases involving soft tissue and other injuries. He is a member of the Illinois State Bar and American Trial Lawyers Associations.

•**Daniel J. Greer,** who has also been selected as a Leading Illinois Attorney, was admitted to the Illinois Bar in 1966. Another graduate of the University of Illinois School of Law, Mr. Greer, a member of the Sangamon County and Illinois State Bar Associations, concentrates in taxation, real estate, and probate law.

Stine, Wolter & Greer strives to provide expert legal services and personal attention to its clients. Together, the firm members are dedicated to effective representation and advocacy. Personal service and a clear explanation of the legal process is recognized as essential.

Additionally, each of the partners is dedicated to extending and sharing his knowledge and experience to the legal community and the community-at-large by participating in local and state legal associations, lecturing frequently on current legal topics and trial tactics, and taking leadership roles in local not-for-profit organizations.

THE LAW OFFICES OF FREDERIC W. NESSLER AND ASSOCIATES
800 Myers Building, Springfield, IL 62701 - Phone: (217) 753-5533, Fax: (217) 753-4631, 800: (800) 727-8010

Since its inception in 1977, The Law Offices of Frederic W. Nessler and Associates has grown in reputation and size as one of the leading firms in central Illinois. The firm limits its practice to personal injury, medical malpractice, workers' compensation, product liability, and wrongful death cases, all handled on a contingency fee basis, and has succeeded in obtaining significant financial recovery for its clients in many cases. Headed by Frederic W. Nessler, the firm now enjoys locations in seven Illinois cities, including Springfield, Decatur, Champaign, Bloomington, Urbana, Peoria, and Chicago.

•**Frederic W. Nessler:** Mr. Nessler, selected as a Leading Illinois Attorney, concentrates his efforts in serious and catastrophic injuries. He has been, and continues to be, a sought-after lecturer on personal injury and workers' compensation law and related topics. Mr. Nessler is a life-long resident of central Illinois and served as a legislative assistant to the late Congressman Edward Madigan, U.S. Congress, served on the Tort Section Council of the Illinois State Bar Association, and has been active with the Illinois Trial Lawyers Association and the Association of Trial Lawyers of America in efforts to protect victims' rights. *See complete biographical profile in the Personal Injury Law: General Chapter.*

•**Gary L. Clark:** An integral member of The Law Offices of Frederic W. Nessler and Associates, Mr. Clark, also selected as a Leading Illinois Attorney, has successfully handled cases in the fields of auto negligence, product and premises liability, and medical malpractice. Mr. Clark is a frequent lecturer on tort law and civil litigation for the Peoria County Bar Association, the Illinois State Bar Association, and the Illinois Institute for Continuing Legal Education. Mr. Clark is a member of the Illinois Trial Lawyers Association, Association of Trial Lawyers of America, and the Illinois State Bar Association. *See complete biographical profile in the Personal Injury Law: Medical & Professional Malpractice Chapter.*

SOUTHERN ILLINOIS

CARR, KOREIN, TILLERY, KUNIN, MONTROY & GLASS
412 Missouri Avenue, East St. Louis, IL 62201 - Phone: (618) 274-0434, Fax: (618) 274-8369, 800: (800) 333-5297

Carr, Korein, Tillery, Kunin, Montroy & Glass is a firm of 19 lawyers, engaged in all aspects of trial practice, advocating the rights of accident victims. All six of the partners were voted Leading Illinois Attorneys by their peers in their respective areas of concentration.

•**Rex Carr** is nationally renowned for landmark verdicts in areas as diverse as products liability, medical malpractice, and libel. He is a member and former President of the prestigious Inner Circle of Advocates. *See complete profiles in the Personal Injury Law: General and Personal Injury Law: Medical & Professional Malpractice Chapters.*

•**Sandor Korein** has been responsible for a large number of the current safety rules and regulations protecting seamen on the navigable inland waterways of the United States. Many of his Jones Act verdicts since the 1960s have spurred towboat operators to correct unseaworthy conditions that injured maritime employees. He is Rivers Counsel for the National Maritime Union. *See complete profile in the Personal Injury Law: Transportation Chapter.*

•**Steve Tillery** has obtained substantial verdicts for victims of medical malpractice and defective products, as well as injured railroad workers. He is Designated Counsel for the United Transportation Union, in recognition of the outstanding verdicts and settlements he has achieved for so many of its members and other Federal Employer's Liability Act plaintiffs. *See complete profile in the Personal Injury Law: Transportation Chapter.*

•**Gerald Montroy** has concentrated in medical malpractice cases since 1980, securing numerous large verdicts and settlements. He has not only handled many cases of serious damage resulting from negligent diagnosis and treatment, but has lectured and written on aspects of medical malpractice litigation to a number of professional groups. *See complete profile in the Personal Injury Law: Medical & Professional Malpractice Chapter.*

•**Mark Glass,** after years of handling a broad range of civil cases, has confined his practice to Illinois workers' compensation. He has served on statewide committees, addressing legislation and other workers' compensation issues, and has conducted seminars on practice before the Illinois Industrial Commission. *See complete profile in the Workers' Compensation Law Chapter.*

•**Joel Kunin** heads a five-lawyer section within the firm, recognized throughout southern Illinois among the leading practitioners in bankruptcy and commercial litigation. *Complete profile will appear in the Business Law Guidebook, which will be published in 1997.*

The support staff includes paralegals, legal assistants, and two full-time nurses. This experienced and well-rounded staff provides comprehensive analysis of all medical legal issues that arise in a personal injury practice.

The firm has offices in East St. Louis, Belleville, and St. Louis.

NELSON, BEMENT, STUBBLEFIELD & LEVENHAGEN, P.C.

420 North High Street, P.O. Box Y, Belleville, IL 62222 - Phone: (618) 277-4000, Fax: (618) 277-1136

Top row: Timothy C. Stubblefield, Gary L. Bement
Bottom row: Robert C. Nelson, David C. Nelson, T. Fritz Levenhagen

The firm of Nelson, Bement, Stubblefield & Levenhagen, P.C., enjoys a reputation as one of the most aggressive and experienced firms in southern Illinois. The firm focuses squarely on litigation, with a concentration in personal injury and workers' compensation law.

Founded by Robert C. Nelson in 1979, the firm now boasts five attorneys. All are professionally active with state and local bar associations. Each attorney is a member of the Illinois Trial Lawyers Association. While a relatively young firm, the attorneys have considerable litigation experience. They practice law throughout southern Illinois and eastern Missouri.

The firm owes much of its success to a particularly dedicated and hard working professional staff, some of whom have worked for the firm as long as 15 years. The firm's staff members count among past leaders in the St. Clair County Legal Professional organization.

The firm demonstrates its strong community presence by sponsoring many community activities, such as the Walk for Cystic Fibrosis, the Southwestern Illinois Epilepsy Association's Summer Stroll, several 10K runs, and a variety of soccer and baseball teams.

•**Robert C. Nelson:** *See complete biographical profile in the Workers' Compensation Law Chapter.*

Gary L. Bement practices in Illinois and Missouri, with a strong emphasis in workers' compensation and personal injury law. He has handled many major criminal and civil trials in his 15 years of practice.

•**Timothy C. Stubblefield:** *See complete biographical profiles in the Civil Appellate Law and Family Law Chapters.*

T. Fritz Levenhagen concentrates exclusively in workers' compensation and personal injury litigation. With over ten years' trial experience, he has become a leading trial lawyer in both southern Illinois and eastern Missouri.

David C. Nelson is an active member of the state bar and has published articles in the *Illinois Bar Journal, Tort Trends,* and *Trial Briefs,* among other professional journals.

APPENDIX B

LEGAL RESOURCES

BAR ASSOCIATIONS

Bar associations are professional groups for attorneys. Bar associations view helping the public as an important part of their mission. The largest bar association in Illinois is the Illinois State Bar Association (ISBA). Each member of the ISBA may also belong to one of the 11 local bar associations. These associations serve their members by providing continuing legal education and a forum for discussing concerns of the legal profession. They also serve the public, providing lawyer referrals, informational booklets and pamphlets, telephone information services, and a variety of public education programs. Most of these services are available at little or no cost.

Members of the public should consider taking advantage of bar association services when they are seeking general information. Although they cannot provide legal advice, bar associations can help people decide whether to pursue a case, what actions to take, and what type of lawyer to contact. A list of bar associations and bar association referral services appear later in this appendix.

The following pamphlets were prepared and published by the Illinois State Bar Association as a public service. Their purpose is to inform citizens of their legal rights and obligations. Consult a lawyer if you have questions about application of the law in a particular case.

Single copies of each of the pamphlets are free to individuals. Spanish language translations are also available. For information on obtaining quantity copies, write or call the ISBA at the following:

Illinois State Bar Association
424 South Second Street
Springfield, IL 62701
Phone: (217) 525-1760
Fax: (217) 525-0712

Adoption
Advice to Newly Marrieds
Auto Accidents
Bankruptcy for Individuals
Buying a Home
Buying on Time

Careers in the Law
Domestic Relations
Estate Planning
General Practitioner
How a Lawyer Computes Fees
Illinois Lawyer Referral Service
Know Your Lawyer
Landlord-Tenant
Q & A About Prepaid Legal Services
Starting a Business
Your Rights if Arrested

ATTORNEY GENERAL'S OFFICE

Attorney General Jim Ryan

Attorney General Jim Ryan serves the citizens of Illinois as the state's chief law officer and top legal official. Charged with these responsibilities, the Attorney General directs a broad range of services dedicated to protecting and assisting the state and its citizens.

As Illinois' chief law enforcement official, Attorney General Jim Ryan leads the statewide fight against crime and violence. He assists local State's Attorneys in the prosecution of major crimes, and heads the Statewide Grand Jury, which indicts and convicts drug dealers and gun runners whose operations cross county lines.

As Illinois' top legal official, Attorney General Jim Ryan prosecutes perpetrators of consumer fraud, enforces environmental laws and regulations, and advocates on behalf of the state's citizens whose interests might otherwise go unheard.

Key Divisions in the Office of the Attorney General and Their Missions

The Office of the Attorney General provides services that cover a broad range of issues, reaching every corner of Illinois.

The Criminal Justice Division helps local State's Attorneys prosecute death penalty cases and other major crimes.

To help put sophisticated criminal operations out of business, the Statewide Grand Jury is charged with prosecuting multi-county drug trafficking and gun running cases.

The Victim Compensation/Grants Bureau takes court costs imposed on convicted defendants and uses the money to help fight crime. The bureau distributes millions of dollars each year in grants to local crime-fighting organizations. The bureau's Victim Compensation Program provides financial help directly to crime victims.

The Consumer Protection Division protects consumers and small businesses who have been victimized by fraud, deception or unfair competition. The Attorney General is a leader in fighting the emerging menace of telecommunications fraud. A network of regional offices throughout Illinois gives citizens immediate access to these services.

The Environmental Enforcement Division protects the health, safety and welfare of citizens through prosecution of environmental laws and regulations.

To serve those whose voices might not otherwise be heard, the Legal Advocacy Division provides information and referral services for seniors, veterans, women and children, disabled citizens, and agricultural advocacy groups.

The Public Interest Division protects Illinois citizens in cases involving civil rights, nursing homes, public utilities, charities, and antitrust violations.

The Attorney General is the lawyer for state government. The Appeals/Opinions and Government Representation Divisions act as the attorney for state agencies and officers.

Office of Attorney General
500 South Second Street
Springfield, IL 62706
Phone: (217) 782-1090
Fax: (217) 782-7046
TDD: (217) 785-2771

Office of Attorney General
100 West Randolph Street
Chicago, IL 60601
Phone: (312) 814-3000
TDD: (312) 814-3374
Fax: (312) 814-2549

Office of Attorney General
1001 East Main
Carbondale, IL 62901
Phone: (618) 457-3505
TDD: (618) 457-5509

Toll-Free Numbers:
Consumer: (800) 252-8666
Senior Citizens: (800) 252-2518
Veterans: (800) 382-3000

As lawyers have grown increasingly concerned about their public image, they have also expanded their efforts to reach out to the public and provide helpful services to consumers. Free information, referrals, and a variety of educational programs are only a telephone call away. Consumers seeking information would be wise to make that call as one of their first steps in pursuing a legal matter.

BAR ASSOCIATIONS

American Bar Association
750 North Lake Shore Drive
Chicago, IL 60611
Phone: (312) 988-5000
Fax: (312) 988-6281
Provides information and telephone numbers of referral services.

Chicago Bar Association
321 South Plymouth Court
Chicago, IL 60604
Phone: (312) 554-2000
Fax: (312) 554-2054
Provides free informational pamphlets, maintains a referral service, administers the free Call-A-Lawyer public information program and senior citizen will program.

Appendix B: Legal Resources

Cook County Bar Association/Community Law Project
188 West Randolph Street, #720
Chicago, IL 60601
Phone: (312) 630-9363
Fax: (312) 630-0983
Maintains a referral service and administers Community Law Project, which provides free legal clinics to low-income persons for legal advice, representation and referrals.

Illinois State Bar Association
Illinois Bar Center
424 South Second Street
Springfield, IL 62701
Phone: (217) 525-1760
Fax: (217) 525-0712
Provides free informational pamphlets, maintains a referral service.

LAWYER REFERRAL SERVICES (GENERAL)

See also Specialized Legal Services (below) for referral services on special legal needs.

Chicago Bar Association
321 South Plymouth Court
Chicago, IL 60604
Phone: (312) 554-2001
Fax: (312) 554-2054
Available to residents in Cook and DuPage Counties; $20 fee for referral to private attorneys. Spanish-speaking intake staff; referral to non-English speaking attorneys available.

Cook County Bar Association
188 West Randolph Street, #720
Chicago, IL 60601
Phone: (312) 630-1157
Fax: (312) 630-0983
Free referrals to private attorneys.

DuPage County Bar Association
126 South County Farm Road
Wheaton, IL 60187
Phone: (708) 653-7779
Fax: (708) 653-7870

Illinois State Bar Association/Lawyer Referral Service
Illinois Bar Center
424 South Second Street
Springfield, IL 62701
Phone: (217) 525-5297
No referrals made to lawyers in Cook, Lake, DuPage, Will, Winnebago, Peoria, and Kane Counties. Referrals to private attorneys; $15 for first half-hour consultation.

Kane County Bar Association
127 South Second Street
P.O. Box 571
Geneva, IL 60134
Phone: (708) 232-6416
Fax: (708) 232-7978

North Suburban Bar Association Lawyer Referral Service
Buffalo Grove
Phone: (708) 564-4800
Referrals to private attorneys; $15 referral fee.

Northwest Suburban Bar Association
515 East Golf Road, #100-101
Arlington Heights, IL 60005
Phone: (708) 290-8070
Fax: (708) 290-8073
Referrals to private attorneys; $20 fee for initial half-hour consultation.

Peoria County Bar Association
1618 First Financial Plaza
Peoria, IL 61602
Phone: (309) 674-1224

Will County Bar Association
63 East Jefferson Street, #202
Joliet, IL 60432
Voice and Fax: (815) 726-0383

Winnebago County Bar Association
321 West State Street, #300
Rockford, IL 61101
Phone: (815) 964-5152
Fax: (815) 964-9091

Women's Bar Association of Illinois
825 Greenbay Road
Suite 270
Wilmette, IL 60091
Phone: (312) 341-8530
Referrals to private attorneys; $25 fee for initial half-hour consultation.

PUBLIC DEFENDERS

Public Defenders Office
Cook County
200 West Adams
Ninth Floor
Chicago, IL 60606
Phone: (312) 609-2040
Fax: (312) 609-8917

Public Defender
McLean County
104 West Front Street, #603
Bloomington, IL 61701
Phone: (309) 888-5235
Fax: (309) 888-5765

Public Defenders Office
Lee County Courthouse
P.O. Box 521
Dixon, IL 61021
Phone: (815) 284-5239

Public Defenders Office
Kane County
37 West 777
Route 38, #200
St. Charles, IL 60175
Phone: (708) 232-5835
Fax: (708) 208-2192

Public Defenders Office
Williamson County Courthouse
Marion, IL 62959
Phone: (618) 997-1301
Fax: (618) 997-8450

SPECIALIZED LEGAL SERVICES

VOLUNTEER ATTORNEYS
Note: Many of the organizations listed under other sub-headings also provide free or low-cost legal services.

American Civil Liberties Union (ACLU)
203 North LaSalle Street, #1405
Chicago, IL 60601
Phone: (312) 201-9740
Fax: (312) 201-9760
Provides free legal representation in civil rights and civil liberties cases that present significant issues or affect a large number of people.

AGRICULTURE
Farmers Legal Action Group
46 East Fourth Street, #1301
St. Paul, MN 55101
Phone: (612) 223-5333
Fax: (612) 223-5335
800: (800) 233-4534
Provides nationwide legal information and services concerning agriculture and farming.

AIDS/HIV/ARC
AIDS Legal Council of Chicago
220 South State Street, #1330
Chicago, IL 60604
Phone: (312) 427-8990
Fax: (312) 427-8419
Provides legal consultation and representation on HIV-related legal matters to persons in Cook County affected by AIDS/HIV.

Land of Lincoln Legal Assistance Foundation
2420 Bloomer Drive
Alton, IL 62002
Phone: (618) 462-0036
Fax: (618) 462-0043
Provides free legal counseling and representation in civil cases for low-income persons in most regions of Illinois.

Illinois American Agricultural Movement
12352 East 2100 Road North
Danville, IL 61834
Works to preserve the family farm.

Farm Law Institute
P.O. Box 196
Carlinville, IL 62626

Appendix B: Legal Resources

PERSONS WITH DISABILITIES
Chicago Bar Association Legal Clinic for the
Disabled, Inc.
448 East Ontario Street
Chicago, IL 60611
Phone: (312) 908-4463
Fax: (312) 908-0866
Provides free legal services in civil matters, especially disability matters, to low-income persons with disabilities.

Legal Assistance Foundation of Chicago
Disability Law Project
343 South Dearborn Street, #700
Chicago, IL 60604
Phone: (312) 341-1070
Fax: (312) 341-1041
Provides legal counseling and representation in civil cases to low-income mentally and physically disabled persons in Chicago.

GAY AND LESBIAN
Horizons Community Legal Services
961 West Montana Street
Chicago, IL 60614
Phone: (312) 929-4357
Provides free legal consultation and referrals to attorneys.

INCARCERATED PERSONS
Chicago Legal Aid to Incarcerated Mothers (CLAIM)
205 West Randolph Street, #830
Chicago, IL 60606
Phone: (312) 332-5537
Fax: (312) 332-2570
Provides legal services in family law matters to imprisoned or formerly imprisoned mothers.

Institute of Women Today
7315 South Yale Avenue
Chicago, IL 60621
Phone: (312) 651-8372
Provides legal services to women incarcerated in the Illinois prison system.

MIGRANT
Legal Assistance Foundation of Chicago
Illinois Migrant Legal Assistance Project
343 South Dearborn Street, #700
Chicago, IL 60604
Phone: (312) 341-1070
Fax: (312) 341-1041
Provides legal counseling and representation to migrant workers in civil cases.

The Council for Disability Rights
176 West Adams Street, #1830
Chicago, IL 60603
Phone: (312) 444-9484
Fax: (312) 444-1977
Provides legal counseling and representation to persons with disabilities.

Lesbian and Gay Bar Association
P.O. Box 06498
Chicago, IL 60606
Phone: (312) 404-9574
Free referrals to gay or lesbian attorneys.

Legal Assistance Foundation of Chicago
Correctional Law Project
343 South Dearborn Street, #700
Chicago, IL 60604
Phone: (312) 341-1070
Fax: (312) 341-1041
Provides legal services to low-income persons confined in the Cook County Jail or the Illinois prison system.

U.S. Department of Labor
Wage-Hour Division
230 South Dearborn Street, #412
Chicago, IL 60604
Phone: (312) 353-8145
Enforces the Migrant Safety and Protection Act.

Legal Resources

SOUTHEAST ASIAN
Chinese Americans Service League
310 West 24th Place
Chicago, IL 60616
Phone: (312) 791-0418
Fax: (312) 791-0509

SPANISH-SPEAKING
Latin American Bar Association
P.O. Box A-3823
Chicago, IL 60690
Phone: (312) 845-1665
Free referrals to private
English/Spanish-speaking attorneys.

Mexican-American Legal Defense and
Educational Fund
542 South Dearborn Street, #750
Chicago, IL 60605
Phone: (312) 427-9363
Fax: (312) 427-9393
Initiates class action suits involving civil rights violations that affect the Hispanic community.

Mujeres Latinas En Accion
1823 West 17th Street
Chicago, IL 60608
Phone: (312) 226-1544
Provides referrals to attorneys and legal services.

WOMEN
Illinois Women's Agenda
Six North Michigan Avenue, #1313
Chicago, IL 60602
Phone: (312) 704-1833
Advocates and protects women's rights in Illinois.

Legal Assistance Foundation of Chicago
Women's Law Project
343 South Dearborn Street, #700
Chicago, IL 60604
Phone: (312) 341-1070
Fax: (312) 341-1041
Provides legal services in civil cases having the potential to affect a large number of poor women.

REGIONAL SERVICES

General legal resources for persons who fall within specific income guidelines or meet other requirements.

COOK & COLLAR COUNTIES
American Civil Liberties Union of Illinois
203 North LaSalle, #1405
Chicago, IL 60601
Phone: (312) 201-9740
Fax: (312) 201-9760

Chicago Volunteer Legal Services Foundation
100 North LaSalle Street, #90
Chicago, IL 60602
Phone: (312) 332-1624
Fax: (312) 332-1460
Provides free legal consultation and representation to low-income persons on civil matters only.

University of Chicago, Legal Aid Office
6020 South University Avenue
Chicago, IL 60637
Phone: (312) 702-9611
Fax: (312) 702-2063

Life Span
P.O. Box 445
Des Plaines, IL 60016
Phone: (312) 824-0382

Cook County Legal Assistance Foundation
Incorporated
1146 Westgate, #200
Oak Park, IL 60301-1055
Phone: (708) 524-2600
Fax: (708) 524-2643

Appendix B: Legal Resources

Will County Legal Assistance
Program, Incorporated
16 West Van Buren, #204
Joliet, IL 60431
Phone: (815) 727-5123
Fax: (815) 727-5152

Legal Aid Center of the DuPage County Bar
126 South County Farm Road
Wheaton, IL 60187
Phone: (708) 653-6212
Fax: (708) 653-6317

NORTHWESTERN ILLINOIS INCLUDING ROCKFORD & QUAD CITIES

Prairie State Legal Services, Incorporated
975 North Main Street
Rockford, IL 61103-7064
Phone: (815) 965-2134
Fax: (815) 965-1081

Student Legal Services
Northern Illinois University
Student Center, Lower Level
Dekalb, IL 60115
Phone: (815) 753-1701
Fax: (815) 753-1871

CENTRAL ILLINOIS

West Central Illinois Legal Assistance
1614 East Knox Street
P.O. Box 1232
Galesburg, IL 61402-1232
Phone: (309) 343-2141
Fax: (309) 343-7647

Land of Lincoln Legal Assistance
Foundation, Incorporated
730 East Vine Street, #214
P.O. Box 2206
Springfield, IL 62705-2206
Phone: (217) 753-3300
Fax: (217) 753-8291

University of Illinois
Student Legal Services
Illini Union, Room 324
1401 West Green Street
Urbana, IL 61801
Phone: (217) 333-9053
Phone: (217) 333-0474

Legal Services Support Center of Illinois
516 East Monroe, #400
Springfield, IL 62701-1451
Phone: (217) 544-0006

SOUTHERN ILLINOIS

Land of Lincoln Legal Assistance
Foundation, Incorporated
2420 Bloomer Drive
Alton, IL 62002
Phone: (618) 462-0036
Fax: (618) 462-0043

Clinical Program
Southern Illinois University, School of Law
104 Lesar Law Building
Carbondale, IL 62901-6821
Phone: (618) 536-4423
Phone: (618) 453-8727

Southern Illinois University
Student Legal Services
Box 1023
Edwardsville, IL 62026-1023
Phone: (618) 692-3355

APPENDIX C

COMMUNITY RESOURCES

GENERAL RESOURCES

COOK & COLLAR COUNTIES

Crisis Intervention
Talkline Help Lines, Inc.
P.O. Box 1321
Elk Grove Village, IL 60007
Talk Line (for adults): (708) 228-6400
Teen Line: (708) 228-TEEN (8336)
Kids Line: (708) 228-KIDS (5437)
Fax: (708) 228-3461

Community Information and Referral Service
560 West Lake Street
Chicago, IL 60661
Phone: (312) 876-0010
Fax: (312) 876-0721
A professional information and referral service supported by the United Way/Crusade of Mercy. Trained and experienced social work consultants link people who need help with qualified service providers.

Lutheran Child and Family Services of Illinois
7620 Madison Street
River Forest, IL 60305
Phone: (708) 771-7180 or (312) 287-4848
Fax: (708) 771-7184

United Way Community Referral Service
560 West Lake Street
Chicago, IL 60661-1499
Phone: (312) 876-0010
800: (800) 564-5733 (Chicago metro area)
Fax: (312) 876-0721

Connection Telephone Crisis Intervention and Referral Service
P.O. Box 906
Libertyville, IL 60048
Hotline: (708) 367-1080
Office: (708) 362-3381

Lake County Urban League
122 Madison Avenue
Waukegan, IL 60085
Phone: (708) 249-3770
Fax: (708) 249-4894

Crisis Intervention
Community Crisis Center
P.O. Box 1390
Elgin, IL 60121
Phone: (708) 697-2380
Fax: (708) 742-4182

American Red Cross
Arlington Heights Center
544 West Northwest Highway
Arlington Heights, IL 60004
Service Center Phone: (708) 255-0703
Suburban Region Phone: (708) 255-9534
Fax: (708) 255-2897

DuPage County Department of Human Resources
Division of Human Services
421 County Farm Road North
Wheaton, IL 60187
Senior Services Phone: (800) 640-3683
800: (800) 942-9412
TDD: (708) 682-6926
Fax: (708) 690-3799

Senior Services Center of Will County
310 North Joliet Street
Joliet, IL 60432
Phone: (815) 723-9713
Fax: (815) 740-4218

Kane County Information
1035 East State Street
Geneva, IL 60134
Phone: (708) 232-7600

Northwestern Illinois Including Rockford & Quad Cities

American Red Cross, Rock River Chapter
727 North Church Street
Rockford, IL 61103
Phone: (815) 963-8471

United Way Services, Inc.
612 North Main Street, #200
Rockford, IL 61101-6929
Phone: (815) 968-5400

Information and Assistance
1905 East Main
Urbana, IL 61801
Phone: (217) 328-5148
Fax: (217) 328-5148

Infoline
P.O. Box 1976
Rockford, IL 61110
Phone: (815) 636-5005
800: (800) 866-3733
Fax: (815) 636-5009

Central Illinois

Springfield Urban League
100 North 11th Street
P.O. Box 3865
Springfield, IL 62708
Phone: (217) 789-0830

United Way of McLean County
201 East Grove, #100
Bloomington, IL 61701
Phone: (309) 828-7383

Path Crisis Center
201 East Grove
Bloomington, IL 61701
Phone: (309) 827-4005

First Call for Help
405 South State Street
Champaign, IL 61820
Phone: (217) 352-6300
TDD: (217) 352-0160
Fax: (217) 352-9512

United Way Help Line
300 Civic Center Plaza, #260
Quincy, IL 62301
Phone: (217) 224-1223
Fax: (217) 222-0911

Your Link to Help
509 West High Street
Peoria, IL 61606
Phone: (309) 674-7140
Fax: (309) 674-1056
800: (800) 338-4636 (within Illinois)
Serving Tri-county area of central Illinois (Peoria, Tazewell, Woodford Counties).

Southern Illinois

Call for Help
9400 Lebanon Road
Edgemont, IL 62203
Phone: (618) 397-0968
Fax: (618) 397-6836

Information and Referral
9400 Lebanon Road
Edgemont, IL 62203
Phone: (618) 397-0996
24-Hour Hotline: (618) 397-0963

Information and Assistance
P.O. Box 631
Effingham, IL 62401
Phone: (217) 347-5569
Elder Abuse: (800) 283-4070
Fax: (217) 347-5590

Catholic Social Services of Belleville
617 South Belt West
Belleville, IL 62220-2482
Phone: (618) 277-0368
Fax: (618) 277-0368
Serves social needs of 28 southern counties.

SPECIALIZED RESOURCES

AFRICAN AMERICAN
Champaign County Urban League
17 Taylor Street
Champaign, IL 61820
Phone: (217) 356-1364

Chicago Urban League
4510 South Michigan Avenue
Chicago, IL 60653
Phone: (312) 285-5800
Fax: (312) 285-7772

Illinois Committee on Black Concerns
411 East Broadway
East St. Louis, IL 62201
Phone: (618) 482-6900

Lake County Urban League
122 Madison Street
Waukegan, IL 60085
Phone: (708) 249-3770

Madison County Urban League
210 William Street
Alton, IL 62002
Phone: (618) 463-1906

Springfield County Urban League
100 North 11th Street
P.O. Box 3865
Springfield, IL 62708
Phone: (217) 789-0830

DOMESTIC ABUSE, ASSAULT, VICTIM SERVICES
Illinois Coalition Against Domestic Violence
730 East Vine Street, #109
Springfield, IL 62703
Phone: (217) 789-2830
Fax: (217) 789-1939
Provides emergency shelter, food, medical care and counseling to victims of domestic violence.

Illinois Coalition Against Sexual Assault
123 South Seventh Street, #500
Springfield, IL 62701
Phone: (217) 753-8229
Fax: (217) 753-8229
Provides services for victims of sexual assault.

Northwest Action Against Rape
415 West Golf Road, #47MST-RAPE
Arlington Heights, IL 60005
Phone: (708) 228-0990
Provides counseling and crisis services.

Parents United, Bolingbrook Chapter
345 Manor Court
Bolingbrook, IL 60439
Phone: (708) 739-0491
Fax: (708) 739-5831
Crisis and long-term support for those affected by child sexual abuse.

Stopping Woman Abuse Now
P.O. Box 176
Olney, IL 62450
Phone: (618) 392-3556
Provides legal and social services to victims of domestic violence in southeastern Illinois.

GAY AND LESBIAN
University of Chicago Gay and Lesbian Alliance
1212 East 59th Street
Room 207
Chicago, IL 60637
Phone: (312) 702-9734
Promotes individual rights; provides support services.

AIDS/HIV/ARC
AIDS Foundation of Chicago
1332 North Halstead
Chicago, IL 60622
Phone: (312) 922-2322
Serves persons with AIDS.

AIDS Pastoral Care Network
4753 North Broadway, #800
Chicago, IL 60640
Phone: (312) 334-5333
Fax: (312) 334-3293
Interfaith support and crisis counseling.

Midwest AIDS Foundation
2202 North Cleveland Street
Chicago, IL 60614
Phone: (312) 772-5958
Provides assistance and support to persons affected by AIDS.

Southeast Asian

Chinese Mutual Aid Association
1100 West Argyle Street
Chicago, IL 60640
Phone: (312) 784-2900
Fax: (312) 784-2984
Provides employment services, counseling and community organizing to Chinese immigrants and refugees.

Southeast Asian Center
1134 West Ainslie
Chicago, IL 60640
Phone: (312) 989-6927
Fax: (312) 989-4871
Fosters self-sufficiency for Southeast Asian immigrants and refugees.

Vietnamese Association of Illinois
5252 North Broadway Street
Chicago, IL 60640
Phone: (312) 728-3700
Fax: (312) 728-0497
Provides employment and immigration services, youth and elderly services and assistance to refugee businesses.

Spanish-Speaking

Centro Hispano Sembrador
921 West State Street
Rockford, IL 61102
Phone: (815) 964-8142
Fax: (815) 968-2808
Provides social services for the Hispanic community.

Mujeres Latinas En Accion
1823 West 17th Street
Chicago, IL 60608
Phone: (312) 226-1544
Fax: (312) 226-2720
Operates domestic violence program, youth advocacy program and parental support groups.

Hispanic Social Service Agency
Lutheran Family and Child Services
3859 West 26th Street
Chicago, IL 60623
Phone: (312) 277-7330

Latino Counseling Service
3225 North Sheffield
Chicago, IL 60657
Phone: (312) 549-5886
Fax: (312) 549-3265

Hispanic AIDS Network
1874 North Milwaukee Avenue
Chicago, IL 60647
Phone: (312) 276-2185

Women

Oasis Women's Center
111 Market Street
Alton, IL 62002
Phone: (618) 465-1978
800: (800) 244-1978
Fax: (618) 465-0749

Kindred Spirit
224 Ridge Avenue
Evanston, IL 60201
Phone: (708) 491-1103

YWCA of Metropolitan Chicago
South Suburban Center
4343 West Lincoln Highway, #210
Matteson, IL 60443
Phone: (708) 748-6600
24-Hour Hotline: (708) 746-5672
Fax: (708) 748-6606
Provides transitions counseling.

Illinois Women's Agenda
Six North Michigan Avenue, Suite 1313
Chicago, IL 60602
Phone: (312) 704-1833
Protects women's rights in Illinois; women's rights advocacy.

APPENDIX D

STATE BAR ASSOCIATIONS

STATE BAR ASSOCIATIONS

It is important to keep in mind that laws can vary drastically from state to state. Rarely is it safe to assume that what holds true under Illinois state law will hold true in another state. A good place to start researching law or attorneys in states other than Illinois is to contact a state bar association in that jurisdiction. Many state bar associations refer callers to member attorneys and several will provide basic summaries of state laws, free of charge. Below is a list of state bar associations around the country. Note that a few states have more than one bar association listed.

Alabama State Bar
415 Dexter Avenue
Montgomery, AL 36104
Phone: (334) 269-1515
Fax: (334) 261-6310

Alaska Bar Association
510 L Street, #602
P.O. Box 100279
Anchorage, AK 99510
Phone: (907) 272-7469
Fax: (907) 272-2932

State Bar of Arizona
111 West Monroe, #1800
Phoenix, AZ 85003-1742
Phone: (602) 252-4804
Fax: (602) 271-4930

Arkansas Bar Association
400 West Markham Street
Little Rock, AR 72201
Phone: (501) 375-4605
800: (800) 509-5668
Fax: (501) 375-4901

State Bar of California
555 Franklin Street
San Francisco, CA 94102
Phone: (415) 561-8200
Fax: (415) 561-8305

The Colorado Bar Association
1900 Grant Street, #950
Denver, CO 80203
Phone: (303) 860-1115
Fax: (303) 894-0821

Connecticut Bar Association
101 Corporate Place
Rocky Hill, CT 06067-1894
Phone: (860) 721-0025
Fax: (860) 257-4125

Delaware State Bar Association
1201 Orange Street, #1201
Wilmington, DE 19801
Phone: (302) 658-5279
Fax: (302) 658-5212

District of Columbia Bar
1250 H Street Northwest
Sixth Floor
Washington, D.C. 20005-3908
Phone: (202) 737-4700
Fax: (202) 626-3471

Bar Association of the District of Columbia
1819 H Street Northwest
12th Floor
Washington, D.C. 20006-3690
Phone: (202) 223-6600
Fax: (202) 293-3388

The Florida Bar
The Florida Bar Center
650 Apalachee Parkway
Tallahassee, FL 32399-2300
Phone: (904) 561-5600
Fax: (904) 561-5827

State Bar of Georgia
50 Hurt Plaza, #800
Atlanta, GA 30303
Phone: (404) 527-8700
Fax: (404) 527-8717

Hawaii State Bar Association
1136 Union Mall
Penthouse One
Honolulu, HI 96813
Phone: (808) 537-1868
Fax: (808) 521-7936

Idaho State Bar
P.O. Box 895
Boise, ID 83701
Phone: (208) 334-4500
Fax: (208) 334-4515

Illinois State Bar Association
424 South Second Street
Springfield, IL 62701
Phone: (217) 525-1760
Fax: (217) 525-0712

Indiana State Bar Association
230 East Ohio Street
Fourth Floor
Indianapolis, IN 46204
Phone: (317) 639-5465
Fax: (317) 266-2588

The Iowa State Bar Association
521 East Locust
Des Moines, IA 50309
Phone: (515) 243-3179
Fax: (515) 243-2511

Kansas Bar Association
P.O. Box 1037
Topeka, KS 66601-1037
Phone: (913) 234-5696
Fax: (913) 234-3813

Kentucky Bar Association
514 West Main Street
Frankfort, KY 40601-1883
Phone: (502) 564-3795
Fax: (502) 564-3225

Louisiana State Bar Association
601 St. Charles Avenue
New Orleans, LA 70130
Phone: (504) 566-1600
Fax: (504) 566-0930

Maine State Bar Association
124 State Street
P.O. Box 788
Augusta, ME 04332
Phone: (207) 622-7523
Fax: (207) 623-0083

Maryland State Bar Association, Inc.
520 West Fayette Street
Baltimore, MD 21201
Phone: (410) 685-7878
Fax: (410) 837-0518

Massachusetts Bar Association
20 West Street
Boston, MA 02111
Phone: (617) 542-3602
Fax: (617) 426-4344

State Bar of Michigan
306 Townsend Street
Lansing, MI 48933-2083
Phone: (517) 372-9030
Fax: (517) 482-6248

Minnesota State Bar Association
514 Nicollet Mall, #300
Minneapolis, MN 55402
Phone: (612) 333-1183
Fax: (612) 333-4927

The Mississippi State Bar
643 North State Street
Jackson, MS 39202
Phone: (601) 948-4471
Fax: (601) 355-8635

The Missouri Bar
326 Monroe Street
P.O. Box 119
Jefferson City, MO 65101
Phone: (573) 635-4128
Fax: (573) 635-2811

State Bar of Montana
46 North Last Chance Gulch
P.O. Box 577
Helena, MT 59624
Phone: (406) 442-7660
Fax: (406) 442-7763

Nebraska State Bar Association
635 South 14th Street
Second Floor
Lincoln, NE 68508
Phone: (402) 475-7091
Fax: (402) 475-7098

State Bar of Nevada
201 Las Vegas Boulevard, #200
Las Vegas, NV 89101
Phone: (702) 382-2200
Fax: (702) 385-2878

New Hampshire Bar Association
112 Pleasant Street
Concord, NH 03301
Phone: (603) 224-6942
Fax: (603) 224-2910

New Jersey State Bar Association
New Jersey Law Center
One Constitution Square
New Brunswick, NJ 08901-1500
Phone: (908) 249-5000
Fax: (908) 249-2815

State Bar of New Mexico
121 Tijeras Street Northeast
Albuquerque, NM 87102
Phone: (505) 842-6132
Fax: (505) 843-8765

New York State Bar Association
One Elk Street
Albany, NY 12207
Phone: (518) 463-3200
Fax: (518) 463-8527

North Carolina State Bar
208 Fayetteville Street Mall
Raleigh, NC 27601
Phone: (919) 828-4620
Fax: (919) 821-9168

North Carolina Bar Association
8000 Western Parkway
Cary, NC 27513
OR: P.O. Box 3688
Cary, NC 27519
Phone: (919) 677-0561
Fax: (919) 677-0761

State Bar Association of North Dakota
515-1/2 East Broadway, #101
Bismarck, ND 58501
OR: P.O. Box 2136
Bismarck, ND 58502
Phone: (701) 255-1404
Fax: (701) 224-1621

Ohio State Bar Association
1700 Lake Shore Drive
Columbus, OH 43216-6562
Phone: (614) 487-2050
Fax: (614) 487-1008

Oklahoma Bar Association
1901 Lincoln Boulevard
Oklahoma City, OK 73105
OR: P.O. Box 53036
Oklahoma City, OK 73152
Phone: (405) 524-2365
Fax: (405) 524-1115

Oregon State Bar
5200 Meadows Road Southwest
P.O. Box 1689
Lake Oswego, OR 97035-0889
Phone: (503) 620-0222
Fax: (503) 684-1366

Pennsylvania Bar Association
100 South Street
Harrisburg, PA 17101
OR: P.O. Box 186
Harrisburg, PA 17108
Phone: (717) 238-6715
Fax: (717) 238-1204

Puerto Rico Bar Association
P.O. Box 1900
San Juan, PR 00903
Phone: (809) 721-3358
Fax: (809) 725-0330

Rhode Island Bar Association
115 Cedar Street
Providence, RI 02903
Phone: (401) 421-5740
Fax: (401) 421-2703

South Carolina Bar
P.O. Box 608
Columbia, SC 29202
Phone: (803) 799-6653
Fax: (803) 799-4118

State Bar of South Dakota
222 East Capital
Pierre, SD 57501
Phone: (605) 224-7554
Fax: (605) 224-0282

Tennessee Bar Association
3622 West End Avenue
Nashville, TN 37205
Phone: (615) 383-7421
Fax: (615) 297-8058

State Bar of Texas
P.O. Box 12487
Austin, TX 78711-2487
Phone: (800) 204-2222
Fax: (512) 463-1475

Utah State Bar
645 South 200 E, #310
Salt Lake City, UT 84111
Phone: (801) 531-9077
Fax: (801) 531-0660

Vermont Bar Association
P.O. Box 100
Montpelier, VT 05601-0100
Phone: (802) 223-2020
Fax: (802) 223-1573

Virginia State Bar
707 East Main Street, #1500
Richmond, VA 23219-2803
Phone: (804) 775-0500
Fax: (804) 775-0501

Virginia Bar Association
701 East Franklin Street, #1120
Richmond, VA 23219
Phone: (804) 644-0041
Fax: (804) 644-0052

Virgin Islands Bar Association
P.O. Box 4108
Christiansted, St. Croix, VI 00822
Phone: (809) 778-7497
Fax: (809) 773-5060

Washington State Bar Association
500 Westin Building
2001 Sixth Avenue
Seattle, WA 98121-2599
Phone: (206) 727-8200
Fax: (206) 727-8320

West Virginia State Bar
2006 Kanawha Boulevard East
Charleston, WV 25311
Phone: (304) 558-2456
Fax: (304) 558-2467

West Virginia Bar Association
P.O. Box 3956
Charleston, WV 25339
Phone: (304) 895-3663

State Bar of Wisconsin
402 West Wilson Street
Madison, WI 53703
Phone: (608) 257-3838
Fax: (608) 257-5502

Wyoming State Bar
500 Randall Avenue
P.O. Box 109
Cheyenne, WY 82001
Phone: (307) 632-9061
Fax: (307) 632-3737

Appendix E

Glossary of Legal Terms & Phrases

Acquittal—The release or discharge of a person who was charged with a crime.

Alternative Dispute Resolution (ADR)—A variety of procedures through which disputing parties can resolve their dispute outside the courtroom. Among the more popular ADR methods are mediation and arbitration.

Affirm—A decision by an appellate court that the judgment of a lower court is correct and should stand.

Answer—A pleading on the part of a defendant in response to a plaintiff's complaint.

Appeal—A complaint to a higher court seeking review and reversal of a lower court's ruling.

Arbitrator—A neutral person either chosen by the parties or the court to resolve a dispute. Arbitrators are the decision makers in an arbitration. An arbitrator hears evidence from all parties involved in a dispute, then issues a decision. An arbitrator has the authority to issue a binding or non-binding decision.

Arraignment—A procedure in the criminal process wherein the accused is informed of the charge(s) pending against him or her and pleads guilty, not guilty, or nolo contendere.

Assault—An intentional and unlawful threat, by word or act, of violence against a victim, where the defendant has the ability to carry out the threat and the victim has a well-founded fear that violence is imminent.

"At-Will" Employment—If an employee's employment contract does not specify a definite term of employment, his or her relationship with the employer is terminable "at will." Either the employer or the employee may terminate the employment relationship at his or her discretion, without any further costs to either party, provided the reasons for termination are not illegal (e.g., race, age, or sex discrimination).

Attorney—Any person who has passed the bar exam and is authorized by the appropriate bar to practice law in a particular jurisdiction. An attorney is regarded as an officer of the court and subject to ethical and professional guidelines. Attorney and lawyer are synonyms.

Bar—A bar or a bar association is a body of attorneys and judges authorized to practice in a particular jurisdiction. A bar can be local, statewide, or national. Bar associations can be voluntary (i.e., an attorney is not required to be a member in order to practice law in the jurisdiction) or mandatory (i.e., every attorney wishing to practice in the jurisdiction must be member). One of the principal responsibilities of a bar association is attorney regulation and assuring that attorneys are abiding by the ethical and professional guidelines governing attorney conduct. Bar associations also serve the public through various services, publications, and public education programs. The largest bar association in Illinois is the Illinois State Bar Association (ISBA).

Battery—The unlawful application of force to another person.

Breach of Contract—The failure of a party to a contract to abide by the terms of the contract. A breach may be minor in nature, in which case the contract may be remedied; or material, in which case the contract is probably destroyed.

Cause of Action—The basis for a lawsuit; a claim (e.g., the negligent practice of medicine resulting in an injury is a cause of action).

Civil—The branch of law pertaining to issues outside of criminal law. For example, lawsuits based on tort or contract are civil lawsuits.

Class Action—A lawsuit brought by a representative plaintiff on behalf of a large number of plaintiffs with the same cause of action. Class action lawsuits benefit both plaintiffs and defendants by consolidating many lawsuits into one.

Common Law—A system of jurisprudence, originating in England and used in the United States, wherein judicial decision making is based upon judicial precedent rather than statutory law.

Glossary of Legal Terms & Phrases

Compensatory Damages—Damages which can be directly attributed to a breach of contract or some tortious activity. Compensatory damages are meant to "compensate" a plaintiff for harm suffered because of action or inaction by the defendant; unlike **punitive damages**, which are meant to "punish" the defendant and are awarded only in instances of malicious or willful misconduct.

Complaint—The legal document filed with the proper court by a plaintiff beginning a lawsuit.

Consideration—A necessary component in the formation of a contract. Consideration is anything of value given in return for a performance or a promise of a performance.

Contract—A promise or a set of promises, the breach of which entitles the non-breaching party to damages. The essential components of a contract are offer, acceptance, and consideration.

Conviction—The legal act whereby a judge or jury declares a defendant guilty of the charges pending.

Counter-Claim—A lawsuit filed by a defendant in response to a plaintiff's lawsuit. A counter-claim is not an answer nor a denial of a plaintiff's claim, but an independent (and related) cause of action.

Crime—A crime is a wrong which affects and is injurious to the public welfare; a wrong for which the state has prescribed a punishment, including fines, imprisonment, or death.

Cross-Examination—The examination of a witness at a trial, hearing, or deposition by the opposing party. The purpose of cross-examination is to test the truth or otherwise develop a witness' testimony. Cross-examination is distinguished from **direct examination,** wherein a witness is examined at a trial, hearing, or deposition by the party producing the witness. The scope of a cross-examination is usually limited by the scope of the direct examination and matters affecting the witness' credibility.

Defamation—An intentional tort whereby the offender harms the reputation of another. Defamation can be in the form of libel (written) or slander (spoken).

Defendant—The subject of a criminal or civil legal proceeding. The defendant in a criminal proceeding is accused by the government of a crime. The defendant in a civil proceeding is accused by the plaintiff of having harmed him or her in some way.

Deposition—A method of pre-trial discovery which consists of a statement of a witness taken in question and answer form and recorded stenographically. One party (through his or her attorney) will depose a witness while the attorney(s) for the other party is present. A deposition can be taken in either a civil or criminal case.

Direct Examination—*See Cross-Examination.*

Discovery—The period in a lawsuit where the parties gather information in preparation for trial. Depositions and interrogatories are the two principal means of discovery.

Due Process—Due process of law is a phrase from the U.S. Constitution. The phrase has taken on two separate but related meanings: procedural and substantive. **Procedural due process** requires that the government provide notice and an opportunity to be heard when depriving a citizen of life, liberty, or property. **Substantive due process** requires that all governmental action be in furtherance of a legitimate government objective and overly burdensome on those it affects.

Durable Power of Attorney—*See Power of Attorney.*

Employee—Any person who works for and is directed by another (the employer) in exchange for compensation; as distinguished from an **independent contractor,** who is not directed by the employer. Employees are entitled to certain state and federal protections such as wage and hour laws, unemployment insurance, and workers' compensation.

Equal Protection—All citizens of the U.S. are entitled to equal protection of the law under the Fourteenth Amendment of the U.S. Constitution. Many state constitutions also guarantee equal protection.

Federal—Of or relating to the national government; as distinguished from state government.

Felony—A criminal classification where the crime is punishable by death (if state has the death penalty) or more than one year imprisonment.

Grand Jury—A panel of citizens summoned to hear evidence as part of the criminal process. A grand jury listens to evidence presented by the government and determines whether the evidence is sufficient to issue an indictment (i.e., a formal written accusation charging one or more persons with a crime).

Hung Jury—*See Jury.*

Independent Contractor—A person who contracts with another to perform a service in exchange for compensation. An independent contractor is not an employee and thus not protected by state and federal wage and hour regulations, entitled to workers' compensation, nor considered an agent of the employer for purposes of liability. The extent of the relationship between an independent contractor and employer is the terms of their contract.

Indictment—*See Grand Jury; Information.*

Appendix E: Glossary of Legal Terms & Phrases

Information—A formal, written accusation charging a person or persons with a crime. All crimes except for capital offenses can be charged with an information. Capital offenses must be charged with an indictment and therefore require the participation of a grand jury.

Intellectual Property—*See Personal Property.*

Intentional Tort—A tort wherein the offender intends the consequences of an act. Examples include defamation, battery, assault, and trespass.

Interrogatory—A pre-trial tool in civil actions in which written questions are served on one party by another, who must make written replies under oath. Interrogatories do not include the opportunity of cross-examination, such as depositions, but they are considered an inexpensive method of gathering information.

Intestate (Intestacy)—To die "intestate" is to die without leaving a valid will. If a person dies intestate, his or her estate is distributed according to a state's intestacy laws. *See Probate.*

Jurisdiction—The power of a court to hear and determine a case. Jurisdiction can be discretionary, in which case a court can decide whether or not it wishes to hear the case; or jurisdiction can be mandatory, in which case a court must hear a case. To have proper jurisdiction over a case, a court must have jurisdiction over both the subject matter of the dispute and the parties to the dispute.

Jurisprudence—The study of law and of legal systems.

Jury—A group of people sworn to decide on the factual issues of a trial, also known as a petit jury; as distinguished from a **grand jury.** Trials by jury can be either criminal or civil in nature. A jury which fails to reach a verdict by whatever degree of agreement is required is a hung jury and the case may be tried again before a different jury.

Law—The rules which govern a person's actions in society. In the U.S., law can be created on both the state and federal level by legislatures, courts, or administrative agencies.

Lawyer—*See Attorney.*

Libel—*See Defamation.*

Limited Liability—A characteristic of a corporation (and a limited partnership) where the owner(s) of the corporation is not personally liable for the debts of the corporation; as distinguished from a **partnership** or **sole proprietorship** where the owner is personally liable for the debts of the business.

Liquidated Damages—An amount stipulated in a contract agreed to by the parties as a reasonable estimation of damages should either of the parties fail to abide by the terms of the contract. A liquidated damages clause is used in contracts where a determination of damages would be difficult in the event of a breach.

Litigation—A legal controversy in the court system initiated by the filing of a complaint by a plaintiff.

Mediator—A neutral third person, chosen by or agreed to by the parties, who attempts to facilitate dispute resolution by promoting discussion between the parties. Unlike an arbitrator or a judge, a mediator has no decision making power. Any resolution arising from a mediation is generally crafted and agreed to by the parties.

Motion—An official request made to a court by a party to a lawsuit asking that the court take a particular course of action.

Naturalization—The process whereby a person born in another country or otherwise reared as an alien is granted U.S. citizenship and the rights and duties of that status.

Negligence—The failure to exercise the degree of care that a reasonable, ordinary, prudent person would exercise under similar circumstances. If a person is found to have negligently caused another harm, he or she may be liable for damages.

Non-Compete Agreement—An agreement between an employer and an employee (or independent contractor) which limits the employee's right to compete with that employee in a given geographic area for a certain period of time. Usually employers ask particularly valuable employees to sign non-compete agreements since the employer could be damaged if the employee left the company to work for a competitor.

Order—A direction by a court regarding some aspect of a lawsuit over which it has jurisdiction. A court may order the parties to do or not do something.

Personal Property—Things which are moveable; as distinguished from **real property,** which is land and/or things fixed upon the land such as buildings and other structures. Personal property is also distinguished from **intellectual property**, which is property created by the mind such as literature and inventions.

Plaintiff—A person who initiates a lawsuit by filing a complaint against a defendant with the proper court.

Glossary of Legal Terms & Phrases

Pleadings—The formal allegations by the parties to a lawsuit of their respective claims and defenses. A complaint is a pleading, as is an **answer.** The purpose of pleadings is to identify and limit those issues which are in dispute. Parties are permitted to amend their pleadings as necessary.

Power of Attorney—A written document in which one person (the principal) authorizes another (the agent) to perform specified acts (usually financial) on his or her behalf. A power of attorney typically dissolves in the event the principal becomes incapacitated. A **durable power of attorney** is a document wherein the principal authorizes the agent to make decisions (including health care decisions) on his or her behalf in the event the principal is incapacitated.

Pre-Trial—The period of time in the process of a lawsuit before the trial. **Discovery** is conducted during pre-trial. Settlement negotiations are also frequently conducted during pre-trial.

Probate—The court-supervised procedure in which the validity of a decedent's (someone who has died) will is determined. If the will is valid, the decedent's estate is distributed pursuant to the terms of the will. If a person dies without a will or the will is invalid, the decedent's estate is distributed pursuant to the state's intestacy laws. All relevant taxes and claims against a decedent's estate are also paid during the probate process.

Procedural Due Process—*See Due Process.*

Prosecutor—A government attorney who prepares and conducts a prosecution of someone charged with a crime. State prosecutors are called district attorneys or county attorneys or county prosecutors. Federal prosecutors are called U.S. attorneys.

Punitive Damages—Compensation in excess of actual or **compensatory damages.** Punitive damages are meant to punish a defendant and are awarded only in instances of malicious or willful misconduct.

Real Property—Land or buildings or structures fixed upon the land. Real property also includes whatever is beneath the land such as minerals, and the area above the land's surface.

Reversal—The setting aside, annulling, or vacating of a lower court's opinion by an appellate court.

Slander—*See Defamation.*

Standard of Proof—The threshold of proof which must be provided in order for a plaintiff or prosecutor to prevail in a trial. In a civil trial, the standard of proof is "by a preponderance of the evidence." That is, a plaintiff must convince a judge or jury by a preponderance of the evidence that a defendant is responsible for whatever the plaintiff claims. Another way of saying a preponderance of the evidence is "more likely than not." In a criminal trial, a prosecutor must convince a jury "beyond a reasonable doubt" that the defendant committed the alleged crime. The criminal standard of proof is higher than that of the civil since in a criminal trial a person's liberty and perhaps his or her life are at stake.

Statute—An act of a legislature pursuant to constitutional authority. A statute may define crimes, create inferior governments, prohibit certain behavior, appropriate public monies, or otherwise direct the conduct of the citizenry within the legislature's jurisdiction.

Statute of Limitations—A statute which sets the period of time in which a criminal or civil lawsuit must be filed. If a lawsuit is not filed within the period set by a statute of limitations, the right to file that lawsuit is lost.

Strict Liability—A tort law theory of recovery in which a defendant is found liable regardless of fault. Strict liability applies to injuries caused by wild animals, ultrahazardous activities, and consumer products.

Strict Scrutiny—A test to determine the constitutional validity of a law or government action which creates a classification of persons or burdens a person's fundamental right. Under this test, which is part of a court's **substantive due process** analysis, the law or government action must be the least intrusive way of achieving some compelling government interest. If the government interest is not compelling or if there is a less intrusive means of achieving the same end, the government activity will be declared unconstitutional. Government actions which undergo a strict scrutiny analysis are rarely found to be constitutional.

Subpoena—A legal document issued by a court which compels the appearance of a witness at a judicial proceeding. A subpoena may also require the production of certain documents, books, papers or other items.

Substantive Due Process—*See Due Process.*

Tort—A wrong committed against another which caused harm and for which the law provides a remedy in civil court. Defamation is an example of a tort; as is negligently damaging someone's property or person.

Trade Secret—Any confidential information, machine, pattern or process which may give its user an advantage in the marketplace. A trade secret is the property of its owner or creator and cannot be divulged without proper authorization.

Trial—The judicial hearing and determination of the disputed issues between the parties to a lawsuit. Trials are conducted in both the civil and criminal legal systems. The judge in a trial decides questions of law (i.e., those questions which require an interpretation of law, whether statute, administrative law, or case law) and, in some cases, will consider the evidence and issue a verdict. This is known as a bench trial. In a trial by jury, the jury considers the evidence and, after deliberating, reaches a verdict.

Trustee—A person who holds legal title to property "in trust" for the benefit of another person.

Vacate—*See Reversal.*

Venue—The proper court for a trial within a particular jurisdiction. For example, assuming a lawsuit is properly brought in state county court, venue determines the county in which the lawsuit should be heard. Parties can petition a court for a change of venue within a jurisdiction if they believe they may not receive a fair trial in the present court or if another court would be more convenient.

Verdict—The judgment of a jury or a judge (if there is no jury) regarding the factual question(s) of a trial.

Visa—A stamp in a person's passport giving a person permission to enter a country. In some cases, citizens of one country may travel to another country for a limited period of time without obtaining a visa.

Voir Dire—The process of selecting a jury for a trial. During a voir dire examination the attorneys for the parties ask prospective jurors questions to determine their qualifications for jury service. Voir dire permits attorneys to "challenge" or excuse prospective jurors they feel are ill-suited for jury service.

Workers' Compensation—A program pursuant to state law which requires most employers to have an insurance policy covering workers who are injured on the job. Eligible workers may be entitled to payments for medical costs, disability, death, or lost wages. Workers' compensation premiums are paid for by the employer and not the employee.

SUBJECT MATTER INDEX

A

Abstract of Title. 287
Abuse 171
Abused and Neglected Child Reporting Act 173
Acceptance, Contracts 27
Adopting a Child from Another Country 32
Adopting Stepchildren 30
Adoption Agencies. 31
Adoption in Illinois 30
Adoption Information Center of Illinois. 33
Adoption Law 30
Adoption Placements and Procedures. 31
Adoptive Parents 30
ADR (Alternative Dispute Resolution). 38
ADR Providers 40
ADR Training and Education. 40
ADR Costs 40
Adultery 168
Affirm. 79
Age Discrimination 134
Age Discrimination in Employment. 118
Age Discrimination in Employment Act of 1967
   (ADEA) 119, 133, 134
Aggravated DUI. 90
Aiding and Abetting. 88, 99
Alcohol and Drug-Related Traffic Offenses 89
Alcoholic Beverages and Vehicles 89
Alien 219
Alimony. 170
Alternative Dispute Resolution (ADR). 38
Americans with Disabilities Act of 1990 (ADA). . . . 133, 134
Annulment, Legal and Religious 171
Answer 12
Antenuptial agreement. 167
Appeal. 77
Appealing an Audit 323
Appeals Courts and Appellate Procedure 77, 79
Appellant. 77
Appellate Decision. 79
Appellee 77
Applying for Social Security Benefits 314
Appointing a Guardian for Children. 152
Arbitration. 39
Arraignment 13
Arson. 12
Art Dealers 54
Artists Contracts 54
Artists' Moral Rights 53
Arts, Entertainment & Intellectual Property Law 49
Assault. 100
Assault and Battery 231
Assessment, Real Estate. 285
Asylees 221
Attempt to Commit a Crime. 88, 99
Attorney Advertising 1
Attorney Fees 5
Attorney Registration and Disciplinary Commission 3
Attorney Reputation. 2
Audit Process. 321
Automatic Citizenship 219
Automobile Accidents 275
Automobile Buyer Protection. 21
Available Benefits 332
Aviation Accidents. 276

B

Bail. 13
Bank Fraud 103
Bankruptcy Code. 62
Bankruptcy Law 62
Bankruptcy Rules of Procedure 62
Bankruptcy, Alternatives 67
Battery. 100
Becoming a Naturalized Citizen. 221
Beneficiary 151
Benefits for Retirees 310
Bilateral Contract. 27
Bill of Rights. 15
Bill of Rights for Victims and Witnesses of Violent
   Crime Act. 105
Blood Alcohol Concentration (BAC) 89
Body of Evidence/Record 79
Breach. 259, 261
Breach of Warranty 231
Bribery 102
Burden of Proof in a Civil Case 11, 229
Burden of Proof in a Criminal Case 12, 229
Burglary. 89, 101

Index F: Subject Matter Index

Business Name Registration. 302
Buying a Home 287
Buying from a Used Car Dealer. 22

C

Capacity of the Parties, Contracts. 28
Certificate of Assumed Name. 302
Changing and Updating Wills 153
Chapter 11, Bankruptcy. 66
Chapter 12, Bankruptcy. 66
Chapter 13, Bankruptcy. 63
Chapter 7, Bankruptcy. 62
Chapter 9, Bankruptcy. 66
Child Abuse. 173
Child Custody 169
Child Labor. 135
Child Pornography. 19, 173
Child Prostitution or Pornography 173
Child Sexual Abuse Prevention Act 173
Child Support 169
Children's Advocacy Center Act 173
Choosing a Lawyer 1
Civil Appellate Law. 77
Civil Cases 11
Civil Jury Trials. 11
Civil Lawsuit 228, 259
Civil Pretrial Process 11
Civil Process 11
Civil Rights. 15
Civil Rights Act of 1964 133
Civil Rights Act of 1991 133
Civil Rights Crimes 89
Civil Rights in the Workplace 133
Claims, Bankruptcy 63
Class Actions. 11
Classifications That Infringe Upon Fundamental
   Rights. 17
Classifications, Government. 16
Closing Arguments 13
Co-Owning Property 286
Codicil. 153
Cold Weather Utility Rule 291
Collection Agencies. 67
Commercial Speech. 19
Commission on Legal Problems for the Elderly,
   American Bar Association. 125
Commitment to a State Institution 121
Common Law Marriage. 167
Comparative Fault 228
Comparative Fault Rule 229
Complaint. 11
Computer Crime 102
Computer Fraud. 102
Computer Tampering 102
Condominiums. 286
Confirmation Hearing 64
Conflicting Trademark. 52
Consent Forms. 261

Consideration. 28
Consignment Agreement 54
Conspiracy. 88, 99
Constitutional Law & Civil Rights. 15
Consulting a Lawyer 4
Consumer Protection 21
Consumer Reporting Agencies. 25
Contingent Fee 6
Contract Breach. 29
Contract Components. 27
Contract Fraud. 28
Contract Law. 27
Contract, Void 28
Contracts Involving the Sale of Real Estate 28, 29
Controlled Substances 101
Copyright. 49
Copyright Infringement 50
Copyright Notice 50
Copyright Office of the Library of Congress 50, 55
Copyright Ownership. 49
Copyright Protection 49
Copyrighted Work 49
Corporation 301
Corporations and Double Taxation. 301
Costs Not Covered by Medicare. 124
Counterclaims 12
Counteroffer 27
Court of Appeals for the Seventh Circuit 79
Covered Employment (RSI). 310
Credit Card Scams. 22
Credit Counselors 67
Credit History 25
Credit Rating. 65
Credit Report. 25
Creditors Meeting 63
Crime Victims' Rights 90, 105
Crimes Causing Harm to Persons. 100
Crimes Causing Harm to Property 89
Criminal Cases. 12, 88, 99
Criminal Codes 88, 99
Criminal Housing Management 289
Criminal Law: DUI & Misdemeanors 88
Criminal Law: Felonies & White Collar Crime 99
Criminal Pretrial Process 12
Criminal Process 12
Criminal Sexual Assault. 100
Cross-Examination. 13

D

Damages 229
DCFS (Department of Children and Family Services . 31, 173
Debt Collection Agencies. 25, 67
Debt Collection Laws 25
Deceptive Collections Practices 103
Declaration of Invalidity of Marriage. 171
Deed Restriction 285
Deeds. 287
Defacement of Property 89

Subject Matter Index

Defamation	53
Defective Products	230
Defendant	11
Defenses	229
Defenses and Punishment	104
Defenses to Contract	28
Degree of Fault	228
Delinquent Acts	90
Department of Public Aid, Division of Child Support Enforcement	175
Deportation	222
Deposition	12
Design Patent	51
Direct Examination	13
Disability Benefits	123, 311
Discovery	12
Discrimination Against Persons with Disabilities	134
Discrimination in Housing	291
Disinheriting a Spouse or Child	152
Dissolution of Marriage	168
Diversity Immigrants	221
Division of Property	170
Divorce	168
Domestic Abuse	171
Domestic Violence	171
Door-to-Door Sales	23
Driving Under the Influence (DUI)	89
Drug and Alcohol Tests and Employment	135
Due Process	17
DUI (Driving Under the Influence)	89
Duress	28
Duty	259
Dying Without a Will	153

E

Early Neutral Evaluation (ENE)	39
Easement	285
Effects of Declaring Bankruptcy	65
Elder Law	118
Embezzlement	102
Employee Access to Personnel Records	137
Employee Resignation	131
Employees' Right to Privacy	136
Employer's First Report of Injury or Illness Form	333
Employer's Right to Terminate Employees	131
Employer–Employee Problems	131
Employment at Will	131
Employment Discrimination	133
Employment Law	131
Employment-Based Immigration	220
Encumbrance	285
Entrapment	104
Entry and Exclusion	221
Equal Employment Opportunity Commission (EEOC)	134
Equal Protection of the Law	15, 16
Error	79
Establishment Clause	19
Estate Planning, Wills & Trusts Law	151

Ethnic Classifications	16
Eviction	290
Exclusive Jurisdiction	8
Exempt Assets, Bankruptcy	62

F

False Imprisonment	231
False Statements	103
Family and Medical Leave Act of 1993 (FMLA)	136
Family Law	167
Family-Based Immigration	221
Fault Divorce	168
Federal Appellate Structure	79
Federal Court of Appeals	10
Federal Courts	9
Federal District Court	9
Federal Drug and Gun Laws	101
Federal Employer Identification Number	302
Federal Employer's Liability Act (FELA)	276
Federal Fair Credit Reporting Act	25
Federal Insurance Contributions Act (FICA)	310
Federal Tax Disputes	320
Federal Trade Commission's Funeral Practices Trade Regulation Rule	25
Federal Used Motor Vehicle Trade Regulation Rule	22
Fees and Expenses, Attorneys	5
FELA (Federal Employer's Liability Act)	276
Felonies	12, 100
Felony Criminal Case	12, 99
FICA (Federal Insurance Contributions Act)	310
Fiduciary Obligations	259
Fifteenth Amendment	18
Fifth Amendment	15, 17
Final Adoption Order	32
Final Judgments	78
Finalizing an Adoption	32
Firearms	101
First Amendment	19
First Degree Murder	12, 100
First Stop Business Information Center	302
Flat Fee	5
FMLA (Family and Medical Leave Act of 1993)	136
Foreclosure	288
Forgery	103
Fourteenth Amendment	15, 17, 18
Franchise	302
Fraud	103
Fraudulent Conveyances	66
Freedom of Expression	53
Freedom of Religion	19
Funerals, Burial and Cremation	24

G

General Accidents and Injuries	231
General Jurisdiction	8

July 1996 389

General Partners 300
General Partnership 299
General Warranty Deed 287
Get-Rich-Quick Schemes 24
Government Administered Benefits 132
Green Card 221
Grounds for Dissolution 168
Guardianship 121

H

Hate Crime 101
Health Maintenance Organization (HMO) 124, 313
Hearing Aid Sales 24
High-Risk Adults with Disabilities 174
Holographic Will 151
Home Ownership 286
Home Solicitations 23
Home Study, Adoption 31
Home Warranties 287
Homestead 286
Homicide 100
Hospital Insurance 124, 312
Hourly Rate 5
How to Hire an Attorney 1
Hung Jury 12

I

IHRA and ADEA, Relationship Between 119
Illegal Confinement 231
Illegal Discrimination 16
Illinois Adoption Act 30
Illinois Appellate Court 9
Illinois Child Care Act 31
Illinois Circuit Courts 9
Illinois Coalition Against Domestic Violence .. 175
Illinois Comprehensive Health Insurance Plan 124, 314
Illinois Constitution 15
Illinois Crime Victims Reparation Board 105
Illinois Criminal Code 89
Illinois Department of Children and Family Services (DCFS) 31, 173
Illinois Department of Children and Family Services, Adoption and Guardianship Section 33
Illinois Department of Children and Family Services, Division of Child Protection 175
Illinois Department of Employment Security 132
Illinois Department of Human Rights 118, 134
Illinois Department of Labor 137
Illinois Department of Public Aid 313
Illinois Department of Public Health, Office of Vital Records 175
Illinois Department of Transportation 275
Illinois Department on Aging 174
Illinois Department on Aging, Division of Older American Services 125

Illinois Domestic Violence Act of 1986 .... 171, 174
Illinois Guardians for Disabled Adults Act 121
Illinois Health Care Surrogate Act 119
Illinois Home Repair Fraud Act 26
Illinois Housing Development Authority 291
Illinois Human Rights Act (IHRA) 89, 118, 139
Illinois Industrial Commission 133, 137
Illinois Lemon Law 21
Illinois Not-For-Profit Dispute Resolution Center Act 38, 40
Illinois Parentage Act 171
Illinois Retaliatory Eviction Act 290
Illinois Safety Responsibility Law 275
Illinois Second Injury Law 333
Illinois State Criminal Code 99
Illinois Supreme Court 9
Illinois Tax Disputes 324
Illinois Used Car Warranty Law 22
Illinois Victims Rights Constitutional Amendment ... 91, 105
Illinois Workers' Compensation Act 232, 331
Illinois' Appellate Structure 80
Illinois' Judicial Systems 8
Illinois' Mandatory Insurance (Motorists) 275
Illinois' New Vehicle Buyer Protection Act 21
Immigrant 219
Immigrant Visas 220
Immigration and Naturalization Service (INS) 219, 222
Immigration Law 219
Implied Warranty of Habitability 287
In-House Collections 25, 67
Independent Administration 155
Independent Contractor Versus Employee 131
Indictment 12
Infringement, Copyright 50
Initial Consultation with an Attorney 4
Initiating an Adoption 31
Injunction 11
Injury 260
(INS) Immigration and Naturalization Service 219, 222
Insider Trading 104
Insurance Fraud 23
Insurance Issues Related to Medicare 124
Intellectual Property 49
Intellectual Property Rights 49
Intent to Commit a Crime 88, 99
Intentional Misconduct 228
Intercountry Adoptions 32
Intermediate Scrutiny 16
Internal Revenue Service (IRS) 320
Interrogatories 12
Interstate Compact on the Placement of Children 31
Intestacy 153
Intimidation 101
Invalid Marriages 171
Invention 50
Investigation of Child Abuse 174
Involuntary Bankruptcy 65
Involuntary Manslaughter 100
Irrevocable Trusts 154
IRS Audit 320

J

Joint Legal Custody	169
Joint Parenting Agreement	169
Joint Physical Custody	169
Joint Tenancy	286
Judgment of Dissolution of Marriage	168
Judgment of Legal Separation	170
Jurisdiction	8
Jury Trial	13
Juvenile Court System	90
Juvenile Gang Violence	90
Juveniles and the Law	90

K

Kidnapping	101

L

Landlord–Tenant Issues	288
Landowner Liability	231
Lead Poisoning Prevention Act	288
Leases	288
Legal Aid	7
Legal Malpractice	259
Legal Separation	171
Libel	53
Lien	285
Limited Jurisdiction	8
Limited Liability Partnership	301
Limited Partners	300
Limited Partnership	300
Liquidated Damages	29
Liquidation Bankruptcy	62
Living Trust (inter vivos trust)	154
Living Will	120

M

Mail Fraud	103
Malpractice Insurance	4
Malpractice Lawsuit	259
Management or Booking Contract	54
Mandatory Appeals	80
Mandatory Arbitration	12
Mandatory Reporters	173
Mandatory Retirement Policies	134
Manslaughter	100
Marital Debts	170
Marital Property	170
Marital Settlement Agreements	168
Maritime Personal Injury	276
Marriage in Illinois	167
Marriage Licenses	167
Maternity Leave	135
Mechanic's Lien	285
Mediation	38
Mediation-Arbitration	39
Medicaid	122, 310, 312
Medical Assistance	312
Medical Insurance	124, 312
Medical Malpractice	260
Medicare	123, 312
Medicare Parts A and B	124, 312
Medigap	313
Mental Injury	173
Military	18
Mini-Trial	39
Minimizing Litigation and Attorney Fees in Divorce Cases	168
Minimum Wage	135
Miranda Warning	12
Misdemeanors	12, 89
Mistake, Duress and Fraud	28
Mistrial	12
Motor Vehicle Accidents	275
Murder	12, 100
Mutual Release Agreement	54

N

National Adoption Information Clearinghouse	33
National Center on Women and Family Law, Inc.	175
National Clearinghouse on Marital and Date Rape	175
National Coalition Against Sexual Assault	105
National Council on Child Abuse and Family Violence	175
National Organization for Victim Assistance	105
National Senior Citizens Law Center	155
Natural or Birth Parents	30
Naturalization	219
Neglect	173
Negligence	228
Negligent Design or Manufacture	230
Neutral Fact-Finding	39
No-Asset Cases, Bankruptcy	63
No-Fault Divorce	168
Non-Custodial Parent	169
Non-Dischargeable Debts	63
Non-Marital Property	170
Nonimmigrant	219
Nonimmigrant Visas	220
Nonprofit Corporation	301
Nonviolent Crimes	102
Notice of Appeal	80

O

Obscene Material	53
Obscenity	19
Obstruction of Justice	103
Offer, Contracts	27

Open Versus Closed Adoption 30
Opening Statement. 13
Order of Protection 172
Overtime Regulations. 135

P

Parol Evidence Rule 28
Partnership. 299
Patent 50
Patent and Trademark Depository Libraries 51, 55
Patent, Searches. 51
Paternity 171
Pay-per-Call Services Consumer Protection Act. 26
Peremptory Challenge 13
Performance 27
Performance Agreement. 54
Perjury. 103
Permanent Resident 219
Personal Injury Law: General. 228
Personal Injury Law: Medical &Professional
   Malpractice. 259
Personal Injury Law: Transportation 275
Personal Jurisdiction 8
Personal Referrals 2
Personal Representative 151
Petition for an Order of Protection 172
Petitioning for Certiorari 80
Petty Offenses 12
Physical Abuse. 173
Physical Custody 169
Physical Problems Caused by Work 332
Plaintiff 11
Planning for Incapacity 152
Plant Patent 51
Plea 13
Plea Bargaining 13
Pleadings. 12
Postnuptial Agreements 168
Power of Attorney 152
Power of Attorney for Health Care. 120
Pre-Sentence Investigation 13
Preferences, Bankruptcy 66
Pregnancy Discrimination 135
Pregnant Workers. 135
Prenuptial or Premarital Agreements 167
Primary Insurance Amount (PIA). 122, 311
Privacy. 18
Private Possession of Obscene Material 19
Prize Mailings 23
Probate 155
Procedural Due Process 17
Process of a Case: Civil & Criminal. 11
Product Liability 230
Professional Malpractice 259
Property Crimes. 101
Protecting Creative Work 49
Proximate Cause 260

Public Search Library of the Patent and Trademark
   Office 51, 52
Punitive Damages 229
Pyramid Schemes 24

Q

Qualified Medicare Beneficiary Program (QMB) . . . 124, 314
Qualifying for Medicaid. 314
Quitclaim Deed 287

R

Racketeer Influenced and Corrupt Organizations
   Act (RICO). 103
Railroad Accidents. 276
Railroad Retirement Benefits 311
Railroad Retirement System 123, 311
Rape 89, 100
Rational Basis Scrutiny 16
Reaffirmation. 63
Real Estate Agents 287
Real Estate Law. 285
Real Estate Taxes. 285
Real Property. 285
Reckless Homicide 100
Record/Body of Evidence 79
Referral Services 2
Refugees 221
Refusing Medical Treatment 18, 20
Registering a Copyright 50
Registering a Trademark 51
Relative Adoption 30
Released on Bail 13
Relevant Experience 4
Remand 79
Rental Contracts 288
Rental Security Deposit 288
Repetitive Stress Injuries 332
Report of Child Abuse or Neglect 173
Requirements for a Valid Will 151
Requirements for Appealing a Decision 78
Rescission 29
Residential Parent 169
Residential Real Estate. 286
Residential Real Property Disclosure Act 287
Respondeat Superior 229
Restitution 90, 105
Restraining Order 11
Restrictions on Wills 152
Result of an Audit 322
Retailer's Occupation Tax Number. 302
Retainer Fees 5
Retaining an Attorney 4
Retirement and Survivors Insurance (RSI) 122, 310
Retirement Assistance 310

Subject Matter Index

Retirement, Survivors, and Disability Health Insurance (RSDHI) 122, 310
Reverse 79
Revocable Trust 154
(RICO) Racketeer Influenced and Corrupt Organizations Act 103
Right of Election 153
Right to Abortion and Contraception 18
Right to Assemble Peacefully 15
Right to be Free from Discrimination 15
Right to Free Speech 15, 19
Right to Practice a Religion Freely 15
Right to Privacy 15, 18
Right to Refuse Medical Treatment 18
Rights Within Marriage 168
Robbery 89, 101
Role of Constitutions 15
RSDHI Disability Insurance 123, 311
RSI (Retirement and Survivors Insurance) 122

S

S Corporation 301
Second Degree Murder 100
Securities and Exchange Act of 1934 104
Securities Fraud 104
Selecting a Jury 13
Selecting Legal Services 1
Self-Defense 104
Seller Disclosures 287
Selling a Home 287
Selling Artwork 54
Selling Used Cars 22
Semi-Suspect Classifications 17
Sentencing Hearing 13
Separation of Church and State 19
Service Mark and Trademark 51
Seventh Circuit Court of Appeals 10
Sex Crimes 89
Sexual Abuse 173
Sexual Exploitation 19
Sexual Harassment 134
Sexual Orientation 18
Sham Marriages 221
Shareholders 301
Shopping Agreement 54
Slander 53
Small Business Law 299
Small Claims Court 14
Social Security 122, 132
Social Security Act in 1935 .... 122, 310
Social Security Law 310
Sole Legal Custody 169
Sole Proprietorship 299
Special Classes of Immigrants 221
Specific Performance 29
Specified Low-Income Medicare Beneficiary Program (SLMB) 124, 314
Spousal Maintenance 170

Spousal Obligations 167
SSI (Supplemental Security Income) 122, 123, 310, 312
Stalking 101
Standards of Scrutiny 16
State Action 18
State and Federal Courts 9
State Courts 9
State Supplemental Payments (SSP) 123, 312
Statute of Frauds 28
Statutes of Limitations 11
Statutory Rape 100
Statutory Share of an Estate 153
Stay, Bankruptcy 63
Strict Liability 228
Strict Product Liability 230
Strict Scrutiny 16
Subject Matter Jurisdiction 8
Sublease 290
Substance Abuse in the Workplace 135
Substantive Due Process 17-18
Suicide 100
Suing the Government 230
Summary Administration 155
Summary Jury Trial 40
Summons 12
Supervised Administration 155
Supplemental Security Income (SSI) 122, 123, 310
Surviving Joint Tenant 152
Suspect Classifications 16

T

Tax Avoidance 320
Tax Court 323
Tax Crimes 104
Tax Evasion 320
Tax Identification Numbers 302
Tax Law 320
Tax-Exempt Status 301
Taxpayer Rights in an IRS Audit 321
Telemarketing Fraud 22
Telephone and Mail Fraud 22
Tenant Damages 289
Tenant Rights 290
Tenants in Common 286
Termination of Marriage 168
Testamentary Trusts 154
Testator 151
Testimony 13
Theft 89, 101
Third Party Lawsuits 261
Three-Day Cooling-Off Law 23
Title Insurance 286
Title to Real Estate 286
Title VII 133, 135
Tort Action 228, 259
Tort Law 228
Townhouses 286
Trademark and Service Mark 51

July 1996 393

Index F: Subject Matter Index

Trademark Registration 51
Trademark Trial and Appeal Board 52
Trademark, Searches 52
Transfers to Avoid Losing an Asset in Bankruptcy 66
Transmission of HIV 100
Trial Process 13
Trusts. 154

U

U.S. Constitution 15
U.S. Supreme Court. 10
Unemployment Benefits. 132
Unemployment Compensation Insurance 132
Uniform Arbitration Act. 39
Uniform Fraudulent Transfer Act 66
Uniform Premarital Agreement Act 167
Unilateral Contract. 27
United States Citizenship 219
United States Department of Commerce, Patent and
    Trademark Office 51, 55
Unrelated Adoption 30
Unsolicited Merchandise Act 23
Utility Patent 50
Utility Suspension 290

V

Validity of a Contract. 28
Variable Contingent Fee. 6
Venue 9
Vicarious Liability 229
Violation of the Conditions of a Visa 222
Violations of Orders of Protection 172
Visa. 219
Visa Categories 220
Visa System. 219
Visitation and Parenting Time 169
Visual Artists Rights Act (VARA) 53
Void and Voidable Marriages 171

W

W-2 Form 321
Wage-Earner Plan, Bankruptcy 63
Wages and Hours. 135
Warrant for Arrest 12
Whistleblowing 136
White Collar Crime 100, 102
Wills 151
Wire fraud 103
Withholding Rent. 289
Work-at-Home Scams 24
Work-Related Injuries 331
Worker's Rights. 131
Workers' Compensation 232
Workers' Compensation Benefit Payments 333
Workers' Compensation Benefits Denied 334
Workers' Compensation Coverage 331
Workers' Compensation Insurance 132
Workers' Compensation Law 331
Workplace Environment. 132
Workplace Injuries. 331
Workplace Rights and Responsibilities. 135
Writ of Error 78
Wrongful Death Lawsuit 229

Z

Zero Tolerance, Blood Alcohol Content 89

INDEX G

ATTORNEY EXTENSIVE EXPERIENCE INDEX

The following is an index of items cited by attorneys in the "Extensive Experience" boxes found in many of the biographical profiles in this *Guidebook*. The purpose of this index is to provide *Guidebook* users with a means of locating profiled Leading Illinois Attorneys with the legal issue-specific experience desired.

When using this index, look for a subject under related categories in the particular area of law. For example, "Custody" may be listed under "Custody Issues" as well as under "Divorce/Custody Issues." Also, search for terms with similar or same meanings. For example, "Maintenance" can be found under "Maintenance Issues" as well as "Support & Maintenance."

- Adoption 189, 203, 211
- Adoption Law & Custody Litigation 36
- Adoption Law Litigation 185
- ADR Process Advice 47
- Age Discrimination Claims .149
- Age/Race/Gender Discrimination 145
- Air Disasters/Train Crashes .281
- Alimony & Child Support Arrearages 204
- Alternative Dispute Resolution 183, 190
- Appeals 190
- Appellate Litigation 241
- Artists, Retrieving Monies Due 61
- Asset Protection 160, 328
- Automobile Accidents 239, 253, 256
  also see Motor Vehicle Accidents
- Aviation 239
- Bankruptcy 329, 330
- Bankruptcy Litigation & Appeals 72
- Bankruptcy Litigation, Complex 74
- Bankruptcy-Creditors 74
- Bankruptcy-Debtors 74
- Bankruptcy, Nondischargeability/Denial of Discharge .73
- Bankruptcy, Preferential Transfers 73
- Bankruptcy, Trial Work 73
- Birth Injuries 266
- Birth Injury Litigation 268
- Birth Trauma 252
- Bus/Vehicular Crashes 281
- Business Disputes 44
- Business Litigation 307, 308
- Business Organizations 162
- Business Reorganization 74
- Business Structure & Planning 328
- Cancer, Failure to Diagnose 252
- Cases Before Human Rights Commission 142
- Casino/Riverboat Injuries 342

- Chapter 7 Bankruptcy 75
- Chapter 7 Cases 71
- Chapter 7, Consumer & Corporation 71
- Chapters 7, 11 & 13 72
- Chapter 11 Cases 71, 76
- Chapter 13, Consumer & Business 71
- Chapter 13 Wage Earner Plan 75
- Charitable Remainder Trusts 166
- Child Abuse & Neglect 206
- Child/Guardian Ad Litem Matters 36, 185
- Children's Rights 197
- Civil Appeals 47, 85
- Civil Rights 148
- Civil Trials 270
- Commercial Litigation 162, 247
- Computer Law 84
- Conflict Resolution Plan Development 46
- Construction Accidents 248, 346
- Construction Site Claims 257
- Copyright Litigation 60
- Corporate Assignments 71
- Criminal Law, Trials Involving Credibility Issues . . .114
- Criminal Matters, Complex 96, 112
- Custody Cases, Contested 202, 214
- Custody 182, 184, 186, 190, 194, 197, 198, 202,
   . . . . .204, 206, 209, 210, 211, 212, 214, 215
- Custody & Property Trials .190
- Custody & Visitation 182, 193, 199, 207, 216, 196
- Custody Mediation 46
- Debt Restructure 74
- Defamation Against Media Defendants 47, 85
- Disability & Minor's Trusts 163
- Disability Discrimination 145
- Discrimination 146
- Dispute Resolution 182
- Dissolution of Marriage 184, 212

Index G: Attorney Extensive Experience Index

- Dissolutions, Contested 182
- Division of Retirement Benefits 204
- Divorce .182, 186, 202, 203, 206
- Divorce & Custody Trials .204
- Divorce Litigation 45, 184, 188, 196, 198, 207, 209
- Divorce Mediation 45, 184
- Divorce, Custody & Related Trials 208
- Divorce-Related Business Evaluations 204
- Divorce/Custody 189
- Domestic Violence 191
- Domestic Violence & Spousal Abuse 208
- Drafting of Wills & Trusts 164
- Drug Offenses 117
- DUI & Misdemeanors 96, 112, 114
- Elder Law 163
- Employee Benefits 330
- Employment Cases, Litigation of 142, 144
- Employment Contracts, Negotiations of 144
- Employment Discharge 216
- Employment Discrimination 143, 146, 148
- Employment Mediation 44
- Entertainment Contracts, Negotiation of 61
- Environmental Issues/Zoning Issues 296
- Estate Administration 164
- Estate Planning 160, 162
- Estate Planning, Trusts & Probate 186
- Estate Tax Returns & Tax Planning 163
- Estates & Wills, Contested 163
- FELA 283
- Family & Divorce Mediation 44
- Family Law & Custody Litigation 185
- Family Law Litigation 36, 195
   also see Matrimonial Law
- Family Law Litigation, Complex 190
- Family Law-Related Matters 188
- Family Law, Trial of Complex Cases 214
- Family Law Valuation Issues, Complex 209
- Farm & Business Estate Planning 164
- Farm Estate Planning 165
- Federal & State Tax Litigation 329
- Federal Civil Rights 47, 85
- Felonies/Misdemeanors, Professionals 114
- Financial Aspects 190
- Financial Disputes 193
- Foreclosure Law 71
- Foreclosures/Evictions/Condemnations 296
- Fraud 112
- Guardianship 129
- Guardianship, Contested 161
- Guardianship of Adults 163
- H Visas/Permanent Residency 226
- Health Care Law 256
- Health Law 165
- Heirship, Contested 163
- Homicide, Reckless 117
- Identification/Division of Assets 193
- Immigration Matters 227
- Insurance Coverage & Acquisitions 307
- Insurance Issues 253
- Intellectual Property Insurance Coverage 60
- IRS Appeals 329
- IRS Defense 328
- J-1 Visa Waivers 226
- Labor & Employment Matters 47
- Large Arbitration Disputes 307
- Legislative Consulting 339
- Lender Liability 76
- Lien & Mortgage Matters .73
- Liquidations & Reorganizations 72
- Living Trusts 161, 165, 166
- Maintenance & Child Support 193
- Maintenance Issues 212
- Maintenance Requests 211
- Malpractice Cases 244
- Malpractice/Products Liability 243
- Marital Property Rights 189
- Matrimonial Law 183, 186, 216
   also see Family Law
- Mediation 194, 195, 202, 211
- Mediator-Alternative Dispute Resolution 243
- Mediators, Training of 46
- Medicaid Issues 129
- Medical Malpractice 239, 240, 241, 248, 253, 268
- Medical Malpractice Defense 84
- Medical Malpractice Litigation 266
- Medical Negligence 246, 253, 266, 270, 280
- Medical Products 273
- Mortgage Banking 73
- Mortgage Foreclosure 76
- Motor Vehicle Accidents 248, 269
   also see Automobile Accidents and Trucks & Motorcycle Cases
- Multi-Party Disputes 47
- Murder & Other Violent Felonies 112
- Murder/Capital Murder 114
- Murder, First & Second Degree 117
- Narcotics Felonies 112
- Narcotics/Violent Crimes .114
- 911 & Paramedic Negligence 243
- Orthopedic/Neurological Causation Issues 345
- "Palimony" 196
- Patent/Trademark/Copyright Application 59
- Patent/Trademark/Copyright Law 59
- Patent/Trademark/Copyright Litigation 59
- Paternity 186, 199, 215
- Paternity & Non-Support .208
- Personal Injury, General 240, 243, 244,
   . . . . .247, 268, 339, 346
- Personal Injury Trial Litigation 241
- Post-Decree Matters (Family Law) 193
- Postjudgment Litigation (Family Law) 196
- Premises Liability (Personal Injury Issues) 257
- Prenuptial Agreements 184, 196
- Prenuptial & Postnuptial Agreements 188
- Probate 330
- Product Liability Defense .84
- Products Liability 239, 240, 241, 244, 246, 249, 250, 255,
   . . . .257, 267, 268, 269, 272, 273, 274, 280, 281, 283, 344
- Professional Malpractice 273
- Professional/Medical Negligence 255
- Property Division 198, 211, 212, 214
- Property Matters 215

- Property Settlements, Complex 207, 214
- Protection, Orders of (Family Law Issues) 203
- Public Employer Labor Relations 217
- Publicity & Packaging, Rights to 61
- Publishing Contracts 60
- Railroad & Truck Accident Cases 239
- Real Estate Closings/Litigation 296
- Real Estate Law 183
- Real Estate Leasing & Acquisitions 308
- Real Estate Reorganization 73
- Removal of Children from Illinois 210
- Removal Petitions 214
- Repetitive Traumas 342
- Representing Health Care Institutions 226
- Retaliatory Discharge ,....................146, 149
- Roll-Over & Air Bags (Personal Injury Issues) 252
- Search & Seizure Matters 114
- Securities & Commodities Law 45
- Separation Agreements, Negotiations of 144
- Sexual Harassment 143, 145, 146
- Shareholder Litigation 76
- Small Business Incorporation 308
- Social Security Disability 346
- Spousal Impoverishment 129
- State Tax Disputes 329
- Support & Maintenance 182
  also see Alimony and Maintenance Issues
- Support/Property Division 199
- Tax Investigations, Criminal & Civil 329
- Tax Litigation 329
- Tax Planning/Connection with Divorce 191
- Tax Structure & Planning 160
- Taxation 186
- Title VII & Human Rights Litigation 149
- Trademarks 227
- Transportation 241, 268
- Transportation Liability 280
- Transportation—Trucking 246
- Truck & Motorcycle Cases 257
  also see Motor Vehicle Accidents
- UCC Article 9 76
- Vehicular Accidents 248
  also see Motor Vehicle Accidents, Automobile Accidents and Truck & Motorcycle Cases
- Vehicular Cases 255
- Vehicle Injuries 243
- Violent Felonies/Narcotics Felonies 96, 112
- Visitation 194, 210
- Visitation/Custody 196
- Vocational Rehabilitation Benefits 345
- Wage Differential Analysis 345
- Wills & Probate 165
- Wills/Trusts Contests 161
- Women's Rights 197
- Workers' Compensation 253
- Workers' Compensation Contested Claims 342
- Wrongful Death 256, 266
- Wrongful Death/Medical Malpractice 269
- Wrongful Discharge 143, 148

Profiled Attorneys Index

Ackerman, Allan A. - *Allan A. Ackerman, P.C.* - Chicago - **(312) 332-2891** 110
Aimen, Julie B. - *Attorney at Law* - Chicago - **(312) 697-0022** 110
Asonye, Uche O. - *Asonye & Associates* - Chicago - **(312) 558-1792** 142, 226
Avgeris, George N. - *George N. Avgeris, Chartered, Attorney at Law* - Hinsdale - **(630) 654-4161** 238
Azulay, J. Daniel - *Azulay & Azulay, P.C.* - Chicago - **(312) 236-6965** 181
Azulay, Y. Judd - *Azulay & Azulay, P.C.* - Chicago - **(312) 832-9200** 227
Badesch, Robert T. - *Davis, Friedman, Zavett, Kane & MacRae* - Chicago - **(312) 782-2220** 181
Bayard, Forrest S. - *Law Offices of Forrest S. Bayard* - Chicago - **(312) 236-3828** 182
Beermann, Jon L. - *Jon L. Beermann & Associates, Ltd.* - Libertyville - **(847) 680-7070** 182
Bell, Brigitte Schmidt - *Brigitte Schmidt Bell, P.C.* - Chicago - **(312) 360-1124** 44, 183
Belz, Edwin J. - *Belz & McWilliams* - Chicago - **(312) 282-9129** 111
Bennett, Margaret A. - *Law Offices of Bennett & Bennett, Ltd.* - Oak Brook - **(630) 573-8800** 183
Berman, Peter J. - *Peter J. Berman, Ltd.* - Chicago - **(312) 408-1114** 45
Bernstein, Arnold - *Attorney at Law* - Arlington Heights - **(847) 394-4017** 266
Biallas, John S. - *Attorney at Law* - St. Charles - **(630) 513-7878** 71
Blan, Kenneth W., Jr. - *Blan Law Offices* - Danville - **(217) 443-5400** 252
Bloom, Marvin - *Marvin Bloom & Associates* - Chicago - **(312) 641-1044** 111
Bowman, John T. - *Bowman & Corday, Ltd.* - Chicago - **(312) 606-9675** 339
Boyle, Charles A. - *Charles A. Boyle & Associates, Ltd.* - Chicago - **(312) 346-4944** 238
Brezina, David C. - *Lee, Mann, Smith, McWilliams, Sweeny & Ohlson* - Chicago - **(312) 368-1300** 59
Broecker, Howard W. - *J•A•M•S/Endispute* - Chicago - **(312) 739-0200**; *Howard W. Broecker & Associates, Ltd.* - Geneva - **(708) 232-1445** 45, 184
Bush, Anna Markley - *Bush & Heise* - Barrington - **(847) 382-4560** 184
Callis, Lance - *Callis, Papa, Jensen, Jackstadt & Halloran, P.C.* - Granite City - **(618) 452-1323** 282
Camic, David E. - *Camic, Johnson, Wilson & Bloom, P.C.* - Aurora - **(630) 859-0135** 96, 112
Carlson, Jon G. - *Carlson Wendler & Sanderson, P.C.* - Edwardsville - **(618) 656-0066** 283
Carr, Rex - *Carr, Korein, Tillery, Kunin, Montroy & Glass* - East St. Louis - **(618) 274-0434** 257, 274
Cassel, Jamie J. Swenson - *Reno, Zahm, Folgate, Lindberg & Powell* - Rockford - **(815) 987-4050** 73
Chamberlin, Darcy J. - *Attorney at Law* - Oak Brook - **(630) 447-2478** 160
Cirignani, Thomas R. - *Thomas R. Cirignani & Associates* - Chicago - **(312) 346-8700** 266
Clancy, Thomas A. - *Clancy & Stevens* - Chicago - **(312) 782-2800** 267
Clark, Gary L. - *The Law Offices of Frederic W. Nessler and Associates* - Peoria - **(309) 673-6404** 272
Clifford, Robert A. - *Clifford Law Offices* - Chicago - **(312) 899-9090** 280
Colombik, Richard M. - *Richard M. Colombik & Associates, P.C.* - Schaumburg - **(847) 619-5700** 160, 328
Corsentino, Anthony P. - *Anthony P. Corsentino, Ltd.* - Peoria - **(309) 676-1073** 210
Cox, A. Clay - *Hayes, Hammer, Miles, Cox & Ginzkey* - Bloomington - **(309) 828-7331** 330
Cullen, George J. - *Cullen, Haskins, Nicholson & Menchetti, P.C.* - Chicago - **(312) 332-2545** 339
Davis, Muller - *Davis, Friedman, Zavett, Kane & MacRae* - Chicago - **(312) 782-2220** 185
DeSanto, James J. - *Law Offices of James J. DeSanto, P.C.* - Libertyville - **(847) 816-8100** 239
Downs, Robert K. - *Downs & Downs, P.C.* - Oak Park (Chicago) - **(708) 848-0700** 36, 185
DuCanto, Joseph N. - *Schiller, DuCanto and Fleck* - Chicago - **(312) 641-5560** 186
Durkin, Kevin P. - *Clifford Law Offices* - Chicago - **(312) 899-9090** 239
Dutton, Janna S. - *Monahan & Cohen* - Chicago - **(312) 774-5220** 129
Ecker, Lori D. - *Kahan & Ecker* - Chicago - **(312) 855-1660** 142
Favaro, Dennis R. - *Thill, Kolodz & Favaro, Ltd.* - Palatine - **(847) 934-0060** 143
Felch, Patricia A. - *ARTSLaw Offices of Patricia A. Felch, P.C.* - Chicago - **(312) 236-0404** 60

Profiled Attorneys Index

Feldman, Howard W. - *Feldman & Wasser* - Springfield - **(217) 544-3403** 210
Fields, Jane F. - *Law Office of Jane F. Fields* - Chicago - **(312) 263-6065** 186
Fleck, Charles J. - *Schiller, DuCanto and Fleck* - Chicago - **(312) 641-5560** 187
Foote, Robert M. - *Murphy, Hupp, Foote, Mielke and Kinnally* - Aurora - **(630) 844-0056** 240
Frankel, Scott J. - *Frankel & Cohen, Attorneys at Law* - Chicago - **(312) 759-9600** 112, 143
Fredrickson, Robert A. - *Reno, Zahm, Folgate, Lindberg & Powell* - Rockford - **(815) 987-4050** 250
Friedman, James T. - *Davis, Friedman, Zavett, Kane & MacRae* - Chicago - **(312) 782-2220** 187
Friedman, Linda D. - *Leng Stowell Friedman & Vernon* - Chicago - **(312) 431-0888** 144
Gibson, Scott B. - *Law Offices of Scott B. Gibson, Ltd.* - Waukegan - **(847) 263-5100** 240
Gilbert, Howard E. - *Howard E. Gilbert & Associates, Ltd.* - Skokie - **(847) 966-6600** 307
Glass, Mark - *Carr, Korein, Tillery, Kunin, Montroy & Glass* - East St. Louis - **(618) 274-0434** 345
Glieberman, Herbert A. - *Herbert A. Glieberman & Associates* - Chicago - **(312) 236-2879** 188
Glimco, Joseph P., III - *Law Offices of Joseph P. Glimco III* - Downers Grove - **(630) 852-3636** 188
Goldberg, Jeffrey M. - *Jeffrey M. Goldberg & Associates, Ltd.* - Chicago - **(312) 236-4146** 268
Goodman, Bruce D. - *Steinberg, Polacek & Goodman* - Chicago - **(312) 782-1386** 268
Gossage, Roza - *Roza Gossage, P.C.* - Belleville - **(618) 277 6800** 216
Grant, Burton F. - *Grant and Grant* - Chicago - **(312) 641-3600** 189
Greenberg, Sharran R. - *Attorney at Law* - Highland Park - **(847) 433-5823** 189, 296
Greer, Daniel J. - *Stine, Wolter & Greer* - Springfield - **(217) 744-1000** 165
Grimsley, Gregg N. - *Carter & Grimsley* - Peoria - **(309) 673-3517** 74
Grund, David I. - *Grund & Starkopf, P.C.* - Chicago - **(312) 616-6600** 190
Hammer, Don C. - *Hayes, Hammer, Miles, Cox & Ginzkey* - Bloomington - **(309) 828-7331** 211
Hannigan, Richard D. - *Richard D. Hannigan, Ltd.* - Mundelein - **(847) 949-1070** 340
Harte, William J. - *William J. Harte, Ltd.* - Chicago - **(312) 726-5015** 241
Harvey, Morris Lane - *Law Offices of Morris Lane Harvey* - Fairfield - **(618) 842-5117** 216
Haskin, Lyle B. - *Lyle B. Haskin & Associates* - Wheaton - **(630) 665-0800** 190
Haskins, Charles G., Jr. - *Cullen, Haskins, Nicholson & Menchetti, P.C.* - Chicago - **(312) 332-2545** 340
Hassakis, Mark D. - *Hassakis & Hassakis, P.C.* - Mt. Vernon - **(618) 244-5335** 257
Hauser, Robert J. - *Sullivan, Smith, Hauser & Noonan, Ltd.* - Waukegan - **(847) 244-0111** 113
Healy, Martin J., Jr. - *Martin J. Healy, Jr. & Associates* - Chicago - **(312) 977-0100** 241
Hebeisen, Keith A. - *Clifford Law Offices* - Chicago - **(312) 899-9090** 269
Hogan, Judy L. - *Judy L. Hogan, P.C., Attorneys and Mediators* - Geneva - **(630) 232-1886** 46
hooks, william h. - *Hooks Law Offices, P.C.* - Chicago - **(312) 553-5252** 114
Hopkins, David H. - *Schiller, DuCanto and Fleck* - Chicago - **(312) 641-5560** 191
Jeep, Markham M. - *Markham M. Jeep, P.C.* - Waukegan - **(847) 360-3300** 341
Jensen, Philip F. - *Hammer, Simon & Jensen* - Galena - **(815) 777-1101** 207, 308
Johnson, Gary V. - *Camic, Johnson, Wilson & Bloom, P.C.* - Aurora - **(630) 859-0135** 97, 114
Jones, Lance T. - *Reid & Jones Law Offices* - Springfield - **(217) 546-1001** 148
Kahan, Penny Nathan - *Kahan & Ecker* - Chicago - **(312) 855-1660** 144
Kalcheim, Michael W. - *Kalcheim, Schatz & Berger* - Chicago - **(312) 782-3456** 191
Kane, Larry R. - *Davis, Friedman, Zavett, Kane & MacRae* - Chicago - **(312) 782-2220** 192
Kaplan, Melvin J. - *Melvin J. Kaplan & Associates* - Chicago - **(312) 294-8989** 71
Katz, Stephen H. - *Schiller, DuCanto and Fleck* - Lake Forest - **(847) 615-8300** 192
Kavensky, Craig L. - *Winstein, Kavensky & Wallace* - Rock Island - **(309) 794-1515** 250, 344
Kelly, Roger J. - *Law Offices of Roger J. Kelly* - Chicago - **(312) 663-3699** 145, 296
Kimnach, Richard A. - *Anesi, Ozmon & Rodin, Ltd.* - Chicago - **(312) 372-3822** 341
Kionka, Edward J. - *Professor of Law* - Carbondale - **(618) 453-8755** 86
Koenig, Philip E. - *Katz, McHard, Balch, Lefstein & Fieweger, P.C.* - Rock Island - **(309) 788-5661** 164
Kohen, Bruce M. - *Anesi, Ozmon & Rodin, Ltd.* - Chicago - **(312) 372-3822** 242
Korein, Sandor - *Carr, Korein, Tillery, Kunin, Montroy & Glass* - East St. Louis - **(618) 274-0434** 284
Koukios, Steven S. - *Koukios & Associates* - Park Ridge - **(847) 299-4440** 72
Kremin, David K. - *David K. Kremin & Associates, A Professional Corporation* - Chicago - **(312) 456-9000** ... 243
Kurowski, John J. - *The Kurowski Law Firm, P.C.* - Belleville (Swansea) - **(618) 277-5500** 217
Lambert, J. Laird - *Attorney at Law* - Rockford - **(815) 969-9800** 297
Lane, Fred - *Lane & Lane* - Chicago - **(312) 332-1400** 243
Lane, Stephen I. - *Lane & Lane* - Chicago - **(312) 332-1400** 244
Latherow, Jerry A. - *Law Office of Jerry A. Latherow* - Chicago - **(312) 372-0052** 244
Leahy, Mary Lee - *Leahy Law Offices* - Springfield - **(217) 522-4411** 149
Levy, David H. - *Kalcheim, Schatz & Berger* - Chicago - **(312) 782-3456** 193
Levy, Steven B. - *Steven B. Levy, Ltd.* - Naperville - **(630) 416-6300** 245
Lichter, Sally - *Voegtle & Lichter* - Libertyville - **(847) 918-9840** 193

Index H: Profiled Attorney Index

Lindner, George P. - *Lindner, Speers & Reuland, P.C.* - Aurora - **(630) 892-8109** 270
Loats, J. Timothy - *Law Offices of J. Timothy Loats* - Aurora - **(630) 898-4200** 342
Lonergan, Susan M. - *Susan M. Lonergan, Attorney at Law, P.C.* - St. Charles - **(630) 513-8600** 194
Lynch, David M. - *Lynch & Bloom, P.C.* - Peoria - **(309) 673-7415** 211
MacRae, Roderick E. - *Davis, Friedman, Zavett, Kane & MacRae* - Chicago - **(312) 782-2220** 194
Malkin, Earle A. - *Law Offices of Earle A. Malkin* - Chicago - **(312) 372-6150** 195
Marcus, Dorene - *Davis, Friedman, Zavett, Kane & MacRae* - Chicago - **(312) 782-2220** 195
Martin, Royal B. - *Martin, Brown & Sullivan, Ltd.* - Chicago - **(312) 360-5000** 115
Mathis, J. Michael - *The Mathis Law Firm* - Peoria - **(309) 692-2600** 130
McCarthy, David H. - *Attorney at Law* - Peoria - **(309) 674-4508** 212
McKenzie, Robert E. - *McKenzie & McKenzie, P.C.* - Chicago - **(312) 714-8040** 329
Metnick, Michael B. - *Metnick, Wise, Cherry & Frazier* - Springfield - **(217) 753-4242** 117, 212, 253
Minchella, Erica Crohn - *Minchella & Porter, Ltd.* - Chicago - **(312) 759-1700** 72
Mirabelli, Enrico J. - *Enrico J. Mirabelli & Associates* - Chicago - **(312) 993-1500** 196
Miroballi, Joseph J. - *Anesi, Ozmon & Rodin, Ltd.* - Chicago - **(312) 372-3822** 270
Montroy, Gerald L. - *Carr, Korein, Tillery, Kunin, Montroy & Glass* - East St. Louis - **(618) 397-9191** 274
Morrison, John J. - *Law Office of John J. Morrison, Ltd.* - Chicago - **(312) 641-3484** 329
Morse, Keith S. - *Attorney at Law* - Rockford - **(815) 967-5000** 208
Mueller, William A. - *The Bankruptcy Center* - Belleville - **(618) 394-0713** 75
Muller, Kurt A. - *The Muller Firm, Ltd.* - Chicago - **(312) 855-9558** 196
Nardulli, Steven - *Stratton and Nardulli* - Springfield - **(217) 528-2183** 213
Nelson, Robert C. - *Nelson, Bement, Stubblefield & Levenhagen, P.C.* - Belleville - **(618) 277-4000** 346
Nessler, Frederic W. - *The Law Offices of Frederic W. Nessler and Associates* - Springfield - **(217) 753-5533** 253
Nicoara, John P. - *Nicoara & Steagall* - Peoria - **(309) 674-6085** 254
Niro, Cheryl I. - *Partridge & Niro, P.C.; Associates in Dispute Resolution, Inc.* - Chicago - **(312) 850-1906** 47
Nolte, Peter B. - *Attorney at Law* - Rockford - **(815) 965-2647** 85
O'Neill, Treva H. - *O'Neill & Proctor* - Carbondale - **(618) 457-3561** 217
Ohlander, Jan H. - *Reno, Zahm, Folgate, Lindberg & Powell* - Rockford - **(815) 987-4050** 251
Oney, Claudia - *Claudia Oney, P.C.* - Chicago - **(312) 782-1900** 145, 197
Ores, Nicholas H. - *Attorney at Law* - Peoria - **(309) 674-5297** 213
Ozmon, Nat P. - *Anesi, Ozmon & Rodin, Ltd.* - Chicago - **(312) 372-3822** 246
Parker, Drew - *Parker & Halliday* - Peoria - **(309) 673-0069** 214
Patterson, Robert B. - *Law Offices of Robert B. Patterson, Ltd.* - Chicago - **(312) 236-0995** 246
Peck, Kerry R. - *Kerry R. Peck & Associates* - Chicago - **(312) 201-0900** 161
Peithmann, William A. - *Peithmann Law Office* - Farmer City - **(309) 928-3390** 165
Pekala, Beverly A. - *The Law Offices of Beverly A. Pekala, P.C.* - Chicago - **(312) 251-0737** 197
Peskind, Steven N. - *Peskind & Peskind, Ltd.* - Aurora - **(630) 844-1263** 198
Presbrey, Kim E. - *Presbrey and Associates, P.C.* - Aurora - **(630) 264-7300** 342
Proctor, Janet C. - *O'Neill & Proctor* - Carbondale - **(618) 457-3561** 218
Provenza, James C. - *James C. Provenza, P.C.* - Glenview - **(847) 729-3939** 161
Rapoport, David E. - *Rapoport & Kupets Law Offices* - Rosemont - **(847) 803-9880** 281
Rawles, Edward H. - *Rawles, O'Byrne, Stanko & Kepley, P.C.* - Champaign - **(217) 352-7661** 255
Reda, Edward E., Jr. - *Reda, Ltd.* - Chicago - **(312) 399-1122** 162
Redfield, John H. - *Attorney at Law* - Skokie - **(847) 966-9920** 72
Reed, Mike - *Law Office of Mike Reed* - Centralia - **(618) 533-0122** 76
Reuland, Timothy J. - *Lindner, Speers & Reuland, P.C.* - Aurora - **(630) 892-8109** 247
Richter, Harold - *Law Offices of Harold Richter* - Lansing - **(708) 862-2299** 198
Rikli, Donald C. - *Attorney at Law* - Highland - **(618) 654-2364** 166
Rinella, Bernard B. - *Rinella and Rinella, Ltd.* - Chicago - **(312) 236-5454** 199
Ritz, Kenneth F. - *Ritz, Willette & Hampilos* - Rockford - **(815) 968-1807** 74
Rodin, Curt N. - *Anesi, Ozmon & Rodin, Ltd.* - Chicago - **(312) 372-3822** 247
Rolewick, David F. - *Rolewick & Gutzke, P.C.* - Wheaton - **(630) 653-1577** 162
Rosenfeld, Howard H. - *Rosenfeld, Rotenberg, Hafron & Shapiro* - Chicago - **(312) 372-6058** 199
Ross, Jay B. - *Jay B. Ross and Associates, P.C.* - Chicago - **(312) 633-9000** 61
Rubens, James L. - *Davis, Friedman, Zavett, Kane & MacRae* - Chicago - **(312) 782-2220** 200
Rubin, Arnold G. - *Law Offices of Arnold G. Rubin, Ltd.* - Chicago - **(312) 899-0022** 343
Ryan, Catherine M. - *Ryan, Miller & Trafelet, P.C.* - Chicago - **(312) 207-1700** 200
Sahlstrom, R. Craig - *Attorney and Counsellor at Law* - Rockford - **(815) 964-4601** 116
Saint, Gale W. - *Saint & Carmichael, P.C.* - Bloomington - **(309) 829-7086** 165
Scanlan, Edmund J. - *Law Offices of Edmund J. Scanlan, Ltd.* - Chicago - **(312) 372-0020** 248
Schaffner, Harry - *Schaffner & Van Der Snick, P.C.* - Geneva - **(630) 232-8900** 201

Profiled Attorneys Index

Schiever, Carey J. - *Carey J. Schiever, Ltd.* - Libertyville - **(847) 680-1123** 163
Schiller, Donald C. - *Schiller, DuCanto and Fleck* - Chicago - **(312) 641-5560** 201
Schlesinger, Gary L. - *Law Office of Gary L. Schlesinger* - Libertyville - **(847) 680-4970** 202
Schwarz, Benedict, II - *Law Offices of Benedict Schwarz II, Ltd.* - West Dundee - **(847) 428-7725** 202
Shancer, Jeffrey M. - *Law Offices of Jeffrey M. Shancer* - Chicago - **(312) 558-5167** 248
Sharp, Terrell Lee - *Law Office of Terry Sharp, P.C.* - Mt. Vernon - **(618) 242-0246** 76
Sheffler, Stephen K. - *Pelini & Sheffler* - Champaign - **(217) 359-6242** 75
Siebert, William Newell - *William Newell Siebert & Associates* - Chicago - **(312) 329-0646** 227
Sigman, Helen - *Helen Sigman & Associates, Ltd.* - Chicago - **(312) 258-8441** 203
Slevin, John A. - *Vonachen, Lawless, Trager & Slevin* - Peoria - **(309) 676-8986** 255
Smith, Robert S., Jr. - *Law Offices of Robert S. Smith, Jr.* - Deerfield - **(847) 945-3455** 163
Speers, Robert L. - *Lindner, Speers & Reuland, P.C.* - Aurora - **(630) 892-8109** 249
Stanko, Glenn A. - *Rawles, O'Byrne, Stanko & Kepley, P.C.* - Champaign - **(217) 352-7661** 149
Stein, Arnold - *Schiller, DuCanto and Fleck* - Chicago - **(312) 641-5560** 203
Stein, Edward I. - *Edward I. Stein, Ltd.* - Northbrook - **(847) 291-4320** 204
Stine, Robert E. - *Stine, Wolter & Greer* - Springfield - **(217) 744-1000** 256
Stogsdill, William J., Jr. - *Law Offices of William J. Stogsdill, Jr., P.C.* - Wheaton - **(630) 462-9500** 204
Stone, Jed - *Law Offices of Jed Stone, Ltd.* - Chicago - **(312) 943-7881** 115
Stowell, Mary - *Leng Stowell Friedman & Vernon* - Chicago - **(312) 431-0888** 146
Strodel, Robert C. - *Law Offices of Robert C. Strodel, Ltd.* - Peoria - **(309) 676-4500** 273
Stubblefield, Timothy C. - *Nelson, Bement, Stubblefield & Levenhagen, P.C.* - Belleville - **(618) 277-4000 or (618) 277-8260** 87, 218
Sutterfield, David W. - *Sutterfield & Johnson, P.C.* - Effingham - **(217) 342-3100** 318
Switzer, Peter S. - *Barrick, Switzer, Long, Balsley & Van Evera* - Rockford - **(815) 962-6611** 208
Tighe, Mary Beth S. - *Attorney at Law* - Park Ridge - **(847) 823-7771** 205
Tillery, Stephen M. - *Carr, Korein, Tillery, Kunin, Montroy & Glass* - Belleville - **(618) 277-1180** 284
Tobin, Craig D. - *Craig D. Tobin & Associates* - Chicago - **(312) 641-1321** 116
Trevino, Fern Niehuss - *Law Office of Fern N. Trevino* - Chicago - **(312) 408-2751** 146
Truemper, William J. - *Truemper, Hollingsworth, Wojtecki, Courtin & Titiner* - Aurora - **(630) 820-8400** 205
VanDemark, Ruth E. - *Law Offices of Ruth E. VanDemark* - Chicago - **(312) 419-7162** 84
Wadington, Robert N. - *Robert N. Wadington & Associates* - Chicago - **(312) 629-2706** 249
Wasser, Stanley N. - *Feldman & Wasser* - Springfield - **(217) 544-3403** 150
Wasserman, Laurie J. - *Law Offices of Laurie J. Wasserman* - Skokie - **(847) 674-7324** 147
Weiler, Rory T. - *Weiler & Noble, P.C.* - Batavia - **(630) 879-3020** 206
Weinstein, Melvin A. - *Melvin A. Weinstein & Associates* - Chicago - **(312) 263-2257** 206
Weissberg, Ariel - *Weissberg and Associates, Ltd.* - Chicago - **(312) 663-0004** 73
Wham, Fred L., III - *Attorney at Law* - Rockford - **(815) 964-6717** 209
Wimmer, John R. - *The Law Offices of John R. Wimmer* - Downers Grove - **(630) 810-0005** 47, 85
Winget, Walter W. - *Winget & Kane* - Peoria - **(309) 674-2310** 214
Winstein, Arthur R. - *Winstein, Kavensky & Wallace* - Rock Island - **(309) 794-1515** 209
Womick, John - *Womick & Associates, Chartered* - Carbondale - **(618) 529-2440** 258
Zavett, Errol - *Davis, Friedman, Zavett, Kane & MacRae* - Chicago - **(312) 782-2220** 207
Zuckerman, Richard Wayne - *Law Offices of Richard W. Zuckerman* - Peoria - **(309) 637-3732** 215